TABLE OF CONTENTS

BASICS **5**
History 5
Climate 6
Dress, Smoking, Tipping 6
Tourist Information and Maps 7
Safety 7
Emergencies 7
Special Resources 7
Notes for Foreigners 8
Media 9
Phones 11
Utilities 11
Seasonal Events 11

TRANSPORTATION **13**
Driving & Automobiles 13
   Auto Registration &
     Driver's Licenses 13
   Automobile Rental 14
   Driving and Parking 14
   Taxis 16
   Transportation for the
     Elderly and Disabled 17
Public Transportation 17
Getting Away 20
   Air Travel 20
   Airport Transportation 21
   Land Travel 22

NEIGHBORHOODS & HOUSING **.23**
Resources 23
Neighborhood Profiles 25

VISITING **39**
Sightseeing 39
Museums 70
Hotels & Inns 72

GETTING SETTLED **79**
Shopping Overview 79
Bookstores 81
CDs & Records 83
Food & Wine 84
Home Furnishings 88
Outlets 92
Specialty Stores 93
Sporting Goods 95
Toys 97

RESTAURANTS **99**
Restaurant Reviews 99
Restaurant Indexes 137
   Types of Cuisine 137
   Special Features 138

ARTS & ENTERTAINMENT ..**139**
Amusements 139
   Entertaining Children 140
   Pro and College Sports 142
Movie Theaters 143
Performing Arts 145
   Classical Music and Opera 145
   Dance 146

.... 161
Bicycling 162
   Mountain Biking 162
   Road Biking 164
Fitness & Health Clubs 166
Golf 168
Parks & Open Space 170
Playground Sports 171
River Rafting 173
Sailing 174
Scuba Diving 176
Sea Kayaking 178
(In-Line) Skating 179
Windsurfing 181

THE BAY AREA
East Bay 183
Marin 217
Peninsula & San Jose 233

GETAWAYS
Mendocino 269
Monterey, Carmel, Big Sur 276
Peninsula Coast 284
Santa Cruz 289
Tahoe 294
Wine Country 301
Yosemite National Park 311

INDEX **317**

MAPS
Northern California 4
San Francisco
   Chinatown 43
   Civic Center, Lower Haight 47
   Financial District, Embarcadero ... 39
   Marina, Pacific Heights 53
   Mission 65
   Nob Hill, Russian Hill 48
   Noe Valley, Castro 62
   Northern Waterfront, North Beach .50
   Richmond, Sunset, Haight,
   Presidio, Golden Gate 56, 57
   SoMa 67
   Union Square 45
Marin 218
Mendocino 270
Monterey, Carmel, Big Sur 277
Peninsula Coast 285
Santa Cruz 289
Tahoe 297
Wine Country 303
Yosemite 313

CREDITS

Series Editor
Peter Massik
Copy Editors
Julie Carlson, Leslie Clagett, Sharon Silva, Stephanie Vollmer
Associate Editors
Jeremy Chipman, Lisa Trottier, Sean Vitali
Cover Design
Big Fish Books
Cover Painting: Joan Brown, *The Dancers in a City #2*.
Courtesy of Noel Neri and Mike Hebel
Cover Photograph Courtesy of Photonika
Contributors
Velvy Appleton, Kim Christensen, Caleb Clark, Sarah Crumb, Jessica Hempel, Holly Erickson, Reena Jana, Suzanne Joyal, Julie Lane, Mimi Lathan Towle, Lysa Allman dba Lyman Productions, Ed McGinty, Chris Merrill, Gwen Mickelson, Steve Moore, Lakenda North, Sharon Silva, Ann Marie Spinelli, Raymond R. Watson

Inside Front Cover map © 1997 Eureka Cartography. Reprinted with permission.
Front Cover Flap map © 1997 Good Life Publications.
Inside Back Cover Map © 1996 Metropolitan Transportation Commission. Reprinted with permission.

Good Life San Francisco Insider's Guide
ISBN 0-886776-04-0 Softcover.
Copyright © 1997 Good Life Publications. All rights reserved.
Interior maps © 1997 Good Life Publications. All rights reserved.
First edition.
Printed in Canada.

All rights reserved. No part of this book may be reproduced or transmitted in any form or by any means, electronic or mechanical, including photocopying, recording, or by any information retrieval system without written permission from the publisher, except for the inclusion of brief quotations in a review.

Although the publisher has made every effort to ensure that the information was correct and verified at press time, the publisher does not assume and hereby disclaims any liability to any party for any loss or damage caused by errors, omissions, or any potential disruption due to labor or financial difficulty, whether such errors or omissions result from negligence, accident, or any other cause.

Please send all comments, corrections, and additions for future editions to:

Good Life Publications
760 Market St., #759
San Francisco, California 94102
(415) 989-1844
(415) 989-3122 fax
glife@aol.com

SPECIAL SALES
Good Life guides are available at bulk discounts for conventions, corporate gifts, fundraising sales premiums, and sales promotions. Special editions, including custom covers, excerpts of existing guides, and corporate imprints, can be created for large orders. For more information, contact Good Life Publications, (888) 989-GOOD.

INTRODUCTION

In the following pages, you will find both humorous and practical information. In the never-ending search for comprehensiveness, we included as much as we could. If we overlooked some gem or gave you a bum steer, let us know! One cautionary note: prices are subject to change without notice (ditto hours of operation), so if you're watching your wallet or watch, play it safe and call ahead.

We hope that you have as much fun using the book as we did putting it together.

KEY TO RATINGS

This guidebook includes easy-to-understand stars and dollar signs for quality and price ratings. Keep in mind that things change. Even well-established businesses close, and changes in staff or ownership can greatly affect quality and price. The ratings in this book are based on information available at press time.

★ Stars

Sights and attractions are rated on the following popular scale of one to three stars.

★   Interesting.

★★   Worth a detour.

★★★   Worth the trip.

Restaurants are rated on the following scale of one to four stars. The star ratings are purely subjective, and based on an overall evaluation of the restaurant, with heavy emphasis on the quality and consistency of the food.

★   Good. Has some interesting, satisfying features and dishes.

★★   Very Good. Has some extraordinary dishes and features.

★★★   Excellent. Has many extraordinary dishes and features.

★★★★ Extraordinary. The best in its class, with consistently exceptional food, service, and atmosphere.

Restaurant Prices

Rating the price of a restaurant meal isn't a science: two groups can go to the same establishment and leave with wildly different checks. Do you order an appetizer, a dessert, or alcohol? These items can double the price of the meal.

Our ratings are based on what it might cost each person to have a reasonable dinner (breakfast or lunch if that's all the restaurant serves) including tax and tip. This means neither splurging nor skimping: Maybe enjoy one drink, split an appetizer, order an entrée, and share a dessert.

¢   A filling meal for $8 or less. In most cases, this refers to taquerias, burger joints, and other places with counter service.

$ $8 to $15 each for dinner. Typically, places that only serve brunch and lunch, ethnic restaurants, and other eateries where main dishes are under $10.

$$ You can get away with spending as little as $15 for dinner or easily go up to $25. Mostly places serving pasta, sushi, or moderately priced meat and seafood dishes.

$$$ Meals run from $25 to $40 per person. Restaurants where there is no escape from ordering entrées priced in the teens, most items are à la carte, and most tables have a bottle of wine.

$$$$ There is no cap on the amount you could spend at these fine dining establishments, but we have them starting at $40 per person. For that blow-out celebration meal (or when someone else is paying).

Northern California

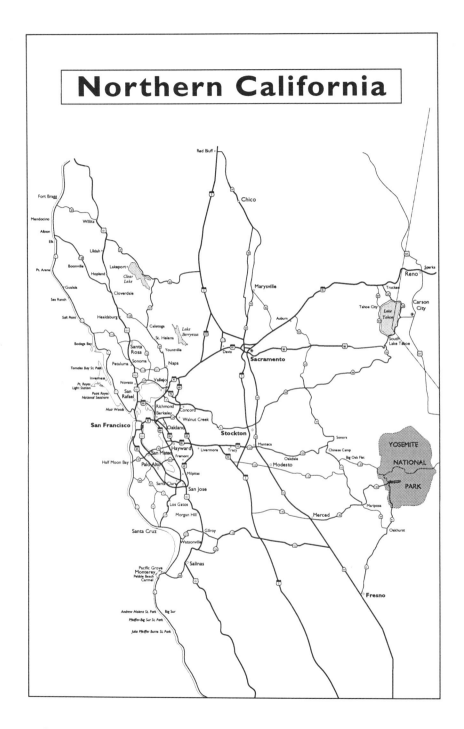

Basics

People flock to San Francisco. It was the gold that first brought them here in droves, but it is the distinctive beauty, the weather, the spirit of diversity and acceptance, the cultural history and rich cultural present that keeps them here and keeps them coming. As a newcomer, you will find San Francisco easy to fall in love with, but perhaps difficult to navigate. This book is a guide for you, to help you with everything from making your new apartment a home to finding out the inside scoop on the best the city has to offer—and where to go when you've had enough.

History

For thousands of years before the first European sailed through the Golden Gate, the area was inhabited by as many as 15,000 Coast Miwok and Ohlone Indians. When the Spanish finally stumbled upon the bay in 1775 (several explorers had passed right by the Golden Gate during the 16th century), they quickly claimed the area for Spain and established a community dubbed "Yerba Buena," or "good herb," for the wild mint that grew in the region. In 1835, after the Spanish had lost control of Mexico, Andrew Jackson made an unsuccessful bid to the newly created Mexican government to purchase Yerba Buena for the U.S. What could not be won with financial negotiations was won with force. The U.S. claimed Yerba Buena in 1846 as a result of its success in the Mexican-American War.

Official U.S. control over tiny Yerba Buena (renamed San Francisco by the Americans) came in 1848, just a week after gold was discovered in the Sierra Nevada Mountains. Although San Francisco was far from the gold mines, the mad rush west boosted its population from several hundred to over 25,000 in under a year. Those were San Francisco's boom years, when the quickly growing city gained a seamy reputation for the scoundrel-filled saloons and brothels crowded into the port area known as the Barbary Coast. By the 1870s, the boom years were over, the Sierra mined out. Nevertheless, the completion of the transcontinental railroad in 1869 assured the city's continued growth.

Yet tumult lay ahead. The Big One hit on April 18, 1906, while the city was sleeping. Estimated at over an eight on the Richter scale, the earthquake and the resulting fires demolished almost the entire city between the port and Van Ness Avenue. In the rush to rebuild, planners installed a simple grid system of streets, completely ignoring the dramatic topography of the city and creating the roller coaster streets for which the city is justly famous. The public works projects of the Depression era gave the city its two main bridges: the Bay Bridge, which opened in 1936, quickly followed by the Golden Gate Bridge, which opened in 1937.

The onset of World War II brought another boom to the Bay Area, as it became the major stepping-off point for military operations in the Pacific. New jobs created by the shipyards drew thousands of people to the area, and many military families that passed through the area returned to settle at the close of the war.

During the post-war years, the city continued its freewheeling ways, becoming the birthplace of the 1950s Beat movement in North Beach and the 1960s hippie scene in Haight-Ashbury. San Francisco's gay community stepped forward to be recognized with the Gay Pride movement, which took off during the 1970s. Elements of all of these movements still flourish throughout the city. Intellectuals and poets crowd the cafés and bars of North Beach and beyond. Along Haight Street, hippies still linger; some have been there since the Summer of Love, others were born during the Reagan years. Rainbow flags shout Gay Pride from rooftops in the Castro, and the community takes over the city once a year during the Gay Pride Parade. This tolerance and diversity has created a modern city that reveals elements of its past at every turn.

BASICS

Climate

California owes much of its dramatic population growth over the past 50 years to its attractive, Mediterranean climate. Generally, you can expect warm days and cool nights all year round. However, there is substantial variation from region to region, month to month, and year to year. The coastal areas along the Pacific bear the brunt of winter storms sweeping off the ocean and are chilled by ocean breezes and fog during spring and summer—especially in San Francisco. The surrounding mountains wring moisture from winter storms, receiving significantly more rainfall than low-lying areas, and even some occasional snow. Because the coastal mountains shelter the bay from the ocean, most inland residents enjoy warm days and moderate rainfall.

The average year-round daily Bay Area temperature is 70 degrees Fahrenheit, with a nighttime low of 45. San Francisco's daily average is only 62 degrees. Inland daytime highs near 100 are common. Almost all rainfall comes between November and April. San Francisco averages more than 20 inches of rain per year; San Jose, less than 14 inches; and parts of Marin, well over 30 inches.

San Francisco's weather will keep you guessing—not only day to day, but hour to hour. A sunny, 80-degree afternoon in the city can quickly turn into a gray 50 degrees when thick banks of fog roll in, leaving many a scantily clad tourist shivering. The unpredictability of the weather means it's always a good idea to dress in layers.

San Franciscans know that they will pay for any hot days with subsequent foggy ones. The fog occurs most often during the summer: It is created offshore when warm, moist air meets the chilly Pacific Ocean. Hot weather inland creates thermal updrafts that draw the fog through the Golden Gate and over the hills. The oceanside half of the city sees more fog than the bayside half: North Beach may enjoy sunny weather while the Richmond shivers under a mantle of fog. Spring and fall are the best seasons, with September and October the most spectacular months.

Averages	Temperature °F		Rainfall
	Max	Min	Inches
January	56	46	4.5
February	59	48	2.8
March	60	49	2.6
April	61	49	1.5
May	63	51	0.4
June	64	53	0.2
July	64	53	0.0
August	65	54	0.1
September	69	56	0.2
October	68	55	1.1
November	63	52	2.5
December	57	47	3.5
Average	63	51	19.3

Dress, Smoking, Tipping

Dress in California is generally casual. Business types wear suits, especially in the financial district, but many companies allow employees to wear "Gap-casual" clothes especially on Friday, often an official dress-down day. Very few restaurants require a coat and tie, although some may object to a full-blown grunge look; otherwise, the only restaurants where you might feel out of place without formal dress are old-style Continental restaurants. This isn't to say San Franciscans don't care about how they look. Many people do dress up for the performing arts, particularly the opera, especially the all-important opening night. Others dress up for a night out in less traditional ways—polyester bell bottoms, Doc Martens, hip-hop baggies.

Smoking generates a considerable amount of controversy in California, but most local governments have now passed regulations restricting smoking in public buildings, work areas, and restaurants. (In fact, San Francisco has plans to ban smoking even in bars starting January 1997.) Look for crowds of people smoking outside doorways, and expect clouds of smoke in those bars and cafés that do allow smoking.

Unless otherwise noted on the menu or the check, restaurants do not include a gratuity on the bill. The standard tip is at least 15 percent of the tab, more for above-average service, less if the service was somehow offensive. It is also customary to tip taxi drivers, airport baggage handlers, parking valets, and most hotel service staff.

CLIMATE

Tourist Information

San Francisco Visitor Information Center: 900 Market St., SF, (415) 391-2000; events hotline, (415) 391-2001. • M-F 9am-5:30pm; Sa 9am-3pm; Su 10am-2pm.

San Francisco Convention and Visitor's Bureau: 201 3rd St., Suite 900, SF, (415) 974-6900. Produces an excellent free map of the city. • M-F 9am-5:30pm.

Safety

Like all big cities in the U.S., San Francisco has its share of seedy areas. You should particularly avoid walking alone at night in the Tenderloin, the Western Addition, Hunters Point, Market Street (especially between Powell and Laguna), and some areas of SoMa; however, people get raped and carjacked even in Pacific Heights, so don't be oblivious to your surroundings. Panhandlers abound even in some of the ritzier areas of downtown, but they are for the most part nonaggressive. Call SAFE at (415) 553-1984 for more information on safety issues.

Emergencies

Dial 911 on any telephone for emergency assistance. To reach the police or fire department for nonemergency questions, use these numbers.

Police: (415) 553-0123.

Fire: (415) 861-8000.

Hospitals: Most emergencies in the city are handled by **San Francisco General Hospital** at 1001 Potrero Ave., SF, (415) 206-8000. Another hospital with a busy 24-hour emergency room is **UCSF Medical Center** at 500 Parnassus Ave., SF, (415) 476-1000. More central to downtown is **Saint Francis Memorial Hospital** at 900 Hyde St., SF, (415) 353-6566.

24-Hour Pharmacies: There are two **Walgreen's Drug Stores** in the city that are open 24 hours, with a pharmacist always on hand. 498 Castro St. (18th St.), SF, (415) 861-6276. • 3201 Divisadero St. (Lombard), SF, (415) 931-6415.

Special Resources

Resources for the Disabled
American Foundation for the Blind: 111 Pine St., Suite 725, SF, (415) 392-4845.
Center for Independent Living: 70 10th St., SF, (415) 863-0581.
Environmental Traveling Companions: Fort Mason, Bldg. C, SF, (415) 474-7662.
Lighthouse for the Blind and Visually Disabled: 214 Van Ness Ave., SF, (415) 431-1481.

Resources for Women
Bay Area Women's & Children's Center: 318 Leavenworth St., SF, (415) 474-2400.
Planned Parenthood: 815 Eddy St., Suite 200, SF, (415) 441-5454.
Rape Crisis Hotline: (415) 647-7273.
San Francisco's Women's Building: 3543 18th St., SF, (415) 431-1180.
Women's Needs Center: 1825 Haight St., SF, (415) 487-5607.

Resources for Gays and Lesbians
Finding out about gay and lesbian groups and activities is not a challenge in San Francisco. Start by flipping through the *Bay Times*, the *Bay Area Reporter*, and *The Sentinel*, the three major free gay publications in the city, which you can find in any gay-oriented café, bar, or bookstore. The Castro, dominated by gay-owned businesses, is the major meeting place in the city, although more so for gay men than for lesbians.

BASICS

Resources for the Elderly
Friendship Line for the Elderly: (415) 752-3778.
Senior Citizen Information Line: (415) 626-1033.

Other Resources
Alumnae Resources: 120 Montgomery St., SF, (415) 274-4700. Resources for career planning and job searches.
Center for African and African-American Art & Culture: 762 Fulton St., SF, (415) 928-8546.
Chinese Cultural Center: Holiday Inn, 750 Kearny St., 3rd Floor, SF, (415) 986-1822.
International Indian Treaty Council: 54 Mint St., Suite 400, SF, (415) 512-1501 (for Native American resources).
Jewish Community Information & Referral: (415) 777-4545.
Mission Cultural Center: 2868 Mission St., SF, (415) 821-1155 (for Latino resources).

Notes for Foreigners

Passports/Visas
Visitors to the U.S. must have a valid passport and many must also have a U.S. visa. Visitors from nations participating in the visa-waiver program (Andorra, Austria, Belgium, Brunei, Denmark, Finland, France, Germany, Iceland, Italy, Japan, Liechtenstein, Luxembourg, Monaco, the Netherlands, New Zealand, Norway, San Marino, Spain, Sweden, Switzerland, and the U.K.) may stay for 90 days without obtaining a visa, but they must come with a round-trip ticket, proof of financial solvency, and a waiver of the right to a hearing of deportation. Visitors from other nations will need to obtain a U.S. visa from the U.S. Consulate in their home country. If you want to apply for an extension of your visa, contact the U.S. Justice Department's **Immigration & Naturalization Service**, 630 Sansome St., SF, (415) 705-4411, M-F 8am-4pm.

Consulates
Foreign consulates in San Francisco include:
Australia: 1 Bush St., SF, (415) 362-6160.
Denmark: 610 Montgomery St., Suite 1440, SF, (415) 391-0100.
France: 540 Bush St., SF, (415) 397-4330.
Germany: 1960 Jackson St., SF, (415) 775-1061.
Ireland: 655 Montgomery St., SF, (415) 392-4214.
Israel: 456 Montgomery St., SF, (415) 398-8885.
Japan: 50 Fremont St., 23rd Floor, SF, (415) 777-3533.
Netherlands: 1 Maritime Plaza, SF, (415) 981-6454.
New Zealand: 1 Maritime Plaza, Suite 700, SF, (415) 399-1455.
Norway: 20 California St., SF, (415) 986-0766.
Sweden: 120 Montgomery St., SF, (415) 788-2631.
Switzerland: 456 Montgomery St., SF, (415) 788-2272.
U.K.: 1 Sansome St., SF, (415) 981-3030.

Money/Foreign Exchange
The quickest way to get money in San Francisco is from one of the ATM machines that abound in the city. Branches of Bank of America and Wells Fargo—the two major banks of the area—are plentiful. However, for exchange of foreign currency you often have to travel to a bank's main branch in the financial district.

NOTES FOR FOREIGNERS

For easier exchange of foreign currency, travelers checks, or wire transfers, try one of the dedicated exchange businesses located throughout the downtown area:
AFEX: 201 Sansome St. (Pine), SF, (415) 781-7683.
American Express: 237 Post St. (Grant/Stockton), SF, (415) 536-2600. • 295 California St. (Battery), SF, (415) 536-2600. • 455 Market St. (1st St.), SF, (415) 536-2600. • 201 Mission St. (Beale/Main), SF, (415) 536-2600.
Thomas Cooke: 75 Geary St. (Kearny/Grant), SF, (800) 287-7362. • Pier 39, 2nd Level (Embarcadero at Beach), SF, (800) 287-7362.

SFO Airport: There are two branches of the Bank of America in the airport, as well as Bank of America and American Express ATMs in every terminal. Foreign exchange is available at the B of A in the international terminal branch daily from 7am to 11pm, and in Boarding Area D daily from 7am to 11pm.

Media

Newspapers

There's no shortage of media in the area, although coverage can be provincial and heavily focused on local issues. In the opinion of many people weaned on the *New York Times*, San Francisco's two daily journalistic offerings suffer in comparison. The larger circulation, morning-edition *Chronicle* is often called the "Comical" for its thin news section, top heavy with wire copy. The afternoon *Examiner* has struggled in recent years, with periodic rumors surfacing of a merger with the *Chronicle* or a shutdown, but it continues to grab readers with its screaming front page of bold, large-point headlines in the tradition of founder William Randolph Hearst. The two papers combine to produce one Sunday edition, which includes the "Datebook" section (better known as the "Pink Pages"), one of the best overall guides to arts and entertainment in the Bay Area.

The *San Jose Mercury News* is the best place to find the inside scoop on Silicon Valley and other high-tech stories. The "Merc" tends to have stories actually written by its reporters. Other area papers of note include the *Oakland Tribune* and the *Contra Costa Times*, both of which are owned by the same company.

There are four major alternative free weeklies. The *Bay Guardian* and *SF Weekly* attempt to outdo each other in their coverage of what's happening in San Francisco, though judging by their contents, the target demographic is an early twenties Mission dweller. *The East Bay Express* covers the East Bay scene, and is notable for its long but generally well-written cover stories. *The Metro* covers the South Bay. All four provide extensive arts and entertainment listings.

Television

2	KTVU	Oakland (Fox)
4	KRON	San Francisco (NBC)
5	KPIX	San Francisco (CBS)
7	KGO	San Francisco (ABC)
9	KQED	San Francisco (PBS)
11	KNTV	San Jose (ABC)
14	KDTV	San Francisco (Univision/Spanish)
20	KOFY	San Francisco (WB)
36	KICU	San Jose (Ind)
44	KBHK	San Francisco (UPN)
54	KTEH	San Jose (PBS)

BASICS

AM Radio

560	KSFO	Often-outrageous right-wing talk.
610	KFRC	Pop music.
680	KNBR	Mostly sports talk. (NBC)
740	KCBS	Round-the-clock news, weather, and traffic. Solid reporting. (CBS)
810	KGO	News/Talk. (ABC)
910	KNEW	Country and western music.
1010	KIQI	Spanish-language programming. ("El grande diez diez")
1550	KPIX	Same as KPIX 95.7 FM.

FM Radio

88.5	KQED	SF's major public radio station. NPR, BBC, and local talk shows.
89.5	KPOO	SF community radio, varied multi-ethnic music. Hard to pick up, worth listening to.
89.7	KFJC	Foothill College radio. Diverse and progressive.
90.1	KZSU	Stanford University radio. Rock, rap, etc.
90.3	KUSF	University of San Francisco radio. Award-winning, diverse, lots of "college" rock.
90.7	KALX	University of California Berkeley radio. Eclectic.
91.1	KCSM	San Mateo pubic radio. Good jazz programming around the clock.
91.7	KALW	"Information Radio." Superb commercial-free programs—NPR, BBC, CBC, and local.
92.3	KSJO	Album Oriented Rock, though more Nirvana than Van Halen.
93.3	KYCY	Country music.
94.1	KPFA	Berkeley public radio and the flagship of the liberal Pacifica network. Diverse music/talk.
94.5	KUFX	"K-Fox", Classic—Jurassic—rock.
94.9	KSAN	Modern country, i.e. Garth Brooks.
95.7	KPIX	News/talk that was "O.J. Radio" during the Simpson trial.
96.5	KOIT	Light rock—*very* light rock—and love songs at night.
97.3	KLLC	"Alice," a new format going after the 20-to-34-year-old female demographic.
98.1	KBGG	"Big 98.1." Mostly 1970s music (yes, this means Bread) but 1980s tunes are moving in, too.
98.5	KOME	San Jose's modern rock station. Howard Stern in the morning.
98.9	KSOL	Spanish language music.
100.9	KKHI	Classical music.
101.3	KIOI	"K101." The closest thing to Adult Contemporary/Top 40 radio in San Francisco.
102.1	KDFC	Very well-programmed commercial classical station.
102.9	KBLX	"Quiet Storm." Another way of saying mellow adult contemporary.
103.7	KKSF	Easy listening, waiting-on-hold music.
104.5	KFOG	Baby Boomer–friendly contemporary and classic rock played by excellent, knowledgeable DJs. Lots of commercials.
104.9	KBRG	Spanish language music.
105.3	KITS	"Live 105." Modern rock/1980s pop. The oldies station for Generation X.
106.1	KMEL	"The People's Station." Rhythm-based dance and lots of rap.
107.7	KYLD	"Wild 107." Like KMEL, with an aggressive "street" image.

Phones

Pacific Bell (800) 974-2355 is the local phone company throughout most of Northern California (GTE serves a few communities) although it was recently purchased by San Antonio-based Southwest Bell Communications. Contact them to establish any new service, but be prepared to pay an exorbitant setup fee of approximately $40 per line plus wiring charges for installation of jacks (you are free to do the wiring yourself or hire a third-party contractor).

California is on the cutting edge of telephone deregulation. The California Public Utilities Commission (CPUC) allows competition among phone companies for local toll calls (intraLATA calls over 16 miles, which are regulated by the CPUC). In addition to Pacific Bell, you can now use AT&T, MCI, Sprint, or any other phone company for these calls, although you will have to dial an access code to use these other services. Similarly, public telephones have been deregulated. Many are owned and operated by Pacific Bell; many others are owned by private companies. While these phones may outwardly look similar to Pacific Bell phones, service can be erratic. Most important, for long-distance calls, many of these other phones connect you to obscure carriers that charge obscene rates. Most local calls cost 20 cents, higher for calls over 16 miles.

In addition, the Bay Area will be getting several new area codes in the near future; in particular, the Peninsula will become code 650 in August 1997. Pay attention to your phone books and bills for updates.

Utilities

Pacific Gas and Electric (PG&E) provides local gas and electric service to most homes in the area, although some towns such as Alameda, Palo Alto, and Santa Clara maintain their own services. Consult your phone book for the local office nearest you. Because the climate is moderate, many homes and apartments are poorly insulated, and you can expect to use heat intermittently from October to April, especially if you live in the hills. Air-conditioning is helpful on many summer days, especially as you move away from the ocean in the East Bay, North Bay, and Peninsula. Most cities are responsible for their own water and garbage services; curbside recycling is common in most communities as landfill space becomes scarce.

Seasonal Events

January-February
Chinese New Year: The city's biggest Chinese cultural event culminates with the Golden Dragon Parade, which winds its way through a thronged Chinatown in late February. Call the Chinatown Chamber of Commerce at (415) 982-3000.

March
St. Patrick's Day Parade: Grab that green shirt out of the back of the closet, order up a tall green beer, and join thousands of others who are doing the same. Much safer than Boston. The parade takes place on Market Street in San Francisco the Sunday before March 17 every year. Call the United Irish Cultural Center at (415) 661-2700.

April
San Francisco International Film Festival: More than 100 films are screened annually at the country's oldest film festival. Centered in the AMC Kabuki 8 Cinemas in Japantown, but with films showing at several other Bay Area locations as well. Call (415) 931-FILM/3456.

Cherry Blossom Festival: The city's annual Japanese cultural festival includes demonstrations, exhibits, and a parade around Japantown. Call (415) 563-2313.

BASICS

May

Cinco de Mayo: During the weekend closest to May 5, the Mission district celebrates the anniversary of Mexico's independence from Spain. Check it out for great music, food, and dance, as well as a colorful Sunday parade. Call (415) 647-8622.

Bay to Breakers: San Francisco's most famous and by far its silliest footrace of the year. Join 70,000 other runners and walkers for this 12-kilometer race from the bay to the ocean. The serious racers show up early and are relaxing in the park before the thousands behind them even leave the Financial District. Don't be alarmed if the runner next to you turns out to be an Elvis impersonator, a giant bagel, or a drag queen in heels. Takes place the third Sunday of May. Call (415) 777-7770.

Carnaval: Memorial Day weekend the Mission district hosts a party, South American style, including bands, dancing, food, and a parade on Sunday. Call (415) 826-1401.

June

San Francisco Lesbian, Gay, Bisexual Transgender Pride Celebration: Locally known as the Gay Pride Parade, this event is always preceded by a week of parties and buildup. The parade itself tends to highlight the more, shall we say, flamboyant side of gay life. Gay and lesbian politicians also come to soak up the crowd's support. Check newspapers for the exact date, or call (415) 864-3733 for more information.

Street Fairs: Beginning in June, there are street fairs throughout the city during the summer, usually with music, food, and booths of local businesses. Call (415) 346-4446.

July

Independence Day: Evening festivities center around the waterfront area. You can count on fireworks and a good array of free music. If you've never seen fireworks in the fog, you've got to check it out. Call (415) 777-8498.

September

Opera in the Park: The one chance you'll have to see free opera in San Francisco, and you don't even have to dress up. The performance consists of selections, not a complete opera. Staged the Sunday after the first performance of the season. Call (415) 861-4008.

Festival de las Americas: A huge festival in the Mission on 24th Street celebrating the independence of eight Latin American countries. With Latino food, bands, crafts, and pride abounding. On a Sunday late in September. Call (415) 826-1401.

San Francisco Blues Festival: Enjoy blues and beautiful weather at Fort Mason's Great Meadow. One-day tickets are $15 in advance, $20 at the door; two-day tickets are $28, advance purchase only. Call (415) 826-6837 or (415) 979-5588.

October

Halloween: This huge, raucous, traditionally queer party has taken place in the Castro for years. Lately, however, the party has outgrown its venue—too many "bridge and tunnel" rowdies—and the organizers moving it to the Civic Center. Check the papers for details. Show up in sequins or a serious costume or prepare to be ostracized as a lowly spectator.

Pumpkin Festival: For a quieter form of entertainment, head south to Half Moon Bay, which hosts an annual festival every October to celebrate the town's most famous crop. Unfortunately, the event is also famous for causing incredible traffic jams.

November-December

In late November, the city dresses up for the holiday season, with strings of lights decorating Union Square and the Embarcadero Buildings. Two temporary outdoor ice skating rinks are set up, one in Union Square and one in Justin Herman Plaza (across from the Ferry Building). It's a great time to wander around downtown to enjoy the spectacle.

Transportation

DRIVING & AUTOMOBILES

Because California is the land of the automobile, it is also the land of automobile regulations. Bringing a car to California from another state has its hassles, not the least of which is the cost. Under state law, if you don't obtain California registration at the Department of Motor Vehicles (DMV) within 20 days of establishing California residency, you face a stiff fine. (You become a resident when you vote, your dependents attend public schools, you file for a home owner's property tax exemption, or you obtain any other privilege or benefit not ordinarily extended to nonresidents.) When you make your home here, you must also get a California driver's license within 10 days (see below). A word to the wise: Wearing a safety belt is required by law in California, and police frequently issue tickets to violators.

Auto Registration & Driver's Licenses

Perhaps you've already heard the horror stories about the DMV—long lines, endless forms, bored and condescending staff. Well, it's all true. Going to the DMV is a long, complicated, and exceedingly frustrating exercise in bureaucracy. But don't lose hope—you can save yourself some of the agony by calling ahead to make an appointment. The DMV is located at 1377 Fell Street in San Francisco, (415) 557-1179. Office hours are M-F 8am-5pm, Th till 6:30pm.

To register your car, you must fill out an application, present a California smog certificate, and show your out-of-state registration and title. The DMV will mail an application if you call ahead. Fill out this form carefully, since it could cost you. For example, if you go to the DMV more than 20 days after the date you claim to have moved here, the DMV will charge a penalty fee. You should also know that your registration cost depends on your car's value; think twice before you brag that your '71 bug is a priceless classic. In general, find out how the DMV will treat any information before you volunteer it. (But remember that making false statements to the DMV is a crime.)

You must also have your car smog checked before you go to the DMV, but not more than 90 days before. Many gas stations and repair shops perform this service. The fees vary from $20 to $50, but all shops must abide by certain rules regarding repairs and retesting on cars that fail the tests. Unfortunately, because California has the strictest auto emissions standards in the nation, most out-of-state cars don't comply with California smog regulations. Even after you get your smog certificate, you'll most likely be required to pay a $300 smog impact fee. The certificate indicates that your car is as clean as it can be; the fee is because your car's best isn't good enough.

And as if this weren't enough, if you bought your car less than 90 days before you entered California, you'll also owe any difference between California's fairly hefty sales tax and the sales tax you paid in the state of purchase.

If you purchase a car from a dealer in California, the dealer is responsible for collecting the fees and submitting the paperwork to the DMV. Within six to eight weeks of purchasing a car, you should receive a registration card from the DMV. If, however, you purchase a car from, say, your next-door neighbor, you are responsible for transferring the vehicle with the DMV within 10 days of purchase.

Driver's Licenses

Driving tests are normally waived for license renewals and holders of valid out-of-state licenses, so relax if you fit that bill. However, if you're applying for a new license and you're at least 18 years old, you may be given a license after you've passed a written

TRANSPORTATION

AAA

You can probably save yourself quite a bit of grief by joining the American Automobile Association, better known nationwide as Triple A and in Northern California as California State Automobile Association (CSAA). CSAA helps you register your car and complete many DMV procedures. They also provide emergency road service—they tow your car, change your tire, deliver fuel if you run out, and get you into your car if you lock yourself out, usually without asking embarrassing questions. They will, however, ask to see your AAA card, so keep it on you or in the car. Other benefits include an information service providing answers to technical questions, diagnostic clinics for low prices, auto maintenance classes, free maps, and traveler's checks. The San Francisco AAA office is located at 150 Van Ness Ave., (415) 565-2012. Open M-F 8:30am-5pm. For help on the road, call (800) 222-4357, daily 24 hrs. Website: http://www.csaa.com.

test on road regulations, a vision test (bring your contacts or glasses), and a driving test. You must also prove you are a legal resident. Driving tests are given by appointment only, so call ahead. You supply the car for the test—in full working condition—as well as a licensed driver to accompany you to the test. The $12 application fee is good for three tries within 12 months. Once you've completed this obstacle course, you're photographed and thumbprinted (or fingerprinted, if you have no thumbs), and let loose on the road.

Automobile Rental

A quick glimpse in the phone book will reveal that there's no shortage of rental car agencies in San Francisco. All of the major national organizations are well represented, as are many smaller agencies. Most agencies are located at the airport, but many maintain operations in the city, especially around Union Square. When comparison shopping, remember that rental rates are as volatile as air fares; expect to pay more during the summer, for instance. Always ask about weekend, frequent flier, student, and AAA discounts. Your rate is usually set when you make the reservation, not when you actually pick up the car, so plan ahead and book during a slow time. Always get your confirmation number, in case the rental agency loses track of your reservation. Keep in mind that many companies require a major credit card. You should also know that if you're under 25, you're a special insurance liability—which may be reflected in an extra surcharge. And if you're under 21, most companies won't even talk to you. Many local governments levy additional car rental taxes of up to $5 per day.

Alamo Rent A Car: (800) 327-9633.
Avis Rent A Car: (800) 831-2847.
Budget Rent-A-Car: (800) 527-0700.
Dollar Rent A Car: (800) 800-4000.
Enterprise Rent-A-Car: (800) 325-8007.
Hertz: (800) 654-3131.
National: (800) 227-7368.

Driving and Parking

Those accustomed to cruising the freeways of Southern California will find that driving in San Francisco is a very different animal. You'll encounter narrow streets, hair-raising hills at every turn, psychotic cab drivers, and oblivious pedestrians. It doesn't help that nearly every neighborhood is being torn up for some sort of construction project. However, before you turn in your keys for good, consider the following tips:

DRIVING & AUTOMOBILES

San Francisco is not a freeway-driving sort of town. There is not a single north/south freeway route through the city: vehicles are deposited onto surface streets and forced to thread their way back to the freeway; in fact, the northern portion of the Central Freeway (Hwy 101), from I-80 to the on- and off-ramps at Oak and Fell streets, will be closed indefinitely for earthquake repairs. The most common north/south routes through the city are along 19th Avenue and Van Ness Avenue. During heavy traffic, little can be done to alleviate this frustration. If you take the Van Ness/101 exit into the city from the south, you may save time by cutting over to Franklin Street to make your way north through the city. In addition, ever since the 1989 Loma Prieta earthquake closed the Embarcadero Freeway, getting to Hwy 101 or I-280 from downtown can be the most time-consuming and frustrating part of a journey. If possible, try to avoid approaching the freeway from downtown between 3:30pm and 6:30pm on weekdays.

The city has several one-way streets with traffic lights timed to allow you to cruise along for 10 to 20 blocks without stopping. Northbound is Franklin; southbound is Gough (a block west of Franklin). Running west is Pine, and east is Bush. Be warned, however, that these streets are well known to every other driver in the city. Further, although the streets ostensibly have three lanes, the right and left lanes are frequently blocked by double-parked, parallel-parked, or otherwise stopped vehicles. (You'll be amazed at how many drivers pull right up behind a vehicle that's about to back into a parking space—blocking access to the space—then sit there blowing their horn.)

In 1995, over 3,000 cars ran out of gas on the Bay Bridge

Parking is the topic of much ranting and raving among San Francisco drivers. Some of the outlying neighborhoods don't have it so bad: parking in Noe Valley, the Richmond, or the Sunset is usually just a matter of taking a turn around the block. Street parking downtown during the day is close to impossible. Hands down, the worst residential neighborhoods for parking in the city are North Beach and Russian Hill. Many inhabitants of these neighborhoods don't move their cars at night for fear they'll never find another space; wealthier residents just park on an out-of-the-way sidewalk and pay the $25 ticket.

Street parking throughout San Francisco is regulated by parking meters, painted curbs, and signs; unless money is no object, pay attention to all of these. Rule number one, don't park in a bus stop zone: although bus drivers never use them, the fine is still $250—no, it's not a typo. Most meters operate from 8am to 6pm Monday through Saturday *and* holidays, and require a lot of change (usually quarters). Many meters are restricted to commercial vehicles at certain times (look for the small yellow signs); the city takes this restriction seriously, so don't park here or you will be ticketed and probably towed. Also pay attention to signs restricting parking (even at meters) during certain hours for street cleaning or rush hour traffic. Curb paint also indicates parking restrictions: red indicates no parking; blue indicates disabled parking only; yellow indicates commercial loading (usually only during daytime hours); green indicates 10-minute parking (which allows you to run into a dry cleaner or perform a similar errand); white indicates passenger loading (hours vary widely, from 24 hours in front of an apartment building to business hours in front of a store).

It's no wonder California pedestrians get hit by cars more often than any others: they wander blindly into streets without checking traffic signals or looking for oncoming cars.

Street parking in most residential neighborhoods is restricted by permit rules indicated by signs. Generally, with a permit you can park all day, virtually every day, on any street—just don't forget to watch out for street cleaning. Without a permit you must move your car every two or three hours for as long as the rules apply: in some neigh-

TRANSPORTATION

borhoods, that can be from 7am to 9pm every day; in others, from 9am to 5pm Monday through Friday. If you don't have a parking garage, you will want to get a permit immediately after finding an apartment. To get a permit, you must prove that both you and your car reside in a neighborhood (usually a signed lease and the car's registration will suffice), as well as pay the annual $21 fee. Each neighborhood has its own annual renewal cycle, and fees are not prorated; if you move on February 1 into a neighborhood where permits renew in March, you will have to pay $21 for February, then another $21 for the next year. Obtain your permit from the Department of Parking and Transportation (DPT) Residential Permit Parking office at 370 Grove St., SF, (415) 554-5000. Open M-F 7:45am-4:45pm, Th until 6pm. If your guests arrive with a car, you can get them a Visitors Permit good for two weeks. (You must do this for them; only legal residents can get permits.) Each two-week permit costs $5.

If you find yourself in despair, eyeing the empty curb in front of a fire hydrant or a bus zone, keep in mind that parking fines can be unexpectedly severe. Under no circumstances should you block a driveway—especially in a rich neighborhood, where residents are particularly territorial: not only will you pay through the nose for the towing, but the necessary visit to the DPT to retrieve your car could cost you your sanity. Also be sure to avoid the wheelchair access curb cuts ($275 ticket), which are cropping up on most street corners in the city and are *not* marked with the familiar blue and white signs.

San Francisco's parking laws also require drivers to curb their wheels when parking on a hill. If you park facing uphill, turn the wheel into the road; if you park facing downhill, turn the wheel into the curb.

San Francisco has many, mostly expensive, parking garages downtown. Rates average $20 per day. Two city garages offer a good deal for short-term parking, charging $1 per hour for the first hour, $2 per hour thereafter: the Sutter-Stockton Garage, on its namesake streets and Bush; and the Ellis-O'Farrell, on its namesake streets between Stockton and Powell. Both garages tend to fill up with shoppers. If you plan to spend a full day downtown and don't mind walking or taking a bus to save money, you can find cheap, plentiful parking south of Market Street near the I-80 elevated freeway. Many self-service lots charge $5 per day. Garages are neither as common nor as expensive outside of downtown, but many restaurants and bars offer valet parking for about $5.

Traffic Information Fastline: (415) 777-1000. Traffic, bridge, and transit information.

Taxis

Taxis in the city are not cheap, and unless you are downtown, are not particularly abundant (most cabbies are at the airport waiting for fares back to town). You may be able to catch a cab at one of the big, downtown hotels: many drivers hang out there waiting for airport fares. Generally, unless you live on a major thoroughfare, you're better off phoning for a cab. During peak hours, especially morning and evening rush hours when it rains, you may not be able to get through to *any* of the companies without auto redial—either the line will be busy or no one will answer—and if you do get through, there could be a 45-minute wait. You can also forget about calling a cab on New Year's Eve, when the cab companies don't seem to answer the phone at all. Most companies encourage calling the night before to reserve a morning cab to the airport. Fares start at $1.70 for the first sixth of a mile; after that, it's 30 cents for every sixth of a mile or every minute of waiting or traffic delay. The typical airport fare from downtown is about $30. Many people add a 10 to 15 percent tip to the fare (or just round up).

City Cab: (415) 468-7200.
DeSoto Cab Company: (415) 673-1414.
Luxor Cab Company: (415) 282-4141.
Veteran's Cab: (415) 552-1300.
Yellow Cab: (415) 626-2345.

PUBLIC TRANSPORTATION

Transportation for the Elderly and Disabled

On Lok: (415) 292-8888, (415) 550-2210. Shuttle service for elderly persons.

San Francisco Paratransit Services: (415) 202-9903. Disabled persons who meet the requirements can make use of this subsidized van and taxi service. You must make a reservation the previous day for the vans.

PUBLIC TRANSPORTATION

The Bay Area has an extensive public transportation network, with many interconnecting systems linking the city to the outlying areas that surround it on three sides. This makes traveling around without a car relatively easy, albeit slow. There's often more than one way to get someplace, so it's definitely worth taking the time to find the fastest or most appropriate route.

If you need information, call the numbers given below. Once you get through the frequently busy phone lines, the operators are usually helpful; most will also mail free timetables and maps within a couple of days. If you're confused about how to get from one place to another, try calling a Visitor Information Center (see Basic Information section).

AC Transit: (510) 839-2882. Alameda County Transit (AC Transit) covers the East Bay from Richmond to Fremont, with stops at every East Bay BART station. Transbay buses run across the Bay Bridge from Oakland to San Francisco's Transbay Terminal, mostly during rush hour. Express routes, which operate only during rush hour, go from downtown Oakland south to the suburbs as far as San Leandro and Hayward.

The fare for Local or Intercity Express buses is $1.25 (youth, seniors, and disabled 60 cents), Transbay routes cost $2.20 (youth, seniors, and disabled $1.10). Monthly passes are $45 for adults ($11 discount), or $75 for a Transbay pass. Local passes can be upgraded to get across the bay by paying $1.10 (55 cents) per journey. Books of 10 local bus tickets cost $10 (discount $5) and are available at local stores; call (800) 559-INFO/4636 for store locations. Transfers are available for an extra 25 cents, and bus-BART transfers can be purchased in BART stations, valid only for the bus stop outside that particular BART station. Generally, buses run every 30 minutes during the day, every 15 minutes during commute hours, and every 30 or 60 minutes evenings and weekends.

BART: (415) 992-2278. Bay Area Rapid Transit (BART) is an efficient way to get from San Francisco to the East Bay, where it runs to Fremont, North Concord, and Richmond; expansion will extend the system to Pleasanton and Pittsburg. Service to the Peninsula currently reaches only as far as Colma, but an airport extension is in the works. Trains run every 15 to 20 minutes, more often during peak hours. Rail service runs daily until about midnight starting at 4am on weekdays, 6am on Saturdays, and 8am on Sundays. Fares range from $1 to $4 for a one-way ticket, and are scheduled to increase again in 1997.

Tickets must be purchased from confusing machines that regularly break down; some give change, others do not (ask other riders for advice if you get confused). You also need your ticket to get out of the system, so don't throw it away after you enter. Hint: bring plenty of crisp dollar bills and assorted change to feed the machines. Most East Bay BART stations have free parking, although the lots fill up early most workdays.

BART connects to MUNI, SamTrans, and Golden Gate Transit in San Francisco, as well as to AC Transit in the East Bay and Santa Clara TA buses in the South Bay. You can connect from CalTrain to BART via MUNI in San Francisco by taking the 15, 30, or 45 bus from the CalTrain station at 4th and Townsend to the Montgomery Street BART station on Market, or if you're going the other way, by taking the 30 or 45 from the Powell Street BART station along 4th Street to the CalTrain station.

TRANSPORTATION

CalTrain: (800) 660-4BUS/4287. CalTrain runs from San Francisco south to San Jose and Gilroy, stopping at stations every two to five miles. Trains run approximately every hour from 5am to 10pm on weekdays, more often during commute hours. Weekend and holiday trains run 6am to 10pm every two hours. On Friday and Saturday nights, the last train south from San Francisco leaves at midnight. The trip from San Francisco to San Jose takes 90 minutes; from San Francisco to Palo Alto it takes an hour. Rush hour express trains cut these times significantly. Parking is available at most stations for a minimal fee.

Fares depend on the distance traveled. For example, the San Francisco to Palo Alto fare is $3.50, while San Francisco to San Jose is $4.50. Regular riders can save with a variety of passes, including ten-ride (valid for 90 days), monthly, weekly, and weekend passes. San Francisco to Palo Alto ten-ride passes cost $29.50, monthly passes run $91.75. Weekend passes for unlimited travel anywhere in the CalTrain system are $8. During the week, if you travel farther than your pass normally allows, you can pay to upgrade. Seniors, the disabled, and youths under 18 get discounts on tickets and monthly passes. If you have a MUNI Fast Pass, you may ride CalTrain free on all journeys that begin and end within San Francisco. An important tip: buy your ticket at the station window if it's open, because CalTrain adds a surcharge if you pay your fare on board when the station is open.

If you have a monthly CalTrain pass, you may *transfer* free to connecting TA buses and get a dollar off *transfers* to SamTrans buses. CalTrain monthly ticket holders can also purchase a Peninsula Pass for $25, which provides free local MUNI, TA, Light Rail, and SamTrans service (not limited to transfers), as well as partial credit for the Dumbarton Express and SamTrans express lines.

The CalTrain terminus in San Francisco is located South of Market at Fourth and Townsend Streets; but be warned, the station is far from downtown. You'll probably want to take a MUNI bus to your final destination. Several buses stop at the station: the 15, 30, 42, and 45, as well as the 80X, 81X, and 82X shuttle buses that operate between the station and downtown only during commute hours. A shuttle bus runs between San Francisco International Airport and the Millbrae station; it meets every train, although connections are better for northbound trains.

Dumbarton Express: (408) 321-2300, (800) 894-9908. The Dumbarton Bridge Express bus runs across its namesake, and is probably the most convenient way to get from the mid-Peninsula to the southern part of the East Bay on weekdays. There is only one route, between Palo Alto and the Union City BART station in the East Bay. It runs weekdays only, hourly during the day and every 15 minutes during rush hour. The fare is $1.50 for adults or $1 for youths; a monthly pass will set you back $60.

Golden Gate Transit: (415) 332-6600. Golden Gate Transit provides bus service in the North Bay and ferry service between Marin and San Francisco. Buses run through Marin, Contra Costa, Sonoma, and San Francisco counties, with weekend routes to Stinson Beach and Point Reyes. Bus routes in San Francisco begin at the Transbay Terminal located at First and Mission. Basic service operates every 15 to 90 minutes, while commute routes from West Marin to San Francisco operate every 2 to 20 minutes. Bus fares vary from $1.25 to $4.50, depending on how far you travel; exact change is required.

Golden Gate Transit also operates two ferry routes across the bay, from San Francisco to Larkspur and San Francisco to Sausalito. Ferries depart San Francisco from the Ferry Building at Embarcadero and Market. During commuter hours only, free shuttles are available to and from the ferry terminals and the surrounding areas in Marin or downtown San Francisco. On weekdays, ferries run every 30 to 60 minutes from 5:30am to 8:25pm. On weekends and holidays, there are five ferries each way, spread between 9:45am and 6pm. The Sausalito ferry departs every 90 minutes, on weekdays from 7am to 7pm; on Saturday, Sunday, and holidays it runs from 11am to 6pm. From Larkspur, the fare is $2.50 on weekdays and $4.25 on weekends and holidays. The ferry from Sausalito costs $4.25 each way.

PUBLIC TRANSPORTATION

MUNI: (415) 673-MUNI/6864. San Franciscans love to hate MUNI. The much maligned system gets its bad rap for its erratic service and surly drivers, yet San Francisco's Municipal Railway is one of the most comprehensive transit systems in the country in terms of geographic coverage: Wherever you are in the city, at least one bus stop is within a two-minute walk. MUNI's system consists mostly of electric buses, with a few diesel buses, five light-rail train routes, and the famous cable cars thrown in for good measure. The historic trolley cars that once appeared all over the city have recently made a reappearance on the Market Street F-Line. The renovated cars add a little panache to the ride from downtown to the Upper Market area. Many bus shelters have a map of the bus lines (although not every bus stop has a shelter); a map of all routes is sold at many convenience and drug stores.

Most buses run from 6am to midnight, although a few commuter buses stop at 6pm. The OWL routes run all night; the commuter (X) lines are fast routes straight downtown during rush hour. Limited (L) buses are faster than regular lines as they only stop at every third or fourth regular stop. Buses run from every two minutes to every 30 minutes during the day; OWL routes usually run about every hour. Timetables are available on the buses, but they are so approximate that most people just go to the bus stop and wait. Be warned, you may be in for the odd-but-infuriating 45-minute wait, especially in the evening.

The train routes (MUNI Metro) run from downtown west along Market Street, branching south and west; the underground trains are typically faster than buses along equivalent routes, although unpleasantly crowded during rush hour.

Bus, light rail, and tram fare is $1 (35 cents for youth/senior/disabled) and includes a transfer, valid for two more rides over the next hour and a half. Exact change is required. A monthly Fast Pass costs $35 for adults and $8 for youth, seniors, and the disabled. The pass is also valid for BART and CalTrain within San Francisco. Cable car fare is $2, and there are no transfers, although most passes can be used.

Red and White Fleet: (800) 229-2784. The Red and White Fleet offers ferry service from Pier 43 1/2 on Fisherman's Wharf in San Francisco to Sausalito, Tiburon, Angel Island, and Alcatraz, and from the Ferry Building at Embarcadero and Market Streets in San Francisco to Tiburon. The 20-minute trip to Tiburon from the Ferry Building runs Monday through Friday during commute hours. Ferries from Fisherman's Wharf are tourist oriented: the Sausalito and Tiburon boats operate from about 11am to 5pm on weekdays and 10:40am to 6pm on weekends and holidays (later during the summer). The Angel Island ferry makes only one trip on weekdays, but makes three on weekends and holidays. Adult tickets to Sausalito and Tiburon cost $5.50 each way; children ages 5 to 11 pay $2.75 each way. Angel Island tickets cost $9 round-trip.

Blue and Gold Fleet: (415) 705-5444. Blue and Gold runs ferries between San Francisco and Vallejo, Alameda, and Oakland. During the week, ferries run between Vallejo and the Ferry Building from 6:30am to 6:35pm, and between Vallejo and Fisherman's Wharf from 8:45am to 7:40pm. Weekends and holidays, ferries run between Vallejo and the Ferry Building from 10am to 6:30pm, and between Vallejo and Fisherman's Wharf from 8:45am to 7:40pm. The crossing takes about an hour each way. One-way tickets cost $7.50 adults, $6 ages 13 to 18, $4 ages 5 to 12. An 18-ride pass is $97, and a monthly pass is $140. In Oakland, ferries leave from Jack London Square and in Alameda from the Main Street Terminal; both locations have free parking. On weekdays, ferries leave about every 90 minutes. They run between the East Bay and the Ferry Building from 6am to 8pm and run to Fisherman's Wharf from 9am to 7pm. On weekends, ferries travel only twice daily, leaving Pier 39 at 8:55am and 4:30pm and the Ferry Building at 9:10am and 4:45pm. They return from Alameda at 10:10am and 5:15pm and leave Oakland at 10am and 5:30pm. The journey takes about 30 minutes. Tickets cost $3.75 each way ($2.50 for disabled and seniors and $1.50 for children 5 to 12 years old).

TRANSPORTATION

SamTrans: (800) 660-4BUS/4287. SamTrans runs throughout San Mateo County, as well as to and from downtown San Francisco, San Francisco International Airport, and games at 3Com Park/Candlestick. Four bus routes go to San Francisco International Airport: the 7B, the 7F, the 3B, and the 3X.

Buses generally run every 30 or 60 minutes beginning at 6am. Many of them stop around 6pm, although several continue until midnight; some run during commute hours only. On Saturdays, the service is sparse; on Sundays, even more so. Bikes are allowed on buses, and there are Park and Ride lots along some routes.

The fare is $1 for regular adult service, 50 cents for youths, 35 cents for the disabled, and 25 cents for seniors. Express service is $1.50, $1.75, or $2 for adults, depending on the route taken, with limited discounts available. Monthly passes can be bought for each different fare, any of which may be upgraded for a single journey by paying the cash difference.

SamTrans connects in various places with BART, CalTrain, AC Transit, Golden Gate Transit, the Dumbarton Express, and the Santa Clara County Transportation Agency. Passes and transfers from some of these companies are valid on certain SamTrans buses.

Santa Clara County TA: (408) 321-2300, (800) 894-9908. The Santa Clara County Transportation Agency (TA) operates both the buses and the Light Rail system within Santa Clara County. The regular adult fare is $1.10, or $1.75 to $2.25 for express commuter services. The youth fare is 55 cents, and seniors and the disabled pay 35 cents. Day passes are also available for twice these amounts. Monthly passes cost $33 for a regular pass, $16.50 for youths, $6 for seniors and the disabled, and $50 or $55 for the two types of express passes. Bus service begins at around 6am. Many buses continue until midnight and some until 2am, but a few stop after commute hours. They run every 15 to 30 minutes, less frequently in the evening. On weekends and holidays, buses start between 7am and 9am; some run until around 6pm and others as late as midnight. Weekend buses run every 30 to 60 minutes.

Light Rail Transit (LRT) currently has just one rail route, from the southern part of San Jose to the Great America Theme Park in Santa Clara. The Light Rail has connections to many bus lines that also connect to CalTrain, SamTrans, AC Transit, BART, Amtrak, and the Dumbarton Bridge Express. Tickets or passes from some of these companies may be accepted as part or full payment toward your TA ticket, and SamTrans accepts TA monthly and day passes as full fare at mutual stops.

GETTING AWAY

Air Travel

San Francisco Airport (SFO): (415) 876-7809, (415) 761-0800. The Bay Area's primary airport, with the most flights and international service, SFO is also one of the nation's busiest airports and a major gateway for flights across the Pacific to Asia and beyond. Look for big crowds and plenty of chaos.

Oakland Airport (OAK): (510) 577-4000. Oakland Airport is much smaller than SFO, but it's convenient to the East Bay, especially with its handy BART connection. OAK also serves bargain airlines like Southwest.

San Jose Airport (SJC): (408) 277-4759. One of the best-kept secrets around, San Jose Airport is close to Silicon Valley and as smaller and easier to negotiate than San Francisco International Airport.

GETTING AWAY

Airport Transportation

Driving and Parking

San Francisco International Airport (SFO) is located 14 miles south of San Francisco and maintains its own transit information line, (800) SFO-2008. Choose your route to SFO depending on your starting point and traffic; bad congestion, especially on Hwy 101 when there is a game at 3Com Park/Candlestick, can cause severe delays. Take Hwy 101 to San Bruno; the airport exit is between Millbrae Avenue and I-380. Or take I-280 to I-380 to Hwy 101 south and follow the signs into the airport (you never actually get on Hwy 101). To get to long-term parking, take the San Bruno Avenue East exit and follow the signs. Free shuttles will take you from the lot to your terminal. The charge is $6 for the first three hours, with a maximum of $11 per day. To get to short-term parking, take the airport exit and follow the signs; prices start at $1 for up to 30 minutes, with a maximum of $22 per day. Private airport parking lots in the area include **Park 'n Fly**, 101 Terminal Court, South SF, (415) 877-0304; **Anza Park & Sky**, 615 Airport Boulevard, Burlingame, (800) 453-9056; **PCA Parking**, 160 Produce Avenue, South SF, (415) 952-5730; and **SkyPark**, 1000 San Mateo Avenue, San Bruno, (415) 875-6655. They offer free shuttles from the lot to the airport terminals.

San Jose International Airport is located along Hwy 101 just north of San Jose; you'll see the airport at Guadalupe Parkway. Turn right off Guadalupe onto Brokaw—Brokaw becomes Airport Boulevard and takes you to the airport. Long-term parking is in the "green" or "yellow" lot on Airport Blvd. north of Terminal A; the charge is 75 cents per half hour, with a maximum of $8 per day. Short-term parking is in Terminal A or across from Terminal C; the charge is 75 cents per half hour, with a maximum of $17 per day. Shuttles to the terminals are available from the lots.

Oakland Airport is located next to the Bay in southwest Oakland, south of Alameda. Primary access is from Highway I-880 via the Hegenberger Road Exit, located south of the Oakland Coliseum; Hegenberger Road takes you to the airport. Long-term parking is $8.25 per day. Short-term parking is 85 cents per half hour with a maximum of $17 per day. Private airport parking lots include **Airpark**, 111 98th Avenue, Oakland, (510) 568-1221; **Park 'n Fly**, 82 98th Avenue, Oakland, (510) 633-0700; and **RBJ Airport Parking**, 106 Hegenberger Road, Oakland, (510) 562-3055.

Public Transportation

See Public Transportation section above for additional information on the companies and routes mentioned here. Four SamTrans bus routes go to **San Francisco International Airport**: the 7B, the 7F, the 3B, and the 3X. In San Francisco, both buses start at the Transbay Terminal at First and Mission Streets. The 7B follows surface streets, takes an hour from San Francisco, and costs $1, while the 7F follows Hwy 101, takes 40 minutes, and costs $1.75. The problem with the 7F is that only hand luggage is allowed between San Francisco and the airport. (Baggage can be taken on the 7B.) The buses run from 6am until midnight. The other two buses, the 3B and the 3X, run from the Daly City BART station to the airport. The 3B follows surface streets to the airport. The 3X follows I-280 and I-380 for most of its route. The adult fare for both buses is $1.

From the Peninsula, the 7F express route stops at SFO on its trip between Palo Alto and San Francisco (baggage is allowed between the airport and Palo Alto). Allow yourself a good hour for the ride from Palo Alto to SFO, or 40 minutes from Redwood City. The 7B local route stops at SFO on its trip between Redwood City and San Francisco. Allow yourself a little over an hour from Redwood City to SFO, 45 minutes from San Mateo. The adult fare for both buses is $1 from the Peninsula to the airport.

CalTrain also serves SFO. Hop a train to the Millbrae Station, then take the free CalTrain shuttle to the terminal building.

San Jose Airport is served by TA Light Rail Transit (LRT) and buses. From the Light Rail Metro/Airport Station in San Jose, catch the free Metro Airport Shuttle on

TRANSPORTATION

the southbound side of First Street. The shuttle runs every 10 minutes from 6am to 8am, then every 15 minutes until 6:48pm. After 6:48pm, you can catch the 10 TA bus. The 10 runs from the Metro/Airport LRT to the airport and the Santa Clara CalTrain station. It runs every 30 minutes during rush hour and every hour at other times. Peninsula residents can reach Santa Clara via either CalTrain or the 22 TA bus, which travels down El Camino from Palo Alto.

BART serves **Oakland Airport** via the Oakland Coliseum Station on the Fremont line. From the station, the AirBART shuttle costs $2 each way and runs about every 10 minutes, less frequently during evenings and weekends. You must have exact change when you get on the shuttle. See Public Transportation section above for information on how to reach BART.

Private Shuttles

Door-to-door airport shuttles are usually faster and simpler than public transportation, but more expensive. Do some research on all the different companies—the best deal depends on your situation. The basic fare from the city to SFO is in the neighborhood of $11 one way for one person. Many shuttles offer discounts when they pick up more than one person at a location; some charge extra if you exceed a baggage limit. Always make reservations well in advance for rides to the airport, and when you do, let the shuttle service know if you have any special luggage requirements, such as a bike or extra baggage.

Airport Connection: (415) 872-2552, (510) 841-0150.

Bay Area Shuttle: (415) 873-7771.

BayPorter Express: (415) 467-1800.

Lorrie's Airport Shuttle: (415) 334-9000.

Marin Airporter: (415) 461-4222.

Marin Door-to-Door: (800) 540-4815.

SFO Airporter: (415) 495-8404.

South and East Bay Airport Shuttle: (800) 548-4664.

Super Shuttle: (415) 558-8500.

Land Travel

Amtrak: (800) USA-RAIL/872-7245. Amtrak connects the Bay Area to the rest of North America via depots in San Jose, Oakland, Berkeley, Emeryville, and Richmond. (There is no station in San Francisco; Amtrak buses take passengers from San Francisco to Oakland.) Those familiar with Amtrak train service between Boston and Washington, D.C., will be mystified by Amtrak's dizzying schedules and amazed at how few actual trains run on the West Coast routes; the majority of service is provided by buses. There are several trains a day from San Jose and Oakland to Sacramento, and several others to the Central Valley. One train goes all the way up the Pacific Coast, from San Diego and Los Angeles through San Jose to Seattle and Vancouver, Canada. Another train runs east from Oakland through Truckee and Reno—passing through spectacular Sierra scenery—on the way to Salt Lake City, Denver, and Chicago. Most long-distance trains require reservations.

Greyhound: (800) 231-2222, (415) 495-1575. Greyhound Bus is an inexpensive alternative. You won't get anywhere in a hurry, but you won't pay through the nose either. Greyhound's San Francisco depot is in the Transbay Terminal at First and Mission. Greyhound's best deals are with the Ameripass, which gives you unlimited rides and an unrestricted schedule for a fixed fee. Make reservations more than two weeks in advance for discounts.

Neighborhoods & Housing

RESOURCES

Everyone wants to live in San Francisco, a fact that is no more apparent than when one is looking for an apartment here. Put simply, housing in the City by the Bay is neither inexpensive nor easy to find. But at the same time, the search for an abode is not as bad as people say. There are great deals and views to steal for those out there unwilling to give up. If you rely solely on the classifieds in the Sunday *San Francisco Examiner and Chronicle* and the weekly *Bay Guardian*, you should know in advance that lots of other people will be doing the same thing. The advertised place that sounds perfect to you is bound to have a line of prospective renters snaking out the door. Good places go fast, so no one resource is the key. Every angle must be exploited. One must live, eat, and breathe apartment hunting until the search is successful.

Here are some practical tips from successful hunters. You'll see them watching you from rounded bay windows, their bare feet on warm hardwood, the fireplace glow flickering off high ceilings, as you trudge up the street to yet another appointment. Creativity and focus are the keys: Carry blank checks with you 24 hours a day so you can be the fastest deposit in the West. Dress neatly and go to the neighborhoods where you want to live. Walk around and look for For Rent signs in the windows, then knock on the manager's door or take down the phone number and call from a nearby booth. Hang out in cafés in areas you would like to call home, and put out the word you're looking for a place to rent. Check bulletin boards at cafés and laundromats for rental listings. Go to the nearest college or university student union and check their apartment files and bulletin boards. Write up a biography describing who you are, what you do, your credit history, and why you are a valuable tenant. (Some folks have even shot home videos to impress a landlord.) And last but not least, offer prospective landlords more money per month or anything else you can provide—gardening, dog walking, lobby sweeping—that will distinguish you from the legions of hunters.

The Bay Area also offers a number of privately owned housing agencies with exclusive listings you won't find in the newspapers (they are usually free to landlords, unlike classifieds). If knowledge is power, these private databases can help in San Francisco's competitive housing market. You will find agency listings far more informative than the two lines of type in a newspaper ad. Descriptions give clients a thorough look at amenities, facilities, and roommate profiles (for those seeking housing-to-share). Learn when the new listings appear and get there that morning.

Try not to stress. After all, countless others have found themselves in your predicament and have made it through. A few tips for newcomers to the market: avail yourself of every resource, be sure to allow at least three months for your search, and be very clear on what you consider life's necessities and what you can do without. Take your time, have faith, and remember, the warm hardwood awaits!

American Property Exchange: 170 Page St. (Octavia), SF, (800) 747-7784; Fax (415) 255-8865; email AMPROPEX@aol.com. A full-service real estate firm with a good stock of furnished and unfurnished rentals. This place caters to an upscale, professional clientele seeking housing convenient to the financial district. Vacancies are available for long- and short-term rentals. Ask an agent about their extensive relocation package specifically designed to take the stress out of your move. If you're on a limited budget, the prices may be too crippling to your wallet.

IMPRESSING A LANDLORD

The pairing between landlord and tenant is similar to that between employer and employee: both sides have a lot to offer and a lot to lose, so mutual suspicion is the rule. When the San Francisco rental market is tight, as it is today, landlords often have the luxury of choosing among many qualified applicants. Renters have a better chance of getting the place of their dreams if they can impress a potential landlord right from the start, thereby ensuring an edge over other applicants. While landlords can't legally discriminate against a potential tenant based on race or religion, they can screen for who they think will be stable and credit-worthy. Your reliability will boil down to a few key issues: references from former landlords (you don't want reports about trashing a previous apartment, then fighting an eviction), and proof you can and will pay rent, including a stable job profile, good income, and a solid credit history. Preparing a package with information addressing these concerns will show prospective landlords you will make an excellent tenant and are serious about finding a good place to live. Obtain a credit report far enough in advance to correct any mistakes, and be prepared to find a cosponsor if you have had a troubled past. Always carry all the information you'll need to fill out an application (bank account number, references, past landlord information). And don't forget to bring your checkbook so you can leave a deposit for that place you really love before 18 other people do.

Community Rentals: 2105 Van Ness Ave. (Pacific), SF, (415) 474-2787. • 470 Castro St. (18th St.), SF, (415) 552-9595. Offers listings for vacancies as well as housing-to-share; although the latter are limited, used primarily by Castro residents seeking same sexual-orientation housemates. Listings are updated daily and organized by neighborhood. Regular memberships, which include both housing-to-share and vacancy listings, are $75 for 60 days. If you do not find housing through the agency (which only happens to one out of every five customers), you are entitled to a $50 refund. If you are only interested in housing-to-share, the fee is $30 for a 60-day membership, in which case access is restricted solely to housing-to-share information.

Metro Rents: 546 Grant Ave. (Pine), SF, (415) 563-RENT/7368; Fax (415) 563-0383. Has extensive listings of apartments and houses for rent. Lists vacancies only and will refer you to Roommate Referral (see listing below) if you are seeking shared housing. The property listings detail amenities such as fireplace, dishwasher, total number of bathrooms, and outside spaces. All aspects of housing are covered in these descriptive listings, including whether the floors have been redone recently, what sort of sunlight you can expect, and if there's a view. Basic 60-day membership is $65. Phone computer search membership is $95. Metro Rents does offer a $40 money-back guarantee should you not find housing through the listings.

Roommate Referral: 610A Cole St. (Haight), SF, (415) 626-0606, (415) 558-9191. The original San Francisco roommate service. If you are seeking housing-to-share or a roommate to share housing, this service will be invaluable. Both in-house listings and dial-up service are available. The listings, organized by neighborhood, offer situations with rents ranging from $200 to $1,000 a month. Profile sheets give an overview of household amenities and the roommates presently entrenched. Many listings offer a profile of the ideal tenant, such as smoker, nonsmoker, pets, cats only, neat freak, whatever. It is best to be ruthlessly honest when filling out your personal profile. Find roommates and households that fit well, rather than taking the "I just want some place to live now" approach. You will have to live with these people, and it will be easier if you all have the same values about bathroom cleanliness. It is free to list vacancies seeking roommates. For those seeking vacancies, $29 will buy you a one-month membership offering phone access to listings and profiles. This service is only available with a touch-tone phone. For $34 you may enroll in the Deluxe Membership, which includes four months of access to in-house listings and one month of the dial-up service.

Roommate Express: 2269 Chestnut St. (Scott), SF, (415) 928-4530, (415) 397-4008. Complete roommate services for residents throughout the Bay Area. Using personality surveys completed by each applicant, a computer-matching system generates a list of compatible roommate opportunities especially for you. This process ensures all roommates will share similar bathroom and kitchen values. There are 70 locations in the Bay Area for in-house research, as well as a 24-hour dial-up service. Membership runs for 60 days. A four-month roommate guarantee is included, in case you run into that *Single White Female* situation. Listing a vacancy will cost you $39, seeking vacancies $44. Prices include application fee, computer matchline service, and deposit.

NEIGHBORHOOD PROFILES

On your first day in San Francisco, you will most likely find yourself at some lookout point, dazzled by a sweeping view of the urban skyline. The city's drop-dead beauty is generally the first thing that strikes newcomers, and from a distant aerie, the hills and architecture blend into a coherent and ravishing whole. Once you get into the streets and start pounding the pavement, however, the web of diversity is what will sustain your attention. San Francisco is a city of neighborhoods, and you can never walk more than a few blocks without seeing a change in scene, architecture, and atmosphere that will keep you enthralled long after you've become a resident yourself.

Every San Franciscan given the opportunity will passionately extol the virtues of his or her neighborhood (and the exceedingly intelligent and hip people who choose to live there), even if he or she can't define exactly where the borders of that neighborhood lie. Each of the following profiles was written by someone who lives in and loves their neighborhood—locals who can tell you what to expect in terms of housing, rent, and parking, as well as who your neighbors will be and where you can look for a café and grocery store.

Keep in mind, though, that many comments about San Francisco communities are relative. It's hard to understand how housing in a neighborhood with a median home price of $350,000 can be called plentiful and affordable. Just remember, San Francisco housing is consistently rated the nation's least affordable. What may seem a good deal by local standards will still seem incredibly expensive compared to other markets.

Still, there are a few general rules about pricing in San Francisco. As you climb the hills, housing tabs go up with the quality of the views. And as the commute from downtown increases, costs shrink (there are some exceptions to this rule, most notably the St. Francis Wood area).

Newcomers tend to gravitate to the neighborhoods in the northeast part of the city—the Marina, North Beach, Russian Hill, Nob Hill, and Pacific Heights—as these

SECURITY DEPOSITS

The Bay Area's tight rental market means that landlords can generally have their way with tenants during negotiations. Security deposits, however, are one area where tenants are protected by a number of state and local laws. What is a security deposit? No matter what the landlord says or the lease reads, state law defines it as "any payment, fee, deposit, or charge" other than the first month's rent paid to a landlord "on or before initial occupancy"; no matter whether it's called last month's rent, a cleaning deposit, or anything else, it's still a security deposit. California law also requires landlords to repay deposits within two weeks of a tenant moving out. If any money is withheld, the charges must be itemized in writing, and landlords cannot withhold money for normal wear and tear (a decidedly vague term). Residents of San Francisco, Berkeley, and Hayward are also entitled to interest, payable annually, on their security deposits. For more information, contact the nonprofit **San Francisco Tenants Union**, 558 Capp St., SF, (415) 282-6622.

NEIGHBORHOODS & HOUSING

are closest to San Francisco's best-known attractions and full of other young newcomers. Don't rule out the lesser-known areas, though, until you've read these profiles and paid a visit yourself. They are often just as habitable and less expensive than the better-known environs—even though they don't have a view of the Golden Gate Bridge.

The following neighborhoods are listed in roughly alphabetical order, with similar adjacent neighborhoods grouped together in one listing. San Franciscans and real estate agents can argue forever about where boundaries lie, however, and many smaller areas have their own names and descriptions not listed here. This is not a definitive map, but instead a good overview of the city's diversity.

Bayview/Hunter's Point

It is astonishing that many people who have lived in San Francisco for years have either never heard of the Bayview/Hunter's Point area or have only heard bad things. Although best known for its low socio-economic and industrial climate, the neighborhood has shown a progressive revitalization in recent years.

Formerly centered around blue-collar industries, the largest being the now-inactive Hunter's Point Naval Shipyard, the area is home primarily to African-Americans and Asian-Americans, and boasts several good restaurants, historical buildings, and two community college campuses. World-famous 3Com/Candlestick Park lies at the southern edge of the neighborhood. Numerous bus lines traverse these blocks, and easy freeway access to both I-280 and Hwy 101 has added to the growth in small businesses and restaurants. A light rail system running along Third Street to the Embarcadero and Fisherman's Wharf is currently in the planning stages. Bayview/Hunter's Point also boasts the warmest weather in the city, sheltered from the ocean and its summer fog and winter storms.

Housing is very affordable, particularly for San Francisco. The average home is under $150,000, and becoming more readily available as redevelopment plans progress. As a result, the area boasts the highest rate of home ownership in the city. Much of the housing construction was tied to the shipyard's growth during World War II and after. Not all areas have been equally revitalized, however, so selectivity is advised when looking around.

Bernal Heights

Bernal Heights has been described as the village at the edge of the Emerald City—a perfect synopsis for what is, in many ways, an idyllic urban corner. Called The Hill by local residents, it is a compact, self-sufficient neighborhood with Old World values and small-town charm. Located south of the Mission, Bernal is also well-protected from the fog, and the hills have kept earthquake damage relatively low.

The rents here are surprisingly affordable, in part because Bernal is not well known. Housing in this neighborhood is not readily available, however, and is quickly snatched up once on the market. You will find both houses and flats—many of wooden clapboard construction reminiscent of the Northeast—along with some small cottages surrounded by private garden space tucked behind larger houses. The average house costs about $300,000. There are some dicey areas where safety is a concern, so look around before you sign that lease.

Cortland Avenue is the main thoroughfare. The MUNI 24 Divisadero bus runs along it, connecting Bernal to BART and the city's northern reaches. The north side of the hill has the most commercial activity.

Bernal is a place where a sense of community thrives. The Bernal Heights Community Center offers workshops in dance and crafts for all ages. Community gardens—like the walk at Virginia Avenue and Winfield Street—are scattered around The Hill. People say hello as you pass on the street, and they care about their neighborhood. Yes, it's a lot like Mayberry RFD, except that it's on the edge of San Francisco, the Emerald City. Besides, how can you not like a neighborhood whose best-known food market is called Good Life Grocery?

Castro/Upper Market

The Castro, located south of Market Street between Church Street and Twin Peaks, is where a substantial number of the city's gay men (and to a much lesser extent, lesbians) have made their home, and is arguably the city's liveliest neighborhood. The Upper Market area, centered around Market Street above Castro, is a quieter residential extension of the neighborhood.

Ten years ago, the Castro scene focused on bars; today it revolves more around gyms, cafés, and juice joints (not that you can't also find less wholesome fun). The neighborhood's current, more mild-mannered nature owes much to the gay population's assimilation into the city at large. There has also been an increase in the number of straight families living in the Castro (although you still won't see many baby strollers in these parts). But don't think that the Castro has gone dull—any given night here will have streets full of people, crowded restaurants and bars, and more beautiful men than you're likely to find anywhere else in the city.

The Castro's many interesting and offbeat shops, cafés, and bars cluster along Market, Castro, and 18th streets. Other byways in the area are primarily residential and fairly quiet. Housing is made up of small apartment buildings, including many beautiful Victorians, and a few single unit homes (especially above Market Street). Apartment prices are fairly high, with $700 studios not uncommon. A typical house will set you back $400,000.

Public transportation in the area is plentiful and convenient. The corner of Market and Castro is right on the underground MUNI line, and there are innumerable buses regularly passing through the area. The newly reinstated F Line, whose retro streetcars run along Market to the Financial District, has added a touch of class to city transportation. Despite this wealth of choices, there is no shortage of people searching for parking, especially along Castro Street.

During the summer, the fog is generally held at bay by Twin Peaks until mid-afternoon, when it pours down into the Castro with a wind that will send you running for a nice, warm latte. Fortunately, you'll never have to go more than a couple of doors to find one.

On the north side of Market Street lies an area known as **Duboce Triangle**, a quiet, tree-lined haven behind a funky Safeway. Bordered by Market Street, Duboce Street, and Buena Vista Park, this neighborhood's arms-length distance from the Castro and the Haight, easy access to public transportation, and moderate housing prices, combined with its well-tended Victorians and some of the healthiest trees in the city, attract a diverse crowd. Residents range from young gay men wanting to be near the action of the Castro to elderly couples who enjoy the proximity to parks and hospitals. With less crime and fewer panhandlers than the nearby lower Haight, this area is an attractive choice for those who want to be near the action, but not mired in it.

Chinatown

Although San Francisco's Chinatown draws hordes of tourists, don't be fooled into thinking the neighborhood resembles a Hollywood movie set. Chinatown is so authentic, in fact, that most people who have not lived in Taiwan, Hong Kong, or mainland China will feel as if they've moved abroad. First-generation immigrants from Asia set the tone here: store signs are commonly written in both Chinese characters and Roman letters, and street conversation is more often in Cantonese than English.

Housing tends toward apartments located above street-level shops. Smaller buildings and single-family homes are more common as you climb up Nob and Russian hills. Prices are moderate, partly because many residents graduate to less-crowded areas as soon as they can afford it, and partly because English-speaking house hunters don't have easy access to the many signs and listings posted only in Chinese. English listings are more common on the neighborhood's borders with Nob Hill, Russian Hill, and North Beach, wedges of real estate where you can find some great deals.

NEIGHBORHOODS & HOUSING

Located next to the heart of downtown and the Financial District, Chinatown is far and away San Francisco's most densely populated neighborhood, with usually pleasant weather and busy street life to match. On Saturday mornings, the markets along Stockton Street teem with shoppers hunting for everything from asparagus and bok choy to shrimp, frogs, and roast duck. Looking for parking can be a maddening experience when the streets are filled with trucks, buses, and pedestrians. Auto theft and vandalism is also quite common; a garage is a must for car owners for that reason and because there is simply no place to park. The downtown commute is just a short walk and bus service is plentiful, making this a great place to live without a car.

Crocker Amazon/Excelsior

These two adjoining neighborhoods, located on the fringe of San Francisco south of I-280, are among the least known of the city, even by natives. Geneva Avenue divides them, acting as the northern border for Crocker Amazon and the southern border for the Excelsior. Together, they are the perfect antithesis to the Marina.

Ethnically diverse, Crocker Amazon residents are generally working class, and have often lived in the neighborhood for years. Close to Daly City, the weather is moderately windy and foggy. Housing is a mix of single- and multi-family units. The average home is in the $230,000 range, with much of the stock constructed in the 1940s on acreage that was once a Spanish land grant. The Excelsior has many of the same features, with a few more sunny days. If you're not meeting native San Franciscans like you had hoped, try this neighborhood. This is where they live. Although it's about as far as you can get from downtown and still be in San Francisco, I-280 and BART pass close by. Nearby McLaren Park and San Bruno Mountain Park are great resources for anyone looking for a quick golf game or a long hike.

Downtown/Financial District/Jackson Square

In San Francisco, downtown living lacks the cachet it may hold in New York, but what it lacks in glamour, it makes up for in convenience. After all, where else can a downtown worker live and walk to the office in under five minutes? The area is also convenient for commuters heading to the East Bay, as it is just a short drive from the Bay Bridge or walk from BART.

Housing consists primarily of posh high-rise condominiums—most with doormen—scattered among the office buildings, the largest of them being the Golden Gateway Center near Sydney Walton Park. (Many of these buildings offer units for rent, as well.) Don't look for any neighborhood feeling. The streets empty at night when the workers head home, and the only food store is the Safeway/Bon Appetit in the Golden Gateway Center. But residents do have an excellent selection of restaurants, especially fine dining establishments catering to the business scene. Reflecting the doorman-high-rise setting, prices are generally high, although many residents feel they get good value for their money with the services and amenities.

Glen Park

A small, beautiful, and friendly community is what you will find just south of Noe Valley in the neighborhood called Glen Park. Easily accessible by I-280 as well as BART, Glen Park is an ethnically diverse area of mostly two- and three-bedroom homes (you will be hard-pressed to find any apartments or other rentals). You might expect such housing to cater only to families, but a look at the demography reveals a mix—singles, couples sans children, and families. Architecturally diverse, there are Victorian, Marina, A-frame, and other styles jumbled together. Formerly a farming area and one of the city's older neighborhoods, Glen Park survived both the 1906 and 1989 earthquakes with little more than a few broken dishes. Very community oriented, most of the residents have lived here for many years.

Home prices are moderate for San Francisco, with the average just under $300,000. Typical of the city, almost every house has a small front yard, if any, but a large backyard. Sometimes a little fog hangs over the rooftops—it generally burns off early in the day—but mostly sunny, warm days prevail. The main commercial drag, Chenery Street, is about five blocks long, and most of Glen Park's eateries and stores are scrunched together along it. A few are situated on Diamond Street, but they soon give way to homes.

One of the best features of the neighborhood is Glen Canyon Park. Besides the usual recreation center, baseball field, and open space you expect in city parks, it boasts two miles of walking and hiking trails through tall, majestic eucalyptus. Unlike some places, the trails and park are both people and dog friendly.

Haight-Ashbury/Cole Valley

Haight-Ashbury is probably the most notorious residential area in the city, but it doesn't really live up to its image. The cheap Victorian flats of yesteryear aren't so cheap anymore, and the sheer volume of tourists and homeless people can sometimes make the area noisy, crowded, and downright aggravating. Nevertheless, its historic reputation and youthful energy keep the Haight popular with young hippie wannabees, creating a sense of community among those who still believe (in spite of Jerry's death).

For those who enjoy the scene, Haight Street offers one of the livelier neighborhood shopping areas, full of restaurants, bars, and retail galore—and without the chichi atmosphere found in many districts. The Victorian architecture on the surrounding streets is also some of the most impressive in the city, although a number of buildings verge on being dilapidated. While rents have gone up plenty since the Summer of Love, they are still moderate by central city standards. Driving and parking can seem nearly impossible—with pedestrians swarming into the streets and available spaces at a bare minimum—but plentiful public transit makes downtown commuting reasonable. Golden Gate Park offers an oasis of calm within easy walking distance. Old-timers complain that crime is a growing concern in the area, highlighted by an increased police presence, but minor drug offenses are the biggest problem.

The area known as Cole Valley is often lumped in with the Haight, but it possesses a charm all its own, as area residents are quick to note. Located up the hillside south of Haight Street, Cole Valley is characterized by shady, hilly streets and a laid-back, quiet atmosphere. The area has a mix of long-time residents and young professionals attracted by the architecture and neighborly feel. Cole Street offers a few lively cafés, restaurants, and retail establishments. The view from Twin Peaks, located just south of the area, is also impressive.

While the traditional Victorian flat can be found throughout Cole Valley, the area also claims a number of more modern dwellings. Single-family homes and apartment buildings are common, and you can find a variety of quaint and attractive living spaces in the medium to upper price range. Prices increase as you go up the hill, with the average abode approaching $500,000 in the nicest areas. Parking is often a hassle, plus there are a number of narrow streets that demand expert parallel-parking skills. Many dwellings come equipped with garages or parking areas, however. Crime is not much of a problem; most lawbreakers hang out closer to Haight Street.

Lakeshore/Park Merced

Lakeshore and Park Merced are located in the city's southwest corner, just south of the Sunset, bordering Lake Merced and the Harding Park Municipal Golf Course. The area more closely resembles Peninsula cities than downtown neighborhoods: the housing is a mix of moderately-priced apartments and single-family homes built after World War II, with a lot of rentals suited to students associated with nearby San Francisco State University. At the other end of the age spectrum, the Park Merced development incorporates several 300-plus condominium-unit buildings that are retirement homes for many seniors.

NEIGHBORHOODS & HOUSING

Life here is centered around local attractions, far removed from distant downtown. A bike and running path parallels Lake Merced Boulevard, which is lined with fragrant eucalyptus trees and shrubs. Ocean Beach, Stern Grove, the San Francisco Zoo, and Stonestown Shopping Center are also nearby. Proximity to the ocean brings lots of fog. Daly City BART station serves downtown commuters.

Marina

Expensive, yuppie, much sought after, and incredibly beautiful all describe the Marina district. Located just off the Bay between busy Lombard Street and Marina Boulevard, this area is popular with both city residents and tourists. The Marina is home to a combination of small, charming, single-family Mediterranean bungalows and large apartment buildings (studio and one-bedroom units are especially common, contributing to the young, single atmosphere). Rents start anywhere from $800 for a studio to well over $3,000 for two bedrooms. Homes average well over $500,000. Street parking is at a premium, but many buildings have garages.

As you might expect, the Marina's popularity declined dramatically after the 1989 earthquake damaged and destroyed many buildings in the neighborhood. Nothing like thousands of people losing everything and a few deaths to kill a real estate market. But memories are short, and once-moribund Chestnut Street has roared back as one of the city's preeminent retail stretches, alive with restaurants, shops, banks, coffee houses, clothing boutiques, delicatessens, and movie theaters. Anything you could possibly want or need is located here, as the young, beautiful, Spandex-clad throngs can attest. (Friday evenings are reportedly singles' night at Marina Safeway. Talk about one-stop shopping!)

Nothing has changed to make it any safer, but like the mermaids of yore, the Marina's siren song proves hard to resist. Other than the vibrant energy that ripples along Chestnut Street, the area's primary attraction is proximity to parks, recreational facilities, and open spaces for outdoor activities: jogging along Marina Green, windsurfing at Crissy Field, tennis at Moscone Center, bicycling across the Golden Gate Bridge, it's all here. The generally favorable weather is also less foggy than San Francisco's other waterfront neighborhoods. The biggest crime issue is CD players stolen from Jeeps or BMWs. Several bus lines service the neighborhood, making downtown commuting convenient for the ambitious young executives who live here.

Mission

The Mission District's character is largely influenced by the rich cultures of Latin America, the ancestral home of much of the neighborhood's population. Taquerias, salsa nightclubs, Brazilian eateries, Mexican piñatas, and Day of the Dead decorations enhance the Mission's flavor. Well sheltered from the ocean fog, the area's relatively steady diet of warm weather adds to the feeling. Artists, musicians, and Generation Xers pepper the mix, creating a unique multicultural, all-inclusive community. The young hipsters have also attracted what is arguably the city's liveliest collection of bars, restaurants, and cafés.

Housing is less expensive than in many other parts of San Francisco, but this is definitely city living. Many apartments offered on the main thoroughfares of Valencia and Mission are above shops. There are wonderful houses and Victorian flats, offering gardens and views, available for rent on any of the neighborhood's abundant side streets, many of which are beautifully tree lined. The jewels are snatched up quickly, so be diligent and act fast once you find what you like. Direct your search for housing west of Mission Street for a safer climate. Crime is a sometime concern in the barrio, especially near the occasional housing project. The typical home goes for a little over $200,000.

A primary drawback to this area is parking. If your accommodations do not come with a driveway or garage, parking can be a bear. Street cleaning regulations and competitors who slide into spots before you can get your blinker on will sometimes leave you circling several blocks. The flip side to this coin, however, is the area's good public transportation, which makes owning a car unnecessary for daily living. BART and several bus lines conveniently traverse the neighborhood, making for an easy downtown commute. You will also find it impossible to hail a cab, but with so much to do and see on every street, and great public transportation to help you do it, who needs one? (Tip: Bartenders, supermarkets, and friendly shopkeepers will usually call a cab for you, if you ask nicely.)

Nob Hill/Russian Hill

Ever since the great 19th-century robber barons built their mansions atop Nob Hill, the area has lived with the Snob Hill sobriquet; neighboring Russian Hill's reputation is only somewhat less intimidating. The local socialite rag, the *Nob Hill Gazette*, doesn't help, with its slogan, "More than an address, an attitude," and its frequent reporting on debutante balls. In reality, the robber-baron mansions burned in the fire following the 1906 quake, and today these quiet neighborhoods have more diversity and less snobbery than Pacific Heights. Chinatown has spread over the years to cover much of the area, bringing many restaurants, sewing shops, and other small businesses. For every luxury high-rise—uniformed doormen and all—there are many modest apartment buildings, small houses, and postquake flats.

Housing prices are as diverse as the buildings, from cheap apartments on the edge of the Tenderloin to penthouses renting for more than most mortgages. Away from the edges, however, the average place is seriously expensive. It's nearly impossible to find a house for less than $400,000, or a one-bedroom apartment for under $1,000 per month. In addition to the famous hilltop views for those lucky enough to afford them, a big draw is the neighborhoods' easy access to downtown—just a short walk—making them a convenient place to live without a car. In fact, parking here is such an incredible nightmare, anyone without a garage frequently regrets owning a car. Many pedestrian stairways through small parks make for pleasant, albeit strenuous strolling. A few buses navigate the hills, but cable cars provide the bulk of public transit, which translates to a charming but slow and expensive way to travel if you don't get a monthly Fast Pass.

The hills and narrow, steep streets discourage through traffic, resulting in many quiet stretches. The primary exception is the steady stream of gawkers who line up on Lombard Street to drive the crooked block between Hyde and Leavenworth streets. Most people do their shopping around the edges of the hills: in Chinatown and North Beach, along California and Polk Streets, or in shopping centers near Fisherman's Wharf. Weather is generally good, as the neighborhoods are far enough east to enjoy sun when the Richmond or even the Marina gets covered. The area is also viewed as relatively safe, making it popular with single women. (Cars are much less safe than people; theft is fairly common.)

Noe Valley

Noe Valley—actually an expansive plateau and steep hills that sit east of Twin Peaks and west of the Mission—has two distinguishing characteristics: first, in this earthquake-jittery metropolis, it is one of the few areas that emerged from the devastating 1906 temblor almost completely unscathed; second, the sidewalks of the main commercial strip, 24th Street between Castro and Church, are usually filled with a bumper crop of baby buggies. Suffice it to say, many bohemian yuppies who have traded in the singles scene for a nice Victorian and a Dr. Spock book live here. Not that *all* of Noe Valley's residents are politically liberal thirtysomething professionals enjoying the small town, nesting atmosphere, however. The area also houses a mix of recent college graduates and longtime residents—including some native San Franciscans—who have watched the inexorable gentrification of what was once a working-class neighborhood.

NEIGHBORHOODS & HOUSING

Although it isn't Pacific Heights yet, housing prices are in the moderate to pricy range, and creeping up. Tales of woe, such as tiny basement studios renting for $700 per month, are becoming common. Little bungalows in the flatter sections often sell for $250,000, with most houses priced in the $500,000 range (don't even ask about the Victorian mansions on Sanchez hilltop).

For residents, Noe Valley's attractions are obvious. It's very sunny (the summer fog tends to hang on the tip of Twin Peaks without dropping down). It has (by this city's warped standards) manageable parking, 24th Street notwithstanding. It's relatively safe, save for the occasional keyed car or burglary. It's easily accessible from downtown by both BART and MUNI, yet feels far enough away from the madding crowd that it could almost be a suburb. (Tourists and residents of other neighborhoods rarely visit.) It's convenient for commuting to the Peninsula, where all the jobs are. It is home to some of the city's most gorgeous Victorian houses—most of them well-kept—and panoramic views. Finally, it's reputed to have excellent public schools for when those baby-buggy passengers are matriculating toward their BMW futures.

North Beach/Telegraph Hill

North Beach is for those who value a good latte and a newspaper in a friendly café on a Sunday morning above money and sex. In other words, the Marina it ain't. This lively borough in the city's northeast corner is full of tourists and an eclectic crowd of resident locals reminiscent of and nostalgic for the Beat poets that thrived here in the late 1950s. If you love cafés, bars, good food, and a central location, this is it. If you like convenient parking, forget it. It offers the city's worst street parking in a city known for its lack of curbside spaces. The people of North Beach range from old Italian families to downtown suits, and from students to the no-visible-means-of-support café goers who always seem to have enough money for a double latte.

The area offers a wide variety of apartments in the moderately expensive price range, many of them built mid-century. In the valley along Columbus Avenue you can find two- to four-bedroom Victorian flats starting at $450 per room. (This is not a place to find studios, although they do exist.) Telegraph Hill—which in real estate terms means the area closer to Coit Tower and the top of the eponymous hill—is more expensive, offering quieter streets, better views, and more modern, better-kept buildings, as well as more single-family homes. The east side of the hill is home to the charming cottages along the Filbert and Greenwich steps, which contrast with the luxury apartment complexes at the base of the hill. Prices fall closer to Bay Street, especially near the North Point housing projects.

North Beach has some notable attractions. If you work downtown, the location is perfect; if not, you can still walk to BART in 20 minutes or take one of the many buses that crisscross the neighborhood. The area is quite safe at night: a few sloppy homeless folks or bunches of young drunk lawyers in love down from Nob Hill is usually about as bad as it gets. There is plenty of local energy along Grant and Columbus avenues, with cafés, bars, restaurants, and bookstores everywhere. You're also only a stone's throw from Chinatown, home to great food and good, cheap produce, and Fisherman's Wharf, where you can find a supermarket and the ferries. Spend a sunny afternoon café hopping, or a night on the town. If you wake up in love, you'll know you're a North Beacher.

Oceanview/Merced/Ingleside

These three districts, more commonly referred to as the OMI, interlock near the southwest corner of San Francisco, just north of Daly City. Bordered by I-280 to the south and east, 19th Avenue to the west, and Holloway Avenue to the north, the neighborhoods are similar. Most homes are two-story single-family residences, priced around $200,000. The affordability has produced a large number of resident homeowners. Many members of the community have been here a long time, some operating businesses near their homes. Several small parks and recreational areas dot the communities and there are numerous schools. Unfortunately, a rising crime rate has afflicted these neighborhoods.

Ocean Avenue is a major thoroughfare, running east and west, and offers a wide variety of shops and restaurants. Eating establishments primarily include Thai, Korean, and Chinese venues, with a smattering of Mexican and some barbecue joints mixed in. As with most of western San Francisco, the weather is frequently foggy, but on clear days the ocean to the west and Mt. Tamalpais north across the Golden Gate Bridge are visible from the hilltop areas. Despite the distance from downtown, one of the OMI's strong points is its access to public transportation; eight major streetcar and bus lines traverse the area and BART runs nearby, connecting to major areas of the city. These neighborhoods feel quite distant from downtown San Francisco—places people go to get away from the crowding and to find more affordable housing.

Pacific Heights/Lower Pacific Heights

This is one of San Francisco's most appealing and expensive neighborhoods, where you can hobnob with both aspiring yuppies and the truly wealthy. A studio apartment here can cost as much as a two-bedroom house elsewhere, and million-dollar homes are the norm. The neighborhood's steep prices also apply to local merchants' wares. Pacific Heights housing—a mixture of mostly classic Victorian flats, luxury high-rise apartments, and single-family mansions, with a few modern buildings thrown in—is in high demand and has low turnover. Expect long lines and huge crowds at any available dwelling listed in the newspaper. If you are lucky enough to be the first applicant, be sure to bring your checkbook and a spotless credit record.

The higher you live on the hill, the more costly—you pay for the stunning bay views—and the quieter. At the foot of the hill's northern slope lies Cow Hollow, where housing is almost as expensive as it is at the higher elevations, the sun is often hidden behind those hills, and yuppies are frequently seen cavorting on busy Union Street. If viewing sailboats isn't as important to you as staying solvent, but you love the neighborhood's youthful energy, try "Pacific Lows." The area roughly between Sacramento Street and Geary Boulevard—part of the Western Addition until gentrification transformed Fillmore Street—is now referred to as Lower Pacific Heights, a reference to both altitude and rents (prices drop and crime increases as you head southwest).

People pay extra to live here for many reasons: the brilliant views from Alta Plaza and Lafayette parks, the elegant homes along quiet streets, the relatively low crime rate (but don't leave that new Jeep Grand Cherokee unprotected), the easy downtown commute, and the beautiful neighbors hanging out on Fillmore and Union streets. The fog frequently hangs over the Richmond just to the west, and even parking is manageable compared to Russian Hill or North Beach. Just don't come to "Specific Whites" for diversity. Nevertheless, the area is a charming one where local merchants offer small-town appeal and friendly neighbors make it a true neighborhood.

Potrero Hill

Perched on the hills south of the city's heart, the Potrero Hill neighborhood offers spectacular panoramic views of downtown, the Oakland-Bay Bridge, Oakland, Alameda, and even 3Com/Candlestick Park, making it a favorite location for filming television shows and movies. Affectionately called The Hill, it is ethnically diverse and family oriented. Many businesses are owned and operated by residents, and many artisans—attracted to warehouse lofts—call it home. It can be quite windy, but lies far enough from the ocean to remain clear and warm during much of the spring and summer, making its various parks and open spaces inviting venues.

Housing here was built primarily during the aftermath of the 1906 quake until the 1930s, and is in the moderate to expensive range for the city. Most apartments run between $700 and $1,500 per month. Homes in this formerly working-class neighborhood are two or three bedrooms and cost $250,000 and up. New condominiums and lofts developed over the past few years sell in the vicinity of $200,000 to $350,000. The southern side of the hill is industrial and less expensive, especially near the housing projects.

Although it feels worlds away from downtown, Potrero's close proximity to other parts of the city is a major draw, and it is serviced by three major bus lines. Two freeways, Hwy 101 and I-280, traverse the neighborhood, and can be noisy for nearby neighbors. Bookstores, restaurants, a health club, delicatessens, markets—including a Good Life Grocery—theater, and a public library enhance the area's self-sufficiency, and friendly neighbors create an appealing small village atmosphere.

Portola

This district, which is often confused with the West Portal area, is a relatively unknown, family-oriented neighborhood of predominantly one- to three-bedroom homes built between 1960 and 1980. Located southwest of the Hwy 101 and I-280 intersection at Silver Avenue, just northwest of 3Com/Candlestick Park, the area's numerous elementary, middle, and high schools keep it attractive for families. Homes are affordable by San Francisco standards, priced around $250,000. There is little new construction, and rentals, which are few, carry pricetags near $850 per month for two bedrooms.

The diversity of the population reflects the overall diversity of San Francisco, a very close-knit hodgepodge of Asian, white (many Italian), African-American, and Latino. Many of the people who live here also own businesses here, and this has contributed to the longevity of the commercial sector as well as the stability of the neighborhood. There are often sunny days, but the area has its fair share of wind and cool temperatures. Portola is accessible from either Bayshore Boulevard, Silver Avenue, Geneva Avenue, or Mission Street, by way of the freeway or bus.

Presidio Heights/Laurel Heights

Quiet and peaceful, the adjoining residential neighborhoods of Presidio Heights and Laurel Heights are so tranquil and reserved you won't necessarily find them marked on a map of San Francisco. Presidio Heights, which borders the southeastern edge of the eponymous former military base, is tony and exclusive (neighbors include Senator Dianne Feinstein, home prices are in the millions). Laurel Heights, which lies just south of Presidio Heights, is more affordable and laid-back. Both are oases of surprisingly nonurban calm smack-dab in the middle of the city. You'll find a variety of architecture in these two areas, ranging from Victorian flats lining Sacramento Street to blocks of identical cubelike modern apartment buildings on the roads branching off of Euclid Avenue. A nice mix of lovely mansions and mini mansions in different period styles can also be found throughout the area, most notably on Clay Street and Jordan Avenue.

The serene atmosphere is perfect for families. Children can play safely in either the Presidio Heights Playground (between Laurel and Walnut, Sacramento and Clay) or the Laurel Hill Playground (off Euclid, between Blake and Collins); the Children's Hospital of San Francisco is nearby, as is a campus of the California Pacific Medical Center (both on California Street). Besides families, many young professionals seeking a more restful environment choose these neighborhoods (not a place for swinging singles). As you might expect given Presidio Heights' prestige and Laurel Heights' affordability, both rental vacancies and properties for sale come few and far between.

For those lucky enough to find a spot, life is convenient. Sacramento Street offers fashionable boutiques, small food markets, coffee shops, and restaurants for all budgets. Laurel Village, a plaza on California Street, features two full-service supermarkets, cafés, and retail stores ranging from Walgreen's to GapKids. The inner Richmond's ethnic markets—and some of its summer fog—are also close by. Parking in both areas is relatively easy by San Francisco standards, presumably because most dwellers have garages for their Jaguars. The Financial District, to the east, and the Pacific Ocean, to the west, are both readily accessible by public transportation via bus service along California Street.

The Richmond/Seacliff

"Richmond District, Where the Pluses Blot Out the Minuses," read a headline in the *San Francisco Chronicle* Real Estate section. A rather innocuous title for an otherwise glowing article listing many pluses and only one minus—fog. A few of the pluses listed were abundance of parking (not in all areas), relatively little crime, excellent schools, convenient downtown commute, and ease of public transportation. That minus, the fog, can blanket the area throughout much of the summer.

Living in the Richmond, aka the Avenues, is like being in a quiet suburb buffered from the rest of the hectic city by the ocean and parks. It is quite large in comparison to other city neighborhoods, and is loosely divided into three sections: Inner Richmond, from Arguello to Park Presidio; Middle Richmond, from Park Presidio to 25th Avenue; and Outer Richmond, from 26th Avenue to Ocean Beach. To the south and west, Golden Gate Park and Ocean Beach provide abundant recreational opportunities and definite borders. To the north, the Richmond merges into two tony enclaves, Seacliff and Lake Street, before meeting Lincoln Park, the Presidio, and the water. To the east, there is no definite border, fading out somewhere between Arguello and Masonic.

Unbelievable rent deals can be found throughout the district—except in Seacliff—but the further west, the cheaper it gets. The Inner Richmond, especially around Lake Street, tends to be a little pricy, but it is still relatively affordable compared to most city neighborhoods. A two bedroom with ocean views, deck, yard, and parking for under $1,000 a month is a benefit to living in the Outer Richmond. Typically, the housing consists of two- or three-story postwar houses and beautiful old Victorians on the north-south avenues, and small apartment buildings or houses on the east-west streets. There are also a few large apartment buildings, especially in the Middle Richmond. An average Richmond house runs $380,000; a typical Seacliff mansion costs close to a million.

Since the late 1800s the Richmond—especially the Middle—has been a popular place for both Russian and Chinese immigrant families to settle, and today it is a melting pot of many cultures. Ethnic diversity and competition keep the selection of restaurants and food stores interesting and the prices low. Most daily needs can be met in the shopping district that runs along Clement Street from Arguello to 26th Avenue and the entire length of Geary Boulevard. Clement Street has an exotic feel because of its throngs of pedestrians and abundance of ethnic restaurants, specialty stores, herb shops, and discount stores. Although the strip is often called Little Chinatown, many other cultures and cuisines are represented, including Korean, Vietnamese, Russian, Middle Eastern, and Irish.

South of Market

San Francisco's South of Market (referred to as SoMa in imitation of New York's SoHo) lies—as one might suspect—south of Market Street in the downtown area. This large section of the city is dominated by warehouses, busy streets, and thundering freeway overpasses, as well as busy Moscone Convention Center and surrounding museums and other cultural outposts. When it is finished, the new baseball stadium for the Giants slated for the China Basin area will be a boon to fans and a traffic nightmare for everyone else. At night, the area's many bars and clubs attract the young and restless.

SoMa's industrial character camouflages a surprising amount of housing. Many of the small side streets and alleys bisecting the neighborhood's enormous blocks

NEIGHBORHOODS & HOUSING

hide low-slung apartment buildings and even some charming Victorians. Warehouse apartments and live-work lofts are also popular, especially with artists and hipsters. The South Beach area next to the bay is home to some very large, modern apartment complexes, creating yuppie oases in the industrial landscape. In addition, a number of senior and low-income housing complexes are scattered throughout. Rents here vary widely depending on the block and building. A one-bedroom apartment can start at $650 and run as high as $1,500.

SoMa's primary attractions are convenience to downtown, access to the Bay Bridge, and alternative chic. There is little of the neighborhood atmosphere found in the rest of the city: corner markets, cafés, and street life are virtually nonexistent. However, warehouse outlet stores are common. SoMa is a great place to get your car fixed, and many bus lines run through the area. But during the day, the area tends to have a high level of noise and auto exhaust. At night, some sections can feel rather desolate, while others seem like a refuge for all the city's homeless, so pick carefully. There aren't many trees or much vegetation either. Parking is highly variable, scarce around workplaces during the day or clubs and restaurants at night, but plentiful during off hours; garages and pay lots are abundant if you're willing to fork over the cash. Anyone who feels that a city isn't a city without the hyper pace will feel at home here.

Sunset

Beneath the Sunset's seemingly endless array of symmetrical blocks and charmless, "brutal aesthetic" two-story houses lies an ethnically diverse neighborhood, rich with fun restaurants, good shopping, and natural beauty. This enormous area of the city stretches from Haight Ashbury to the Ocean and from Golden Gate Park to Lake Merced. The eastern portion, called the Inner Sunset, has the oldest housing and the most street life; proximity to the University of California Medical Center attracts lots of students and medical types, all of whom help keep Irving Street between Arguello and Ninth Avenue fairly bustling with restaurants, bars, coffee houses, and shops. Farther south and west the streets tend to be treeless, windswept boulevards, lined with houses mass-produced between the wars. This middle-class neighborhood was traditionally Irish—producing some boxing heroes who were loudly cheered in local pubs—but has recently attracted a diverse mix of young families, many escaping crowded Chinatown. The area closest to the ocean attracts plenty of surfers with a laid-back, California hippie attitude. Recent construction in this area includes larger apartment buildings.

Generally reasonable housing prices and abundant parking are strong draws. A typical house costs $300,000. Otherwise, most of the Sunset's main attractions lie along its perimeter. To the north, Golden Gate Park is an incredible neighborhood resource. To the south, the San Francisco Zoo makes a popular spot for family outings. To the west, Ocean Beach is a broad playground for those rare warm days. (Fog regularly blankets the Sunset, one of the area's biggest drawbacks.)

Most restaurants and stores are concentrated along Irving and Judah streets and 9th Avenue. The Sunset's large Asian population accounts for some of the best ethnic eateries in San Francisco. The neighborhood also offers a good selection of market shopping, from supermarkets to health-food stores to the many Asian groceries that line Irving Street between 19th and 25th avenues. The neighborhood is well-served by MUNI streetcars and buses, although it is a long commute to a downtown job.

Tenderloin/Civic Center

The Tenderloin section of San Francisco has a bad reputation among many city residents. Viewed as one of the least desirable places to live, a quick visit does little to dispel its skid row image: winos, hookers, and drug dealers abound. The Tenderloin's only attractions are cheap rents—$400 for a studio—and proximity to downtown, but the rents are low for a reason. In addition to the questionable street scene, many of the apartment buildings are in serious need of repairs. Unsurprisingly, crime is a problem here, and the area should be approached with caution after dark. The abundance of cheap housing in the area is attractive for many of the foreign immigrants who settle here until they can afford to go elsewhere, but you get what you pay for. A transition zone between the Tenderloin and Nob Hill—known in real estate listings as the "Tendernob"—on the northwest side of Union Square has much less blight and rents are still moderate.

Twin Peaks/Diamond Heights

People live in Twin Peaks for the views—and the vistas are truly spectacular. Tour buses full of visitors come year-round to take in the panorama from the overlook atop Twin Peaks Boulevard. Be warned, however: it is extremely windy on that perch—a quality common to the neighborhood. Of equal appeal to residents is the neighborhood's combination of tree-lined suburban security and city convenience. Centrally located, Twin Peaks is no more than a 15-minute drive to Golden Gate Park or the ocean for recreation and less than 5 minutes to the Castro, Noe Valley, and Inner Sunset for shopping and entertainment.

With the exception of a few major thoroughfares, neighborhood streets are extremely quiet and primarily residential. Living spaces consist mainly of two-story contemporary townhouses and small apartment buildings clustered on the hills. Rental and purchase rates are comparable to those in the nearby Sunset. The better the view from your living room window, however, the more you will pay. Although you don't need to have a car to get around, having one makes living in Twin Peaks more convenient, and parking is plentiful. If public transportation is your mode, MUNI buses will take you to virtually every nearby neighborhood; you can ride directly to the Castro, Church Street, West Portal, and Forest Hills MUNI stations, as well as the Glen Park and Balboa Park BART stations. There are also a few parks in addition to the tops of the peaks themselves. For a quiet, scenic (although often foggy) oasis in the middle of the bustling city, Twin Peaks can't be beat.

Corner markets and cafés are scarce in Twin Peaks, but the area boasts a couple of suburban wonders for one-stop shopping and errand running. At Diamond Heights Center, you can do your banking, drop off your dry cleaning, visit the post office, get your prescriptions filled, rent a video, and buy fixings for dinner (this Safeway is legendary, drawing San Franciscans from far and wide to its clean, well-stocked aisles).

Visitacion Valley

Like the other neighborhoods at the city's southern edge, this is something of a forgotten area. Running alongside Hwy 101 about 15 minutes south of downtown, Visitation Valley is easily accessible by car but less so by MUNI. It doesn't have a reputation as one of the safer neighborhoods in the city, although things are slowly improving. The community is home to many working-class families, historically African-American but today more ethnically diverse (residents are warily learning to live together). Close to Candlestick Park, Visitacion Valley is frequently foggy and windy. Most homes were built in the 1920s, and rentals, which are scarce, run between $700 and $800 per month for two bedrooms. The average home costs around $160,000.

Western Addition/Hayes Valley/Lower Haight/Alamo Square

The Western Addition occupies a large expanse in the middle of San Francisco just south of Pacific Heights. Many sections of the neighborhood have different names, especially those on the edges, reflecting the area's diversity and somewhat fragmented personality. Like Pacific Heights, the area has scores of beautiful Victorians that were spared from the ravages of the Great Fire following the 1906 earthquake

NEIGHBORHOODS & HOUSING

(although many others were destroyed by ill-advised urban renewal programs). Unlike its tony northern neighbor, the Western Addition has a decidedly middle-class reputation and relatively reasonable housing prices; large apartment buildings and public housing projects are mixed in with the Victorians. Denizens include African-American families and retirees—many of whom have lived in the neighborhood since World War II; young bohemians who share large, affordable railway flats; and professionals who are fixing up ramshackle Victorians or condo-izing.

Capitalizing on fame from postcards and such, the area near Alamo Square gets its own real estate listings and slightly higher rents; it is reputedly the quietest part of the neighborhood. The Lower Haight, centered around Haight and Fillmore streets, is one of neighborhood's funkiest sections, alive with ultrahip clubs and ethnic restaurants but with a slightly downtrodden edge. Hayes Valley, located along Hayes Street west of Franklin Street, is an up-and-coming area. Rescued from eternal gloom when the 1989 earthquake led the city to tear down the freeway overpass, Hayes Valley emerged as a funky, eclectic, and vibrant area. In late spring and summer of 1996, the city closed down the nearby Hayes Valley housing projects and is slated to build new housing on the same land. San Francisco's Japantown lies along the Western Addition's northern edge—assimilation has left it quite small—next to the Fillmore, where gentrification north of Geary has earned the new name Lower Pacific Heights.

In addition to reasonable housing prices, the Western Addition offers a quick downtown commute—Geary has incredible bus service—and many parks and playgrounds (even Golden Gate Park is close). The center of the 'hood is somewhat short on retail activity and accompanying street life, however. Divisadero and Fillmore streets have some stores, restaurants, and bars; Hayes Valley is littered with new galleries, cafés, art-furniture shops, and vintage stores; and The Fillmore Center at the intersection of Fillmore and Geary Streets provides many strip-mall basics, including a Safeway.

West Portal/St. Francis Wood

Quiet and friendly, West Portal is nestled on the west side of Twin Peaks, creating a quintessential small town in the big city. The main street is West Portal Avenue, with about five blocks of retail activity. Construction in 1917 of the Twin Peaks Tunnel, now the West Portal MUNI Station, connected the area with downtown, leading to its growth. Housing is primarily single-family residences, built in the 1930s, in the $360,000 range, and very few rental units. The numerous schools in and around the area make the neighborhood family oriented, with people of various ethnic groups residing here—many of them all of their lives; however, there has also been some gentrification over the years.

West Portal's closest neighbor is St. Francis Wood, an exclusive neighborhood of large homes influenced architecturally by the Spanish hacienda. Because of the size, price—average $600,000—and absolutely beautiful location—amid tall trees with spectacular views—of these homes, their residents are typically the well-to-do, including celebrities and government officials. During the summer, they can enjoy the performances—Shakespeare, Mozart, Verdi—at nearby Stern Grove.

The weather for both areas is typical of western San Francisco—frequently foggy, especially during the summer. The streets, many intersecting at funky angles, offer incredible views of the ocean and neighboring communities. One of the best things about these neighborhoods is that, despite their distance from downtown, they're easily accessible: three streetcar lines and many buses pass through, and car owners have only a short distance to 19th Avenue and I-280. (A more scenic approach follows Market Street from downtown, converging with and winding down West Portal Avenue.)

Visiting

SIGHTSEEING

The real sights and attractions of San Francisco are not the museums and monuments, but the neighborhoods themselves, each with its own character and identity. To glimpse the unique charm of each area, and to avoid parking nightmares, travel by foot—and be ready to climb the city's famous hills.

Embarcadero ★

(BART/MUNI: Embarcadero. Cable Car: California. F trolley. Buses: 42 Downtown Loop, 1 California, 41 Union, 15 Third, and many on Market St.)

Along the downtown waterfront, the **Embarcadero** (Spanish for "wharf") has seen a recent revival. Freed from the shadow of the Embarcadero Freeway, which was torn down after being severely damaged in the 1989 Loma Prieta earthquake, the strip is now a sunny esplanade filled with joggers, bikers, and skaters who praise the demise of the concrete overhead at the same time frustrated commuters curse it. The city is investing heavily in the area, installing lighting and rows of palm trees as part of a beautification effort. There is also construction underway to introduce public transportation on the roadway.

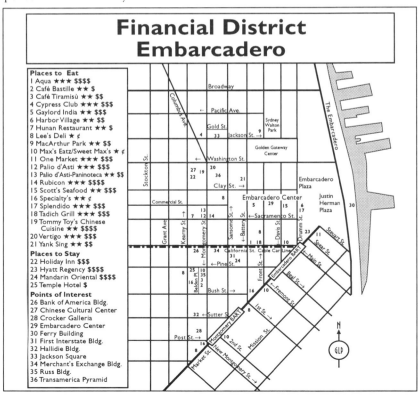

Financial District Embarcadero

Places to Eat
1 Aqua ★★★ $$$$
2 Café Bastille ★★ $
3 Café Tiramisù ★★ $$
4 Cypress Club ★★★ $$$
5 Gaylord India ★★ $$$
6 Harbor Village ★★ $$
7 Hunan Restaurant ★★ $
8 Lee's Deli ★ ¢
9 MacArthur Park ★★ $$
10 Max's Eatz/Sweet Max's ★ ¢
11 One Market ★★★ $$$
12 Palio d'Asti ★★★ $$$
13 Palio d'Asti-Paninoteca ★★ $$
14 Rubicon ★★★ $$$$
15 Scott's Seafood ★★ $$$
16 Specialty's ★★ ¢
17 Splendido ★★★ $$$
18 Tadich Grill ★★★ $$$
19 Tommy Toy's Chinese Cuisine ★★ $$$$
20 Vertigo ★★★ $$$
21 Yank Sing ★★ $$

Places to Stay
22 Holiday Inn $$$
23 Hyatt Regency $$$$
24 Mandarin Oriental $$$$
25 Temple Hotel $

Points of Interest
26 Bank of America Bldg.
27 Chinese Cultural Center
28 Crocker Galleria
29 Embarcadero Center
30 Ferry Building
31 First Interstate Bldg.
32 Hallidie Bldg.
33 Jackson Square
34 Merchant's Exchange Bldg.
35 Russ Bldg.
36 Transamerica Pyramid

VISITING

Ferry Building: Embarcadero at the foot of Market St. The building's elegant clock tower (modeled on the cathedral tower in Seville, Spain), was once the tallest structure in the city. For years after the 1989 quake, the hands remained frozen at 5:01 and the flagpole skewed at an odd angle, a reminder of the temblor's effects.

Embarcadero Center: Four blocks from Drumm to Battery between Clay and Sacramento sts. Consisting of four office towers, the lowest three levels of this center have shops and restaurants that cater to downtown workers. In an effort to attract more shoppers and diners, the center is building a **Sky Deck** indoor/outdoor viewing area on the 41st floor of Embarcadero One. Opening fall 1996, it should be open Tu-F 5pm-10pm; Sa-Su 10am-10pm.

1 TO 3 DAYS TO SEE SAN FRANCISCO

San Francisco is primarily a walking city, although visitors unaccustomed to climbing its steep hills may find them rather strenuous. Trust us, *it's worth the effort*. Many of the sights suggested here are within walking distance of one another. For others, a bus or taxi ride will usually prove less expensive and frustrating than driving and parking. All of the sights mentioned below are described in more detail in other sections of the book.

Day One: Begin with a **cable car ride** to **Chinatown**; all the lines pass near the neighborhood. (Plan on getting an early start, before 9:30am, to avoid long lines! Buy a day pass so you can hop on for short rides later in the day.) Begin with some **dim sum** for breakfast at Dol Ho. As you wander in Chinatown, stroll down Stockton, Pacific, or Washington streets to enjoy the exotic flavor of local life.

Columbus Avenue roughly divides Chinatown from **North Beach**, historically the Italian part of town. Before crossing over, literary types will want to stop at City Lights bookstore and Vesuvio Café to peek at these two landmarks of the Beat movement. Columbus and Grant avenues are both lined with cafés and interesting shops. If you're hungry, have lunch at Mario's Bohemian Cigar Store or one of the other cafés; if not, have a cappuccino and grab a sandwich-to-go from a neighborhood deli. Hike up **Telegraph Hill** to **Coit Tower** and enjoy the stunning views, then go inside the tower to see the murals.

Descend east via the **Filbert** or **Greenwich steps**. From Levis Plaza at the bottom of the hill, walk north to Embarcadero and west to Pier 43, where you can catch a **boat tour of the bay** with either the Red & White Fleet or the Blue & Gold Fleet. If you have to wait a little for your boat, check out the **sea lions** on the docks west of Pier 39. After the tour, bypass the wharf's touristy offerings—stop at Ghirardelli for an ice-cream sundae if you can't resist—and head to the **San Francisco Art Institute** to check out the Diego Rivera mural, student art, and the café with a great view.

Walk up the crooked part of **Lombard Street** between Leavenworth and Hyde Streets to see the famous gardens (much better to see on foot than in a car, traffic can be atrocious). Stroll over to charming **Macondray Lane**, and enjoy the views and **stairways** atop Vallejo Street between Jones and Taylor. Push on to the top of **Nob Hill**, where you can visit Grace Cathedral and the famous hotels. Rest up with an expensive cocktail atop the Fairmont—don't miss a ride to the top in the glass elevator—or the recently redone Mark Hopkins bar, or enjoy a campy happy-hour umbrella drink in the Fairmont's Tonga Room.

From the intersection of California and Powell streets, grab any of the cable car lines for a ride to dinner or back to your hotel. Chinatown is still close. You are also still close to North Beach. If you prefer highbrow culture, catch a play at one of the theaters near Union Square.

Financial District ★

(BART/MUNI: Montgomery. Cable Car: California. F trolley. Buses: 1 California, 2 Clement, 3 Jackson, 4 Sutter, 15 Third, 41 Union, 42 Downtown Loop, and many on Market St.)

Every weekday, hordes of smartly dressed workers pour into the Financial District, making a beeline to their offices without pausing to take a look at their surroundings. If you happen to have the luxury of not working here, however, a leisurely stroll through these streets can uncover a treasure trove of architectural and historical gems. For, despite its sheer wall of modern edifices, this district holds more artifacts of the city's early history than any other area. Driving and parking here during the day, especially at rush hour, can be all but impossible—don't do it. Fortunately, the area is also the hub of San Francisco's public transportation network.

In the days when gold coming down from the Sierra had to be measured and valued, San Francisco's early bankers established themselves along Montgomery Street, and they have never left. Today, Montgomery is known as Wall Street of the West for the numerous financial and banking giants to be found here. If you're interested in San Francisco's 18th-century history, stop by one of several small museums supported by the banks that house them.

Day Two: Start with a morning in the beautiful **San Francisco Museum of Modern Art**. Have lunch in the museum cafe or grab a sandwich in a nearby shop and enjoy it in **Yerba Buena Gardens**, where, on a sunny day, you are likely to catch a free performance of some sort.

Then head up to the northern waterfront for an early afternoon visit to **Alcatraz**. The cable car is the most scenic means of transport, but if the lines are long, take a bus or cab. Also, make sure you reserve Alcatraz ferry tickets a couple of days in advance, and do get the audio tour. After the tour, head west along the waterfront through **Fort Mason**, the **Marina**, and the **Presidio** to San Francisco's legendary **Golden Gate Bridge**, a long but beautiful hike if you're on foot.

If you are driving or biking, continue along Lincoln Boulevard to the **Legion of Honor** in **Lincoln Park**, a beautiful museum housing the city's European art collection. Even if you don't go inside, the views are heavenly, especially from the nearby Coastal Trail. Enjoying a **sunset** on a clear evening from any vista point between the Golden Gate Bridge and Lincoln Park will have you looking for an apartment in San Francisco before dinner.

Day Three: Begin with a tour of the **murals** in the **Mission District**. **Mission Dolores**, the oldest building in San Francisco, is only a couple of blocks away, as are the many neighborhood thrift stores. For an early lunch, grab a burrito or taco, then head to the **Haight** for a walk through the remains of the Summer of Love. Wander along Haight Street from Masonic Street toward the park, taking in the strange stores and characters along the way. (*Warning:* if you give money to all the bedraggled teenagers along the way, by the time you reach the park you will have to beg for money yourself.) If you didn't grab that burrito in the Mission, stop at Cha Cha Cha for lunch and avoid the dinnertime wait.

Spend the afternoon exploring **Golden Gate Park**'s many attractions. You may want to rent Rollerblades or a bicycle at one of the shops near Haight and Stanyan streets—you will never make it all the way through the park on foot.

In the evening, choose from San Francisco's myriad selection of nighttime hot spots for dinner and barhopping. The Mission and the South of Market have many of the hottest spots to eat and drink. The Lower Haight continues to attract a well-pierced cross section of slackers. And the Castro is a good starting point for any exploration of Gay San Francisco; as you walk around the area, stop in at A Different Light bookstore.

VISITING

Jackson Square: After a visit to the frenetic Financial District, wandering here offers a return to tranquility. Not actually a square, but rather the area bordered by Montgomery, Sansome, Jackson, and Gold streets, it is best approached by aimless wandering, rather than rigid sightseeing. This area was the Barbary Coast of San Francisco's early days, known for its brothels and bars (where soldiers were often Shanghaied into involuntary service on some ship headed for the Orient). Today, it contains some of the few downtown buildings to survive the 1906 quake, appropriately filled with antique shops—great for window shopping, even if you can't afford the $20,000 Persian rug on display.

Transamerica Building ★: Montgomery Street between Washington and Clay. By far the most famous downtown landmark, this 48-story pyramid gives the city's skyline its most distinctive landmark. Locals who at first hated the building (after all, it was built by a Los Angeles firm), have by now adopted it as their own. From an economic standpoint, the structure was disastrously planned: its tapering shape allows for only a few choice offices on the pricy upper floors, and the top 212 feet are purely ornamental—beautifully lit at night, but unrentable. In a recent move to get a little more out of the building, the Transamerica Corporation converted a public lookout point on the 27th floor into office space. Uninvited visitors are politely but firmly shown the elevator down. The adjacent **redwood park** is a cool and quiet place to picnic.

Bank of America: 555 California St. (Montgomery). To see many of today's financiers, check out this looming, dark, jagged landmark. In the plaza in front of the building sits a chunk of black marble titled *Transcendence*. B of A (as many San Franciscans call the bank) displays pieces of its impressive modern art collection on the lobby walls. If you're set on catching the spectacular **view ★★** from the top, you'll probably have to shell out some cash for a drink or meal at the **Carnelian Room** on the 52nd floor; brunch is an affordable way to enjoy the panorama.

First Interstate Building ★★: 222 Sansome St. (Pine/California). Possibly the best view to be had downtown. The top floors of this building house the posh Mandarin Oriental Hotel, which is made up of two towers linked on each floor by a glassed-in bridge. While the public is not exactly invited to go wandering about the hotel's hallways, if you're reasonably well dressed and respectful, you might well be able to sneak a peek.

Russ Building: 235 Montgomery St. (Bush/Pine). Those homesick for Chicago will want to take a look at this neo-Gothic high-rise modeled after the creepy and famous Chicago Tribune building.

Hallidie Building: 130 Sutter St. (Kearny/Montgomery). This shimmery tower claims to be the first building with a curtain-wall glass facade, an element that presages today's glass skyscrapers. Its delicate fire escapes and metal lattice give the structure something of an industrial wedding-cake look.

Merchants' Exchange Building: 465 California St. (Sansome/Montgomery). Inside this former commercial center of the young city you'll find a series of 19th-century paintings by William Coulter depicting the history of the port of San Francisco.

Chinatown ★★★

(Cable Car: California, Powell-Mason, and Powell-Hyde. Buses: 1 California, 15 Third, 30 Stockton, 41 Union, 45 Union-Stockton, 83 Pacific.)

You'll instantly know when you've entered Chinatown: the ornate **Chinatown Gateway**, an elaborate structure with photogenic menacing dragons, marks the main tourist entrance at the corner of Grant Avenue and Bush Street, and the streets suddenly take on the bustle, color, and richness of Asia. Chinatown was created when virulent racism in the late 1800s forced immigrants to band together for self-protection (they were also prohibited from living elsewhere). Inhabited largely by first-generation immigrants—continually replenished by new arrivals—street life has a decidedly foreign feel, with many conversations and signs in Chinese.

CHINATOWN

Chinese Cultural Center: Holiday Inn, 750 Kearny St., (415) 986-1822. Stop by to get your bearings, and pick up listings of sights and current events. • Tu-Sa 10am-4pm.

Portsmouth Square: Kearny St. between Clay and Washington. Originally a social center of the Spanish Village Yerba Buena, it is still a neighborhood center where many older men gather to smoke, gossip, and play cards.

Grant Avenue ★★: between Bush and Broadway. Although now largely geared toward tourists, Grant Avenue is the main thoroughfare in Chinatown. It is lined with some outstanding Chinese architecture and many interesting shops filled with everything from tourist trinkets and housewares to cameras and electronics. Some particularly intriguing spots are the **Chinatown Kite Shop** (717 Grant) and the **Wok Shop** (718 Grant). Farther up the street is **Ten Ren's** (949 Grant), a distinguished tea store with a vast storehouse of leaves, roots, and flowers. **Li Po Lounge** (916 Grant) and **Buddha Lounge** (901 Grant) are just two of the local hangouts, both with friendly bartenders. **Golden Gate Fortune Cookie Factory** (56 Ross Alley, enter from Jackson or Washington between Stockton and Grant) is a fun spot to explore the making of these crunchy treats; the x-rated fortunes are guaranteed to bring a blush and an adolescent laugh. To see Chinatown locals, poke around Grant Avenue between Jackson Street and Broadway, among the many food markets.

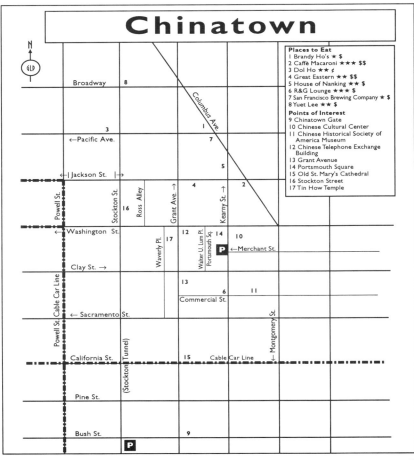

VISITING

Stockton Street ★★: between Sacramento and Vallejo sts. Here you can pick up all kinds of fresh seafood and produce, and anything from live frogs and Chinese pornography to ginseng. To view a truly authentic centerpiece of Chinese culture, climb the long staircase to visit the **Tin How Temple**, 125 Waverly, off Clay between Stockton and Grant, (415) 391-4841, founded in 1852 to honor the Goddess of Heaven, the protectress of travelers. It is open to visitors; leave a small donation before you descend.

Chinese Telephone Exchange Building: 743 Washington St. (Kearny/Grant). Although it looks like a pagoda, the building was originally the Pacific Telephone and Telegraph Exchange serving Chinatown; now it is a branch of the Bank of Canton.

Chinese Historical Society of America Museum: 650 Commercial St. (Kearny/Montgomery), (415) 391-1188. Museum dedicated to Chinese pioneers in California and to the establishment of Chinese-American Culture in America. M-Th 10am-2pm. Free.

St. Mary's Cathedral: 600 California St. (Grant). This quaint brick building predates the 1906 quake and was San Francisco's first Catholic church.

FINE ART, FREE FOOD

Wondering what the established names, rising stars, and hopelessly obscure in the Bay Area art world are up to? There's a good way to find out that doesn't cost any money, doesn't involve much walking around, and will fill your stomach and quench your thirst at the same time. It's called **First Thursday**. The first Thursday of each month is when San Francisco's major downtown art galleries host free receptions. They are open to the public and celebrate the galleries' newest installations. The range of exhibits runs from the bizarre to the sublime. But whatever kind of art captures your fancy, there is something for everyone. Best of all, wine and hors d'oeuvres are usually served during the receptions, which generally run from 5pm to 7:30pm. It's also a great way to people watch, especially those smartly dressed Beautiful People who tend to populate the local art scene. Many of the galleries are wonderful to look at, too, with wooden floors, high ceilings, and natural lighting.

The major galleries that host First Thursday receptions are all located within a two-block radius of one another, just east of Union Square. For more information, call the San Francisco Art Dealers Association at (415) 626-7498.

Gallery Paule Anglim: 14 Geary St., (415) 433-2710
Fraenkel Gallery: 49 Geary St., (415) 981-2661
Haines Gallery: 49 Geary St., (415) 397-8114
Robert Koch Gallery: 49 Geary St., (415) 421-0122
Stephen Wirtz Gallery: 49 Geary St., (415) 433-6879
George Krevsky Fine Art: 77 Geary St., (415) 397-9748
Rena Bransten Gallery: 77 Geary St., (415) 982-3292
Olga Dollar Gallery: 210 Post. St., (415) 398-2297
Edith Caldwell Gallery: 251 Post St., (415) 989-5414
Braunstein-Quay Gallery: 250 Sutter St., (415) 392-5532
Contemporary Realist Gallery: 250 Sutter St., (415) 362-7152
Shapiro Gallery: 250 Sutter St., (415) 398-6655
Dorothy Weiss Gallery: 256 Sutter St., (415) 397-3611
Erickson and Elins Gallery: 345 Sutter St., (415) 981-1080

Union Square ★

(BART/MUNI: Powell. Cable Car: Powell-Mason and Powell-Hyde. F trolley. Buses: 2 Clement, 3 Jackson, 4 Sutter, 30 Stockton, 41 Union, 45 Union-Stockton, 38 Geary, and many on Market St.)

Union Square, framed by Geary, Powell, Post, and Stockton streets, is an enclave of palm trees and park benches swarming with tourists, shoppers, pigeons, and homeless people. It was named for the pro-Union rallies held here during the Civil War, and the looming Dewey Monument at its center commemorates a Spanish-American War victory. For a quick overview of downtown, ride the **glass elevators** ★ to the top of the posh **St. Francis Hotel** on the Powell side of the square.

The **Cable Car Turnaround** (see Transportation chapter) at Powell and Market streets serves as ground zero for the area's many tourists. Appropriately, the **San Francisco Visitor Information Center** (415) 391-2000 is located nearby, on the plaza's lower level. Driving and parking in this congested area are difficult at best. Fortunately, public transit options are plentiful. If you do drive, the best parking deal is at the **Sutter-Stockton Garage** (entrances on Stockton and Bush streets); the **Ellis-O'Farrell Garage** (entrances on Ellis and O'Farrell streets) has similar rates. The **Union Square Garage** (entrances on Post and Geary streets) has reasonable night rates.

Union Square Shopping ★★: Most people come to Union Square to stay in the many hotels and to shop. Historically, large department stores and small, unique boutiques dominated the area, but an increasing number of chain specialty operations have

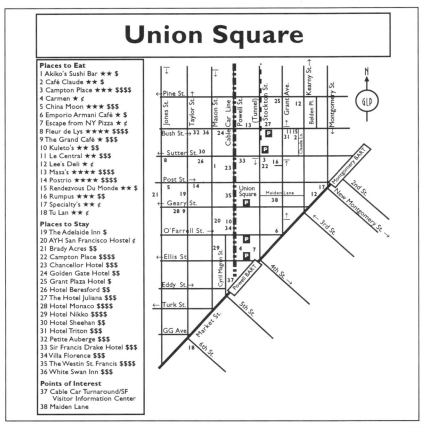

VISITING

moved in, making the area resemble a downtown shopping mall. Among the famous stores on the square are **Macy's**, **Neiman-Marcus**, **Saks Fifth Avenue**, **Hermes**, **Tiffany**, **Bally**, and—just so you don't think it's all high fashion—a **Disney Store**, **Borders Books & Music**, and **Niketown**. Nearby entries include San Francisco's own **Gump's** (135 Post), plus **F.A.O. Schwartz** (48 Stockton), **Williams-Sonoma** (150 Post), **Virgin Megastore** (2 Stockton), and **The Gap** (890 Market). The best way to experience this area is to start early (ensuring a space in the Sutter-Stockton parking garage) and walk the streets radiating from Union Square. To complete the scene, visit the stylish **San Francisco Centre** (Market and 5th streets), which features a spiral escalator and anchor tenants **J. Crew**, **Ann Taylor**, and **Nordstrom**.

Other notable spots found around Union Square include the city's own **Wilkes-Bashford** (375 Sutter), which suits many of the city's business elite and celebrities, and **Emporio Armani** (1 Grant), located in a striking Roman-style building that once housed a bank. The latter also features Armani-designed food at a chic café within the store. For more expensive Armani, visit the **Giorgio Armani Boutique** (278 Post), one of the few stores in America showcasing Armani's top-of-the-line Black Label line. Drop in at the world-class **Fraenkel Gallery** and the interesting **Stephen Wirtz Gallery**, as well as several other located in the building at 49 Geary. These galleries host a variety of modern work, including some interesting photography. Serious gallery goers should pick up the *Gallery Guide*, a free publication that lists exhibition schedules for the city's major galleries, some located around Union Square.

Maiden Lane: just off Stockton St. between Post and Geary. Filled with warehouse-sized brothels prior to the 1906 quake, Maiden Lane today attracts high-style women to chichi Old World boutiques like **Chanel** (No. 155). Newcomers like **Metier** (No. 50), which sells clothes and trendy jewelry by local designers, are also worth checking out. Don't miss the **Circle Gallery** building (No. 140), designed by Frank Lloyd Wright.

Theater district: centered around Geary St. west of Union Square. Many of San Francisco's theaters are located near Union Square. Make sure to see what's on the bill at the renowned **American Conservatory Theater.** Check the "Datebook" section of the Sunday *San Francisco Examiner and Chronicle* (called the pink pages by locals) for a comprehensive listing of shows and information on how to buy tickets. For low-priced tickets, try **TIX Bay Area**, formerly **STBS**, east side of Union Square, (415) 433-STBS/7827, where half-price tickets for some shows are available the day of the show (see Arts & Entertainment chapter).

Tenderloin: between the Civic Center and Union Square. Although best known as skid row, this seedy area offers some ultra-hip urban gems beyond the crack and prostitutes. See Bars & Clubs and Restaurants sections for local highlights.

Civic Center ★

(BART/MUNI: Civic Center. MUNI: Civic Center and Van Ness. F trolley. Buses: 5 Fulton, 19 Polk, 21 Hayes, 26 Valencia, 42 Downtown Loop, 47 Van Ness, 49 Van Ness-Mission, and many on Market St.)

The **Civic Center** area houses many city and state government buildings. Most of the historic buildings were constructed after the 1906 quake in the Beaux Arts style as part of a grand plan to enhance San Francisco's stature—although 1996 saw most of them boarded up while they undergo seismic retrofitting in the wake of the 1989 quake. **City Hall**, at the center of the area surrounded by Van Ness Avenue, McAllister, Polk, and Grove streets, is capped by an impressive dome modeled after that of St. Peter's in the Vatican. Across Van Ness Avenue, the **Veterans Building**, former site of the Museum of Modern Art, houses Herbst Theater and part of the **San Francisco Arts Commission Gallery** (see below). **War Memorial Opera House** is home to the city's opera and ballet companies. The building will be closed for earthquake construction work until September 1997 (see Arts & Entertainment chapter). On the northwest corner of Van Ness and Grove lies **Louise M. Davies Symphony Hall**, an elegant mod-

CIVIC CENTER

ern addition to the architecture of the neighborhood; the name tells its purpose. East across Grove Street, the **San Francisco Arts Commission Gallery** hosts city-sponsored art shows featuring works by local artists. Neighboring Civic Auditorium has been renamed the **Bill Graham Civic Auditorium** after the legendary San Francisco rock concert promoter. The auditorium is used for live music performances (as well as for part of the San Francisco Opera 1996-97 season), while adjoining **Brooks Exhibit Hall** hosts conventions. The **old Main Library**, which sits one-half block north, was severely damaged in the 1989 quake; ironically, it replaced a former library destroyed in the 1906 quake. When renovation is eventually completed, it will become the new home to the Asian Art Museum. Just across Hyde Street, **United Nations Plaza** is home to the Heart of the City Farmers' Market on Wednesdays and Sundays, as well as a substantial homeless encampment. In the other direction, across Larkin Street, **Civic Center Plaza** is a somewhat barren square popular for holding protests. The **California State Building**, on the northwest corner of Van Ness and McAllister, was designed by the same architects as Davies Hall, and has a similar exterior.

San Francisco Public Library ★★ Fulton St. at Larkin. In April 1996, the city installed its main branch in a grand new building with impressive interior architecture, particularly the skylit atrium. More famous for its high-tech tools than for its book collection—a library of the future here today—the new structure has been swamped with visitors. The library boasts a number of special interest collections serving the city's diverse community, a children's center with an outdoor terrace, and a treasure trove of resources on San Francisco history.

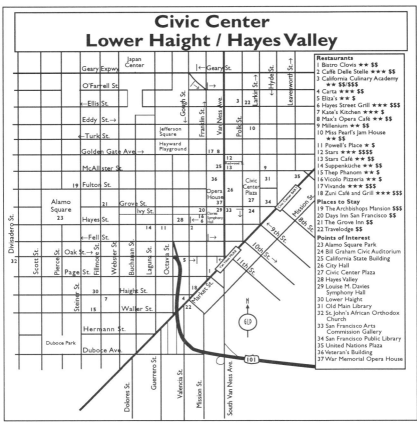

VISITING
Nob Hill ★★

(Cable Car: California, Powell-Mason, and Powell-Hyde. Buses: 1 California, 12 Folsom, 19 Polk, 27 Bryant, 41 Union, 45 Union-Stockton, 83 Pacific.)

A few words may come to mind when first asked to describe **Nob Hill**: pretentious, diverse, quaint. This is a charming residential area offering true urban living with a European flair. These qualities are found not only in the architecture of the buildings nestled along narrow streets, but also in the local businesses.

Top of Nob Hill ★★: California St. between Mason and Taylor. The site of the Big Four hotels: **Stanford Court, Mark Hopkins, Fairmont,** and **Huntington**, named for the railroad and silver barons whose mansions graced the hill until their demise in the 1906 earthquake and fire. **The Pacific-Union Club**, an elegant brownstone at the top of Nob Hill, is the only remnant of those elite structures, and is now a private club for old-money San Franciscans. For an amazing view, visit the **Top of the Mark ★★** atop the **Mark Hopkins Hotel** or the **Crown Room ★★★** atop the **Fairmont Hotel ★** (the exterior **glass elevator ★★★** to the Crown Room is incredible) and relax in comfort by the piano bar with an expensive cocktail. If you go to either one during a

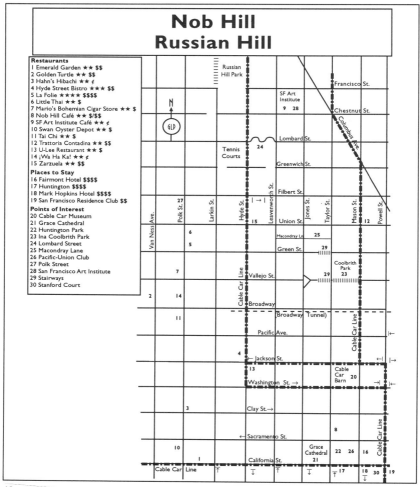

slow time, you can usually rubberneck without staying for a drink or a meal. While you're in the Fairmont, stop in at the campy **Tonga Room** ★ and enjoy the mechanical tropical storm and floating band while sipping exotic drinks (see Bars & Clubs section). Many of the hotel's halls display interesting historical photos and painting with an emphasis on images showing destruction from the 1906 quake. In the center of the block, play on the swing sets or relax on the grass in **Huntington Park.**

Grace Cathedral ★: 1501 Taylor St. (California), (415) 776-6611. This Episcopalian cathedral is one of San Francisco's greatest architectural jewels. Climb the grand staircase that leads you to a copy of Ghiberti's bronze doors to the Baptistry in Florence, Italy. The interior walls are covered with the usual gilded saints and other religious figures, as well as less typical murals and stained glass depicting the history of San Francisco and America from Sir Francis Drake to astronaut John Glenn. Extremely informative tours daily at 1pm (weekdays are the best). Go to the 11am service on Sunday morning to catch the choir's amazing performances.

Cable Car Museum: 1201 Mason St. (Washington), (415) 474-1887. A small museum of cable-car history (see Museums section).

Russian Hill ★★

(Cable Car: Powell-Mason and Powell-Hyde. Buses: 12 Folsom, 19 Polk, 27 Bryant, 41 Union, 45 Union-Stockton, 83 Pacific.)

Russian Hill is a quiet, residential neighborhood full of wonderful restaurants, shops, and cafés, very similar to Nob Hill in its simple charm. While wandering the area, check out the many pedestrian streets. **Macondray Lane** is a woodsy lane with delightful cottage houses; enter from Jones between Union and Green streets and go south. Both Green and Vallejo streets have **stairways** ★ between Jones and Mason streets (use caution when passing at night); a park at the top of Vallejo Street just east of Jones offers incredible **views** ★★ and a tiny patch of grass for a picnic.

Lombard Street ★★: between Hyde and Leavenworth sts. The primary tourist attraction in the area is a drive or walk down what's known as The Crookedest Street in the World, a serpentine brick road lined with magnificent flower gardens and beautiful homes. If you drive, go early or risk a long wait in traffic sure to burn your clutch.

San Francisco Art Institute ★★: 800 Chestnut St. (Jones), (415) 771-7020. San Francisco's oldest art school is also a great place to visit: enjoy student exhibits while wandering through the Spanish courtyard, check out the mural by institute teacher Diego Rivera (follow the signs), visit the two galleries with regularly changing shows, and then go up to the rooftop café for an inexpensive lunch surrounded by angular art students and incredible bay **views** ★★★.

Polk Street: Along the main retail strip for Russian and Nob Hills one can find great little boutiques, antique shops, book stores, and wonderful secondhand clothing emporiums such as **Buffalo Exchange** (1800 Polk). Stop at any one of the numerous cafés and enjoy a latte, read a book, play a game, or just have coffee talk. See the restaurant section for a list of the many fine local restaurants. Nightlife is hopping in this area (see Bars & Clubs).

North Beach/Telegraph Hill ★★

(Buses: 15 Third, 30 Stockton, 41 Union, 45 Union-Stockton.)

North Beach is San Francisco's little Italy, where sand and parking are a state of mind—you'll find neither today—the city's cradle of cafés, its repository of restaurants (and a bevy of bars). The Italian population dates back to the late 1800s, and, although Chinatown has expanded into North Beach, the old influence remains. In the 1950s and 1960s, beats such as Lenny Bruce, Jack Kerouac, and Allen Ginsberg came for the cheap rents—long gone—and hung out at places like **Vesuvio Café** (255 Columbus) and were published by Lawrence Ferlinghetti's **City Lights**

VISITING

Bookstore next door (261 Columbus). The combination of the Italians' love of life and the beat poets' dramatic energy spices up the area to this day. Throw a balled-up napkin over your shoulder in a North Beach café and you'll hit a writer. Although tourism is a neighborhood mainstay, tourist attractions are few. Other than visiting Coit Tower (see below), most people come to soak up the neighborhood atmosphere and enjoy the cafés, restaurants, and bars.

Columbus & Grant Avenues ★★: Columbus Avenue is a main drag in North Beach, lined with countless cafés, pastry shops, and Italian restaurants. Grant Avenue is another major thoroughfare, with plenty of blues bars, cafés, restaurants, and eclectic retail stores. **Quantity Postcards** has both streets covered with two locations (1441 Grant and 507 Columbus). It has the best selection of postcards in the city, with subjects ranging from the historical to the perverse, as well as wacky funhouse props to play with. If you visit North Beach during the day, check out **Figoni Hardware** (1351 Grant), a heartwarming emporium that doubles as a museum.

Washington Square Park ★: Union St. and Columbus Ave. North Beach's patch of green, where neighborhood residents mingle with park residents (homeless) and tourists. The park is dominated by **Saints Peter and Paul Catholic Church**, which was founded in 1884 and was the first Italian parish established in the United States, as well as the backdrop for Joe DiMaggio and Marilyn Monroe's wedding photos. The church towers are beautifully lit at night. **Liguria Bakery** (1700 Stockton) makes the city's best focaccia (go early in the day before they run out). Just north is the **Maybeck Building** (1736 Stockton), a beautiful example of the local architect's shingle style; inside are offices.

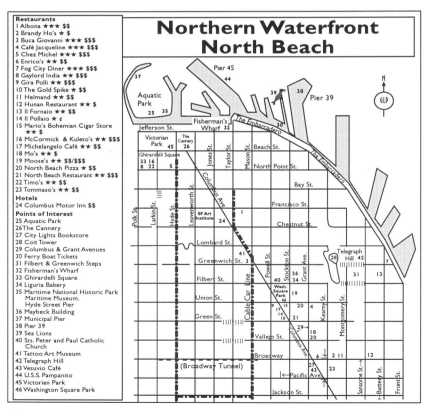

Telegraph Hill ★★★: Access via Lombard, Filbert, and Greenwich sts. The hill, which stands northeast of the neighborhood's restaurants and cafés, is crowned by **Coit Tower**, one of the city's great landmarks, and is named for the semaphore that operated on the summit between 1850 and 1890, to announce approaching ships. The **views ★★★** from the top are spectacular. The tower was funded by a bequest of Lillie Hitchcock Coit and honors San Francisco's fire fighters (she was an honorary member of a Engine Company No. 5). The lobby walls are covered with **WPA murals ★★** by local artists, many students and associates of Diego Rivera. The social realist murals depict life in California, many of them strong critiques on contemporary society, and they caused quite a row before the tower's opening. A short elevator ride (415) 362-0808 costing $3 takes you to the tower's summit; the vantage point is spectacular, but the views are generally better from outside, where they are unobstructed by dirty windows. Open 10am-7pm. Like everything in North Beach it's better to walk than to drive—the small parking lot fills quickly, creating massive traffic jams on the approach roads—but the view is worth the huff up the hill.

Filbert Steps ★★★: To enjoy the real secret of North Beach and get a taste of San Francisco's uniqueness, take one of the paths leading down the east side of Telegraph Hill to the Embarcadero piers. Although generally called the Filbert Steps, both Filbert and Greenwich streets descend the hill in a series of quaint stairways through Hobbit-like houses surrounded by gardens bursting with flowers and hiding friendly cats (and sometimes the city's flock of wild parrots). This is the only part of North Beach to survive the 1906 quake. At the corner of Filbert and Montgomery streets, Humphrey Bogart fans can see the Art Deco building that was featured in the film *Dark Passage*. Levi's Plaza sits at the bottom of the hill.

Northern Waterfront ★★★

(Cable Cars: Powell-Hyde and Powell-Taylor. Buses: 15 Third, 19 Polk, 30 Stockton, 42 Downtown Loop.)

Throngs of tourists can always be found in the area surrounding Fisherman's Wharf—the city's most popular tourist attraction—shopping or waiting in line for ferries to **Angel Island**, **Alcatraz**, and **Sausalito**, so if crowds aren't to your liking, stay away. But while most of the land-based sights are decidedly tacky, the bay and waterfront offer some fascinating activities: a bay cruise, a sea lion colony, and historical ships. Keep an eye on your wallet—pickpockets lurk everywhere.

Alcatraz ★★★: One of the most frequented tourist attractions in San Francisco, Alcatraz has held many of the most infamous high-risk prisoners in our nation's history. During the period between 1937 and 1963, this tiny island housed Al Capone, Machine Gun Kelly, and Robert "Birdman" Stroud, among, of course, many others.

Set in the center of the bay, The Rock has always had an eerie quality. In 1963, as the cost of upkeep for the decaying prison skyrocketed, the government shut it down. In the second half of the decade, the island was occupied for a short period by a group of Native Americans who claimed an inherent right to the land. Today, however, The Rock is owned by the National Park Service, and open to the public.

Tickets for the ferry ride and for the tour are available from **Red & White Fleet** (415) 546-2896 for information and (415) 546-2700 for tickets. A ferry ticket alone costs $6.75 adults, $5 seniors, $3.50 ages 5-11, but most people choose to purchase the ferry and tour together for $10 adults, $8.25 seniors, $4.95 ages 5-11. Available in several languages, the 35-minute, self-guided audiocassette tour is well worth the cost. It includes accounts by former inmates and prison guards, as well as an overview of the history of the island. Tickets should be purchased several days in advance either by reporting to the office between 8:30am and 5pm or by phone (there is a $2 service charge for tickets ordered over the phone). Ferries depart from Pier 41 at half-hour intervals between 9:30am and 2:15pm (4:15pm, June through August). You are invited to stay as long as you like on the island; the last returning ferry departs at 6pm.

VISITING

Bay Cruise ★★★: A cruise around the bay can give you a beautiful view of the city and surrounding area. There are two ferry lines that offer rides beneath the bridge, along the bay, and around Alcatraz: **Red & White Fleet** boats depart from Pier 43 1/2 beginning at 10:50am and running until 6:05pm at fairly regular intervals. The fares run $16 for adults, $12 for seniors aged 62 and over, 12-18, and active military, and $8 for children 5-11. Fares include rental of an audiocassette tour—available in a variety of languages—lasting just under an hour. Tickets can be purchased at the pier or by phone (800) 229-2784 between 7am and 7pm (there is a service charge for phone orders). **Blue & Gold Fleet** runs Monday through Thursday from 10am-7pm and weekends from 10am-6pm. Cruises depart at hourly intervals (half-hour intervals during the early afternoon). It is not necessary to purchase tickets in advance, although it is a good idea in the summer. Fares run $16 for adults, and $8 for seniors 62 and over, children 5-18, and active military. Tours include a 75-minute narrated tour; the extra time allows the Blue & Gold tour to circle under the Bay Bridge. *Note:* Bring warm clothes on any bay trip, the frigid winds off the water are bone chilling.

Sea Lions ★★★: One of the most popular and interesting sights here is the sea lions that have taken over a number of docks in the marina on the west side of Pier 39. The animals drive the boatkeepers crazy with their incessant barking and pungent odor. A thrilling sight in the middle of a busy city.

Fisherman's Wharf: Embarcadero between Stockton and Polk sts. At one time, Fisherman's Wharf was the center of San Francisco's commercial fishing industry. Today, you can still spot fishing boats plying the harbor or unloading their catch at the docks, but for the most part the wharf area, with its Wax Museum, Guinness Book of Records display, and innumerable T-shirt and souvenir shops, serves the tourist industry. **Pier 39** itself is a modern shopping area built on an old pier. It looks like a historic street and is a favorite spot to watch street performers. The stores sell mostly tourist items of the T-shirt-and-cotton-candy variety. **Underwater World**, is a new aquarium (see Amusements section).

Across the street, **Boudin's Bakery** (156 Jefferson) continues to turn out sourdough bread as it has since 1849—although not originally in this space. A large window lets you view the process. A short distance west on Jefferson, you can pick up small, pricy samples of crab, squid, and other seafood from a group of retail fish peddlers. Continue west on Jefferson to **The Cannery** (2801 Leavenworth), a former Del Monte peach canning plant converted into a shopping center. **Ghirardelli Square** is nearby at 900 North Point. Originally a woolen mill during the Civil War, it later became the chocolate factory for which it is named. The current **Ghirardelli Chocolate Manufactory** is an old-fashioned ice cream parlor with long lines, high prices, great fudge, and examples of historic chocolate-making machines—the real factory is now in the East Bay. Ghirardelli Square itself offers yet another shopping center, although this one is much more upscale than Pier 39. Beach Street and **Victorian Park** are popular with tourists and peddlers (and hustlers) catering to tourists.

> *"Pier 39 is like a Roach Motel for tourists, to keep people with bad taste off San Francisco streets."* —
> **Rob Morse**, SF Examiner.

Maritime National Historic Park ★: Much of the waterfront west of Pier 43 is part of an outdoor historic park with restored ships, a World War II submarine, and a museum (see Museums section). **Aquatic Park**, on the shore just north of Ghirardelli Square, is a protected cove with a beach used primarily by the members of the Dolphin Club, a group of ocean swimmers who take a famous cold dip every New Year's. For a good view of the city and a peek at the salty fishermen of the wharf, take a walk along the **municipal pier** several hundred yards west of Aquatic Park at the foot of Van Ness Avenue.

The Marina ★★

(Buses: 22 Fillmore, 28 19th Ave., 30 Stockton, 42 Downtown Loop, 47 Van Ness, 49 Van Ness-Mission.)

Although the Marina is primarily a residential district, the waterfront—yes, there really are marinas—between Fort Mason and the Palace of Fine Arts is one of prettiest spots in the city and a great place for a picnic, stroll, Rollerblade outing, or easy bike ride. Inland you can wander attractive residential streets and visit one of San Francisco's premier yuppie retail strips, Chestnut Street.

Fort Mason ★: at the foot of Laguna St. at Marina Blvd. Although it was under the watchful eye of U.S. Army from the 1850s until the 1970s, Fort Mason is now part of the **Golden Gate National Recreational Area** (GGNRA is headquartered here). The long warehouse-type buildings that line the water's edge house numerous crafts

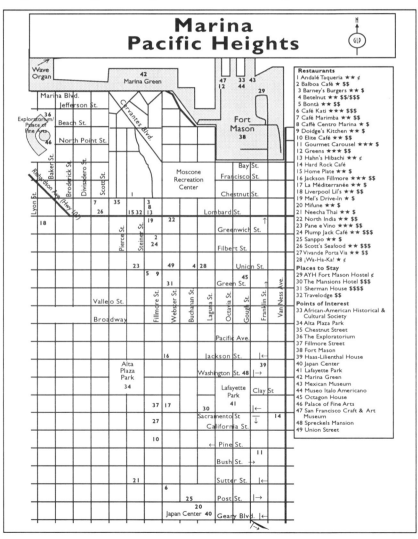

stores, theaters, and museums showcasing the ethnic diversity of the city (see Museums section for more on the **African-American Cultural Society** and the **Craft and Folk Art, Italo-American,** and **Mexican museums**). Start your exploration with a wonderful vegetarian meal at **Greens** (see review). **Book Bay Bookstore** (415-771-1076) sells inexpensive used books to raise money for the San Francisco Public Library. Inland up the hill, you'll find a beautiful **park** ★ good for picnicking and sunbathing, as well as an **AYH Youth Hostel** popular with budget tourists.

Marina Green ★★: waterfront between Fort Mason and Baker St. From Fort Mason it's fun to jump on your bike or Rollerblades—walking also works—and head west along the Marina Green pathway toward the Golden Gate Bridge. From kite flyers to runners, dog walkers, bike riders, and boat lovers, this strip has something for everyone. The grassy patch near the entrance to the Presidio is popular with volleyball players. A local artist uses the adjacent stone wall as a gallery for his sand sculptures—usually of mermaids. Take a walk out on the peninsula behind the Yacht Club and look for **the wave organ**, a series of benches and ceramic tubes embedded in the rocks that magnify the sounds of the sea. The shoreline continues west into the Presidio (see below).

Palace of Fine Arts ★★: Lyon St. and Marina Blvd., (415) 561-0360. The Palace, designed by Bernard Maybeck, is the only remnant of the 1915 Panama-Pacific International Exposition. The exposition, organized to celebrate the opening of the Panama Canal, was hosted by San Francisco to show the world how well it had recovered after the 1906 quake. Ironically, it was constructed on landfill and was never intended for permanent settlement—even today's structure is a reconstruction of the plaster-and-wood original—which is why the surrounding neighborhood suffered so much damage in the 1989 quake (few visible scars remain). The building is spectacular, possibly upstaged only by the beautiful man-made lagoon and fountain that adorn its exterior—equally popular with visitors, wedding photographers, folks seeking a spot to snooze for a bit, pigeons, seagulls, and ducks. The **Exploratorium** ★★ (see Museums section) is a hands-on science and technology museum with something for everyone.

Chestnut Street ★: between Fillmore and Broderick sts. To rest and recharge, wander past the many restaurants, cafés, and shops along the neighborhood's main retail strip. If architecture is your fancy, you will enjoy meandering through the surrounding windy streets, taking in the beauty of the many 1920s-style luxury apartment buildings and Mediterranean-inspired stucco homes.

Pacific Heights/Japantown ★★

(Buses: 1 California, 2 Clement, 3 Jackson, 4 Sutter, 12 Folsom, 22 Fillmore, 38 Geary, 41 Union, 45 Union-Stockton, 47 Van Ness, 49 Van Ness-Mission.)

Pacific Heights, a ritzy residential neighborhood perched atop one of San Francisco's hills, is a favorite place to see San Francisco Bay in panorama and to view some of the city's most dazzling architecture. The north side of the hill leads down to the Marina, passing through an area centered around **Union Street** known as Cow Hollow, a bucolic pasture in the 1800s.

Victorians ★★: You can walk for hours on these quiet streets, gawking at the many well-preserved homes and sprawling mansions. The area boasts many Victorians because it was primarily developed at the end of the last century—the height of the Victorian period—and it was behind the main fire line when the 1906 quake burned almost everything east of Van Ness Avenue.

Haas-Lilienthal House ★: 2007 Franklin St., (415) 441-3004. Short of befriending a wealthy local, your best chance of seeing the inside of a Victorian is to visit this Queen Anne mansion built in 1886. Presently owned by the Foundation for San Francisco's Architectural Heritage, it's the only Victorian house open to the public, and comes complete with period furniture. You can visit the house for an hour-long tour on Wednesday noon-4pm and on Sunday 11am-5pm. The admission fee is $5 adults, $3 kids under 12 and seniors over 65. Walking tours of the neighborhood leave from the museum entrance at 12:30 on Sundays. The fee is $5 adults, $3 kids and seniors.

Spreckels Mansion: 2080 Washington St. (Gough). This mansion, built in 1912 by sugar baron Adolph Spreckels and his wife, Alma, is now the private residence of pulp-novelist Danielle Steele. The adjacent block of Octavia Street is paved with bricks.

Parks ★: There are several hilltop parks for gazing at the **views**. On Sacramento and Laguna streets is **Lafayette Park ★**, which has a terrific view of Russian Hill and the Bay Bridge. **Alta Plaza Park ★** at Jackson and Steiner Streets provides a cityscape view and has public tennis courts and a playground. (Be sure to take a look at the quaint Victorians lining its south side and the mansions along the north side.) For a picnic, pick up a baguette, cheese, and other fixings at the **California Street Creamery** (2413 California). For a more elaborate basket, try **Grand Central Market** (2435 California).

Shopping ★: Fillmore, Union, and Sacramento streets are the main retail strips in the area—each a boutique browser's paradise. Fillmore between Sutter and Jackson is where yuppie comfortably meets upscale grunge, with a mix of cafés, restaurants, and shops. Union Street between Gough and Steiner has a mix of jewelry, clothing, and furniture stores suited to Pacific Heights' gentry. Sacramento Street between Presidio and Spruce has many antique stores.

Japantown: Post Street between Webster and Laguna sts. The area is centered around the prominent **Japan Center** complex, a small, 1960s shopping center that houses many shops selling Japanese goods. The rather spare outdoor Peace Plaza is home to a large concrete pagoda. The block on Buchanan Street between Post and Sutter streets is a pedestrian mall. There are also a number of Japanese restaurants and grocery stores in the vicinity, as well as a handful of community churches and local civic organizations. The popular **Kabuki Movie Theater** (see Movies section) and **Kabuki Hot Springs** are in the neighborhood. Many Japanese Americans lived here until they were interned during World War II, but the area never regained its original population. The Cherry Blossom Festival is held in April.

The Golden Gate ★★★

(Buses: 1 California, 2 Clement, 18 46th Ave., 28 19th Ave., 29 Sunset, 31 Balboa, 38 Geary, 43 Masonic, 76 Marin Headlands.)

The northwestern portion of San Francisco has a long list of attractions, starting with the Golden Gate Bridge. Although the bridge is San Francisco's most recognizable landmark, the natural surroundings are what are most impressive. Much of the land ringing the entrance from the ocean to the bay remained relatively undeveloped as part of military installations guarding the area since the late 1700s. Over the years, a sizable chunk of these installations have been converted to parkland; the Presidio, a vast military expanse surrounding the bridge's south anchor, is still in the process of being handed over to the Park Service; much of this area's future remains uncertain.

Golden Gate Bridge ★★★: The Art Deco suspension bridge, constructed from 1933 to 1937, stretches 1.6 miles, excluding approach ramps. Parking areas on both sides accommodate the hordes of tourists who come to enjoy the beautiful views of the bay, the city, and the surrounding hillsides from the bridge (parking areas on the west side of the bridge are less congested, and it's easy to walk under the span to the other side). Most tourists congregate around the **Visitors Center** located at the southeast entrance near the toll booths. A sidewalk along the east side of the bridge lets pedestrians **walk ★★★** as far across as they can manage (bring warm clothes, as the winds can be fierce). While the views are great, the noise and exhaust can be overwhelming when traffic is heavy.

VISITING

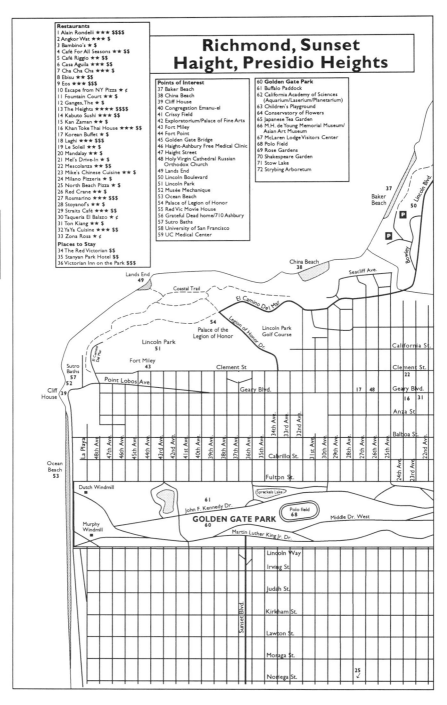

THE GOLDEN GATE

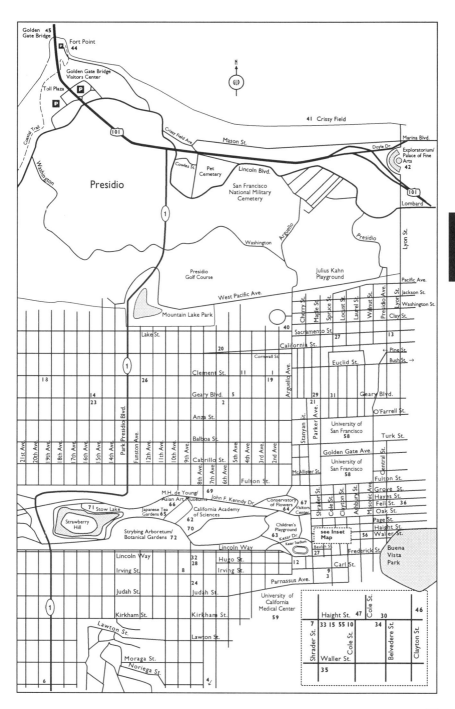

VISITING

Presidio ★★★: This former military-base-turned-park has the potential to be an incredible resource for San Francisco visitors and residents. Although it is now run by the National Park Service, many funding issues remain to be worked out in Congress. The Park Service is currently in the process cleaning up the military's toxic waste sites, tearing down structurally unsound buildings, and restoring many areas to their natural habitat. While the construction can be a bit disconcerting, there are still acres of shady groves and miles of shoreline offering beaches and spectacular views, as well as a golf course (see Golfing section).

The northeast section of the Presidio along **Crissy Field** ★ features a long stretch of beach along the bay, a favorite launch spot for windsurfers (see Sports & the Great Outdoors chapter) and an excellent spot for a jog, picnic, or sunset stroll. The Park Service has made restoring this area to its natural habitat a priority. Mason Street, the road running parallel to the beach, is a favorite flat spot for beginning in-line skaters. Crissy Field continues west to the Golden Gate Bridge. Although the trail directly up to the bridge is closed, you can follow the road around; this area has great spots to watch spectacular sunsets, particularly if you stay away from the highway.

Fort Point ★: (415) 556-1693. An historic structure located under the bridge. You can take an audio tour of this site, the only Civil War fort on the West Coast. Watch daring surfers catch precarious waves off the point. W-Su 10am-5pm. Audio Tour $2.50 adults, $1 ages 12 and under.

Lincoln Boulevard ★★★: This sizable thoroughfare skirts the Presidio's western edge, providing spectacular **views** ★★★ of the Golden Gate. From the small parking areas located on the boulevard, you can head off on one of the many narrow pathways that meander along the cliffs. Lincoln Boulevard becomes El Camino del Mar when you leave the Presidio and enter Seacliff, a district that contains many elegant Mediterranean-style homes. Pause at the corner of El Camino del Mar and 25th Avenue to look at the **sinkhole** that swallowed a mansion in 1995. As you head west, stop at Baker Beach or China Beach for a little sunbathing (see Beaches section).

Lincoln Park ★★★: This park, which occupies the northwest corner of San Francisco, has two faces: the perfectly manicured golf course and the rugged coastline. **The Coastal Trail** ★★★ runs west from El Camino del Mar at the park's eastern edge—where it borders the golf course—winding around a rugged point called **Lands End** to Seal Rocks near the Sutro Baths, ending at Ocean Beach. It offers exquisite **views** ★★★ of the Golden Gate Bridge and the Marin Headlands. Lincoln Park is also home to the newly restored **Palace of the Legion of Honor** ★★★ (see Museums section). In addition to a reputable collection, the museum boasts a stunning exterior and a beautiful setting. Be sure to walk around the parking lot to see the moving **Holocaust sculpture** ★★★ and the **views** ★★★ of the Golden Gate.

Expansive **Ocean Beach** ★ occupies the city's western edge (see Beaches section). Perched at the northern end of Ocean Beach is the classic **Cliff House,** 1090 Point Lobos, at the end of Geary Boulevard, (415) 386-1170, oozing with San Francisco history and trivia. In 1853, this was the site of the first wire that stretched over the vast sand dunes (now the Richmond District) to Telegraph Hill, where it announced incoming ships to merchants. Ten years later the original Cliff House was built, only to burn and be rebuilt two more times. The only access to this destination was a privately owned four-mile toll road (now Geary Boulevard). Today the Cliff House building houses a touristy restaurant with **beautiful views** ★★ (a good place for a drink), a camera obscura, the Musée Mecanique (see Museums section), and a Park Service Visitor Center (415) 556-8642; open 10am-5pm. Also in the late 1800s, Adolph Sutro built a huge indoor-outdoor swimming pool called **Sutro Baths** right next to the Cliff House; it was closed in the 1950s and burned in the mid-1960s. Its ruins are visible today. Sutro Heights Park, across the Great Highway and up the hill, harbors a charming Victorian kiosk. Despite its cobbled-together state, the area remains an attraction for tourists and locals alike.

Golden Gate Park ★★★

(MUNI: N-Judah. Buses: 5 Fulton, 7 Haight, 18 46th Ave., 21 Hayes, 28 19th Ave., 29 Sunset, 33 Stanyan, 37 Corbett, 44 O'Shaughnessy, 71 Haight-Noriega.)

Who would have thought it possible in 1870 that a 1,017-acre plot of windswept sand dunes could be transformed into a lush green park? With the vision and guidance of William Hammond Hall, a young civil engineer, and his successor, planner John McLaren, a whole new ecological system was born and has grown to become a verdant wonderland. Spanning three miles east to west and nine blocks north to south, Golden Gate Park is a city treasure, inviting enthusiasts of life to sample nature, sports, and culture: in addition to verdant pathways, the park houses some of the city's largest museums as well as an eclectic collection of attractions and sports facilities. If in-line skating or biking is your thing, a trip to the park on Sundays is a must. Traffic on John F. Kennedy Drive east of 19th Avenue is blocked off so those on man-powered wheels can glide down the park streets in peace. The atmosphere at Golden Gate Park on Sundays is like a huge party (see Sports & and the Great Outdoors chapter).

The park has more than 50 entryways, from the Great Highway at the west end of the park to the eastern boundary at Stanyan Street. The best way to start is with the *Map & Guide to Golden Gate Park*, found at the **McLaren Lodge Visitors Center** (415) 666-7200 on John F. Kennedy Drive near Stanyan Street on the eastern edge of the park. Open daily 8am-5pm. (Most of the bike rental or sport shops on Haight and Stanyan streets also sell the map.)

The centrally located Music Concourse is flanked by two of Golden Gate Park's most famous attractions: the **California Academy of Sciences** and the **M.H. de Young Memorial Museum**. The de Young building houses both the **Asian Art Museum** (which is slated to move when its new Civic Center home has finished undergoing retrofitting) and a large collection of American and British art (see Museums section). As the park was originally created for strollers who wanted a respite from the frenetic pace of city life, there are hundreds of paths to explore.

Japanese Tea Garden ★★: Music Concourse, (415) 666-7200. The famous—and popular—garden offers a beautiful setting where you can lose yourself in Zen contemplation of pagodas, bonsai trees, and expensive tea. It's best visited on a rainy spring day. Open 10am-6:30pm daily; $2.50 adults, $1 children and seniors.

Strybing Arboretum ★: M.L. King, Jr. Dr. between 9th and 19th aves., just south of the Music Concourse, (415) 661-1316. A walk through the countless varieties of plants and flowers here can be particularly pleasant on a spring day. Vision-impaired visitors will enjoy the **Garden of Fragrance**; its plants are specifically selected for scent and texture.

Rose Gardens ★: J.F. Kennedy Dr. near 8th Ave. A wonderful collection of these flowering beauties in a variety of colors and sizes.

Conservatory of Flowers: J.F. Kennedy Dr. near Arguello Blvd. Currently closed to the public as storms and old age have settled it into a state of deterioration without money to halt the descent. The elegant glass-and-wood Victorian greenhouse dating from 1879 is fronted by beautiful gardens.

Stow Lake ★: located near the middle of the park just west of the Music Concourse. An artificial lake popular with strollers and those who like taking a rowboat out on the water (boats available for rent). **Strawberry Hill**, a rise in the middle of Stow Lake, is the highest point in the park. An attractive waterfall cascades down the hill into the lake.

Children's Playground: off Kezar Dr. A favorite spot to climb, swing, and slide (make sure to visit the carousel, a Herschel-Spillman restored to its original splendor, complete with horses, frogs, and zebras. Open June-Sept 10am-5pm and October-May on Th-Su 10am-4pm. $1 adults and 25 cents kids.

Other Park Attractions: The **Shakespeare Garden** (behind the Academy of Sciences) contains plants and flowers figuring in Shakespeare's works. The **Buffalo Paddock**, on John F. Kennedy Drive at the west end of the park, is a large section of land reserved

VISITING

for a small bison herd. Just east of the paddock you'll find **Spreckels Lake**, where you can watch members of the Model Yacht Club sail their miniature boats. Continuing west on Kennedy Drive, you reach the **Dutch Windmill** surrounded by a colorful tulip garden. The windmill originally drove a pump used for irrigating the park. If you continue on the drive and cross the Great Highway, there's parking along **Ocean Beach** (see Beaches section). The **Polo Field** fills the middle of the western half of the park. Forget any images of idle gentry lounging here; this area has been home to musical gatherings since the great Human Be-In and the Summer of Love.

The Haight ★★

(MUNI: N-Judah. Buses: 6 Parnassus, 7 Haight, 33 Stanyan, 37 Corbett, 71 Haight-Noriega.)

The Haight Ashbury was the center of the mid-1960s hippie utopia, but a lot has changed in 30 years. The Haight's heyday was in 1967, when the Human Be-In and the Gathering of the Tribes were held at the Golden Gate Park Polo Field. Over 20,000 people gathered to listen to Timothy Leary, Jerry Rubin, the Jefferson Airplane, and the Grateful Dead. The Haight has gradually matured since those days—there's a Gap store on the corner of Haight and Ashbury—but it hasn't lost its 1960s feel. When Grateful Dead guitarist Jerry Garcia died in 1995, the streets filled with groups of fans—many of whom weren't even born by the Summer of Love—grieving around makeshift shrines. You'll also find a mix of local residents: students; young, affluent professionals and homeowners; black-clad, pierced hipsters; and an enclave of 1960s holdouts, petty drug dealers, and aggressive panhandlers.

The area, now called the Upper Haight, runs along Haight Street from Golden Gate Park to Central Avenue, and contains the famous intersection of Haight and Ashbury. Part of the area's charm lies in the large and detailed **Victorian homes**, many of which have been beautifully restored in luscious color schemes. The best house viewing is actually on the blocks north and south of Haight; cross-street Masonic Avenue is also a good spot. Most famous of the lot is **710 Ashbury Street**, former communal home of the Grateful Dead. Country Joe McDonald and Janis Joplin both lived right up the street, at 612 and 635 Ashbury, respectively. All are private homes now, so don't bother the current occupants.

Haight Street ★: The main retail strip is a kind of informal shopping mall of the offbeat, with an interesting collection of stores, cafés, restaurants, and bars. Since many shops are as unique inside as their storefronts suggest, wandering up and down the street until you expire from sensory overload seems to be the best strategy. You'll find an especially large selection of funky clothing stores, with both new and used threads, including such places as **Daljeets** (1744 Haight), a punk-rock fashion haven that

---

THE ANARCHIST

The essence of a Haight Street drowsy with patchouli incense and a certain kind of drug is found at The Anarchist, at Haight and Masonic. This bookstore, run by a collective of volunteers, is the trading post of information on subjects ranging from the battle to legalize marijuana to the CIA's role in JFK's assassination—and there is no attempt to hide partisanship. Fans of experimental literature can find Beckett, Miller, Nin, Kerouac, and other such writers. The last remnants of the seriously left wing know The Anarchist as a Mecca for underground and desktop publications, many written and produced by members of the local community. The dominant theme of these publications, not surprisingly, is that the American government is the enemy of the people. Visitors will find the store volunteers and clientele, who range from political activists to conspiracy buffs to the slightly unhinged, to be excellent sources of the kind of information not readily found at a neighborhood library.

claims to have "The Largest Selection of Thi-Hi Boots." Music still plays an important role in the Haight. **Reckless Records** and **Recycled Records** are two good outlets (see Record Stores section). The **Haight/Ashbury Music Center** (1540 Haight) has a broad selection of new and used instruments and equipment, and the occasional professional musician can be spotted here stocking up. For a bit of the unusual, check out the **Bound Together Book Collective** (see Sidebar).

The Haight has a long history of being a place to get wasted, and if you're craving a few drinks, you'll find many fine watering holes where you can quench your thirst and catch live music (see Clubs, Bar, & Live Music section). If you're in need of a smoke, be sure to stop by the **Ashbury Tobacco Center** (1524 Haight). You'll find plenty of posters, pipes, T-shirts, and tobacco supplies.

Western Addition/Hayes Valley ★

(Buses: 5 Fulton, 6 Parnassus, 7 Haight, 16AX, 16BX Noriega Express, 21 Hayes, 22 Fillmore, 24 Divisadero, 38 Geary, 71 Haight-Noriega.)

A centrally located, predominantly residential region of the city, the Western Addition is remarkable for its many stunning Victorian mansions and row houses.

Alamo Square Park ★: between Fulton, Hayes, Scott, and Steiner sts. In the surrounding streets, some 300 Victorian buildings were saved from the flames following the 1906 quake by the fire line at Van Ness Avenue. From the park, where refugees camped in 1906, one can see the world famous **view ★**, captured on many postcards and book covers, of the Painted Ladies—a row of prim, pastel Victorians—in front of today's skyscraper skyline. On the corner of Steiner and Fulton is **The Archbishop's Mansion,** which is just what the building was. Now it is a bed and breakfast where every suite is decorated in an operatic theme. A steep stroll up Fulton Street leads to the **Westerfeld House** (1198 Fulton). The builder of the St. Francis and Palace hotels lived here in the late 1800s. Later a white Russian consular corps took up residence in this particularly well-painted and elegant specimen. In the 1960s, it became a crash pad of sorts where Charles Manson is said to have roomed for a while. Catercorner is the **Alamo Square Bed and Breakfast** at Scott and Fulton. **Chateau Tivoli** (1057 Steiner) is considered one of the most elaborate Victorians in San Francisco. It's so varied in colors and cupolas you probably won't take in all the details the first time you see it. One handsome Italianate Victorian at 1321 Scott Street bears a plaque claiming that at the site, in 1897, nothing at all happened.

St. John's African Orthodox Church: 351 Divisadero (Oak), (415) 621-4054. This house of worship offers a Sunday morning jazz service at 11:45am. Come early for the best seats, as there is always a crowd. The service stretches to about three hours.

Lower Haight: The area centered around the intersection of Haight and Fillmore has an interesting cross section of skaters, ravers, rappers, and bohemians, most attracted by large flats and relatively low rents. The Lower Haight primarily offers sightseers a glimpse of young, hip, ultra-urban life (caution is advised when walking through this area at night). Haight and Fillmore streets are filled with an odd assortment of funky stores, cafés, restaurants, and bars. A pub or club crawl at night will keep you busy (see Bars & Clubs section).

Hayes Valley ★: Hayes btwn. Franklin and Laguna sts. This up-and-coming area was rescued from eternal gloom when the earthquake of 1989 forced the city to tear down the freeway overhead. Hayes Valley has emerged as a funky, eclectic, and vibrant area. The five blocks or so are littered with new galleries, art-furniture shops, and vintage stores. At the **San Francisco Performing Arts Library and Museum,** 399 Grove Street, (415) 255-4800, take a peek at whatever exhibit is up. Open Tu, Th, F 10am-5pm, W noon-7pm, Sa noon-4pm. Free. As you walk, you will pass several trendy clothing and shoe stores, jewelry and leather good shops. Stroll from Hayes and Franklin to Market Street. These few blocks are filled with antique stores and vintage furniture shops whose wares range from Art Deco and 1950s furniture to Old West artifacts, faux and true.

VISITING

The Castro ★

(MUNI: Castro. F Trolley. Buses: 8 Market, 24 Divisadero, 33 Stanyan, 35 Eureka, 37 Corbett.)

The Castro, the heart of San Francisco's gay community since the 1970s, is never a dull place to wander. Best of all, however, you won't need to worry about a strict agenda since there are no real "sights," per se. You'll find most of the stores, restaurants, and bars along Market, Castro, and 18th streets. The surrounding area has many well-tended Victorian homes with rainbow flags proudly displayed.

Harvey Milk Plaza: If you get to the Castro by MUNI, you will come up to street level at the corner of Market and Castro at **Harvey Milk Plaza**, named after the Castro camera store owner who became the first openly gay elected city official, only to be assassinated along with Mayor George Moscone in 1978 by conservative and disgruntled ex-city supervisor Dan White. To this day, Harvey Milk remains a local hero, and the date of his assassination is always marked by a candlelight procession from Harvey Milk Plaza to City Hall, where the murder took place.

NAMES Project Foundation ★★: 2362A Market St. (Castro), (415) 882-5500. For insight into the community spirit that has gathered force in the face of the AIDS cri-

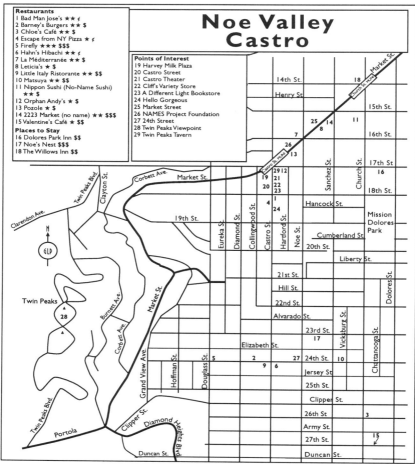

THE CASTRO

sis, pay a visit to the headquarters of the organization that has sponsored the creation of a gigantic quilt made up of individual panels created in memory of AIDS victims by their lovers, friends, or family. Sections of the quilt are often on display around the country, but it has become too large to be exhibited as a whole. In the showroom, you can see thousands of individual panels and learn more about the quilt project. Open daily noon-5pm. Free.

Twin Peaks Tavern: 401 Castro St. (Market). Known for being the first gay bar with a facade of windows, a good-bye kiss to the days when such places had to be tucked away in back alleys to avoid police raids. Today, the bar is better known by the young-and-beautiful set as the "glass coffin," for the older crowd that frequents this spot.

Castro Theater: 429 Castro St. (Market/18th St.). One of the city's favorite movie theaters, loved equally for its magnificent, over-the-top baroque interior, its unpredictable lineup (see Movies section).

Castro and 18th Streets: Known as the "gayest four corners in the world," there is never a dull moment on the southeast corner, dubbed Hibernia Beach for the bank that once stood here (now home to a Bank of America) and the shirtless men who tend to gather in front of it.

Castro and Market Streets: Many area stores capture the neighborhood flavor. At the indispensable **Cliff's Variety Store** (479 Castro) you can pick up any of your basic items, from a wrench to a red feather boa. Next door, **A Different Light** is the only bookstore in the city devoted solely to gay and lesbian literature. **Does Your Mother Know . . .** (4079 18th Street) offers a wide selection of cards for every occasion, except, strangely enough, for coming out to your parents. **The Midnight Sun** (4069 18th Street) is a popular gay video bar where a rapt audience watches *Melrose, 90210*, and anything else that comes across the oversized screens placed around the bar. Fans of Barbra Streisand will not want to pass by **Hello Gorgeous** (549 Castro), a museum-gallery-store wholly dedicated to the many facets and fashions of Barb. Check out the look-alike mannequin in the front window.

Along Market Street, innumerable restaurants, cafés, and shops have sprung up over the years, but the most popular of these is still the long-enduring **Café Flore** (2298 Market). This is the place to be seen reading Descartes or, if you're not into the brainy image, to put on an ultra-cool pair of sunglasses and go for the pretty look. Later in the evening, **The Café** (2367 Market) is a popular bar, especially good if you're up for dancing (see Bars & Clubs section). This stretch of Market is also one of the best places to scout for music, especially vinyl (see Record Stores section). Once you're stocked up on music, head to **Gauntlet** (2377 Market), where the staff will gladly assist you with all of your body piercing needs. Local restaurants cater to the late-night tendencies of their clientele, and there are several 24-hour eateries that will never turn you away. **Sparky's Diner** (242 Church) and **Bagdad Café** (2295 Market) offer good, greasy food at any hour.

Noe Valley ★

(MUNI: J-Church. Buses: 24 Divisadero, 35 Eureka, 37 Corbett, 48 Quintara/24th.)

Noe Valley sits on the ridge south of the Castro. A neighborhood first and a tourist destination second (and a distant second at that), Noe Valley's sights are few, consisting mostly of views and Victorians. Stair climbers should check out any number of promenades to catch exceptional scenery, especially **Sanchez between 20th and 21st streets**, or **Liberty between Castro and Noe**. Those driving a car might wish to re-create the drive down **22nd Street between Sanchez and Church** that Goldie Hawn and Chevy Chase took in *Foul Play* (at a slower speed, of course).

Twin Peaks ★★: Tour buses full of visitors come year-round to take in the spectacular **view** of the city (on a clear day) from the city's highest lookout point, at the top of Twin Peaks (take Twin Peaks Drive off of Portola Drive). From this vantage, you can

VISITING

see the Marin Headlands and Golden Gate Bridge to the north, downtown San Francisco, the bay, and Oakland to the east, and the San Mateo bridge to the south. Another beautiful and popular panorama of the city can be viewed from the pull-off on Portola Drive just down from the intersection of Burnett Avenue and Clipper Street. At sunrise and on clear evenings, professional photographers line up to capture the city's beauty for posterity and postcards.

24th Street: Although some shops and restaurant are scattered along Church, Castro, and a few other streets, 24th Street is definitely the consumer epicenter of Noe Valley. Boutiques and tiny independent shops are happily the norm here, rather than the exception. Look for a bounty of book and record stores. Of course, food lovers have numerous choices, with many cafés, specialty stores, and restaurants. **Spinelli Coffee Co.** (3966 24th Street), where the caffeine keeps conversation lively, often looks to be social ground zero for Noe Valley. A more refined place to imbibe hot drinks is **Lovejoy's Tea Room and Antiques** (1195 Church Street), full of lace curtains, plush sofas, and British elegance. For a touch of serious local flavor, drop by the **Rat and Raven** (Noe and 24th streets) on Sunday nights to sip a bargain beer while you watch *The Simpsons*.

The Mission ★

(BART: 16th St. and 24th St. Buses: 9 San Bruno, 12 Folsom, 14 Mission, 26 Valencia, 27 Bryant, 33 Stanyan, 48 Quintara/24th, 53 Southern Heights, 67 Bernal Heights.)

The Mission District, named for Mision San Francisco De Asis (aka Mission Dolores), was established as a Spanish settlement in 1776, four days before the signing of the Declaration of Independence. That spirit of freedom lives on in this neighborhood on the south side of San Francisco. Populated predominately by families of Latin American descent, the Mission is also home to many artists, musicians, and others seeking the liberty to express themselves while paying less rent than in other areas.

Although there are only a few formal tourist attractions, there are plenty of ways to enjoy the Mission: a window-shopping stroll along Valencia to visit the many thrift stores, sunbathing in the park, or maybe just having coffee in a hip café. The Mission is on the sunny side of San Francisco: when the summer fog rolls over the rest of the city, the Mission frequently still lies in full sun. The area isn't the city's safest, however, and visitors should be cautious at night, especially north of 16th Street and east of Mission Street.

Festivals for **Day of the Dead** happen around Halloween, complete with a drumled procession through the streets (check with the Mission Cultural Center for details). **Carnaval** happens the last Sunday in May and fills the streets with costume-clad revelers swaying to music that could be live or DJ and from any nation. Contingents represent a mix of nations, including Brazil, Cuba, Haiti, Trinidad and Tobago, and the Bahamas.

Mission Dolores ★: Dolores and 16th St., (415) 621-8203. Built in 1791, this is the oldest building in San Francisco, with furnishings accumulated over the last 200 years. The cemetery is particularly captivating, as is the small collection of artifacts on display in the modest museum.

Dolores Street: This rolling boulevard has an attractive median with grass and palm trees and is lined with some nice Victorian homes. **Dolores Park** (18th Street and Dolores) offers incredible skyline views of San Francisco, as well as tennis courts, great people watching, and a full playground for kids (nighttime attracts less savory types).

Murals ★★: A favorite neighborhood activity is viewing the more than 60 murals sited in various spots throughout the Mission. There's a concentration of excellent murals on 24th Street between Folsom and Potrero, with some of the best tucked away on Balmy Alley, a narrow lane next to the **Mission Neighborhood Center** (3013 24th Street). Don't miss the gripping mural painted, perhaps ironically, on **St. Peter's Church** (corner of 24th and Florida streets). In 1995, work by over 500 artists

THE MISSION

was completed on the magnificent mural lining two sides of the **Women's Building** (18th Street between Valencia and Guerrero). **Organized walking tours** are hosted by **Precita Eyes** (348 Precita). Stop in any time and, for a $1 donation, receive a map of the mural locations for a self-guided tour. A guided tour leaves on Saturdays at 1pm ($4 adults, $3 seniors, $1 students under 18), covers 70 murals in an eight-block walk, and may inspire you to take one of Precita Eyes's affordable mural painting classes.

Galeria de la Raza: 2857 24th St. (Bryant), (415) 826-8009. Experience the local art scene on a smaller scale at this gallery, which shows local and international Latino artwork. The gallery's adjacent shop sells Mexican and South American folk art at reasonable prices.

Mission Cultural Center: 2868 Mission St. (24th St./25th St.), (415) 821-1155. In addition to showing artwork, Mission Cultural Center itself is an object of art, covered with an enormous, vivid mural. This neighborhood center houses an active theater and a large gallery, and offers dance classes from countries around the globe. Try some Brazilian samba or, if you are more inclined, the home arts classes will teach you how to re-cane and repaint your needy furniture.

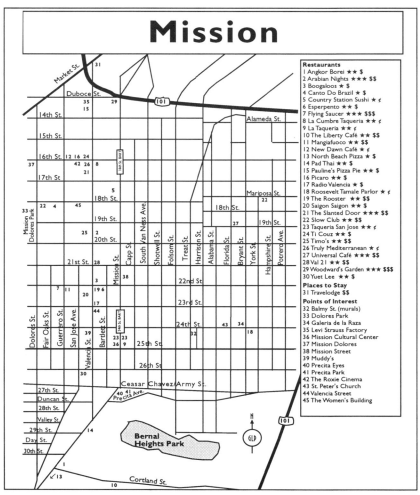

VISITING

Mission and Valencia Streets ★: Mission and Valencia streets are lined with fruit and vegetable stands offering a rich selection of fruits and vegetables from all over the world. Some of the best outlets are at Valencia and 22nd, Valencia and 16th, and Mission and 26th. The area is also home to some of the city's best and most diverse restaurants (see Restaurants chapter).

Mission nightlife is equally interesting, with many excellent bars, clubs, and cafés offering everything from a quiet game of pool to cutting-edge local music (see Clubs, Bars, & Live Music). If you are in the mood for a movie, the **Roxie** (see Movies section) screens an interesting array of films. **Muddy's** (1304 Valencia), which is not to be confused with **Muddy Waters**, hosts a weekly Wednesday Night Game Night: Scrabble, checkers, you name it. You can bring your own board or settle into some friendly competition with a friend-not-yet-met. (Tip: A great way to meet people if you're new in town. But don't steal from the Monopoly bank if you expect to make friends and influence people.)

Some local stores, in true San Francisco style, cater to unique tastes. Be sure to browse in **Modern Times Bookstore** (888 Valencia), which has a particularly good selection of books dealing with political and social issues. **Good Vibrations** (1210 Valencia) carries a selection of sensual accessories in a women-friendly, nurturing environment.

Thrift Stores ★: If these are a passion for you, you'll be spending most of your time in the Mission. **Captain Jack's** (866 Valencia) has an incredible selection of clothing, shoes, and accessories, while **Hocus Pocus** (900 Valencia) has more antiques, collectibles, and furnishings than you can imagine. We dare you to walk out empty-handed. **Classic Consignment** (867 Valencia), **Harrington Brothers Antiques** (599 Valencia), and **Upstairs Downstairs** (890 Valencia) primarily offer refinished 1920s to 1950s furnishings. **Sensacional** (3615 18th Street) has as-is furnishings at unbelievable prices. Don't be dismayed by the sign out front that says "This junk is for sale." There are good treasures buried in that pile. **ThriftTown** (2101 Mission), though incredibly large, does not offer the competitive pricing you would expect from a Salvation Army. The selection is vast, however, with items ranging from wedding dresses to washing machines. **Gypsy Honeymoon** (1201 Guerrero) has a taste for the macabre, as well as furnishings and fashions. **Community Thrift** (625 Valencia) has everything you need to start a new house: toasters, coasters, and roasters at unbelievably thrifty prices along with furnishings, clothing, dishes, magazines, and more. Well worth a look, even if you are usually antithrift.

South of Market ★

(MUNI/BART: Embarcadero, Montgomery, Powell, and Civic Center. F Trolley. Buses: 1 California, 9X San Bruno, 12 Folsom, 14 Mission, 14X Mission, 15 Third, 19 Polk, 27 Bryant, 30 Stockton, 42 Downtown Loop, 45 Union-Stockton, and many on Market St.)

Like Dr. Jekyll and Mr. Hyde, South of Market (SoMa, after New York's SoHo) leads a double life. By day, it's the hardworking, blue-collar backbone of the city's economy. The streets are lined with warehouses, auto-repair shops, building-supply wholesalers, and a growing number of clothing factory outlets. It is also home to a slew of film and video concerns and to a steadily increasing network of cyberspace-related operations that have earned the name **multimedia gulch**. After dark, however, South of Market metamorphoses into the liveliest and most diverse night scene in San Francisco, complete with arty cafés, upscale restaurants, crowded bars, and swinging dance clubs (as well as some unsavory stretches straight out of *Blade Runner*). The eastern edge of SoMa along the bay is a continuation of the Embarcadero esplanade, a pleasant, flat spot for a bicycling or Rollerblading. The city is building a new **baseball park** for the Giants on the southern edge of the Embarcadero near China Basin. As most downtown traffic passes through SoMa on its way to the freeway, traffic here can be merciless during rush hour. On the other hand, as you move south of Market Street, you can find plentiful self-serve parking lots with reasonable rates.

SOUTH OF MARKET

In the late 1800s, SoMa was at the bustling center of San Francisco life. It was also one of the areas hardest hit by the 1906 quake and fire. **South Park**, a quaint, English-style square between Second, Third, Bryant, and Brannan streets is one of the few remnants of SoMa's past. A slightly newer relic, **Rincon Center**, on Spear between Mission and Howard, is a small shopping center built around an historic Art Deco post office. The airy center court is topped by a sunroof from which a waterfall cascades soothingly. The developers preserved the original murals depicting San Francisco history.

Numerous outposts serve good food and great coffee. **Brain Wash** (1122 Folsom at 7th Street) best captures the area's unique mixture of industry and social life with its self-service laundry, coffee shop, and grill. Nearby there's the European **Kaffe Kreuzberg** (289 9th Street), where "the coffee is really black."

The 11th Street corridor at Folsom is the hub of SoMa nightlife. Although many never get beyond the concentration of bars and clubs at 11th and Folsom, this area represents just the tip of the iceberg that is South-of-Market nightlife. If you head down Folsom in the direction of First Street, you'll encounter dozens of nightspots (see Bars & Clubs section). Before heading out to the clubs, hit one of the many restaurants in the area—some of the best food in the city can be found here (see Restaurants section).

Yerba Buena Gardens ★★: between Third, Fourth, Folsom, and Mission streets. The city has actively promoted the development of this arts and cultural hub around **Moscone Convention Center.** The area above the convention center's northern half forms the center of the complex. Outside, lush lawns, water sculptures, pavilions, and

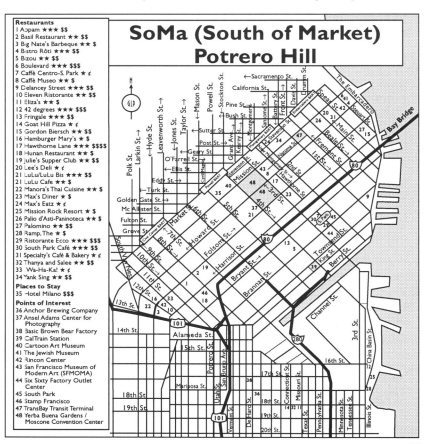

VISITING

benches mark the landscape, a perfect setting for a picnic while enjoying one of the many free alfresco performances. The buildings house theaters and art galleries. A large children's center and an imposing Sony entertainment complex are planned for the site. Many museums now surround the area, including the dramatic new **San Francisco Museum of Modern Art (SFMOMA)**, **Ansel Adams Center for Photography**, and **Cartoon Art Museum** (see Museums section).

Outlets: South of Market is home to a number of discount art, craft, and clothing stores. If you are willing to explore a little bit, some bargains can come your way. Many of the outlets sell maps to all the others—once you find the underground network, you've hit it big. **Gunne Sax** (35 Stanford Street) has a discount outlet for formal clothes; if you prefer to make your own designs, they also carry fabrics. **Winterland Productions** makes most of the rock and roll T-shirts you see at concerts; they have an outlet called **Rock Express** (350 Spear Street). Indoor-exercise types should buy cheap leggings and body suits at **City Lights** (333 9th Street). The famed **Esprit Outlet** (499 Illinois Street) has a selection that outlet shoppers only dream

CHEAP THRILLS

Golden Gate Park can swallow you for days at a time. Bring sneakers, a bike, or Rollerblades and prepare for an adventure (if you don't have the latter, a short rental is a reasonable splurge). There are plenty of opportunities for pick-up Frisbee, soccer, or softball, and the park offers free tennis lessons (although you may have to pay for court space). See Sports. While you are in the area, wander along Haight Street and be sure to pass by the former residences of the Grateful Dead (710 Ashbury) and Janis Joplin (635 Ashbury).

Check out the tour of its over 60 **Mission District murals** offered through Precita Eyes. For a $1 donation, you can pick up a map for a walking tour, or if you feel like splurging, show up at 1pm on Saturdays for a $4 guided tour ($3 seniors, $1 under 18). See San Francisco Sightseeing, The Mission.

Stern Grove plays host to a summer concert series on Sunday afternoons that includes companies such as the San Francisco Symphony Orchestra and the San Francisco Opera. The concerts begin at 2pm, but the crowds arrive early. The truly view-thirsty begin arriving at 9am. Bring a picnic lunch—maybe even a breakfast—and enjoy the sunshine (or sometimes the fog) and the show.

The Fairmont and the Saint Francis hotels offer great views of the city from their **glass elevators**. For no charge, you can take a ride to the top. See San Francisco Sightseeing—Union Square and Nob Hill.

The **Anchor Brewery** gives you free tours and free beers—all you have to do is make the reservation. See San Francisco Sightseeing, Potrero Hill.

Golden Gate Transit ferries between San Francisco and Larkspur primarily serve commuters, and the 50-minute ride costs only $2.50 each way on weekdays. There's not much to see at the Larkspur ferry terminal, but the round-trip journey is by far the least expensive way to enjoy a couple of hours on the Bay. See Transportation chapter.

Unfortunately this isn't DC, and most of the museums around here have hefty entrance fees. But several area museums offer free and discount days each month:

S. F. Museum of Modern Art: first Tuesday 10am-6pm, half-price Thursday 6-9pm.
Asian Art Museum: first Wednesday 10am-8:45pm.
California Academy of Sciences: first Wednesday 10am-5pm.
Yerba Buena Center for the Arts: first Thursday 6-8pm.
Exploratorium: first Wednesday 10am-9:30pm.
M.H. de Young Museum: first Wednesday 10am-8:45pm.
Mexican Museum: first Wednesday noon-8pm.
Museo Italoamericano: first Wednesday noon-8pm.

about, although the prices there don't really match the fantasy. And for one-stop outlet shopping, the **Six Sixty Factory Outlet Center** at, of course, 660 3rd Street, gives you a variety of outlet options.

Potrero Hill ★

(Buses: 22 Fillmore, 48 Quintara/24th, 53 Southern Heights.)

Potrero Hill is not on the tourist map, but this should not dissuade you from visiting two great landmarks.

Basic Brown Bear Factory: 444 DeHaro St. (17th St./Mariposa), (415) 626-0781. One of the few remaining manufacturers of stuffed animals in America, this cuddly spot sells stuffed bears of various sizes, shapes, and "personalities," as well as bear "skins" for stuffing. • Open M-Sa 10am-5pm, Su 12pm-5pm; drop in tours are M-F at 1pm and 2pm, Sa 11am and 1pm; group tours can be arranged for nine or more. All tours are free.

Anchor Brewing Company ★★: 1705 Mariposa St. (De Haro), (415) 863-8350. This is a stop that beer lovers can't afford to miss—the home of San Francisco's celebrated Anchor Steam. After a brief history of beer production, you are lead through each area of the production line. The 45-minute tour ends with the best part—samples! Pours are generous and include all beers except the special Christmas ale. Anyone may take the free tour, but 21 and over is required to sample the wares. • M at 2pm, Tu-F at 11am and 2pm; advance reservations required.

Bayview/Hunters Point ★

(Buses: 9 San Bruno, 15 Third, 19 Polk, 23 Monterey, 24 Divisadero, 29 Sunset, 44 O'Shaughnessy, 54 Felton.)

Like many neighborhoods in the city, Bayview/Hunters Point offers spectacular views from atop the many hills that feed into Third Street. One can see the South Bay, Oakland, and Alameda in one sweep of the eye.

Hunters Point Naval Base ★: east end of Evans St. Now that the base is inactive, many of its buildings and barracks are utilized as studios, making this one of the city's largest concentrations of artists. Open studios are held annually for the general public, during which an incredible wealth of Bay Area talent is on display.

Bayview Opera House: 4705 Third St. (Oakdale/Newcomb), (415) 824-0386. Built in 1888, this is the oldest theater in San Francisco. Declared the city's Ace Historic Landmark, it now operates as a community center under the Arts Commission's Neighborhood Arts Program. In addition to sponsoring afterschool programs for children, it also showcases community events such as Afro-centered theater and dance productions.

TOP 10 TOURIST ATTRACTIONS

The average tourist spends $130.40 a day during his or her visit, and $11.75 is devoted to entertainment and sightseeing. Where are these folks spending their money?

1. Fisherman's Wharf: 81%
2. Chinatown: 74%
3. Golden Gate Bridge: 73%
4. Union Square: 65%
5. Cable Cars: 65%
6. Golden Gate Park: 56%
7. Alcatraz: 42%
8. Museums/galleries: 35%
9. Union Street: 25%
10. Broadway/North Beach: 25%

VISITING
MUSEUMS

Golden Gate Park is home to the M.H. de Young and Asian Art Museums and the Academy of Sciences. Museum frequenters note: membership in the **Museum Society** (415) 750-3636 entitles you and a friend to a year's free admission to both the de Young and Asian Art museums. Fort Mason houses several smaller museums that spotlight particular cultures, while the Yerba Buena Center for the Arts in the South of Market area is the city's new and comprehensive home for the arts.

Academy of Sciences: Tea Garden Dr., Golden Gate Park, SF, (415) 750-7145. Morrison Planetarium: (415) 750-7141. Laserium: (415) 750-7138. San Francisco's main science museum. The attractions include a "safe quake," a simulation of the 1906 earthquake; a frozen great white shark, and the Discovery Room for Children, which is filled with interactive exhibits. Academy admission includes entry to the **Steinhart Aquarium**, located in the same building. Watch dolphins, seals, and thousands of other fish and aquatic creatures cruise in tanks. Call for animal feeding schedules. The Academy also houses the **Morrison Planetarium**, which features celestially oriented planetarium shows and entertainment-oriented Laserium shows. Admission to Planetarium is separate. • Labor Day-Memorial Day, daily 10am-5pm; Memorial Day-Labor Day, daily 10am-6pm. $7 adults; $4 ages 12-17; $1.50 ages 6-11; children under 6 free. Free first W of month. Morrison Planetarium: General admission plus $2.50 adults; $1.25 ages 6-17 and seniors; children under 6 free. Laserium: Th-Su evenings, call for times and matinee shows. $7 adults; $5 ages 6-12; $6 matinee.

African-American Historical and Cultural Society: Bldg. C, Fort Mason (Buchanan St. at Marina Blvd.), SF, (415) 441-0640. Displays African, African-American, and Caribbean artwork. • Tu-Su 11am-5pm; first W of month noon-7pm. $3 adults and seniors; $2 children.

Asian Art Museum: Tea Garden Dr., Golden Gate Park, SF, (415) 668-8921. Located in the same building as the de Young, the Asian Art Museum contains an important permanent collection of paintings and ceramics from all Asian countries. Because of limited space, only a small portion of the collection is on display at a time, so exhibits are small and frequently rotated. The museum will move into the old Main Library when a large earthquake retrofit is completed. • W-Su 10am-4:45pm; first W of month 10am-8:45pm. $6 adults; $4 seniors; $3 ages 12-17; under age 12 free. Free first W of month.

Cable Car Museum: 1201 Mason St. (Washington), SF, (415) 474-1887. A tiny museum which houses three antique cable cars, including the world's first (built in 1873), and the cable winding machinery that's still used to run the cars. • Daily 10am-5pm (summer until 6pm). Free.

California Palace of the Legion of Honor: Lincoln Park, 34th Ave. and Clement St., SF, (415) 750-3600. Looking buffed and polished after a recent renovation, the Legion houses a collection of European art impressive in scope, yet manageable in size. Beaux Arts galleries lit by skylights gracefully frame works ranging from Medieval to Postimpressionist. Makes for a great afternoon for art lovers and is a must-see for any fan of Rodin sculptures. Downstairs, the Achenbach Foundation for Graphic Arts displays the Bay Area's largest print collection—frequently changing to protect the fragile works. • Tu-Su 10am-4:45pm; first Sa of month 10am-8:45pm. $6 adults; $4 seniors; $3 ages 12-17. Free second W of month.

Cartoon Art Museum: 814 Mission St. (4th St./5th St.), SF, (415) 546-3922. A collection of newspaper strips, animation stills, comic books, and political cartoons illustrating the history of the craft, from a Hogarth engraving to present-day "funnies." • W-F 11am-5pm; Sa 10am-5pm; Su 1-5pm. $3.50 adults; $2.50 students and seniors; $1.50 children under 12; children under 6 free. Free first W of month.

Chinese Cultural Center: Holiday Inn, 750 Kearny St. (Washington), SF, (415) 986-1822. Features changing exhibits of everything from Chinese-American history to calligraphy. Fun to visit during Chinese New Year. • Tu-Sa 10am-4pm; Su noon-4pm. Free.

MUSEUMS

Exploratorium: 3601 Lyon St. (Marina Blvd.), SF, (415) 561-0360 (recorded information); Tactile Dome (415) 561-0362. Located at the breathtakingly scenic Palace of Fine Arts (dangerously close to the road that leads you without return towards the Golden Gate Bridge, check your map before going) the Exploratorium is an internationally acclaimed museum of science, art, and human perception, featuring over 650 interactive exhibits, including a distorted room, an indoor tornado, and the popular Shadow Box—all designed to help people of all ages and backgrounds understand natural phenomena. • Labor Day-Memorial Day: Tu, Th-Su 10am-5pm; W 10am-9:30pm. Memorial Day-Labor Day: Th-Tu 10am-6pm, W until 9:30pm. $9 adults; $7 seniors and students; $5 disabled and children 5-17; $2.50 children ages 3-5; free under age 3. First Wednesday of each month free. Tactile Dome: $12 during museum hours (includes Exploratorium admission); $10 after hours Tu, Th, F. Reservations are necessary.

The Friends of Photography and Ansel Adams Center: 250 4th St. (Folsom/Howard), SF, (415) 495-7000. Houses works by Adams and exhibits works by other photographers. • Tu-Su 11am-5pm; 11am-8pm first Th of month. $4 adults; $3 students; $2 ages 13-17 and seniors; children under 12 free.

Jewish Museum: 121 Steuart St. (Mission/Howard), SF, (415) 543-8880. Features changing exhibits of Jewish art and artifacts from all over the world. • Su 11am-6pm; M-W noon-6pm; Th noon-8pm. $5 adults; $2.50 students and seniors. Free first M of month.

Mexican Museum: Bldg. D, Fort Mason (Buchanan St. at Marina Blvd.), SF, (415) 441-0404. A collection numbering 9,000 works divided into galleries of pre-Hispanic, colonial, folk, Mexican, and Mexican-American art. • W-Su noon-5pm; first W of month noon-8pm. $3 adults; $2 students and seniors; under age 10 free. Free first W of month.

Musée Mecanique: Cliff House, 1090 Point Lobos Ave. (Great Hwy.), SF, (415) 386-1170. A re-creation of a tacky, turn-of-the-century arcade, where the mechanical attractions include fortune tellers, elaborate moving toothpick architecture constructed by Alcatraz inmates, and hysterical laughing ladies. (Warning: racist caricatures abound.) • M-F 11am-7pm; Sa-Su, Hol 10am-7pm. Free.

Museo Italo Americano: Bldg. C, Fort Mason, SF, (415) 673-2200. Contains a permanent collection of Italian and Italian-American modern art, and presents four special exhibits a year. • W-Su noon-5pm. $2 adults; $1 students; free ages 12 and under.

Maritime National Historical Park: extends from Aquatic Park at Polk Street to Fisherman's Wharf at Taylor Street, SF, (415) 556-3002. Museum: Beach St. and Polk St. An historic park encompassing parts of the northern waterfront. Within the park, the **Maritime Museum** at the northern foot of Polk Street houses models and photos of historical ships. Outside, at the **Hyde Street Pier**, explore three 19th-century ships—a sidewheel ferry, a lumber schooner, and a square rigger. • Museum: Daily 10am-5pm. Free. Hyde Street Pier: Labor Day-Memorial Day, Daily 9:30am-5pm; Memorial Day-Labor Day, Daily 10am-6pm. $2 adults; $1 ages 12-17; free under 12 and seniors.

M.H. de Young Memorial Museum: Tea Garden Dr., Golden Gate Park, SF, (415) 750-3600. The de Young, 44 galleries strong, features a recently expanded collection of American art from the colonial period to the mid-20th century—the finest collection west of the Mississippi—along with exhibits featuring the arts and crafts of Africa, Oceania, the Americas, and England. The de Young also offers tours, workshops, children's classes, and occasional films, often free. • W-Su 10am-4:45pm; first W of month 10am-8:45pm. $6 adults; $4 seniors; $3 ages 12-17; free ages 11 and under. Free first W of month. Free Walkman-guided tours.

San Francisco Craft and Folk Art Museum: Bldg. A, Fort Mason (Buchanan St. at Marina Blvd.), SF, (415) 775-0990. The only museum of its kind in Northern California, this San Francisco original hosts six exhibitions a year on subjects ranging from African-American quilt making to Haitian steel-drum sculpture. • Tu-F 11am-5pm; Sa 10am-5pm; Su 11am-5pm. $1 adults; 50¢ seniors and ages 12-17; free ages 11 and under. Also free every Sa 10am-noon and first W of month 11am-7pm.

VISITING

San Francisco Museum of Modern Art: 151 3rd St. (Mission/Howard), SF, (415) 357-4000. The museum recently moved to a large, stunning new home near Yerba Buena Center in the SoMa district where it draws an incredible stream of visitors. Although the permanent collection includes works by virtually every major 20th-century artist, including Calder, Klee, Matisse, and Pollack, it doesn't live up to the world-class architecture, lacking the depth and breadth; some of the most interesting pieces are by California artists such as Richard Diebenkorn and Wayne Thiebaud. Nevertheless, the fascinating array of exhibits ranges from visions of futuristic cities created by Japan's leading architects to a pop sculpture of Michael Jackson and his chimpanzee, created by Jeff Koons. • Tu-Su 11am-6pm; Th until 9pm. $7 adults; $3.50 students and seniors; under 14 free with adult. Half-price Th 6-9pm; free first Tu of month.

Stamp Francisco: 466 8th St. (Harrison/Bryant), SF, (415) 252-5975. The only rubber stamp museum in the world, Stamp Francisco houses the largest collection of antique rubber stamps in the U.S. and a gallery dedicated to performance art, eraser carvings, rubber stamp art, and mail art. Limited edition, hand-bound stamp art books and 1,800 rubber stamps are manufactured in the on-site factory and sold in the adjacent shop or by mail order. • M-F 10am-5pm; Sa 11am-3pm. Free.

Tattoo Art Museum: 841 Columbus St. (Greenwich/Lombard), SF, (415) 775-4991. The country's only museum devoted to body graphics displays tattoo equipment, flashes (advertisements), and exhibits on tattoo use in other cultures. • M-Th noon-9pm; F-Sa noon-10pm; Su noon-8pm. Free.

U.S.S. Pampanito: Pier 45, Fisherman's Wharf (Embarcadero at Taylor St.), SF, (415) 929-0202. Explore a World War II submarine in this part of the National Maritime Historic Park. Labor Day-Memorial Day: Daily 9am-6pm; Memorial Day-Labor Day: Su-Th 9am-6pm; F-Sa 9am-8pm. $5 adults; $3 ages 6-12 and seniors; free ages 5 and under. $15 family rate includes 2 adults and 4 children.

Yerba Buena Center for the Arts: 701 Mission St. (3rd St.), SF, (415) 978-ARTS/2787. The Center for the Arts Gallery is bright, open, and spacious. There is no permanent collection, so exhibits change regularly. The gallery shares its elegant space with a screening room for documentaries, films, and video presentations, a café, and a gift shop selling goods made by local and international artisans. • Tu-Su 11am-6pm; first Th of month 11am-8pm. $4 adults; $2 students, seniors and children. Children under 5 free. (More for special events.) Free first Th of month 6pm-8pm.

HOTELS & INNS

The vast majority of hotel rooms are located downtown in the Financial District and Union Square areas since these locations are convenient to the Moscone Center for business travelers and conventioneers. However, it's expensive to park in downtown San Francisco, it can be desolate at night, and it lacks the charm of the city's neighborhoods. Nob Hill represents a good compromise between proximity to the financial district and to nighttime activities.

Several expensive, bland hotels and motels are crowded around Fisherman's Wharf, where you will mainly encounter other tourists. Many moderately priced, fifties-style motels are located along Lombard Street in the Marina; while this location is convenient to the Golden Gate Bridge and the Fort Mason waterfront, Lombard Street is busy and loud; try to get a back room facing away from the street if you stay here.

To best enjoy San Francisco's charm, consider staying in one of the residential neighborhoods, where you can mingle with the locals.

Prices listed below show a general range covering singles, doubles, and suites. Prices at an establishment can vary quite dramatically depending on the room and the season. Always ask about specials: weekend, frequent flier, AAA, seniors, and so forth.

The Adelaide Inn $: 5 Isadora Duncan Ln. (off Taylor btwn. Geary/Post), SF, (415) 441-2261; fax (415) 441-0161. From its extremely steep staircase to its shared baths,

HOTELS & INNS

this is a true Continental *pensione*, tucked away on a quiet Theater District alley. For rock-bottom prices, you'll get one of 18 worn-looking rooms with bare-bones furniture and a small TV. (There's a pay phone in the foyer.) A complimentary continental breakfast is served in the dining room, where the young, largely European, chain-smoking clientele gather. The ambience is sure to bring a nostalgic tear to the eye of any former year-abroad student. $38-$52.

Amsterdam Hotel $$: 749 Taylor St. (Sutter/Bush), SF, (415) 673-3277. Basic, affordable hotel popular with foreign tourists. $69-$129. Parking is $13 extra.

The Archbishops Mansion $$$: 1000 Fulton St. (Steiner), SF, (415) 563-7872, (800) 543-5820; fax (415) 885-3193. One of the finest hotels of any size in San Francisco, the Archbishops Mansion is a popular place for honeymooners. Built in 1904 for the archbishop himself, this elegant mansion on Alamo Square features a beautiful French parlor, deep-stained wood cornices, oriental rugs galore, an enormous staircase lit by a stained-glass skylight, and a piano once owned by Noel Coward. The rooms have traditional fireplaces, partially canopied beds, and French antiques; the suites feature double tubs, lovely views, and sitting areas. A complimentary continental breakfast is brought to your room in the morning, and wine is served in the afternoon. Advance reservations recommended. $129-$385)

AYH Fort Mason Hostel ¢: Fort Mason, Franklin St. at Bay St., SF, (415) 771-7277. This budget-priced hostel, located in the Marina's Golden Gate National Recreation Area, overlooks the Golden Gate Bridge and is convenient to Fisherman's Wharf, the Marina, and Pacific Heights. Of course, you'll have to sleep in dormitory quarters and live with a few simple regulations, but it's worth it for the beautiful scenery. $14 a night for members and nonmembers.

AYH San Francisco Hostel ¢: 312 Mason St. (O'Farrell/Geary), SF, (415) 788-5604. The downtown youth hostel is close to BART and Union Square and costs $16 a night for members and $19 for nonmembers. People under 18 years of age stay for half price, but must be accompanied by someone at least 18 years old.

Brady Acres $$: 649 Jones St. (Post/Geary), SF, (415) 929-8033, (800) 627-2396. The name conjures up rural, homey imagery, and despite being three blocks from the bustle of Union Square, personable proprietor Deborah Liane Brady makes good on the promise of comfort in a cozy setting. The 25 recently remodeled studio rooms are individually (and tastefully) decorated, with enough cupboards and kitchen amenities (refrigerator, microwave, coffeemaker, toaster, plus utensils) to encourage cooking. Each studio also has a color TV, cassette player, and a private-line telephone with answering machine. The private baths are tiny but newly tiled and clean. An especially good choice for those staying a week, as special deals apply. $50-$85.

Campton Place $$$$: 340 Stockton St. (Sutter), SF, (415) 781-5555 This Union Square luxury hotel is renowned for its restaurant (celebrity chef Bradley Ogden established his reputation here) and for its tasteful, understated atmosphere. The Campton staff manages to create an intimate and romantic atmosphere that is quite a contrast to most large hotels in this area. $220-$330.

Chancellor Hotel $$$: 433 Powell St. (Post), SF, (415) 362-2004, (800) 428-4748; Fax (415) 362-1403. Columnist Herb Caen has raved that this hotel is the best bargain in Union Square, and he's probably right. A hundred and twenty-seven pristine, stylish rooms, many with terrific views of the square, feature queen or twin beds with phones and private baths. There are also ceiling fans for those rare hot days. Neighborhood parking, complimentary health club, and a location that can't be beat make this an attractive choice for anyone on an expense account. Call for special package deals on "slow days" or off-season, which often include breakfast or free parking. $105-$125.

Columbus Motor Inn $$: 1075 Columbus Ave. (Chestnut/Francisco), SF, (415) 885-1492. If you prefer an American feel, the Columbus Motor Inn is a reasonable option. Located near Fisherman's Wharf and with free parking. $78-$97.

VISITING

Days Inn San Francisco $$: 465 Grove St. (Franklin), SF, (415) 864-4040, (800) 325-2525. The San Francisco Days Inn is just what you'd expect from a national motel chain—comfortable, affordable, nondescript rooms with ample free parking for guests. The neighborhood is a no-man's land between Civic Center and the Western Addition, but it feels safe, and the Opera House is two blocks away. $75-$105.

Dolores Park Inn $$: 3641 17th St. (Church/Dolores), SF, (415) 621-0482. Former airline employee Bernie Vielwerth has run this gorgeous, ornate B&B since 1987. Chock full of fine antiques and Oriental rugs, the two-story Italianate Victorian mansion was built in 1874 by the Dorland family and features a subtropical garden in front, a sunny patio in back, and twin lion statues guarding the entry. No wonder celebrities like Tom Cruise have chosen to stay here. Rooms have queen-size beds, color TVs, clock radios, and shared baths. Full breakfast served. Two-night minimum stay. German and Spanish spoken. $65-$165.

The Fairmont Hotel $$$$: 950 Mason St. (California/Sacramento), SF, (415) 772-5000; fax (415) 781-3929. The Fairmont Hotel, whose stone façade gained notoriety in the 1980s when it was used in the opening credits of the TV series *Hotel,* is routinely rated the best in San Francisco. If you judge a hotel by the common facilities, this is certainly true: The lobby is an impressive space, with golden marble columns, a grand staircase, world-class art, and plush red velvet chairs. The rooms, however, vary in size, degree of luxury, and view. Eight lounges and restaurants are scattered around the building, including the kitschy Tonga Room (see Bars section), the after-dinner New Orleans Room, and the top-floor Crown Restaurant, which is reached by riding a glass elevator with truly breathtaking views. There are plenty of meeting rooms and a fitness club as well. Room rates begin at $200 and spiral upward from there.

Golden Gate Hotel $$: 775 Bush St. (Powell/Mason), SF, (415) 392-3702, (800) 835-1118; fax (415) 392-6202. Midway between Union Square and Nob Hill lies this cozy, 23-room B&B, which may be the best value in the city. Wicker furniture, brightly painted walls, antique claw-foot tubs, and an original 1913 birdcage elevator add to the ambience, overseen by a friendly and helpful management. The European-style rooms with a double bed and separate bath are a real bargain; the larger queen or twin rooms include a private bath. Continental breakfast and afternoon tea are included. $65-$89.

Grant Plaza Hotel $: 465 Grant Ave. (Pine), SF, (415) 434-3883, (800) 472-6899; Fax (415) 434-3886. For those seeking the basics, the Grant Plaza is a perfectly adequate choice. Not to be confused with the much dingier Grant Hotel around the corner, the Grant Plaza Hotel is a bargain considering that it's located just off Union Square and close to the Chinatown Gateway. The small but spotless Holiday Inn-style rooms include private baths, direct-dial phones, and color TVs. The top floor features stained-glass windows and skylights in the hallway. $45-$57.

The Grove Inn $$: 890 Grove St. (Fillmore), SF, (415) 929-0780, (800) 829-0780. The Grove Inn, a charming 15-room Victorian located one block from Alamo Square, is a historic landmark dating back to the late 1880s. Current owner Klaus Zimmerman completely refurbished the place in 1983, and now welcomes guests from all over the world to his large and sunny rooms with bay windows and plenty of flowers. There is a shared bath, although some rooms do have showers, and all have a phone and TV. Complimentary continental breakfast is served in the front dining room. The neighborhood is somewhat dicey, but off-street parking is available. $70-$85.

Holiday Inn $$$: 750 Kearny St. (Washington), SF, (800) 465 4329, (415) 433-6600. The Holiday Inn offers a major chain experience at several different locations in and near San Francisco. Your best choice is located in Chinatown, which is officially called the Holiday Inn Financial District. Whatever you call this hotel, the location is great, within walking distance of Downtown and North Beach. Amenities include free passes to a fitness center and a rooftop pool made famous by the opening scene in *Dirty Harry.* $120-$170.

HOTELS & INNS

Hotel Beresford $$: 635 Sutter St. (Mason), SF, (415) 673-9900, (800) 533-6533; Fax (415) 474-0449. This is one of the more underrated hotels in the city, and an especially good deal for families, since children under 12 stay free. The warmly lit rooms have a subtle, tasteful decor with private baths, honor bars, phones, and color TVs. Downstairs features a Victorian parlor and the White Horse Tavern, a startlingly authentic British pub. Continental breakfast is included, and there is an adjacent public garage. $89-$99 (family rates $104-$109). Discount for senior citizens and AAA members.

The Hotel Juliana $$$: 590 Bush St. (Stockton), SF, (415) 392-2540, (800) 372-8800 for CA, (800) 328-3880 for USA; Fax (415) 391-8447. *Lifestyles of the Rich and Famous* gadabout Robin Leach has put his seal of approval on this recently refurbished upscale hotel. Elegant-yet-simple decor abounds, from the plush sofas in the lobby to the pastel, classically furnished rooms. Although the target clientele is clearly corporate travelers, tourists will also enjoy the complimentary limousine service, drinks (coffee and tea in the morning, wine at night), and breakfast. All rooms include color TVs, stocked mini-refrigerators, voice mail, and more. $119-$179.

Hotel Milano $$$: 55 Fifth St. (Mission), SF, (415) 543-8555, (800) 398-7555; Fax (415) 543-5843. This hip, ultramodern hotel in located in a not-so-desirable location just South of Market. But its 108 rooms are some of the most expansive in the city and include phone with voice mail and modem capabilities, honor bar, in-room safe, soundproof windows, and TVs. Certain rooms even have bidets and Jacuzzi jets in the bath. There's also a large fitness center with the ubiquitous StairMaster and floor-to-ceiling mirrors. The hotel's stylish restaurant and bar, Bistro M, is adjacent to the tan-walled and sleekly furnished lobby, and there are meeting rooms for the many business travelers who stay here. The staff is pleasant and relaxed. Breakfast not included. $129-$189.

Hotel Monaco $$$$: 501 Geary St. (Taylor), SF, (415) 292-0100, (800) 214-4220; fax (415) 292-0111. The newly restored Hotel Monaco, located just off Union Square, boasts opulent decor and unusual furnishings, set against bright, primary-colored walls and marble floors. It's also chock full of all the amenities a business traveler could want: room service, valet parking, on-site fitness center, and more. However, all this doesn't come cheap. Meeting rooms and banquet facilities are available, and the stylish Grand Café Restaurant is located on the ground floor. $170-$355

Hotel Nikko $$$$: 222 Mason St. (Ellis/O'Farrell), SF, (415) 394-1111. Visiting film and artsy types often select the Hotel Nikko, which is located directly across the street from Glide Memorial Church and features an indoor pool with a glass ceiling. Open until 10pm, the pool is complemented by both wet and dry saunas. $195-$1400.

Hotel Sheehan $$: 620 Sutter St. (Mason/Taylor), SF, (800) 848-1529, (415) 775-6500. The Hotel Sheehan offers a good deal for downtown San Francisco: For as little as $59 you get a room for two in a real hotel just a few blocks from Union Square. Parking across the street is also reasonable. All this plus a pool. $59-$119.

Hotel Triton $$$: 342 Grant Ave. (Bush), SF, (415) 394-0500, (800) 433-6611; Fax (415) 394-0555. Interior-design buffs will think they've died and gone to heaven at the Hotel Triton, where every last lamp, table, bed, and chair is a work of art. No two rooms are the same, and a typical one looks more Magritte than Motel 6. Beyond the off-the-charts hip quotient, it's full of amenities like honor bars, cable TVs, room service, valet parking, and an on-site health facility. The cafe and restaurant are on the ground floor. $135-$255 and up.

Huntington $$$$: 1075 California St. (Taylor), SF, (415) 474-5400. Much less well known than the other two bigger hotels on the top of Nob Hill, the Huntington is the local's pick. It is smaller and less suited to large business events, but for luxury and atmosphere, it's hard to beat. Rooms vary in quality and price, so look before you chose. $170-$240.

VISITING

Hyatt-Regency $$$$: Embarcadero Center Five, Drumm St. at Market St., SF, (800) 233-1234, (415) 788-1234. For business people operating in the financial district, the Hyatt-Regency Embarcadero offers a great location at the foot of Market and California Streets. The accommodating staff adds to the attraction of this architecturally appealing hotel. Although the neighborhood is dead at night, this is the easiest place to get a cab in the whole state. $169-$325.

Mandarin Oriental $$$$: 222 Sansome St. (Pine/California), SF; (415) 885-0999. A favorite among the investment banking community, the Mandarin Oriental occupies ten floors in the First Interstate building on Sansome. Great views of the bay and city are accented by exquisite and subtle Japanese decor. Guests can use the Bay Club, the premier health facility in the city, for only $15 per day. $285-$1400.

The Mansions Hotel $$$: 2220 Sacramento St. (Laguna/Buchanan), SF, (415) 929-9444. A singular lodging experience in a city full of interesting hotels, the Mansions is a century-old historical landmark that's quirky, cozy, opulent, packed with more "stuff" than a museum, and to top it all off, (apparently) haunted. Those staying here might never see the city because one could easily spend hours exploring all the common rooms: the restaurant featuring the largest continuous scene of stained glass ever created; the parlor full of historic documents; the International Pig Museum; the Billiard Room with a giant dollhouse against the wall; and the velvet-drenched Music Room, home to a nightly magic show performance (complimentary for guests). Barbara Streisand is one of many famous guests who have been taken in by the Mansions charms. Private baths. Limited number of TVs for in-room use. Breakfast included. Reservations recommended. Rooms $89-$175, expansive suites $250-$350.

Mark Hopkins Intercontinental Hotel $$$$: 1 Nob Hill (California/Mason), SF, (415) 392-3434; fax (415) 421-3302. For sheer physical location, few hotels in the world rival the Mark Hopkins, which sits atop the peak of Nob Hill, an imposing L-shaped lion overlooking the city. The airy, chandeliered lobby is small but usually packed with business types or conventioneers (though the hotel has, in its storied history, hosted everyone from Judy Garland to Nikita Khruschev). The 390 guest rooms, many with outstanding views, have a functional but pleasant style, and come well equipped with color TV, mini-bar, and private bath. Limousine service, 24-hour room service, and an in-house fitness room are also available. Fourteen function rooms host various meetings. Glorious views and drinks can be had on the 19th floor at the world-famous Top of the Mark Lounge. Not surprisingly, you'll pay dearly for all this privilege: rooms start at $180, and the luxury suites can top a cool grand.

Noe's Nest $$$: 3973 23rd St. (Sanchez/Noe), SF, (415) 821-0751. If Noe's Nest looks like a private home from the outside, that's because it is; the owner is a former Brooklyn schoolteacher who's also a licensed masseuse. Her Noe Valley retreat is split into five rooms with cable TV, VCR, and private phone lines, along with private baths. The more expensive Penthouse room also has a steam room, deck, and washer/dryer, while the Garden room has its own fireplace and hot tub. There's also a hot tub shed in the woodsy back garden for guests. An enormous buffet breakfast is served in the kitchen each morning, and numerous other amenities are available. $85-$145.

Ocean Park Motel $$: 2690 46th Ave. (Sloat), SF, (415) 566-7020. If you have an insatiable urge to stay within strolling distance of the Pacific Ocean and the terminus of the L-Taraval streetcar line, then this is the place. The first motel built in the city, back in 1937, the Ocean Park today is a restored collection of streamlined Art Deco buildings centered around a grassy courtyard, with an outdoor (enclosed) hot tub and children's play area on the periphery. The 24 units have modern interiors and range in size from small boxes with a queen-size bed, TV, and shower, to two-room suites with fully equipped kitchens. Mark and Victoria Duffet, who have owned the place since 1977, are friendly and relaxed. Prices vary depending on the season, but generally range from $60 to $120.

HOTELS & INNS

Petite Auberge $$$: 863 Bush St. (Mason/Taylor), SF, (415) 928-6000, (800) 365-3004; fax (415) 775-5717. Owned by the same people who run the White Swan Inn a few door down, this charming inn is decorated with a French theme, with plenty of terra-cotta tiling and country-rustic furniture, earth-toned painted walls, and hand-crafted armoires. The private baths in each of the 26 guest rooms are somewhat smaller than at the White Swan, but the attention to detail is equally superb. A country breakfast is served downstairs in the café, which opens out onto a small garden, and plenty of amenities are available. $110-$220.

The Red Victorian $$: 1665 Haight St. (Cole), SF, (415) 864-1978; fax (415) 863-3293. The "Red Vic" Peace Center is a unique B&B, a tranquil oasis in the general chaos of the Upper Haight. For those who seek spiritual peace as well as a good night's rest, here are 18 guest rooms, each with its own theme and design—ranging from the tiny, economy Butterfly Room with its canopied double bed and corner sink (share the "Love Bath" outside), to the Redwood Forest room queen bed and private bath), to the Peacock Suite, an exceptionally large and popular spot for honeymooners. Continental breakfast is included, while walking tours and "life enhancement consultants" are also available. The smiling staff is wonderfully earnest. There's a minimum stay of two to three nights on weekends and holidays; big discounts for longer stays. $76-$200.

San Francisco Residence Club $$: 851 California St. (Powell), SF, (415) 421-2220; fax (415) 421-2335. More like a prep-school dormitory than a hotel, the SFRC is a popular place for international students and business people staying for an extended period of time. Its genteel atmosphere of wood-paneled dens and thick-carpeted hallways befits its location near the top of Nob Hill. Rooms are priced depending on size, view (some overlook the bay), and level of amenities (shared, half- or private baths). All guests receive complimentary breakfast and dinner. Laundry facilities are available. $38-$95, with cheaper weekly and monthly rates.

Sherman House $$$$: 2160 Green St. (Webster/Fillmore), SF, (415) 563-3600. Built in 1876, this beautiful Victorian mansion located in tony Pacific Heights nicely survived both the 1906 and 1989 quakes. Luxuriously decorated rooms, a fine chef, and a professional, personable staff make this charming spot one of the city's most sought-after destinations. With only 12 rooms, the hotel recommends making reservations months in advance for popular weekends. $295-$825.

Sir Francis Drake Hotel $$$: 450 Powell St. (Sutter), SF, (415) 392-7755, (800) 227-5480; fax (415) 677-9341. A 1928 historic landmark that sits mere feet from Union Square, the Sir Francis Drake attracts business travelers as well as an international set. The dramatic staircase leading up to the glittering lobby of mirrors, marble, and chandeliers hints at the elegance within, but the rooms are relatively affordable given the location. Most feature cherry wood and mahogany furniture, air-conditioning, cable TV, telephones with voice mail, and a clock radio. Scala's Bistro is on the ground floor, and Harry Denton's Starlite Room, with its spectacular views of the city and the bay, is on the top floor.. Reservations recommended. $109-$218.

Stanyan Park Hotel $$: 750 Stanyan St. (Waller), SF, (415) 751-1000. Located near Golden Gate Park, the Stanyan Park Hotel offers standard rooms or suites that include a kitchen. This is a great deal for people who like to do some of their own cooking or prefer to be away from downtown. $78-$120

Temple Hotel $: 469 Pine St. (Kearny/Montgomery), SF, (415) 781-2565. Those with a yearning for deep shag carpeting and (with luck) a perfect view of the Bank of America building need look no further. This old-time hotel appeals to budget travelers—especially European backpackers—who are willing to look beyond the sagging beds and lack of amenities. The rooms are basic but clean and come with sinks. The financial district location is dreary at night, but only a block away from Chinatown. Stays of three days or longer are discounted 20 percent from the already ridiculously cheap daily rates of $30 to $35 for a room with shared bath and $40 to $45 for a room with a private bath. Breakfast not included.

VISITING

Travelodge $$: 790 Ellis St. (Polk), SF, (415) 775-7612; fax (415) 567-1328. • 1707 Market St. (Valencia), SF, (415) 621-6775; fax (415) 621-4305. • 2230 Lombard St. (Steiner), SF, (415) 922-3900; fax (415) 921-4795. • Central Reservations: (800) 578-7878. It's reassuring to know that if ever you have an attack of the blands while searching for a place to stay, the king-size-bed-and-cable-TV world of Travelodge is always there. There are three locations in the city, the only real variable being the neighborhood; therefore, the best choice is Lombard Street, both the safest and cheapest. $59-$89; rates vary from season to season and location to location, so call ahead. Breakfast not included. Free parking.

Victorian Inn on the Park $$$: 301 Lyon St. (Fell), SF, (415) 931-1830, (800) 435-1967; fax (415) 931-1830. This enormous Victorian across the street from the Panhandle features a warm atmosphere reminiscent of 1890s elegance (at 1990s prices). Guest rooms are simultaneously cozy and ample, full of touches like frilly lace curtains, Victorian furniture, and poster beds; each one includes a private bathroom, and TVs are provided by request. The common areas of the house are almost as interesting: dark hallways with deep red carpeting, a gloriously ornate sitting room and library, and an oak-paneled dining room where a generous continental breakfast is served each morning. The neighborhood, however, is somewhat nondescript. $99-$320.

Villa Florence $$$: 225 Powell St. (Geary/O'Farrell), SF, (415) 397-7700, (800) 553-4411; Fax (415) 397-1006. The Villa Florence offers centrally located, Italian-themed elegance in a turn-of-the-century building. Marble columns, a huge fireplace, plush sofas, and a tromp l'oeil mural of the hotel's namesake city grace the lobby, while the rooms are a riot of florals, with matching chairs, bedsheets, and even curtains. Each features an honor bar, TV, air-conditioning, and private bath. A continental breakfast is available, but consider heading downstairs to the acclaimed Kuleto's Restaurant in the lobby. $135-$250.

The Westin St. Francis $$$$: 335 Powell St. (Geary), SF, (415) 397-7000, (800) 228-3000; fax (415) 774-0124. An incredible, jaw-dropping hotel at incredible, jaw-dropping prices. The spectacular lobby, with gold-leafed cornices, Tiffany chandeliers, oriental rugs, and enormous marble columns, is bigger than some B&Bs. The glass elevators in the modern wing rise 32 floors over Union Square with a great view of the entire downtown. The rooms are well appointed with TVs, phones, honor bars, and private baths. Breakfast included. $195-$1700.

White Swan Inn $$$: 845 Bush St. (Mason/Taylor), SF, (415) 775-1755, (800) 999-9570; fax (415) 775-5717. Part of a statewide collection of country inns, the White Swan's richly decorated Laura Ashley-style interior will make you'll swear you're in England instead of Nob Hill. Rooms are swathed in rose-printed wallpaper and feature mahogany poster beds, lace curtains, and mantle clocks over the fireplaces. A gracious staff serves a complimentary country breakfast in the elegant basement parlor, which is a adjacent to a wood-paneled library straight out of *Masterpiece Theatre*. Books, magazines, newspapers, afternoon tea, concierge, and countless other amenities are available. $145-$250; ask about special deals.

The Willows Inn $$: 710 14th St. (near Church/Market intersection), SF, (415) 431-4770; Fax (415) 431-5295. Even though it's self-described as "gay-oriented," owing to its proximity to the Castro, this relaxing inn welcomes a diverse and international clientele with rustic willow furnishings and Laura Ashley bedding. Each room has a phone, alarm clock/radio, and robes to wear to the separate bath facilities. A healthy breakfast and a morning newspaper are brought to your room; sherry and chocolates are served at night. Off-street parking is available, and reservations are recommended for weekends, holidays, and the Gay Pride parade. $70-$96.

Getting Settled

SHOPPING OVERVIEW

As with most other aspects of life in San Francisco, the neighborhoods define the shopping scene. Instead of going to the mall, San Franciscans go to the neighborhoods. Each has its own character and enough hidden treasures to keep a determined shopaholic deep in debt. The following descriptions of the city's top shopping districts should get you started, but there's more to each area. Hours vary widely from business to business, but a good general rule is to expect stores to be open Monday through Friday from 10am to between 6pm and 9pm (usually the bigger the store, the longer the hours); Saturdays, from 10am to 6pm; Sundays, from noon to 5pm.

Union Square is the city's premier shopping destination. Socialites and bargain hunters alike head here whenever the shopping bug strikes. The square itself is lined with major department stores such as Macy's, Saks Fifth Avenue, and Neiman Marcus. The area's streets are also packed with everything from tony boutiques such as Chanel and Agnès B. to tacky tourist outlets to galleries galore. Most tourists come to ride the cable cars, look for celebrities at Planet Hollywood, find outrageous toys in FAO Schwarz, and cruise the many shops that sell San Francisco memorabilia.

Mall denizens can head for Union Square's **Crocker Galleria**, an upscale urban version of a shopping mall, which houses the country's second-largest Ralph Lauren Polo store, and the **San Francisco Shopping Centre** on nearby Market Street, which is anchored by a four-level Nordstrom. Comprised of five separate but connected indoor/outdoor "mall" buildings, the **Embarcadero Center** caters to a busy financial district professional crowd. Shops line the lower three levels of Embarcadero 1-4, and include a variety of clothing, book, and gift stores. European Newsstand carries magazines and newspapers from around the world, and Coach Gifts sells very expensive purses, briefcases, and assorted leather and suede goods. Well-known names like Pottery Barn and The Gap are also among the lineup here. There is also a great abundance of eateries at every price range, but many are open only for lunch.

Situated on Jackson Street near the Transamerica Pyramid at the north end of the financial district, **Jackson Square** has a chic and expensive collection of antique stores housed in historic brick buildings. Although the prices may be prohibitive, the window shopping is unsurpassed. If antique silver, European furniture, Persian rugs, and paintings are not on your shopping list, head for Arch, a fabulous art supply store selling quirky cards, gifts, and picture frames.

Just on the border of Union Square is **Chinatown**, which is like a world apart. Lively crowds bustle along Stockton, Jackson, Washington, and Pacific Streets performing their daily shopping ritual at the innumerable vegetable, meat, and fish shops. Grant Avenue caters to tourists, with cameras and video equipment, luggage and leather goods, knickknacks, tourist memorabilia, and even gemstones for sale. A number of smaller stores throughout the neighborhood stock herbal cure-alls, including the ubiquitous ginseng.

North Beach maintains a very distinct Italian flavor. Mixed in with the Italian cafés and restaurants is a diverse mix of bookstores, small clothing boutiques, and shops. This is a great place to pick up culinary treats, with the smell of fresh focaccia bread, biscotti, and pastries wafting through the streets at every turn. In recent years, Grant Avenue has become a hotbed of fashion, with notable stops including MAC, Grand (partly owned by Mayor Willie Brown's son), and Slips, the city's best upholstery and fabric shop. Other shops to investigate include Biordi, a family operation that imports hand-painted Italian ceramics; City Lights, the most beloved bookstore in the city and also the former haunt of the Beatniks; and Eclectix, which stocks all sorts of fine-arts posters.

GETTING SETTLED

Chestnut Street west of Fillmore Street is the center of the Marina's day and night life. Although there are few destination spots along the street, clothing, housewares, sporting goods, and knickknacks are abundant and easy to find, and there are numerous cafés and restaurants for a mid-spree pick-me-up. Upscale shops full of housewares, clothing, cards, and gifts cater to the young, health-conscious crowd that prevails in the Marina.

Sandwiched between Pacific Heights and the Marina, **Union Street**, not to be confused with Union Square, is part yuppie, part gentry, with a mix of boutiques emphasizing chic women's clothing, furniture, and personal pampering. The young and beautiful cruise the sidewalks, updating their already gargantuan wardrobes, while the older, yet still beautiful, cruise right along with them, beautiful children in tow. Don't worry about shopping fatigue: every few doors the stores are punctuated by cafés, yogurt shops, and juice bars.

Fillmore Street is another fun place to hang out and shop for an afternoon, with its eclectic collection of small boutiques for clothing, furniture, and housewares. Between Jackson and Post Street are stores like Betsy Johnson and Ms. Dewson's Hats; the street is also dotted with secondhand clothing shops full of great vintage clothing and hidden gems waiting to be discovered.

Primarily contained within a large, rather sterile, indoor mall, **Japantown** encompasses Japanese bookstores, restaurants, and clothing and housewares stores. Look for Japanese books and stationery at Goshadco Company, and books, magazines, and CDs (in English and Japanese) at Kinokuniya Bookstore. A variety of stores feature Japanese art, artifacts, and plates and utensils. The Miyako Ice Cream Shop is an old-fashioned confectioner's shop serving several varieties of ice cream.

Along **Haight Street**, Woodstock, the 1960s, and leather still rule. Thirty years after its heyday, this area still pays homage to its famous past. Try shopping for used clothes at Aardvark's Odd Ark or Buffalo Exchange. For music, investigate Zebra Records or Reckless Records, both of which buy, sell, and accept trade-ins. A number of coffeehouses give shoppers an opportunity to relax and take in Gen-X slacker life. Great Expectations Bookstore sells literature, psychology, and mythology-oriented books as well as T-shirts, while Pipe Dreams caters to stoners young and old.

Wild and rambunctious, the **Castro** shopping district meets the needs of neighborhood residents and also caters to visitors making a pilgrimage to this gay Mecca. Most shopping is located on Castro Street south of Market and along Market Street east of Castro. Chic men's boutiques coexist with numerous used-clothing outlets. This district also has, per capita, the highest number of upscale sunglasses stores in the city. For the reader, A Different Light Bookstore carries a wide variety of books by and about gays and lesbians. Numerous boutiques, too quirky and varied to categorize, abound.

The **Mission District** is a great place to shop for antiques and used clothing in the many funky outlets. The stores here reflect the ethnic diversity of the neighborhood, with produce markets selling foods from Mexico, South and Central America, and other Latin American countries. Casa Lucas Market specializes in Central American produce and imported cheeses, and the Lucky Pork Store offers many varieties of meats. Don't miss the Dominguez Mexican Bakery. Sensual and self-help books, videos, adult toys, and safe-sex supplies are available at Good Vibrations, the best sex shop in the city. La Casa Del Libro (The Book House) has books from a multitude of Latino writers and countries, as does Modern Times Bookstore.

South-of-Market, or "SoMa," is dominated by retail stores, restaurants, and dance clubs. At the center of the new civic development in SoMa, the Yerba Buena Gardens Museum Store has magazines, tourist memorabilia, books, posters, and the famous gardens across the street. This area has more outlets and discount warehouse stores than any other in the city, including wholesale apparel warehouses like Bay Marketing Company and Russell Imports, as well as Burlington Coat Factory and the Shoe Pavilion, which sell items for the whole family at discount prices. The Flower Mart sells fresh and silk flowers, plants, pottery, and decorations at wholesale prices to the public.

BOOKSTORES

San Franciscans are justifiably proud of the city's large selection of bookstores. Here a bookstore is not just a place to buy the latest best-selling roman à clef or diet book, but also a destination for a couple on a date to browse the shelves and assess each other's tastes. It's the perfect complement to café hopping.

A Clean Well Lighted Place for Books: 601 Van Ness Ave. (Golden Gate), SF, (415) 441-6670. As its name implies, this bookstore is a pleasant place to browse through a large selection of books, tapes, and magazines, as well as a good selection of sale books. It hosts frequent author appearances.

Alexander's Books: 50 2nd St. (Market/Mission), SF, (415) 495-2992. Alexander's boasts three floors of books, with an especially good selection of children's literature.

B. Dalton Bookseller: 200 Kearny St. (Sutter), SF, (415) 956-2850. • 2 Embarcadero Center, SF, (415) 982-4278. This national chain offers a 15 percent discount card for frequent customers.

Barnes and Noble: 2550 Taylor St. (Bay/Northpoint), SF, (415) 292-6762. Yet another national chain with a general selection of books, this store also sells discounted hardcovers and bestsellers.

Books Inc.: 3515 California St. (Locust), SF, (415) 221-3666. • 2275 Market St. (16th/Noe), (415) 864-6777. This local chain is one of the oldest booksellers in California, although it has been closing old locations and opening new ones. A quarter of its stock is always marked 50 to 90 percent off. Chefs should investigate the substantial cookbook selection.

Booksmith: 1644 Haight St. (Clayton/Cole), SF, (415) 863-8688. This large neighborhood store features literary, sci-fi, mystery, and photography books.

Borders Books & Music: 400 Post St. (Powell), SF, (415) 837-1145. This enormous outlet of a national chain has a café, a wide selection of books, CDs, and tapes, and regular author readings and musical events.

Browser Books: 2195 Fillmore St. (Sacramento), SF, (415) 567-8027. The devoted staff of Browser's gives old-fashioned service to their many repeat customers. Literary, philosophy, and psychology books are emphasized at this cozy store, where late hours and strategically placed chairs invite browsing.

City Lights: 261 Columbus Ave. (Broadway/Pacific), SF, (415) 362-8193. San Francisco's pride and joy among bookstores, City Lights is run by veteran beat poet Lawrence Ferlinghetti. Conveniently located near the cafés and bars of North Beach, it's prime browsing territory for appropriate coffeehouse reading material. City Lights specializes in literary titles and also publishes cutting-edge works. If you can only make it to one bookstore, this is the one you should see.

Crown Books: 1591 Sloat Blvd. (Riverton), SF, (415) 664-1774. • 1700 Van Ness Ave. (Sacramento), SF, (415) 441-7479. National chain.

Richard Hilkert: 333 Hayes St. (Franklin/Gough), SF, (415) 863-3339. Through the Dutch door of this charming, old-fashioned bookshop, you'll find new and used books with an emphasis on design, arts, travel, and cooking.

Rizzoli: 117 Post St. (Kearny/Grant), SF, (415) 984-0225. The San Francisco retail outlet of the famous New York art-book publisher, Rizzoli sells gorgeous art books—including many by other publishers—as well as local interest titles. The elegant, mahogany-paneled store also features an espresso bar.

Solar Lights: 2068 Union St. (Buchanan/Webster), SF, (415) 567-3206. This subterranean Cow Hollow hangout specializes in contemporary literature, travel, and New Age books. They do out-of-print searches, too.

GETTING SETTLED

Stacey's: 581 Market St. (1st St./2nd St.), SF, (415) 421-4687. This mini-chain of general bookstores is an excellent resource for professionals, with extensive reference-book sections covering computers, business topics, and medical subjects.

Tillman Place Bookshop: 8 Tillman Place (off Grant btwn. Sutter and Post), SF, (415) 392-4668. This tiny, tweedy, denlike shop in an alleyway sells mostly academic works and serious literature. It's like stepping into another world.

Waldenbooks: 4 Embarcadero Center (Drumm/Sacramento), SF, (415) 397-8181. • 255 West Portal Ave. (14th Ave./Vicente), SF, (415) 664-7596. This national chain features smaller, neighborhood stores.

Specialty

A Different Light: 489 Castro St. (Market/18th St.), SF, (415) 431-0891. A community clearinghouse as well as a bookstore specializing in gay and lesbian literature, this shop offers free readings and other events two or three times a week.

Ansel Adams Center for Photography Bookstore: 250 4th St. (Howard/Folsom), SF, (415) 495-7242. Located in the Ansel Adams Center for Photography Museum, this small shop has the broadest selection of photography books in the city. You don't have to pay the museum fee to browse the books, calendars, and postcards.

Charlotte's Web: 2278 Union St. (Fillmore/Steiner), SF, (415) 441-4700. For a small but tasteful selection of children's books in an atmosphere catering to the neighboring Pacific Heights matrons, look no further. They also offer story hours.

EastWind: 1435 Stockton St. (Columbus/Vallejo), SF, (415) 772-5899. EastWind carries Chinese, Asian, and Asian-American books and authors, and books on Asian medicine, martial arts, and religions.

European Bookstore: 925 Larkin St. (Geary/Post), SF, (415) 474-0626. Europhiles will be pleased by the selection of literature, travel books, and magazines in many languages here, as well as instructional tapes, books, and ESL materials.

Kinokuniya: Japan Center, 1581 Webster St. (Post/Geary), SF, (415) 567-7625. This store offers a huge array of Japanese books, including children's titles in both Japanese and English.

Marcus Books: 1712 Fillmore St. (Post), SF, (415) 346-4222. Named for Jamaican black nationalist Marcus Garvey, this bookstore sells titles with black and African-American subjects and authors.

Modern Times: 888 Valencia St. (19th St./20th St.), SF, (415) 282-9246. This Mission District shop specializes in political and multicultural books in English and Spanish.

Mystery Bookstore: 4175 24th St. (Castro/Diamond), SF, (415) 282-7444. The detective and mystery books offered here range from paperbacks that you can read on the beach to collectibles that you would keep covered in plastic.

Used

Aardvark: 227 Church St. (Market/15th St.), SF, (415) 552-6733. The range of titles bought and sold here includes art, cooking, literary, sci-fi, and mystery books.

Acorn: 740 Polk St. (Eddy/Ellis), SF, (415) 563-1736. Acorn sells old books, collectibles, and pre-1940s magazines. They will perform worldwide searches for that hard-to-find book you're looking for.

Beat Books: 552 Hayes St. (Laguna/Octavia), SF, (415) 554-0435. Handsomely decorated with yellow walls, black-painted bookshelves, and plenty of seating options, this shop features warm service and a wide range of used books with an emphasis on lesbian and gay authors and subjects.

Carroll's: 1193 Church St. (23rd St./24th St.), SF, (415) 647-3020. Carroll's offers a broad selection of vintage paperbacks, art books, and literary titles along with some new books, all on display against a backdrop of exotic bird twitterings. Next door is a teashop where you can peruse your purchases.

Columbus Books: 540 Broadway (Columbus/Kearny), SF, (415) 986-3872. An archetypal, gigantic used bookstore with lots of dusty nooks and corners filled with a great selection of almost any kind of book. If the experience becomes too highbrow, duck next door into one of the nearby sex shops.

Dog Eared Books: 1173 Valencia St. (22nd St./23rd St.), SF, (415) 282-1901. Yet another stop for used and new books and music, this Mission District bookstore is a favorite with the Valencia Street set.

Green Apple: 506 Clement St. (6th Ave.), SF, (415) 387-2272. Green Apple overflows with new, used, and marked-down books on a full range of subjects.

Phoenix: 3850 24th St. (Vicksburg), SF, (415) 821-3477. Phoenix offers friendly, unpretentious service for a regular clientele and also buys, sells, and trades books and music. The store specializes in art, photography, literature, queer, and gender studies and has a good remainder selection.

CDS & RECORDS

Aquarius Records: 1055 Valencia St. (21st St./22nd St.), SF, (415) 647-2272. This Noe Valley institution has just moved to a larger, brighter space in the Mission from which it sells some great alternative and underground releases. A wonderfully enthusiastic staff loves turning customers on to its favorite artists. Good, hard-to-find vinyl, too.

Bay Area Records and Tapes: 1409 Polk St. (Pine), SF, (415) 441-9093. Browse through the large selection of CDs, tapes, videos, and LPs at this well-stocked shop.

Groove Merchant Records: 687 Haight St. (Steiner/Pierce), SF, (415) 252-5766. The rhythmically inclined will be pleased with the selection of ambient, acid jazz, world beat, and dance music here.

Grooves: 1797 Market St. (McCoppin), SF, (415) 436-9933. This is the place to go for vinyl, including classic rock, soul, soundtracks, jazz, rarities, and collectibles.

Jack's Record Cellar: 254 Scott St. (Haight/Page), SF, (415) 431-3047. The selection here includes jazz, blues, vocals, R&B, rockabilly, country, and international, as well as old 45s and 78s.

Let It Be Records: 2434 Judah St. (29th Ave./30th Ave.), SF, (415) 681-2113. Featuring Beatles memorabilia and rare and out-of-print records, this store is a required stop on any Beatles fan's itinerary.

Medium Rare Records: 2310 Market St. (Noe/Castro), SF, (415) 255-RARE/7273. As advertised, this shop is a storehouse of obscure, unusual, and—since it's located in the Castro—downright campy albums, selling everything from show tunes and soundtracks to pop and jazz vocalists.

Open Mind Music: 342 Divisadero St. (Oak/Page), SF, (415) 621-2244. Fans of esoteric music, including funk, reggae, jazz, and ambient, should investigate this shop.

Reckless Records: 1401 Haight St. (Masonic), SF, (415) 431-3434. Your basic Haight Street emporium, this shop sells independent rock, T-shirts, used CDs, tapes, and LPs.

Record Finder: 258 Noe St. (Market), SF, (415) 431-4443. The "anti-Tower" is located right around the corner from the chain's Castro locale and offers lots of vinyl, both new and used, and an impressive selection of underground rock singles, all at very reasonable prices.

Recycled Records: 1377 Haight St. (Masonic/Central), SF, (415) 626-4075. A Haight Street institution, this shop features used records and CDs.

GETTING SETTLED

Revolver Records: 520 Clement St. (6th Ave./7th Ave.), SF, (415) 386-6128. As its name suggests, this shop specializes in spreading the music, buying, selling, and trading a wide variety of genres.

Ritmo Latino: 2401 Mission St. (20th St.), SF, (415) 824-8556. Spanish speakers and would-be Latinos alike can find a wide variety of Spanish-language records at this Mission District shop.

Rocket Records: 1377 9th Ave. (Judah), SF, (415) 664-2324. This rock-oriented shop is a good source for new and used CDs, records and tapes, imports, and collectibles.

Streetlight Records: 3979 24th St. (Noe), SF, (415) 282-3550. • 2350 Market St. (Castro/Noe), SF, (415) 282-8000. An excellent independent record store with two city locations, this chain features a diverse selection, many rock obscurities, bargain prices on used CDs, and a helpful staff.

Tower Records: 2525 Jones St. (Columbus), SF, (415) 885-0500 (classical annex across the street at 2568 Jones St., (415) 441-4880. • 2280 Market St. (Noe), SF, (415) 621-0588. • Stonestown Galleria, 19th Ave. and Winston Dr., SF, (415) 681-2001. • **Outlet** 660 3rd St. (Brannan/Townsend), SF, (415) 957-9660. America's hippest record chain has three stores in the city, though the North Beach address is the largest. Tower has made its name with a comprehensive all-around selection, knowledgeable staff, quirky book and magazine selection, and (in general) better prices than Virgin. The **Tower Outlet**, located on Third Street in SoMa, sells back-catalog albums and remainder records at tremendous discounts.

Virgin Megastore: 2 Stockton St. (Market), SF, (415) 397-4525. The newest chain to hit downtown is also the biggest: 53,000 square feet of space are devoted to Sir Richard Branson's house of music, video, books, and multimedia. There's also a café. This store even has its own DJ booth, and there are over sixty listening stations where you can sample any track off a new CD before purchasing. The pop/rock section, which engulfs the ground floor, is good and, not surprisingly, UK imports are readily available, usually within a few days after their European release.

West Side Records: 1819 Polk St. (Jackson/Washington), SF, (415) 441-4519. Located on café-lined Polk Street, this shop specializes in vintage LPs.

Wherehouse: 1303 Van Ness Ave. (Sutter), SF, (415) 346-1978. • 2083 Union St. (Buchanan/Webster), SF, (415) 346-0944. • 3301 Geary Blvd. (Parker), SF, (415) 751-3711. • 2110 Chestnut St. (Steiner), SF, (415) 567-7884. Since this large, faceless chain recently filed for Chapter 11 reorganization, its days may be numbered. Although the chain caters mostly to those seeking mainstream bestsellers, it does trade in used CDs and cassettes, so it's always possible to find a reasonably priced gem.

FOOD & WINE

The San Francisco grocery scene is dominated by Safeway (megachain Lucky Foods also has a local presence, but most stores are in the suburbs). In addition to the giants, Cala Foods, Bell Market, and Andronico's are local chains with an area presence; Cala and Bell are mainstream, while Andronico's is upscale.

Most neighborhoods also have smaller, independent supermarkets, as well as a range of specialty, ethnic, and health food stores. In almost every neighborhood there are small corner stores every block or two offering an eclectic selection of life's daily essentials—milk, toilet paper, beer. They are usually family run, very friendly, and the kind of place where you can pick up something on credit in an emergency or leave an extra key to your house. The goods cost more than at a larger place, but the convenience is worth it. Finally, virtually any store in California can sell alcoholic beverages, so don't be surprised to see a beer cooler in your drug store or rare, expensive wines in your neighborhood supermarket.

There are also two **Farmers' Markets**, one at Civic Center Plaza, Market Street between 7th and 8th streets, (415) 558-9455, on Sunday and Wednesday mornings and another one at the Embarcadero Ferry Plaza, Market Street at Embarcadero, (510) 528-0987, on Saturday and Tuesday mornings. The Ferry Plaza Farmers' Market boasts an extensive selection of producers selling seasonal fruits, vegetables, and flowers, much of it organically grown. Other offerings include fish, meats, eggs, bread, pastries, cheese, and olive oil. Restaurant LuLu and the Hayes Street Grill both operate stands where you can indulge in fabulous Hobb's bacon and tomato sandwiches, grilled salmon sandwiches, and peach lemonade.

Andronico's: 1200 Irving St. (Funston), SF, (415) 661-3220. The Bay Area's premier upscale grocer offers an excellent selection of meats and seafood. The produce section features a number of ethnic goods; the cheese selection is outstanding; and the gourmet items are as good as you will find in many specialty stores.

Specialty Markets

San Francisco's ethnic diversity supports an incredible abundance of specialty markets. For Asian produce, sauces, seasonings, fish, and meat, head for Grant Avenue or Stockton Street in Chinatown, or Clement Street in the Richmond District. Further west on Clement Street you'll find stores jammed with Russian and Mediterranean specialties. The supermarkets in Japantown carry virtually everything you'll need for Japanese cooking or snacking. For Mexican and Central American foods, the Mission District, Twenty-Fourth Street in particular, abounds with grocers selling tortillas, chilies, beans, and Mexican fruits and beverages.

Beverages & More: 201 Bayshore Blvd. (Oakdale), SF, (415) 648-1233. This is the place for shoppers with champagne tastes and beer budgets. The prices here are some of the most competitive in the Bay Area, and the selection is out of this world. Beers can be found in an array of bottles, colors, and shades, as well as a variety of hard liquors, snacks, and pastas and sauces.

California Street Creamery: 2413 California St. (Fillmore/Steiner), SF, (415) 929-8610. A great selection of cheese, pâté, and other charcuterie is offered here, as well as wonderful pastries from some of the Bay Area's best bakeries.

Casa Lucas Market: 2934 24th St. (Harrison/Treat), SF, (415) 826-4334. Casa Lucas Market is the premier destination for all your Latin American provision needs.

Cost Plus Imports: 2552 Taylor St. (Bay), SF, (415) 928-6200. Connoisseurs will appreciate this bargain Mecca for fine wines, coffees, teas, and imported foods.

Country Cheese: 415 Divisadero St. (Oak), SF, (415) 621-8130. The hallmark here is outrageously low prices on domestic and imported cheeses, dried fruits, grains, pastas, nuts, spices, gourmet items, and fresh bread.

Greek American Food Imports: 223 Valencia St. (14th St.), SF, (415) 864-0978. This is a good place to stock up for cocktail-party food: including Greek olives, wines, oil, filo, feta, vine leaves, and baked goods.

Haig's Delicacies: 642 Clement St. (8th Ave.), SF, (415) 752-6283. A simply wonderful store filled with good things: The variety of Indian goods is outstanding, as well as the array of Southeast Asian products. A small selection of cheeses and pastries rounds out the offerings.

Happy Supermarket: 400 Clement St. (5th Ave.), SF, (415) 221-3195. For Asian groceries, this is the most complete source in the Clement shopping district. Happy features a complete butcher, an excellent produce section, a complete line of Chinese products, and a selection of Southeast Asian foods.

Leonard's 2001: 2001 Polk St. (Pacific), SF, (415) 921-2001. This friendly shop is an excellent source for grains, dried pastas, dried spices, with over 150 types of cheeses available. Unfortunately, cheeses are sold only in large blocks.

GETTING SETTLED

Lucca Delicatessen: 2120 Chestnut St. (Steiner), SF, (415) 921-7873. Given the dearth of quality provision stores in the Marina, Lucca stands out as an oasis. Overworked neighborhood yuppies flock here for the homemade ravioli, the ultimate convenience meal. You'll also find a small cheese selection, excellent cold cuts, Acme bread, a small selection of wines, and Italian olive oils.

May Wah Supermarket: 1230 Stockton St. (Broadway), SF, (415) 433-3095. • 547 Clement St. (6th Ave./7th Ave.), SF, (415) 668-2583. A highlight of any visit to Chinatown is a stop at this large and bustling Asian market. The Chinese goods include various rice and wheat noodles, black bean sauces, hoisin sauce, and spices. The selection of Indonesian, Thai, and Malaysian canned goods and bottled products is outstanding. The produce section is well stocked with Asian vegetables, and Chinese cookware and tableware are available.

Noah's Bagels: Locations throughout San Francisco. Noah's has attracted almost fanatical devotion from fans of its almost-but-not-quite New York bagels and its extensive array of bagel fixings. There are Noah's Bagel shops in every central neighborhood in San Francisco.

Prudente: 1462 Grant Ave. (Union), SF, (415) 421-0757. Better known by its former name, **Iacopi Deli** (Leo Rossi retired and sold the business), this deli continues to sell excellent, pricy housemade sausages, tortas, cold cuts, and cheeses, as well as imported Italian packaged foods such as pasta and boxed tomatoes. Great Italian sandwiches.

Rainbow Grocery: 1745 Folsom St. (13th St.), SF, (415) 863-0620. This longtime Mission district favorite recently relocated to a new, larger store with much more parking. A mostly organic and health food store, Rainbow Grocery stocks an eclectic mix of goods, ranging from fresh produce and herbs to bulk goods, candles, vitamins, and books.

Real Food Company: 1023 Stanyan St. (Carl), SF, (415) 564-2800. • 2140 Polk St. (Broadway/Vallejo), SF, (415) 673-7420. • 3939 24th St. (Noe/Sanchez), SF, (415) 282-9500. San Francisco's mini chain of health food stores, Real Food carries a beautiful selection of organic produce and unusual vegetables plus dozens of gourmet oils, vinegars, jams, and bulk grains and spices, as well as fresh and packaged baked goods. At the Stanyan and Polk locations there are restaurant-delis for take-out and eat-in. The Polk Street location sells organic meats, fish, and poultry. Unfortunately, the prices have earned the chain the name "Really expensive food company," and the healthful goods don't seem to have given employees peace of mind—they range from apathetic to hostile.

San Bruno Supermarket: 2480 San Bruno Ave. (Carl), SF, (415) 468-5788. A gem of a supermarket, this one-stop Asian shopping experience offers an excellent produce section, complete with fresh galangal, Thai eggplant, Japanese squash, bitter melon, and various Chinese cabbages, as well as a good meat department stocking beef, pork, lamb, chicken, and fresh fish.

Say Cheese: 856 Cole St. (Carl/Frederick), SF, (415) 665-5020. One of the premier cheese shops in the Bay Area, They stock well over a hundred cheeses. Some of the harder to find cheeses are Mascarpone, Manchego, Majón, and Huntsman Cheddar.

Shenson's: 5120 Geary Blvd. (15th Ave.), SF, (415) 751-4699. Homesick New Yorkers will appreciate this traditional Jewish deli, with cases full of corned beef, pastrami, lox, whitefish, herring, macaroons, *schmaltz*, chopped chicken liver, and knishes, as well as matzo ball soup.

Some Like It Hot: 3208 Scott St. (Lombard/Chestnut), SF, (415) 441-7468. The ultimate hot-foods destination, the store sells dozens of hot sauces from Jamaica, Costa Rica, Mexico, the United States, Sri Lanka, Morocco, Indonesia, Thailand, China, and India. While there are no fresh chilies, the selection of dried chilies is extraordinary.

FOOD & WINE

Super Koyama: 1790 Sutter St. (Buchanan), SF, (415) 921-6529. A pristine shop stocking all the essentials for Japanese cooking, Super Koyama has both fresh and frozen fish for sushi and sashimi, a small produce section, pastries, Japanese canned goods, crackers, candies, beverages, and condiments.

Tel Aviv Kosher Meats: 2445 Irving St. (26th Ave.), SF, (415) 661-7588. The name says it all here: cold cuts, salads, knishes, piroshkis, matzo ball soup, chopped chicken liver—in short, the works.

Trader Joe's: 555 9th St. (Bryant/Brannan), SF, (415) 863-1292. One of the most reasonably priced gourmet outlets around, Trader Joe's offers natural foods, frozen seafood, chips, dried fruit and nuts, and specialty items, as well as a wide variety of discount-priced wine and beer.

Whole Foods: 1765 California St., SF, (415) 674-0500. The newest location of this gourmet health food store is an instant success, providing customers with an abundant variety of organic foods in a soothing shopping experience. Among the offerings are a fresh seafood section, organic and conventionally grown produce, a variety of bulk rices, whole grains and granolas, a bakery and deli, a meat market featuring organic meat and homemade sausages, and a great selection of wine and beer—plus more than a hundred parking spots.

Bakeries

Just Desserts: Locations throughout San Francisco. The well-loved and ubiquitous Just Desserts chain sells its cakes, tarts, muffins, cookies, pies, and special items at its own cafés as well as other outlets. Don't miss their fresh berry pies when they are in season.

Liguria Bakery: 1700 Stockton St. (Filbert), SF, (415) 421-3786. This small storefront makes the city's best focaccia. Most of its business is wholesale to restaurants and delis (including many of its North Beach neighbors), and it frequently run out of items for retail sale early in the day. Skip the pizza flavor, instead opt for the plain or onion.

Stella: 466 Columbus Ave. (Green/Vallejo), SF, (415) 986-2914. A classic selection of pastries and cookies is offered here, as well as coffee for those who want to sit and enjoy their purchases pronto.

Victoria Pastry Company: 1362 Stockton St. (Vallejo), SF, (415) 781-2015. This bakery specializes in wedding cakes, *Gâteau St. Honoré* in particular, almond tortes, and a wide array of French and Italian cookies. At Christmastime, they bake traditional Italian goodies like *pannetone* and *torrone*.

Word of Mouth Patisserie: 1480 Fulton St. (Broderick/Baker), SF, (415) 346-9034. Although this shop specializes in wedding cakes, it also offers scones, *küchens*, lighter-than-air turnovers and cupcakes, and various sweetmeats to take out or eat with coffee on the premises. Open to public only F-Su.

Coffee & Tea

Caffè Trieste: 609 Vallejo St. (Grant), SF, (415) 982-2605. This moody beat-era café serves the best cappuccino in town, but somehow the beans from the roastery never taste as good at home.

Graffeo Coffee: 735 Columbus St. (Filbert/Greenwich), SF, (415) 986-2429. At this San Francisco institution, it's simple: Do you want light or dark or decaf made from South American, Southeast Asian, or Central American beans?

Peet's Coffee and Tea: Locations throughout San Francisco. Alfred Peet introduced Bay Area residents to premium coffee and tea blends from all over the world long before Starbucks took over the West Coast. The stores also sell a good selection of espresso makers, mugs, and teakettles.

Pure T: 2238 Polk St. (Green), SF, (415) 441-7878. This pleasant, zenlike tea salon stocks a wide assortment of prettily packaged teas: green, black, scented, and herbal, and also sells delicate cookies and a large selection of tea ice creams and sorbets.

GETTING SETTLED

Spinelli: Locations throughout San Francisco. A San Francisco native born in 1984, this chain sells "full city roast"—dark roasted—coffee. Their in-store brew is known for its strength. They also sell very good teas and fresh pastries, as well as coffee and tea brewing accoutrements.

Wine and Beer

Coit Liquors: 585 Columbus Ave. (Union), SF, (415) 986-4036. Located smack in the heart of North Beach, this small store is packed with a good selection of wine and beer at very competitive prices, including a good mix of wines from California, France, and Italy, as well as a few items from other countries. The salespeople dispense knowledgeable advice.

D&M Liquors: 2200 Fillmore St., (Sacramento), SF, (415) 346-1325. Famous during the 1980s for selling gray-market Champagne (the real French stuff) at spectacularly low prices, D&M still offers some of the area's best Champagne deals. The selection of still wines is more limited, and pricing is not as aggressively cut-rate, but this shop is still a must-visit before any New Year's Eve party. The salespeople are highly opinionated, but not everyone will agree with their taste.

Jug Shop: 1567 Pacific Ave., (Polk/Larkin), SF, (415) 885-2922. A large, all-purpose liquor store with an extensive selection of wines, good prices, and parking. California wines fill one wall, while crates and cases of French, Australian, Italian, Spanish, and Chilean wines cover the floor. Wines from a few other countries round out the selection. There's usually someone around with an opinion to offer, and the shop also hosts tastings to help you develop your own. Plenty of beer at good prices.

Plump Jack: 3201 Fillmore St. (Greenwich), SF, (415) 346-9870. The first installation of the Getty brother's empire in the Marina's Bermuda Triangle, Plump Jack offers an intelligent selection for a Pacific Heights clientele. Prices are reasonable, although slightly higher than the clubs, but the location, atmosphere, and service earn points.

Wine Club: 953 Harrison St., (5th St./6th St.), SF, (415) 512-9086. One of the premier wine outlets, this SoMa shop sells discounted high-end wines in a bare-bones warehouse atmosphere. The selection is ever-changing, but emphasizes higher-end California, French, and Italian wines. A tasting bar will help you make your picks.

HOME FURNISHINGS

General Purpose Stores

Bed and Bath Superstore: 555 9th St. (Harrison/Bryant), SF, (415) 252-0490. The name is self-explanatory—shop for bargains on bedding, towels, and bathroom accessories here, as well as nightstands, shelves, and the like. You can also find a wide selection of cookware, plates, and glassware, plus that incredible city commodity—free parking.

Butterfield West: 164 Utah St. (Alameda/15th St.), SF, (415) 861-7500. If you're looking to inject a little more drama into your shopping experience, or want to find something with a little more character than you'll find at your average department or discount store, join the ranks of the auction junkies that converge on every third Monday at Butterfield West. The Monday sales are a clearinghouse for all of the items which don't merit being shown in one of Butterfield's "Collections" or "Fine" sales, where you couldn't afford anything anyway. Come on the weekend prior to view the warehouse, full of everything from couches to paintings, books to china. Sift through the junk to find the gem that will perfect your decor. You can leave a written bid on the weekend, which will be read off during the auction as though you were there, or better yet, come to the auction and fight it out in person with your competitors. There is no minimum bid, so you can pick up some great deals if you're diligent, but be warned: a 15 percent "buyer's commission" in addition to sales tax will be tacked onto whatever you bid, so do your math before you raise that paddle.

HOME FURNISHINGS

Cost Plus Imports: 2552 Taylor St. (Bay), SF, (415) 928-6200. • 785 Serramonte Blvd. (Junipero Serra), Colma, (415) 994-7090. Cost Plus Imports is a discount store with reasonably priced furniture and kitchenware. Several types of kitchen tables are available, as well as rattan sofas and chairs. The collection of odd knickknacks, including huge paper fans and ethnic figurines, is a must-see.

Crate and Barrel: 125 Grant Ave. (Post/Berry), SF, (415) 986-4000. • **Outlet store**: 1785 4th St. (Hearst/Virginia), Berkeley, (510) 528-5500. Crate and Barrel is your best bet for a broad array of reasonably priced kitchenware. The store is packed to the gills with tableware, cooking utensils, table linens, and other kitchen items. They also have a limited selection of kitchen appliances and furniture. Service is excellent. If you're a true bargain shopper and don't mind a jaunt, check out the Crate and Barrel Outlet store (see Outlets below).

Fillamento: 2185 Fillmore St. (California/Sacramento), SF, (415) 931-2224. Go to Fillamento for the hippest home furnishings in town. It's the place for the latest designs, with an angular, ultra-refined product line that is strikingly elegant. The store's main focus is decorative accessories such as lamps and picture frames, but it also stocks furniture, bedding, tableware, toiletries, and domestic-comfort items like pajamas and day books. Expect to spend a chunk here (lamps range from $150 to $200, couches from $1,500 to $2,300), but don't expect particularly attentive service.

Macy's: Union Square, Stockton and O'Farrell sts., SF, (415) 397-3333. • Stonestown Galleria, 19th Ave. and Winston Dr., SF, (415) 753-4000. • 1 Serramonte Center, Serramonte and Callan Blvd., Daly City, (415) 994-3333. Macy's has everything you could possibly want for your home. Go to **The Cellar at Macy's** for an excellent selection of kitchenware, appliances, pots and pans, dinnerware, and glassware. Check around on the other floors for a wide selection of bone china and crystal, towels and bathroom furnishings, bed linen, beds, and a wide range of carpets and rugs. Most Macy's departments are understaffed, which means you may have to struggle to find someone who will take your money. Plans are under way for a Macy's home furnishings store in the I. Magnin building on Union Square.

Pier 1 Imports: 3535 Geary Blvd. (Stanyan), SF, (415) 387-6642 • 101 Colma Blvd. (Junipero/Serra), Colma, (415) 755-6600. Pier 1 specializes in wicker baskets and wood furniture, but it also offers basic glassware and dishes, rugs, and so forth. While not as cheap as some other outlets, there's lots of variety and stylish offerings at Pier 1.

Pottery Barn: 2100 Chestnut St. (Steiner), SF, (415) 441-1787. • One Embarcadero Center (Battery and Sacramento), SF, (415) 788-6810. • Stonestown Galleria, 19th Ave. and Winston Dr., SF, (415) 731-1863. Pottery Barn stocks everything necessary to outfit your space with the latest rustic styles and trendy upscale versions of the basics: glassware and dishware, lamps and rugs, candles, frames, vases, chests, wine racks, big cushy couches and chairs, and sturdy wood dining room tables. The Chestnut Street store also has a "design studio," where the store's employees can help you outfit your space, discussing floors, finishes, windows, tables and chairs, and lighting. Prices aren't cheap, but the offerings are stylish, and a well-chosen piece here and there could add a nice note of class to a room. Note that only the Chestnut Street store has furniture items; the other stores stock mainly dishware, glassware, candles, and smaller items.

Price Costco: 450 10th St. (Bryant), SF, (415) 626-4288. The two giants of warehouse shopping, Costco and Price Club, merged to form Price Costco. The transformation is not yet complete, so each store may go by any one of the three names. You have to be a member to shop at Price Costco, but the big plus is the terrific prices, as many things are sold in bulk. Yet the stock, which ranges from stereos to barbecues to dish soap, can be very random. The brand choice is very limited as well. While prices can be low, service is nonexistent, as is customer support if something goes wrong with your purchase.

Target: 5001 Junipero Serra Blvd. (Serramonte), Colma, (415) 992-8433. Target is a treasure chest of reasonably priced household necessities, offering cheap towels, pots

GETTING SETTLED

and pans, plastic anythings, and basic furniture; you can count on them to outfit your bedroom, bathroom, and kitchen for less money than almost anywhere else. Look for all the kitchen and bathroom accessories you could ever want—plates, glasses, cooking utensils, soap holders, shower caddies, and shower curtains galore. Target's furniture is mostly along the line of shelving units, nightstands, and chairs made of either lightweight wood or plastic, mostly unassembled.

Whole Earth Access: 401 Bayshore Blvd. (Cortland/Oakdale), SF, (415) 285-5244. Whole Earth Access is Sears for the New Age crowd, with a bit of everything the modern family needs to get started, from jeans to housewares to furniture. It stocks a small selection of functional, low-priced furniture, with an emphasis on mattresses and home-office items. A trip to Whole Earth Access can yield a cornucopia of stylish housewares: reasonably priced dishware and glasses, cutting boards, Cuisinarts, blenders, and so on, as well as a decent selection of electronics: audio, video, communications, and so forth. A recent reorganization led to some store closings and a reduction in product lines carried.

Z Gallerie: San Francisco Centre, 865 Market St. (5th St.), SF, (415) 495-7121. • Stonestown Galleria, 19th Ave. and Winston Dr., SF, (415) 664-7891. • 2071 Union St. (Webster/Buchanan), SF, (415) 346-9000. • 2154 Union St. (Fillmore), SF, (415) 567-4891. • 1465 Haight St. (Masonic/Ashbury), SF, (415) 863-7466. Wherever there are yuppies, there's Z Gallerie: one of the Bay Area's premier purveyor of housewares and decorative items. Among the stylish and distinctive wares are dishware, glassware, flatware, overstuffed couches and funky chairs, beds, coffee and dining tables, bath products, and a wide variety of framed and unframed art posters.

Furniture

Basic Bookshelves Too: 555 Hayes St. (Gough/Octavia), SF, (415) 863-5864. This nononsense store offer fine unfinished furniture, made-to-order pieces, and wooden desks and bookcases painted in mouth-watering shades.

Discount Depot: 520 Haight St. (Fillmore/Steiner), SF, (415) 552-1474. This basic home-furnishings store is packed with futons, mattresses, furnishings, and linens at low prices.

The Futon Gallery Plus: 3401 Geary Blvd. (Beaumont), SF, (415) 750-1492. For an upscale line of futons (with an especially wide selection of frames and covers) and excellent service, look no further.

The Futon Shop: 810 Van Ness Ave. (Eddy), SF, (415) 563-8866. If you're looking for a large selection of futons and frames and a self-service atmosphere, the Futon Shop is the ticket.

Harrington Bros. Inc.: 599 Valencia St. (17th St.), SF, (415) 861-7300. Harrington Bros. offers a wide variety of used furniture and is a good starting point for exploring the Mission District's many secondhand shops.

Limn: 290 Townsend St. (4th St.), SF, (415) 543-5466. The city's best-known location for cutting-edge designer furniture, Limn offers wares from Ligne Roset, Herman Miller, and many esoteric European manufacturers. Bargain hunters can find instant gratification and discounts on one-of-a-kind showroom items. Even if you can't afford a $5,000-dollar-couch, it's worth a visit here just to see some stunning art furniture.

Mattress Discounters: 1350 Van Ness Ave. (Bush), SF, (415) 567-6288. • 4550 Geary Blvd. (10th Ave.), SF, (415) 752-7911. Mattress Discounters stocks a wide range of mattresses, including national brands and discounted products.

Mike Furniture: 2142 Fillmore St. (Sacramento), SF, (415) 567-2700. Well-known designer Mike Moore sells his chic, California-style furniture here, nicely filling the furniture niche between department stores and studio designers. Moore specializes in overscale couches, armchairs, and clean-lined accessories.

HOME FURNISHINGS

Nest: 2300 Fillmore St. (Clay), SF, (415) 292-6199. This charming Fillmore Street shop sells quirky garden furniture, retro dishware, jewelry, and antiques. Well worth a visit.

Thomas Moser Cabinetmakers: 3395 Sacramento St. (Presidio/Walnut), (415) 931-8131. This showroom displays the elegant, Shaker-inspired wooden furniture advertised in such magazines as *The New Yorker*. Not for the faint of wallet.

Zinc Details: 1905 Fillmore St. (Pine/Bush), SF, (415) 776-2100. Visit Zinc Details when you get a hankering for modern retro-contemporary classics for the home—colored glass vases, groovy lamps, 1950s-style futuristic dining furniture, and novelties, including artwork by local artists.

Zonal: 568 Hayes St. (Octavia/Laguna), SF, (415) 255-9307. Located in hip Hayes Valley, Zonal has made its name selling ultra-distressed furnishings: weather-beaten garden furniture, old porch swings, and rusty sconces.

Housewares

Affordable Essentials: 518 Haight St. (Fillmore), SF, (415) 703-0128. All the mundane household goods—cleaning supplies, cleaning tools, paper items—can be found here at very good prices.

Cliff's Variety: 479 Castro St. (18th St./Market), SF, (415) 431-5365. Cliff's Variety offers fashionable basics for the home, lamps, toys, and fun little gewgaws.

City Discount: 2436 Polk St. (Union/Filbert), SF, (415) 771-4649. The remedy for Williams-Sonoma overload, this small storefront is crammed with an odd collection of useful items at bargain prices. The whatever-fell-off-the-truck merchandise consists primarily of restaurant supplies and includes gourmet foodstuffs (tiny jars of jam, industrial-size sized ketchup, tubes of anchovy paste), kitchenware galore (knives, pots, pans, utensils), basic plates, glasses, flatware, candles, sponges, and more.

Cookin': 339 Divisadero St. (Page/Oak), SF, (415) 861-1854. Recycled gourmet appurtenances are sold here in an old-time hardware-store atmosphere. Everything from dozens of dainty demitasses to basic cast iron pots, cutesy collectable salt and pepper shakers, and nutmeg graters. If it belongs in a kitchen or a pantry, you will find it here.

SFMOMA Museum Store: 151 3rd St. (Mission/Howard), SF, (415) 357-4035. For those who like artistic housewares, the SFMOMA gift store offers a small selection of artist-designed gadgets ranging from tea kettles and corkscrews to plates and silverware. Prices reflect the products' hand-crafted nature.

Strouds: 731 Market St. (3rd St./4th St.), SF, (415) 979-0460. Strouds stores offer an incredible variety of bed and bath items: sheets, comforters, pillows, towels, and bedroom and bathroom accessories. Watch for their frequent sales.

Williams-Sonoma: 2 Embarcadero Center (Sacramento and Front), SF, (415) 421-2033. • San Francisco Centre, 865 Market St. (5th St.), SF, (415) 546-0171. • Stonestown Galleria, 19th Ave. and Winston Dr., SF, (415) 681-5525. • 150 Post St. (Grant/Stockton), SF, (415) 362-6904. Gorgeous copper pots, a wide variety of kitchen gadgetry, tableware, and glassware are all featured at these specialty stores. Prices are on the high side, but so is the quality.

Thrift Stores

Thrift stores sell donated items of varying quality at low prices, while consignment stores are more picky about the goods they sell and consequently charge more. Consignment shops will also sell your unwanted things for a percentage. Also consider checking out one of **Butterfield West**'s auctions (see description under General Purpose Stores above). Finally, pick up a copy of *Rummaging Through Northern California*, a free directory of resale shops available at many thrift shops, for more ideas.

GETTING SETTLED

Discovery Shop: 1827 Union St. (Octavia/Laguna), SF, (415) 929-8053. If you're in the market for a mink coat or a designer dress, visit the Discovery Shop. The wares at this store are amazingly tasteful and include everything from clothes to furniture to used magazines. Prices are higher than the usual thrift store, but sales are out of this world.

Goodwill: 1700 Haight St. (Cole), SF, (415) 387-1192. • 820 Clement St. (9th Ave./10th Ave.), SF, (415) 668-3635. • 1700 Fillmore St. (Post), SF, (415) 441-2159. • 822 Geary St. (Larkin/Hyde), SF, (415) 922-0405. • 2279 Mission St. (19th St.), SF, (415) 826-5759. • 3801 3rd St. (Evans), SF, (415) 641-4470. • 241 10th St. (Howard/Folsom), SF, (415) 252-1677. This national institution, known for offering a large selection of goods at low prices, has many area outlets.

Salvation Army: 1185 Sutter St. (Polk), SF, (415) 771-3818. • 1509 Valencia St. (26th St.), SF, (415) 695-8040. In addition to used clothing, the Salvation Army offers secondhand couches, fridges, mattresses, desks, and more, all at very low prices.

Savers: 2840 Geneva Ave. (Oriente), Daly City, (415) 468-0646. This store offers a good selection of general housewares. For $3, you can walk away with a Chinese wok, and for 99 cents each, you can assemble a decent set of glasses.

Flea Markets and Garage Sales

The classified ads in the local papers are a great resource for surprise finds. You'll see listings of secondhand goods, the week's flea markets and garage sales, and sometimes even a freebie section. Go early for the best selection.

OUTLETS

Crate & Barrel: 1785 4th St. (Hearst/Virginia), Berkeley, (510) 528-5500. The Crate and Barrel Outlet offers out-of-season, discontinued, and (occasionally) damaged goods from their retail stores. The markdowns are less generous (25 to 30 percent) than most outlets, but they can add up if you're trying to furnish an entire house.

Esprit Factory Outlet: 499 Illinois St. (16th St.), SF, (415) 957-2550. San Francisco's most dynamic outlet store is filled with high-tech displays and merchandise at 30 to 75 percent off department-store prices.

Gunne Sax: 35 Stanford St. (Brannan), SF, (415) 495-3326. In the market for formalwear? Gunne Sax's outlet (the biggest user of lace in the country) has a wide selection of evening dresses and evening ware at good prices.

Marina Square in San Leandro: Marina Square, (I-880 at Marina Blvd.), San Leandro. This East Bay mall has outlet stores for **The Gap** and **Eddie Bauer**, a discount publishers' outlet, and more. There's also a **Nordstrom Rack** clearance center replete with dresses and stylish men's suits—all recent store rejects at great markdowns.

North Face Outlet: 1325 Howard St. (9th St./10th St.), SF, (415) 626-6444. • 1238 5th St. (Gilman), Berkeley, (510) 526-3530. The North Face Outlet features sportswear, outerwear, skiwear, and trustworthy equipment at discounted prices. However, there are usually no warranties on outlet goods, something to consider before making any serious investments.

Factory Stores at Nut Tree: I-80 at 505 Orange Dr., Nut Tree exit, Vacaville, (707) 447-5755. At this giant collection of outlets, the 50 stores range from **Benetton** to **Bugle Boy**.

Outlets at Gilroy: Hwy 101 at Leavesley Rd. (Hwy 152) exit, Gilroy, (408) 842-3729. Next door to the Pacific West Outlet Center, Outlets at Gilroy offers over 70 outlets.

Pacific West Outlet Center: Hwy 101 at Leavesley Rd. (Hwy 152) exit, Gilroy, (408) 847-4155. Pacific West offers **Liz Claiborne** and the **Nike Factory Store**, as well as 50 designer outlets and a wonderful kitchenware discount store. Carloads of bargain hunters flock here, so prepare for full-contact shopping.

Six Sixty Center: 660 3rd St. (Brannan/Townsend), SF, (415) 227-0464. Lesser known manufactures such as **Dress Market** and **Carole's Shoe Heaven** sell their wares in this SoMa outlet center.

SPECIALTY STORES

Bernal Heights

Living Pieces: 307 Cortland Ave. (Bocana), SF, (415) 285-9617. An eclectic range of items is on display here, from velvet dresses, Christian Dior sunglasses, used dishes, and rocking chairs to turn-of-the-century wall adornments.

Custom Leather Shop: 813 Cortland Ave. (Gates/Ellsworth), SF, (415) 826-5089. The last of a dying breed, this shop makes custom shoes as well as belts, purses, and sandals.

Las Road Runners: 511 Cortland Ave. (Andover), SF, (415) 641-0402. For dishware, kitchen utensils, dolls, and more all under one roof, head for this outpost.

Cooperative Popular Teodosia: 430A Cortland Ave. (Andover), SF, (415) 642-9223, (800) 731-5865. A group of more than 150 local artists and craftspeople show their wares at this colorful gallery. Among the wares are dream catchers, mirrors, moon-shaped pillows, Guatemalan flutes, jewelry, even a carved chess board.

Heartfelt: 436 Cortland Ave. (Andover), SF, (415) 648-1380. All sorts of lighthearted items can be found at Heartfelt, including marbles, kissing-couple double candles, and squirmy plastic toys.

Castro

DYMK: 4079 18th St. (Castro/Noe), SF, (415) 864-3160. DYMK stands for "Does Your Mother Know," and maybe she shouldn't—the store stocks explicit gay-male-themed greeting cards. No minors are allowed.

Main Line: 516 Castro St. (18th St.), SF, (415) 863-7811. • 1928 Fillmore St. (Bush/Pine), SF, (415) 563-4438. Shop Main Line for lava lamps and other novelties, plus end tables, candles and candle holders, jewelry, and cards.

Mercury Mail Order: 4084 18th St. (Castro/Hartford), SF, (415) 621-1188. Only in San Francisco . . . Mercury is a mail-order and retail store supplying leather, lubricants, condoms, and other autoerotic necessities.

Uncle Mame: 2193 Market St. (15th St.), SF, (415) 626-1953. Uncle Mame is an adult toy store/museum dedicated to pop culture nostalgia. Look here for Oscar Meyer wiener whistles, Jetson-family rubber stamps, and Mr. Peanut salt-and-pepper shakers.

Haight

Gargoyle: 1324 Haight St. (Central/Masonic), SF, (415) 552-7393. A haven for the pierced and black-clad fetishist crowd, Gargoyle features a "Dark Collection of Things Terrifying and Lovely." Pick up jewelry, candles, incense, herbs, stationery, gargoyle-themed knickknacks, and other gothic gewgaws infused with morbid overtones.

Gargoyle Beads: 1310 Haight St. (Central/Masonic), SF, (415) 552-GARG/4274. Gargoyle stocks every kind of bead, chain, cord, clasp, and wire for jewelry making, plus various amulets, jewelry, and jewelry-making tools.

Mascara Club: 1408 Haight St. (Masonic), SF, (415) 863-2837. Mascara Club is the perfect shop to find a little pick-me-up. It's a tiny place filled with funny cards, colorful novelties, psychedelia, groovy candles, picture frames, clocks, plastic toys, watches, and cool little lamps.

PlaNetweavers: 1573 Haight St. (Clayton), SF, (415) 864-4415. A treasure trove for upscale gifts with an international flavor, such as decorative masks, bongo drums, candles, toiletries, incense, attractive jewelry boxes and clocks, quality leatherbound journals, stationery and cards, books, tapestries, and T-shirts.

GETTING SETTLED

Positively Haight Street: 1157 Masonic Ave. (Haight/Page), SF, (800) 870-8878, (415) ALA-TRIP/252-8747. Where the Grateful Dead will not fade away. A clothing and gift store brimming with tie-dyed tapestries, vintage posters, men's and women's imported fashions, hemp clothing, handcrafted smoking accessories, candles, jewelry, incense, Grateful Dead merchandise, and a selection of more than 200 printed T-shirts.

Fillmore

Cedanna: 1925 Fillmore St. (Pine/Bush), SF, (415) 474-7152. A gallery and store for "artful living," Cedanna provides hours of browsing entertainment. The store also carries an elegant collection of functional works by artists (about half local), from a crushed-glass-encrusted telephone table to a wrought-iron twisting CD tower, plus toiletries, artsy books, jewelry, and iron sculpture.

Main Line: 1928 Fillmore St. (Pine/Bush), SF, (415) 563-GIFT/4438. • 516 Castro St. (18th), SF, (415) 863-7811. Main Line offers toys for the urban professional, from the tasteless and ultra-tacky ("California Earthquake in a Can" and worse) to the hip and functional (couches, coffee and end tables) to the beautiful (jewelry and handicrafts).

Nile Trading Co.: 1856 Fillmore St. (Sutter/Bush), SF, (415) 776-2233. As the name of the shop suggests, this store carries African objets d'art, jewelry, hats, and clothing.

Surprise Party!: 1900A Fillmore St. (Bush), SF, (415) 928-1885. This tiny shop carries beautiful shells, beads, coral, and silver jewelry.

Financial District

Arch: 407 Jackson St. (Sansome), SF, (415) 433-2724. In the shadow of the Transamerica Pyramid, amid the serenity of this little stretch of Jackson Street populated by stately antiques galleries, small architectural bookstores, and rug merchants, you'll find Arch, an architectural and graphic design materials store that also carries unique stationery and other cool items like intricate picture frames.

Hayes Valley

The African Outlet: 524 Octavia St. (Hayes/Grove), SF, (415) 864-EKPO/3576. Self-billed as "the coolest and hardest store in the nation" and "the only authentic authorized African store in the nation," the tiny African Outlet is home to African goods, brilliantly colored and patterned fabrics, men's, women's, and children's fashions, and treasures for your walls, shelves, head, neck, arms, and feet.

Art Options: 372 Hayes St. (Gough/Franklin), SF, (415) 252-8334. One of a number of galleries along Hayes Street between Franklin and Buchanan in Hayes Valley, Art Options displays a clean-lined selection of artists' works in glass, ceramics, and wood, as well as paintings and handmade jewelry.

Curios and Candles: 289 Divisadero St. (Haight/Page), SF, (415) 863-5669. This busy place offers readings and occult items, an array of herbs and herbal teas from deer's tongue to chamomile, incense and candles, earrings, books on the occult and spirituality, and greeting cards. The sales assistants are prohibited from dispensing medical advice about their herbs, but they're happy to give you information on casting spells.

The Magical Trinket: 524 Hayes St. (Octavia/Laguna), SF, (415) 626-0764. The Magical Trinket is the place to head for an extensive selection of beads, baubles, bangles, and jewelry-making stuff. The store also offers workshops in bead making and other crafts—call for a class schedule.

Marina

Earthsake: 2076 Chestnut St. (Fillmore/Steiner), SF, (415) 441-2896. Earthsake calls itself a store with "products that make a difference." Indeed, everything at Earthsake is eco-friendly or recycled—check out the little welded animals made from the salvaged metal of abandoned cars—and some of it is handmade by artists. The store stocks furniture, clothing, and various objets d'art.

Forbeadin': 2381 Chestnut St. (Scott/Divisadero), SF, (415) 923-1414. This tiny store in the Marina is a good source for gemstones, beads, medallions, and amulets.

Laurel's Treasures and Toys: 2258 Chestnut St. (Scott/Pierce), SF, (415) 441-5952. Every inch of this closet-sized store is jam packed with little goodies: scarves, vests, jewelry, umbrellas, and novelty books.

Red Rose Gallerie: 2251 Chestnut St. (Scott/Pierce), SF, (415) 776-6871. For a true California experience, visit Red Rose Gallerie, which specializes in "empowering products for body, mind and spirit." Every ilk of Eastern-inspired spiritual gift can be found here, from tiny, elegant clay teapots to healing gemstones and books on how to achieve a Zen state of mind. To receive a catalog of the store's products, call (800) 374-5505.

Mission

Botanica Yoruba: 998 Valencia St. (21st St.), SF, (415) 826-4967. Botanica Yoruba offers spiritual consulting, incense, and herbs. It's also the place to head for various religious aids such as "black water" or "bear fat," beads, and devotional candles.

Flax: 1699 Market St. (Valencia), SF, (415) 552-2355. San Francisco's premier spot for art supplies, Flax carries a wide array of pens, brushes, inks, paint, and portfolios, as well as an unbelievable selection of papers, including stationery, gift wrap, and handmade specialty papers. This is the place for artistic invitations or announcements.

Three Eighty One: 381 Guerrero St. (15th St./16th St.), SF, (415) 621-3830. A self-described "spiritual bizarre" featuring curios and things mystical and spooky. You can also find kitschy knickknacks, odd candles (like the ones in the shape of a hand, with five wicks), trendy T-shirts, religious-themed amulets, and Jesus imagery.

Upstairs Downstairs: 890 Valencia St. (20th St.), SF, (415) 647-4211. An "antiques department store," Upstairs Downstairs carries a selection of funky 1950s Americana; downstairs is like your grandma's basement, packed with chunky old furniture and huge 1950s fast-food signage. Prices are moderate and the tackiness is unbeatable.

Union Street

The Americas: 1977 Union St. (Buchanan/Laguna), SF, (415) 921-4600, (800) ARTI-FAX/278-4329. The Americas is a vivid little eye-catcher, featuring beautiful, brilliantly colored kachinas and folk and tribal art from both North and South America.

Bishop's: 2266 Union St. (Steiner/Fillmore), SF, (415) 673-1292. Bishop's calls itself "a not-so-general general store," and indeed, you won't find flour and provisions here—you will find tin toys, women's and men's clothing, cards and paper products, and assorted doodads.

Kozo: 1969-A Union St. (Buchanan/Laguna), SF, (415) 351-2114. • 531 Castro St. (18th St./19th St.), SF, (415) 621-0869. Visit Kozo when you need any kind of decorative paper or are looking for elegant stationery to give as a gift. The store is gorgeous, filled with neatly organized, extraordinarily ornate handmade decorative papers, books of stationery, and blank books. Kozo also offers bookbinding services.

SPORTING GOODS

General Purpose

Any Mountain: 737 Market St. (3rd St./4th St.), SF, (415) 284-9990. Too broad to be a specialty store but too specialized to be a general store, Any Mountain has a great selection of ski and snowboard equipment and apparel, Rollerblades, and even some camping equipment. Beyond that, you'd better look elsewhere. No rentals.

Dave Sullivan's Sport Shop: 5323 Geary Blvd. (17th Ave./18th Ave.), SF, (415) 751-7070. This mom-and-pop establishment is especially good for fishing, skiing, and

GETTING SETTLED

camping equipment. Ski and snowboard rentals are offered at a reasonable price, as are the sundry items that most places leave out (like jackets and ski racks). A wide array of camping equipment and group summer games rentals make this a great place when you feel like trying something new (bocce ball, anyone?).

G&M Sales: 1667 Market St. (Gough), SF, (415) 863-2855. The biggest sporting goods store in the city, with enough toys to tempt even the most determined couch potato. Great place to stock up for camping, fishing, and skiing. The cavernous second floor has more tents on display than you thought you'd ever see in one room; the emphasis is on RV-type goods. Like Dave Sullivan, if you want it, they rent it—both summer and winter equipment. They leave nothing out: not the ski gloves, not the ice chest, nothing.

Lombardi Sports: 1600 Jackson St. (Polk), SF, (415) 771-0600. A good source for most items, unless you're looking for *highly* specialized equipment. The store boasts large skiing, bicycling, and camping departments, and also rents skis and snowboards.

Play It Again Sports: 45 West Portal Ave. (Ulloa), SF, (415) 753-3049. A cheap alternative for those who aren't ready to shell out big bucks for new equipment. Here, used equipment gets a second chance. Bring in that dusty stair-stepper you're never going to use, and trade it in for something you will. They take in all types of equipment on trade-for-credit, consignment or—if you've got something really good—cash. Rental skis are also available at reasonable prices. Play It Again has sixteen locations throughout the Bay Area, so call around and see if they've what you're looking for.

Specialty

Cool World Sports: 2426 California St. (Fillmore/Steiner), SF, (415) 928-3639. A high-end selection of ski and snowboarding equipment and hard-to-find European lines of outdoor apparel are the hallmarks of this store. Although they don't rent basic skis, you can demo better ones for a fee if you're thinking of upgrading. A computerized foot scanner takes custom boot fitting into the next century. Snowboard rentals are reasonable, and you're promised brand-new equipment.

Don Sherwood Golf & Tennis World: 320 Grant Ave. (Sutter), SF, (415) 989-5000. This legendary sporting goods store offers the best-quality (and the largest) selection in the city, a full range of services, including club adjustment and racquet restringing, and an extremely helpful staff. Try out your racquet in the practice tunnel, equipped with a ball server, or demo one for $10 for five days. You can't demo golf clubs, but you can give them a whack at the practice net in the store. Check out the line of golf and tennis clothes, which will keep you looking like a pro, even when your swing speaks the truth.

Fry's Warehouse Golf & Tennis: 164 Marco Way (South Airport), South SF, (415) 583-5034. This discount warehouse, located near the airport, does a large tourist business, but natives also stop by on their way out of town to spiff up their image for that first drive or serve.

FTC Ski & Sports: 1586 Bush St. (Franklin/Van Ness), SF, (415) 673-8363. A full-service ski and snowboard shop with a sampling of other goods, including in-line skates and tennis racquets. You can rent skis and boards or demo them and apply the charge to the purchase of new equipment.

Golf Mart: Target shopping mall, 4937 Junipero Serra Blvd. (Serramonte), Colma, (415) 994-4653. Even if you're not sure what you want, you can probably find it in this warehouse crammed with golf-related equipment. The stock runs the gamut, from beginner sets to pro clubs. Try them out at the in-store practice net.

Hoy's Sports: 1632 Haight St. (Clayton/Cole), SF, (415) 252-5370. The unbeatable selection of athletic shoes here is definitely worth a look.

Marmot Mountain Works: 3049 Adeline St. (Ashby), Berkeley, (510) 849-0735. • 901 Sir Francis Drake Blvd., Kentfield, (415) 454-8543. Fully loaded outdoor stores with a particularly good selection of technical mountaineering gear and backcountry ski equipment. The friendly, knowledgeable staff clearly uses the merchandise. They have great end-of-season sales. If you can't afford to buy, check out the extensive rental program.

North Face: 180 Post St. (Grant/Kearny), SF, (415) 433-3223. • Outlet: 1325 Howard St. (9th St./10th St.), SF, (415) 626-6444. Located amid the perfume-and-handbag boutiques around Union Square, this shop attracts a hardier clientele. The sales reps are prepared to arm you for even the most serious mountain trek with their specialized gear and clothing for rockclimbing, backpacking, and trekking. For the adventurer on a more restricted budget, try the **North Face Outlet** in SoMa. Savings are not huge, but it's worth a look if you're shopping in the off season (see Outlets above).

On the Run: 1310 9th Ave. (Irving), SF, (415) 665-5311. The new, larger location of this store is still dedicated to walkers, power-walkers, joggers, and marathon runners of every speed and intensity. In addition to running and aerobic shoes, they also carry walking shoes by Rockport and others.

Patagonia: 770 North Point St. (Hyde/Leavenworth), SF, (415) 771-2050. This store showcases Patagonia's full catalog of beautiful, pricy outdoor apparel, some sleeping bags, backpacks, walking and hiking shoes, and a good library of outdoor books.

REI: 1338 San Pablo Ave. (Gilman), Berkeley, (510) 527-4140. • 1119 Industrial Rd. (Holly), San Carlos, (415) 508-2330. If you're stocking up on camping equipment or looking for the perfect backpack, it's worth driving for REI's informed staff and huge selection. The stores also sell kayaks, bikes, canoes, and Bay Area maps. The selection of rental equipment, both for the slopes and for camping, is excellent, and you get a better deal if you become a member ($15 for lifetime membership).

SFO Snowboarding: 618 Shrader St. (Haight/Waller), SF, (415) 386-1666. The traditional skier will find no satisfaction here. SFO rents and sells snowboards only. Great selection ranging from your basic board to ones that will make you the envy of everyone on the mountain (yeah, we know, you're too cool to care about that).

Ski Circus: 3121 Laguna St. (Greenwich/Lombard), SF, (415) 922-5257. A full-service shop for the serious skier, Ski Circus offers a full line of middle- to high-end ski equipment and apparel, as well as custom boot fitting and ski tune-ups. Pick up weekend ski rentals on Thursday and head for the hills. Open October-May.

Swiss Ski Sports: 559 Clay St. (Montgomery/Sansome), SF, (415) 434-0322. This top-quality ski shop focuses primarily on ski equipment and apparel in the winter and is closed in the summer. High-end skis, snowboards, and clothing are available for sale or rental. The excellent staff—some with authentic European accents—will help you prepare for the slopes.

Tennis Shack-Baysport: 3375 Sacramento St. (Presidio/Walnut), SF, (415) 928-2255. Browse through the small selection of racquets displayed in a nontraditional, laid-back atmosphere and check out the bulletin board of players looking for partners and adversaries.

TOYS

Ark Toys Books & Crafts: 3845 24th St. (Church/Sanchez), SF, (415) 821-1257. Tasteful wooden toys, cards, books, and games are sold here. The owner of the Ark is a founder of the Waldorf School, and the store used to be located in the school.

Basic Brown Bears: 444 De Haro St. (17th St./Mariposa), SF, (415) 626-0781. Basic Brown Bears is a field-trip destination for many local school (and preschool) kids. Not only can you buy their bears at reasonable prices but you can also stuff your own.

GETTING SETTLED

Cliff's Variety: 479 Castro St. (18th St./Market), SF, (415) 431-5365. Cliff's Variety is really a hardware store, but parents will appreciate its eclectic selection of obscure and usually affordable toys and games for kids of all ages.

Exploratorium Store: 3601 Lyon St. (Marina Blvd.), SF, (415) 561-0390, (415) 561-0393 (mail order). For playful educational toys, check out the Exploratorium Store, which you can access without paying admission to the museum. Aside from a huge assortment of standard chemistry sets and science books, you can find bubble gum-making kits that teach kids about rubber trees in the rainforest and reusable exploding cap-balls that teach parents the limits of patience, as well as a great assortment of plastic insects, Wild Planet Toys, and fun educational books and games.

FAO Schwarz Fifth Ave.: 48 Stockton St. (O'Farrell), SF, (415) 394-8700. For an upscale toy shopping experience, check out the enormous FAO Schwarz store near Union Square. Look for the store's famous selection of stuffed animals, books, and dolls, as well as an array of more lowbrow Saturday-morning plastic toys (prices are generally higher than Toys R Us). Many come just to gawk at exotic and expensive playthings sold to the scions of the rich and famous.

Hearth Song: 3505 California St. (Laurel/Spruce), SF, (415) 397-9900. Hearth Song has a wide assortment of quality nontoxic arts and crafts supplies, wooden toys and puppets, and dolls. As their ad says, "Toys that run on imagination." Hearthsong's selection better suits older children, as many of their art supplies and toys include small pieces or sharp edges. The wares are a bit pricy, and the quality does not always match the price.

Imaginarium: 3535 California St. (Laurel/Spruce), SF, (415) 387-9885. • Stonestown Galleria, 19th Ave. and Winston Dr., SF, (415) 566-4111. The science kits, art projects, and learning toys here are fantastic, from infant crib toys and plush animals through young adult computer games. Competitive prices to boot.

Jeffrey's Toys: 7 3rd St. (Market), SF, (415) 546-6551. Very convenient for downtown workers, Jeffrey's is located near the financial district. It stocks everything from wind-up dung beetles to teddy bears with their own castles, Hello Kitty paraphernalia, hatching dinosaur egg-puppets, and odd-shaped Slinkies. Jeffrey's also has two walls devoted to comic books.

Kinder Toys: 1974 Union St. (Laguna/Buchanan), SF, (415) 673-1780. Kinder Toys offers a great selection of wooden toys and cloth puppets from Europe. Their selection includes high-quality puzzles, trains, and pull toys. Look for the great, homemade Ferris wheel in the front window. Kids are encouraged to play here.

Toys R Us: 555 9th St. (Bryant/Brannan), (415) 252-0607. • 2675 Geary Blvd. (Masonic), SF, (415) 931-8896. If you are craving the latest in plastic, prepackaged, made-in-China toys, Toys R Us is never far away. They have two locations in San Francisco proper, and five more in nearby towns. The selection of mass-market toys—from classic games to anything your little ones saw on Saturday morning—and prices are hard to beat, although service is minimal. They also have a good selection of baby items and furniture.

Wound About: Pier 39 (Embarcadero), SF, (415) 986-8697. If you decide to brave Fisherman's Wharf, be sure to allow plenty of time to explore Wound About, which offers a full spectrum of windup and mechanical toys. For a few bucks you can choose from every shape of little plastic bug, car, robot, or animal. Big spenders can invest in a variety of battery-operated squeaking and squawking pigs, gorillas, little puppy dogs, and even Godzillas.

Restaurants

Akiko's Sushi Bar ★★ $ Union Sq.: 542 Mason St. (Post/Sutter), (415) 989-8218. With only four small tables and a few places at the sushi bar, Akiko's will never become a major destination, although the food is certainly worthy. Glistening fresh sushi (ask for albacore if it's available), savory *udon*, and low, low prices make this hole-in-the-wall a find among the Union Square restaurants. Service from the husband-and-wife team is polite but disorganized—don't come if you're rushing to make a curtain. Not much decor, with Formica tables and a fish tank. • M-Sa 11:30am-9:30pm.

Alain Rondelli ★★★ $$$$ Richmond: 126 Clement St. (2nd Ave./3rd Ave.), (415) 387-0408 Dressed to the nines, customers arriving at Alain Rondelli might at first feel a little awkward in this neighborhood that is better known for its ethnic eateries. They'll feel more at home once they are seated in the understated dining room and presented with a menu offering a reassuring array of sophisticated contemporary French dishes. The namesake chef earned his stars at the late revered Ernie's before striking out on his own, and critics and diners have been oohing and aahing from the beginning. Start with a foie gras, fig, and warm brioche appetizer to get in the mood, then sample such creations as crisp skinned salmon with lemon and mint or oxtail braised in red wine, tapioca, and young carrots. Tasting menus allow the whole table to share the complete experience without passing plates. Usually the food is as delicate and refined as you'd expect in such a high-ticket spot, and the service is sure to please. But, ineffably, you don't always leave feeling you've experienced culinary nirvana. Reservations recommended. • Tu-Th, Su 5:30-10pm; F-Sa 5:30-10:30pm.

Albona ★★★ $$ North Beach: 545 Francisco St. (Taylor/Mason), (415) 441-1040. Named after the owner's hometown on the Istrian Peninsula (the point of land that sticks out below Trieste across the Adriatic from Venice), this eatery serves a menu that meshes cuisines of Central Europe and Italy into a unique table. Delicacies include homemade ravioli stuffed with nuts and cheeses, fried gnocchi in a savory sauce with bits of sirloin, and lamb in pomegranate sauce. Everything is memorable here, including the service, which is very friendly. All of the pastas and desserts are made on the premises. Reservations recommended. • Tu-Sa 5-10pm.

Andalé Taqueria ★★ ¢ Marina: 2150 Chestnut St. (Steiner/Pierce), (415) 749-0506. See Peninsula/San Jose section for review. • M-Th 11am-10pm; F 11am-11pm; Sa-Su 9:30am-10pm.

Angkor Borei ★★ $ Mission: 3471 Mission St. (Cortland/30th St.), (415) 550-8417. Located on the edge of the Mission, this modest restaurant offers an unusual dining experience at reasonable prices. Start off with the cold Cambodian noodles served with a mild fish-lime sauce or fresh spinach leaves that you stuff with various fillings and dip in a mysterious tart sauce. Curries make an excellent main-course choice, or go for the asparagus or spinach in oyster sauce. Adventurous diners should try the *ahmohk* (fish curry mousse served in a banana leaf). For dessert, order mango slices with sweet rice or banana fritters with ice cream. • M-Sa 11am-3pm, 5-10pm; Su 5-10pm.

Angkor Wat ★★★ $ Richmond: 4217 Geary Blvd. (6th Ave.), (415) 221-7887. This is probably the only restaurant in San Francisco that serves a soup (*samlaw machhou kroeung krahorm,* chicken and pineapple simmered in lemongrass broth) for which the Pope's personal cook requested the recipe, after the Pontiff himself ate here on a visit. Host Charlie Sar, chef and owner of this beautifully decorated Cambodian palace, is effusive and eager to recommend dishes; if you go late on a (rare) slow evening, he'll virtually guide you through the meal. Aside from the soup, which is darn near mandatory to order, recommendations include the gourmet duck curry and the incredible Cambodian five-spices shark. It's hard to go wrong with any dish, so expertly do they mix ingredients into a delectable whole; there are fine vegetarian choices as well. Classical Cambodian dancing is performed on Fridays and Saturdays. • M-Th 11am-2:30pm, 5-10pm; F-Sa 11am-2:30pm, 5-10:30pm; Su 5-10pm.

Appam ★★★ $$ SoMa: 1261 Folsom St. (8th St./9th St.), (415) 626-2798. Some of the best Indian food in the city is served at this elegant SoMa eatery. The dining room is dimly lit and romantic. Curries are prepared *dum phukt* style, cooked under a crust in a specially made clay pot that allows them to steam gently. Sit out back under the gazebo on warm evenings. • Daily 5:30-10pm.

Aqua ★★★ $$$$ Fin. Dist.: 252 California St. (Front/Battery), (415) 956-9662. This is one of the city's most glittery, stylish seafood restaurants. Enter the gleaming, mirrored dining room through an unmarked facade; you'll know you're in the right place by the fish-tail door handle and the glamorous patrons. Exquisitely prepared and beautifully presented fish is the order of the day. Try the lobster, potato gnocchi, or the grilled swordfish. Jacket and tie preferred for men. Reservations recommended. • M-Th 11:30am-2:15pm, 5:30-10pm; F 11:30am-2:15pm, 5:30-10:30pm; Sa 5:30-10:30pm.

Arabian Nights ★★★ $$ Mission: 811 Valencia St. (19th St./20th St.), (415) 821-9747. It's a Middle Eastern restaurant! It's a bar! It's a museum of Arabian carpets, mural scenes, and exquisite decorations! Arabian Nights is all three at once, so when the live music is blasting (and it does) and the staff belly dancer is doing her thing, don't expect to be able to carry on much of a conversation, let alone a quiet one. If you can get beyond the stylish, jaw-dropping riches of the L-shaped room, however, and can get used to sitting on floor cushions, the superb fare deserves attention. Start with the delicious *baba ghanouj* (just the right consistency) or grilled quails as an appetizer; move on to the other-worldly "sultan's pleasure" (rack of lamb with herbs, couscous, and rice), the vegetarian plate of 40 thieves (hummus, falafel, and so on), or the excellent shish kebab, with very large cubes of meat. Finish off the filling meal with a dessert of baklava and Turkish coffee or mint tea. Efficient and friendly staff. The dining gets quite crowded on weekends. • Tu-Th 6-11pm; F-Sa 6pm-midnight (happy hour light menu 3-8pm).

Bad Man Jose's ★★ ¢ Castro: 4077 18th St. (Noe/Castro), (415) 861-1706. California healthy goes south of the border at Bad Man Jose's. Whole-wheat tortillas and red cabbage begin to separate this from the average burrito-to-go shop. The burritos are truly huge—possibly a two-person meal, depending on your appetite—the garden veggie tacos are fantastic. The decor boasts some incredibly cool metal work; check out the salamander door handle. A quick, inexpensive, satisfying meal when you're on the go. No credit cards. • Daily 11am-11pm.

(Plump Jack) Balboa Café ★ $$ Pacific Heights: 3199 Fillmore St. (Greenwich), (415) 921-3944.The Balboa was a packed singles bar 20 years ago when Harry Denton earned celebrity as the city's most charismatic bartender. In the 1980s, when Jeremiah Tower was cooking here pre-Stars, the place got a reputation for food—pub grub raised to new heights. The latest owners, the team behind the celebrated Plump Jack Cafe, have reinvigorated the bar and revived the kitchen. The diverse patrons enjoy meals of burgers, pasta, or a delicious spicy skirt steak, perhaps topped off by one of the homey desserts, which range from pies to frosted animal cookies. • Daily 11am-10:30pm.

Bambino's ★ $ Haight: 945 Cole St. (Parnassus/Carl), (415) 731-1343. Although they make plenty of tasty pizzas for pickup and delivery, Bambino's is also a good Italian restaurant in its own right, a cozy storefront with frilly lace curtains and virgin-white tablecloths. The enormous pasta servings (which follow the copious amounts of bread placed at each table) are generally excellent, especially angel hair with sun-dried tomatoes, mushrooms, zucchini, and caramelized red onions. Appetizers and salads are good as well, and you have to like a place that offers rock shrimp as a pizza topping. A popular place for neighborhood residents and a nice surprise for anyone just visiting. • Su-Th 11am-11pm; F-Sa 11am-midnight.

SAN FRANCISCO RESTAURANTS A-B

Barney's ★★ $ Marina: 3344 Steiner St. (Lombard/Chestnut), (415) 563-0307. • Noe Valley: 4138 24th St. (Castro/Diamond), (415) 282-7770. This popular chain of Bay Area hamburger joints consistently wins awards from the local weeklies, all proudly displayed on the walls. The secret is Barney's marvelous, generous toppings. The guacamole burger comes with a huge mound of fresh, spicy guacamole, while the Baja burger has enough bacon to feed two for breakfast. The burgers themselves are large, although cooking can be inconsistent. Healthy diners can substitute chicken, turkey, tofu, or garden burgers. (You can get your calories with spicy fries and a chocolate shake.) The bright, casual storefronts attract lines of boisterous postfraternity types. Outdoor patios for Sunday afternoon relaxing. No credit cards. • M-Th 11am-9:30pm; F 11am-10pm; Sa 10am-10pm; Su 10am-9pm (later in summer).

Basil Restaurant & Bar ★★ $$ SoMa: 1175 Folsom St. (7th St./8th St.), (415) 552-8999. Hands down, San Francisco's most stylish Thai restaurant, sporting a plate-glass facade, sleek, curved bar, hardwood floors, mod brass silverware, and wall of glass blocks. The menu also goes beyond the usual, *yum ped*, warm duck salad with watercress and lettuce; *hoi pad ped*, Prince Edward Island mussels with a roasted chili sauce; and *pla rad gang*, charbroiled salmon served over a curry basil sauce. Dishes combine fresh ingredients with the archetypal Thai balance of sweet, sour, and spicy, although prepare for some surprises: the chicken and coconut milk soup, for example, uses coconut milk sparingly, allowing galangal and other aromatic seasonings to dominate. The fancy decoration doesn't come cheap: prices are steep by Thai restaurant standards. • M-Th 11:30am-3pm, 5-10pm; F 11:30am-3pm, 5-11pm; Sa 5-11pm; Su 5-9:30pm.

Betelnut ★★ $$/$$$ Pacific Heights: 2030 Union St. (Buchanan/Webster), (415) 929-8855. This riotously popular place is an Asian snack palace and beer house. Grazing food, tidbits to accompany drinks, a light lunch, a late-afternoon or late-night snack, or even dinner: all can be had here. Chinese, Thai, Vietnamese, Japanese, and less frequently seen specialties from Malaysia and Singapore are eaten by shoppers, tourists, and the Union Street weekend crowds at the sidewalk tables, in the lively bar, in a seating area where you can see the chefs at work, or in a spacious back space where larger groups are seated. • Su-Th 11:30am-11pm; F-Sa 11:30am-midnight.

Big Nate's Barbeque ★★ $ SoMa: 1665 Folsom St. (12th St./13th St.), (415) 861-4242. If you aren't from the South, you've probably never had barbecue like this. It's spicy, hot, tangy, and finger-licking good. Drop the fork and knife, but pick up extra napkins. Former Golden State Warrior star Big Nate Thurmond has found a second calling after basketball. Barbecued chicken, barbecued ribs, coleslaw, and corn muffins that'll make you reach back into the basket for more. This is down-home southern cuisine at its best: Sit down and worry about your waistline later. By the way, Big Nate has a stand at the ballpark to satisfy the 'Q needs of Giants fans, and this operation will also deliver to your home or office. It just doesn't get more convenient than that. • M-Sa 11am-10pm; Su noon-10pm.

Bistro Clovis ★★ $$ Civic Center: 1596 Market St. (Franklin St.), (415) 864-0231. A *très charmant* French eatery located on Market Street, with an emphasis on wine tasting. Authentic French specialties are served at reasonable prices, and the interior is spacious and airy, with an unmistakable Gallic feel (the owner, chef, and wait staff are all French). A trio of different wines is available for tastings each night, some for a mere four or five dollars. All in all, *très raisonable*. • M-Sa 11:30am-2:30pm, 5-11pm.

Bistro Rôti ★★★ $$ SoMa: 155 Steuart St. (Mission/Howard), (415) 495-6500. On the block of Steuart Street that has become a serious restaurant row, head straight to Rôti for delicious bistro fare. There, in a charming, convivial space highlighted by a beautiful long bar, you can watch rabbits and chickens slowly roasting on a spit in the fabulous open hearth. Menu highlights include great roast chicken and tasty fish. Look to the well-made cocktails and extensive wine list for your beverages. Request a table by the window and enjoy the view of San Francisco Bay. Reservations recommended. • M-Th 11:30am-10pm; F 11:30am-11pm; Sa 5-11pm; Su 5-10pm.

SAN FRANCISCO RESTAURANTS

Bizou ★★ $$ SoMa: 598 4th St. (Brannan), (415) 543-2222. At Bizou—"little kiss"— chef Loretta Keller has created a rustic European menu, serving what's fresh at the market, from just-caught sardines and sand dabs to broccoli rabe. Other authentic— and unusual—specialties include tender beef cheeks and sea-fresh skate (delicious but difficult to eat by some accounts). Pastas are more run-of-the-mill. Few restaurants generate such widely disparate comments about the food: some love it, some hate it, although everyone seems to love the fried green beans with fig sauce. Apparently enough love this place to fill the cramped tables and create a loud, chaotic atmosphere most nights. (This, of course, has led to horror stories about service, including waiting 40 minutes for a glass of wine, which finally arrived after the main course had been eaten). • M-Th 11:30am-2:30pm, 5:30-10pm; F 11:30am-2:30pm, 5:30pm-10:30pm; Sa 5:30pm-10:30pm.

Bontà ★★ $$ Pacific Heights: 2223 Union St. (Fillmore/Steiner), (415) 929-0407. Excellent food and friendly service make this cozy Italian restaurant, specializing in homemade pastas and Roman cuisine, a real find. Try the smoked mozzarella with mushrooms for an appetizer, or the deep-fried three-cheese baby calzone. There is a tempting array of main courses to choose from, each ample enough for the moderately hungry. Pastas, such as *fettuccine sapori* or *fettuccine di mare*, are excellent, and among the meat and seafood dishes the *saltimbocca alla romana* and *lombata di vitello* are outstanding. Be sure to save room for dessert: the fabulous tiramisù is huge. Bontà only seats about 50 people, so call ahead for reservations. • Tu-Th 5:30-10pm; F-Sa 5:30-10pm; Su 5-10pm.

Boogaloos ★ $ Mission: 3296 22nd St. (Valencia), (415) 824-3211. A popular hangout for frisky young Mission-aries, especially on weekend mornings and afternoons, when the wait just to get inside is usually long. Everyone, it seems, wants to see and be seen at this eclectically decorated corner locale, with its bright, multicolored walls lined with abstract art and its columns filled with mosaics made out of busted plates. It doesn't hurt that the food is very cheap, very filling, and quite good. Carnivores will love the succulent jerked pork chops with fried plantains, fish lovers should be around when the special is thresher shark, and any self-respecting late riser will enjoy the tofu scramble breakfast or the temple of spuds (which is exactly what it sounds like, topped with melted cheese). Alas, service can be spacy and indifferent more often than not. • Su-Tu 8am-3:30pm; W-Th 8am-3:30pm, 5-10pm; F-Sa 8am-3:30pm, 5-11pm.

Boulevard ★★★ $$$ SoMa: 1 Mission St. (Steuart), (415) 543-6084. Another instant hit for the ubiquitous Pat Kuleto. The dramatic decor in the historic Audiffred Building overlooking the bay updates the Parisian brasserie with such trademark Kuleto touches as an open kitchen, alabaster lighting fixtures, and sweeping views. The French theme contrasts with chef Nancy Oakes eclectic California cuisine, which might feature such starters as lobster skillet cake with herb chantilly, mussels steamed in a Thai broth with crispy calamari, or rare ahi tuna with cucumber noodles and wasabi dressing. Main dishes can be as simple as oven-roasted chicken with mashed potatoes or as elaborately wrought as roast duck breast with champagne Parmesan risotto, chanterelle mushrooms, roasted tomatoes, and a salad of duck cracklings and chervil. The large dining room and lively scene enhance the restaurant's celebratory feeling. Reservations recommended. • M-F 11:30am-10:30pm; Sa-Su 5:30-10:30pm.

Brandy Ho's ★ $ Chinatown: 217 Columbus Ave. (Pacific/Broadway), (415) 788-7527. • North Beach: 450 Broadway (Montgomery/Kearny), (415) 362-6268. You'll be tempted to call the Columbus Street branch Brandy Joe's, it looks so much like your typical Joe's Italian restaurant: black-and-white tile floors, polished granite tabletops, and the trademark counter in front of the open kitchen (the sauté stations have been replaced by woks). After you taste the incendiary Hunan cooking, you'll be tempted to call the fire department. The young non-Chinese crowd comes for the larger-than-life flavors. The specialty is the flavorful house-smoked ham, chicken, and duck, which would do any southerner proud. The Broadway locale is all neon and glitz. • Chinatown: Su-Th 11:30am-11pm; F-Sa 11:30am-midnight. • NB: Daily 11:30am-11pm.

SAN FRANCISCO RESTAURANTS B-C

Buca Giovanni ★★★ $$$ North Beach: 800 Greenwich St. (Columbus/Mason), (415) 776-7766. An old-style northern Italian restaurant for people who eat pasta as a *secondo piatto*. All the foodies go here, as do well-informed tourists and old North Beach families (although none with small children in tow). Giovanni Leoni's marvelous menu offers a wide range of salads, many unusual pastas, risotto, seafood, rabbit, game dishes, lamb, veal, and beef. Rabbit with grappa, prosciutto, and oyster mushrooms or lamb with black olives and capers exemplify dishes to tantalize the jaded palate. Count on everything being well prepared. Go with a hearty appetite: You'll start with the *salsa rossa* and chewy bread, but pace yourself to save room for a gooey dessert. The below-street-level setting is cavelike (*buca* means "cave") but pleasant, and the Old World service is casually professional. Reservations recommended. • Tu-Th 6:30-10pm; F-Sa 5:30-10:30pm.

Café Bastille ★★ $ Fin. Dist.: 22 Belden St. (Pine/Bush), (415) 986-5673. Wish you could be whisked away on an impromptu trip to France? Dining at Café Bastille is the next best thing. With its charming alleyway location (complete with outdoor seating under umbrellas), official Paris-style address plaque, and large amount of French spoken by staff and patrons alike, Café Bastille is a perfect destination for Francophiles. The savory crepes—filled with chicken or ratatouille for dinner, with chocolate for dessert—transport you directly to France, as does the pâté with cornichons; the ahi tuna appetizer is a tasty reminder that you are still in California. Jazz and DJ dancing most nights. • M-F 11am-11pm; Sa 11am-2pm.

Café Claude ★★ $ Union Sq.: 7 Claude Ln. (off Bush btwn. Grant/Kearny), (415) 392-3505. So Gallic, from the music, to the food, to the charming waiters. The atmosphere is airy and open, with French posters and original art on the walls. On nice days, tables are set out in the alley for that Parisian sidewalk-café feel. The espresso bar serves latte in a bowl, just like in the old country. For lunch or dinner, be sure to try the onion soup and huge Caesar salad, or such typical French standbys as a *croque monsieur* or a baguette sandwich. The desserts are worth sampling, too. Don't miss glimpsing the antique zinc bar brought over from Paris. Tucked into a little alley off of Bush, it's well hidden but worth the search. Live jazz most nights. • M-F 8am-10pm; Sa 10am-10pm.

Café for All Seasons ★★ $$ Sunset: 150 W. Portal Ave. (Vicente/14th Ave.), (415) 665-0900. One of the busiest restaurants in this remote part of San Francisco. At lunch the menu features California and American standards like Cobb salad, a hamburger with excellent fries, and assorted pastas; at dinner try pork scallops with a mustard cream sauce for a light version of the Germanic standby, or chicken with artichoke hearts in light cream. The heavenly desserts include pumpkin pie and triple-chocolate cake. The open kitchen and bright interior blend well with the fare. You may have to wait for a table Friday and Saturday evenings when reservations are taken. • M-Th 11:30am-2:30pm, 5:30-9:30pm; F 11:30am-2:30pm, 5-9:30pm; Sa 10am-2:30pm, 5-9:30pm; Su 9am-2:30pm, 5-8:30pm.

Café Jacqueline ★★★ $$$ North Beach: 1454 Grant Ave. (Green/Union), (415) 981-5565. One of the city's more romantic eateries, with fresh flowers and candles on the tables. Jacqueline specializes in made-to-order soufflés. The spinach tends to be a bit watery, so go for the mushroom or the corn, ginger, and garlic special instead. And don't skip dessert! The chocolate-raspberry soufflé is beyond decadent. Despite the romantic ambience, this is a risky place for a first date: soufflé production can be excruciatingly slow, especially if conversation fails (order soup or salad to while away the time). The wine list is painfully overpriced; consider bringing your own and paying corkage. • W-Su 5:30-11pm.

Café Kati ★★★ $$$ Pacific Heights: 1963 Sutter St. (Fillmore/Webster), (415) 775-7313. Make sure you're feeling daring when you venture to Café Kati, which bills itself as featuring cuisine that marries flavors and foods from the Asia-Pacific region with those of the West. Many of the offerings are exotic and mysterious, beginning with the *papadam* (a large crispy Indian cracker) and cucumber dipping sauce that arrive on your table in lieu of bread and butter. Curious appetizers such as mango rolls (wrapped in rice paper) and adventurous main courses such as a trio of "Hawaiian seafoods" (ask your waiter for an explanation) make you feel like a gastronomic Indiana Jones. There is a clever element of the familiar, however—garlic mashed potatoes, lightly breaded pork loin—that adds to the surprise of Café Kati's unique menu. The desserts, namely the "warm and gooey chocolate cake" (its real name!) and the butterscotch pudding, are dramatically presented with tiaralike clouds of spun sugar crowning them. Reservations recommended. • Tu-Su 5:30-10pm.

Café Marimba ★★ $$ Marina: 2317 Chestnut St. (Scott/Divisadero), (415) 776-1506. A sizzling mix of inspired Mexican dishes and Chestnut Street nightlife, Café Marimba is one of the see and be seen spots in the Marina. The house drinks, like habanero martinis or Brazilian *batidas* (an alcoholic *agua fresca*), are potent but smooth and keep the crowd lively. Chips come with two kinds of homemade salsas, such as *rojo* and *el copil*. Main courses vary from light side dishes, including squash blossom quesadillas, to one of several hearty chicken moles. The side dishes of drunken beans, rice, and plantains and grilled corn are tasty and inexpensive. • M 5:30-11pm; Tu-Th, Su 11:30am-11pm; F-Sa 11:30am-midnight.

Café Riggio ★★ $$ Richmond: 4112 Geary Blvd. (5th Ave./6th Ave.), (415) 221-2114. Wonderful Italian fare and seafood prepared with a light, modern touch. The aroma of garlic is ever present. Lively, young, upbeat atmosphere in attractive dining rooms. Full bar. • M-Th 5-10pm; F-Sa 5-11pm; Su 4:30-10pm.

Café Tiramisù ★★ $$ Fin. Dist.: 28 Belden Pl. (Bush/Pine), (415) 421-7044. Want to go to Italy now? Head for Tiramisù, owned by two charming brothers from Italy. The Italian waiters, wall paintings, and outdoor dining will make you feel like you're in a little neighborhood trattoria in Roma. While the rustic food is very good, the atmosphere and the attitudes are the real winners here. Finish your meal with a little grappa before leaving *la dolce vita* and returning home. • M-F 11:30am-3pm, 5:30-10:30pm; Sa 5-10:30pm.

Caffè Centro Marina ★ $$ Marina: 3340 Steiner St. (Lombard/Chestnut), (415) 202-0100. At this casual and pleasant Marina hangout you can select one of a number of European journals lying around, then sit for a snack in the garden, nibble something at the bar, sip a latte on the sidewalk, or dine at a table in the dining area. The fare is standard; a good burger, a big basket of tasty fries, pastas, chicken, risotto, and changing specials. Service is extremely friendly; if you eat by yourself you won't feel alone. • Tu-Th 6-11pm; F 6-10pm; Sa 9:30am-2:30pm, 6-10pm; Su 9:30am-2:30pm, 5:30-9:30pm.

Caffè Centro South Park ★ ¢ SoMa: 102 South Park (2nd St./3rd St.), (415) 882-1500. Facing South Park's lunchtime picnickers and playground, this relaxing, sunny spot is a place to play dominos while sipping a glass of wine or to eavesdrop on the multimedia types who work nearby. Caffè Centro serves the usual coffees, teas, sandwiches, salads, quiches, and frittatas. Stop here for coffee and a pastry after shopping the fashion outlet stores that litter the area. Cash only. • M-F 7:30am-6:30pm; Sa 9am-4pm.

Caffè delle Stelle ★★★ $$ Hayes Valley: 395 Hayes St. (Gough), (415) 252-1110. A popular spot in the ultracool Hayes Valley neighborhood, Caffè delle Stelle serves rustic Italian cuisine at reasonable prices. The modest interior feels like an authentic Italian trattoria—even after moving down the block to Vince's former location—and the eclectic clientele ranges from stylish Euro types to doggedly determined foodies. Everything on the menu is a safe bet. Order one of the unusual pasta dishes with a glass of rough country wine. • M-Th 11:30am-2:30pm, 5-10pm; F-Sa 11:30am-2:30pm, 5-11pm.

Caffè Macaroni ★★★ $$ Chinatown: 59 Columbus Ave. (Jackson), (415) 956-9737. Nouvelle-rustic southern Italian food is served in this *tiny*, funky interior. Tall patrons should try to sit downstairs (the upstairs dining area has perilously low ceilings), where sponge-painted walls, lots of plants, and closely spaced tables make for an intimate atmosphere. Don't miss the antipasto plate, which includes assorted marinated vegetables, or the excellent veal shank. Portions are on the small side, so order up. Loud music and friendly, overly helpful waiters. No credit cards or dinner reservations taken. • M-F 11:30am-2:30pm, 5:30-10pm; Sa 5:30-10pm.

Caffè Museo ★★ $ SoMa: 151 3rd St. (Mission/Howard), (415) 357-4500. A casual street-level café in the spectacular new Museum of Modern Art. Good breakfast and lunch dishes are served at fair prices. Like the museum, this café is a cut above, with lots of style. Try the panini (the orange-roasted chicken with carmelized onions is good), wonderful salads, and excellent pastries. No table service; you stand in line, order, and the food is delivered to your table. Also like the museum, it can be crowded on weekends. • Tu-W, F-Su 10am-6pm; Th 10am-9pm.

California Culinary Academy ★★ $$/$$$ Civic Center: 625 Polk St. (Ellis/O'Farrell), (415) 771-3536. Sit down for a relaxing meal created by the famous chefs of tomorrow. Right now you can taste their succulent creations for less than $20 many nights; after graduation, watch out! The academy boasts two dining rooms, one formal, one more casual. Each has a multicultural menu of delectables trying to outshine the other. The smells will leave you swooning and the tastes will quiet all conversation to a hushed "hmmmm," but the wait may leave you fuming. These are, after all, chefs in training: the food is the highlight; the service you must just suffer through. Your best bet is to plan on a two-hour wait between salad and main dish and have no pressing appointments. Then sit back, have another glass of wine, and enjoy. You can always browse in the gift shop if you get too bored. Reservations required. • M-F 11:30am-1:30pm; 6-8pm.

Campton Place ★★★ $$$$ Union Sq.: 340 Stockton St. (Post/Sutter), (415) 781-5555. A beautiful restaurant in a beautiful hotel. The dining room is sumptuous and peaceful, the crowd rich and well dressed, and the food almost as good as the high prices. The kitchen is renowned for what many think is the best breakfast in town, including warm house-baked corn sticks with sweet butter for every table and some of the most memorable corned beef hash this side of the Pierre in New York. Also try the excellent version of eggs Benedict with an orange hollandaise. Superb service. Go during the Christmas season, when the hotel and restaurant are imaginatively decorated. A small bar adjoining the dining room offers excellent bar food and reasonably priced—for the deluxe setting—wines and cocktails. The perfect resting spot after shopping around Union Square or an ideal meeting place for a drink before the theater. Reservations and jacket and tie recommended. • M-Th 7-10:30am, 11:30am-2pm, 6-10pm; F 7-10:30am, 11:30am-2pm, 5:30-10:30pm; Sa 8-11am, noon-2pm, 5:30-10:30pm; Su 10am-2pm, 6-9:30pm

Canto Do Brazil ★ $ Mission: 3621 18th St. (Guerrero), (415) 626-8727. This pleasant Brazilian restaurant near Dolores Park serves meals with a home-cooked flavor. Although a bit on the greasy side, the appetizers are very good, notably the *mandioca frita* (fried yucca with vinaigrette sauce). Main dishes include the savory *galinha na cerveja* (half chicken marinated in dark beer). The hungrier you come the better: main dishes arrive with a motherlode of rice and beans. On Saturdays, the kitchen dishes up Brazil's national dish, *feijoada*, a stew of black beans, ham, beef, and garlic; at eight dollars, it's the most expensive thing on the menu. If the music isn't too loud, it's a fun atmosphere between walls splashed in green and yellow. • M-F 11am-10pm; Sa-Su noon-11pm.

Carmen ★ ¢ Union Sq.: 110 Powell St. (O'Farrell/Ellis), (415) 397-9535. Without a doubt, the best food deal in an area dominated by tourist traps. Carmen serves heaping portions of almost-Mission-district-taqueria-quality favorites. Although the place still looks like the old-time bar it once was, with dark wood wainscoting, chrome-and-black-Naugahyde bar stools, and a tile floor, the hanging piñatas and blaring Latin pop music remind the mix of local workers and lucky tourists that they won't get Shanghaied here. No credit cards. • M-Sa 7am-10pm; Su 7am-9pm.

SAN FRANCISCO RESTAURANTS

Carta ★★★ $$ Civic Center: 1772 Market St. (Gough/Octavia), (415) 863-3516. Although the description—inconvenient location, dicey parking, far from elegant inside, a menu based on the cuisine of a different single country or region each month—doesn't encourage you to drop everything and head there, please go to Carta! These people really know how to cook, and you'll enjoy dishes you'll never get elsewhere. Culinary venues have included Greece, Provence, and India. Tables in the small storefront are sandwiched between one counter looking out on Market Street's new trolleys and another looking into the open kitchen. Prices are fair and service is good. A unique restaurant in its combination of quality, price, and daring. • Tu-F noon-3pm, 6-11pm; Sa 6-11pm; Su 10am-2pm, 6-11pm.

Casa Aguila ★★★ $$ Sunset: 1240 Noriega St. (19th Ave./20th Ave.), (415) 661-5593. This Sunset District hole-in-the-wall has year-round Yuletide spirit (note the dusty Christmas decorations) and serves up some of the tastiest Mexican grub in San Francisco. The portions are enormous and the prices reasonable. Try the pork enchiladas, the chiles rellenos, the tamales, the extra-fruity sangria—and anything else on the extensive menu, for that matter, since it's all good. The service is efficient and friendly, although on weekends the line can be long (yes, it's been discovered). Sign up for a table and hang out in the seedy bar (with pool table) next door while you wait. • Daily 11:30am-3:30pm, 5-9:30pm.

Cha Cha Cha ★★★ $ Haight: 1801 Haight St. (Shrader), (415) 386-5758. You *will* have to wait for a table—two hours is not uncommon—at this swinging Caribbean restaurant in the Haight, but it's a small inconvenience considering the quirky, palate-tingling food that comes out of the kitchen. Most items are tapas sized, so order a selection and share. Shrimp in creamy Cajun coconut sauce is sublime, as are fried plantains, seafood specials, and just about everything else on the menu. The kooky, witch-doctorish decor adds to the experience. The yuppies have definitely invaded, sending the prices up. But it's still one of the city's best meals. If you're feeling daring, ask Russ to do his tablecloth trick. Swing by to put your name on the wait list, then go enjoy the Haight scene; they keep your name at the top if you miss your turn. No credit cards. • Su-Th 11:30am-4pm, 5-11pm; F 11:30am-4pm, 5-11:30pm; Sa 11:30am-4pm, 5-11:30pm.

Chez Michel ★★★ $$$ Fisherman's Wharf: 804 North Point St. (Hyde), (415) 775-7036. Owner Michel Elkaim believes in reincarnation: after a successful 18-year run, he closed Chez Michel, only to reopen 8 years later. Perhaps his sophisticated restaurant will add life to the Fisherman's Wharf restaurant scene. The warm, gregarious owner, with a mane of white hair, oversees a pleasant dining room decorated with light wood, bright windows, and a bar, and establishes *très sympathique* service. Simply prepared traditional French bistro plates might include duck confit, various *galettes*, and seafood in puff pastry. • Su-Th 5-10:30pm; F-Sa 5-11pm.

China Moon ★★★ $$$ Fin. Dist.: 639 Post St. (Jones/Taylor), (415) 775-4789. Exquisite renditions of classic and not-so-classic Chinese dishes are served at this tiny, elegant former-diner-turned-gourmet-restaurant. The decor consists of glorious flower arrangements, moon-shaped hanging lamps, and the original diner booths and soda fountain. Appetizers are a delight, especially the spring rolls and the unusual eggplant. Or try the China Moon chicken salad, a melange of chicken, black sesame seeds, shredded carrot, and daikon radish dressed in a Dijon vinaigrette. For dessert, homemade ginger ice cream is the only fitting conclusion. • Daily 5:30-10pm.

Chloe's Café ★★ $ Noe Valley: 1399 Church St. (26th St.), (415) 648-4116. This tiny corner café, one of the best-kept secrets in town, is well known to Noe Valley residents, who happily wait upward of an hour on weekends for a table and the chance to eat Chloe's exquisite brunch. Along with the obligatory coffee and freshly squeezed o.j., recommendations would include any of the scrambled-egg dishes with a heap of home fries and choice of fresh breads; the mouth-watering applewood sausage; the wonderful banana walnut pancakes; or the amazing cinnamon croissant

French toast. Healthful sandwiches and salads are available for lunch. Service is attentive and quick, and eating here on a sun-splashed morning feels like the epitome of a civilized existence. • M-F 8am-3pm; Sa-Su 8am-4pm.

Country Station Sushi Café ★ ¢ Mission: 2140 Mission Ave. (17th St./18th St.), (415) 861-0972. They do indeed serve Japanese food here, but that's where the similarities with any other sushi place in town end. The cooks act like harried short-order chefs, there's a wall rack full of magazines, and the music of choice is straight out of a Tarantino film. Still, the sushi is good and very cheap (a 30-piece party plate is only $13), the *udon* noodles are filling, and the *yakitori* chicken is a great side dish. Reservations are accepted, so don't underestimate its popularity. • M-Th 5-10pm; F-Sa 5-11pm. - *haven't been here, but heard it's top*

Cypress Club ★★★ $$$ Fin. Dist.: 500 Jackson St. (Columbus/Montgomery), (415) 296-8555. A visiting Bostonian described the interior of this supper club as "biological punk." Strange, anthropomorphic shapes dominate the interior; a copper door frame resembles a pair of balloon-shaped legs, and curvy purple velvet banquettes have a Jetsonesque appeal. The menu includes luxurious, well-prepared fare such as seared paillard of venison, grilled vegetable sandwiches, and fabulous braised sweetbreads. If you're not springing for dinner, have a drink at the bar and observe the scene. • Su-Th 5:30-10pm; F-Sa 5:30-11pm.

Delancey Street Restaurant ★★★ $$ SoMa: 600 Embarcadero (Brannan), (415) 512-5179. Good food and good deeds join at Delancey Street. The restaurant is a project of the Delancey Street Foundation, which works to help people who have hit rock bottom begin new, productive lives. With the assistance of numerous Bay Area restaurateurs, program members have created a bright, cheerful restaurant with a down-home flavor. The sleek corner space, done up with burnished copper, warm wood wainscoting, and pastel upholstery offers spectacular views of the Bay Bridge (especially from the glass-sheltered patio). The eclectic food reflects the backgrounds of the staff and the consulting chefs. Choose from a multicultural array of dishes such as *spanakopitta*, salmon mousse with lemon dill cream sauce, barbecued ribs, grilled ahi tuna with mango ginger glaze, creole gumbo, or pot roast. A large rotisserie turns out a range of roasted meats. Health-conscious diners always have a selection of low-fat, low-sodium dishes. Above average service. • Tu-Su 11am-11pm (high tea 3-5:30pm).

Doidge's Kitchen ★★ $ Pacific Heights: 2217 Union St. (Fillmore/Steiner), (415) 921-2149. If you're looking for a quintessential Sunday brunch—any day of the week—you'll find it at Doidge's Kitchen. Craving fluffy French toast or a heaping mound of pancakes? A comforting plate of eggs Benedict with just the right amount of hollandaise? Doidge's has found a way to perfect these classics. If only the seating system was equally well engineered. Expect to wait for a table even if you've made reservations. Perhaps it's the homey atmosphere—complete with faded wall coverings and curtains that seem to have been picked out by some universal mom—that encourages patrons to linger over their hash browns and toast. • M-F 8am-1:45pm; Sa-Su 8am-2:45pm.

Dol Ho ★★ ¢ Chinatown: 808 Pacific Ave. (Stockton), (415) 392-2828. A classic dim sum dive, right in the heart of Chinatown, Dol Ho provides a good alternative to the large, glamorous, and more expensive restaurants dominating San Francisco's dumpling lunch scene. Most everything is good, from the steamed pork buns to the shrimp in translucent wrappers to the shark fin dumplings. Ingredients are fresh, particularly the pungent ginger and scallions. The restaurant is small, so the food is still hot when the cart gets to your table, and popular with neighborhood locals. A remodel added a shocking green tile facade and brightened the pink walls. No credit cards. • Daily 7am-5pm.

Ebisu ★★ $$ Sunset: 1283 9th Ave. (Irving), (415) 566-1770. Top-notch sushi has made this bare-bones eatery a local favorite; expect a line most nights. Friendly, boisterous sushi chefs entertain the crowd at the sushi bar where the long list of daily specials is in plain view. Well-worn screens divide the rest of the dining room into

SAN FRANCISCO RESTAURANTS

Japanese and American rooms. Limber guests remove their shoes and sit on tatami mats, Japanese style, while older, stiffer diners sit in chairs at tables. • M-W 11:30am-2pm, 5-10pm; Th-F 11:30am-2pm, 5-midnight; Sa 5-midnight.

Eleven Ristorante & Bar ★★ $$ SoMa: 374 11th St. (Folsom/Harrison), (415) 431-3337. Cool jazz and hot pasta! This South-of-Market gem offers a hip dining experience. Wrought iron and trompe l'oeil wall paintings create an ancient Roman feel; the hostesses' hip huggers and navel jewels are decidedly '90s funk; and the music says '40s, a hot night at the Apollo. All in all, a great combination. The extensive wine list includes a nice range of vintages by the glass at all price levels. Choose from contemporary Italian dishes such as pizza with Gorgonzola, roasted potatoes, and caramelized onions or chicken with balsamic vinegar, black olives, and onions. The cheese ravioli with arugula are a standout. Beware, you may overeat on bread: it's just too good to stop until your meal comes and then you realize it's too late. Bring your appetite and your attitude. • M-Th 6-11pm; F-Sa 6pm-midnight.

The Elite Café ★★ $$ Pacific Heights: 2049 Fillmore St. (Pine/California), (415) 346-8668. The Elite Café has the look of that "great place to meet for a drink." Originally constructed in the 1920s, the inviting space offers large private wooden booths—pull the curtains for that clandestine rendezvous—along one wall for groups, a long counter along the other for singles, and cramped small tables in the middle for everybody else. A trendsetting place when it opened in 1981 during the '80s Cajun rage, it's been packing in yuppies and tourists ever since. The Cajun and creole standards—blackened meat and fish, gumbo—can be pretty good, but the kitchen is terribly inconsistent. While you're waiting for a table, or if you are just meeting for that drink, indulge in the reasonably priced oysters at the raw bar. The staff varies from friendly to elitist. • M-Sa 5-11pm; Su 10am-3pm; 5-10pm.

Eliza's ★★ $ Hayes Valley: 205 Oak St. (Gough/Octavia), (415) 621-4819. • Potrero Hill: 1457 18th St. (Connecticut/Missouri), (415) 648-9999. An unlikely name for a Chinese restaurant, but it doesn't fool those in search of the city's latest bargain in well-prepared Asian fare. At locations in Hayes Valley and on Potrero Hill, Eliza's delivers a host of appealing dishes with fresh ingredients and strong spices. Celery salad is a tasty and unusual appetizer. Main dishes include all the usuals plus lesser-known but successful offerings like minced chicken with deep-fried basil. • HV: M-Sa 11am-9pm. • PH: Daily 11am-3pm, 5-9:45pm.

Emerald Garden ★★ $$ Nob Hill: 1550 California St. (Larkin/Polk), (415) 673-1155. Wonderful, refined Vietnamese food is served in this stylish venue tucked between two buildings in the lower Nob Hill area. The interior features silk palms, soft light, and black glass tabletops—this is Rick's Café Americain teleported to LA. You'll savor the rich curries, the pungent grilled Saigon-style pork chop, or anything else on the French-influenced Vietnamese menu. Friendly service, but sappy music. Validated parking nearby. Reservations recommended. • M-Th 11:30am-2:30pm, 5-10pm; F 11:30am-2:30pm, 5-10:30pm; Sa 5pm-10:30pm; Su 5-10pm.

Emporio Armani Express Café ★ $ Union Sq.: 1 Grant St. (O'Farrell), (415) 677-9010. Although the chichi upstairs restaurant closed, Emporio Armani still offers their café—smack-dab in the middle of this upscale retail establishment, in a stunning marble rotunda—for customers and browsers alike. The menu is as streamlined as Armani's signature pared-down style: salads, sandwiches, and espresso drinks are the main offerings. The carpaccio is as tasteful as an Armani suit; those hoping to fit into the sleek designer clothes hanging from nearby racks can sample the daily antipasti specials. Even if all you can afford is a latte during your visit, it's worth it to sit at the café's counter, sip your drink, and soak up the glamorous atmosphere. Sidewalk seating, popular with tourists, adds to the Euro ambience. • M-Sa 11:30am-4:30pm, Su noon-4:30pm.

Enrico's ★★ $$ North Beach: 504 Broadway (Kearny), (415) 982-6223. Inside there is a bar where regulars who began drinking at Enrico's in its first incarnation still imbibe.

Diners sit at marble-topped tables and banquettes along art-filled walls and eat tasty California-Italian meals, listen to live music, or just graze on small dishes like garlic mashed potatoes or cockles and mussels. The outdoor patio—San Francisco's first sidewalk café—heated with lamps against chilly summer nights is a prime people-watching place. The sightings aren't what they used to be: the beatniks, hippies, and punks have disappeared into the past while Broadway has filled with seedy strip joints, but it's still a good spot to have a drink. • Su-Th noon-11pm; F-Sa noon-midnight (bar open until 1:30am).

Eos ★★★ $$$ Haight: 901 Cole St. (Carl), (415) 566-3063. At this bustling new outpost of fusion cuisine, head chef Arnold Wong cooks in an open kitchen that, along with the rest of the sharp, stripped-down dining area (exposed pipes, wooden beams, cylindrical lighting, and black matte tables are among the touches), feels like an artist's work space. The style is fitting, because the dishes are as colorful, textured and carefully arranged as a painted canvas. Start with the appetizers, small and expensive but essential: the shiitake mushroom dumplings and rock shrimp cakes are exceptional. The best of the entrées are the organic skirt steak (mouth-watering slices of meat marinated in Chimay ale), the tea-smoked duck breast, and the pan-roasted local salmon. Original side dishes such as a feta cheese croquette and the wasabi mashed potatoes point to Wong's ingenious mix of European and Asian tastes. Don't miss dessert: the hot crisp of the day is enough to feed two, but you may want one for yourself. Many excellent wines are available to complement the meal, or to enjoy at the adjoining wine bar. The staff is good, although they are still having trouble seating reserved tables promptly, which is about the only drawback to an otherwise excellent eating experience. • M-W 5:30-11pm; Th-Sa 5:30-midnight; Su 5-10pm.

Escape from N.Y. Pizza ★ ¢ Union Sq.: 7 Stockton St. (O'Farrell/Ellis), (415) 421-0700. • Haight: 1737 Haight St. (Cole/Shrader), (415) 668-5577. • Castro: 508 Castro St. (18th St./19th St.), (415) 252-1515. Escape to New York with authentic thin-crust pizza, complete with tangy tomato sauce. The menu includes the usual pepperoni, mushrooms, and sausage, as well as many concessions to California taste: flavorful pesto ("not found in New York!" notes the menu), artichokes, sun-dried tomatoes, and broccoli. The menu offers little else: soda, beer, and a few overpriced salads. These stripped-down counter-service operations are the perfect quick stop while making the rounds shopping or clubbing. If you prefer your digs to theirs, call for delivery. No credit cards. • Union Sq.: M-Th 10:30am-11pm; F-Sa 10:30am-midnight; Su 11:30am-8pm. • Haight: M-W 11:30am-1am; Th-Sa 11:30am-2am; Su noon-midnight. • Castro: M-W 11:30am-1am; Th-Sa 11:30am-2am; Su 11:30am-1am.

Esperpento ★★ $ Mission: 3295 22nd St. (Mission/Valencia), (415) 282-8867. A boisterous crowd flocks to this quirky, brightly painted tapas restaurant, so expect a wait if you go on a weekend night. Try the grilled squid, marinated pork, mussels in a red-pepper vinaigrette, or potatoes served with hot chile sauce—the perfect antidote to a foggy San Francisco evening. No credit cards. • M-Th noon-3pm, 5-10pm; F-Sa noon-3pm, 5-10:30pm; Su noon-10:30pm.

Firefly ★★★ $$$ Noe Valley: 4288 24th St. (Douglas), (415) 821-7652. Firefly is one of the hottest restaurants in town, and no wonder. Few others manage to combine professionalism, in both the cooking and the service, with a relaxed neighborhood climate that includes country curtains, wall moldings, and a real colonial hutch. The food is eclectic and excellent. Appetizers such as grilled polenta or Thai salmon cakes are small for the price but tasty. Main courses are triumphs of presentation and conceal explosions of taste: try the pepper-seared top sirloin steak or the gigantic bayou gumbo with spiced duck breast. The decadent desserts—sorbet, shortcake, a towering ice cream brownie sundae—top it all off. It may cost a bit, but a truly exceptional meal can be had here. Reservations recommended. • Daily 5:30-9:30pm.

Fleur de Lys ★★★★ $$$$ Union Sq.: 777 Sutter St. (Taylor/Jones), (415) 673-7779. You might expect to be let down by a restaurant that has been heralded for years by critics, chefs, and foodies as one of San Francisco's shining stars. Experiencing Fleur de Lys firsthand, however, is enough to convert any cynic. Situated in a surprisingly seedy block of Sutter Street (on the edge of the Tenderloin), the elegant interior, dimly lit to a velvety, romantic darkness, is a welcome oasis of luxury in an ultraurban landscape. Contemporary French fare is the specialty: standout items include a silky New York State foie gras and a smooth chilled cucumber soup with vodka sorbet and caviar as appetizers; salmon served with wild mushrooms and a classic cut of filet mignon are sure-bet pleasers for main courses. More exotic meats such as squab, duck, and venison are also often on the menu. Desserts are the crowning glory of a Fleur de Lys feast. On one evening, the chocolate crème brûlée with caramelized banana was so delicious that it soothed the sting of the considerable bill that arrived soon afterward. Book your reservations for Friday and Saturday two or three weeks in advance. Tie optional but jacket required for gentlemen. • M-Th 6-9pm; F-Sa 5:30-10:30pm.

Flying Saucer ★★★ $$$ Mission: 1000 Guerrero St. (22nd St.), (415) 641-9955. Some of the most celestial food in San Francisco is served here in a Jetsons junk-store atmosphere. Choose from luxurious foie gras, homemade smoked oysters, or any of the other fabulous starters, and move on to a superb blackened catfish, ultrasophisticated duck confit, or house-smoked pork loin. Culinary accents are Asian, and the platter-sized dinner plates—two can easily share—come decked out with a dizzying array of garnishes, all delightfully seasoned with mysterious flavors. Out-of-this-world desserts like three sorbets on a macadamia nut shell arrive on huge plates dusted with sparkling blue sugar. Reservations recommended. • Tu-Sa 5:30-9:30pm; Su 6-9pm.

Fog City Diner ★★★ $$$ Fisherman's Wharf: 1300 Battery St. (Embarcadero/Greenwich), (415) 982-2000. The slick interior of this popular San Francisco institution only marginally resembles a diner, with its black leatherette banquettes, gleaming chrome fixtures, and polished wood accents. The eclectic menu is full of tantalizing choices: cornsticks flecked with red pepper, grilled cheese-stuffed pasilla peppers, terrific chicken pot pie, and a diner chili dog. Portions are less than abundant, and it's hard to narrow your decisions, so order a selection and share. The clatter from the kitchen can be deafening, and the wait can be long. • Su-Th 11:30am-11pm; F-Sa 11:30am-midnight.

42 degrees ★★★ $$$ SoMa: 235 16th St. (3rd St./Illinois), (415) 777-5558. James Moffat has a way with out-of-the-way warehouses. A partner in the industrial district Slow Club, he has turned the former Caffè Esprit into a sleek dinner spot serving California comfort food along with jazz music until midnight. The softly lit downstairs seating area is lined by an open kitchen along one wall and a deco bar along another. Giant roll-up warehouse doors in front open onto a patio where lunch is served during warm weather. The upstairs balcony offers bay views and enormous curved banquettes for festive small groups. The menu changes weekly, but generously portioned dinners might include roasted lamb chops heaped on celery root mashed potatoes, grilled salmon with white beans and chanterelle mushrooms, or rigatoni with tuna, black olives, and toasted garlic. Grazers can pick from tapas-sized chalkboard specials such as herb-roasted potatoes with aïoli; pizzetta with roasted potatoes, Fontina, and dry chilies; or a charcuterie plate. • M-Tu 11:30am-3pm; W-Th 11:30am-3pm, 7-11pm; F 11:30am-3pm, 7pm-1am; Sa 7pm-1am.

Fountain Court ★★ $ Richmond: 354 Clement St. (5th Ave.), (415) 668-1100. Fountain Court is always busy and packed, a sure sign of success in a neighborhood where fierce competition among Asian eateries prevails. This restaurant both respects authentic Chinese culinary traditions and satisfies the health-conscious palate by using only the best ingredients. While the specials are always worth investigating, don't miss the spinach with bean curd skin, eggplant with basil, or vegetarian steamed pot stickers. If you happen to live in the neighborhood, the management will throw in a free order of fried rice or chow mein with a minimum-delivery order of $15. • Daily 11am-3pm, 5-10pm.

SAN FRANCISCO RESTAURANTS F-G

Fringale ★★★ $$ SoMa: 570 4th St. (Bryant/Brannan), (415) 543-0573. This sophisticated, sleek bistro located in the netherworld between Market Street and the Caltrain station is oh-so-French. The waiters speak in exaggerated accents (you may ask yourself, "Is this guy for real?"), the menu features classic French fare such as bouillabaisse and cassoulet, and you begin to feel like an Ugly American. But the food is very good, simple, and reasonably priced, and the scene is fun to observe. • M-F 11:30am-3pm, 5:30-10:30pm; Sa 5:30-10:30pm.

The Ganges ★ $ Sunset: 775 Frederick St. (Arguello), (415) 661-7290. The Ganges is a great place to go after a yoga class to maintain your relaxed, healthful spirit. Nestled in a storefront facing Kezar Stadium, The Ganges serves an Indian vegetarian menu with some 15 curries. You can order a curry as part of one of the special combination meals, which are also good for sampling the various chutneys, dals, and *pakoras* on the menu. (The meals are priced from $9.50 to $13.50, depending on size.) The cuisine hails from the Surat region of India and offers such specialties as bananas stuffed with coconut, cilantro, chilies, and ginger. Vegans will appreciate the many dishes that are sugar and dairy free. Befitting the obscure location, the atmosphere is hushed and peaceful. On Fridays and Saturdays, tabla or sitar music lulls diners into a state of meditation. Cash only. Reservations recommended. • Tu-Sa 5-10pm.

Gaylord India ★★ $$$ Embarcadero: 1 Embarcadero Center (Sacramento/Clay/Front/Battery), (415) 397-7775. • Fisherman's Wharf: Ghirardelli Square, 900 North Point St. (Polk/Larkin), (415) 771-8822. Chicken *tikka*, tandoori chicken done to perfection, and garlic *nan* and onion *kulchas* warm from the oven are but a few of the highlights at this elegant, expensive Indian establishment. The elaborate menu covers almost all north Indian dishes, including a savory lamb curry served with fragrant basmati rice and delectable cucumber-yogurt *raita*. Order a Bombay beer to wash down your exotic meal. • Embarcadero: M-Th 11:30am-2:45pm, 5-10pm; F-Sa 11:30am-2:45pm, 5-10:30pm; Su 5-10pm. • FW: M-Sa 11:45am-1:45pm, 5-10:45pm; Su noon-2:45pm, 5-10:45pm.

Gira Polli ★★ $$$ (Take-out $) North Beach: 659 Union St. (Columbus/Powell), (415) 434-GIRA/4472. The name says it all—"turning chicken." This is the place for lemon-and-rosemary-scented chicken roasted on a spit over an open fire. In the heart of North Beach, kitty-corner to Washington Square Park, this tiny, chic eatery has a huge fireplace and a congenial owner, who is usually on hand to help pour the Chianti. The chicken is incredible, as are the Palermo potatoes. Friday and Saturday nights are crowded; even with reservations, expect a wait, or take advantage of the early take-out special. • Daily 4:30-9:30pm.

Goat Hill Pizza ★ ¢ Potrero Hill: 300 Connecticut St. (18th St.), (415) 647-7676. Thin-crusted pizza with a great sweet sauce is the draw here; try the Mediterranean-style pie with feta and olives, and wash it down with a pitcher of Anchor Steam. Regular-Joe pizza parlor ambience and good view of the city are draws. An easy stop on your way in or out of the city. • Daily 11:30am-10:30pm.

The Gold Spike ★ $$ North Beach: 527 Columbus Ave. (Green/Union), (415) 421-4591. This 75-year-old family establishment is immediately recognizable by its funky decor. Doesn't every Italian restaurant line its walls with business cards, dollar bills, and moose heads? A reasonably priced family-style eatery known for its five-course meals, Gold Spike has created a name for itself with a few simple specialties: chicken Marsala, cioppino, Italian pot roast. In some ways it is like eating in a cave, but it's unique and atmospheric. • M, Tu-Th, 5-10pm; F-Sa 5-10:30pm; Su 4:30-9:45pm.

Golden Turtle ★★ $$ Russian Hill: 2211 Van Ness St. (Broadway/Vallejo), (415) 441-4419. The city's most celebrated Vietnamese food is served in this attractive dining room that's decorated with tree branches and twinkling lights. Try the imperial rolls stuffed with minced pork and shrimp and the five-spice chicken. • Tu-Su 5-11pm.

SAN FRANCISCO RESTAURANTS

Gordon Biersch Brewing Company ★★ $$ SoMa: 2 Harrison St. (Embarcadero), (415) 243-8246. See Peninsula/San Jose section for review of other locations. The enormous San Francisco branch occupies a prime spot in the beautifully restored Hills Brothers building. The young, loud singles scene makes the lively Palo Alto and San Jose locations appear stone dead by comparison. • Daily 11am-3pm, 5-10pm (Bar til 2am).

Gourmet Carousel ★★★ $ Pacific Heights: 1559 Franklin St. (Pine), (415) 771-2044. Newly redecorated with wood paneling and mirrors throughout (after being badly damaged in a police shootout on Franklin and a fire before that), Gourmet Carousel remains a clean and basic Chinese restaurant. The food, however, is anything but basic. The Sichuan curry noodles (which the waitress said contained no vegetables) arrive teeming with a tasty assortment of carrots, onions, celery, and tender shrimp and tossed with just the right amount of spicy yellow curry. Also try the pot stickers or egg rolls, crisp on the outside, soft and doughy when you bite down, and full of crunchy vegetables. If good food isn't enough to get you to stop in, maybe low prices and large portions will win you over. • Tu-Sa 11:30am-9:30pm; Su 4-9:30pm.

The Grand Café ★ $$$ Union Sq.: Hotel Monaco, 501 Geary St. (Taylor), (415) 292-0101. Few restaurants look as nice as this one, with its high ceilings, warm yellow columns, chandeliers like upside-down wedding cakes, and exquisite tiling. Toulose paintings and modernist flair aside, the food is a mixed bag: appetizers like steamed mussels with saffron and leeks shine, while many main dishes such as oven-roasted chicken or scallops and risotto, lacking a distinct taste, fall flat. In addition, service can be somewhat distracted. There is, however, a nice bar and nondining setting near the front entrance (which also serves snacks late), so drinks and dessert might be the best bet for those with a slim wallet. • M-Th 7-10:30am, 11:30am-3pm, 5-10pm; F 7-10:30am, 11:30am-3pm, 5-11pm; Sa-Su 8-10:30am, 11:30am-2:30pm, 5-11pm.

Great Eastern ★★ $$ Chinatown: 649 Jackson St. (Kearny/Grant), (415) 986-2500. A Chinatown hot spot for Cantonese seafood. The neon board on the back wall lists the night's fresh catch, most of which are swimming (or hopping) in large tanks nearby. Neighborhood families crowd around large tables for pricy, authentic feasts of octopus and pork feet with jellyfish, sea conch and geoduck clams with yellow chives, sliced steelhead, and clams with black bean sauce. A few smaller tables serve non-Asian customers who can order the more familiar kung pao chicken or beef with broccoli; seafood is clearly the highlight, although soups and chow mein dishes are also quite good. The brightly lit two-level restaurant sports upscale white-linen-black-lacquer decor with attentive service to match. • Su-Th 11am-1am; F-Sa 11am-3am.

Greens ★★★ $$ Marina: Fort Mason Center, Bldg. A (Buchanan St. at Marina Blvd.), (415) 771-6222. Sympathetic, soothing Greens has been catering to vegetarians for over ten years from a light, airy dining room with a panoramic view of the marina and Golden Gate Bridge. The only creatures you'll find with spines in this place are the diners. Affiliated with the Green Gulch Zen Center, much of the produce served at the restaurant comes from the center's famous farm. While it's vegetarian, you would hardly guess from the surprisingly rich creations—cheese and crème fraîche are kitchen favorites. The menu changes periodically, but you might find delectable corn fritters, a southwestern corn tart, or pasta and pizza. Excellent wine list. Reserve a table far in advance; Saturday nights there's an expensive prix fixe menu. The to-go counter serves soups, salads, and sandwiches. • M 5:30-9:30pm; Tu-F 11:30am-2pm, 5:30-9:30pm; Sa 11:30am-2:30pm, 6-9:30pm; Su 10am-2pm. To-go counter M-F 8am-9:30pm; Sa 8am-4:30pm; Su 9am-3:30pm.

Hahn's Hibachi ★★ ¢ Nob Hill: 1710 Polk St. (Clay/Washington), (415) 776-1095. • Marina: 3318 Steiner St. (Lombard/Chestnut), (415) 931-6284. • Noe Valley: 1345 Castro St. (24th St.) (415) 642-8151. A warning accompanies the barbecued chicken that Hahn's Hibachi is best known for: "Danger... World Famous and Extremely Addictive—Really—Support Groups are Available." The chicken *does* have a cult status, and is also available frozen in bulk to carry home. The chicken's secret is its distinctive sweet and spicy flavor—the flavor of traditional Korean barbecue. Hahn's serves up beef, pork, and shrimp cloaked in the same secret in a variety of styles and combinations, from kabobs to sandwiches topped with melted Jack cheese. Other Asian dishes, from *udon* to tempura, are available. The atmosphere at Hahn's is a little rushed, cramped, and fast foody, but gargantuan portions quickly served keep folks coming back in droves. No credit cards. • Marina: Daily 11am-10pm. • NV: M-Sa 11am-10pm; Su 11am-9pm.

Hamburger Mary's ★ $ SoMa: 1582 Folsom St. (12th St.), (415) 626-1985. This SoMa institution is perfect for a quick meal before hitting the clubs. Not surprisingly, burgers (choose from beef or tofu) are the house specialty. You can also get breakfast all day long. The atmosphere is cluttered junk collector, the patrons are fascinating to watch (especially after nightfall), and the home fries are deliciously spicy. Decorated with garage-sale bargains (including a toilet seat hanging over the wait station), Hamburger Mary's is famous for its offbeat atmosphere. This is the type of place where the wait staff and patrons compete to see who has more tattoos. • M-Th 11:30am-1am; F 11:30am-2am; Sa 10am-2am; Su 10am-1am.

Harbor Village ★★ $$ Embarcadero: 4 Embarcadero Center (Clay/Drumm), (415) 781-8833. This flourishing restaurant serves up some of San Francisco's best dim sum in a truly elegant setting. The large hall, usually packed with Asian families and businessmen, boasts rows of linen-covered tables set amid plush carpeting and dark wood furnishings. The plentiful carts come laden with a large variety of pristine dumplings and such, all of very high quality. The restaurant is a branch of a Hong Kong operation, and the dinner menu includes a full selection of pricy seafood specialties—fresh from the tanks—as well as delightful chow mein. The formal wait staff responds better if you order in Chinese. Reservations recommended. • M-F 11am-2:30pm, 5:30-9:30pm; Sa 10:30am-2:30pm, 5:30-9:30pm; Su 10am-2:30pm, 5:30-9:30pm.

Hawthorne Lane ★★★ $$$$ SoMa: 22 Hawthorne St. (Howard/Folsom), (415) 777-9779. A new sensation from the husband-and-wife chef team of Anne and David Gingrass formerly of Postrio. The location is highly unlikely for one of the city's most celebrated new eateries: the ground floor of the Crown Point Press building on an alley hidden between Second, Third, Howard, and Folsom streets. An enormous bar area with tables makes it easy to sample starters such as tempura vegetables and Postrio-like gourmet pizzas without reserving a table in the dining room weeks in advance (although competition for bar seats can be plenty fierce). Plus, the bar allows you to order not only from its menu, but from the dining room menu as well. With such a great range of selections possible, the bar scene may be enough for you, although some folks just swoon over the chance to sit in the stunning dining room. The huge hall offers good views of the line chefs and the beautiful artworks printed by Crown Point over the years. The food expands upon the East-West California cuisine the chefs developed at Postrio, from foie gras to grilled beef to halibut with cellophane noodles. The outsized wine list matches the surroundings. • Restaurant: M-Th 11:30am-2pm, 5:30-10pm; F 11:30am-2pm, 5:30-11pm; Sa 5:30-11pm; Su 5:30-10pm. Bar/Café: M-F 2:30pm-midnight; Sa-Su 5:30pm-midnight.

Hayes Street Grill ★★★ $$$ Hayes Valley: 320 Hayes St. (Franklin/Gough), (415) 863-5545. Hayes Street is one of the city's best seafood restaurants. Order Chinese-menu style from a series of lists: first, pick your cooking method (grilled, sautéed, fried); then, choose the fish from the day's fresh offerings (if your heart is set on something in particular, reserve it quickly before they run out); finally, pick a sauce: herbed butter, tomatillo salsa, hollandaise. The salads are quite good (especially greens with warm goat cheese and hazelnuts), and the French fries are famous. Landlubbers can get burgers and other meats. The spare brasserie setting is a bit clubby—brass rails, wood, forest green appointments, signed photos of stars—with professional service to match. • M-Th 11:30am-2pm, 5-9:30pm; F 11:30am-2pm, 5:30-10:30pm; Sa 5:30-10:30pm; Su 5-8:30pm.

SAN FRANCISCO RESTAURANTS

The Heights ★★★★ $$$$ Presidio Heights: 3235 Sacramento St. (Presidio/Lyon), (415) 474-8890. An elegant and expensive restaurant in a converted Pacific Heights home. The austerely elegant decor includes simple white walls, beautiful floral arrangements, and red tile floors; the small dining rooms look out over a pretty herb garden. Charles Solomon's exquisite, contemporary French cuisine with California flourishes is based on the freshest and best luxury foods, including a liberal use of foie gras, truffles, and lobster. Choose from à la carte selections or go with the prix fixe tasting menu and let the chef make the decisions. Attentive, unpretentious service makes this is the perfect spot for a special romantic occasion. Reservations recommended. • Tu-Su 5:30-9pm.

Helmand ★★ $$ North Beach: 430 Broadway (Montgomery/Kearny), (415) 362-0641. Afghani food in North Beach? Strange but true. The Beats would surely have approved of the excellent exotic food served at this elegant spot. Start with the *kaddo borawni* (baby pumpkin served with yogurt and garlic sauce), and move on to *chopan* (grilled lamb served on flat bread). A selection of vegetarian specialties will please nonmeat eaters. Reservations required. • Daily 5:30-10pm.

Home Plate ★★ $ Marina: 2274 Lombard St. (Steiner/Pierce), (415) 922-4663. One of the city's most popular breakfast spots, Home Plate attracts hoards of beautiful, hungry yuppies for weekend brunch. Put your name on the list, sit in the sun on the sidewalk, and watch traffic plow along Lombard Street, then crowd into a table in a bright, bare little room. Your endurance will be rewarded when you dive into the eggs Benedict, pancakes heaped with fresh fruit, turkey bacon and avocado omelet, or a similar delight. You can always find an empty table and a waitress not on the verge of a nervous breakdown if you go early or during the week, although you won't get to admire the happy loving Marina couples who met the night before. (If you call ahead they will add your name to the waiting list.) • Daily 7am-4pm.

House of Nanking ★★ $ Chinatown: 919 Kearny St. (Jackson/Columbus), (415) 421-1429. This riotously popular restaurant in the heart of Chinatown always has an hour-long line snaking outside (although they recently expanded into the space next door). This is the kind of place where the waiter tries to order for you, perhaps because the menu only lists a sampling of what the kitchen produces. The crowds flock here for the excellent renditions of Chinese specialties updated with American and Southeast Asian influences. No credit cards. • M-Sa noon-10pm; Su 4-10pm.

Hunan Restaurant ★★ $ Fisherman's Wharf: 924 Sansome St. (Broadway/Vallejo), (415) 956-7727. • Fin. Dist.: 674 Sacramento St. (Kearny/Montgomery), (415) 788-2234. • SoMa: 1016 Bryant St. (8th St./9th St.), (415) 861-5808. This is the restaurant that introduced Hunan food to the Bay Area. They pack them in, but the incendiary food remains high quality, especially the Chinese chicken salad and the harvest pork. The cavernous dining rooms at the Sansome Street location are nothing to write home about, and service is abrupt at best, but the place is worth a visit. Two other branches spread the fire. • FW: Daily 11:30am-9:30pm. • Fin. Dist.: M-F 9:30am-5:30pm. • SoMa: M-F 11:30am-9pm.

Hyde Street Bistro ★★★ $$ Russian Hill: 1521 Hyde St. (Pacific/Jackson), (415) 441-7778. A comfortable, unpretentious neighborhood bistro serving some of the area's best food. The sponged pastel paint and lively local art on the walls don't quite obscure vestigial structural elements: an acoustic tile ceiling and fluorescent lighting fixtures are casually ignored relics of a more modest past. The elegant food blends Austrian and northern Italian influences in wonderful combinations; try the pungently spiced tomato soup, spaetzle with scallops in cream sauce, or the garlicky roast Sonoma chicken. Romantic diners should request the table in the tiny alcove. Limited but reasonably priced wine list. Reservations recommended. • Daily 5:30-10:30pm.

Il Fornaio ★★ $$ Fisherman's Wharf: 1265 Battery St. (Greenwich/Filbert), 986-0100. Sure it seems like you can find an Il Fornaio in almost any California city, but unlike most chain restaurants, each Il Fornaio provides a unique dining experience. The San

Francisco locale boasts high-style Tuscan decor—marble, tile, soaring ceilings—and a charming outdoor patio. No wonder Il Fornaio dominates the pizza, pasta, and pesto market. The *piadina al vegetali*, pizza bread with grilled vegetables, is a great lunch item. All of the pastas are excellent, especially the *tagliolini alla capresante*, thin flat pasta with scallops, shiitake mushrooms, and pesto. If you love food, sit at the counter where you can watch and smell every dish being prepared. (An added benefit for those on a low budget: since 70 percent of taste is smell, the counter seating provides a high satisfaction to dollar ratio.) Save room for dessert. • M-Th 7-10:30am, 11:30am-11pm; F 7-10:30am, 11:30am-midnight; Sa 9am-midnight; Su 9am-11pm.

Il Pollaio ★ ¢ North Beach: 555 Columbus Ave. (Union/Green), (415) 362-7727. If your pocket is feeling a little emptier than Gira Polli will allow, this is a good second choice just around the corner. The dinerlike Il Pollaio, squeezed into a small triangular-shaped storefront, does not rate high on the ambience scale. But the fresh-grilled chickens, a quarter or a half, are hot, good, quick, and inexpensive. For under six bucks, you can get a salad and a half chicken, which is not bad in the City by the Bay. • M-Sa 11:30am-9pm.

Jackson Fillmore Trattoria ★★★ $$ Pacific Heights: 2506 Fillmore St. (Jackson), (415) 346-5288. An inviting neighborhood place, highly recommended by loyal patrons. The decor is nothing special, just a storefront with white walls, basic furniture, and a friendly local clientele. The menu is rustic Italian with California touches. Risotto and a delicious *bruschetta* are good choices, although seafood is the bestseller here—don't miss the salmon in sage butter. Most tables seat four, and reservations are taken only for groups of three or more—highly recommended—so single diners and couples will have to wait for the chance table (you might end up sharing) or a seat at the counter overlooking the open kitchen. Service has brightened with the addition of some Cha Cha Cha refugees. • M 5:30-10pm; Tu-Th 5:30pm-10:30pm; F-Sa 5:30-11pm; Su 5-10pm.

Julie's Supper Club ★★ $$ SoMa: 1123 Folsom St. (7th St./8th St.), (415) 861-0707. A pink vinyl-upholstered bar, '50s-style Holiday Inn lamps, and good, reasonably priced food make this swinging SoMa spot a worthy destination for kitsch lovers. The menu includes fun appetizers and side dishes—everything from fries to eggplant to grilled chicken with corn soufflé, as well as a '90s version of wontons. Eat to the beat of Frank Sinatra and the Neville Brothers while you survey the scene. Save room for dessert. Expect prompt service and a hopping bar scene. • M 5:30-10pm; Tu-W 5-10pm; Th 5-11pm; F-Sa 5-11:30pm.

Kabuto Sushi ★★★ $$ Richmond: 5116 Geary Blvd. (15th Ave./16th Ave.), (415) 752-5652. A diverse crowd agrees that Kabuto has some of the best sushi in town. While there's plenty of seating in the spare dining room, many diners prefer waiting for a seat at the sushi bar, where they will be welcomed and entertained by owner-chef Sachio Kojima. This generous, creative soul will whip up all the usual stuff, as well as delightful creative combinations (not always on the menu, trust him if you feel brave), with a frenzy of enthusiastic energy. Don't be surprised if he slips you a complimentary sample of something to gain your confidence. The menu also includes the usual array of cooked Japanese standards. • Tu-Sa 5:30-11pm.

Kan Zaman ★★ $ Haight: 1793 Haight St. (Shrader), (415) 751-9656. A reasonably priced Middle Eastern restaurant in the riotous Upper Haight, serving fine food amidst fake palm trees and exquisite murals, with floor seating on cushions available. The specialties include *imijadare*, a vegetarian shish kebab, and *bahdoucea*, a terrific milky dip for pita bread. To sample many different dishes, order the Mediterranean plate, with healthy portions of hummus, *baba ghanoush*, tabbouleh, and falafel. For a novel dessert of sorts, head to the bar and try the apple-, honey- or apricot-flavored tobacco, which is smoked through hookahs. Diners on weekend evenings may be lucky enough to catch a free performance by a belly dancer. • M 5pm-midnight; Tu-Th noon-midnight; F-Sa noon-2am; Su noon-midnight.

SAN FRANCISCO RESTAURANTS

Kate's Kitchen ★★★ $ Hayes Valley: 471 Haight St. (Webster/Fillmore), (415) 626-3984. This bare-bones Lower Haight eatery serves up some of the biggest and best breakfasts in town to a hip crowd of well-pierced slackers. Weekend mornings the sidewalk fills with the hungry and hungover waiting for a table and a heaping plate of some down-home specialty. The red flannel hash with giant chunks of corned beef, potatoes, onions, and celery looks more like a New England dinner; it dwarfs the two eggs on top. The famous cornmeal pancakes and orange-spiced French toast come with real maple syrup; fresh fruit toppings add even more bulk. And don't miss the hush puppies (deep-fried cornmeal) with pooh butter. Homey soups and sandwiches carry the menu into the lunch hour. The linoleum floor, closely packed tables with stapled-on red-and-white-checkered vinyl tablecloths, and coolly casual staff make a relaxed beginning to the day. No credit cards. • M-F 8am-2:45pm; Sa-Su 9am-3:45pm.

Khan Toke Thai House ★★★ $$ Richmond: 5937 Geary Blvd. (23rd Ave./24th Ave.), (415) 668-6654. One spoonful of Khan Toke's stratospheric chicken coconut soup and you'll know you're eating at a great Thai restaurant. This Richmond district eatery requires its customers to take off their shoes before entering the teakwood dining rooms and to sit, in traditional style, on the floors surrounded by exotic decorations on the walls and woven dinner mats and real roses on the tables. Ambience aside, the real highlights are the tasty dishes: try the superb *rama long grong* (beef with spinach topped with peanut sauce), the subtle *yom pla muk* (squid with salad, chili, lemongrass, and mint leaves), or the pad Thai. After dinner, check out the small outdoor garden in back. Not surprisingly, this rare combination of wonderful service, atmosphere, and food means a one-hour wait on weekend evenings is common. • M-F 8am-2:45pm; Sa-Su 9am-3:45pm.

Korean Buffet ★ $ Richmond: 6314 Geary Blvd. (27th Ave./28th Ave.), (415) 221-0685. Unusual, impeccably fresh dishes are served in this authentic eatery patronized by people who know their Korean food. There's a grill at every table, which should be enough of a hint that the patrons do their own cooking here. (It probably isn't the best choice for a first date.) Servers light the fire and pour the water, but otherwise you're on your own with the $13.99 all-you-can-eat barbecue buffet. Choose from beef, chicken, squid, and various other meats, plus kimchi, rice, salads and mandarin orange slices. The meats are nicely marinated and not too tough, either. Worth the price for those with a large appetite. Definitely a place for culinary experimentation. • Daily 11am-3pm, 5-10pm.

Kuleto's Restaurant ★★ $$ Union Sq.: 221 Powell St. (Geary/O'Farrell), (415) 397-7720. Named for the restaurant's designer, the ubiquitous Pat Kuleto, the trattoria is loaded with signature Kuleto touches: tortoiseshell-patterned light fixtures, softly buffed dark wood, a roaring wood-fired oven. The two-level dining area affords views of the sauté chefs juggling pans over leaping flames. The once cutting-edge menu reprises favorites such as salmon-filled ravioli with asparagus and lemon cream sauce and risotto primavera. The homemade focaccia that comes with lunch and dinner is excellent, as are grilled seafood specials, but pastas tend to be heavy and the food can be inconsistent. Nevertheless, good cheer pervades the always bustling scene, especially at the long, narrow bar area (perfect for pretheater antipasti). The newer Burlingame location has also been an instant hit. • M-F 7am-11pm; Sa-Su 8am-11pm.

La Cumbre Taqueria ★★ ¢ Mission: 515 Valencia St. (16th St./17th St.), (415) 863-8205. A cheap, authentic burrito joint in the heart of the Mission. Red tile floors, murals on the walls, and lots of seating at the rustic wooden tables. You might need to wait in line during the lunch rush hour, but it's worth it. Very good, very large burritos, especially those constructed with ingredients off the grill. Watch the hot sauce, though. It's deadly! Cash only. • M-Sa 11am-10pm; Su noon-9pm.

La Folie ★★★★ $$$$ Russian Hill: 2316 Polk St. (Union/Green), (415) 776-5577. A great standard bearer of contemporary French cooking in San Francisco, with prices to match. La Folie should be one of the top choices when the boss says "Treat yourself and a date to dinner on me." Chef Roland Passot's superbly presented creations are flavorful and interesting without being eccentric or merely bizarre; rich sauces burst with flavor. Each night Passot offers a tasting menu—less expensive Monday through Thursday—and a la carte selections consistently featuring foie gras, lobster, and game. The light dining room relies on tawny tile, wood, and painted clouds floating across a sky-blue ceiling to create an intimate environment without the somber, fussy feeling typical in four-star restaurants (in fact, it can be quite loud and bustling). Suitably expensive wine list. Reservations recommended. • M-Sa 5:30-10:30pm.

La Méditerranée ★★ $ Pacific Heights: 2210 Fillmore St. (Sacramento/Clay), (415) 921-2956. • Castro: 288 Noe St. (Market/16th St.), (415) 431-7210. These unassuming eateries may look like neighborhood holes-in-the-wall, but are well worth a visit. The Mediterranean specialties are delicious, and the *meze* combination platter for two—available regular or vegetarian—gives first timers an introduction to the flavorful cuisine. Be sure to try the chicken pomegranate and the chicken Cilicia. A perfect place for a low-budget evening with friends, even the wine list is amazingly reasonable. No reservations, so expect a wait at peak times. • PH: M-Th 11am-10pm; F 11am-11pm; Sa 11am-11pm. • Castro: Tu-Th, Su 11am-10pm; F-Sa 11am-11pm.

La Taqueria ★★ ¢ Mission: 2889 Mission St. (24th St./25th St.), (415) 285-7117. Perhaps the area's most beloved taqueria, always packed with lively neighborhood patrons from families to workers to young hipsters. The scrambling counter staff frantically chops and cooks to stay ahead of the crowd. They've been filling their excellent tacos, burritos, and quesadillas with house-made meats, salsas, and vegetables since long before the chains popularized fresh Mex. La Cumbre has the edge on *carne asada*, but La Taqueria's succulent chicken, pork, and spicy chorizo are second to none. Standard Mexican fast-food decor with mural-covered stucco walls, tile floors and counters, picnic tables, and a loud jukebox. The sunny front patio offers a good view of this busy neighborhood. No credit cards. • M-Sa 11am-9pm; Su 11am-8pm.

Laghi ★★★ $$$ Richmond: 1801 Clement St. (19th Ave.), (415) 386-6266. This popular Clement Street Italian looks ordinary, but the food and service are first-rate. You won't find better rabbit anywhere, and specialty dishes such as risotto with black truffles truly shine. The delicious bread and pasta are homemade by the chef's wife. The Italian wine list is very good and reasonably priced; desserts are strong, with the tiramisù particularly good. Reservations recommended. • Tu-Sa 5-9:30pm; Su 5-8:30pm.

Le Central ★★ $$$ Union Sq.: 453 Bush St. (Grant/Kearny), (415) 391-2233. An attractively authentic but over-the-hill French bistro near the Financial district. The kitchen turns out all the French standards—*steak pommes frites*, roast chicken, and cassoulet—although they can taste a little too familiar after all these years. Herb Caen, Willie Brown, Wilkes Bashford, and other well-known locals still appear regularly, as do many downtown power lunchers. A good-looking zinc bar, cramped tables, and casually professional service enhance the Parisian atmosphere, however predictable the formula has become. • Tu-Sa 5-9:30pm; Su 5-8:30pm.

Le Soleil ★★ $ Richmond: 133 Clement St. (2nd Ave./3rd Ave.), (415) 668-4848. Found near the eastern end of the Richmond, Le Soleil is among the best of the many ethnic eateries in the neighborhood. The decor is light and airy, and the place is generally full with Vietnamese of all ages and a smattering of other locals. The dishes, like five-spice chicken and lemongrass beef, are fresh tasting and packed with flavor. Start your meal off with shrimp wrapped in sugarcane. • Su-Th 11am-10pm; F-Sa 11am-10:30pm.

Lee's Deli ★ ¢ Fin. Dist.: 343 Kearny St. (Pine/Bush), (415) 986-1052. • Fin. Dist.: 525 Market St. (entrance faces 1st St.), (415) 777-9352. • Fin. Dist.: 648 Market St. (Montgomery/Kearny), (415) 421-0648. • Fin. Dist.: 222 Front St. (California/Sacramento), (415) 433-3222. • Fin. Dist.: 475 Sansome St. (Sacramento/Clay), (415) 391-4740. • SoMa: 123 Mission St. (Main), (415) 986-1230. This chain of take-out shops owns the downtown lunch market. Indeed, they

SAN FRANCISCO RESTAURANTS

probably make more sandwiches than everybody else combined. Long lines get chewed up in minutes by workers churning out sandwiches at prices you can't believe for downtown San Francisco. How about egg, tuna, or chicken salad for two and change? Most surprising at these prices are the large portions of fresh ingredients: look for thick slices of turkey breast from birds they roast themselves daily, pink roast beef, and real bacon slices. The breads are supermarket-style loaves, but that enhances the homey feel of a peanut butter and jelly or liverwurst sandwich. No credit cards. • Kearny: M-F 6:30am-3:30pm. • 525 Market: M-F 6:30am-5:45pm; Sa 8am-4pm. • 648 Market: M-Sa 6am-6pm. • Front: M-F 6:30am-5pm. • Sansome: M-F 6:30am-4pm. • SoMa: M-F 6am-4pm.

Leticia's ★ $ Castro: 2247 Market St. (Sanchez/Noe), (415) 621-0441. Leticia's has hip, rock-formationlike booths, dim lighting, and the best (self-proclaimed) margaritas in town, but falls dramatically short on taste. The margaritas are more ice than anything else. The food is bland and unmemorable—the black bean mole is a safe bet—and service comes with an attitude. In short, come for the convivial atmosphere, but go to the Mission for authentic Mexican specialties and save yourself some money. • Su-Th 11am-11:30pm; F-Sa 11am-midnight.

The Liberty Café ★★ $$ Mission: 410 Cortland Ave. (Bennington/Andover), (415) 695-8777. This cute neighborhood storefront serves simple all-American favorites with modern improvements, such as grilled cheese on challah bread, gourmet pizzas, and the crowning glory, chicken pot pie. Their steak is among the best around, but more adventurous ethnic dishes like plantains and black beans can be bland. Breads and rolls are house-made using organic ingredients. There is a nice array of reasonably priced wines well suited to the food. Hardwood floors, light wood furniture, and white tablecloths make for an unpretentious hangout, although booming popularity is creating a bit of a scene and long waits (they don't take reservations). This child-friendly place offers tasteful wooden high chairs for little diners. • Tu-F 11:30am-3pm, 5:30-9:30pm; Sa 9:30am-2:30pm, 5:30-9pm; Su 10am-2pm.

Little Italy Ristorante ★★ $$ Noe Valley: 4109 24th St. (Castro), (415) 821-1515. Most everything aside from the drinks and desserts is smothered in garlic here, but luckily, it's all terrific, served in a warm and cozy atmosphere of exposed wood beams and checkered tablecloths. Choice appetizers include fried mozzarella marinara and the heavenly stuffed mushrooms. The pasta dishes are largely variations on spaghetti, but that includes a house special with prawns, garlic, oil, and anchovies. The class act of the main dishes just might be the juicy pork chops parmigiana. Vegetable dishes are also available, as are numerous fine wines. There's an excellent wait staff to boot, making this a truly fine dining experience. • M 5:30-10pm; Tu-Th 5:30-10:30pm; F-Sa 5:30-11pm; Su 5-10pm.

Little Thai ★★ $ Russian Hill: 2348 Polk St. (Green/Union), (415) 771-5544. This unpretentious little gem boasts house specials that are always worth consideration. But some excellent standard plates merit your attention, too, such as the pad Thai, *com guy* soup, or eggplant with ground chicken and basil (even better if you request whole pieces of chicken or tofu instead of the ground chicken). The staff is attentive without smothering and will accommodate almost any request. The one small dining room, packed with Thai standard-issue glass-and-pink-cloth-topped tables, gets crowded during peak hours, but the turnover is fast enough to prevent long lines. Forewarned is forearmed: some dishes can be fiery hot, so request mild if your taste buds can't take the heat. • M 5:30-10pm; Tu-Th 5:30-10:30pm; F-Sa 5:30-11pm; Su 5-10pm.

Liverpool Lil's ★★ $$ Pacific Heights: 2942 Lyon St. (Lombard/Greenwich), (415) 921-6664. A traditional British public house, Liverpool Lil's is cozy, comfortable, and more than just a great place to slurp down a beer with friends. Its menu selection is quite broad and very satisfying: in the bar area, there are Thai kabobs, baked Brie, or baby pizzas, among other finger foods; and in the restaurant, daily specials range from pasta to fish dishes. Weekend brunches at Lil's are a great alternative to the "hair of the dog" hangover cure that some of the pub's regular patrons indulge in. The eggs Benedict and eggs Florentine are poached to perfection, served with a mild hollandaise, home fries, and fresh fruit. At any time of day, you can order the hearty Lil's burger, topped with cheese, mushrooms, and onions—definitely one of the best burgers in town. • M-Sa 11am-1am; Su 11am-1am (lighter menu after midnight M-Sa; after 11pm Su).

LuLu ★★★ $$ SoMa: 816 Folsom St. (4th St./5th St.), (415) 495-5775. This grand café has captured the fancy of San Francisco's discriminating epicureans with its intriguing Mediterranean menu. The large, open dining room, done up in muted shades of blue and gray, encourages people watching. The food deserves your full attention, though, especially side dishes like olive-oil mashed potatoes and grilled asparagus with shaved Parmesan and lemon. Main dishes are equally alluring, in particular anything off the grill. And don't overlook the mussels cooked on an iron griddle. Prices are reasonable, but service can be uneven; expect a wait, even with reservations. • M-Th 7-11am, 11:30am-10:45pm; F 7-11am, 11:30am-11:45pm; Sa-Su 9-11am, 11:30am-11:45pm.

LuLu Bis ★★★ $$$/ LuLu Café ★★ $ SoMa: 816 Folsom St. (4th St./5th St.), (415) 495-5775. Adjoining either side of LuLu are its two recent siblings, LuLu Bis and LuLu Café. LuLu Bis, a long, narrow space, has a warmth that is missing from the chaotic scene next door. The country-style service adds to the cozy charm; vegetables and side dishes are served family-style, in a large bowl in the middle of the table. The delicious fava bean and baby artichoke salad has been a staple first course, with Mediterranean fish, pasta, and meat completing the menu. Each night choose from two prix fixe menus ($33 and $35) and à la carte selections. At the other end of the building is the café, the most informal of the three eateries. Open all day, it offers breakfast fare, as well as light starters such as pizzas, deep-fried artichokes with aioli and a full raw bar. • LuLu Bis: Daily 5:45-10pm. • LuLu Café: M-Th 6am-10:30pm; F-Sa 6am-11:30pm; Su 9am-10:30pm.

MacArthur Park ★★ $$ Fin. Dist.: 607 Front St. (Jackson), (415) 398-5700. See Peninsula/San Jose section for review of the Palo Alto location. The San Francisco location's atmospheric brick hall fits its historic Jackson Square location well, and the large bar area booms with reveling suits and skirts at happy hour, but the food is better at the Palo Alto original. • M-Th 11:30am-10pm; F 11:30am-11pm; Sa 5-11pm; Su 4:30-10pm.

Mandalay ★★ $ Richmond: 4348 California St. (6th Ave.), (415) 386-3895. Unusual, delicious Burmese food is served within this simple, attractive dining room. Try the ginger salad, the curried prawns, and the fish salad with garlic. The brave of palate may want to try the *lap pat dok*, marinated tea leaves tossed with an assortment of condiments. Or try the Mandalay squid served on spinach with hot-and-sour sauce. • Daily 11:30am-9:30pm.

Mangiafuoco ★★ $$ Mission: 1001 Guerrero St. (22nd St.), (415) 206-9881. Yet another sizzling restaurant in the Mission. Mangiafuoco ("fire eater" in Italian) bases its short menu around a large fire-breathing brick oven visible in the open kitchen. A young, lively, and loud crowd packs into this trendy but cramped little dining room for the festive spirit and excellent grilled and oven-baked specialties (don't miss the lamb or seafood in parchment). Well-done pasta dishes complement the grilled choices. Start with an excellent carpaccio. Reservations recommended. No credit cards. • Su-Th 5:30-10:30pm; F-Sa 5:30-11:30pm.

Manora's Thai Cuisine ★★ $ SoMa: 1600 Folsom St. (12th St.), (415) 861-6224. Manora's serves a full range of Thai specialties and excellent seafood—don't miss the combination grilled on skewers—and rich curries, with such interesting specials as fried soft-shell crabs with tamarind sauce. The restaurant has a perpetual crowd of SoMa party types waiting at the bar for one of the closely packed tables. Reservations accepted for groups of four or more. • M-F 11:30am-2:30pm, 5:30-10:30pm; Sa 5:30-10:30pm; Su 5-10pm.

SAN FRANCISCO RESTAURANTS

Mario's Bohemian Cigar Store ★★ $ North Beach: 566 Columbus Ave. (Union), (415) 362-0536. • Russian Hill: 2209 Polk St. (Vallejo/Green), (415) 776-8226. Mario's is a good example of a restaurateur's ingenuity in the face of an adverse floor plan. Wedged into the triangular space where Columbus meets Union, the restaurant is not very welcoming from the outside, but take a seat at the bar (or wherever possible) and soak up the authentic Italian atmosphere. Both the cappuccino and mocha are excellent, the focaccia sandwiches and cannelloni are authentic, and the beer selection is decent. The larger new branch on Polk Street has an expanded menu of pizza and pasta. Cash only. • NB: M-Sa 10am-midnight, Su 10am-11pm. • RH: M-Th 10am-midnight; F-Sa 10am-1am; Su 10am-midnight.

Masa's ★★★★ $$$$ Union Sq.: 648 Bush St. (Powell/Stockton), (415) 989-7154. Just about perfect, and very expensive. Many call Masa's San Francisco's best restaurant. The new deep red walls are a bit somber, but the food and the wines are still sparkling. The five-and seven-course menus ($68 and $75, respectively) are full of dishes that shimmer with imagination and thrill with deep flavors. Opt for the seven smallish tasting courses, which offer such choices as a succulent foie gras and a beautiful squab in its own juices. The service is impeccable and quite friendly, with no arrogance. Reserve at least two weeks ahead. • Tu-Sa 6-9:30pm.

Matsuya ★★ $$ Noe Valley: 3856 24th St. (Vicksburg), (415) 282-7989. From the steaming hot towels before the meal to the eager questioning from grandmotherly owner (and server) Fusae Ponne after it, this Noe Valley hole-in-the-wall is about as authentic as Japanese restaurants come. A chef makes sushi for those at the bar or one of the few tables, while Ponne keeps the giant bottles of Asahi and Sapporo beer flowing during dinner. Choose from numerous, filling combos of sushi or sashimi, or get the full menu experience from the Matsuya ($10) or Special ($16) dinners. *Donburi* (a bowl of rice with topping) and *gyoza* (tasty shrimp-filled pot stickers) are also available. Sometimes closed without explanation, so it's best to call ahead. • M-Sa 4-11pm.

Max's Diner ★ $ SoMa: 311 3rd St. (Folsom), (415) 546-MAXS/6297. Max's Opera Café with a '50s diner theme and no singing. • M-Th 11am-10pm; F-Sa 11am-midnight; Su 11am-10pm.

Max's Eatz/Sweet Max's ★ ¢ Embarcadero: 30 Fremont St. (Mission/Market), (415) 543-8777. • Fin. Dist.: 595 2nd St. (Market St.), (415) 896-MAXS/6297. • Fin. Dist.: 1 California St. (Market), (415) 781-MAXS/6297. • Fin. Dist.: 235 Montgomery (Pine/Bush), (415) 398-MAXS/6297. Gargantuan portions are the hallmark of these busy New York–style deli/bakeries. From the football-sized stuffed potatoes to the sandwiches stacked so high with corned beef that you can hardly fit your mouth around them, everything on the menu is calculated to make you feel positively Lilliputian. Save room for dessert; the choices are outrageous. The downtown locations are popular lunch spots for the working crowd. The Fremont Street location has a bar and serves light eats into the evening. • Fremont: M-F 6am-2pm, 4:30-7:30pm. • Second: M-F 6am-2pm. • California: M-F 6am-3pm. • Montgomery: M-F 6am-2pm.

Max's Opera Café ★★ $$ Civic Center: 601 Van Ness Ave. (Golden Gate), (415) 771-7300 (take-out 771-7301). The kind of high camp that draws a crowd in Miami Beach works here, too. The brassy, boastful menu starts with New York-style chopped liver and corned beef sandwiches and then goes ballistic with sweet-and-sour duck and pasta galore. Not everything works perfectly, but it's always tasty and interesting. Best to take a doggie bag for the main course to save room for Sweet Max's larger-than-life desserts. The name refers to the singing wait staff, who perform everything from show tunes to opera starting at 7pm each night. Decor is glitzy deli. • M 11:30am-10pm; Tu-Th 11:30am-midnight; F-Sa 11:30am-1am; Su 11:30am-11pm.

McCormick & Kuleto's Seafood ★★ $$$ Fisherman's Wharf: Ghirardelli Square, 900 North Point St. (Polk/Larkin), (415) 929-1730. This huge restaurant has something for almost everyone. At the top back, with an entrance of its own, a nook with a sports bar feel serves beer and crab cakes to patrons wearing baseball caps and shorts. One

SAN FRANCISCO RESTAURANTS M

level down, diners enjoying a magnificent Golden Gate vista can order an array of café food—crusty sourdough, old-fashioned shrimp cocktails, a wide selection of oysters—while serious drinkers can imbibe at the long bar. The lowest level's more formal white-clothed dining room offers full dinners of pasta and seafood. Simple fish dishes tend to be the best. The view is as beautiful on foggy days as on sunny days. • M-Sa 11:30am-11pm; Su 10:30am-11pm.

Mel's Drive-In ★ $ Richmond: 3355 Geary Blvd. (Parker/Stanyan), (415) 387-2244. • Marina: 2165 Lombard St. (Fillmore/Steiner), (415) 921-3039. Mel's is part of the movement to recapture the glory of the '50s, with coin-op jukeboxes at every table and a menu with favorites like meat loaf sandwiches and bread pudding. A popular late-night hangout, especially with teens, Mel's is perfect for a milk shake after the movies and is a fun place to go with a group. The more health-conscious will be relieved to see turkey burgers and salads on the menu in addition to the burgers, dogs, and fries. Whatever you choose, be sure to save room for dessert. Apple pie, root beer floats, and hot fudge all guarantee a sugar high. No credit cards. • Richmond: Su-Th 6am-1am; F-Sa 6am-3am. • Marina: Su-Th 6am-3am; F-Sa 24 hours (from F 6am through M 3am).

Mescolanza ★★ $$ Richmond: 2221 Clement St. (23rd Ave./24th Ave.), (415) 668-2221. A simply decorated and simply wonderful Italian restaurant located in a storefront way out in the Richmond. An order of tomatoes with fresh mozzarella is a nice light appetizer to start, as is the *insalata* Mescolanza; hungrier patrons will prefer the hearty antipasti. For entrees, all the pasta choices are excellent, and are surprisingly rich without being too heavy; try their heavenly *linguine alla carbonara* or fettuccine with pesto. For meat eaters, the veal Marsala is also recommended, and there's usually a seafood special. Desserts are meant to be sinful. The portions are generous and moderately priced, and the staff is prompt and very friendly, adding to the warm neighborhood feel. • Daily 5-10pm.

Michelangelo Café ★★ $$ North Beach: 579 Columbus Ave. (Union/Green), (415) 986-4058. Turning off Columbus Street into Michelangelo is like walking into Italy, or at least Little Italy. Michelangelo offers customers authentic Italian-American style and a menu full of such reliable favorites as prosciutto-wrapped melon, fettuccine with pesto, and shrimp scampi. Michelangelo also fulfills the old-fashioned ideal of treating customers like family. (Much of the art on the cluttered walls looks to have been painted by family members.) Wine is served in pitchers, Botticelli-inspired faces glow from the tabletops, sauces leave you wanting more to taste (no matter how full you are), and biscotti and orange slices come with your coffee. Just like you always wanted home to be—at a reasonable price. No credit cards. • M-Sa 5-11pm; Su 3-10pm.

Mifune ★★ $ Pacific Heights: Japantown Center, 1737 Post St. (Buchanan/Webster), (415) 922-0337. For a quick, cheap noodle fix, head for Mifune in Japantown. Choose from *udon* or *soba* noodles served any which way: in broth plain, in broth topped with tempura, or served cold on a lacquer tray with dipping sauces and tempura. The decor is nothing to write home about, but the noodles are worth the trip. • Su-Th 11am-9:30pm; F-Sa 11am-10pm.

Mike's Chinese Cuisine ★★ $ Richmond: 5145 Geary Blvd. (15th Ave./16th Ave.), (415) 752-0120. The lines of local Chinese residents that form around mealtime in the lobby are a sure sign that Mike's is big favorite in the neighborhood. The sauces have a particularly clean and healthful appeal. The chicken salad is excellent, as are the pot stickers, hot-and-sour soup, and bean cake with black mushrooms. Indeed, most of the items on the menu are delicious. Don't miss the boiled wontons and noodles—a delectable Asian carbo load. • W-M 4:30-9:30pm.

Milano Pizzeria ★ $ Sunset: 1330 9th Ave. (Irving/Judah), (415) 665-3773. In the never-ending search for true New York–style pizza in San Francisco, many people feel that this Sunset spot comes awfully close. Choose from the regular selection of toppings, or try some of the "special creations" like The True Greek, featuring cold feta and cucumbers, or the artery-hardening meat special of salami, pepperoni, sausage, and beef. Sandwiches, salads, main dishes, and pastas are also available. Delivery until 1am. • Daily noon-midnight.

Millennium ★★ $$ Civic Center: 246 McAllister St. (Hyde/Larkin), (415) 487-9800. For those who find Green's heavy use of cream and cheese unacceptable, Millenium should be the answer, the next step in vegetarian cooking. Specializing primarily in organic vegan cooking, which avoids all animal products and the fats and oils that generally accompany them, Millenium presents a menu filled with salads, vegetables, and numerous faux concoctions. After a Caesar salad (they will include cheese on request), choose dishes such as grilled portobello mushrooms with sweet Moroccan dressing, a gyro made with seitan instead of pressed lamb, a "steak" of soy or seitan in a mushroom and Marsala sauce, or an unambiguous macro (as in biotic) plate that includes a mushroom, bean, and onion stew with grains, tofu, kale, broccoli, seaweed salad, and house pickle. A list of organic wines completes the healthful menu. The bright upscale dining room in the old Abigail Hotel features black-and-white floor tiles, sponged cream walls, and large floral arrangements. Reservations required on weekends. • Tu-F 11:30am-2:30pm, 5-10pm; Sa-Su 5-10pm.

Miss Pearl's Jam House ★★ $$ Civic Center: 601 Eddy St. (Polk/Larkin), (415) 775-5267. Popular with the swanky young set, Miss Pearl's serves Caribbean specialties like jerk chicken in a tropical, fun-filled ambience. Try the blackened beef fillet served over black beans and roasted peppers. The bartenders make the best rum drinks around. At Sunday brunch there's outdoor seating around the aqua pool, Miami Beach style (bring your bathing suit and take a dip). Live music Thursdays through Saturdays. • W-Th 6-10pm; F-Sa 6-11pm; Su 11am-2:30pm, 5-9:30pm.

Mission Rock Resort ★ $ SoMa: 817 China Basin Blvd. (Mariposa/3rd St.), (415) 621-5538. The food at this burger joint is nothing to crow about (although the sea gulls might disagree), but the views of the bay and the funky biker ambience make up for the kitchen's lapses. A good place to while away a Sunday afternoon is on the upstairs outdoor deck with a cup of diner coffee. Outdoor barbecues depend on the weather, as do the restaurant hours—keep in mind that rain may close the place down. Live blues and jazz Friday through Sunday afternoons. • Upstairs on deck: daily 10am-3pm; downstairs take-out counter: 7am-6pm.

Mo's ★★ $ North Beach: 1322 Grant Ave. (Vallejo/Green), (415) 788-3779. Mo's proves that there's more to North Beach than pasta. Knowledgeable San Franciscans come to this modest eatery for one of the city's best burgers. Mo's grills seven-ounce slabs of prime chuck to perfection over an open flame for that backyard barbecue flavor (only Mo's doesn't overcook them the way most garden chefs do). A good assortment of toppings includes American, Gruyère, and blue cheeses, sautéed mushrooms, and barbecue sauce. Other, equally delicious menu items have an international flavor: grilled chicken breast with Thai curry paste, Mediterranean lamb burger, grilled eggplant with pesto and Parmesan on focaccia. A thick shake goes perfectly with the spicy fries—just don't tell your cardiologist. Bare-bones diner decor, complete with black-and-white tile and chrome-tube furniture. • M-Th 11:30am-10:30pm; F 11:30am-11:30pm; Sa 9am-11:30pm; Su 9am-10:30pm.

Moose's ★★ $$/$$$ North Beach: 1652 Stockton St. (Union/Filbert), (415) 989-7800. It's unclear whether Moose's large front window was designed to allow diners to admire Washington Square or passersby to admire the see-and-be-seen crowd wheeling and dealing over pizza, pasta, and cocktails. Everywhere you turn there's something to look at: cooks bustle in the large open kitchen visible behind a counter on one wall and through a glass window along another, while singles mingle at the narrow bar along the third. The upscale interior—with a white tile floor and green marble cocktail tables in front and green carpeting and white tablecloths in the main area—and convivial atmosphere make the place seem like Star's for the masses. The menu includes such Cal-Italian favorites as wood-fired gourmet pizzas, simple pastas, grilled salmon, and pork chops, but most patrons come for the lively energy, not the food. Reservations recommended. • M-Th 11:30am-11pm; F-Sa 11:30am-midnight; Su 10:30am-11pm.

Neecha Thai ★★ $ Pacific Heights: 2100 Sutter St. (Steiner), (415) 922-9419. This neighborhood Thai restaurant lies hidden just a block off busy Fillmore, which keeps crowds to a minimum. Everything but the seafood is above average, with an especially large selection of vegetarian appetizers and entrées featuring bright, fresh ingredients and spices. The smooth, rich duck in red curry with pineapple will have you swooning. You will be treated to typically solicitous service in a cozy, dimly lit dining room that looks better than the rec-room wood and brick paneling should. A long bench perfect for dining alone runs along a wall of windows looking out on a quiet street. Traditional Thai instrumental music provides a soothing, psychedelic background. • M-F 11am-3pm, 5-10pm; Sa-Su 5-10pm.

New Dawn Café ★ ¢ Mission: 3174 16th St. (Guerrero), no phone. With knickknacks strewn everywhere, the menu written in lipstick on a broken mirror, mismatched chairs, and United Airlines utensils, some may find that eating here is kind of like dining in someone's garage. But the rock-bottom prices and enormous servings will appeal to bohemian Mission types, or to those who wished they were. New Dawn's specialty is big breakfasts for big hangovers: biscuits the size of softballs, congealed bacon, eggs, pancakes, and some of the best home fries anywhere. (An order of the veggie home fries will feed the entire table.) The staff is somewhat aloof (some servers have been seen wearing Bermuda shorts and thongs); once having ordered and paid at the counter, though, the wait to eat isn't very long. Beware the punk rock playing in the background and the giant stuffed animal leaning over the plush corner booth. • M-Tu 8:30am-2:30pm; W-Su 8:30am-8:30pm.

Nippon Sushi (No Name) ★★ $ Castro: 314 Church St. (15th St./16th St.), no phone. You'll have to work to find this place (the nondescript storefront is unmarked, just look for the line of people waiting outside), but your trouble will be well rewarded. Impeccably fresh, very inexpensive sushi is the specialty; the nine-piece *nigiri* combination is a steal. Sit at one of the eight tables or take a stool at the sushi bar, and if you'd like a Kirin to go with your meal, stop in at the corner deli—Nippon is strictly BYOB. Cash only. • M-Sa 5:30-9pm.

Nob Hill Café ★★ $/$$ Nob Hill: 1152 Taylor St. (Sacramento/Clay), (415) 776-6500. It's surprising to find one of San Francisco's most affordable trattorias in the shadow of Nob Hill's plush hotels and condos. But each night, neighborhood denizens line up for heaping plates of pasta like penne with a spicy tomato cream sauce or for a thin-crust pizza priced at only $8. Entrées posted on the permanent specials board invariably include chicken, sole, and calamari in a tangy piccata sauce served with a mound of pasta and crunchy al dente vegetable—a deal for $11. The calamari steak is so tender you'll forget lesser, rubbery renditions. Two schizophrenic dining rooms share the same cramped kitchen and wait staff, but otherwise look like separate restaurants: the original spare space sports mauve-and-tan tabletops and a view of the scrambling chefs; the newer Vicino has deep green walls, green tabletops, and a terra-cotta tile floor. A couple of sidewalk tables are popular for dessert and coffee. Service is friendly, but tends to be disorganized, especially when events at the nearby Masonic Hall attract big crowds. • Daily 11am-10pm.

North Beach Pizza ★ $ North Beach: 1499 Grant Ave. (Union), (415) 433-2444. • North Beach: 1310 Grant Ave. (Vallejo/Green), (415) 433-1818. • Mission: 4787 Mission St. (Excelsior), (415) 586-1400. • Haight (take-out only): 800 Stanyan (Beulah), (415) 751-2300. • Sunset (take-out only): 3054 Taraval (41st Ave.), (415) 242-9100. The celebrated chain of San Francisco pizza parlors is loud and energized, with lots of families and large groups in attendance. Toppings are sometimes hidden between the gooey cheese and chewy crust, which can make for some surprises. The menu includes other Italian favorites, but stick to the pizza—pastas are only fair and tend to be salty. The green, red, and white color scheme is true to the Italian flag—

although the place is run by Italians from Brazil—and booth seating provides a modicum of intimacy. Service is good, although it can be rushed when the place is packed and lines are long. Skip the lines and call for delivery; the chain is very efficient and even has take-out only locations. • Grant (Union): Su-Th 11am-1am; F-Sa 11am-3am.• Grant (Vallejo/Green): M-Th 5-11pm; F-Sa 11am-1am; Su 11am-11pm. • Mission: M-Sa 11am-11pm; Su noon-11pm. • Haight: Daily 24 hours. • Sunset: Su-Th 4-11pm; F-Sa 4pm-midnight.

North Beach Restaurant ★★ $$$ North Beach: 1512 Stockton St. (Green/Union), (415) 392-1700. Firmly believing that "the two most important things in life are nutrition and the propagation of the species," owner Lorenzo Petroni and chef Bruno Orsi have dedicated themselves to serving fine Tuscan cuisine. Fiercely patriotic, they refuse to use French parsley for garnishing, and thus use bay leaves instead. The pasta portions are generous, and the fork-tender meats, especially the veal scaloppine with pine nuts and mushrooms, are in a class by themselves. The restaurant was recently remodeled, finally updating the Prohibition-era decor. The wine list has been voted in the top 100 by *Wine Spectator* Magazine. • Daily 11:30am-11:45pm.

North India Restaurant ★★ $$ Pacific Heights: 3131 Webster St. (Lombard), (415) 931-1556. Popular consensus has it that North India serves the best tandooris around: mouth-watering, with the freshest ingredients, and imaginatively presented. It's best to stick to those regional specialties, since the curries tend to be thin. In addition, the portions are somewhat smaller than at other Indian restaurants. Still, there are a few deals, like the $9.95 prix fixe, which includes soup, *nan*, condiments, basmati rice, and an entrée. The wealthier famished might enjoy the traditional feast ($22.95 per person), which embraces a bit of nearly everything on the menu. Most anyone will like the genteel atmosphere and hushed conversations, fine service, and the sight of cooks working at the tandoor through a glass window. • M-F 11:30am-2:30pm, 5-10:30pm; Sa 5-10:30pm; Su 4:30-10pm.

One Market Restaurant ★★★ $$$ Embarcadero: 1 Market St. (Steuart), (415) 777-5577. Bradley Ogden's large venture in One Market Plaza has a dining room that overlooks the bay, but, unlike Ogden's famed Lark Creek Inn, has a somewhat corporate feel. The food is still great, though. The menu changes daily and might include grilled Norwegian salmon with artichoke ragout, grilled barbecued pork loin, or oak-grilled chicken breast with crispy wild mushrooms. Desserts could include chilled apricot and plum compote with champagne sabayon, root-beer-float *granita,* or chocolate brioche bread pudding. Reservations recommended. • M-Th 11:30am-2pm, 5:30-9:15pm; F 11:30am-2pm, 5:30-9:45pm; Sa 5-9:45pm; Su 10am-2pm, 5-8:45pm.

Orphan Andy's ★ $ Castro: 3991-A 17th St. (Castro), (415) 864-9795. This is true diner cuisine, where you can get crispy fries, juicy burgers, pancakes, or eggs at any hour. If your arteries aren't up to chicken fried steak or pork chops, try a veggie burger. Orphan Andy's also carries a line of Just Desserts' sinful baked goods. And don't forget the shakes—diner food's not the same without them. Vinyl booths and a jukebox complete the picture. Does it get any better than this? All-night service in the heart of the Castro means there can be a line after club closing time on the weekends. Cash only. • Daily 24 hours (closed Thanksgiving and Christmas).

Pad Thai ★★ $ Mission: 3259 Mission St. (Duncan/29th St.), (415) 285-4210. Great Thai in the Mission. The lace curtains and the small white building stamp this place with the feeling of a bed and breakfast. The food, however, is authentic Thai. The namesake pad Thai is some of the best San Francisco has to offer. For a real treat, go for the chicken *gaeng daeng* (chicken, bamboo shoots, and red pepper in a red coconut curry sauce). Excellent service and reasonable prices add to the cozy dining experience. • M-F 11am-10pm; Sa-Su noon-10pm.

Palio d'Asti ★★★ $$$ Fin. Dist.: 640 Sacramento St. (Montgomery/Kearny), (415) 395-9800. • Downtown (Paninoteca $$): 505 Montgomery St. (Commercial/Sacramento),

(415) 362-6900. • SoMa (Paninoteca $$): 201 Mission St. (Beale/Main), (415) 979-0451. Named for the annual bareback horse races of Asti, Italy, which are celebrated in the restaurant's colorful hanging banners. The formal concrete-and-glass dining space includes stone columns and multileveled ceilings. Owner Gianni Fassio, who used to run the landmark Blue Fox, presents a changing menu of hearty regional Italian specialties. For a real treat try the ravioli filled with Fontina cheese or braised rabbit; for lighter fare, order sautéed spinach, sun-dried tomatoes, and mozzarella on focaccia. The two Paninoteca operations serve quicker, lighter dishes in more modern, sparser settings. At these or at the main restaurant, the dining experience is always one of excellent service, making these stops favorites with the business lunch crowd. • Sacramento: M-F 11:30am-9:30pm. • Montgomery: M-F 7am-4pm. • SoMa: M-F 6:30am-3:30pm.

Palomino ★★ $$ SoMa: 345 Spear St. (Harrison/Folsom), (415) 512-7400. This is a place where all the senses are stimulated: colorful Matisse reproductions and tantalizing smells from the wood-burning hearth greet you at the door; the people are friendly and the California-Mediterranean food is delicious (try the Brie and sun-dried tomato pizza or anything from the rotisserie); and in true San Francisco style, the bay view from the slick dining room is breathtaking! Out-of-town guests will love it. • M-Th 11:30am-2:30pm, 5-10pm; F 11:30am-2:30pm, 5-11pm; Sa 5-11pm; Su 5-10pm (light menu served in the bar M-Th until 11pm, F-Sa until 1am).

Pane e Vino ★★★ $$ Pacific Heights: 3011 Steiner St. (Union), (415) 346-2111. This perfect neighborhood trattoria serves simple, classic Italian dishes like *vitello tonnato*, gnocchi, antipasto, and a great tiramisù. The interior is rustic and inviting: a long wooden table divides the dining area and holds wildflower arrangements, hunks of Parmesan, and bowls of antipasti. Service is friendly and professional. Reservations are essential, although you may still have to wait before being seated. • M-Th 11:30am-2:30pm, 5-10pm; F-Sa 11:30am-2:30pm, 5-10:30pm; Su 5-10pm.

Pauline's Pizza Pie ★★ $ Mission: 260 Valencia St. (14th St./Duboce), (415) 552-2050. In a friendly, cheery setting, Pauline's has found the right mix of gourmet and traditional pizza making. The toppings don't overwhelm, but they do give the pizzas some new taste dimensions. Specials include combinations like *tasso* (smoked pork shoulder) and *gremolata* (garlic, parsley, and lemon) or braised leeks, Kalamata olives, garlic, and tarragon. The salads are also fresh and inventive. • Tu-Sa 5-10pm.

Picaro ★★ $ Mission: 3120 16th St. (Valencia/Guerrero), (415) 431-4089. The same folks who run the wildly popular Esperpento run this festive, brightly painted tapas bar. In fact, after visiting both, it's impossible to keep the names straight, since the menus are identical. Picaro is bigger; it's more spacious and doesn't yet have Esperpento's waiting line. Picaro also has a long, Spanish-style tapas bar where patrons can drink sherry and nibble *bocadillas*. Dishes are authentically heavy on olive oil and garlic: green beans in garlic, fried calamari with *alioli* (Catalan garlic mayonnaise), chicken in garlic, and mussels in a garlicky red-pepper vinaigrette. Gather a group and share—no one else will come near you. The paella is disappointing, and leisurely service prevails. A good selection of cheap Spanish wines. Cash only. • M-F 11am-3pm, 5-10pm; Sa-Su 11am-3pm, 5-11pm (later if busy).

Plump Jack Café ★★ $$$ Pacific Heights: 3127 Fillmore St. (Filbert/Greenwich), (415) 563-4755. A new sensation off Union Street from the people who started the wine store of the same name a few doors away. The management team includes two of Gordon Getty's sons, which resulted in immediate fanfare and the patronage of the Pacific Heights set. Wine prices are incredible, the result of the tie-in to the wine store (they basically sell for retail). The food is an eclectic assortment of trendy California-Mediterranean dishes, and has improved dramatically since new chef Maria Helm came over from the Sherman House. The restaurant has two dining areas, a sleekly somber front area done in black and taupe and a private back room. Reservations recommended. • M-F 11:30am-2pm, 5:30-10pm; Sa 5:30-10pm.

SAN FRANCISCO RESTAURANTS

Postrio ★★★★ $$$$ Union Sq.: Prescott Hotel, 545 Post St. (Taylor/Mason), (415) 776-7825. Strictly a splurge experience, Postrio has been a hit since the moment it opened. An upscale business crowd flocks here to sample celebrity chef Wolfgang Puck's cuisine. If you're a nobody (and odds are you fit this description) you may be relegated to a corner table and treated like a nuisance. But if you're a dedicated restaurant goer with a strong ego, this is a must-stop on your itinerary. The haute California cuisine with an Asian twist is superb (it should be considering the prices); grab a table in the bar and try the gourmet pizzas Puck is known for. Reservations required and jacket and tie preferred for gentlemen at dinner. • M-W 7-10am, 11:30am-2pm, 5:30-10pm; Th-F 7-10am, 11:30am-2pm, 5:30-10:30pm; Sa 9am-2pm, 5:30-10:30pm; Su 9am-2pm, 5:30-10pm.

Powell's Place ★ $ Civic Center: 511 Hayes St. (Octavia/Laguna), (415) 863-1404. You won't find down-home southern cooking like this just anywhere in tony San Francisco. Most people come to Powell's for the fried chicken, crispy on the outside, juicy on the inside; order it by the piece or with a complete dinner that includes airy corn muffins and homey side dishes like mashed potatoes and greens. Other menu items run from barbecued beef ribs, chitterlings, meat loaf, and hamburgers to well-salted canned vegetables, although nothing else matches the chicken. Breakfast is served well into the afternoon. The minimal decor might be described as Victorian rec room: high ceilings, peach walls, and linoleum. A steady stream of customers drifts through, occasionally putting Aretha, B.B. King, or Miles to work on the jukebox. • Daily 9am-11pm.

Pozole ★ $ Castro: 2337 Market St. (Castro/Noe), (415) 626-2666. One of the most visually intriguing eateries around: the walls are painted in colorful cartoon hues, plaster figurines sit atop pillars, and dressed-up skeletons hang on the walls. (It's Day of the Dead meets the Castro.) As for the Mexican food served within, it looks great and tastes pretty good, too. Try the chicken-filled burrito Mexicano or the cactus-filled burrito Californiano; both are part of the menu devoted to low-fat dishes. Also recommended are the mushroom and red pepper quesadilla Baja, and the *tamal de Oaxaca*, a vegetarian dish topped with a mango-orange sauce. The moderate portions are served by a healthy-looking and pleasant wait staff. No credit cards. • M-Th 4-11pm; F-Sa noon-midnight; Su noon-11pm.

R & G Lounge ★★ $ Chinatown: 631 Kearny St. (Clay/Sacramento), (415) 982-7877. When you walk up to the door you may think this an unlikely eatery, but go on downstairs. It's loud. It's bright. It's linoleum and Formica. And the food—authentic Cantonese—is incredible! Follow the locals and order seafood and vegetable dishes such as stir-fried water spinach, pepper-and-salt prawns, and oyster claypot from a big menu that includes four-color photographs of some of the offerings. (Many popular dishes are not on the English menu, so look around and point at what other people are eating.) Popular with Chinese families, it's great for big groups. The many large tables are equipped with lazy Susans for easy access, so sharing is mandatory. The upstairs dining room is corporate upscale—muted gray carpet, shoji screens—with large round tables for group events. • Daily 11am-9:30pm.

Radio Valencia ★ $ Mission: 1199 Valencia St.(23rd St.), (415) 826-1199. This café with a coffeehouse feel has always been a casual place, one where people just dropped by for a bite. But when a city fire truck just dropped in—through the front window—in mid-1995, it was forced to close for repairs. They have since re-opened and are doing what they do best: cooking up great healthful dishes like vegan pizzas, sandwiches on mouth-watering focaccia, expansive and filling salads, and the always-invigorating soup du jour. A great selection of beverages, like the supreme Mexican hot cocoa, is available to wash down the meal. Live music on weekends. • M-F 5pm-midnight; Sa-Su noon-midnight.

The Ramp ★ $ SoMa: 855 China Basin Blvd. (Mariposa off 3rd St.), (415) 621-2378. The most popular of the several waterfront bars in the abandoned warehouse section of SoMa, The Ramp is San Francisco's premier postfraternal party spot. On weeknights, this vast, outdoor concrete slab of a bar is regularly booked for informal, semi-private, very drunken dance parties. On weekend mornings it's the perfect post-blowout brunch place, serving generous portions of fried hangover food. Bring sunglasses, and be prepared to wait for a table. Weekday al fresco lunches are a less crowded, relaxing escape. Live music Thursday and Friday evenings, Saturday and Sunday afternoons. • Daily 8am-3:30pm (appetizers available M-F 5-7:30pm; barbecue/appetizers Sa-Su 3:30-7:30pm).

Red Crane ★★ $ Richmond: 1115 Clement St. (12th Ave./Funston), (415) 751-7226. If you like vegetarian Chinese food, you *must* get out to Red Crane. Satisfying, healthful, and delicious, the dishes here are large enough to conquer any hunger without the notorious heavy oil found in many Chinese restaurants. The decor is to-be-expected-tacky, but you're not paying for design at these prices. Notable offerings, which include both vegetarian and seafood specialties, include prawns in lobster sauce, spicy eggplant, black mushrooms and greens, Chinese cabbage with ginger sauce, and vegetarian chicken with cashew nuts. The vegetarian pot stickers—a black fungus mixture tucked into a doughy wrap—is ideal for sharing (or eat a half order by yourself) as you wait for the rest of your meal. • Daily 11:30am-10pm.

Rendezvous du Monde ★★ $ Union Sq.: 431 Bush St. (Grant/Kearny), (415) 392-3332. If you're not up to the aggressively French scene around the corner at Café Claude, try a low-key lunch at this cheery café. Like Claude, Du Monde also sports a few outdoor tables in an alley, and occasional waiters with heavy French accents. But the light menu is more pan-Mediterranean, offering a mix of salads, pasta, and focaccia sandwiches with such grilled fillings as eggplant, chicken breast, or ground beef. The front half of the dining room is bright and cheery; the back half around a corner is a moodier retreat. Not a good place to gossip loudly, as tables are tightly placed. • M 8:30am-3:30pm; Tu-F 8:30am-3:30pm, 5:30-9:30pm; Sa 11am-3:30pm, 5:30-9:30pm.

Ristorante Ecco ★★★ $$$ SoMa: 101 South Park Ave. (Bryant/Brannan), (415) 495-3291. A fine place to impress out-of-town visitors with your knowledge of out-of-the-way, trendy eateries. Located in the heart of the pleasant and decidedly hip South Park neighborhood, the restaurant's interior is spacious and modern, with a view of the park from the front dining room. Moderately priced, well-prepared Italian specialties emerge from the kitchen. Reservations recommended. • M-F 11:30am-2:30pm, 6-10pm; Sa 6-10pm.

Roosevelt Tamale Parlor ★ ¢ Mission: 2817 24th St. (York/Bryant), (415) 550-9213. The granddaddy of all cheap eats in the Mission. With its dim and cozy dining room, Roosevelt's is the kind of place to settle in for several beers and a good feed. Portions are enormous, and the atmosphere very relaxed and friendly. Risk taking with the menu is not encouraged. This is a tamale parlor. No credit cards. • Tu-Sa 10am-9:45pm; Su 10am-8:45pm.

The Rooster ★★ $$ Mission: 1101 Valencia St. (22nd St.), (415) 824-1222. The Rooster describes its cuisine as country cooking from around the world. This includes such hearty dishes as spicy Louisiana gumbo laden with chicken and sausage, Catalonian seafood stew, or beef Bourguignon. Lest you think everything on the menu is geared toward chilly nights, appetizers include a Thai-inspired calamari salad and vegetarian pot stickers. The long dining room wraps around a couple of corners, creating small, intimate spaces; low lighting, sponged ocher walls filled with zany mirrors, dark wood furniture, and a rough concrete floor enhance the moody ambience. Mission-district-hip service prevails. • Su-Th 5:30-10pm; F-Sa 5:30-11pm.

Rosmarino ★★★ $$$ Presidio Heights: 3665 Sacramento St. (Locust/Spruce), (415) 931-7710. A pricy Mediterranean bistro located down a narrow alley off outer Sacramento Street. The crowd is upper crust and well dressed; the food is very good indeed, including on one night a beautifully fresh salmon fillet poached in a broth redolent of fresh herbs and vegetables. Pastas are simple and satisfying. Some good

SAN FRANCISCO RESTAURANTS

wines from Oregon and Italy are your best choices, unless you like to pay $50 for a one-year-old California Chardonnay. Despite the chic setting, some very lively good cheer flows through this place. When the fog retreats, take a table in the comfy courtyard. • Tu-Sa 11:30am-2pm, 5:30-10pm; Su 10am-2pm.

Rubicon ★★★ $$$$ Fin. Dist.: 558 Sacramento St. (Sansome/Montgomery), (415) 434-4100. Traci des Jardins is slinging great hash at this upscale, narrow, two-story celebrity restaurant just off Montgomery Street. It's her food—the superb roast chicken, her excellent lamb, the wonderful herbs and intense flavors—that matters here, not the overtouted celeb investors, Francis Ford Coppola, Robin Williams, and Robert DeNiro, who rarely show up anyway. The industrial brick decor feels less intimidating downstairs; the larger upstairs has a slightly Siberian air to it. Service is generally good. The wine list is extraordinary but high priced (the restaurant is named for Niebaum-Coppola's proprietary red blend). • M-F 11:30am-2:30pm, 5:30pm-10:30pm; Sa 5:30pm-10:30pm.

Rumpus ★★★ $$ Union Sq.: 1 Tillman Pl. (Grant/Stockton), (415) 421-2300. An exciting American bistro only a block off Union Square. It's open late and the food is excellent and relatively inexpensive, especially at lunch. Try the succulent roast chicken, the lusty lamb shank, or the juicy veal chop; interesting appetizers include a piquant onion tart and tasty dolmas. Don't miss ordering some of the fine but less well-known wines featured here, such as McDowell Syrah. The sommelier, Jack, one of the restaurant's greatest assets, is very friendly and very knowledgeable, so put him to work. Reservations recommended. • M-Th 11:30am-2:30pm, 5:30-10pm; F 11:30am-2:30pm, 5:30-11pm; Sa 5:30-11pm; Su 5:30-10pm.

Saigon Saigon ★★ $ Mission: 1132 Valencia St. (22nd St./23rd St.), (415) 206-9635. Excellent Vietnamese food is served at this modest but attractive Mission eatery. White tablecloths, flowers, and plants distinguish the dining room from the usual Formica-heavy Vietnamese eatery. Try the garlic or lemongrass prawns, the crispy rainbow trout, or the papaya beef salad. • M-F 11:30am-2:30pm, 5:30-10pm; Sa 5:30-10pm; Su 5:30-9:30pm.

San Francisco Art Institute Café ★★ ¢ Russian Hill: 800 Chestnut St. (Jones/Leavenworth), (415) 749-4567. Impress friends from out of town by taking them to this ultrahip cafeteria. Located on the futuristic concrete rooftop of San Francisco's oldest art school, patrons enjoy some of the best views of the bay anywhere in town, without having to pay a premium. Rub shoulders with angular artists in Armani eyewear scrounging quarters to get wired on espresso drinks while you fill up on salads, sandwiches, and sinfully delicious baked goods. Hot food ranges from eggs to bean stews to pasta. Cash only. • M-Th 8am-9pm; F 8am-4pm; Sa 9am-2pm (hours vary with school term).

San Francisco Brewing Company ★ $ Chinatown: 155 Columbus Ave. (Pacific), (415) 434-3344. The rumor is that the brewing company has a menu somewhere, but the brewed-on-site beer is what people come for. The interior dates from 1907, with a long mahogany bar, dark wood tables, and a mix of scruffy locals and a few suits. If you can get hold of a menu, try the delicious onion rings or go all out and get a platter of fried calamari, onion rings, and clams. Live music ranging from traditional bluegrass to funky reggae many nights. • M-W noon-9pm; Th-Sa noon-10pm; Su noon-7pm.

Sanppo ★★ $ Pacific Heights: 1702 Post St. (Buchanan), (415) 346-3486. A Japantown standby, serving a complete range of Japanese specialties without sacrificing quality on any. Sushi and sashimi use clean, fresh fish and well-seasoned rice. Customers rave about the light and crunchy tempura. Heaping bowls of soup use rich broths and toothsome noodles. Teriyaki, *shabu shabu*, deep-fried cutlets, and more also appear on the menu. Generous portions and moderate prices—a bit higher for sushi—keep Sanppo among the more reasonable Japantown establishments. The dining room, heavy on potted plants and shoji screens, is split into two small sections by the partially open kitchen. When it's busy, small groups may have to share one of the large tables. Service can be somewhat disorganized. • Tu-Sa 11:30am-9:50pm; Su 3-9:50pm.

Scott's Seafood Grill and Bar ★★ $$$ Embarcadero: 3 Embarcadero Center (Sacramento at Drumm), (415) 981-0622. • Marina: 2400 Lombard St. (Scott), (415) 563-8988. A Bay Area chain of elegantly furnished restaurants with tasteful maritime art on the walls and plenty of room between tables to allow for private conversation or just serious concentration on the well-stocked menu. The Massachusetts fisherman's stew could feed a minor fleet, while the cornmeal-grilled catfish jambalaya will please the most finicky seafood connoisseur. Service is relaxed, to put it kindly, but you'll be glad for the extra time to savor every tender morsel. The original Lombard Street location is run separately by one of the founders. • Fin. Dist.: M-Th 11am-10pm; F-Sa 11am-11pm; Su 4:30-9:30pm. • Marina: Daily 11:30am-10pm.

The Slanted Door ★★★ $$ Mission: 584 Valencia St. (16th St./17th St.), (415) 861-8032. One of the hottest new eateries in the Mission, The Slanted Door, a high-ceilinged bilevel room romantically decked out in light green walls, iron railings, wooden floors, and quirky wall art, brilliantly melds Vietnamese and French styles. The food looks and tastes terrific. Sumptuous appetizers include the perfect Vietnamese crepes or fresh spring rolls in peanut sauce. Entrée highlights range from incredibly sweet chicken simmered in caramel sauce and ginger to shrimp with glass noodles to pork stir-fried with jicama strips. Desserts are not quite as good, but the tropical ice creams (litchi or jackfruit) are worth a try. Servings are fairly large and prices are surprisingly moderate. Service is pleasant and attentive. The only downside is that the wait to be seated can seem eternal (even with a reservation), a compliment to the popularity of the place. • Tu-Su 11:30am-3:30pm, 5:30-10pm.

Slow Club ★★ $$ Mission: 2501 Mariposa St. (Hampshire), (415) 241-9390. Located in an urban no-man's-land, this chic, postindustrial café appeals to the artistic set who flocks here after hours to quaff Red Hook on tap and indulge in Niman-Schell burgers and fries. The Mediterranean-style food is uniformly well done, imaginative, and generously proportioned. Media types from the *Bay Guardian* and KQED (both nearby) have made this their lunchtime canteen. • M 7am-3:30pm; Tu-F 7am-11pm; Sa 6:30pm-midnight.

South Park Café ★★★ $$ SoMa: 108 South Park Ave. (2nd St./3rd St.), (415) 495-7275. For those contemplating film careers, we hear that Philip Kaufman (of *The Unbearable Lightness of Being* and *Henry and June* fame) has frequented this classic French café. Pale yellow walls, morning sunlight, and European newspapers make this an attractive brunch spot. Or go during cocktail hour and sample the excellent tapas, which include golden fried potatoes with aioli and anchovy toasts. For dinner, try the fabulous mussels or the duck. Reservations recommended. • M-F 7:30am-10pm; Sa 6-10pm.

Specialty's Café and Bakery ★ ¢ Fin. Dist.: 312 Kearny St. (Bush/Pine), no phone. • Fin. Dist.: 22 Battery St. (Market), no phone. • Fin. Dist.: 1 Post St. (Market), no phone. • SoMa: 150 Spear St. (Howard/Mission), (415) 512-9550 (all phone orders). • Specials of the day hotline (415) 896-BAKE/2253. In sharp contrast to the bread standards of the Lee's Deli empire, these sandwich shops concentrate on their incredible home-baked breads. Sandwiches come on thick, still-warm slices from such varied loaves as herb, potato, multigrain, and cheese. The wide variety of fillings ranges from the standard turkey, roast beef, and ham to curried chicken salad and vegetarian. Unfortunately, portions vary from hearty to skimpy, and lunch lines move slowly. To ensure you get your fill, indulge in a thick, gooey chocolate chip cookie. Delicious breakfast goodies emerging from the bakery include muffins, scones, and giant, moist cinnamon rolls. No credit cards. • M-F 6am-6pm (Post St. until 7pm).

SAN FRANCISCO RESTAURANTS

Splendido ★★★ $$$ Embarcadero: 4 Embarcadero Center (Sacramento at Drumm), (415) 986-3222. Drift into the Mediterranean right from the Embarcadero. Pat Kuleto's design incorporates stone walls, rough-hewn beams, romantic dining alcoves, and hand-painted Italian tiles, sure to quiet your frantic energy. Nibble warm bread dipped in seasoned olive oil and balsamic vinegar while you browse the extensive wine list. As you gaze out the window, ignore the Ferry Building clock and just smell the wood-burning oven firing another perfect pizza. Relaxed diners tuck into pan-Mediterranean specialties such as polenta with wild mushrooms, ravioli with prosciutto and mascarpone, seared tuna salad with Kalamata olive vinaigrette, and vegetable curry with couscous. Solicitous waiters enhance this comfortable, delicious dining experience. Reservations required. • M-F 11:30am-2:30pm, 5:30-9:30pm; Sa-Su 5:30-9:30pm (bar menu between lunch and dinner).

Stars ★★★ $$$$ Civic Center: 555 Golden Gate Ave. (Van Ness/Polk), (415) 861-7827. San Francisco's much-loved grand café is as sizzling as ever. The glamorous dining room, decorated with framed French posters and a long, polished wooden bar, attracts a glittering crowd of sophisticates and a smattering of tourists along for the ride. The food can be overwrought, although some dishes are perfection, like the seared salmon served on a bed of lentils or the perfectly cooked steak served with a cognac sauce. If the prices are out of your stratosphere, head to Stars Café, which serves good food in a less formal atmosphere. Reservations recommended. • M-F 11am-2:30pm, 5:30-10pm; Sa-Su 5:30-10pm (lighter fare 10-11pm).

Stars Café ★★ $$ Civic Center: 500 Van Ness Ave. (McAllister), (415) 861-4344. When it first opened, Stars Café offered one of the city's better dining values: streamlined versions of superstar chef Jememiah Tower's innovative California cuisine in a more intimate environment. But prices at Star's Junior have been rising, Tower seems to be focusing his energy on his newer ventures (to the detriment of the food), and the large new location lacks the original's charm. But if you don't get lost in nostalgia, you can still enjoy a hint of Tower's cooking talent in an energetic, upscale bistro setting with first-rate service. • Su-Th 11:30am-9:30pm; F-Sa 11:30am-10:30pm (Hours can vary with performances.).

Stoyanof's Café and Restaurant ★★ $ Sunset: 1240 9th Ave. (Lincoln/Irving), (415) 664-3664. Greek cuisine served in an unpretentious wood-beamed dining room with an open kitchen. The ceiling is painted a dazzling blue to remind you of whence the cuisine originates. Stoyanof's is popular with an older neighborhood crowd. Shish kebab is a mainstay on the menu, but the Greek specialties wrapped in filo dough are the real standouts. Try the *spanakopita* (spinach filling) or *tiropetes* (cheese filling). There are a wealth of exotic appetizers—dolmas, tabbouleh, and the like—from which you can assemble a tapas-style meal. Lunch, served cafeteria style, is informal and inexpensive. • Tu-Th 10:30am-4:30pm, 5-9:30pm; F-Sa 10:30am-4:30pm, 5-10pm; Su 10:30am-9pm.

Straits Café ★★★ $$ Richmond: 3300 Geary Blvd. (Parker), (415) 668-1783. It looks like a hip European bistro, with wood shutters, airy lighting and smooth jazz playing over the sound system, but this café is known for its Singaporean menu, a blend of Indian, Malay, and Chinese dishes. The servings are on the small side given the price, so be sure to order appetizers. Start with *poh pia* (spring rolls), *kway pati* (stuffed pastry shells), or lamb soup; all are delicious. For the main course, the highlights include *ayam rendang*, a crisp chicken simmered in a dry curry sauce, and the mouthwatering *ikam panggang*, a grilled boneless trout wrapped in banana leaf that is generally acknowledged to be one of the best seafood dishes in the city. Service is cheerful and attentive. • Su-Th 11:30am-10pm; F-Sa 11:30am-11pm.

Suppenküche ★★ $$ Hayes Valley: 601 Hayes St. (Laguna), (415) 252-9289. Suppenküche brings new respect to German cooking. Opened by a wandering German design student, this fashionable beer hall serves food to take the chill off any summer night, as well as a range of unusual German brews on tap and by the bottle. Seating is family style around long pine tables, so expect to make a few friends through the course of the meal. For starters, there is always a vegetarian soup, and the house salad is a large portion of slaw and cut vegetables. The mains are authentic renditions of traditional dishes such as *sauerbraten* and *jager schnitzel*. They come with delicious accompaniments like spaetzle or panfried potatoes. The strudel will keep you coming back. • Sa-Su 10am-3pm, 5-10pm; M-F 5-10pm.

Swan Oyster Depot ★★ $ Nob Hill: 1517 Polk St. (California/Sacramento), (415) 673-1101. This classic luncheonette serves great chowder and freshly shucked oysters. Nothing but a counter and a few stools. No credit cards. • M-Sa 8am-5:30pm.

Tadich Grill ★★★ $$$ Fin. Dist.: 240 California St. (Battery/Front), (415) 391-1849. This California landmark has been a part of San Francisco dining for nearly a century and a half—the menu gives all the historic details—and things are still done the old-fashioned way here. Brass, wood, and uniformed waiters help maintain the 1850s atmosphere; excellent old-style service and food complete the illusion. Choose a seat in the main dining room, at the long wooden counter, or in a private, curtained alcove reminiscent of cigar-filled back rooms. Fresh seafood—charcoal broiled, panfried, or sautéed—has been the main draw all these years, and the food is still wonderful if a bit retro. Enjoy such timeless classics as oyster stew, broiled halibut steak, or the memorable calamari steak with garlic butter sauce. Homemade tartar sauce accompanies deep-fried dishes, and a martini precedes many a meal. This is a traditional American, time-machine trip that shouldn't be missed. Perfect for parents, out-of-town guests, and nostalgic food lovers. Reasonably priced wine list favors better-known California vineyards. • M-F 11am-9:30pm; Sa 11:30am-9:30pm.

Tai Chi ★★ $ Nob Hill: 2031 Polk St. (Pacific/Broadway), (415) 441-6758. Tai Chi has gained a loyal following among neighborhood denizens who come for consistently good renditions of spicy American Chinese food. Every table has an order of the signature General's chicken, deep-fried nuggets bathed in a heavenly sticky-brown garlic sauce. Most other dishes popular with Americans are well done—moo shu chicken, pot stickers, chow mein—as are the iron plate combinations. Hot-and-sour soup, however, is heavy and murky. The dining area is divided into three small, bright rooms; large groups (usually with screaming children) go in the back, where waiters often forget them. Service is otherwise brusque, with soup, appetizer, and main arriving nearly simultaneously. • M-Sa 11:30am-10pm; Su 4-10pm.

Taqueria El Balazo ★ ¢ Haight: 1654 Haight St. (Belvedere), (415) 864-8608. A brightly colored taqueria that has ample seating for its hip (and hippie) clientele. Service is at the counter only, but is assembly-line efficient. Choices include the usual Mexican fare of tacos, burritos, and quesadillas, but the specials are noteworthy, including the Deadhead monikered Bob's Burrito (with garlic, zucchini, and mushroom) and Jerry's Burrito (with fresh tender cactus and Mexican goat cheese). Even with a fresh fruit drink, it's hard to spend more than five dollars on a filling meal. An inconspicuous guitar player occasionally performs. No credit cards. • Su-Th 10:30am-11pm; F-Sa 10:30am-1am.

Taqueria San Jose ★★ ¢ Mission: 2830 Mission St. (24th St./25th St.), (415) 282-0203. • Mission: 2839 Mission St. (24th St./25th St.), (415) 282-0283. When you're tired of taquerias serving bland heaps of undifferentiated filler, head to this pair of taquerias for a culinary awakening. The long list of well-prepared taco and burrito fillings includes the standard beef and chicken, plus authentic specialties such as *al pastor* (barbecued pork), chorizo sausage, tongue, and brain. Tacos come heaped with meat, finely diced onion, fresh shredded cilantro, and hot sauce. Burritos are equally well packed with more of the same plus rice and plump pinto beans. Each table has bowls of fresh, hand-cut tomato salsa loaded with bright green chili peppers and a fiery tomatillo salsa. Wash it all down with excellent *agua frescas* like *tamarindo* and *horchata*. The decor is typical taqueria: a spare, bright hall with tile floor, Formica tables, murals on the walls, and a loud jukebox. *Menudo* is the weekend specialty. Cash only. • Daily 8am-1am.

SAN FRANCISCO RESTAURANTS

Thanya and Salee ★★ $$ Potrero Hill: 1469 18th St. (Connecticut), (415) 647-6469. With many exquisitely decorated Thai restaurants around town, the plain green carpet, white tablecloth, and oak bar motif here may (along with the lackadaisical service) disappoint some customers. Nevertheless, the kitchen is capable of some fine dishes, especially those with seafood. *Mieng kum* (shrimp, ginger, and coconut in spinach leaves) makes a wonderful appetizer, and *tom kha talay* soup (squid, shrimp, and oysters) is a real treat, served in a doughnut-shaped bowl heated by Sterno in the center. *Gai ga prow*, sautéed chicken with spicy green peppers, is also recommended. The fried banana with ice cream will nicely round out your meal. Moderately sized portions. • Daily 11am-3pm, 5:30-10:30pm.

Thep Phanom ★★ $ Hayes Valley: 400 Waller St. (Fillmore), (415) 431-2526. Possessing one of the most pleasant and inviting interiors of any Thai restaurant in the Bay Area, Thep Phanom has a standout menu as well. A long list of tasty salad dishes provides more ways to get your vegetables than many Thai eateries, and the nightly specials board lists fresh, interesting offerings. One regular favorite is The Weeping Lady, a delectable combination of minced chicken, garlic, chilies, and fresh basil served over broiled Japanese eggplant. • M-Su 5:30-10:30pm.

Ti Couz ★★ $ Mission: 3108 Sixteenth St. (Valencia/Guerrero), (415) 252-7373. A charming Breton-style crêperie, Ti Couz serves an array of classic and delicious crêpes. With its white stucco walls crisscrossed with dark wood beams, French-country tables and chairs, and photographs of peasants from Brittany, Ti Couz is an enchanting spot to indulge your Gallic fantasies. Savory crêpe fillings range from ratatouille to Gruyère to salmon. The onion soup is excellent, as are the salads. Missing a dessert crêpe here—Nutella, white chocolate, poached pears, fresh whipped cream—is a crime; the possibilities are as endless as they are delicious. • M-F 11am-11pm; Sa 10am-11pm; Su 10am-10pm.

Timo's ★★ $$ Mission: 842 Valencia St. (19th St./20th St.), (415) 647-0558. • Fisherman's Wharf: 900 North Point St. (Larkin), (415) 440-1200. Timo's fun and funky decor sports bright yellow, green, and purple paint in abundance and all the waiters sprout goatees (although efficiency isn't their strong point). The long list of well-executed tapas includes traditional Spanish favorites like *tortilla española* (a fluffy egg and potato omelet) and roasted potatoes with *alioli* (Catalan garlic mayonnaise), as well as crosscultural hybrids like cassoulet of duck confit and *biftec al chipotle* (a New Mexico-style grilled steak served with Jack cheese and chipotle sauce on black beans). If they're in season, don't miss the grilled asparagus with *romesco* sauce (Catalan chili, tomato, and almond sauce). Plenty of sherry, sangria, beer on tap, and affordable table wines complete the experience. • Mission: Su-W 5-10:30pm; Th-Sa 5-11:30pm. • Wharf: Daily noon-10:30pm.

Tommaso's ★★ $$ North Beach: 1042 Kearny St. (Broadway/Jackson), (415) 398-9696. Don't be deterred by the sleazy strip joints and peep shows as you hunt down this pizza joint, located in the midst of San Francisco's finest collection of smut houses. Behind a heavy wooden door and down a flight of stairs you'll find a dark, shadowy interior with Italian wall murals. Traditional thin-crusted Italian pizzas have been cooked in the wood-burning oven here for over 60 years. The fewer toppings the better, in order to taste the wonderful tomato sauce. Be sure to try one of the cold vegetable salads (asparagus, if it's in season). If you feel like dining with the locals—this is one of Francis Ford Coppola's favorite spots—this is the place to be. • Tu-Sa 5-10:30pm; Su 4-9:45pm.

Tommy Toy's Cuisine Chinoise ★★ $$$$ Fin. Dist.: 655 Montgomery St. (Washington/Clay), (415) 397-4888. Tommy Toy's calls itself an *haute Chinoise* restaurant in the same class as Masa's and Fleur de Lys. It more closely resembles what you would get if a marketing exec decided to create a Chinese restaurant suitable for a high-powered business get-together. The glamorous lacquered furnishings, dim lighting, well-spaced tables, and obsequious service will make visiting dignitaries feel like imperialist conquerors. The food is primarily well-prepared and elegantly presented

Chinese favorites like pot stickers, scallops in Hunan garlic-chili sauce, and Peking duck. Big eaters looking for the complete experience should go for the multicourse prix fixe meals. Wine list suited to expense accounts. Reservations recommended; jacket and tie required for dinner. • M-F 11:30am-2:30pm, 6-9:30pm; Sa-Su 6-10pm.

Ton Kiang ★★ $ Richmond: 5821 Geary Blvd. (22nd Ave./23rd Ave.), (415) 387-8273. • Richmond: 3148 Geary Blvd. (Spruce), (415) 752-4440. This pair of eateries specializes in Hakka cuisine, famous for wine sauces, pickled vegetables, and claypot dishes. Ignore the specialization. The menu includes dishes from all over China, and execution is consistently good. Start with superior egg rolls, crunchy with fresh vegetables. Choose from an abundant list of seafood dishes: crab in black bean sauce, pepper-and-salt prawns, trout with ginger and scallions, and spicy Sichuan squid. Braised tofu specialties feature airy chunks of tofu, superior fillings, and hearty sauces. Good vegetable dishes, too. Prices are a bit higher than your average dive. The Spruce branch has the bright-red-and-gold-dragon-phoenix Chinese restaurant look; the 22nd Avenue branch is more restrained, with carpeting and pastel colors. The latter branch serves famous dim sum daily. The aggressively friendly staff serves a neighborly clientele. • 5821 Geary: M-Th 10:30am-10pm; F-Su 10:30am-10:30pm. • 3148 Geary: Su-Th 11am-10pm; F-Sa 11am-10:30pm.

Trattoria Contadina ★★ $$ Russian Hill: 1800 Mason St. (Union), (415) 982-5728. Prepare to wait—even if you have a reservation—for a meal at this warm, family-run restaurant with consistently good food and service. Have a glass of wine at the bar to get in the mood for the best *tortellini con panna* this side of Florence. Although the tables are close together, this is still a good place for anything from an intimate dinner for two to a large party. Reservations recommended. • Su-Th 6-10pm; F-Sa 6-11pm.

Truly Mediterranean ★ ¢ Mission: 3109 16th St. (Valencia), (415) 252-PITA/7482. Roxie Cinema regulars and Mission barflys truly appreciate Truly Mediterranean—a tiny fast-food joint that serves up falafel, shawerma, hummus, and even Philly cheese steaks. Aside from the comical counter staff, what makes this Middle Eastern food rise above the crop is the preparation: the sandwiches are filled, rolled burrito style, and then grilled briefly. The hot sauce is as advertised. A soda or garlic-mint yogurt will round out a sumptuous, delicious, incredibly cheap meal. A few stools inside and two tables outside, to watch the hipsters walk by. • M-Sa 11am-midnight; Su 11am-10pm.

Tu Lan ★★ ¢ Union Sq.: 8 6th St. (Market/Mission), (415) 626-0927. *Chronicle* writer Herb Caen once called Sixth Street the dirtiest and most dangerous in the entire city. He has also dined at Tu Lan, located on Sixth Street just south of Market. According to the menu, so has Julia Child; even the *Examiner* food critic Jim Wood has been seen there enjoying lunch with friends. Squeamish diners tempted to experience this diva of dives take a cab and tell the driver to pick them up after they finish. Once seated inside (lunchtime gets busy so go a little early or late), enjoy their cold tofu rolls (tofu, rice noodles, bean sprout, and mint rolled in rice paper) or lemon beef salad. The noodle dishes are excellent, as are the entrées. One very popular dish, *pho*, is a beef noodle soup with spirit. No credit cards. • M-Sa 11am-9pm.

2223 Market (No Name) ★★ $$$ Castro: 2223 Market St. (Sanchez/Noe), (415) 431-0692. Although undoubtedly the easiest restaurant in the city to *find*, Cypress Club proprietor John Cunin's addition to the Castro dining scene is a much harder place to snare a table. Even with a reservation (recommended), be prepared to wait awhile (the kitchen can also be slow). This place has been packing in a hip, prosperous clientele drawn to refined American cuisine. The appetizers are small and very expensive, but the grilled prawns in pancetta, at least, are worth it at twice the price. Main courses are better sized and include grilled ahi tuna, succulent Sonoma lamb, and juicy roasted chicken with outstanding onion rings and garlic mashed potatoes. For dessert, try the caramelized banana tart. The wait staff, if you don't mind a firm touch of Attitude, is tip-top; they'll even fold over your crumpled napkin while you are off visiting the bathroom. The sparse, open dining room, with dark wooden floors, ivory walls, and warm utilitarian lighting, affects a Quaker-like humbleness that fits the restaurant's name but doesn't do justice to the food. The cacophonous space makes conversation a trial. • M-Tu 11:30am-2pm, 6-10pm; W-F 11:30am-2pm, 6-11pm; Sa 6-11pm; Su 10am-2:30pm, 5:30-10pm.

U-Lee Restaurant ★★ $ Russian Hill: 1468 Hyde St. (Jackson), (415) 771-9774. This has got to be the best deal in San Francisco. Where else can you feast on a Chinese banquet for less than $10? (Well, maybe there are cheaper places, but we doubt they're as good.) The tiny storefront space can only accommodate 10 tables, so the atmosphere is cozy and convivial. The decor is of the basic Formica-tabletop school of design, and portions are huge. Order any of the soups, chow meins, and the pot stickers the size of dinosaur eggs. Shrimp and asparagus with black bean sauce is a delight. Cash only. • Tu-Su 11am-9pm.

Universal Café ★★★ $$ Mission: 2814 19th St. (Bryant/Florida), (415) 821-4608. This sleek, stylish café started as a coffee roastery, but the zoning laws made it easier to become a full-service restaurant. Universal switches from a café in the day to a full-scale restaurant at night. The fresh-made soups and grilled sandwiches make a filling lunch; for dinner try one of the flat bread appetizers (either with caramelized onions or *brandade* and tomatoes) and any of the grilled main courses. Reservations recommended. • Tu-F 7:30am-2:30pm, 6-10pm; Sa-Su 9am-2:30pm, 6-10pm.

Val 21 ★★ $$ Mission: 995 Valencia St. (21st St.), (415) 821-6622. Design-studio hip, with Swiss track lighting, a corrugated metal awning over the bar, and tabletops stained grass green. The menu reflects the cutting-edge attitude, with such plates as vegetarian *pozole* with *pipián* pesto, fillet of wild salmon with Asian black bean sauce, and marinated tofu with vegetables and an almond-miso-peanut sauce (your taste buds might experience culture shock, but don't worry; it's good for them). Reservations recommended. • M-Th 5:30-10pm; F 5:30-10:30pm; Sa 10am-1:30pm, 5:30-10:30pm; Su 10am-1:30pm, 5:30-10pm.

Valentine's Café ★ $$ Noe Valley: 1793 Church St. (30th St.), (415) 285-2257. While the atmosphere of warm, yellow lighting and ivory walls is certainly relaxing at this home-style vegetarian restaurant in the far reaches of Noe Valley, the food is hit-and-miss. It is also somewhat overpriced, given the serving sizes and the ingredients—all the dishes are meatless. (The kitchen takes notable pride in the fact that any milk and eggs used here are "hormone- and antibiotic-free.") The best bets are the Italian entrées such as a fine cannelloni or penne gratin, both of which tend to be a lot more invigorating to the taste buds than the bland North Indian plate or the jambalaya. The potstickers filled with wild mushrooms make a good appetizer. Dessert is mostly forgettable. Service is mixed. • Tu 6-9:30pm; W-Th 11am-2:30pm, 6-9:30pm; F 11am-2:30pm, 6-10pm; Sa 6-10pm; Su 6-9:30pm.

Vertigo ★★★ $$$ Fin. Dist.: 600 Montgomery St. (Clay/Washington), (415) 433-7250. One of the city's hottest new restaurants since it opened in early 1995, Vertigo's popularity has risen to dizzying heights. The restaurant is located on the ground floor of the Transamerica Tower, San Francisco's tallest building, and diners may swoon like Jimmy Stewart in Hitchcock's namesake classic when they gaze up at the pyramid through the skylights. The dining room makes the most of the dramatic location: A multilevel design surrounds the pyramid's structural pillars with a swirl of rich wood, burgundy carpeting, futuristic alabaster light fixtures, bright murals, and views of the building's neighboring redwood grove. The crowds' frenetic energy bounces through the loud space, creating a general feeling of joie de vivre. Chef Mark Lusardi, formerly of Aqua and Rubicon, has put together an exciting menu of cutting-edge California cuisine, mingling French, Asian, and Italian influences in elaborately presented creations. Highlights include his tuna carpaccio niçoise, grilled beef fillet in a red wine sauce, and braised sea bass. An excellent but pricy wine list offers plenty of choices to complement your meal. Reservations recommended. • M-Th 11:30am-2:30pm, 5:30-10pm; F 11:30am-2:30pm, 5:30-10:30pm; Sa 5:30-10:30pm.

SAN FRANCISCO RESTAURANTS U-W

Vicolo Pizzeria ★★ $ Hayes Valley: 20 Ivy St. (Franklin), (415) 863-2382. More of a café than a restaurant (you order at the counter), Vicolo serves some of the best gourmet pizza in the city. The key is a thin, crisp cornmeal crust, upon which are placed fresh vegetable and meat toppings, all perfectly cooked without the normal heavy, oily taste. All of the daily varieties are bound to be good, but be sure to try the andouille, a heavenly mix of spicy sausage, scallions, and smoked mozzarella. Slices are small but surprisingly filling, and a full pie is sufficient for three or even four people. Vicolo also offers calzones, focaccia sandwiches, a soup-of-the-day, and salads. You eat all of this in an upscale setting beneath cathedral ceilings and sleek steel-grid windows, but be warned: it gets very crowded in the evenings. • Su-Tu 11:30am-10pm; W-Th 11:30am-10:30pm; F-Sa 11:30am-11:30pm.

Vivande ★★★ $$$ Civic Center: 670 Golden Gate Ave. (Van Ness/Franklin), (415) 673-9245. Chef Carlo Middione, who gained wide recognition for his culinary skills at his casual restaurant and deli operation on Fillmore, has brought his lusty southern Italian cooking to the elegant Opera Plaza dining room formerly occupied by Modesto Lanzone. The large, ornate space glows with orange and yellow lamp shades that illuminate dark wood furniture and earth-toned fabrics. As with his other location, the rustic homemade pasta and risotto dishes are winners; so, too, are the hearty meats like lamb chops and osso buco. The extensive wine list presents a varied selection of Italy's best wines. Reservations recommended. • Daily 11:30am-midnight (tea 2:30-5:30pm; light late menu 10:30pm-midnight).

Vivande Porta Via ★★ $$ Pacific Heights: 2125 Fillmore St. (Sacramento/California), (415) 346-4430. This unlikely venue is actually a combination gourmet food store and Italian restaurant. A brick wall covered with beautiful, hand-painted Italian tiles (for sale, like many furnishings) lines one side of the cramped dining area, a deli counter the other. The food is imaginative and authoritatively Italian. Owner Carlo Middione is a noted writer on Italian cuisine, and his menus include wonderful pastas and risottos, excellent lamb chops, and a superb version of the classic Tuscan side dish of white beans with olive oil. One of our favorite Italian restaurants in San Francisco. An added benefit of Middione's deli/restaurant: you can purchase many of his ingredients—and even finished creations—to enjoy at home or on a picnic. • Daily 11:30am-10pm.

¡Wa-Ha-Ka! ★ ¢ SoMa: 1489 Folsom St. (11th St.), (415) 861-1410. • Russian Hill: 2141 Polk St. (Broadway/Vallejo), (415) 775-1055. • Pacific Heights: 1980 Union St. (Buchanan), (415) 775-4145. This trio of taquerias exude youthful energy, drawing hungry nighttime revelers from the surrounding bars. Bright, industrial decor sports warehouse-high ceilings, rough concrete walls and floor, mismatched wooden tables and chairs, and Mexican billboard murals—"Disfruta Tecate!" blares one. Their unique addition to the fresh-Mex scene is surprisingly authentic fish tacos: tender fried fish fingers on soft corn tortillas and a bed of shredded purple cabbage. The homemade salsas are fresh and delicious. No credit cards. • SoMa: M-W 11:30am-10pm; Th 11:30am-11pm; F-Sa 11:30am-1am; Su 5-10pm. • RH: M-Th 11:30am-10pm; F 11:30am-11pm; Sa 11am-11pm; Su 11am-10pm. • PH: M-W 11:30am-10pm; Th 11:30an-11pm; F 11:30am-midnight; Sa 11am-midnight; Su 11am-11pm.

Woodward's Garden ★★★ $$$ Mission: 1700 Mission St. (Duboce), (415) 621-7122. Incongruous locale notwithstanding (it's located beneath the freeway), this unpretentious yet elegant little restaurant serves up the most phenomenal California cuisine this side of Chez Panisse. Cooks Dana Tommasino and Margie Conrad (formerly of Greens and Postrio) create works of art on a plate, mixing different textures and tastes in the same dish with aplomb. Although the menu is limited and often changes, you'll be sure to find mouth-watering appetizers like grilled nectarines in Gorgonzola; enormous main dishes like pork chops with garlic mashed potatoes, apple slices and greens; and out-of-this-world desserts like blueberry and lemon crème brûlée. Add to this great wines, good service, and an unhurried atmosphere amid mismatched hotel service tableware, and you'll easily forget what's outside the door. Reservations are a must. No credit cards. • W-Su dinner seatings at 6pm, 6:30pm, 8pm, and 8:30pm.

SAN FRANCISCO RESTAURANTS

YaYa Cuisine ★★★ $$ Sunset: 1220 9th Ave. (Lincoln Way), (415) 566-6966. The elegant, trendily decorated dining room signals the high-style food to come. Exotic Middle Eastern creations with a California twist are the specialty of chef Yahya Salih, who whips up a mean pomegranate sauce. Try the appetizer of mini ravioli stuffed with dates and topped with Parmesan cheese, walnuts, olive oil, and roasted red peppers. Follow up the raviolis with a succulent lamb *biriani* served with lemony cream sauce. • Tu-Th, Su 5:30-9:30pm; F-Sa 5:30-10pm.

Yank Sing ★★ $$ **(Take-Out $)** Fin. Dist.: 427 Battery St. (Clay/Washington), (415) 781-1111. • SoMa: 49 Stevenson St. (1st St./2nd St.), (415) 541-4949. One of San Francisco's most famous dim sum houses, Yank Sing has two locations giving easy lunch access to downtown workers. The food is available two ways: sit in the restaurant's giant, white-tablecloth-formal dining room and choose elegantly presented, authentic specialties from roving carts, or sit at your desk and slurp them out of a plastic container. The upscale setting is perfect for lunch meetings or a romantic midday rendezvous, and prices reasonable. Efficient take-out operations offer fast food at low prices. Yank Sing features an extensive selection appealing to Asian and non-Asian customers alike (don't miss the roast duck). Go early for the best selection: as closing time approaches, the same unpopular carts keep appearing. • Fin. Dist.: M-F 11am-3pm; Sa-Su 10am-4pm. • SoMa: M-F 11am-3pm.

Yuet Lee ★★ $ Chinatown: 1300 Stockton St. (Broadway), (415) 982-6020. • Mission: 3601 26th St. (San Jose/Valencia/Guerrero), (415) 550-8998. This place has all the hallmarks of a dive—bright lights, Formica tables, and brusque service—but the Cantonese seafood is arguably unmatched for freshness and flavor. Try the clams in black bean sauce, the pepper-and-salt roast squid or prawns, and any other seafood items on the menu. Also good are the vegetable dishes, Peking spareribs, and claypots, especially the one combining oysters and scallions. Alas, the soup and noodle dishes are disappointing. Don't sit downstairs in the Chinatown branch; it's dreary. Cash only in Chinatown; credit cards accepted at 26th Street branch. • Chinatown: W-M 11am-3am. • Mission: Su-Th 11am-3pm; 5-9:30pm; F-Sa 11am-3pm, 5-10:30pm.

Zarzuela ★★ $$ Russian Hill: 2000 Hyde St. (Union), (415) 346-0800. The name derives from a Spanish musical variety show and is also the name of a Catalonian seafood stew. All the favorite hot and cold Spanish tapas dishes—salty ham, savory squid, *tortilla española*, chorizo—and main dishes such as paella and, naturally, zarzuela are served along with sangria and sherry in this crowded restaurant right off the Hyde Street cable car line. There may be a slight wait during rush hours (they don't take reservations). It's sunny and much less crowded for a late-afternoon graze. • M-Th noon-10:30pm; F-Sa noon-11pm.

Zona Rosa ★ ¢ Haight: 1797 Haight St. (Shrader), (415) 668-7711. Starving students and people on limited budgets have discovered Zona Rosa, a great deal for authentic Mexican food. For a few dollars you can feast on one of the biggest burritos imaginable. Food is served cafeteria style. The meat is cooked in front of you, and vegetarians will find a large selection of meatless entrées. *Churros*, fresh fruit drinks, and other tasty snack items are also served. No credit cards. • Su-Th 11am-10:30pm; F-Sa 11am-11pm.

Zuni Café and Grill ★★★ $$$ Civic Center: 1658 Market St. (Gough/Franklin), (415) 552-2522. A die-hard temple of Mediterranean cuisine frequented by the artsy set, with a few advertising and business types mixed in. It looks very New Mexico, with a wood-fired adobe fireplace, a long copper bar, mismatched chairs, and lots of serapes thrown about. The best selection of oysters around, sold by the piece and served over shaved ice with seaweed garnish. Interesting preparations include house-cured anchovies with Parmesan and celery, or a divine whole roast chicken for two served with Tuscan bread salad. Slow service with a bad attitude unless you're a regular. Reservations recommended. • Tu-Sa 7:30am-midnight; Su 7:30am-11pm.

SAN FRANCISCO RESTAURANT INDEX

TYPES OF CUISINE

AMERICAN
Bad Man Jose's ★★ ¢
Balboa Café ★ $$
California Culinary Acad. ★★ $$
Chloe's Café ★★ $
Delancey Street ★★★ $$
Doidge's Kitchen ★★ $
Elite Café, The ★★ $$
Home Plate ★★ $
Julie's Supper Club ★★ $$
Kate's Kitchen ★★★ $
Lee's Deli ★ ¢
Liberty Café, The ★★ $$
Liverpool Lil's ★★ $$
MacArthur Park ★★ $$
Max's Diner ★ $
Max's Eatz/Sweet Max's ★ ¢
Max's Opera Café ★★ $$
McCormick & Kuleto's ★★ $$$
Mel's Drive-In ★ $
New Dawn Café ★ ¢
One Market ★★★ $$$
Orphan Andy's ★ $
Powell's Place ★ $
Specialty's Café & Bakery ★ ¢

BARBECUE
Big Nate's Barbeque ★★ $
MacArthur Park ★★ $$

BURGERS
Barney's ★★ $
Hamburger Mary's ★ $
Liverpool Lil's ★★ $$
Mission Rock Resort ★ $
Mo's ★★ $
Ramp, The ★ $
SF Brewing Company ★ $

CAFÉ
Boogaloos ★ ¢
Café Bastille ★★ $
Café Claude ★★ $
Caffè Centro-S. Park ★ ¢
Caffè Museo ★★ $
Emporio Armani Café ★ $
Enrico's Café ★★ $$
LuLu Café ★★ $
Mario's Bohemian ★★ $
Radio Valencia ★ $
Rendezvous Du Monde ★★ $
SF Art Institute Café ★★ ¢

CALIFORNIA/ECLECTIC
Bistro Rôti ★★★ $$
Boulevard ★★★ $$$
Café For All Seasons ★★ $$
Café Kati ★★★ $$$
Caffè Centro-Marina ★ $$
Campton Place ★★★ $$$$
Carta ★★★ $$
China Moon ★★★ $$$
Cypress Club ★★★ $$$
Eos ★★★ $$$
Firefly ★★★ $$$
Flying Saucer ★★★ $$$
Fog City Diner ★★★ $$$
42 degrees ★★★ $$$
Gordon Biersch ★★ $$
Grand Café ★ $$$
Greens ★★★ $$
Hawthorne Lane ★★★ $$$$
LuLu ★★★ $$
Moose's ★★ $$/$$$
One Market ★★★ $$$
Plump Jack Café ★★ $$$
Postrio ★★★★ $$$$
Rooster, The ★★ $$
Rubicon ★★★ $$$$
Rumpus ★★ $$
Slow Club ★★ $$
Stars ★★★ $$$$
Stars Café ★★ $$
2223 Market (No Name) ★★ $$$
Universal Café ★★★ $$
Val 21 ★★ $$
Vertigo ★★★ $$$
Woodward's Garden ★★★ $$$
Zuni Café & Grill ★★★ $$$

CHINESE
Betelnut ★★ $$/$$$
Brandy Ho's ★ $
China Moon ★★★ $$$
Dol Ho ★★ ¢
Eliza's ★★ $
Fountain Court ★★ $
Gourmet Carousel ★★★ $
Great Eastern ★★ $$
Harbor Village ★★ $$
House of Nanking ★★ $
Hunan Restaurant ★★ $
Mike's Chinese Cuisine ★★ $
R&G Lounge ★★ $
Red Crane ★★ $
Tai Chi ★★ $
Tommy Toy's ★★ $$$$
Ton Kiang ★★ $
U-Lee Restaurant ★★ $
Yank Sing ★★ $$
Yuet Lee ★★ $

CONTINENTAL
Albona ★★★ $$
California Culinary Acad. ★★ $$
Enrico's Café ★★ $$
Liverpool Lil's ★★ $$

FRENCH
Alain Rondelli ★★★ $$$$
Bistro Clovis ★★ $$
Bistro Rôti ★★★ $$
Bizou ★★ $$
Café Bastille ★★ $
Café Jacqueline ★★★ $$$
California Culinary Acad. ★★ $$
Chez Michel ★★★ $$$
Fleur de Lys ★★★★ $$$$
Fringale ★★★ $$
Heights, The ★★★★ $$$$
La Folie ★★★★ $$$$
Le Central ★★ $$$
Le Trou ★★★ $$
Masa's ★★★★ $$$$
South Park Café ★★★ $$
Ti Couz ★★ $

GERMAN/AUSTRIAN
Hyde Street Bistro ★★★ $$
Suppenküche ★★ $

INDIAN
Appam ★★★ $$
Ganges, The ★ $
Gaylord India ★★ $$$
North India ★★ $$

ITALIAN
Bambino's ★ $
Bontà ★★ $$
Buca Giovanni ★★★ $$$
Café Riggio ★★ $$
Café Tiramisù ★★ $$
Caffè Delle Stelle ★★★ $$
Caffè Macaroni ★★★ $$
Eleven Ristorante ★★ $$
Enrico's Café ★★ $$
Gira Polli ★★ $$
Gold Spike, The ★ $$
Il Fornaio ★★ $$
Il Pollaio ★ ¢
Jackson Fillmore ★★★ $$
Kuleto's Restaurant ★★ $$
Laghi ★★★ $$$
Little Italy Ristorante ★★ $$
Mangiafuoco ★★ $$
Mescolanza ★★ $$
Michaelangelo Café ★★ $$
Moose's ★★ $$/$$$
Nob Hill Café ★★ $
North Beach Restaurant ★★ $$$
Palio d'Asti ★★★ $$$
Palio d'Asti-Paninoteca ★★ $
Palomino ★★ $$
Pane e Vino ★★★ $$
Ristorante Ecco ★★★ $$$
Rosmarino ★★★ $$$
Splendido ★★★ $$$
Tommaso's ★★ $$
Trattoria Contadina ★★ $$
Vivande ★★★ $$$
Vivande Porta Via ★★ $$

JAPANESE
Akiko's Sushi Bar ★★ $
Country Station Sushi ★ ¢
Ebisu ★★ $$
Kabuto Sushi ★★★ $$
Matsuya ★★ $$
Mifune ★★ $
Nippon Sushi (No-Name) ★★ $
Sanppo ★★ $

137

SAN FRANCISCO RESTAURANTS

LATIN AMERICAN/ MEXICAN
Andalé Taqueria ★★ ¢
Bad Man Jose's ★★ ¢
Café Marimba ★★ $
Canto Do Brazil ★ $
Carmen ★ ¢
Casa Aguila ★★★ $$
Cha Cha Cha ★★★ $
Il Pollaio ★ ¢
La Cumbre ★★ ¢
La Taqueria ★★ ¢
Leticia's ★ $
Miss Pearl's Jam House ★★ $$
Pozole ★ $
Roosevelt Tamale Parlor ★ ¢
Taqueria El Balazo ★ ¢
Taqueria San Jose ★★ ¢
Wa-Ha-Ka! ★ ¢
Zona Rosa ★ ¢

MEDITERRANEAN
LuLu/LuLu Bis ★★★ $$
Rendezvous Du Monde ★★ $
Rooster, The ★★ $
Rosmarino ★★★ $$$
Splendido ★★★ $$$

MIDDLE EASTERN
Arabian Nights ★★★ $$
Helmand ★★ $$
Kan Zaman ★★ $
La Méditerranée ★★ $
Stoyanof's ★★ $
Truly Mediterranean ★ ¢
YaYa Cuisine ★★★ $$

PIZZA
Escape from NY Pizza ★ ¢
Goat Hill Pizza ★ ¢
Milano Pizzeria ★ $
North Beach Pizza ★ $
Pauline's Pizza Pie ★★ $
Tommaso's ★★ $
Vicolo Pizzeria ★★ $

SEAFOOD
Aqua ★★★ $$$$
Elite Café, The ★★ $$
Hayes Street Grill ★★★ $$$
McCormick & Kuleto's ★★ $$$
Scott's Seafood ★★ $$$
Swan Oyster Depot ★★ $
Tadich Grill ★★★ $$$

SOUTHEAST ASIAN
Angkor Borei ★ $
Angkor Wat ★★★ $
Basil Restaurant ★★ $$
Betelnut ★★ $$/$$$
Café Kati ★★★ $$$
Emerald Garden ★★ $$
Golden Turtle ★★ $$
Hahn's Hibachi ★★ ¢
Khan Toke Thai House ★★★ $$
Korea Buffet ★ $

Le Soleil ★★ $
Little Thai ★★ $
Mandalay ★★ $
Manora's Thai Cuisine ★★ $
Neecha Thai ★★ $
Pad Thai ★★ $
Saigon Saigon ★★ $
Slanted Door ★★★ $$
Straits Café ★★★ $$
Thanya and Salee ★★ $$
Thep Phanom ★★ $
Tu Lan ★★ ¢

SPANISH
Esperpento ★★ $
Picaro ★★ $
Timo's ★★ $$
Zarzuela ★★ $$

VEGETARIAN
Fountain Court ★★ $
Ganges, The ★ $
Greens ★★★ $$
Millennium ★★ $$
Red Crane ★★ $
Valentine's Café ★ $$

SPECIAL FEATURES

CHILD FRIENDLY
Barney's ★★ $
Delancey Street ★★★ $$
Dol Ho ★★ ¢
Eliza's ★★ $
Fountain Court ★★ $
Goat Hill Pizza ★ ¢
Gold Spike, The ★ $
Great Eastern ★★ $$
Harbor Village ★★ $$
Il Pollaio ★ ¢
Liberty Café, The ★★ $$
MacArthur Park ★★ $$
Max's Diner ★ $
McCormick & Kuleto's ★★ $$$
Mel's Drive-In ★ $
Mifune ★★ $
Mo's ★★ $
Orphan Andy's ★ $
Powell's Place ★ $
R&G Lounge ★★ $
Tai Chi ★★ $
Taqueria San Jose ★★ ¢
Tommaso's ★★ $$
Ton Kiang ★★ $
Yuet Lee ★★ $

OUTDOOR SEATING
Andalé Taqueria ★★ ¢
Barney's ★★ $
Betelnut ★★ $$/$$$
Bistro Rôti ★★★ $$
Café Bastille ★★ $
Café Claude ★★ $
Café Tiramisù ★★ $$
Caffè Centro-Marina ★ $$

Caffè Centro-S. Park ★ ¢
Chloe's Café ★★ $
Delancey Street ★★★ $$
Emporio Armani Café ★ $
Enrico's Café ★★ $$
42 degrees ★★★ $$$
Il Fornaio ★★ $$
La Taqueria ★★ ¢
Mario's Bohemian ★★ $
Miss Pearl's Jam House ★★ $$
Mission Rock Resort ★ $
Nob Hill Café ★★ $
Ramp, The ★ $
Rendezvous Du Monde ★★ $
Rosmarino ★★★ $$$
SF Art Institute Café ★★ ¢
Stoyanof's ★★ $
Universal Café ★★★ $$

ROMANTIC
Alain Rondelli ★★★ $$$$
Albona ★★★ $$
Appam ★★★ $$
Bistro Clovis ★★ $$
Boulevard ★★★ $$$
Café Jacqueline ★★★ $$$
Emerald Garden ★★ $$
Fleur de Lys ★★★★ $$$$
42 degrees ★★★ $$$
Heights, The ★★★★ $$$$
Helmand ★★ $$
Hyde Street Bistro ★★★ $$
Khan Toke Thai House ★★★ $$
La Folie ★★★★ $$$$
Pad Thai ★★ $
Pane e Vino ★★★ $$
Plump Jack Café ★★ $$$
Rooster, The ★★ $
Rosmarino ★★★ $$$
South Park Café ★★★ $$
Splendido ★★★ $$$
Thep Phanom ★★ $

VIEWS
Bistro Rôti ★★★ $$
Boulevard ★★★ $$$
Delancey Street ★★★ $$
Gordon Biersch ★★ $$
Greens ★★★ $$
McCormick & Kuleto's ★★ $$$
Mission Rock Resort ★ $
Palomino ★★ $$
Ramp, The ★ $
SF Art Institute Café ★★ ¢
Splendido ★★★ $$$

Arts and Entertainment

AMUSEMENTS

Bay Meadows: 2600 S. Delaware St. (Hillsdale), San Mateo, (415) 574-7223. See Peninsula Amusements.

Chalkers: Rincon Center, 101 Spear St. (Mission), SF, (415) 512-0450. A slightly swankier affair than your average billiards parlor, it has a full bar and serves burgers and appetizers. Frequented by the financial district set. They also offer lessons, either private or in groups, by their resident "pro." • M-F 11:30am-2am; Sa-Su 2pm-2am. Prices vary according to number of people and time of day.

Family Billiards: 2807 Geary Blvd. (Wood/Collins), SF, (415) 931-1115. Despite the name, no one under the age of 18 is allowed. Adult family members, however, can play to their heart's content on any one of 19 tables. The snack bar will sustain you game after game. • Su-Th 11:30am-2am; F-Sa 11:30am-4am.

Golden Gate Stables: Golden Gate Park, SF, (415) 668-7360. Guided rides through the park. • 1 hour for $20. Call for reservations.

Grand Slam USA: 5892 Christie Ave. (Powell), Emeryville, (510) 652-4487. When the weather's bad, or you're just not feeling like a full-fledged game of baseball or softball, Grand Slam lets you make hit after hit in their large, indoor batting cages. Try anything from a nice, easy lob to a raging 80mph fastball. For the less sporty types, try out the air hockey tables and video games. • M-Sa 11am-10pm; Su 11am-7pm.

(Paramount's) Great America: Great America Pkwy., Santa Clara, (408) 988-1800. (Take Hwy 101 South to Great America Parkway exit.) See Peninsula Amusements.

Great Entertainer: 975 Bryant St. (7th St./8th St.), SF, (415) 861-8833. Try your hand at one of 40 pool tables in this cavernous hall. When you get tired of that, take a turn into the full arcade and play until your thumb can do no more. They also have ping-pong, darts, and shuffleboard. With a full bar and menu, you'll find no reason to leave. • Su-Th 11am-2am; F-Sa 11am-3am.

Hollywood Billiards: 61 Golden Gate Ave. (Jones), SF, (415) 252-9643. For fun that never ends, you can rely on this pool hall that never closes. Prices vary according to time of day and number of players. Try Tuesday and Thursday nights, when you and your friends can play for three hours for only $10. Fully stocked bar, and a limited menu. • Daily 24 hours. $3/hr. per person.

Mar Vista Stables: 2152 Skyline Blvd. (John Daly), Daly City, (415) 991-4224. For $20 per person per hour, they'll fix you up with a trusty steed and a guide, and then set you loose to ride along the coast. • Daily 9am-4pm.

Mission Cliffs: 2295 Harrison St. (19th St.), SF, (415) 550-0515. All the adventure of scaling a sheer mountain wall, but without the worry of whether you're going to encounter a rattlesnake or a rainstorm. Their 30 climbing walls (some over 50-feet tall) will test your nerves and give you a workout that will make you scoff at the mere mortals working out on the gym equipment below. Also with a bouldering area—a not-so-high, not-so-steep form of rock climbing that you can do without the ropes. They offer lessons at every level, as well as guided climbs on some of the Bay Area's

ARTS & ENTERTAINMENT

more daunting monoliths. • M, W, F 6:30am-10pm; Tu, Th 11am-10pm; Sa-Su 10am-6pm. Membership is $100 initiation and $50 per month. Or buy a 10 visit pass for $100, and if you still want to join at the end of 10 visits, they'll waive the initiation fee.

Namcoland: Pier 39 (Embarcadero), SF, (415) 399-1909. Opening at 10am every day, they stay as late as you keep playing. With a full range of video games, carnival games and rides, and chances to win big prizes at skeeball, who can stay away? • Su-Th 10am-9pm; F-Sa 10am-11pm.

Presidio Bowling: Presidio Bldg. 93, Montgomery St. (Moraga), SF, (415) 561-2695. Once reserved for the officers who were lucky enough to be stationed in this most desirable of army bases, it is now open to all civilian types, regardless of rank. Offers 12 lanes and a snack bar serving basic grub and beer and wine. • Su-Th 8am-11pm; F-Sa 8am-1am. $1.50/game before 6pm; $2.50/game after 6pm.

Raging Waters: Lake Cunningham Regional Park, 2333 South White Rd. (Tully/Capitol), San Jose, (408) 270-8000. See Peninsula Amusements.

South Beach Billiards: 270 Brannan St. (2nd St.), SF, (415) 495-5939. A friendly place South of Market. Bring some friends and rent a table, or challenge the hotshot on the next table for true glory. When you tire of pool, you can try the indoor bocce ball court. The best deal is Monday night, when you and your friends can play all night for $10 total. Has a full bar and deli food. • Daily noon-2am.

Windsor Waterworks & Slides: 8225 Conde Ln. (Shiloh), Windsor, (707) 838-7760. See Marin Amusements.

Entertaining Children

San Francisco holds plenty of both old-fashioned and innovative ways to keep the little ones amused. Below is a selective sampling of free or low-cost activities (for kids and adults) that get everyone out of the house and away from the computer or TV. Look for many more activities listed in other sections of the Guide. Many of the activities listed in the Amusements section are sure-fire kid pleasers, as are many museums. A wide range of entertaining family destinations can be found in the radius around San Francisco as well, from Marin to the South and East Bay. Try the majestic Muir Woods; Ardenwood Historical Farm in Fremont, where staff and volunteers wear Victorian clothing and visitors can ride in horse-drawn trains and wagons; or visit San Jose's Happy Hollow Park, right in the heart of the city, where you'll find a miniature train and a few other rides.

San Francisco boasts many picturesque **playgrounds** that reflect the unique character of many of the City's colorful neighborhoods. Some of the best: South Park, a charming oasis found South of Market, is home to a playground with a quaint, old-fashioned feel; Julius Kahn Playground is surrounded by the lush woods of the Presidio; the Children's Playground in Golden Gate Park boasts a handsomely restored carousel. Families can also engage in many active pursuits at Golden Gate Park—boat and bicycle rentals are available at Stow Lake; at Golden Gate Park Stables, kids and their parents can saddle up for group trail rides. Scattered throughout San Francisco are smaller parks where kids and parents can play outside. A particularly scenic outdoor spot is Marina Green, with spectacular views of the Golden Gate Bridge—an excellent open area for kite flying or playing soccer.

For newcomers to San Francisco (and visiting friends with children), an excellent introduction to the City's fun spots from a kid's point of view can be arranged with **The Buddy System,** (415) 648-3330, a service offering personal tour guides hosting educational trips to museums and other attractions. For a bedtime story any time of day, call "Dial a Story" at (415) 437-4880, a free service of the San Francisco Public Library.

Academy of Sciences: (includes Steinhart Aquarium, Morrison Planetarium, and the Natural History Museum) Golden Gate Park, SF, (415) 750-7145. See Museums section for additional information.

AMUSEMENTS

Bay Area Discovery Museum: 557 East Fort Baker (Alexander Ave. to East Rd.), Sausalito, (415) 487-4398. See Marin Amusements.

Cartoon Art Museum: 814 Mission St. (4th St./5th St.), 2nd Floor, SF, (415) 546-3922. A children's gallery is included in this unusual museum. See Museums section for additional information.

Discovery Zone: 280 Metro Center, 123 Colma Blvd. (Junipero Serra), Colma, (415) 992-7777. • 2541 S. El Camino Real (Hwy 84/5th Ave.), Redwood City, (415) 568-4386. • 648 Blossom Hill Rd. (Hwy 85), San Jose, (408) 225-4386. Children absolutely love these indoor fun centers. Each is filled with a variety of soft, brightly colored structures that kids can jump on, crawl through, slide down, or play with. Toddlers even have their own area. There is also an arcade for less strenuous stimulation, and a snack bar to recharge with pizza and popcorn. Socks are required. • Su-Th 10am-8pm; F 10am-9pm; Sa 9am-9pm. Weekdays pay child's age up to $4.99; weekends $2.99 ages 2 and under; $5.99 ages 3-12. Free for parents.

Exploratorium: 3601 Lyon St. (Marina), SF, (415) 561-0362 (recorded information); (415) 561-0362 (Tactile Dome). An incredible hands-on science museum. See Museums section for additional information.

The Jungle Fun and Adventure: 955 9th St. (Brannan/Bryant), SF, (415) 552-4386. Kids go wild in this adventurous (and safe) indoor play facility, where they can fly on track glides and swim through ball pools. A fun place for "birthday safaris," the Jungle encourages development of physical and social skills for youngsters. A café features wholesome foods, including made-to-order pizzas. • Su-Th 10am-8pm; F 10am-9pm; Sa 9am-9pm; Su 10am-8pm. $3.95 ages 0-3; $4.95 over age 3.

Hidden Villa: Rhus Ridge Rd. (off Moody Rd.), Los Altos Hills, (415) 949-8660. See Peninsula Amusements.

Lawrence Hall of Science: Middle Centennial Dr., UC Berkeley Campus, (510) 642-5133. See East Bay Chapter for additional information.

Malibu Castle: 320 Blomquist St., Redwood City, (415) 367-1905. (Hwy 101 to Seaport Blvd., exit east to Blomquist). See Peninsula Amusements.

Malibu Grand Prix: 340 Blomquist St., Redwood City, (415) 366-6442. See Peninsula Amusements.

Marine World Africa: Marine World Pkwy. (I-80 and Hwy 37), Vallejo, (707) 643-6722. For zoological entertainment, take a trip to Marine World Africa USA in Vallejo, sort of a combination Sea World and zoo. Learn about dolphins, whales, seals, and other sea life as you wander through the aquarium and tide pools. Their much-touted Shark Experience does give you a new angle on these solemn, graceful creatures as you walk along a Plexiglas walkway right under them. The park also has hundreds of land-roaming animals like monkeys, tigers, and elephants; not to mention the airborne ones like parrots, toucans, and cockatoos. In addition to the furs and fins, check out the water-ski and boat show. Some of the world's best skiers excite and delight daily with cuts, jumps, tricks, and flips in their own style of high-octane water ballet. • Labor Day-Memorial Day: W-Su 9:30am-5pm; Memorial Day-Labor Day: Daily 9:30am-6pm. $25.95 adults; $17.95 ages 4-12; free ages 3 and under; $21.95 seniors. Parking $4. Accessible via Blue & Gold ferry and BART.

Monterey Bay Aquarium: 886 Cannery Row, Monterey, (408) 648-4888, (800) 756-3737. See Monterey Chapter for additional information.

Oakland Zoo: 9777 Golf Links Rd. (off I-80), Oakland, (510) 632-9523. See East Bay Chapter for additional information.

San Francisco Zoo: Sloat Blvd. at 45th Ave. (next to Lake Merced), SF, (415) 753-7061. This zoo features animals in re-creations of their natural habitats, although some claim the cages are on the small side. The Primate Discovery Center is a center-

ARTS & ENTERTAINMENT

piece of the zoo, although, by flaw or fluke, there seems to be an escape every few years. Other highlights include penguins, lions, tigers, and koala bears (Oh, my!). A train ride gives a quick overview. • Daily 10am-5pm. $7 adults, $3.50 seniors and kids age 12-15, $1 kids age 6-11.

Scandia Family Fun Center: 5301 Redwood Rd. (Rohnert Pk. Expwy.), Rohnert Park, (707) 584-1361. One of the great joys of the 'burbs, this freeway-side place has a full 36-hole miniature golf course, batting cages, video games, and all the other cheap fun you had as a kid. • M-F 10am-10pm; Sa-Su 10am-11pm. $5.50 adults; $3.50 ages 6-12 for a round of golf; $1.50 for 22 pitches.

Underwater World: Pier 39 (Embarcadero and Beach), SF, (415) 623-5300. Opened in April 1996, this aquarium takes you on a moving walkway through underwater see-through tunnels under the bay to get a fish-eye view of the local aquatic life. • Daily 9am-9pm. $12.95 adults; $9.95 seniors; $6.50 ages 3-11; under 3 free.

Pro and College Sports

Baseball

Oakland Athletics: Oakland Coliseum, Oakland, (I-880 to Hegenberger Rd. exit or BART to Coliseum station), (510) 638-0500.

San Francisco Giants: 3Com/Candlestick Park, Daly City, (Hwy 101 to 3Com/Candlestick exit), (415) 467-8000.

Basketball

Cal Bears: Harmon Gym, UC Berkeley Campus, Ashby at Telegraph, Berkeley, (800) GO BEARS/462-3277. Also plays three games at San Francisco's Cow Palace.

Golden State Warriors: Oakland Coliseum, Oakland, (I-880 to Hegenberger Rd. exit or BART to Coliseum station), (510) 986-2236. Note that for the 96-97 season, the Warriors will be playing at the San Jose Arena (W. Santa Clara and Autumn, San Jose) while the Coliseum undergoes renovation.

Summer Pro-Am League: Kezar Pavilion, Stanyan St. at Beulah St. (by Golden Gate Park), SF. Watch some present and future NBA stars (past participants include Jason Kidd and Gary Payton) take on local playground legends on weekday evenings during the summer. Free admission.

Stanford Cardinal: Maples Stadium, Stanford Campus, (800) BEAT CAL/232-8225.

Football

Cal Bears: Memorial Stadium, UC Berkeley Campus, (800) GO BEARS/462-3277.

Oakland Raiders: Oakland Coliseum, Oakland, (I-880 to Hegenberger Rd. exit or BART to Coliseum station), (800) 949-2626.

San Francisco 49ers: 3Com/Candlestick Park, Daly City, (Hwy 101 to 3Com/Candlestick exit), (415) 468-2249.

Stanford Cardinal: Stanford Stadium, Stanford Campus, (800) BEAT CAL/232-8225.

Hockey

San Jose Sharks: San Jose Arena (W. Santa Clara and Autumn sts.), San Jose, (800) 366-4423.

Soccer

San Jose Clash: Spartan Stadium, 7th St. at Alma Ave., San Jose State Univ., San Jose, (408) 241-9922.

MOVIE THEATERS

Like the rest of the country, multiplexes dominate the mainstream Hollywood movie scene. However, unlike the rest of the country, the Bay Area is an alternative film Mecca. The demand for variety in cinema is high, and there are plenty of venues to fill that demand. Both individual theaters, such as the Roxie, and chains, like Landmark Theaters, sell discount cards entitling card holders to a discount on movies. You can dial (415) 777-FILM for a quick and handy computer listing of the next and nearest showtime of your favorite flick.

Alexandria: 5400 Geary Blvd. (18th Ave.), SF, (415) 752-5100. First-run films.

Alhambra: 2330 Polk St. (Union/Green), SF, (415) 775-2137. First-run films.

Balboa: 3630 Balboa St. (38th Ave.), SF, (415) 221-8184. Second-run films.

(Landmark) Bridge: 3010 Geary Blvd. (Blake), SF, (415) 352-0810. Art-house, independent, and foreign films.

Cinema 21: 2141 Chestnut St. (Steiner/Pierce), SF, (415) 921-6720. A huge, one-screen theater with comfy rocking seats, almost like watching from the Lazy-Boy at home. First-run films.

(Landmark) Clay: 2261 Fillmore St. (Clay), SF, (415) 352-0810. A cool, art-house theater in Pacific Heights known for its long runs. Tea, coffee and the like served in the lobby. Independent and foreign films.

(UA) Coronet: 3575 Geary Blvd. (Stanyan/Arguello), SF, (415) 752-4400. Known for its blockbuster runs. You will find lines around the block during the opening weekend of the high action, big money, Hollywood hits they show here. A huge theater with excellent sound (it's very loud). First-run films.

(Landmark) Embarcadero Center: 1 Embarcadero Center (Sacramento and Battery), SF, (415) 352-0810. This hip new art-house sports a stylish modern interior and has an espresso bar in the lobby. So you can get a cup of joe and watch the show, daddy-o. Art-house, independent, and foreign films. Free parking in the garage below w/validation (After 5pm M-F; all day Sa-Su).

Four Star: 2200 Clement St. (23rd Ave.), SF, (415) 666-3488. Small theaters, a little rundown, but the price is right. Cool place to see a matinee. Second-run films.

(UA) Galaxy: 1285 Sutter St. (Van Ness), SF, (415) 474-8700. Your standard multiplex, but without the mall attached. First-run films. Reduced parking price at the nearby Quality Hotel.

(Landmark) Gateway: 215 Jackson St. (Battery/Front), SF, (415) 352-0810. Dark and dingy but in a stylish kinda way, with lots of character. Coolest staff in town. Art-house, independent, and foreign films.

Geneva Drive-In: 607 Carter St. (Geneva), Daly City, (415) 587-2884. Double features are the ticket, but don't forget to bring a car.

(AMC) Kabuki: 1881 Post St. (Fillmore), SF, (415) 931-9800. Home of the San Francisco International Film Festival, this multistory, multiplex is a great place to see a movie (many bargain matinees available). Screens vary from huge to large-screen-TV-sized, depending on the run of the film. Standard popcorn concession staffed by cheerless automatons on the second floor as well as a café on the third floor. The Kabuki also hosts the National Asian American Film Festival in early March. First-run films. Parking in the garage below with validation (Free after 5pm, 50 cents all day Sa-Su).

(Landmark) Lumiere: 1572 California St. (Polk/Larkin), SF, (415) 352-0810. One of the premiere art-house theaters in the city in terms of showings, but the auditorium is flat, and the seats extend too close to the screen—go early or bring a chiropractor. Art-house, independent, and foreign films. Reduced parking at the Holiday Inn at Van Ness & California.

ARTS & ENTERTAINMENT

(UA) Metro: 2055 Union St. (Webster/Buchanan), SF, (415) 931-1685. First-run films.

Northpoint: 2290 Powell St. (Bay), SF, (415) 403-8186. Huge theater, enormous screen. The theater seats 1000, and the screen is bigger than a bread truck. First-run films.

(Landmark) Opera Plaza: 601 Van Ness Ave. (Golden Gate), SF, (415) 352-0810. Arthouse, independent, and foreign films, usually late-run (some are already available on video).

Presidio: 2340 Chestnut St. (Scott/Divisadero), SF, (415) 922-1318. First-run films.

Regency I & II: Regency I: 1320 Van Ness Ave. (Sutter), SF, (415) 885-6773. Regency II: 1268 Sutter St. (Van Ness), SF, (415) 776-8054. First-run films. Reduced parking at the Holiday Inn and the Quality Hotel in the vicinity.

Royal: 1529 Polk St. (California/Sacramento), SF, (415) 474-0353. First-run films. Reduced parking at the Holiday Inn at Van Ness & California.

St. Francis: 965 Market St. (5th St./6th St.), SF, (415) 362-4822. Low-priced films in a seedy neighborhood. Second-run films.

Vogue: 3290 Sacramento St. (Presidio), SF, (415) 221-8183. First-run films.

Alternative Theaters & Rep Houses

Artists' Television Access: 922 Valencia St. (20th St./21st St.), SF, (415) 824-3890. This independently run, experimental theater is about as alternative as it gets. Run by filmmakers, it is a great place to see films you will never see anywhere else. Showcases independent works by local and not-so-local artists that deal with alternative, political, and humorous subjects. You can even sign up for a film class after the show. $5 donation for each show.

The Casting Couch: 950 Battery St. (Green/Vallejo), SF, (415) 986-7001. This microcinema is modeled after a Hollywood studio-type screening room. Get there early and check out their gourmet snack menu, which will be served to you at your seat. The theater features classic and cult films that can be comfortably viewed from the many couches, love seats, or armchairs that fill the room (thus the name). A great place for a date. Also available for private parties, private screenings, or business meetings. $8.50.

Castro: 429 Castro St. (Market/18th St.), SF, (415) 621-6120. The best theater in the city, the Castro theater is an experience no matter what is playing. This historic and beautifully ornate theater shows a wide cross section of classic, foreign, and cult favorites, as well as director's anthologies, on one of the biggest screens in the city. The shows are often preceded by live pipe organ music emanating from a grand Wurlitzer that slowly descends into the orchestra pit as the curtain opens. The Castro is the host to the Annual Lesbian and Gay Film Festival.

Cole Hall Cinema: UCSF Campus, 513 Parnassus Ave. (Arguello), SF, (415) 476-2542. Cool films in a college atmosphere. Call for showtimes. $3.50 all shows.

Depot: Ceasar Chavez Student Center, SFSU Campus, 1650 Holloway Ave. (19th Ave.), SF, (415) 338-1842. Limited showings. Call for showtimes. • Free.

Goethe-Institut: 530 Bush St. (Grant/Stockton), SF, (415) 391-0370. The Goethe-Institut houses a cultural center, library, and auditorium. Screens classics and thematic programs on Tuesdays and Thursdays. M-Th 9am-5pm; F 9am-3:30pm.

Red Vic Moviehouse: 1727 Haight St. (Cole/Shrader), SF, (415) 668-3994. This Haight Street institution is hard to miss: it's big, it's red, it's a movie house. The Red Vic shows a variety of just about every type of film out there, usually in short runs, as short as one night only. Insiders know this place for its funky red bench seats and huge bowls of popcorn. For the adventurous, or just plain weird of taste, there is the popcorn condiment bar that features brewer's yeast, f garlic, tamarind, and dill, as well as the standby salt and butter. Get there early as lines and sellouts are often a fact of life at the Vic.

Roxie: 3117 16th St. (Valencia/Guerrero), SF, (415) 863-1087. In this Mission area movie house you are bound be sitting next to a local filmmaker. They are here to see political, cult films, documentaries, genre and director's anthologies, and possibly their own films. Check out their cool programming calendar. The Roxie is also host to the Film Arts Festival.

San Francisco Art Institute: 800 Chestnut St. (Jones), SF, (415) 749-4545. The Institute is the home to S.F. Cinematheque on Sundays, which shows a variety of art films. Call for showtimes.

Total Mobile Home microCinema: 51 McCoppin St. (Market/Valencia), SF, (415) 431-4007. A small alternative theater that showcases local filmmakers and their works. The filmmakers are often on hand to introduce their films and answer questions. Call for showtimes.

PERFORMING ARTS

Few places in the country possess the cultural riches of the Bay Area. And the offerings fit any taste or budget. You can see dance, attend the theater, or hear music in the luxurious surroundings of old-style theaters, sitting in the pew of a cathedral, or on a blanket in a park. In addition to the (mostly) San Francisco performances listed below, check out the many other excellent companies in the East Bay, San Jose, Peninsula, and Marin.

Classical Music and Opera

Companies

Chanticleer: (415) 896-5866. A men's choral group.

Midsummer Mozart: (415) 392-4400. A popular summertime series playing in various Bay Area locations. Performances are mostly, but not exclusively, Mozart.

Philharmonia Baroque: (415) 391-5252. Baroque music conducted by Nicholas McGegan.

Pocket Opera: 333 Kearny St., #703, SF, (415) 989-1853; tickets (415) 989-1855. Performs accessible, contemporary English renditions of operas. Venues vary.

San Francisco Contemporary Music Players: (415) 252-6235. This group plays the likes of Stockhausen and Ornstein.

San Francisco Opera: 301 Van Ness Ave. (Grove), SF, (415) 864-3330. One of the best opera companies in the world, and one of the oldest in the country. The ticket prices reflect this status: single seats run from about $35 to well over $100. Performances usually take place in the grand War Memorial Opera House, where the sound is good even in the least expensive seats far in the back and on the sides. Supertitles projected above the stage make it easy to follow the plots of foreign-language operas, and opera glasses are available for rent. *Note:* Until earthquake retrofit construction is completed at the Opera House in September 1997, performances will take place at the Civic Auditorium at 99 Grove Street and at the Orpheum Theatre at 1192 Market Street.

San Francisco Performances: (415) 392-4400. You can call this number for information on a variety of classical concerts at several venues.

San Francisco Symphony: Louise M. Davies Symphony Hall, 201 Van Ness Ave. (Hayes/Grove), SF, (415) 431-5400. The excellent San Francisco Symphony performs a full and varied schedule and attracts several world-class soloists and guest conductors each season. Tickets cost around $20-$70, but you can also get non-reserved bench seats behind the orchestra (facing the conductor) if the performance

ARTS & ENTERTAINMENT

doesn't feature a chorus; discount tickets go on sale two hours prior to performance, and you can only buy two at a time. Acoustics are generally better in the center seats of elegant Davies Symphony Hall, which also plays host to some of the greatest orchestras in the world, including the Leipziger Gewandhaus Orchestra and the Boston Symphony. Tickets to guest orchestras usually cost more than San Francisco Symphony performances. Bay Area residents can also take advantage of the free summer performances given by the Symphony in Stern Grove.

Vox Animae: (415) 292-7463. The newest addition to San Francisco's vocal ensembles perform a cappella Renaissance music at various venues around the city. Tickets range from $10-$12.

Performance Series

Grace Cathedral Concerts: 1100 California St. (Taylor), SF, (415) 749-6350. Choral music, organ concerts, chamber, and other music is presented in the glorious surroundings of the Cathedral. Some candlelit performances.

Old First Church: 1751 Sacramento St. (Polk/Van Ness), SF, (415) 474-1608. Friday evenings and Sunday afternoons classical, world music, and jazz performers offer you their fare for under $10.

Old St. Mary's Noontime Concerts: 660 California St. (Grant), SF, (415) 288-3840. At 12:30pm every Tuesday and Thursday afternoon of the year, a wide variety of classical performers offer tourists, those seeking a special lunch hour escape, and music lovers from throughout the city an hour's worth of music in one of San Francisco's oldest churches. $3 is recommended as a donation.

Performances at Six: 3 Embarcadero Center (Sacramento and Front), Third Level, EC Cabaret, SF, (415) 398-6449. Every Thursday evening from October to May, $6 will buy you a glass of wine or mineral water and an hour of jazz, classical, or world music by local artists.

San Francisco Community Music Center: 544 Capp St. (20th St./21st St.), SF, (415) 647-6015. The center offers a full range of musical instruction to people of all ages as well as free or low-cost concerts performed by faculty and other professionals in association with San Francisco Performances. The evening concerts, which usually last an hour, are combined with conversation by and with the performers.

San Francisco Conservatory of Music: 1201 Ortega St. (19th Ave.), SF, (415) 759-3475, Music Line (415) 759-3477. The conservatory presents regular events during school days. Opera, orchestra, and chamber music are presented by students, faculty, and visitors. You can hear instruments showcased that you never get to hear elsewhere.

Dance

Dancer's Group/Footwork: 3321 22nd St. (Valencia/Guerrero), SF, (415) 648-4848, (415) 824-5044. Performances by local groups such as Footwork and Joe Goode Performance Group.

Neva Russian Dance Ensemble: (415) 563-7362. Based in San Francisco at the Russian Center, this 24-dancer troupe also works with visiting artists from Georgia, Poland, Lebanon, and Ireland.

ODC Performance Gallery: 3153 17th St. (Shotwell/S. Van Ness), SF, (415) 863-9834, 863-1173. Balkan Dance, Underbelly Dance Company, and Margaret Jenkins Dance Co. are housed and perform here.

Rosa Montoya Bailes Flamencos: (415) 824-1960. One performance each spring, and classes year-round.

San Francisco Ballet: 455 Franklin St. (Grove/Fulton), SF, (415) 861-5600. The War Memorial Opera House is home to the San Francisco Ballet, a major company and

PERFORMING ARTS

the oldest in the country. Uncritical audiences lap up the traditional favorites and romantic new pieces choreographed by Danish director Helgi Tommassen, but critics drool over the contemporary pieces by a variety of guest choreographers. The American Ballet Theater and other world-class touring ballet companies, such as the Kirov and Joffrey, also make frequent appearances at the Opera House. Until seismic retrofitting is complete (and cushy new seats installed), the Opera House will remain dark. The S.F. Ballet will scatter its charms, performing at the Palace of Fine Arts, Zellerbach Auditorium in Berkeley, Yerba Buena Center for the Arts, and outdoors at Stern Grove during the so-called summer. Pack a picnic and either a straw hat (if it's sunny) or lap robes (if it's foggy).

Smuin Ballet: (415) 978-ARTS/2787. Former director of the San Francisco Ballet, Michael Smuin, choreographs for this company, which performs at Yerba Buena Center for the Arts.

Theater

TIX Bay Area (formerly STBS): Union Square, Stockton St. (Post/Geary), SF, (415) 433-7827. This small kiosk is a full-service box office serving most of the city's theaters and performances. It also offers day-of-show, half-price tickets to many events. Half-price tickets are *cash only*, and any tickets for Sunday and Monday shows must be purchased by Saturday. • Tu-Th 11am-6pm; F-Sa 11am-7pm.

ACT (American Conservatory Theater): 450 Geary St. (Mason/Taylor), SF, (415) 749-2228. San Francisco's premier theater company, ACT maintains the Stage Door Theater on Mason, the grandly renovated Geary Theater (on Geary) for major productions, and also presents staged readings. Expect controversial productions from ACT's director Carey Perloff with works ranging from *Hecuba* to *Angels in America*. Famous alumni include Denzel Washington and Annette Bening.

Asian American Theater: (415) 440-5545. Plays and performance pieces by and about Asian Americans.

Beach Blanket Babylon: 678 Beach St. (Hyde/Leavenworth), SF, (415) 421-4222. This beloved San Francisco institution offers ever-changing, highly polished musical revues poking fun at contemporary popular culture. Reserve tickets far in advance.

Curran Theater: 445 Geary St. (Taylor/Mason), SF, (415) 474-3800. The Best of Broadway series brings traveling Broadway productions such as the never-ending *Phantom of the Opera* to the Curran.

Josie's Cabaret: 3583 16th St. (Market), SF, (415) 861-7933. Gay and lesbian acts, many cutting edge and experimental.

Latin American Theatre Artists: (415) 439-2425. Promotes Latino theater from indigenous roots to classic and contemporary theater. Readings, children's shows, and full productions held at Intersection for the Arts and Mission Cultural Center.

Lorraine Hansberry Theater: 620 Sutter St. (Mason/Taylor), SF, (415) 474-8800. This small theater primarily produces African-American productions, from standards like *The Colored Museum* to comical and biting contemporary pieces.

Magic Theatre: Building A, Fort Mason Center, Buchanan St. at Marina Blvd., SF, (415) 441-8822. One of the best places to catch contemporary experimental theater in the city. Look for high-quality productions of works by playwrights like Sam Shepard (before *The Right Stuff*).

The Marsh: 1062 Valencia St. (21st St./22nd St.), SF, (415) 641-0235. The Marsh calls itself a "breeding ground for new theater." It doesn't cost much, at $6 to $15, to see works while they're incubating. They have children's theater workshops, too.

ARTS & ENTERTAINMENT

New Conservatory Theatre Centre: 25 Van Ness Ave. (Market), Lower Lobby, SF, (415) 861-8972. They stage new, musical, lesbian and gay, and also traditional theater pieces. The premises also boast an art gallery.

San Francisco Mime Troupe: 855 Treat St. (21st St./22nd St.), SF, (415) 285-1717. Park information: (415) 285-1720. The world-renowned troupe is not precisely mime, comedy, theater, or performance art, yet combines elements of each. Check out the entertaining and socially relevant shows seen outdoors in various Bay Area parks during the warmer months.

San Francisco Shakespeare Festival: (415) 666-2221. It's free. It's in Golden Gate Park every Saturday and Sunday at 1:30pm in September near the Conservatory of Flowers. First come, first served seating. Bring a blanket and a lunch hamper. Additional performances throughout the Bay Area.

Theatre Artaud: 450 Florida St. (17th St./Mariposa), SF, (415) 621-7797. Presents a good mix of avant-garde and contemporary dance, drama, and multimedia performance. Those prone to acrophobia might not appreciate the scaffolding-like seating. Groups such as Contraband, visitors such as Donald Byrd.

Theatre Rhinoceros: 2926 16th St. (S. Van Ness/Capp), SF, (415) 861-5079. San Francisco's premier gay theater.

Venues

Actors Theatre: 533 Sutter St. (Powell/Mason), SF, (415) 296-9179. Open seating.
Bayfront Theatre: Fort Mason, Building B, (Marina/Buchanan), SF, (415) 441-3400.
Bindlestiff Studio: 185 6th St. (Mission/Howard), SF, (415) 974-1167.
Cable Car Theatre: 430 Mason St. (Post/Geary), SF, (415) 956-8497. Plays, solo performances, musicals, gay friendly, S.F. performer showcases.
Cowell Theatre: Fort Mason, Pier 2, (Marina and Buchanan), SF, (415) 441-3400. Dance performance, comedy, concerts.
Exit Theatre: 156 Eddy St. (Mason/Taylor), SF, (415) 673-3847.
Golden Gate Theatre: Golden Gate Ave. at Taylor St., SF, (415) 474-3800. Big, mainstream shows like Andrew Lloyd Webber's *Music of the Night.*
Intersection for the Arts: 446 Valencia St. (15th St./16th St.), SF, (415) 626-2787. Plays, dance, humor, poetry, readings, new music, literary readings.
Marine's Memorial Theatre: 609 Sutter St. (Mason/Taylor), SF, (415) 771-6900. Presents eclectic performances. Beware of cramped access and insufficient restrooms.
Multi Ethnic Theatre: 953 De Haro St. (20th St./22nd St.), SF, (415) 550-8761. Works like *Purlie Victorious.*
Next Stage Theatre: Trinity Episcopal Church, 1668 Bush St. (enter on Gough at Bush), SF, (415) 885-6763, (415) 921-6430. Performances, classes, and workshops.
Phoenix Theatre: 310 8th St. (Folsom), SF, (415) 621-4423. From Shakespeare to Coward.

NIGHTLIFE

Even for a city of 720,000 residents, San Francisco has a mind-bogglingly large number of bars and clubs. Some say it has the finest selection in the country. There are few types of night owls who are left unprovided for, whether tastes run upscale or downscale, crowded or quiet, bottled domestic beer or exotic mixed drinks, cool jazz or white-hot punk rock. Each and every neighborhood has at least a few hangouts which are noteworthy, and some have so many good ones that you wouldn't need to venture further afield.

Great sources for finding out what's happening each night are Sunday's *San Francisco Chronicle-Examiner's* "Pink Pages," the *Bay Guardian,* and the *SF Weekly.* You

NIGHTLIFE

might want to call **BASS Tickets** at (510) 762-2277 or (408) 998-2277 for information on ticket availability for bigger shows and a listing of events. For a phone listing of hip hop, acid jazz, house, and other dance-oriented music—at both bars and roving parties—call the **Be-at-Line** (415) 626-4087.

The legal drinking age in California is 21 (most bars and clubs check identification religiously). Some night spots, especially those with live entertainment, have "All Ages" nights, when the age requirement drops to 18; those over 21 can get their hands stamped to purchase liquor.

The following is merely a sampling of what's out there and is, by no means, complete.

Bars & Clubs

Albion Club: 3139 16th St. (Valencia/Guerrero), SF, (415) 552-8558. A real dress-down bar that is the epitome of the Mission bohemia scene—locals tend to glare at strangers coming into this bar. Black leather booths, black walls, fake plaster pillars, and blood-red industrial carpeting speak volumes about what kind of clientele comes here. (That, and the "service for the sick" sign in neon over the bar.) Anchor Steam and Pete's Wicked Ale on tap. A jukebox that's always in tune with dynamite singles plus three pool tables and pinball in the back.

Bahia Cabana: 1600 Market St. (Franklin), SF, (415) 861-4202. Salsa bar and restaurant that's always hopping, seven nights a week, whether it's Latin house, techno/trance, or live Brazilian bands kicking out the jams. Elongated narrow space feels distinctly tropical and celebratory, and the crowds are always there to dance up a storm on weekends. Happy hour Tu-Th 7-9pm, with free appetizers.

Balboa Café and Grill: 3199 Fillmore St. (Greenwich), SF, (415) 922-4595. This place has been here since 1914, and it feels like a real saloon, with antique drop lighting, brass railings, and wood paneling. A dining room sits in back. Full Sail Ale and Spaten are among the brews on tap. Very conducive to quiet, relaxed conversation.

Bimbo's 365 Club: 1025 Columbus Ave. (Chestnut), SF, (415) 474-0365. An exquisite, cavernous nightclub/lounge that is the living definition of swank. With candles and red-tablecloth seating, a giant disco ball in the center of the ballroom, and a tropical fish tank behind both bars in the back—don't miss the mermaid when she appears in one—it's no wonder that Bimbo's tends to program lots of gigs with *faux*-swing orchestras and kitschy space-age bachelor pad bands. Sadly, it is only open when there's live music, which is generally on weekend nights. Be sure to dress up— the Cocktail Nation crowd that worships here always does.

The Bitter End: 441 Clement St. (5th Ave./6th Ave.), SF, (415) 221-9538. Irish-themed bar in the Richmond with an upper level balcony and pool tables overlooking the bar. A mounted deer head, a roaring fireplace, and a *giant* screen TV round out the decor. Newcastle, Red Hook, and others on tap served up by a very friendly barstaff. Gets crowded on weekend nights and loud, too: they blast the jukebox. Attracts a young, multiethnic crowd.

Black Thorn: 834 Irving St. (9th Ave./10th Ave.), SF, (415) 564-6627. With its low ceilings, dim lighting, and painted wooden benches, this is the truest Irish pub in the Sunset. Stouts like Murphy's and Guinness are on tap, pictures of Ireland line the walls, and the color scheme is green and white—get the picture? There's a small dance floor where disco takes place Thursdays and Sundays, with live Irish music on Fridays and Saturdays. No cover charge.

Blues: 2125 Lombard St. (Fillmore/Steiner), SF, (415) 771-2583. Regular acts play da blooz amidst the dark leopard skin booths and round formica tables. Velvet paintings of half-naked women grace the walls, so some may wish to keep their eyes focused on the stage. And some may not. Napa Red, Sierra Nevada, and the watery domestics on tap. Cover charge for the bands Thursday, Friday, Saturday, and Sunday.

ARTS & ENTERTAINMENT

Bottom of the Hill: 1233 17th St. (Texas/Missouri), SF, (415) 621-4455. A small rock club at the foot of Potrero Hill that attracts local bands and up-and-coming national acts. (It's also usually the first place to see heavily hyped acts from the U.K.) Quirky wall decor inside skews your perspective even before the drinking starts. A tiny stage means that even sold-out shows are intimate affairs. Pool tables in back, outdoor patio to catch a breath of fresh air. Serves good burgers and other grub, including the all-you-can-eat barbecue during Sunday afternoon gigs.

Bruno's: 2389 Mission St. (19th St./20th St.), SF, (415) 550-7455. Bruno's has been a Mission mainstay for ages, but since its renovation in 1995, the demographic of the crowd has skewed younger and hipper. Maybe that's because the place now looks like a cross between a 1960s bachelor pad and a suburban steakhouse. One half of the place, with gorgeous rounded leather booths, is, in fact, a restaurant. The other half is made up of a long bar with white Naugahyde stools, and a colorfully lit lounge featuring jazz and avant-garde bands performing nightly. Red Hook and ESB on tap, and yes, they do serve cocktails.

Café Babar: 994 Guerrero St. (22nd St.), SF, (415) 282-6789. A relaxing neighborhood corner bar consisting of three connected spaces: a large room done up in a vintage/moderne motif, a dimly lit back room with wooden benches, and a tiny curved bar space. Lots of fruity beers available. Also with a pool table, a small computer hooked up to other bars on the Internet, and a DJ on weekends who spins funk and acid jazz to add to the Bohemian mood. Very young Mission clientele.

Café Du Nord: 2170 Market St. (Church/Sanchez), SF, (415) 979-6545. Basement-level bar that is almost as beautifully decked out as the people who come here. Lots of red velvet, finely buffed wooden floors, and private corner tables. Live music, from salsa on Tuesdays (with free lessons!) to jazz and swing on Saturdays. No cover before 8pm. $2 martinis and Manhattans during happy hour (4-7pm daily).

Chameleon: 853 Valencia St. (19th St./20th St.), SF, (415) 821-1891. A wide open Mission hangout with black velvet paintings, glitter upholstered chairs, and lots of other cheesy furnishings. Everything from Devil Mountain beer to hot sake available; all pints are $2.25 during happy hour. Showcases local rock bands—they're willing to give almost anyone a shot at the stage. Don't forget your earplugs.

Club Deluxe: 1509 Haight St. (Ashbury), SF, (415) 552-6949. For those into the cocktail/lounge scene, this is the place: an art deco bar lit by neon, with sleek formica tables and black leather booths. The crowd tends to dress the part, too, with lots of vintage clothing to be seen. Boogie-woogie piano music or cool jazz Wednesdays, Fridays, Saturdays, and Sundays. Reputedly serves the best Bloody Marys in San Francisco.

Club 181: 181 Eddy St. (Taylor/Mason), SF, (415) 673-8181. The strangest juxtaposition in town: in the heart of the grimy Tenderloin lies this plushly decorated dinner club/dance spot with a tough dress code and the beautiful people who meet it. House and funk music are the sounds of choice most nights. Cover charge.

Dalva: 3121 16th St. (Valencia/Guerrero), SF, (415) 252-7740. "We serve only nice people," warns the sign inside, so keep on your best behavior. A designer bar of sorts, with tan-colored walls, lots of wood, and a sleek, faux-aged interior that has a Mediterranean feel to it. Anchor, Full Sail, and others on tap, plus bottled beers like Chimay Red (brewed by Belgian trappist monks). Fireplace and Anglophile's jukebox in the back. Happy hour Sa-Th 5-8pm, F 2-7pm.

DNA Lounge: 375 11th St. (Folsom/Harrison), SF, (415) 626-1409. DNA is the epitome of the "11th St. Scene," which is why people either love SoMa or hate it. A warehouse club that features a large stage, a horseshoe bar, and a perimeter balcony with comfy sofas, DNA caters to the "bridge-and-tunnel" crowd from the East Bay with 70s cover bands and 80s dance nights, although they occasionally invite edgy rock bands in for a show—reminiscent of their past as an industrial hangout. The cover charge on weekends runs about $10, and drinks are not cheap.

NIGHTLIFE

DV 8: 55 Natoma St. (off 1st St. btwn. Mission/Howard), SF (415) 957-1730. A labyrinth of rooms and bars within one huge warehouse with multiple entrances and exits. This cement club is dark and smoky, offering an air of mystery which is instantly killed by the *loud* DJ dance music. Each room features a different sound. Specialty nights throughout the week attract different types of crowds. Call for weekly schedule.

Eddie Rickenbacker's: 133 2nd St. (Mission/Howard), SF, (415) 543-3498. Spacious, wood-paneled and ornate, Rickenbacker's looks like the type of place Al Capone and his cronies would hang out at if this were in Chicago. Except this is in San Francisco, so there are decorative touches like actual custom mortocycles hanging from the ceiling, plus a model train set that regularly takes a trip around the room. Anchor, Bass, and Sierra among the beers on tap. Happy hour features a very generous, varied collection of appetizers brought to each table free of charge. Full meals are also available.

The Edinburgh Castle: 950 Geary St. (Hyde/Larkin), SF, (415) 885-4074. Great Scot! Not so much a castle as a veritable Viking beer hall, with a large bar and sitting area that sits under awnings beneath a wooden balcony that overlooks everything. Also, pool tables, darts, and a completely separate upstairs room that hosts rock and country bands in a casual, intimate space. Twenty beers on tap. Mouthwatering fish and chips. And, it should go without saying, single malt Scotches. Live music Wednesday through Saturday at 9:30pm.

El Rio: 3158 Mission St. (Ceasar Chavez, née Army), SF, (415) 282-3325. Located in the netherworld between Bernal Heights and the Mission, a casual hangout that gets very crowded on weekends. Salsa bands play in the spacious beer garden Wednesdays, Fridays and Saturdays. Oyster special on Friday nights. Games run the gamut from a pool table with tan-colored felt to an indoor shuffleboard. Drinks are cheap, and what else would one expect from a place that advertises itself as "your dive"?

Elbo Room: 647 Valencia St. (17th St./18th St.), SF, (415) 552-7788. One of the finest looking bars in the city, with a wavy formica top, wooden arches, and candles to enhance the mood lighting. Upstairs, Elbo Room hosts bands ranging from ambient jazz to rap/funk for a modest cover charge. Beers on tap include Red Hook and Guinness. Liquor, like the heavenly Laphroaoig Scotch, is also abundant. Two pool tables in the back. Extremely crowded on weekends as Generation X moves in. (Be prepared to rub elbows with scensters because you'll find them here. If you're a hep cat, you can hang here comfortably.)

Eleven Ristorante + Bar: 374 11th St. (Folsom/Harrison), SF, (415) 431-3337. A hip Italian restaurant and jazz bar in the heart of the SoMa scene. Wrought-iron railings and *trompe l'oeil* murals add to a spare, Roman feel. The band plays on a platform above the kitchen.

500 Club: 500 Guerrero St. (17th St.), SF, (415) 861-2500. A great locals' bar with Pabst and Jaeger on tap. Good prices per pint with friendly bartenders who will give you free popcorn if you look like you've had one too many. Cool, retro style with a pool table in a separate room. If you're willing to share a large booth, you may meet some interesting characters and make lifelong friends. The jukebox rocks. The giant neon martini sign flashing outside is enough reason to drop in.

Gordon Biersch: 2 Harrison St. (Embarcadero), SF, (415) 243-8246. This enormous branch of the successful brewpub chain occupies a prime spot in the beautifully restored Hills Brothers building. Young, loud, single suits and skirts flock here after work for serious mingling.

Grant and Green: 1371 Grant Ave. (Green), SF, (415) 693-9565. Located, coincidentally, on the corner of Grant and Green. A dark, sparsely furnished bar that is purely for drinking and dancing. Attracts a mix of bikers in leather and yuppies looking for the bluesy rock played live many nights. Good microbrews on tap.

ARTS & ENTERTAINMENT

Harrington's Bar and Grill: 245 Front St. (California/Sacramento), SF, (415) 392-7595. Large Irish bar that takes up two rooms in the Financial District, with plenty of booths and long tables for when the entire office comes after work. Guinness, Sierra Nevada, and Bass are just some of the items on tap. Pub food is served, and large pretzels with mustard are gratis during the afternoon rush. Every four years, ex-pat suits play hooky to watch the World Cup here.

Harry Denton's Starlight Room: Sir Francis Drake Hotel, 450 Powell St. (Post/Sutter), SF, (415) 392-7755. Twenty-one floors above Union Square, this rooftop bar is only for the well-dressed and wealthy, but is a great place to have a romantic cocktail or happy hour drink if you've got a few extra bucks. Live music is presented for the evening's entertainment (usually jazz). Lots of Oriental rugs, red velvet drapes, and gilded fittings complement the real star of the show—a breathtaking view south, east and west, especially at sunset.

Hi-Ball Lounge: 473 Broadway (Kearny/Montgomery), SF, (415) 397-9464. The key word here is "lounge," as it reflects the mid-90s retro-Cocktail Revival trend among the city's young clubbers. Red velvet booths, dark circular candlelit tables, and a preponderance of Y-shaped glasses will tip anyone off to what sort of people hang out here. Live jazz and swing most nights, preceeded by the "Mondo Martini Happy Hour" Thursday and Friday evenings from 5-9pm.

Horseshoe Tavern: 2024 Chesnut St. (Fillmore/Steiner), SF, (415) 346-1430. A very old-time neighborhood bar that serves 14 beers on tap. A big screen TV hangs over the bar, and sports trophies are placed on the shelves. Attracts a young and lively crowd, but shows a lower-key side to the Marina.

Hotel Utah Saloon Bistro: 500 4th St. (Bryant), SF, (415) 421-8308. This bi-level old bar exudes a hint of Wild West decor with no hint of a cowboy—or hotel—anywhere. Bartenders behind a massive mahogany bar serve up good pints along with delicious bar fare including vegetarian chili, chips, and spicy salsa. Small stage featuring open mike Mondays where the local talent often surpasses signed acts. Bring plenty of quarters for the "Buzz Ball" machine—chocolate-covered espresso beans!

Ireland's 32: 3920 Geary Blvd. (3rd Ave.), SF, (415) 386-6173. First things first: it is not a good idea to walk in here waving a Union Jack flag. This is the IRA/Sinn Fein pub of record in San Francisco, as the paraphernalia scattered everywhere will attest. The crowd is actually mixed but skews towards the middle-aged and older. Not heavy on microbrews, but plenty of Guinness and Murphy's. Two levels, with a pool table upstairs. Live music during the week. Gaelic football on TV Sunday mornings.

Jack's Bar: 1601 Fillmore St. (Geary), SF, (415) 567-3227. It's not the down-home bar it used to be, but then the Fillmore isn't the Western Addition anymore. Newly remodeled, Jack's features several cozy booths in a modern-meets-retro dive atmosphere. Black and white checkered tile dance floor with mirrored disco ball for either live music—often blues—or DJ beats. Full bar with over 100 beers. A perfect spot for either pre- or post-Fillmore live shows. Tuesday night is live comedy night. Not the safest area at night.

Jacks Elixir: 3200 16th St. (Guerrero), SF, (415) 552-1633. One of the most popular spots in the entire Mission. In business since 1932, there are just stools and window tables for decor, a checkerboard lineoleum floor, and over 60 beers on tap. Pints are generally $3.50. Bloody Mary Sunday has the "Best in the Mission" for $4.50, but beer is really the raison d'être of this corner bar.

Johnny Love's: 1500 Broadway (Polk), SF, (415) 931-6053. *The* pickup joint in town for young, urban professionals, at least according to legend. An enormous bar and dance floor under a high ceiling—which is fortunate because lots of people here end up dancing on tables. It's that kind of place. DJ plays 70s music on Saturday nights. The line to get in usually runs halfway down the block. Unspoken dress code: Oxford shirts and Dockers for men, clingy dresses or miniskirts for women.

NIGHTLIFE

Kate O'Brien's: 579 Howard St. (1st St./2nd St.), SF, (415) 882-7240. Sometimes it seems like every last neighborhood in the city has at least one Irish bar, and this is "north" SoMa's entry. It's dimly lit, with a very high ceiling swathed in rock posters and hanging chandeliers, naturalistic brick walls featuring various knickknacks from the Old Country, and long wooden benches at the line of tables. Guinness and other familiar brews on tap. Come for Sunday brunch when there's a traditional Irish breakfast, free glass of mimosa and the sounds of a live blues band.

Kezar: 900 Cole St. (Carl), SF, (415) 681-7678. A relaxed corner bar that would look straight out of a beer ad if not for the preponderance of skeletons painted on the dark interior walls. Attracts students and the upscale Cole Valley clientele. Anchor, Sierra, and other microbrews on tap. Great burgers, too. Somewhat slow service.

Kilowatt Club: 3160 16th St. (Valencia/Guerrero), SF, (415) 861-2595. Housed in an old firehouse, this has become an alternative rock Mecca since it opened on the ashes of the Firehouse a couple of years ago. Lots of well-known local bands, and many up-and-coming national acts play on weekends. (There is no cover charge on weeknights.) Pints are generally under $4, pitchers are $8 at happy hour, pool tables are only 50 cents a game, and even earplugs are under a buck. A cheap place to hang out and listen to great music.

La Rondalla: 901 Valencia St. (20th St.), SF, (415) 647-7474. One entrance leads to the restaurant, but you'll want to take the entrance that leads to the curvy bar with fake wood paneling, leather backed bar stools (!), fake wood paneling, and Christmas lights. They've been playing mariachi music here every night for almost 30 years, and it'll sound great while drinking their popular margaritas. Bottled beers are also available.

Last Day Saloon: 406 Clement St. (5th Ave./6th Ave.), SF, (415) 387-6343. A huge, two-story bar and music venue; on quiet Clement Street at night, you hear it before you see it. The upstairs is where to go for the bands; an eclectic booking policy brings in lots of different types of music. (One wall is filled with the names of the bands who have graced the stage throughout the club's history—Foghat once played here.) Downstairs is the hopping bar scene, with numerous microbrews on tap, pool tables, a jukebox, and a casually dressed crowd.

Latin American Club: 3286 22nd St. (Valencia/Mission), SF, (415) 647-2732. Divey, dark, loud place that is here to do little more than serve beer—just how the regular patrons like it. Large, bizarre paintings hang on the wall opposite the bar, and in between is a group of tables and chairs, and that's about it. Pool table by the front window, cozy alcove in the back. Young and hip crowd. A giant red neon sign that says, simply, "Sin," is visible only to those sitting inside.

Li Po Cocktail Lounge: 916 Grant St. (Washington/Jackson), SF, (415) 982-0072. The coolest bar in Chinatown: a Buddha shrine behind the bar, cheap red leather booths (including a claustrophobic alcove/grotto), an original Pac Man video game in the corner, and disco music from another era. If the bartender doesn't try to get you to join him for a game of cards, he'll carefully pour the mixed drink of your choice (including a screwdriver made up of five parts vodka and one part orange Gatorade). Watch the stairs to the bathroom in the basement; they're black diamond if you're sober, double black diamond if you're not.

Little Shamrock: 807 Lincoln Ave. (9th Ave.), SF, (415) 661-0060. The second oldest bar in the city is also one of the coziest. Located across the street from Golden Gate Park, this worn bar features plush sofa seating, marble coffee tables, stained glass decor, old highback chairs, and plenty of nooks and crannies to sit and nurse your drink. Hallway leads to a dart room in back. Anchor and Newcastle Brown on tap.

Lone Palm: 3394 22nd St. (Guerrero), SF, (415) 648-0109. A swank cocktail bar with white tablecloths, neon, and a baby grand piano in the corner. When crowded (and it often is), it attracts a lot of Mission retro/vintage clothing types; but when it's quiet, it's inexplicably eerie, and feels straight out of *Twin Peaks*. Serves up great looking martinis.

ARTS & ENTERTAINMENT

Lucky 13: 2140 Market St. (Church/Sanchez), SF, (415) 487-1313. If you're not put off by the imposing, Germanic red-and-black colored facade outside, Lucky 13 is a very happening hangout spot inside. Long and narrow, lit only by red light bulbs, with upper level seating along two walls (great for people watching), the bar attracts a young, leather jacket-clad contingent and blasts the rock-n-roll from the jukebox as a soundtrack. Good variety of microbrews. Pool table, but of course.

Mad Dog in the Fog: 530 Haight St. (Fillmore/Steiner), SF, (415) 626-7279. England-on-Haight: the walls are full of soccer club banners, there's a true English garden in the back, and, yes, they do serve bangers and mash. Beers served include the wonderful Boddington's and Old Peculiar. Comfortable chairs all around in a bare-bones environment. Not surprisingly, lots of Brits hang out here along with the pierced Lower Haight kids. Open mike night on Tuesday, and a *very* serious darts league.

Mick's Lounge: 2513 Van Ness Ave. (Union), SF, (415) 928-0404. Mick's is a great place to lounge when checking out local bands. Comfortable atmosphere, full bar with huge selection of draught beers, and cocktail service. Bi-level with pool table upstairs. Packs 'em in Thursday through Saturday, but this joint is most appealing on a crowd-free night while comfortably watching the bands from a table.

Myles O'Reilly's Pub: 622 Green St. (Columbus/Powell), SF, (415) 989-6222. An Irish bar in North Beach? It sounds like it couldn't work, and yet former Fiddler's Green barman Myles O'Reilly pulls it off beautifully. There's a bar in one half of the room, and an unpretentious dining area in the other. The walls are full of Irish-related mementos, including a mural that pays tribute to some of Ireland's most famous sons (and daughters). Add great food, great beers, and a lively yet easygoing crowd, and it makes for a nice place to start, or finish, or fill, an evening.

Nickie's BBQ: 460 Haight St. (Webster/Fillmore), SF, (415) 621-6508. If Nickie's looks way too small on the outside to be a dance club, that's because it is. The bar and the dance floor are one, and especially on weekends they are sardine-packed with sweaty folk getting down to 70s funk, hip hop, Middle Eastern/African/Asian world beat, or some other eclectic mix of music provided by superb DJs. The crowd is vibrant and diverse, one nation under a groove. Wide selection of domestic and imported beers, if you can find an open space to drink it.

Noc Noc: 557 Haight St. (Fillmore/Steiner), SF, (415) 861-5811. Arguably the weirdest interior of any bar in the city: a mixture of aircraft sheet metal, hieroglyphics, and painted papier-mâché cover the walls, tiny TVs show blank blue screens, and throw pillow seats are scattered amongst the various nooks and crannies—Dr. Who meets Dr. Seuss, basically. A small but solid beer selection, plus wines and pretzels. A DJ hidden behind a booth in the corner plays acid jazz and ambient music for the suitably hipster crowd.

(Bobby's) Owl Tree: 601 Post St. (Taylor), SF, (415) 776-9344. Owls, owls everywhere: paintings of them on the walls, stained glass versions of them in the windows, and stuffed ones behind a glass case. As if that weren't surreal enough, this smoky Tenderloin bar features a women's room seemingly designed for midgets, as well as plush red Naugahyde chairs, a traffic light behind the bar, and a clientele that runs from straight-laced businessmen to bewildered tourists, and everyone in between. Bottled beer only, plus cocktails. Peggy Lee and Frank Sinatra on the jukebox.

Paradise Lounge: 1501 Folsom St. (11th St.), SF, (415) 861-6906. More like a house than a lounge, what with its numerous "spaces" for the bar, the various performance stages, or just the drinking corners. A young, with-it crowd comes here to check out reggae, hip hop, accoustic, or hard rock—it depends on the show. Right next door, connected by a short hallway, lies a recently opened warehouse-sized space called the **Transmission Theater**. It looks like it should be hosting a square dance, but the art videos playing on large screens hanging from two of the walls betray the experimental, eclectic nature of the acts who play/perform here. Like Incredibly Strange Wrestling, for example. Upper loft area faces 11th Street, and is a good place to relax.

NIGHTLIFE

Paragon Bar and Café: 3251 Scott St. (Chestnut/Lombard), SF, (415) 922-2456. Like a Zima ad come to life: smartly dressed yuppie/Marina types check each other out, and on Sunday nights, check out live jazz. Surfboards cover the ceiling and walls. Also serves food. Lots of ex-frat boys.

Pier 23: Pier 23 (Embarcadero at Front), SF, (415) 362-5125. Medium-sized wooden shack that has been transformed into a drinking and dancing establishment. Live bands perform salsa, New Orleans R&B, reggae, and jazz depending on the day of the week. Cover charge is usually very reasonable, given the location. Best of all, there's an outdoor patio where you can spread out and gaze at the Bay under the starry night sky. No music on Mondays.

The Pig & Whistle: 2801 Geary Blvd. (Wood/Collins), SF, (415) 885-4779. A Richmond hangout for British and Irish ex-pats, along with anyone else who drops by. Wooden floors, roomy front area, pool table in the back. Over 20 British bitters are on tap, written up on a giant blackboard behind the bar. They take their darts *very* seriously here.

The Plough & Stars: 116 Clement St. (2nd Ave./3rd Ave.), SF, (415) 751-1122. In a city full of authentic Irish bars, this is as close to the Old Sod as they come: long wooden tables and benches, dim lighting, sparse decoration, and an unobtrusive performance stage in the back. A mellow, ruddy-faced crowd enjoys pool, darts, and traditional Irish music most nights (cover charge on weekends) whilst drinking Guinness, Murphy's, or one of the other heavy beers on tap.

Red Jack Saloon: 131 Bay St (Stockton/Kearny), SF, (415) 989-0700. Voted "Best Neighborhood Bar in North Beach," this cozy place features a jukebox, a pinball machine, and a very competitive darts league. Specials on drinks six days a week, including pint-sized margaritas on Monday nights! Very busy during happy hour.

Red Room: 827 Sutter St. (Jones/Leavenworth), SF, (415) 346-7666. The ultimate in retro-cocktail cool. The name says it all: everything in this lounge is red: the silk curtains, vinyl and ultrasuede 40s furniture, hardwood floors, postmodern lights, and even a wall of stacked bottles—filled with red liquid.

Savoy Tivoli: 1434 Grant St. (Green/Union), SF, (415) 362-7023. An enormous bar that takes up two large storefronts and has room for three pool tables. Two brass bars, a heated open patio area, and a youthful crowd that takes over on weekend nights are some of the highlights of this rockin' place.

Sol y Luna: 475 Sacramento St. (Sansome/Battery), SF, (415) 296-8191. A sleek, lively Latin supper club that's just getting going when the rest of the Financial District has gone home for the night. Young professionals and well-dressed partyers are the crowd, and it has a reputation as a pickup joint. Come to dance regardless, because everyone else will be, especially when the front patio becomes a world beat crush of bodies on Friday nights. Flamenco, Latin jazz, and salsa are the main entertainment between Wednesdays and Sundays. Cover charge.

Spec's 12 Adler Museum Café: 12 Saroyan Pl. (off Columbus Ave. btwn. Broadway/Pacific), SF, (415) 421-4112. This jovial North Beach dive-in-an-alleyway attracts a diverse clientele of equal parts ancient regulars and curious visitors. The main attraction is not the range of drinks—only Budweiser on tap and a few bottled beers; this is a hard liquor place, it would seem—but rather the memorabilia that fills up all available wall, ceiling and, on occasion, floor space. Sent in by people from all over the world, these knickknacks include, among other things, a gold toilet plunger, a Pacific Island license plate, a skull, and an unidentified garden implement. Best to go during happy hour when it is less crowded, so you can see all there is to see.

330 Ritch Street: 330 Ritch St. (off Brannan or Bryant btwn. 3rd St./4th St.), SF, (415) 541-9574. Tucked away in an alley South of Market, this surprisingly large supper club offers good food, full bar, a variety of on-tap beers, and lively dancing. A hot spot for the *Wired* crowd after-hours. Also a great place to rent out for private functions.

ARTS & ENTERTAINMENT

Tonga Room: In the Fairmont Hotel, 950 Mason St. (California/Sacramento), bar entrance on California St., SF, (415) 772-5278. Those who love kitsch swear by this tropical themed hall: thatched hut roofs, palm trees, and an Olympic-sized pool with a floating stage on which the house band performs nightly. Plus, every half-hour there are simulated lightning-and-thunderstorms that have to be seen to be believed. Best to go during happy hour (5-7pm) when the mai-tais and daiquiris are discounted and there is an all-you-can-eat buffet for only $5.

Toronado: 547 Haight St. (Fillmore/Steiner), SF, (415) 863-2276. For beer connoisseurs, this place is heaven: upwards of 40 beers on tap, and countless bottled ones from all around the world. Basic decor, with stools in the front and tables in the back room. Very cool CD jukebox. Absolutely filled to capacity most evenings after 10pm. Don't miss the "Twist of Fate" bitter, or try one of the excellent offerings from the numerous local microbreweries.

Tosca Café: 242 Columbus Ave. (Broadway/Pacific), SF, (415) 986-9651. Elegant without being pricy, refined without being stuffy, relaxed without being a dive, Tosca is perhaps the classiest bar in the city, at least when there's no room-shaking, low rumbling bass coming from the Palladium disco next door (go early). Dark walls, a high ceiling, giant red leather booths and formica tables, a long wooden bar, and operatic arias playing in the background. Pool table in a back room. Ancient jukebox. Bottled beers like Anchor Steam are served, plus cocktails as mixed by the professional bartenders—the house special is a potent coffee drink. Crowded only on weekends, great for hushed conversation most weeknights. Actor Nicholas Cage has been sighted here.

Trad'r Sam: 6150 Geary Blvd. (25th Ave./26th Ave.), SF, (415) 221-0773. The Richmond home of umbrella drinks: from the Singapore Sling, through the Moscow Mule, to the New Orleans Fog Cutter, and many more. There's a horseshoe bar in the center of this mid-sized room, with bamboo-framed, floral-print sofa booths against the walls. Drinks run close to five bucks except during happy hour (Sunday-Thursday 4pm to 7pm). Free popcorn and bags of chips are the sustenance here.

Trocadero Night Club & Restaurant: 520 4th St. (Bryant/Brannan), SF, (415) 495-6620. Huge club with cave-like atmosphere drawing caveman mentality crowd—a bit hip-grunge. Do not miss Bondage a Go-Go upstairs every Wednesday night, featuring amateur S&M (chips, dips, chains, whips) and caged go-go dancing downstairs. DJ spins alternative and techno dance beats.

20 Tank Brewery: 316 11th St. (Folsom/Harrison), SF, (415) 255-9455. Slightly hipper than your average brewpub is this popular place located in San Francisco's SoMa area and frequented by young flannel-clad single types.

Union Street Ale House: 1980 Union St. (Laguna/Buchanan), SF, (415) 921-0300. Basement-level pickup joint once described as "Ground Zero for Lust." Pool tables and darts are in the back, but the real action is at the big bar up front catering to the twenty-somethings who pack the place nightly. Excellent beer selection, from Pintail PSB to Anderson Valley. REM and Pearl Jam are usually blasting from the stereo system.

Up & Down Club: 1151 Folsom St. (7th St./8th St.), SF, (415) 626-2388. Two separate bars under one swell name. Down offers more than up at this chic jazz supper club owned by Erin Turlington (keep your eyes open for her supermodel sister, who is known to drop in on occasion). Simple but sleek downstairs bar charmed by golden walls and candlelight. Upstairs is more of a "gimme a beer, Mac!" joint with sticky-in-the-heat vinyl booths and loud DJ music.

Vesuvio Café: 255 Columbus Ave. (Broadway/Pacific), SF, (415) 362-3370. Once the infamous watering hole for Jack Kerouac and his friends during the late 50s and early 60s (the famous City Lights Bookstore lies across "Kerouac Alley" from here), now the hangout spot for 90s Beats and assorted literary wanna-Beats. Two levels, low ceilings, and walls full of San Francisco history; it's virtually a museum/bar.

CALIFORNIA BEER

Since the mid-1980s, beer has become the drink of choice for many, and Northern California has been a leader in providing its residents with quality suds from local microbreweries. It's a throwback to the turn of the century, when every city had its own brewery. Microbrewery beer is generally sold in bars and liquor stores, although most breweries have tours and tasting rooms. By comparison, brewpubs manufacture smaller quantities of premium brew and usually sell it only in their own bar, pub, or restaurant.

Microbreweries

Anchor Brewing Company: 1705 Mariposa St. (DeHaro), SF, (415) 863-8350. The oldest microbrewery in the Bay Area started during the Gold Rush. Nearly bankrupt in the early 1970s, Anchor was revived after its purchase by Fritz Maytag (heir to the appliance fortune), and today creates five different types of beer. Make a reservation for one of their free tours—they're great fun.

Anderson Valley Brewing Co.: 14081 Hwy 128, Boonville, (707) 895-2337. Try their beers at the bar, and then make your money talk at the retail store. They also have a restaurant. They just built a new brewery, and if you ask nicely, they'll probably give you a tour.

Anheuser-Busch: 3101 Busch Dr. (Abernathy), Fairfield, (707) 429-2000. If you're the sort who doesn't like too much flavor to get in the way of your beer, you can always come here to taste beer the way it used to be, before microbrews started their meddling. They offer free, 45-minute tours every hour from 9am-4pm Tu-Sa. The tour includes free tastings of some of the world's best-known brews.

Mendocino Brewing Co.: 13351 S. Hwy 101, Hopland, (707) 744-1015. They have a gift shop, as well as an adjoining bar and restaurant. Tours of the brewery are by appointment only.

Sierra Nevada: 1075 E. 20th St., Chico, (916) 893-3520. Hardly a microbrewery anymore—their production and distribution has grown wildly over the last few years. Stop by Tuesday through Friday at 2:30pm or Saturday between noon and 3pm for a brewery tour. They also have a bar, restaurant, and gift shop.

Brewpubs

The Bison Brewery: See Berkeley Bar listing.

Gordon Biersch: See Bar listing.

Jupiter: See Berkeley Bar listing.

Lyon's Brewery: Town & Country Shopping Ctr., 7294 San Ramon Rd., Dublin, (510) 829-9071. Judy Ashworth serves Northern California's best selection of microbrewed beer on tap in a big, dark hall with loud music and plenty of pool tables (although she doesn't serve her own beer).

San Francisco Brewing Company: 155 Columbus Ave. (Pacific), SF, (415) 434-3344. Between the Financial District and North Beach, this is a wood-bar and burgers-and-fries brewpub; live music entertains while you enjoy your pint. $1 10-oz. pints during happy hour, 4-6pm.

The Tied House: See Peninsula Bar listing.

Triple Rock: See Berkeley Bar listing.

20 Tank Brewery: See Bar listing.

ARTS & ENTERTAINMENT

Gay & Lesbian Bars

The popular clubs change names depending on the night and the crowd they're hosting. Check the local free weeklies for current DJs and themes; try the *Bay Area Reporter* (BAR), the *Sentinel*, or *Odyssey Magazine*, which has separate listings for men's and women's parties and bars. For literature and current rave and party postings go to **A Different Light Bookstore** at 489 Castro Street in San Francisco, (415) 431-0891.

The Box: 715 Harrison St. (3rd St.), SF, (415) 972-8087. Thursday night at the old Dreamland space in SOMA, 9pm-2am, $6 cover. The home of house and funk, if you will. This diverse space has two parts. In front by the entrance is what could be called the "funk" room, a small dance floor with a balcony overlooking the space. Further into the building is the house music area complete with a lively light system, "Box" dancers, and a stage for those interested in attention.

The Café: 2367 Market (17th St./Castro), SF, (415) 861-3846. Open nightly from 12:30pm-2am (busiest Fridays and Satudays—always a line to get in), no cover. One of the best and cheapest ways to go when it comes to dancing in the city. Once the zenith of lesbian socializing and mingling, only to be taken over by the city's gay male population, this bar remains quite popular across the board. The music consists of pure high-energy house with minor variations. In the early part of the evening, there is pool for enthusiastic players. All night long, the patio and balcony are open for a break from the hot time inside. And friendly bartenders!

Casanova's: 527 Valencia St. (16th St./17th St.), (415) 863-9328. A place to go for the gay and the grungy; there's not much glamour to be had. The closest things to heels and snobbery in this place are the fun drag queens serving hors d'oeuvres, which consist of crackers and Cheese Whiz. The most spectacular feature of this little alternative nook in the Mission area is definitely the music: anything from Stevie Wonder to the Bedrock Twist. Fairly friendly crowd, and you'll trip over the live dancers. Casanova's holds two big parties: **Baby Judy's** on Wednesday nights hosts a variety of different music as well as its variety of people. Laid-back yet quirky, this party runs from 10pm-2am. Sunday night is ladies night with the **Muff Dive**. Wild dance music never grows too heavy. Both parties have a $3 cover—all other nights are free.

Café Flore: 2298 Market St. (Noe), (415) 621-8579. Although it is not a club, Café Flore definitely maintains a scene. Complete with everything from alcoholic drinks to iced coffee to squid over pasta, this café is a great place to sit back for awhile. With everyone from flaunting body builders to lesbian punks, Flore contains its own mini-drama. And if it's hard to find an empty table, introduce yourself to someone with an extra seat. Open Su-Th 7:30am-11:30pm; F-Sa 7:30am-midnight.

Club Townsend: 177 Townsend St. (2nd St./3rd St.), (415) 974-1156. Hosts two of the biggest weekend parties for the queer scene in SoMa: **Club Universe** is their Saturday party, running 9:30pm-7am, $10 cover. This is the largest gay dance space in town. Once a diverse haven of joy for gay, bisexual, and straight clubbing San Franciscans, the atmosphere has transformed into the strictly gay male genre, complete with snobbery and shirtless beef boys. Any time a space has a nickname like "Club Unitard," watch out! Some more attractive aspects: there's a different theme practically every Saturday, and the lighting and music are intense. Well worth your visit for the big club experience. **Pleasuredome** takes the floor on Sundays. Pleasuredome's front dance bar caters to the "boy"-ish crowd with house music and "smart drinks." Travel through the black-lycra time tunnel to the back dance bar, which sports a spinning, mirrored ball, and mustaches. (Need we say more?) In addition, Club Townsend holds rotating dance parties throughout the week.

The Coco Club: 139 8th St. (entrance on Minna btwn. Mission/Howard), SF, (415) 626-2337. Also known as Comme Nous. Saturdays, 9pm-2am, $5 cover. One can experience live music and performances at this little cool joint for women. The atmosphere is completely euphoric, having the power to soothe the mind and move the

NIGHTLIFE

body. After you enter the double doors out front, it's downstairs to a cellar—with the deco of a late 60s bar complete with ocean shell light fixtures and deep red curtains. Though mainly a lesbian bar, all are, and feel, welcomed.

Deco: 510 Larkin St. (Turk), SF, (415) 441-4007. A fun little dance joint right between the Civic Center and the Tenderloin. Not the most affluent area in town, but once you get past the entrance, the experience can be a treat. Full bar in the front parallels a good-size dance floor. The back room consists of two pool tables. Down on the basement level, there's a "mellow" lounge. This cozy nook features a DJ spinning softer grooves. The upper level plays what is known as "trip-hop." The crowd is mixed (boys and girls), though mostly male. Deco hosts a variety of parties, and covers vary according to party.

End Up: 401 Harrison St. (6th St.), SF, (415) 487-6277. A publication circulating through the local area for the past few years is entitled *I Found God at the End Up*. True to its name, after a long night's clubbing, when there is no place left to go, this is your place to End Up. Open almost all the time, with different parties seemingly every few hours—call their phone line for details. Huge space with an outdoor patio.

The Giraffe Video Lounge: 1131 Polk St. (Post/Sutter), SF, (415) 474-1702. F-Sa, 5pm-2am, free. This bar sparkles and glistens in comparison with its lower Polk Street locale. Although there is generous space for dancing, shooting pool (only until they move the table to accommodate dancing), or just sitting at the bar (where you can watch the video screens hanging from either corner), you can't help but think you should explore further: the illusion of faux space, courtesy of the many wall mirrors, makes it seem like the bar goes on forever. Friendly bartenders and the relaxed atmosphere draws a mainly older gay male crowd, though women (real and faux) can be seen as well. Go for a drink and admire the lovely hardwood floors!

The Lion Pub: 2062 Divisadero St. (Sacramento), SF, (415) 567-6565. Wednesday is Macho Night at the Lion Pub, a small, hidden, neighborhood hangout in Pacific Heights, with margaritas at $3. Thursdays have the $2 blow job special. And on Friday night, men begin to gather as early as 6pm. This has become the hangout for the 30- to 40-year-old crowd.

The Phoenix: 482 Castro St. (18th St.), SF, (415) 552-6827. 5pm-2am, $1 cover F-Sa. Open practically every night of the week, but really jumps on weekends. Located in the heart of the Castro, people pour in to dance despite the lack of room—they could use a little more space. The house music spun by the DJs leaves you no choice but to move. Talk about packin' 'em in. The crowd consists of a mixed, but predominantly male, crowd.

Sizzybar at the Powerhouse: 1347 Folsom St. (9th St./10th St.), SF, (415) 552-8689. Thursdays, 10pm-2am, $3 cover. This place is known to be "diva free," and it certainly lives up to that reputation: hard-core, roughen, guys for days. A cozy space with a dark upper-level dance floor and a mirrored wall for those who'd rather watch themselves feel the beat—and watch it happen. Most of the music played is of the alternative-80s variety. Pinball and videos for other entertainment.

The Stud: 399 9th St. (Harrison), SF, (415) 863-6623. Nightly. There is a pool table in the front, while the dance floor stretches fairly deep into the back. Monday night is Funk night with no cover. The crowd gets into it so much that the earth literally moves. While mixed, the majority of the clientele are gay men. Tuesday night is Drag night or Trannyshack, with a $2 cover. Come in your best pumps and don't forget your mink. Wednesday nights are Oldies to Modern, $3 cover. Thursday is White Trash night, $1 cover. Yes, even bands like Whitesnake and Kiss move the mountains of gay folk. Try to get there on a Harley to impress many patrons. Friday is known as Nemesis, $2 cover. For all industrial/alternative music lovers who thought it went out with the 80s, it lives on at Nemesis. Finally, on Saturdays, it's Lowrider, until 3am. A mix of queer boy and girl ruffians with some other folks dance to trip-hop/industrial; fun and festive.

ARTS & ENTERTAINMENT

Major Bay Area Venues

Concord Pavilion: Ygnacio Valley Rd. (off Hwy 680), Concord, (510) 676-8742. Large, outdoor amphitheater featuring major-label performers spring through fall. Attracts country western acts in addition to traditional rock. Capacity: 12,500.

The Fillmore: 1805 Geary St. (Fillmore), SF, (415) 346-6000, show info; (415) 346-3000, office. A bi-level music hall with great acoustics and small-theater appeal. Inside, photos and posters memorialize its famous late-60s, early-70s psychedelic extravaganzas with the Dead, Joplin, and the Airplane. Bars on both floors with a separate dining area on second floor. Decent pasta and fried food to eat during a show. A great place to see your favorite band before they get too big and play at Shoreline. Capacity: 1,100.

Great American Music Hall: 859 O'Farrell St. (Polk/Larkin), SF, (415) 885-0750. A traditional theater—complete with balcony, table seating, cocktail and bar food service, good acoustics, and lots of smoke—now used for contemporary music shows. The acoustics are superb. Attracts a wide variety of bands and singers, from jazz to country to rock, usually nationally or internationally known acts on tour. Arrive early for good seating to see the really hot acts. Capacity: 600.

Greek Theatre: Gayley Rd. (Hearst/Bancroft), UC Berkeley Campus, Berkeley, (510) 642-0527. As the name implies, the Greek is both elegant and old, and also a very pretty outdoor amphitheater. Hosts a popular spring and summer concert series featuring major-label acts, with an emphasis on folk-rockers like Tracy Chapman. The seating is designed so that each audience member has a killer view of the stage. Bring a blanket to cushion the concrete seats. Better acoustics down low. Capacity: 8,500.

Kaiser Arena: 10 10th St. (Fallon), Oakland, (510) 238-7765. A fairly large arena that highlights standbys like Little Feat and Tower of Power. Capacity: 8,000.

Lively Arts at Stanford: Stanford Univ., Stanford, (415) 723-2551. The Stanford Concert Network brings professional acts like Shawn Colvin to campus every year, usually at very low prices. The intimate, outdoor **Frost Amphitheater** holds occasional concerts, but most well-known groups play at gloomy **Memorial Auditorium** when they come to campus. Capacity: Frost 3,000; Memorial Auditorium 1,700.

Oakland Coliseum and Stadium: 7000 Coliseum Way (off Hwy 880 at Hegenberger), Oakland, (510) 639-7700. Major Bay Area concerts come to the Oakland Coliseum (the indoor basketball arena) and the Oakland Stadium (the huge outdoor stadium). Accessible via BART. Capacity: Arena 15,000; Stadium 65,000.

Shoreline Amphitheatre: Shoreline Blvd. (Amphitheatre), Mountain View, (415) 967-4040. Large outdoor amphitheater hosting a varied lineup of major acts performing spring through fall. Reserved seating down low, general admission on the lawn further back, with large video monitors set up so you can see the band. Generally pleasant, but it was built on landfill, and you can occasionally smell it. Capacity: 20,000.

Slim's: 333 11th St. (Folsom/Harrison), SF, (415) 522-0333. One of the big-time music venues in the city, Slim's (owned by singer Boz Scaggs) hosts a very wide variety of performers in a space that is always SRO when a nationally known act comes to town. Large floor allows most any punter a clear view of the stage, and there's a balcony space in the rear to nurse your drink. Attracts wildly different crowds depending on who's playing.

Villa Montalvo: 15400 Montalvo Rd. (Saratoga-Los Gatos Rd.), Saratoga, (408) 741-3421. Smaller outdoor amphitheater on historic estate. Hosts a variety of summer performances, from music to drama to children's shows. Capacity: 800.

The Warfield: 982 Market St. (5th St./6th St.), SF, (415) 775-7722, general info;. (415) 775-9949, directions; (415) 567-2060, office. One of the best places in the area to see a show. This beautiful old theater will surprise you when you walk in from its grimy surroundings, with old-style decor, food and cocktails delivered to the tables on the floor, and traditional theater seating (reserved) in the balcony. Dance floor on the bottom level with a pit in front of stage. The Warfield presents everything from Dylan to Dinosaur Jr. Capacity: 2,000.

Sports & the Great Outdoors

BEACHES

The beaches surrounding San Francisco are an underused resource. San Franciscans cringe at being associated with Southern California beach culture, and the coast also has a reputation for being foggy and chilly, which discourages many residents from cluttering up the open space. Nevertheless, there are numerous beautiful beaches all along the northern California coast. The beaches listed below fall within city limits, perfect for a quick escape. Ocean, Baker, and China Beach are all accessible by MUNI—the best mode of transportation on a crowded day when parking becomes as scarce as the hot weather. For information on additional beaches, see the **Peninsula Coast**, **Santa Cruz**, and **Marin** sections (Santa Cruz beaches are the best for swimming).

Baker Beach: Bowley St. off Lincoln Blvd., SF, (415) 666-7200. MUNI bus 29. Baker Beach reaches right under the Golden Gate Bridge. Although bigger than China Beach, it's still a rather small stretch of sand. The steep shoreline and strong riptides make this a dangerous place to swim. Clothing-optional on the eastern end (closest to the bridge). There are two parking lots, picnic tables, and public restrooms; despite the general barren state of this park, on a sunny day it can be a human zoo.

China Beach: Seacliff Ave. at 29th Ave., SF. MUNI bus 29. This small protected cove, named for the Chinese fisherman who camped here during the early 1860s and 1870s, is located below the mansions of the Seacliff district. Swimming is possible if

---

NUDE BEACHES

If you're itching to be bare, the *Bay Guardian*'s annual guide to nude beaches shows Northern California provides 102 locations to bathe and sun in the nude. Here is a sampling of the favorites:

Land's End Beach: Located within the Golden Gate National Recreation Area (GGNRA), this beach sports a small crowd (30 people per day) of mostly gay men.

North Baker Beach: Also in GGNRA, this beach attracts up to 500 people a day.

Devil's Slide: Described as California's safest beach, the stretch of sand located in San Mateo County is never too crowded.

Bonny Doon Beach: Located in Santa Cruz County, this sunny cove provides many naturists—male and female, gay and straight—with an enjoyable sunshine-filled day.

Garrapata Beach: South of Carmel, this is Monterey's best nude beach. Ignore the postings prohibiting public nudity, and join the crowd.

Muir Beach: Look no further for a super clothing-optional day in Marin County. The little cove just north of the more public section is a haven free of trails, cops, and poison oak.

Lilies Beach: Located on a river in Mendocino, this beach can be tricky to get to, but it is worth the effort. With anywhere from 50 to 100 visitors (mostly nude), this sandy spot is full of sun.

you can stand the cold water; this is also a semisecret launching place for surfers going to Dead Mans, an infamous surf spot. A bathhouse (dating back to the 1930s) adds to the charm of this cove, offering changing rooms and showers, drinking water, restrooms, and a protected roof deck where you can get out of the wind.

Ocean Beach: Great Hwy. between Geary Blvd. and Sloat Blvd., SF. MUNI L, N, many buses. Although Ocean Beach runs the length of San Francisco's western edge and is readily accessible, it is desolate most of the year. Besides a few sketchy characters who seem to have ambled their way west to the end of the continent, the usual beachgoers are surfers, runners, kite flyers, and dog walkers. It's true that it's rarely warm or calm enough to swim, but each season still offers a unique beauty. It's a great place to watch a sunset or an oncoming storm, and expert surfers love the winter storm swells. During hot weather, especially in Indian summer (San Francisco's true summer running from the end of August through October), this tranquil coastline is transformed into "Zuma North." At low tide, the beach stretches more than four miles in length. Heading north from Ocean Beach, a trail circles inland, winding around a point called Lands End. Side trails lead to several remote, tiny beaches accessible only on foot.

BICYCLING

Mountain Biking

The sport of mountain biking was invented just north of San Francisco on the slopes of Mt. Tam, and the area has a reputation as a riding Mecca; reality falls somewhat short of reputation. The city of San Francisco itself offers little off-road riding. You can noodle around some paths in the Presidio, Golden Gate Park, and Lincoln Park near Lands End, but the real riding is beyond city limits. The good news for mountain bikers is that the surrounding area is loaded with parks and open-space preserves with extensive, well-maintained trail networks. The bad news is that mountain bikers are not welcome in many of these areas. In an act of "eco-Buchananism," landowners, hikers, and equestrians unhappy with the dramatic growth in trail use occasioned by the sport are dedicated to eradicating it from "their" playground. The following rides are just a sampling of what's available locally; most bike stores carry a good selection of detailed maps showing which trails are open to bikers.

Marin

Marin offers the only convenient mountain biking for San Francisco residents who want to ride from home rather than drive to some trailhead. Strong riders with good range can find many rides accessible without a car; going to the top of Mt. Tam via the Old Railroad Grade is a good trip. Weaker riders may tire before seeing much dirt—stick to the Conzelman and Battery Road area of the Headlands. The **Bicycle Trails Council of Marin** (415) 456-7512 has been fighting hard to preserve trail access for mountain bikers.

Marin Headlands: Combines some of the area's best fire roads, most beautiful scenery, and most hostile hikers and equestrians. Also the most convenient riding for San Francisco residents, with some trails just across the bridge off Conzelman Road (look out for the hordes of tourists in cars); but when the fog rolls in and the wind howls (most of the time), it feels wonderfully isolated. The few trails still open to bicycles climb the steep slopes of the area's many deep valleys, connecting Rodeo Valley, Gerbode Valley, Tennessee Valley, and Green Gulch. If you drive, there are numerous parking areas, many just gravel pull-outs for a few cars. Good starting points include the visitors center and nearby rodeo lagoon (try Miwok and Bobcat trails); and Tennessee Valley (Ridge Road is a challenging climb).

Mount Tamalpais: Mountain biking's birthplace, Mt. Tam offers an incredible expanse of trails down its sloping shoulders, although all have speed limits and some are one-way. The majority of Mt. Tam is controlled by the Marin Municipal Water

BICYCLING

District (see below); the remainder is divided among Mt. Tam State Park, Muir Woods (no biking), and private land. One popular ride, the Old Railroad Grade, climbs steadily from downtown Mill Valley—follow West Blithedale Avenue away from downtown—to the peak's summit 2,600 feet above. Many other trails are accessible from parking areas off Panoramic Highway (Old Stage Road is good) and Pantoll Road.

Marin Municipal Water District: This agency, responsible for providing Marin's potable water, controls an enormous expanse of land, including most of Mt. Tam, and has the same speed limits and other restrictions on trail use. Most access is from the streets of surrounding communities such as Larkspur, Kentfield, Ross, and Fairfax, although there is a pay parking lot at the end of Sky Oaks Road off Bolinas-Fairfax Road. The residents of these communities have been increasingly hostile to mountain bikers from other areas, so park carefully and obey traffic signals on streets. Some excellent trails begin at Phoenix Lake, accessible from the end of Lagunitas Road in the town of Ross: Eldridge Grade Trail leads all the way up Mt. Tam (pay attention to one-way restrictions); for an easier ride, climb Worn Springs Trail to the top of Bald Hill, less than half Mt. Tam's height.

East Bay

The Berkeley hills aren't very kind to mountain bikers, mostly because there isn't much open space where they're permitted. But, if you just have to take a ride after class or on the weekend, some of the East Bay parks will work well enough. A few good resources in the area can help you in this endeavor. **The Bicycle Trails Council of the East Bay** (510) 933-2942 is a great place to find out about trails and biking events.

Redwood Regional Park: For an easy introduction to East Bay riding, try this eight-mile loop through the redwoods. Take the Stream Trail to West Ridge Trail to East Ridge Trail back to the Canyon Trail to the Stream Trail to the starting point. Begin at Redwood Gate, located on Redwood Rd. off Skyline Blvd. on the ridge east of Oakland.

Tilden Park/Wildcat Canyon Park: For more of a challenge, ride the trails between these two parks. The Lone Oak parking area in Tilden park—off Central Park Drive—is a good starting point. The Loop Road Trail leads to Wildcat Canyon Park (stay on the loop trail around Tilden Nature Area) for the longest rides. Nimitz Way is paved most of the way, but offers incredible views and is a good connector trail.

EBMUD: These lands east of Tilden Park offer good riding branching off the Abrigo Valley Trail in Briones Park. The park entrance is located on Bear Creek Road, which is off Camino Pablo Road north of Orinda on Hwy 24.

Peninsula

Of the park agencies on the Peninsula, San Mateo County is the least friendly toward mountain bikers, limiting them to major service roads with few exceptions. California State Parks limits bikes primarily to fire roads (bikes are allowed on some trails). The Mid-Peninsula Open Space District and Santa Clara County allow bikes on many of their single-track trails, especially in the less-busy parks.

Long Ridge Open Space Preserve: This small preserve offers some of the best legal single-track riding on the Peninsula. The trails roll along a ridge parallel to Skyline Boulevard between Page Mill Road and Hwy 9 through a mix of oak-filled canyons and grassy knolls, reaching overlooks with terrific views. Parking and the trailhead are on the west side of Skyline Boulevard, three miles south of Page Mill. Look for the Long Ridge/Peters Creek trail. The trails wind and roll along the ridgetop to an intersection with Skyline Boulevard. Strong riders can continue across Skyline into Upper Stevens Creek County Park.

Montebello Road: The views on this ride are spectacular. Park at Stevens Creek Reservoir off Stevens Canyon Road in the hills above Cupertino. From the parking lot, Montebello Road is a sharp right turn off Stevens Canyon Road another quarter mile up. The first stretch is a good indicator of what lies ahead: grades as steep as 15

SPORTS & THE GREAT OUTDOORS

percent. Nestled among the acres of vineyards at the top is Ridge Winery, vintner of some of California's best reds. The paved portion of Montebello comes to an end not far above the winery and gives way after a few bends to real dirt. The trail climbs approximately 2,000 feet in eight miles up to the top of Black Mountain, one of the highest points on the Peninsula. To return, continue along Montebello to a junction with the Indian Creek Trail—a long, bumpy traverse down a steep hillside. At the bottom turn left on the Canyon Trail toward Stevens Canyon and Saratoga Gap. The final thrill of this trail is where it cuts across a washed-out section of old Stevens Canyon Road. Crossing really isn't difficult, but don't look down until after you're across. A short way down you'll hit paved Stevens Canyon Road—a great wind-down road along a shaded creek. The road joins Mt. Eden Road, which cuts sharply off to the right. Turn left to stay on Stevens Canyon.

Purisima Creek Redwoods Open Space Preserve: This large park offers some long, steep descents through redwood, tan oak, and madrone groves. The preserve is on the west side of Skyline Drive, less than half a mile north of Kings Mountain Road and Tunitas Creek Road. Purisima Creek Trail drops rapidly down from the ridge to wind westward along the banks of Purisima Creek. On your descent you'll pass lumberman's clearings now filled with lilacs and tan oak trees. When you reach the preserve's western entrance, turn right to take Harkins Trail up to chaparral-covered Harkins Ridge, then turn right on Soda Gulch Trail to return to Purisima. Turn left and climb back to your car.

Road Biking

San Francisco

As with mountain biking, road biking within San Francisco's city limits can be difficult. While there are plenty of roads, there are also plenty of pesky automobiles, pedestrians, stoplights, and potholes. Generally, city riding is best left to professionals: bike messengers and commuters. A short jaunt around town or Golden Gate Park can be fun, but for a full spandex and cleats experience, get out of town.

Northern Waterfront: The one great ride in San Francisco follows the northern and western waterfront. Start at Fort Mason and ride along Marina Green to Crissy Field in the Presidio, then follow Mason Street towards the bridge. At the end of Mason Street, turn left on Crissy Field Avenue, then turn right on Cowles Street and right again on Lincoln Boulevard. Lincoln winds all the way through the Presidio to the exclusive Seacliff district, offering spectacular views along the way (check out the famous sinkhole that swallowed a mansion when you get to Seacliff). Lincoln Boulevard becomes El Camino del Mar as it winds through Seacliff to Lincoln Park, then becomes Legion of Honor Drive as you pass the Palace of the Legion of Honor museum. At the edge of the park, turn right on Clement Street and follow it to the end where a short jog left will connect you with Point Lobos Avenue. Turn right on Point Lobos and follow it past the Sutro Baths and Cliff House restaurant to the Great Highway along Ocean Beach. You can follow Great Highway south along the beach to Lake Merced. For variety on the return trip, turn east into Golden Gate Park from Great Highway onto J. F. Kennedy Drive (look for the windmill), and follow J. F. Kennedy Drive to Conservatory Drive to the Arguello Street exit. Arguello leads north to the Presidio back to Crissy Field.

Marin

With lots of open space, well-paved roads, and relatively few cars (especially weekdays), Marin is a cyclist's paradise. San Franciscans can easily ride across the bridge and leave their cars at home. Novice riders can even take a ferry back to the city from Sausalito or Tiburon. The further north and west you go, the fewer cars and the more beautiful.

BICYCLING

Tiburon: People love this ride because much of it is on a path with no cars, and Tiburon offers good restaurants for a leisurely lunch and a ferry back to San Francisco. Pick up the path on Bridgeway Boulevard at the north end of Sausalito and then follow it along Bay to East Blithedale Avenue. Turn right and follow it across Hwy 101, where it become Tiburon Boulevard, all the way to Tiburon, partly on a path.

Mt. Tam: A macho rite of passage for many a cyclist, this challenging route climbs 2,600-foot Mt. Tam, offering brilliant views from the top. Mt. Tam can be approached from all over Marin, but ultimately, most routes follow Panoramic Highway to Pantoll Road to East Ridgecrest Boulevard.

West Marin: For a much longer, more remote ride create your own loop among the pastoral roads of western Marin. Any route that includes these roads is a sure winner: Lucas Valley Road, Nicasio Valley Road, Petaluma-Point Reyes Road, Petaluma Marshall Road, Fairfax-Bolinas Road, Hwy 1 north of Olema, and Sir Francis Drake Boulevard north of San Geronimo.

East Bay

Whether descending from a ridgetop perch high in the hills, or winding through enchanting redwood forests, East Bay cycling offers immense visual variation and physical challenge. After your first ride through the area's striking natural and metropolitan vistas, you'll understand why these roads attract recreational road biking enthusiasts and national-level competitors alike. The hills which run along the east edge of Oakland, Berkeley, Kensington, El Cerrito, and Richmond are particularly strenuous for bikers—weekend warriors should pace themselves accordingly. If you prefer easier rides, follow routes closer to the Bay.

Popular roads include Arlington Avenue above Kensington near Wildcat Regional Park; Spruce Street and Wildcat Canyon Road above North Berkeley near Tilden Regional Park (Cañon Drive and Central Park Drive take riders into Tilden); Nimitz Way, a four-mile section of the East Bay Skyline National Trail that runs north and south along San Pablo Ridge in Tilden; San Pablo Dam Road and Wildcat Canyon Roads near San Pablo Reservoir east of Tilden and Wildcat Canyon Regional Parks; Grizzly Peak Boulevard, Old Tunnel Road, and Fish Ranch Road in the area above the Caldecott Tunnel where the 1991 fire started; Camino Pablo Road and Moraga Way, Canyon Road, and Pinehurst Road in the Moraga Valley beyond the East Bay Regional Parks; Skyline Boulevard and Redwood Road near Redwood Regional Park.

Peninsula

One of the nation's premier road riding spots, the winding roads west of I-280 provide an incredible array of challenging routes for road bikers.

Cañada Road: Flat, expansive Cañada Road is a cruising ground for beginners and a proving ground for triathletes and time trialists. Running parallel to I-280 from Hwy 84 in Woodside north to Hwy 92 near San Mateo, this out-and-back route clings to the eastern edge of the San Andreas Rift with views of the Santa Cruz mountains and Crystal Springs Reservoir. Begin at Woodside Road (Hwy 84) about one mile west of I-280. Cañada Road is closed to cars on the first and third Sunday of the month from April to October, making it a fine stretch for an exhaust-free ride. (15 miles to Hwy 92.)

Kings Mountain Road: Kings Mountain Road climbs to Skyline Boulevard from Woodside to the north of Hwy 84. It is ideal for fast descents and relaxed climbs. Begin on Hwy 84 in Woodside and head west until you see Kings Mountain Road branching off to the right (about 0.7 miles). The climb begins after you pass the historic Woodside Store at Tripp Road, and winds upward past hidden mansions and through Huddart Park. From the summit at Skyline, descend the way you came or consider taking Skyline five miles south to Hwy 84.

Old La Honda Road: An area favorite, narrow Old La Honda Road climbs from Portola Valley to Skyline Boulevard. It heads west from Portola Road about a mile south of Sand Hill Road, making a twisting ascent through stands of oak and redwood to Skyline. Minimal traffic and patched, uneven pavement combined with dense vegetation make for a peaceful, if strenuous, climb. At the top, enjoy panoramic views of the bay and ocean from Windy Hill (0.3 miles south on Skyline), then continue north on Skyline to Hwy 84. Turn right on Hwy 84 to Portola Road (first right at the bottom) back to your starting point. (19 miles)

Portola Valley Loop: Probably the area's best-known cycling route, the Portola Valley loop is a pleasant, mildly hilly circuit passing along the stables and woods of this tranquil community. Due to its popularity, Portola Road's wide shoulders generally whir with the passage of shiny, spandex-clad cyclists. Start at the intersection of Alpine Road and Sand Hill Road. Follow Sand Hill west across I-280 and around the western edge of Jasper Ridge Preserve, where it merges into Portola Road. Pass through Portola Valley and go left onto Alpine Road, which leads back to Sand Hill Road. (12 miles)

Rentals

There are a few places to rent bikes in the bay area. The standard rate is between $5 and $9 an hour with a normal day rate of $25 for a 21-speed bike worthy of most mountain trails. Angel Island also has its own rental program. For information, call (415) 897-0715.

Blazing Saddles Bike Rentals: 1095 Columbus Ave. (Francisco), SF, (415) 202-8888.
Golden Gate Park Skate & Bike: 3038 Fulton St. (6th Ave.), SF, (415) 668-1117.
Park Cyclery: 1865 Haight St. (Stanyan), SF, (415) 751-RENT/7368.
Marina Cyclery: 330 Steiner St. (Lombard/Chestnut), SF, (415) 929-7135.
Missing Link Co-op: 1988 Shattuck Ave. (Hearst), Berkeley, (510) 843-7471.
Caesar's Cyclery: 29 San Anselmo Ave, San Anselmo, (415) 258-9920.

FITNESS & HEALTH CLUBS

Advantage Fitness: 3741 Buchanan St. (Marina/Bay), SF (415) 563-3535. This facility offers three floors of high-tech fitness equipment, including free weights and cardiovascular machines. The environment here is upscale professional with a country club air. The second floor houses a full physical therapy clinic and prescription therapy center where members receive therapy for sports medicine, industrial accident, and personal injury. Pilates training, low impact aerobics, body sculpting, and yoga are offered on the third floor, where members can also benefit from nutrition classes augmented by a full kitchen and mobile catering cart. Locker rooms are well kept and stocked with toiletries.

Bay Club: 150 Greenwich St. (Sansome/Battery), SF, (415) 433-2200. This 75,000-square-foot club is undoubtedly San Francisco's most sophisticated and well-equipped. Where else can you have your shoes shined while you sign up for the golf tournament and wine tasting class before storing your valuables in a safe deposit box. You can play volleyball, basketball, rooftop tennis, and squash, or talk sales strategies in the conference room. There are more than 20 trainers and an on-site physical therapy clinic. Although the club is leviathan in size, the environment is tame and relaxing. After turning a few laps in the pool, you can have a sandwich and salad in the deli and look over the calendar of events which shows an aggressive social calendar and a multitude of classes. The Bay Club is part of chain of clubs throughout the Bay Area, and even has a separate, smaller facility with the same name in the Bank of America building.

Cole Valley Fitness: 957 Cole St. (Cole/Parnassus), SF, (415) 665-3330. A friendly neighborhood facility for those who live out in the Haight or Sunset. They offer the standard aerobics conditioning and strength training equipment, including free weights. Personal training is available, but don't expect anyone to wash your workout clothes for you or rub your aching back.

FITNESS & HEALTH CLUBS

Market Street Gym: 2301 Market St. (Noe/Market), SF, (415) 626-4488. An integral part of community life in the Castro district. Before getting started, members can belly up to the juice bar for a carbo load while checking out the progressive environment. There are two free weight areas complemented with various other body sculpting machines; the cardiovascular equipment is perched in the front windows where you can watch—or show off for—the passersby.

Muscle System: 2275 Market St. (Noe/Sanchez), SF, (415) 863-4700. • 364 Hayes St. (Franklin/Gough), SF, (415) 863-4701. One of the city's best assortments of free weights and bodybuilding equipment can be found at these all-male gyms. Here you'll find lots of plates, dumbbells, barbells, and cable systems machines; the padding on each machine and bench is rawhide leather, giving the place a rugged feel. There is sufficient cardiovascular equipment at each location, but it seems to take a back seat to muscle cell growth. Tanning beds are also on-site, as well as sauna and Jacuzzi privileges.

Pinnacle Fitness: 61 New Montgomery St. (Market/Mission), SF, (415) 543-1110. An upscale option for the financial district crowd. The churn and whir of challenged cardiovascular equipment and heavy breathing creates the din drifting over the balcony of the second floor here. There's nothing like staring up into a 120 pieces of high-tech equipment to stir the blood. Downstairs you'll find the spacious aerobics room where a multitude of classes is offered, including beginning and advanced Pilates, yoga, hi/low impact, and body sculpting. If you're extremely tense, go a few rounds on the heavy bag and then collapse into the massage room.

San Francisco Athletic Club: 1755 O'Farrell St. (Fillmore), SF, (415) 776-2260. Buried in the Fillmore Center apartment complex, this club provides a surprising oasis in a busy neighborhood. A five-lane pool is center stage in this relaxing subterranean environment. On one side of the pool you'll find a spacious aerobics room with a boxing station; on the other, you'll find an exercise room dominated by cardiovascular machines. There are squash, racquetball, and basketball courts and an adequate free weight room. Better living seminars range from "Healthy Cooking" to "Preventing a Torn Rotator Cuff." Before adjourning to the steam room, sauna, or spa, kick back in front of the large screen television in the lounge and have something refreshing from the juice bar.

University of San Francisco Koret Center: Parker and Turk sts., SF, (415) 666-6821. The modern-looking Koret Center offers a full-service athletic facility with two full basketball courts, racquetball, and swimming pool. Personal trainers are provided and will help you develop a fitness program. Many aerobics classes are offered as well as martial arts instruction. The free weight area is moderately supplied, and there are ample Cybex and Nautilus machines. Their outdoor adventures programs offers seasonal activities including camping, skiing, and kayaking.

24 Hour Nautilus: 350 Bay St. (Powell/Mason), SF, (415) 395-9595. • 100 California St. (Davis), Ste. 200, SF, (415) 434-5080. • 1200 Van Ness Ave. (Post), SF, (415) 776-2200. • 303 2nd St. (Folsom), SF, (415) 543-7808. The facility on Bay is a perfect fix for the fitness junkie where milieu takes a back seat to equipment; however, the din of fitness here can be a little overwhelming. There's not much in the way of machinery they don't have here; unfortunately, it's all packed into one room. The aerobics room has a "floating" hardwood surface for joint preservation and carries a class of 34 sessions per week. If you can't exercise your brain and heart at the same time, take a mental break and play some Nintendo by remote control as you ride the Lifecycles (no joke). The locker rooms are what you'd expect given the traffic. The other locations downtown and on Van Ness offer less of the same. The environment at the latter is not as overwhelming, but expect to wait for machines during peak hours (lunch and happy hour). However, rumor has it you may find a date while you wait in the abdomen area or in the coed steam room, sauna, or whirlpool. Beware of the aggressive sales force and billing plan.

SPORTS & THE GREAT OUTDOORS

Women's Training Center: 2164 Market St. (Church/Sanchez), SF, (415) 864-6835. A small but adequate facility for women can be found at the Women's Training Center. Personal training is the focus here, whether you're interested in strength training, fitness conditioning, or bodybuilding. Although small, there are locker and shower facilities and a sauna.

YMCA: 220 Golden Gate St. (Leavenworth), SF, (415) 885-0460. • 1530 Buchanan St. (Webster/Laguna), SF, (415) 931-9622. • 855 Sacramento St. (Stockton/Grant), SF, (415) 982-8801. • 169 Steuart St. (Mission/Howard), SF, (415) 957-1940. The Central YMCA epitomizes the YMCA objective of developing spirit, body, and mind. In their nine-story location in the Tenderloin, members will find they can engage in anything from bodybuilding to HIV/AIDS Wellness Programs. The staff and volunteers are friendly and helpful and eager to make the enormous facility seem like a neighborhood club. Members have access to the basketball court, free weights and resistance machines, swimming pool, and a cornucopia of classes and programs. Here are a few: 20 different aerobics classes, swimming lessons, strength training, racquetball, karate, after-school programs, senior programs, literacy school, and much more. Other locations around the city offer similar programs and services on a smaller scale, each attracting a local clientele.

GOLF

Golfers the world over maintain that playing the courses of Northern California is an experience just this side of heaven. San Francisco abounds with courses both affordable and breathtaking, while the Monterey Bay area is home to the most famous places: Pebble Beach, Cypress Point, and Spyglass.

Chuck Corica Golf Course: One Clubhouse Memorial Rd., Alameda, (510) 522-4321. A great set of muni courses with something for everyone—including two 18-hole courses and a 9-hole, par 3 course. The layout is flat, but challenging. If you like to hit for distance, try the Jack Clark Course. • Public, Two Par 71, 18-hole courses; One Par 27, 9-hole course, Driving range. Greens fee (for 18 holes): M-F $21, Sa-Su $24; for residents M-F $11; Sa-Su $14. Cart fee: $18.

Crystal Springs Golf Club: 6650 Golf Course Dr., Burlingame, (415) 342-0603. A public course located at the edge of the Santa Cruz Mountains overlooking the San Francisco Watershed. • Public, 18 Holes, Par 72. Greens fee: M-F $30; Sa-Su $45. Cart Fee: $12 for double; $15 for single.

Golden Gate Park Golf Course: Golden Gate Park (at 45th Ave.), SF, (415) 751-8987. This short, par three course in Golden Gate Park is a great place for beginners to try out their swing and for more experienced players to sharpen up their short game. The tight fairways require a steady hand. Fog often becomes a factor in this oceanside course, as does the wind when you shoot toward the ocean off the fifth tee. Play is first come, first served. • Public, 9 Holes, Par 27. Greens fee: M-F $10; Sa-Su $13; with resident card M-F $6; Sa-Su $8. No carts available.

Half Moon Bay Golf Links: 2000 Fairway Dr., Half Moon Bay, (415) 726-4438. This public course is a favorite of all who've played it—expensive, but worth it. Located on the coast, it meanders by beautiful homes and is well known for its final hole running downhill on the cliffs along the ocean. On a windy day this hole will challenge any level of golfer, as will the par three 17th where you hit toward the ocean. Truly a pleasure to play. • Public, 18 Holes, Par 72. Greens fee: M-Th $80; F $90; Sa-Su, Hol. $100. Prices include cart fee.

Harding Park: 99 Harding Rd., SF, (415) 664-4690. One of the busiest courses in Northern California, Harding is a challenging 18-hole course surrounded by Lake Merced. It's fairly flat, but heavily guarded by trees. They accept reservations one week in advance of play. • Public, 18 Holes, Par 72, Driving range. Greens fee: M-F $26; Sa-Su $31; with resident card M-F $17; Sa-Su $20. Cart fee: $22.

GOLF

Lincoln Park Golf Course: 34th Ave. and Clement St., SF, (415) 221-9911. With a prime location overlooking the Golden Gate, this course wraps around the Legion of Honor and runs along the cliffs over the ocean. Between the hills, the curves, and the wind, you'll have your hands full. A breathtaking view off of the 17th tee makes it all worthwhile. Call 750-GOLF/4653 six days in advance for reservations. • Public, 18 Holes, Par 68. Greens fee: M-F $23; Sa-Su $27; with resident card M-F $15; Sa-Su $18. Cart fee: $11 per player.

Mission Bay Golf Center: 1200 6th St. (Channel), SF, (415) 431-PUTT/7888. This is *not* a golf course, but with a double-decker driving range, putting green, and pitching green, it's a great place to come to sharpen up your skills. They offer group or private lessons for every level. On soggy weekends, this place is packed with disgruntled golfers. • Daily 7am-11pm. $7 for bucket of balls.

Olympic Club: 599 Skyline Blvd., SF, (415) 587-4800. If you know someone who is a member of this private club, it would be worth your while to make nice with them to get you on the course. Three striking courses are included within this immaculately maintained club, where the pros play when they come to town. The Lake Course is among the top 10 in the country and has hosted three U.S. Opens. The Ocean Course is shorter and tighter, with the added challenges of wind and fog. The scenic, nine-hole Cliffs Course is a new addition to the club. • Private, Two 18-Hole courses, One 9-Hole course, Driving range. Members and guests only.

Pacific Grove Golf Links: 77 Asilomar Blvd., Pacific Grove, (408) 648-3175, (408) 648-3177. A fun public course with two different nines. With some noteworthy holes along the ocean, Pacific Grove is reasonably priced compared to its close neighbors on 17-Mile Drive. • Public, 18 Holes, Par 70. Greens fee: M-Th $24; F-Su, holidays $28. Cart fee: $23. Reservations taken seven days a week beginning at 6:50am.

Palo Alto Golf Course: 1875 Embarcadero Rd., Palo Alto, (415) 856-0881. On the Bay next to the Palo Alto Baylands, this moderately priced muni course is for long hitters. Like a number of courses in this area, it often takes on a totally different character in the afternoon when the wind can really blow. If you don't like high winds, play in the morning—especially in a tournament! Greens fee: M-F $20; Sa-Su $24. Cart fee: $20.

Peacock Gap Golf and Country Club: 333 Biscayne Dr., San Rafael, (415) 453-3111. This flat, sprawling course is very forgiving, but watch out for the creek which meanders through the course. This is a semiprivate course that allows nonmembers to make reservations starting at noon on Thursday for the weekend. • Semiprivate, 18 Holes, Par 71, Driving range. Greens fee: M-Th $27; F $30, Sa-Su $35. Cart fee: $22 (Carts are mandatory before noon on the weekend). Golf spikes are mandatory.

Pebble Beach Golf Links: 17-Mile Dr., Pebble Beach, (408) 624-6611. Words cannot really do justice to the experience of playing this world-famous course. With eight holes skirting the ocean, lush fairways, tough and very fast greens, and breathtaking scenery, golfers travel from all over the world to fulfill their dreams of playing at Pebble, and really pay for it. Probably the only course in the world where the experience is more important than the score! • Resort/Public play accepted, 18 Holes, Par 72. Greens fee: $195 guests, $245 nonguests. Price includes cart fee. Reservations recommended.

Presidio Golf Club: 300 Finley Rd. (in the Presidio), SF, (415) 561-4653. In the fall of 1995, this course opened to the public for the first time since its creation in 1895. Since the army has relinquished control of the course, it has been run by Arnold Palmer's management company, which is in the process of making some major improvements, including a new clubhouse and irrigation system. The course commands dramatic views of the city and is surrounded by eucalyptus and cypress trees. The layout is hilly and challenging, with fog and wind frequently sweeping over the course. People will come from far and wide to play this course, so make a reservation early. • Public, 18 Holes, Par 72, Driving range. Greens fee: M-F $25; Sa-Su $35. Cart fee: $16 for one person, $22 for two people.

SPORTS & THE GREAT OUTDOORS

(The Links at) Spanish Bay: 2700 17-Mile Dr., Pebble Beach, (408) 624-6611. The newest addition to the wonders of the 17-Mile Drive. This public course was designed in the style of the famous British links courses. If you like a difficult course, with lots of sand, wind, and rough, a game here is a must. There are plenty of accommodations for vacations or overnight stays. • Public/Resort, 18 Holes, Par 72. Greens fee: $135 for guests, $165 nonguests. Prices include cart fee. Reservations recommended two months in advance.

Spyglass Hill Golf Course: Stevenson Dr. and Spyglass Hill Rd., Pebble Beach, (408) 624-6611. Part of the renowned trio from the old Crosby Clambake (together with Pebble Beach and Cypress Point), Spyglass Hill is semiprivate, with public play accepted. From challenging holes to very fast tricky greens, to say nothing of the weather, this course can humble the best. A must for the avid golfer. • Semiprivate/Resort. 18 Holes, Par 72. Public play accepted. Greens fee: $150 guests, $195 nonguests. Price includes cart fee.

Tilden Park Golf Course: Grizzly Peak Blvd. and Shasta Rd., Berkeley, (510) 848-7373. Twisting its way through the Berkeley hills, this is a tricky course with plenty of hazards of every variety. The first tee has you looking straight uphill at a daunting par 4. During the summer, the fog rolls in during the evening, adding yet another dimension to the challenge. Reservations available seven days in advance. • Public, 18 Holes, Par 70, Driving range. Greens fee: M-F $21; Sa-Su $30. Cart fee: $11.

PARKS & OPEN SPACE

By city standards, San Francisco has abundant access to parks and open space. Within city limits, in addition to the many small neighborhood parks, Golden Gate Park, the Presidio, Lincoln Park, Fort Funston, Lake Merced, Glen Canyon Park, and John McLaren Park offer ample opportunity to escape traffic and smog. For information on additional nearby parks, see the Peninsula, East Bay, and Marin sections.

Golden Gate Park: San Francisco's equivalent to New York's Central Park. This enormous resource offers acres of green. You can park your car along on streets within the park or the streets around the edges. See Sightseeing section for additional information.

Presidio: This former military base turned park has the potential to be an incredible resource for San Francisco visitors and residents. See Sightseeing section for more information.

Lincoln Park: Acres of open space along the coast in the northwest corner of San Francisco. See Sightseeing section for more information.

BAY-TO-BREAKERS

For the full San Francisco experience, do not miss this event of events, the 7.46-mile running race through San Francisco known as the Bay-to-Breakers. On the third Sunday in May over 70,000 runners, walkers, and general oddballs from all over the world come to make the trek from the bay, at Spear and Howard streets, through the flatter portions of the city and Golden Gate Park to the ocean (hence the name). Entrants include serious, Olympic-quality competitors and serious club-level runners who lead the pack, as well as costume-clad revelers for whom it is more parade than race. Of particular interest is the centipede competition, open to groups of 13. There are strict rules for these groups, including mandatory antennae and a stinger for the tail runner. The race follows a weekend of exciting events, including a costume contest, a health expo, a huge pasta feed, and of course, the post-race party. In order to participate in this event or for more detailed information, call the Bay-to-Breakers hotline at (415) 777-7773 beginning in February or March.

PARKS & OPEN SPACE

PLAYGROUND SPORTS

Several of the health and fitness clubs mentioned above offer organized and team-oriented athletics. However, if you would prefer a little diversity in your cross-training experience, here are a few options.

Basketball

Here are some of the local playgrounds where you are most likely to find a game. The hours indicate when you are most likely to find other people. For league information, contact either Mission Rec Center at (415) 695-5012 or Eureka Valley Rec Center at (415) 554-9528. For information about late-night basketball, contact the Potrero Hill Rec Center at (415) 585-6337.

Alice Marble Playground: Greenwich and Hyde sts. Here is a less-frequented court that sits high atop Russian Hill. The rims are soft—some would say shaky—and the court wide; sunny days will draw a crowd of banker- and lawyer-types. • Sa-Su 11am.

Grattan Playground: Alma at Stanyan sts.. The court here is long and wide; it's not recommended for those with hangovers. However, if you're ready for some fast break action and a diversity of skill levels that matches the city itself, try it out. The rims are soft, and the action in the paint can be intense. • M-F 5pm; Sa 11am; Su 9am.

James Lick Middle School: 1220 Noe St. (Clipper/25th St.). There are two full courts, which helps mitigate the wait during busy times. The short courts facilitate fast breaking, although cherry-picking is frowned upon. Familiar faces show up regularly, and they don't care for sloppy play. • M-F 5pm; Sa-Su 10am.

Julius Kahn Park: West Pacific Ave. (Presidio/Arguello), in the Presidio. The rims here are reportedly a little low, so bring your legs or be dunked upon. Games on weekends are full-court affairs, less populated on weeknights. • M-F 5pm; Sa-Su 10am.

Moscone Recreation Center: Chestnut and Laguna sts. There are lights here so at night you can watch your soft jumper bounce off the unforgiving double rims like a softball on a milk can; occasionally ferocious crosswinds further keep your jumper in check. Nonetheless, plenty show up here to do battle in the paint. On the opposite side of the park (Bay and Webster sts.) there is another outdoor court offering fierce competition and less wind. • M-F 5pm; Sa-Su 10am.

Panhandle: Fell and Clayton sts. Depending on which ex-high school All Stars show up, the games here can be above the rim. However, if you detect a funny smelling smoke wafting across the court, things may be more low-key. • M-F 5pm; Sa-Su 11am.

Soccer

There are several soccer leagues in the Bay Area. Competition for inclusion is fierce.
Latin Soccer League: (510) 732-6804.
Pleasanton Adult Sunday Soccer League: (510) 426-PASS/7277.
San Francisco Coed Recreational Soccer League: (415) 330-8900.
San Francisco Soccer League: (415) 863-8892.
The Golden Gate Women's Soccer League: Contact Ashley Young at (510) 658-8337.

Softball

For information on spring and summer leagues, call the **San Francisco Recreation and Park Department** at (415) 753-7022. The various fields around the city can also be reserved for private affairs; call the above number for more information.

SPORTS & THE GREAT OUTDOORS

Tennis

There are 130 public tennis courts in San Francisco at various parks, playgrounds, and recreation centers. Unfortunately, the demand for these courts can be ferocious—especially when Wimbledon or the U.S. Open is on TV. Only the courts at Golden Gate Park can be reserved in advance by individuals. For reservation information call either the reservations line at (415) 753-7101 or the courts at (415) 753-7001. The Parks Department also offers free tennis lessons to adults and children on a year-round basis. Here is a list of locations with three or more courts; other court locations can be obtained by calling (415) 753-7032.

Alice Marble: Greenwich and Hyde sts. Three courts.

Alta Plaza: Jackson and Steiner sts. Three courts.

Angelo Rossi: Arguello Blvd. and Edward St. Three courts, practice wall.

George Moscone: Chestnut and Buchanan sts. Four courts.

Golden Gate Park: (415) 753-7001. 21 courts. These courts can be, and usually are, reserved in advance; call ahead. $4-6 reservation fee.

James B. Moffet: 26th Ave. and Vicente St. Four courts.

John P. Murphy: 1960 9th Ave. Three courts, practice wall.

Julius Kahn: Spruce St. and Pacific Ave. in Presidio. Four courts.

Margaret O. Dupont: 30th Ave. (California/Clement). Four courts, practice wall.

Midtown Terrace: Clarendon Dr. and Olympia Way. Four courts.

Mission Dolores Park: 18th and Dolores sts. Six courts.

Mountain Lake: 12th Ave. north of Lake St. Four courts.

North Beach: Lombard and Mason sts. Three courts, lights, practice wall.

Ultimate Frisbee

Ultimate Frisbee is more than a game in the Bay Area; as even the pickup players will tell you, it's a way of life. For information concerning leagues in the area, you can contact the **Ultimate Players Association** (800) UPA-4384 or the Cal Sport Club Program at (510) 643-8024. Leagues can be very competitive, and the best way to find out about them is to join in on a pickup game at any of the parks in the area. The most notable ones include:

Sharon Meadows: Off Kezar Dr. in Golden Gate Park just west of Stanyan St. Tuesday and Thursday evenings from 5:30pm until sundown; also late mornings on weekends.

Julius Kahn Playground: Spruce St. and Pacific Ave. South east corner of the Presidio. Wednesday evenings and Saturday mornings.

Willard Park: Derby St. and Regent St., Berkeley. Friday nights after 6pm.

Oakland Tech High School: 4351 Broadway (43rd Street), Oakland.

Other Clubs

San Francisco has many other socially oriented sports clubs; try **Golden Gate Sport and Social Club** at (415) 921-1233 or **San Francisco Urban Professionals Athletic League** at (415) 431-6339.

RIVER RAFTING

The first questions of rafting are which rivers and which seasons to choose. All rivers are rated on an international scale of rafting difficulty from one to five (Class One means "barely moving," and Class Five is for experts only). The rafting season as a whole extends from March or April until September or October, depending on snow melt and reservoir release. Trips can run from an afternoon to a month, and multiple-day trips often combine rafting with camping, hiking, or other wilderness activities. No matter what kind of trip you take, reservations should be made well in advance. In preparation, talk to your guide about what you'll need to pack. For a free directory of California river outfitters, call **California Outdoors** (800) 552-3625.

Access to Adventure: (800) 441-9463. This outfit offers special theme tours, such as Western, Romance, and Polynesian Luau, as well as discounts on their runs through Northern and Central California. $69-$320; group discounts available.

All Outdoors Whitewater Trips: 1250 Pine St., #103, Walnut Creek, (510) 932-8993, (800) 247-2387. A large, interesting outfit with trips to 10 rivers in Northern California. Local trips offer bed-and-breakfast stays on the South Fork of the American and wilderness camping with runs on the American, Stanislaus, Klamath, Merced, Tuolumne, and Salmon Rivers. $74-$429; group discounts available.

American River Recreation: (916) 622-6802, (800) 333-RAFT/7238. Charters from the Bay Area for large groups. Trips include the South, Middle, and North Forks of the American River as well as the Merced. $59-$500; group discounts available.

Beyond Limits Adventures: (209) 869-6060, (800) 234-RAFT/7238. Beyond Limits runs tours in California's Gold Country on the American, Merced, Kaweah, Stanislaus, and Yuba Rivers. $49-$296; group and midweek discounts available.

Cache Canyon White Water River Trips: (800) 796-3091. Absolutely the best deal in the Bay Area if you're just looking for a day trip—the two-person raft, courtesy transportation, even a free Budweiser (after the trip!) is under $30 per person. More involved, more expensive two-day trips also available. Self-guided, Class Three river, and beautiful scenery to boot. $20-$100.

Cal Adventures: 3201 Bancroft Way, Berkeley, (510) 642-4000. Cal Adventures always has competitively priced trips, including a one-day trip to the South Fork of the American River. It can get overcrowded, but the well-trained guides will maneuver your boat through any sticky situation. $76-$86; group discounts available.

Environmental Traveling Companions (ETC): Fort Mason Center, Bldg. C, Buchanan St. at Marina Blvd., SF, (415) 474-7662. This fascinating all-volunteer operation organizes a variety of water adventures for people with disabilities (as well as the able-bodied), ages 12 and up. ETC will take you on trips all over Northern California as well as Colorado and Utah. $45 and up; reservations required.

OARS: (800) 346-OARS/6277, (209) 736-4677. OARS is a well-reputed outfit with rafts on many rivers throughout the western United States, such as the Tuolumne, Merced, Kern, and Rogue Rivers. $49-$2,600.

Tributary Whitewater Tours: (800) 672-3846, (916) 346-6812. Rafts on most of the California rivers. They offer over 20 trips that cover most of the major Northern California waterways. Student and group discounts are available. $60-$330. Web site: http://www.oars.com.

Whitewater Connections: (800) 336-7238, (916) 622-6446. Unusual trips combining rafting with sailing, horseback riding, parasailing, and hot-air ballooning. They will arrange a charter bus for Bay Area groups. $59-$479; group discounts available.

SPORTS & THE GREAT OUTDOORS
SAILING

Where to Sail

The Bay Area provides some of the best sailing in the world. The Bay's major **harbors—San Francisco, Sausalito, Alameda, Berkeley, Richmond**—provide the best access to the central part of the bay. Richmond has better access to San Pablo Bay, which is shallower and less windy. Alameda presents some challenges—including a lengthy estuary and a large wind hole just south of the Bay Bridge. South of the Bay Bridge, try **South Beach** (just south of the bridge), **Oyster Point** (South San Francisco), **Coyote Point** (San Mateo), and **Redwood City**. On the East Bay shore, check out the **Ballena Bay Harbor** just south of the Alameda Naval Air Station, and the **San Leandro Harbor** further to the south.

Some protected areas of the Bay and outlying lagoons are ideal for sailing smaller boats: **Shoreline, Parkside Aquatic,** and the **Leo Ryan Parks** on the Peninsula; **Berkeley Marina's South Sailing Basin;** and Oakland's **Lake Merritt**.

There are many different programs available for those interested in sailing. Bay Area **yacht clubs** are operated for the benefit of members and their guests. **Private sailing clubs** own boats which are available for charter, either skippered or bareboat. With a skippered charter, the charter company supplies both the skipper and boat. Most can only carry six passengers, but **Chardonnay Charters** has a vessel qualified to carry a greater passenger load. Experienced skippers can reserve a bareboat charter, which lets you control your own day on the bay. (Many clubs require American Sailing Association Certification or equivalent experience; it's best to get checked out a couple of days before you intend to sail.) The least expensive charters are those which take place at regularly scheduled times and set their prices on a per-person basis. Reserve early. **Sailing schools** that aren't club-affiliated also provide a viable introduction to sailing, although they are typically reserved for small boats (ideal for learning the basics). One of the best ways to get plugged into the local sailing network is to pick up an edition of *Latitude 38* (415) 383-8200, which publishes lists of crews looking for boats, and skippers looking for crews.

Resources

Note: Clubs and associations should be contacted before visiting in person. Most operate around the clock, with main business hours M-F 8am-6pm.

U.S. Coast Guard NorCal Region: Yerba Buena Island, (415) 399-3400.

Equipment

North Sails: 2415 Mariner Sq., Alameda, (800) 626-9996.

West Marine Products: 850 San Antonio Rd., Palo Alto, (415) 494-6660. • 2200 Livingston St., Oakland, (510) 532-5230. • 295 Harbor Dr., Sausalito, (415) 332-0202. • 2450 17th Ave., Santa Cruz, (408) 476-1800. • 608 Dubuque Ave., South San Francisco, (415) 873-4044.

Harbors

(Note: numerous independent marinas may exist within one harbor)

Berkeley Harbor: 201 University Ave., Berkeley, (510) 644-6376.
Ballena Bay Harbor: 1150 Ballena Blvd., Ste. 111, Alameda, (510) 523-5528.
Half Moon Bay Harbor: 1 Johnson Pier, Half Moon Bay, (415) 726-5727.
Monterey Harbor: City Hall, Care of the Harbor Master, Monterey, (408) 646-3950.
Moss Landing Harbor: P.O. Box 10, Moss Landing, (408) 633-2461.
Oyster Point Harbor: Marina Blvd., South SF, (415) 952-0808.

SAILING

Redwood City Harbor: 1 Uccelli Blvd., Redwood City, (415) 366-0922.
Richmond Harbor: Cutting Blvd., Richmond, (510) 237-9554.
San Leandro Harbor: 40 San Leandro Marina, (510) 357-7447.
Santa Cruz Harbor: 135 5th Ave., Santa Cruz, (408) 475-6161.
South Beach Harbor: Pier 40, off the Embarcadero, (415) 495-4911.

Private Sailing Clubs and Schools

Cal Sailing Club: Berkeley Marina, University Ave., Berkeley, (510) 287-5905. This organization is run by volunteers, including their instructors. It is the least expensive way to get out on the Bay, so call for details. Their membership rates are excellent, they give lessons, and run the organization like an aquatic co-op.

Cass Charters and Sailing School: 1702 Bridgeway, Sausalito, (415) 332-6789. They offer lessons on 22- to 35-foot boats, and offer rentals on a range of sizes.

Chardonnay Charters: 704 Soquel Ave., Santa Cruz, (408) 423-1213. They offer a whale watching charter as well as rent a Santa Cruz 70 but do not offer lessons.

Club Nautique Alameda: 1150 Ballena Blvd. (Suite #161), Alameda, (510) 865-4700. Offers lessons on 25-foot boats and larger.

Club Nautique Sausalito: 100 Gate Six Rd., Sausalito, (415) 332-8001.

Foster City Recreational Department: 650 Shell Blvd., Foster City, (415) 345-5731. The department holds small-boat sailing classes during the summer months. Classes are taught in the nicely landscaped Leo Ryan Park, although they are not offered as frequently as those run by outfits solely dedicated to sailing; no rental service.

Lake Merritt Sailboat House: 568 Bellevue Ave., Lakeside Park, Oakland, (510) 444-3807. Located on Lake Merritt in Oakland's Lakeside Park, this quaint setting seems totally removed from the nearby downtown. There's a year-round rental and lesson programs for small boats.

O.C.S.C. San Francisco Bay Sailing School: 1 Spinnaker Way, Berkeley, (510) 843-4200. Located at the western end of University Avenue. They teach on bigger boats from 24 to 44 feet.

Rendezvous Charters: Pier 40, South Beach Harbor, SF, (415) 543-7333. Offers lessons on 22- to 40-foot boats. Bareboat, skipper, and private charters available.

Spinnaker Sailing Mountain View: 3160 N. Shoreline Blvd., Shoreline Regional Park, Mountain View, (415) 965-7474. Spinnaker offers rentals, children's sailing camps, and small-boat courses at Shoreline Park in Mountain View. Web site: http://www.spinsail.com.

Spinnaker Sailing Redwood City: 451 Seaport Ct., Redwood City, (415) 363-1390. This is the place where Spinnaker teaches big-boat sailing courses and rents charters on the bay. Web site: http://www.spinsail.com.

Spinnaker Sailing San Mateo: 1 Seal St., Parkside Aquatic Park, San Mateo, (415) 570-7331. In San Mateo, look for rentals, children's sailing camps, and small-boat courses at Parkside Aquatic Park. Web site: http://www.spinsail.com.

Universities

UC Berkeley's Cal Adventures: 2310 Bancroft Ave., Berkeley, (510) 642-4000. Their flexible and inexpensive programs are open to all, even nonstudents. Classes and rentals are available through the UC Aquatic Center (at the Berkeley Marina); the rental program is open to those who have completed their intermediate course or the equivalent. Sailing privileges are open to graduates of more advanced courses.

UC Santa Cruz: E. Field House, Santa Cruz, (408) 459-2531. Similar to Cal Adventures, UC SC also allows certified skippers to bring along guests for a small fee.

SPORTS & THE GREAT OUTDOORS

Yacht Clubs
Berkeley Yacht Club: 1 Seawall Dr., Berkeley, (510) 540-9167.
Coyote Point Yacht Club: Coyote Point Dr., San Mateo, (415) 347-6730.
Encinal Yacht Club: 1251 Pacific Marina, Alameda, (510) 522-3272.
Richmond Yacht Club: 351 Brickyard Cove, Point Richmond, (510) 237-2821.
Saint Francis Yacht Club: Marina Blvd., SF, (415) 563-6363.
San Francisco Yacht Club: 98 Beach Rd., Belvedere, (415) 435-9133.
Santa Cruz Yacht Club: 244 4th Ave., Santa Cruz, (408) 425-0690.
Sequoia Yacht Club: 451 Seaport Ct., Redwood City, (415) 361-9472.

SCUBA DIVING

Some of the world's best diving can be found off the Northern California coast—the water, rich in nutrients carried by upwellings and currents, supports a wide variety of marine life. Our giant kelp forests are famous throughout the world, and there's even a good chance that a friendly seal might bump into you on your next dive.

General Information
Monterey Bay Harbormaster: (408) 646-3950.
Destinet State Park Reservation System: (800) 444-7275.
Divers Alert Network (DAN), National Hotline: (919) 684-8111.

Where to Dive
Some of the best and most convenient dive sites in the Bay Area are in Monterey, Pacific Grove, and Carmel. There is also some great diving along the northern coast in Sonoma and Mendocino Counties. The diving along the north coast is generally at an intermediate to advanced level, with trickier entries than the dives in Monterey. Skin diving for abalone is also a very popular sport in this region. As a general rule, the further north you go, the thinner the crowds and the more abundant the abalone, so stay over and make a weekend of it. When deciding where to make a dive, be sure to consult *Diving and Snorkeling Guide to Northern California and the Monterey Peninsula*, by Steve Rosenberg, which gives detailed descriptions of dives all along the coast. Also worth a look is *California Diver*, available at local dive shops.

Shore Diving
Point Lobos State Reserve, four miles south of Carmel on Hwy 1, is a great place to begin diving. The shore entry into **Whaler's Cove** is easy, and the cove itself has a nice kelp bed and wonderful trough covered with invertebrates. **Bluefish Cove** is right nearby, a deeper dive. Diving in the Reserve is limited, so reservations are recommended—call the Destinet State Park Reservation System. The cost is $3 per diver.

Lover's Point is one of the safest and easiest dives in the Monterey Bay area, although no diving is allowed after 11:30am in the summer, making it a popular night diving spot. There are three places to enter from the beach, but Lover's Point Beach is the safest and easiest entry and exit. Another calm spot to dive in Monterey is the **Breakwater**, but it is often crowded. At its deepest, it descends to about 60 feet off the rock reef down to the sandy sea floor and is teeming with life—sea lemons are a common sight. To get there, go to Foam Street at the start of Cannery Row. Parking is available at the dock and costs only $1.

Only those experienced with surf entries and exits should try **Monastery Beach**. There is a large kelp forest community at both ends of this reef, and a plenitude of

SCUBA DIVING

wildlife, but absolutely don't dive if it's rough and choppy—the area is known as Mortuary Beach.

Along the northern coast, **Timber Cove**, 13 miles north of Jenner on Hwy 1, has some kelp beds which are often frequented by seals. With a small dive shop and warm showers, this spot is well-appointed for the diver. Abalone are abundant here. Further north along Hwy 1 in Little River, **Van Damme State Park** has clear waters and an impressive fern canyon. The protected cove makes for an easy entry, and the ocean swell is generally calm. Camping and showers are available. **Russian Gulch**, 10 miles south of Ft. Bragg on Hwy 1, is a protected cove with an abundance of legal-sized abalone (those over seven inches in diameter). Call (707) 937-5804 for camping reservations.

Boat Diving

If you can't find a protected entry and are tired of braving the surf and the surge, most of the area dive shops have boat trips or listings for companies operating in the area.

Wharf #2 and the **Eel Grass Bed** is an easy, shallow dive at the north end of Figueroa Street in Monterey. Access is by boat only and requires the permission of the Harbor master. Be sure to check out the Eel Grass Beds, which are some 30 feet from the pilings. Located between Pescadero Point and Cypress Point, **the Pinnacles** is a boat dive site regarded as one of the best in the area. On a sunny day, the combination of kelp and rocky pinnacles make the scenery quite dramatic. The area is part of the Carmel Bay Ecological Reserve, so no collecting or spear fishing is permitted.

Cemetery Reef, north of Timber Cove on Hwy 1 in Sonoma County, is a long offshore reef accessible by boat. Only advanced divers should attempt this dive, but those who do will be well-rewarded.

Equipment and Lessons

Prices listed at end of each listing are for weekend scuba rental (all gear included).

Aquarius Dive Shop: 32 Cannery Row, The Breakwater, Monterey, (408) 375-6605. • Rental: 2240 Del Monte Ave., Monterey, (408) 375-1933. A good supply of rentals, though reservations are recommended for weekend use. They sponsor a chocolate abalone dive each March. $65.

Bamboo Reef: 584 4th St., SF, (415) 362-6694. • 614 Lighthouse Ave., Monterey, (408) 372-1685. The oldest dive shop in northern California carries a complete spectrum of diving gear. They offer instruction certified by both NAUI and PADI, and continuing diving programs for advanced divers. $61-$90.

Cal Drive & Travel: 1750 6th St., Berkeley, (510) 524-3248. Offers both NAUI and PADI certification and carries most brands of equipment. Performs routine maintenance on regulator and tanks, and organizes diving trips. $38, not incl. snorkel gear.

Dive Quest: 2875 Glascock St., Oakland, (510) 535-2415. • 1500 Monument Blvd., Concord, (510) 827-2822. Offers a complete rental and service program, PADI certification, and classes for all skill levels. Their travel department runs weekend trips to the Channel Islands. $85 per weekend.

Monterey Bay Wetsuits: 207 Hoffman Ave., Monterey, (408) 375-7848. Monterey Bay makes custom wet- and dry-suits for all water sports, and even does repairs and mending. They also sell "no-name" equipment manufactured by leading international brands at bargain prices.

Scuba Unlimited: 651 Howard St., SF, (415) 777-DIVE/3483. A PADI five-star Instructional Dive Center with classes ranging from entry level to Instructor Level Certification. The center carries one of the broadest ranges of scuba equipment in the Bay Area, and also features well-maintained rental equipment and repair services. $66.

SPORTS & THE GREAT OUTDOORS

SEA KAYAKING

Sea kayaking is a sport that you can do safely with a minimum of instruction—sea kayaks are both stable and easy to paddle. If you already know what you're doing, check out the sites listed below. If you want to try it out before committing, many operators have basic programs that will put you and your friends out on the water with a minimum of hassle. As you improve, you can join organized trips to a variety of destinations throughout Northern California. The full moon trips are particularly popular!

Kayaking Sites

With the ocean and the Bay all around us, kayaking sites are abundant. For beginners, the sheltered bays and coves of San Francisco Bay are convenient starting points. The generally quiet waters of **Richardson Bay** between Sausalito and Tiburon and the **Oakland Estuary** both work well. Other typically calm areas include **Bolinas Lagoon** (near Stinson Beach in Marin) and **Tomales Bay** (by Point Reyes). Also look for kayaking operations on the **Russian, Gualala, Albion,** and **Big Rivers.** From these sites you can move on to more exposed parts of the bay and ocean. Yet don't overestimate your ability: the huge swells, ripping tidal currents, and huge ships all pose a formidable challenge. **Half Moon Bay** has a core group of enthusiasts. In **Santa Cruz,** the ocean is beautiful: blue, clear, and almost warm. One of the most popular kayaking destinations, **Monterey Bay,** offers excellent opportunities to view the area's abundant wildlife.

Kayak Rentals and Instruction

Adventure Sports: 303 Potrero St., Santa Cruz, (408) 458-DO-IT/3648. Rents kayaks, along with other water toys, and offers lessons for paddlers of all levels. Beginners are required to take an introductory class in basic paddling and safety before going out in a enclosed boat. Rentals $25/day off-site for experienced kayakers. Same day rental $15/day.

Adventures by the Sea: 299 Cannery Row, Monterey, (408) 372-1807. $25 per person per day; includes lessons and equipment.

BlueWaters Ocean Kayak Tours: 328 Bayview St., San Rafael, (415) 456-8956. BlueWaters specializes in tours and doesn't rent their boats for any other purpose, but their tours include one-day or overnight trips throughout Northern California and special moonlight paddles. Tours $45-$69/day; discounts for groups of six or more. Web site: http://www.bwkayak.com.

Cal Adventures: Office located at 2301 Bancroft Ave., Berkeley, (510) 642-4000. Rowing center at South Basin of the Berkeley Marina. Cal Adventures offers instruction and equipment for reasonable prices, a variety of classes for all levels, and even off-site rentals. Introductory classes are offered almost every weekend and cover basic equipment, safety, paddling techniques, and rescues. Call for class dates and times. Prices $55/students to $65/community. Reservations recommended.

California Canoe and Kayak: 409 Water St., Oakland, (510) 893-7833. Also provides instruction and equipment for reasonable prices, a variety of classes for all levels, and off-site rentals. Introductory classes are offered almost every weekend, which cover basic equipment, safety, paddling techniques, and rescues. Classes given on the Bay for all levels. Then take one of their guided group paddles, especially to Angel Island. $79 intro safety class required for renting. Reservations accepted. Web site: http://www.calkayak.com.

Environmental Traveling Companions (ETC): Fort Mason Center, Bldg. C, Buchanan St. at Marina Blvd., SF, (415) 474-7662. This fascinating all-volunteer operation organizes a variety of water adventures for people with disabilities (as well as the able-bod-

SEA KAYAKING

ied). "Benefit trips" available for students and others (prices vary). Tours start at $35 per day for students.

Gualala Kayak: 39175 Hwy 1, Suite E (behind Don Berard Associates, east side of Hwy 1), Gualala, (707) 884-4705. Located in the middle of Gualala, this outfit offers river or ocean kayaking with self-guided tours that include kayaks, paddles, and life vests. Rates $25/person half day, $35 full day; midweek and group discounts available.

Monterey Bay Kayaks: 693 Del Monte Ave., Monterey, (800) 649-KELP/5357. Offers excellent instruction and a full line of kayaks for rental or purchase. Classes are designed to elevate you beyond mere paddling to enjoying the water and wildlife. The company also organizes special outings—whale watches, trips to bird and wildlife sanctuaries. $25/day with 20-minute orientation. Reservations recommended on weekends. Web site: http://montereykayaks.com/tour.

Sea Trek Ocean Kayaking Center: Schoonmaker Point Marina, Sausalito, (415) 488-1000. Will qualify you to paddle at any kayaking location after a full day of lessons. They teach formal safety lessons on the quiet Richardson and Tomales Bays; from there you can move on to novice and expert daytime trips and night tours of the Bay on the full moon. Full-day introductory lessons $90; tour prices vary.

IN-LINE SKATING

In-line skating has become an increasingly popular sport in the last few years, keeping emergency rooms busy. Shops offering skates for daily and hourly rentals, classes, and even books on the best rollerblading trails have all surfaced to assist the novice through the nuances of a burgeoning sport. As always, San Francisco offers something for everyone: scenic, relaxing stretches, hills, curb jumps, and flat lands for figures and marathon mileage. In-line hockey has also added some texture to the scene. Call Bladium for more information on joining a league.

Where to Skate

Bladium In-Line Hockey Stadium: 1050 3rd St. (nr. Mission Rock Marina), SF, (415) 442-5060. *The* place to go for indoor in-line hockey in the city. They have open rink from 11am-4pm, when you can come and practice your technique. When you're ready for the real deal, come at 4pm for the daily pickup game, or call for the evening league schedule. They've got a sports bar for post-game bragging and a pro shop for stocking up on the essentials. • M-F 11am-midnight; Sa-Su 8am-midnight. Membership is $35. Open rink for members $5. They'll let you try open rink once without a membership. League games are charged by the team.

Embarcadero: An excellent beginner trail runs along The Embarcadero between South Beach and Pier 39. Cruising along the waterfront with Coit Tower and Bay Bridge views, this path offers a respite for suit-wearing thrashers in the Financial District. Riding along the esplanade, you can avoid traffic obstacles—including the new MUNI tracks—and the newly paved road is so wide that four can ride abreast at times. The foot traffic lightens somewhat on the weekends. Once you reach Pier 39, you will have to loop back towards the Bay Bridge or risk colliding with hordes of tourists and small children.

Golden Gate Park: One of the most favored in-line havens in the city. Sunday is definitely the best day for a park skate, when J. F. Kennedy Drive east of Park Presidio is reserved for bicyclists, skaters, and pedestrians—sans automobiles. It's your opportunity to own the road. There are some side hills for a serious leg workout, a slalom course to test your agility, and a would-be disco roller rink near the Conservatory to test grace and timing.

SPORTS & THE GREAT OUTDOORS

BLADERUNNERS

On Fridays at 8:30pm, in-line skaters can join a moving party in front of the Ferry Building at the intersection of Embarcadero and Market streets, the departure point for a skate-a-thon without a cause, except the pure exhilaration of the sport. Skaters, led by David Miles, a leader of the San Francisco skate scene and an incredible in-line dancer, follow the Embarcadero en route to the Marina and the Presidio, then loop around the city before following Townsend Street back to the starting point. Since 1989, skaters have met here weekly with the highest recorded number at 600. The scene includes people of all races, ages, shapes, and sizes, and everybody is invited to join, although the skate does involve some of San Francisco's milder hills (inexperienced skaters take note!).

Marina Green/Presidio: A flat path winds along the water from Fort Mason to Crissy Field in the Presidio. Sailboats, blue waves, and stunning Bay views provide a spectacular backdrop for postcard California living, although on sunny weekends you may be too busy dodging fellow athletes to catch the view. This is an excellent trail for beginners. The path is flat, well paved, and free from automotive traffic.

The Presidio: This former military base now offers some of San Francisco's best in-line skating. Beginners have Mason Street, a wide, flat road along Crissy Field (enter from Marina Boulevard) for cruising; a couple of parking lots are good for practicing turns and crossovers. More advanced skaters can head south into the hills for twists and thrills: the streets get progressively steeper and more dangerous as you head away from the Bay.

Great Highway: Another cool ride starts in Golden Gate Park and follows J. F. Kennedy Drive to the Great Highway. Continue south along the coast to Lake Merced. Tired yet? Didn't think so. Take a cruise around Lake Merced—preferably counter clockwise, which will allow you to face on-coming traffic, avoid some hairy intersections and take you uphill through a steep, traffic-infested intersection. (No matter how good you are, we all know these babies do not stop on a dime.)

Equipment and Lessons

Golden Gate Park Skates & Bikes: 3038 Fulton St. (6th Ave./7th Ave.), SF, (415) 668-1117. With a prime location right across the street from Golden Gate Park, they rent skates for reasonable prices. They also sell a small selection of Rollerblade products. Especially popular on Sundays, when the nearby part of the park is closed to traffic. $6/hr.

Marina Skate & Snowboard: 2271 Chestnut St. (Scott/Pierce), SF, (415) 567-8400. Located in the Marina, this in-line rental and retail shop has the distinct advantage of access to the Marina Green—free of major intersections or hills. $5.50/hr.

Nu Vo: 3108 Fillmore St. (Filbert/Greenwich), SF, (415) 771-6886. Their helpful staff on wheels will fit you with a pair of Rollerblade brand in-line rentals, and teach you how to use them. They also sell Rollerblade skates and accessories. Ask about the Monday Night Extreme Skate. $7/hr., $10/two hrs.

Skate Pro Sports: 2549 Irving St. (26th Ave./27th Ave.), SF, (415) 752-8776. This shop services the opposite side of the park from Golden Gate Skates. Besides maintaining a busy in-line rental business, they also sell in-line and ice skates. They'll arrange a skating lesson for you at your request. A good source for ice hockey equipment. $5/hr.

Skates on Haight: 1818 Haight St. (Stanyan/Shrader), SF, (415) 752-8375. Another rental place with quick access to the park. Sells and rents in-line skates and also offers beginner lessons with overnight rentals. You can pick up the skates the night before, then show up in the morning for your lesson. Call for times and availability. $7/hr.

WINDSURFING

Few areas in the United States have as many breezy days, abundant launch spots, terrific views, and well-stocked windsurfing shops as the Bay Area; it's an ideal place for the avid windsurfers who regularly color our waters. As a general rule, winds pick up in mid-to late-afternoon and die down as the sun starts to set. The best wind is usually on the leading edge of an advancing fog bank; once the fog settles in, it tends to choke off the wind. The summer season (May-July) sees the best wind. You'll need a wet suit year-round in the Bay and the Pacific, as water temperatures are normally low enough to induce hypothermia.

Places to Sail

Most of the beginner and intermediate spots listed will have good wind on clear days in the late spring and summer. On those days when San Francisco's famous fog just refuses to recede, you'll have better luck finding the breezes inland. Call the on-site rental locations for water, wind conditions, and the hours best suited to your skill level.

Beginning to Intermediate

Alameda's Crown Memorial State Beach: This sheltered location with side-onshore winds that push you back to shore has an easy launch that leads directly to the sandy-bottomed sailing site—a great place to practice waterstarts. From I-880 exit west on High St. Take a right on Hwy 61, then a left on Shoreline Dr., which turns into Westline Drive. Crown Beach is on the left side of the road.

Lake Del Valle State Park (Livermore): This inland lake is a beginner's paradise with rentals, lessons, and facilities on-site. Take I-580 east to Livermore Ave., which turns into Tesla Rd. Go right at Mines Rd. and follow the signs.

Intermediate to Advanced

Berkeley Marina: A tricky launch from the sheltered pier at the Marina leads to the main sailing area. Full facilities and plenty of parking can be found at the west end of University Ave. in Berkeley, with on-site lessons and rentals by Cal Adventures. Launch from the piers adjacent to the Cal Adventures yard (follow the signs).

Candlestick Point: The flat-water speed sailing conditions here are ideal for learning and refining jibing technique, although the gusty winds that tend to blow side-off-shore can be hazardous, and the rocky launch spot is a minor nuisance. Take the 3Com/Candlestick Park exit off Hwy 101 and stay right until you see the park entrance. The sailing area is at the south end of the parking lot.

Coyote Point Regional Park: Some of the most consistent winds in the bay, with conditions that vary from moderate winds and flat water near shore to powerful wind-driven chop further out. Excellent facilities with a $4 per car entry fee. Hwy 101 to the Dore Ave. exit., left at off-ramp and follow signs to entrance.

Crissy Field: This is a thrilling spot to sail with large swells and amazing views of the city, the Marin headlands, and the Golden Gate Bridge. Expect to contend with frigid waters, strong tides, howling winds, and immense ships. Enter the Presidio in San Francisco from Marina Blvd. across from the St. Francis Yacht Club and continue straight. Once inside the gate, take the first street to your right and follow it to the beach.

Half Moon Bay Harbor: Flat-water sailing during the winter and summer months. Head south for wavesailing. In Half Moon Bay, a few miles north of the Hwy 92 intersection.

Rio Vista/Windy Cove: This warm-weather, fresh-water sailing spot gets crowded at early morning. The best winds blow from dawn to 10am, and again in the late after-

SPORTS & THE GREAT OUTDOORS

noon. Take I-580 east to Hwy 24 east through the Caldecott Tunnel. Then take I-680 north, to Hwy 242 west, to Hwy 4 west toward Antioch/Stockton. Cross the Antioch toll bridge and continue until the next bridge (Brannan Isld. State Bridge). Windy Cove is located just across this second bridge on the left side of the road.

San Luis Reservoir: Expect extreme (15 to 40 knots) winds from 5am to 10am at this popular freshwater site. The reservoir is approximately 20 miles east of the Hwy 101/152 interchange in Gilroy; just follow the signs.

Waddell Creek State Park: Check out one of Northern California's most celebrated wavesailing playgrounds. Only advanced sailors should try; you must pay an admission fee from Memorial Day through Labor Day. Located about 45 minutes south of Half Moon Bay on Hwy 1; watch for the signs.

Lessons and Retail Shops

ASD: 302 Lang Rd., Burlingame, (415) 348-8485. Caters to the high-end sailor with custom board manufacturing and repairs.

Berkeley Boardsports: 843 Gilman St. (San Pablo), Berkeley, (510) 527-7873. Offers lessons and demos at Alameda's Crown Beach; the store has a wide selection.

Cal Adventures: 2301 Bancroft Way, Berkeley, (510) 642-4000. One of the best buys in the area, Cal Adventures is located on the UC campus but opens all courses to the public at low prices. After completing a beginner's course, students are eligible to buy a two-month, $100 pass that provides unlimited use of all equipment during recreational hours.

City Front Sailboards: 2936 Lyon St. (Lombard/Greenwich), SF, (415) 929-7873. A small but well-stocked shop with custom and retail equipment.

California Windsurfing: 650 Shell Blvd., Foster City, (415) 594-0335. Offers lessons and rentals.

Delta Windsurf Company: 3729 West Sherman Island Rd., Rio Vista, (916) 777-2299. A great retail store and launch site on the shore of one of Rio Vista's most popular sailing spots.

Helm Ski & Windsurf: 333 N. Amphlett Blvd., San Mateo, (415) 344-2711. A full-service shop that hosts swap meets in the summer.

San Francisco School of Windsurfing: Lake Merced (off of 19th Ave.), SF (beginner and intermediate); or Candlestick Point (advanced), SF, (415) 753-3235. A complete range of lessons are available, as well as demo days and windsurfing camps. Completion of a $95 basic course earns you WIA beginner's certification. Advanced classes are offered at Candlestick, where there are also on-site rentals.

Spinnaker Sailing: Shoreline Lake, Shoreline Park, Mountain View, (415) 965-7474. • Port of Redwood City, (415) 363-1390. • Parkside Aquatic Center, San Mateo, (415) 570-7331. Complete WIA certification facilities with a great rental program, besides the beginning course for $130 they offer advanced lessons, and instructor-certification courses. If you don't pass the test after the first course, you may repeat it until you do.

Windsurf Del Valle: 391 Livermore Ave., Livermore, (510) 455-4008. Beginning and intermediate sailors are taught in lessons geared to new participants of the sport.

Windsurf Bicycle Warehouse: 428 S. Airport Blvd., South SF, (415) 588-1714, (800) 628-4599. Production and hybrid equipment, high-end hardware, and an attentive staff.

East Bay

The East Bay complements San Francisco with many qualities that the city lacks, including a spunky, blue-collar spirit; a world-class university with its concomitant intellectual ferment; and burgeoning suburbs. The region runs along the eastern side of San Francisco Bay, stretching from the Carquinez Strait in the north to San Jose in the south; its inland boundary has gradually expanded with the suburban sprawl across the hills to encompass the towns of Walnut Creek, Concord, Pleasanton, and even Livermore—locales technically quite removed from the bay, indeed. Oakland and Berkeley remain the East Bay's most interesting and important communities, together providing a locus for industry, culture, and entertainment.

Basic Information

Oakland Convention & Visitors Authority: 550 10th St. #214 (Broadway), Oakland, (510) 839-9000. • M-F 8:30am-5pm.

Berkeley Chamber of Commerce: 1834 University Ave. (M.L. King), Berkeley, (510) 549-7000. • M-F 9:30am-noon, 1:30pm-4pm.

TRANSPORTATION

Arrival & Departure

By car, the principal route from San Francisco to the East Bay is I-80 over the San Francisco-Oakland Bay Bridge (popularly known as the Bay Bridge). The bridge is notorious for its horrible traffic jams, a situation that will be exacerbated over the next several years as construction to make the span more seismically sound and to replace nearby freeways proceeds. The $1 toll is collected only in the westbound direction.

After reaching the Oakland shore, the highway divides into a number of branches threading throughout the East Bay and beyond. I-80 continues northeast along the bay to Berkeley, eventually heading to Sacramento, Lake Tahoe, and Nevada. I-580 West briefly follows I-80 north through Berkeley before forking west via the Richmond-San Rafael Bridge to Marin County. I-580 East runs southeast towards Hayward, Dublin, and Livermore, continuing into the Central Valley south of Stockton. Off I-580 East near downtown Oakland, Hwy 24 and I-980 peel off, the former running northeast through the Caldecott Tunnel (another traffic nightmare) to Walnut Creek, where it meets I-680; the latter runs southbound around downtown Oakland and becomes one with I-880 (the Nimitz Freeway), the main route to San Jose. (Before the 1989 earthquake, I-880 intersected I-80 near the foot of the Bay Bridge. Currently, this route is undergoing reconstruction, and drivers should expect to encounter traffic delays and detours for some time to come.)

Amtrak: (800) USA-RAIL/872-7245. Amtrak has stations in Berkeley, Oakland, Emeryville, Richmond, Fremont, and Martinez. Trains do not run into San Francisco—passengers take a shuttle bus from the East Bay. The Oakland station is in Jack London Square where Broadway meets the bay near Second Street. The Berkeley station is at Third Street and University Avenue, a short bus ride from downtown and the UC Campus. The Richmond station is conveniently located next to a BART station at 16th Street and MacDonald Avenue.

Greyhound Bus: (800) 231-2222, (510) 832-4730. The Oakland terminal is located just north of downtown at 2103 San Pablo Avenue (on the corner of 20th Street) in a marginally safe area.

EAST BAY

Airports

Of the Bay Area's three airports, the Oakland facility (OAK) is the most convenient for East Bay-bound visitors—especially those planning to use public transportation. It offers a plethora of budget flights; discount airlines like Southwest fly primarily from Oakland rather than the more hectic and distant San Francisco Airport (SFO), which is the hub for more international carriers. San Jose Airport (SJC) is a last resort: it's small, and getting there is a logistical challenge in itself, especially without a car.

See the Transportation chapter for more information about these airports and options for reaching them.

By Public Transportation

Taking public transportation to OAK is reasonably simple. Take the BART Fremont line to Oakland Coliseum station. At curbside, transfer to the Air-BART shuttle bus ($2 in exact change), which leaves every ten minutes for the airport terminals.

Mass transit to the San Francisco airport is a considerably more difficult process, especially if you are trying to maneuver a cache of suitcases. Take BART into San Francisco and transfer to one of the four SamTrans buses (7B, 7F, 3B, 3X) that go to SFO. To connect to the 7B or 7F lines, get off at the Embarcadero BART station and walk a few blocks southwest to the Transbay Terminal on Mission Street between First and Fremont streets. To reach the 3B or 3X bus lines, ride BART all the way to Daly City. A more reliable option is to take BART to the Embarcadero station and catch the **SFO Airporter** (415) 495-8404 bus from the Hyatt Regency (Market and Drumm streets) for $9 (Children $5). It departs approximately every 30 minutes from 5:20am to 11:05pm.

The journey to San Jose Airport via public transport takes at least two and a half hours—it's wise to bring a good book. Two options here: Either take BART into San Francisco, hop on CalTrain to Santa Clara where you'll catch the TA bus to the airport; or take BART to Fremont, catch a TA bus to downtown San Jose, and transfer to the light rail and then a shuttle bus. For additional information, see Public Transportation section of Transportation chapter.

By Private Shuttle

Although getting to Oakland Airport on public transportation is relatively simple, you may consider calling one of the following shuttle services if you can't deal with lugging your bags on BART. Many services will take you to SFO or SJC as well, but call in advance to make sure.

RBJ Shuttle: (510) 562-3055.
South and East Bay Airport Shuttle: (800) 548-4664.

By Taxi

Travelers in groups or with larger budgets can splurge on a taxi or limousine ride. A cab to the Oakland airport runs about $25-$30, to San Francisco $30-$40, and to San Jose $60 and up. Limos are even more expensive, so unless you have an extravagant expense account, forget those champagne wishes and caviar dreams.

Public Transportation

The East Bay is served primarily by **BART** (Bay Area Rapid Transit) and **AC** (Alameda County) **Transit**. BART trains provide regional transit throughout the East Bay and San Francisco. AC Transit operates the bus system throughout Alameda County, from Richmond to Fremont as well as service across the Bay Bridge; recent budget problems have led to service cuts, including an end to late-night transbay service.

When the Loma Prieta earthquake temporarily closed the Bay Bridge, ferry service between the East Bay and San Francisco was reinstated for the first time since the bridge was constructed in 1936. Boats continue to sail from Alameda, Oakland, and Vallejo to San Francisco. (See Transportation chapter for additional information on routes and fares.)

UC Berkeley Transit Information: (510) 642-5149; UC Davis Shuttle (916) 752-8287; UC San Francisco Shuttle (415) 476-1511; UC Santa Cruz Shuttle (408) 459-2803. UC Berkeley Walk Service: 642-WALK/9255. For destinations close to campus, UC Berkeley offers several public shuttles for under a dollar. The **Local Shuttle** runs weekdays from the campus to the downtown Berkeley BART station; vehicles depart from the Bank of America building on Shattuck Avenue every ten minutes. The **Hill Shuttle** leaves Hearst Mining Circle every half hour and meanders up to the Lawrence Hall of Science, the Botanical Gardens, and Strawberry Canyon. The free **Safety Shuttle** runs every evening during the school year: to north side every half hour, between the Berkeley BART stop and campus at the same interval, and to the libraries and residence halls every 20 minutes (after 10pm, every ten minutes). Stop by the **ASUC Information Desk** in the student union at Bancroft and Telegraph avenues for a schedule or call the **UC Berkeley Transit Operations** information line for details. The school also supplies a free escort service for anyone traveling a reasonable distance to or from the campus at night—call and an escort will respond within 15 minutes. If you're traveling to other UC institutions, you may be able to catch a ride on one of the inter-campus shuttles (you must be a student, faculty, or staff participating in a UC-related activity to ride the buses to the Davis or Santa Cruz schools).

Berkeley Trip Commute Store: 2033 Center St. (Milvia), Berkeley, (510) 644-7665. Carries loads of Berkeley and Bay Area transportation info, including options on campus. • M-W, F 8:30am-5:30pm; Th 9am-6pm.

NEIGHBORHOODS & HOUSING

If you're moving to the East Bay, you won't be alone: the area's population has been growing rapidly. The lands spreading to the north, east, and south from the Bay Bridge have been exploited for acres of affordable (by Bay Area standards, at least) housing, although this growth has created its share of faceless bedroom communities, not to mention some loathsome traffic snarls. Still, many people feel they get more for their money in the East Bay than in San Francisco, Marin, or on the Peninsula. And BART gives the East Bay an edge for those commuting to jobs in downtown San Francisco. As to be expected, housing up in the hills costs more than in the flats and valleys, whether it's the Berkeley slopes or those of Orinda or Danville.

Berkeley

Berkeley is best approached as a collection of distinct neighborhoods. **Southside**, flanking the lower edge of the UC campus around Telegraph Avenue and Bancroft Way, bustles with bookstores, espresso bars, pizza parlors, and a small taste of what Berkeley was like during its radical heyday. This is the most popular area for students seeking school-year housing, with accommodations becoming more expensive the closer one gets to the campus. Residents cope with such unpleasantries as dirty streets and petty thievery, but if you must be close to the action and don't mind spending two months trying to find an apartment, then Southside is your kind of place.

The Oakland/Berkeley firestorm of 1991 destroyed many lovely homes and several apartment complexes in the **Claremont** district, a hillside enclave southeast of the university; as a result, housing here is still in transition, i.e., under construction. The unburned areas do offer some in-laws and living options with single families, as well as work exchanges and sublets. Prices are high, but the area is truly lovely, with exceptional views across the Bay.

Just east of Claremont you'll find **Elmwood**, the hub of which is College Avenue near Ashby and Alcatraz avenues. Cleaner than Southside but still relatively close to campus, Elmwood is full of large houses and apartment buildings where you can find moderately priced lodging. One of the oldest neighborhoods in Berkeley, Elmwood is also one of its nicest places to live.

EAST BAY

South Berkeley, the city's poorest section, is a primarily residential area of smaller houses and apartment complexes. Although it is relatively run-down in spots, this flat, open region is popular with some families and students on budgets who don't mind a bit of a trek to campus.

The **Flatlands** comprises Berkeley's geographic center and is well populated with cats and VW buses. It features some affordable apartment houses, as well as a large number of modest homes for single families or groups of students. You can find some good real estate deals here, although this family-oriented area isn't quite as cutting edge as some of the city's other neighborhoods.

In the **West Berkeley/Oceanview** district, west of downtown, you'll find an appealing mix of light industry and residential properties. Many students and artists have settled in converted warehouses near the freeway, giving the area a funky, SoHo feel. A booming but cultured shopping district is centered around Fourth Street.

North of University Avenue, you move into **Westbrae**, a comfortable, established neighborhood. Perhaps because it's a fair distance to campus and downtown, Westbrae is a little slice of middle-class reality. Single-family houses dominate the streets, with only a few apartment complexes to be seen.

North Berkeley revolves around the so-called **Gourmet Ghetto**, the stretch of Shattuck Avenue roughly bounded by Virginia and Eunice streets, where you will find excellent cafés, bakeries, a cheese shop, a wine store, a fruit and vegetable market, a New York-style deli, and numerous restaurants. This upscale area is popular with Berkeley natives. There are a good number of multi-unit buildings in the vicinity, and rental homes tend to be on the cozy side.

Northside, which, logically, borders the northern edge of the university at Euclid and Hearst, is much more sedate than Southside. Close to campus, there are lots of student apartments and co-ops; further out, you'll run into more expensive detached homes. A significant number of grad students and professors live in this relatively safe neighborhood on a long-term basis, making apartments appreciably harder to find.

The **Berkeley Hills** provide a magnificent survey of San Francisco and the Golden Gate Bridge. Some of the East Bay's finest estates are tucked away in these hills. The views from the winding, steep streets are spectacular—and so are the mortgages. Apartments are rare here, but you may find the occasional cottage or in-law unit in a private home. Tilden Park is nearby, but few buses run through the area, so getting around without a car can be a challenge.

The main thoroughfare of **Thousand Oaks** is Solano Avenue, thick with more fine restaurants, coffee houses, and bookstores. The Solano Avenue corridor is home to a large portion of the UC faculty because of its pleasant, domesticated atmosphere. Most of the housing consists of single-family homes, with students snatching up the few vacant apartments and commuting to campus on public transportation.

Oakland

Oakland's neighborhoods are very diverse, ranging from expensive houses in the hills to run-down dumps in the middle of gang turf, so be careful where you look. Abutting the Berkeley border, **Rockridge** is a safe and very pleasant neighborhood convenient to a major BART station as well as being an easy (aka, flat) bike ride to campus—two qualities that make this part of town popular with a mix of students and professionals. There are many comfortable apartments in pretty bungalows, cottages, and lovely early century homes.

Situated above Rockridge in the Oakland hills, **Montclair** has primarily single-family homes (look for in-law accommodations) and a sprinkling of apartments. Transportation is somewhat problematic here for those without cars, and rents are steep, making this area more suited to couples with kids than to students and grads. Slightly south sits **Piedmont**, an extremely affluent, independent town—one of the wealthiest in the entire Bay Area, in fact—which is wholly surrounded by Oakland. The residences (not a few of them falling into the mansion category) are large and gracious, and not surprisingly, asking prices are formidable. There is a strong sense of community here, and the city services (parks, schools, police, etc.) are enviable.

In the heart of Oakland, the area encircling **Lake Merritt** is a best-of-both-worlds option for those who enjoy city life but still crave fast access to a natural setting. There is a wide variety of character-laden apartment buildings dating from the 1920s up to the 1950s throughout the neighborhood, as well as a couple of BART stations. Rents are reasonable, albeit slightly more expensive than in some other parts of the urban center.

In the environs of **Piedmont Avenue** above MacArthur Boulevard, you'll find tasteful homes and quaint cottages at decent rates. The Avenue itself is full of shops and cafés, though the feeling it exudes is much more familial than forward. By contrast, **Northwest Oakland** is a run-down and sometimes dangerous place to live, but many students flock to it for its cheap quarters and convenient transport to campus.

Surrounding Communities

Emeryville is a growing, funky burg. A little plot parallel to I-80 and sandwiched between Oakland and Berkeley, it is an interesting mix of factories, luxury condominiums, artist's studios, lofts, a few groovy restaurants and cafés, and mega-shopping centers. Its census claims the most artists per capita in the United States, though with only 4,300 residents, this is not a terribly significant statistical feat. Rents are generally lower here, and finding a place to live is not a problem. Shared live/work spaces and tiny Victorians are the most popular housing arrangements.

Due north of Berkeley, **Albany** is a small, quiet area with some nice shops and cafés gracing its predominately residential streets. Albany conjures the classic image of small-town America: quaint and sleepy. Housing consists mostly of small single family homes and apartment buildings built in the 1940s and 50s.

El Cerrito is a strictly residential town. Recently, it has found favor with students because of its rock-bottom rents and high vacancy rates. El Cerrito is a good 20-minute bike ride from downtown Berkeley and the UC campus.

The cost of living in **Richmond** is lower than in the rest of the East Bay. However, the city is not as safe or aesthetically pleasing as other communities in the area. On the plus side, BART is close, and the Point Richmond neighborhood is an interesting alternative hideaway with restaurants, bars, and bay views.

SIGHTS & ATTRACTIONS

Berkeley ★

Berkeley looms large in the national psyche. Tourists picture it as a hippie haven, incoming students envision ivory towers, and long-time residents cling to a more pastoral image of the hillside rose gardens they played in as children. Berkeley indeed has many faces. As any tour guide will tell you, the city offers a wide range of environments and settings, some just as weird as the people in Wauwatosa, Wisconsin think they are, others as serene and beautiful as anything Walt Whitman ever hoped to see.

University of California, Berkeley ★: bounded by Bancroft Way, Oxford St., and Hearst Ave., (510) 642-5215. The university campus, intellectual heart and soul of the city, encompasses many extremes. Step onto **Sproul Plaza**, epicenter of the infamous Free Speech Movement of the 1960s and more modern protests, and you'll instantly become a player in a unique urban theater. Pseudo philosophers spout theories, street people sleep on benches, serious academic types mill about, and bands of Japanese tourists roam freely in search of the exotic. On Sproul, you can never be sure which person is the tenured professor and which is the unemployed poet, but the guessing game is endlessly amusing. **Lower Sproul** usually hosts a more intimate crowd—the odd little statue of the Cal bear mascot is a perennial attendee, as are the weekend groups of highly entertaining drum and bongo players. Hike on through

EAST BAY

Sather Gate to take a breather in more bucolic environs. Take a left to wander through calm eucalyptus groves along picturesque **Strawberry Creek**, or head straight to investigate the classic architecture and marble pillars of the world-renowned **Doe Library**. Upstairs you'll find a stunning reference room exuding an impressive aura of knowledge, and downstairs you can wander into the **Morrison Library** with its cozy armchairs and Sunday papers. No visit to campus can be complete without a stroll through **Faculty Glade**, nestled between the picturesque **Men's Faculty Club** and the music buildings, **Morrison** and **Hertz Halls**, sometimes catching an impromptu string quartet en route. If you've befriended one of the many canines that apparently thinks the campus is one big dog house, it's also a perfect place to throw a few sticks. While the central part of the campus sits in a compact area, the school actually extends far to the east, past the Lawrence Hall of Science and the Botanical Gardens to the open space in the hills above.

Visitor Information Center: 101 University Hall, 2200 University Ave., (510) 642-5215. The source for campus maps, information, and organized tours. Also offers a pamphlet outlining a self-guided trek. • M-F 8:30am-4:30pm; Sa 10am-4pm.

Botanical Gardens ★: Lower Centennial Dr., (510) 642-3343. Over 30 acres of flora from all over the world. The gardens are threaded with hiking trails that lead through the surrounding hills. • Daily 9am-4:45pm. Visitor Center, daily 10am-4pm.

The Campanile ★: Sather Tower, (510) 642-3666. Berkeley's most recognizable landmark, Sather Tower is modeled after the structure in St. Mark's Square in Venice. For a great view, take a fun trip to the top (after the elevator ride, there are 38 steps to climb to the observation deck). At 307 feet, you'll be the highest thing around (and in this town, that's saying something). A carillon of 61 bells, saber-toothed tiger bones, and other artifacts from the La Brea Tar Pits are housed here. • M-Sa 10am-3:30pm; Su 10am-2pm. $.50 elevator charge.

Lawrence Hall of Science: Middle Centennial Dr., (510) 642-5132, (510) 642-5133. See "Entertaining Children" below.

Museum of Paleontology: Earth Sciences Bldg. (McCone Hall), (510) 642-1821. Those with a fetish for fossils should visit the Museum of Paleontology on the ground floor of the earth sciences building. A dinosaur lover's haven, it's not exactly Jurassic Park, but makes for an engrossing afternoon amusement for the kids. • M-Th 9am-10pm; F-Su 9am-5pm. Free.

Phoebe Apperson Hearst Museum of Anthropology: 103 Kroeber Hall, Bancroft Way at College Ave., (510) 642-3681. An archeological and anthropological treasure trove. Only a small portion of the huge collection can be displayed at a time. Highlights include tools made by Ishi, the native American who encountered an anthropologist in 1911 in Northern California and was the subject of extensive study until his death in

---

THE NAKED MEN AND WOMEN

Hang out on Telegraph Avenue long enough and you'll see every fashion statement around, including the recent clothing comment of "No thanks, none for me." The cry for the freedom of the skin was first uttered by Andrew Martinez, aka "The Naked Man," in his former career as a UC Berkeley student. Andrew has since been suspended for his anti-wardrobe activities and begun appearing nationwide to speak for his cause. Other nudists have followed suit and come out into the streets and the Berkeley City Council chambers in support of their freedom to unveil. Three naked adults appeared on Shattuck one summer afternoon pushing a baby carriage between them. They caused some slight traffic problems, but no one noticed if the baby was wearing any clothes. Whether it's just a passing fad or the start of a new age of Aquarius, the row has been enough to make anyone stop and contemplate. "To clothe or not to clothe"—in Berkeley, that is the question.

SIGHTS & ATTRACTIONS

1916. He was believed to be the last survivor of his pre-industrial society, the Yahi. Inquire about special programs, and don't miss the bookstore. • M-W, F 10am-4:30pm; Th 10am-9pm; Sa-Su noon-4:30pm. Admission $2; $1.50 seniors; $.50 children.

University Art Museum and Pacific Film Archive: 2626 Bancroft Way, Berkeley, (510) 642-0808. Cutting-edge expressions fill Berkeley's art museum, a dramatic modern building heavy on concrete and glass. The galleries showcase 20th-century painting, sculpture, and photography—it boasts the world's largest public collection of works by Hans Hofmann, a gift from the artist used to help found the museum—and also displays works by European and Asian masters. The museum is home to the Pacific Film Archive, a resource of more than 6,000 films, with Japanese and Soviet cinema, animation, and American avant-garde celluloid well represented. • W-Su 11am-5pm; Th 11am-9pm. Free 11am-noon and Th 5pm-9pm. Admission $6; $4 seniors and non-UC students; free for UC students and children under 12.

Southside ★★: Telegraph Avenue south of campus. The campus atmosphere spills over into this ghetto of student life—a land of tunes and tomes, croissants and cappuccinos. Follow famed **Telegraph Avenue** south from Sproul Plaza through the maze of tie-dye T-shirt vendors and other persistent artisans, and discover some of the Bay Area's best bookstores, record emporiums, and coffee houses along the way (see the Bookstore, Record Store, and Restaurant sections below for descriptions of the many offerings, especially **Cody's Books** and **Rasputin's Records**). As you shoulder through the crowds, protesters will ask for your signature, panhandlers will seek your patronage, and countless delicious restaurants will tempt your tummy. Although long-time residents can't handle the Telegraph experience for any prolonged period of time, it's an exhilarating place no one should miss—and don't forget **People's Park**, located at Telegraph and Haste on one of the most hotly contested pieces of university land in history. At present, the homeless population and the communal gardens share space with the school's outdoor volleyball courts. Rumors abound that UC will eventually erect dormitories on the site, but stories to that effect have been around since the 60s (as have more than a few of Telegraph's denizens). Nearby you'll find noted local architect Bernard Maybeck's most famous work, the **First Church of Christ Scientist** (2619 Dwight Way). Telegraph is liveliest on the weekends, so if you're driving in, you'll have to cash in all your parking karma to find a space in the residential neighborhoods southwest of the area—or else resort to one of the garages.

Judah Magnes Museum: 2911 Russell St., Berkeley, (510) 549-6950. This historic mansion in the Claremont district houses the largest permanent collection of Judaica in California. Highlights include ceremonial items, fine contemporary works by Jewish artists from around the world, as well as a rare-book and manuscript library. • Su-Th 10am-4pm. Free.

North Berkeley: The area just north of the UC Berkeley campus is known as, you guessed it, **Northside**, the smaller mirror image of Southside. Its proximity to campus gives it a student feel, but on this side of town the air is quieter, full of classical music and lofty thoughts from the nearby **Graduate Theological Seminary** (2400 Ridge Rd.). The coffee houses serve more mature undergraduates and graduates, and the hilly neighborhood streets are cleaner and less crowded with apartment houses. **Codornices Park**, at 1201 Euclid Avenue, is well-known to both families with toddlers and young couples with Frisbees. Just across the Euclid lies the inspiring **Berkeley Rose Garden ★**, nestled in a natural amphitheater with westward views of Mt. Tamalpais and the Golden Gate Bridge. Some 250 species of roses cascade down terraces and trellises to a pool at the bottom. The flowers are in bloom from late spring into early fall. There are few finer places to watch a sunset.

To the east you'll find the hills of **North Berkeley**. Built on a smaller scale than the Claremont area, North Berkeley is home to many Berkeley faculty and professionals. The streets are narrow and winding, the homes are gorgeous and expensive, and the views are breathtaking. It's a great neighborhood for a romantic stroll; there are lots of hidden paths and overgrown stairways, and you might even see deer nibbling on shrub-

EAST BAY

bery at dusk. A long string of parks and green spaces runs north-south along the spine of the hills to the east. **Tilden Park** ★, located just above North Berkeley, is a wondrous natural world unto itself. (See Entertaining Children below.) Serious mountain bikers and hikers should also consider adjacent **Wildcat Canyon Park** and **EBMUD (East Bay Municipal Utility District)** watershed land (the latter for hikers only).

Downtown, West Berkeley, and the Berkeley Marina: Just west of the campus lies the **downtown** district of Berkeley. Plagued by the sluggish economy and a persistent homeless problem, the business and civic center has a mixed atmosphere of wacky small town spirit and depression. Excellent restaurants, movie theaters, and a host of other entertaining options promise a rewarding night out. Parking is not particularly easy, but if you're taking mass transit, the Berkeley BART station is right in the midst of downtown at the corner of Shattuck and Center streets—look for the horde of teenagers hanging out. The commercial area and its endless brigade of photocopy shops and restaurants extends south down Shattuck Avenue into Oakland. University Avenue is also a busy commercial street, lined with all manner of motels, auto parts stores, eateries, and ethnic shops.

West Berkeley borders the bay, and has been an increasingly exciting scene in recent years. A number of good restaurants have sprung into being around **Fourth Street** at the foot of University Avenue, and discerning diners have been flocking here accordingly. West Berkeley also hides numerous outlet stores in its warehouses and factories, making the area well worth a visit for serious shoppers, as well.

The light-industrial area east of I-80 is becoming popular with artsy types, and Heinz Avenue is becoming something of an artistic thoroughfare. **Aquatic Park** parallels the freeway from just north of Ashby Avenue to just south of University Avenue. It's much too close to I-80's congestion and noxious fumes to give a true sense of the outdoors, but there is a bike path and a variety of migrating shorebirds to get to know.

Takara Sake: 708 Addison St., (510) 540-8250. A large producer of this Japanese rice wine, supplying much of what is consumed in America. Free tasting.

Kala Institute: 1060 Heinz Ave., (510) 549-2977. Located in a renovated Heinz Catsup factory, Kala hosts changing exhibits of outstanding printmakers. • Tu-F 11am-5pm.

Artworks Foundry and Gallery: 729 Heinz Ave., (510) 644-2735. A good place to check out emerging local sculptors' works. Huge metal, stone, and mixed media pieces are housed here behind the Magic Garden Center. • M-Th 8am-5:30pm; F 8am-noon.

Urban Sculpture Garden: Fifth and Harrison sts. "Urban" is the operative word here, "garden" being a euphemism for this industrial wasteland next to a truck yard. You should park in the truck lot, wear long pants and long sleeves, and absolutely not come alone—the neighborhood is excessively creepy. The sculpture, however, is quite good, though much of it is obscured by thriving weeds. Visit only during the day.

BERKELEY

Wondering where Berkeley got its name? It all started with an Anglo-Irishman named George Berkeley, a philosopher, writer, and Bishop of Cloyne. Berkeley was a frustrated explorer who wrote a poem called "Destiny of America," which contains the prophetic line "Westward the course of empire takes its way." Bishop Berkeley never actually made it to America, let alone the Wild West. But one of his admirers arrived in California a couple of hundred years after Berkeley wrote his poem: the Reverend Henry Durant, a missionary with an interest in higher education. After opening the Contra Costa Academy in Oakland, Durant decided that the saloon-filled streets of that town were not an appropriate setting for a New England–style college. In 1855 he moved the operation to farmland in what is now Berkeley. In 1866 the officers of the College of California decided to call the projected town Berkeley, in honor of George's high-minded pursuits.

SIGHTS & ATTRACTIONS

Berkeley Marina: University Ave. west of I-80. Everyone should know about this hidden jewel of Berkeley. Follow University Avenue west past the freeway, and you'll find yourself on a peninsula surrounded by breathtaking vistas of San Francisco and the Golden Gate Bridge. Explore this lovely little area with its pleasant playgrounds and rock-filled inlets, catch fish with the locals, or dine on a chili dog while watching the waves.

Oakland

Oakland has neither Berkeley's reputation nor its tourist industry; it's a small but vital city struggling to survive America's metro-area woes. The recently returned professional football Raiders embody Oakland's rough, scrappy character. Nevertheless, its neighborhoods offer some interesting sights, strolls, and historical landmarks.

Downtown: Oakland's central business district has been striving to become an urban renewal success story—and just might achieve that goal. The landscape consists of a handful of corporate skyscrapers of varying vintage (including the headquarters for hometown hero Clorox) and the sylvan Lake Merritt. **Lake Merritt** and its **Lakeside Park** are a breath of fresh air smack in the middle of Oakland. By no means strenuous, a walk around the lake's perimeter is both scenic and healthful, though after dark you may find it safer to take your constitutional indoors. Lakeside Park lies on the north shore of the water, with such amusements as picnic tables, boat rentals, gardens, and occasional free concerts. Each June, the **Festival at the Lake** draws throngs of people to experience live bands, crafts booths, and ample good eats. The park also houses **Children's Fairyland** (see Entertaining Children below).

Downtown Oakland also contains a vibrant **Chinatown,** with many excellent restaurants and fascinating specialty shops, most of which lie between Eighth and Ninth and Franklin and Harrison streets. Three other notable downtown landmarks are the towering **Oakland Tribune Building**—former home to the daily paper of that name—at 13th and Franklin; **City Hall** at Fourth Street and Broadway, an imposing Beaux Arts granite edifice; and **Preservation Park** at 12th Street and Martin Luther King Jr. Way, a stylistically diverse collection of Victorian-era buildings that were moved out of harm's way during downtown redevelopment and set aside as a reminder of Oakland's elegant past.

The Oakland Museum ★★: 1000 Oak St., Oakland, (510) 238-3401. The Oakland Museum, dubbed the "California Smithsonian," is a modern structure surrounded by terraced gardens, fish ponds, and outdoor pathways. Visitors can journey through an Ohlone Indian village, hark back to the bawdy times of the Gold Rush, discover the awesome power of California's earthquakes, and relive the rocking story of the counterculture. The Gallery of California Art features more than 550 works spanning the state's visual and crafts heritage, while the Hall of California Ecology presents biotic zones from ocean to high desert. Cowell Hall contains artifacts and objects from 1848 to the 20th century. Kids love sitting on the massive sculptured redwood burl ring entitled *The Planet,* which represents the tripartite focus of the museum: the Golden State's art, history, and ecology. • W-Sa 10am-5pm; Su noon-7pm. $5; $3 for seniors and students; free 5 and under; free Su 4-7pm. Reasonable parking in garage daily 8am-6pm. Wheelchair access on Tenth and Folsom St.

Paramount Theatre: 2025 Broadway, Oakland, (510) 893-2300. Oakland's premiere performing arts venue is a gorgeous art deco movie palace designed in 1931 by architect Timothy Pflueger. The acclaimed Oakland Ballet, the Oakland-East Bay Symphony, and various touring music and theater groups now tread these venerable boards, in addition to the popular screenings of Hollywood classic films and mighty Wurlitzer recitals.

Jack London Village/Jack London Square: Embarcadero between Alice Street and Broadway. A favorite with out-of-towners, this renovated wharf overlooks the bustling Port of Oakland and houses a variety of shops, restaurants, and museums. Its namesake famous author spent much of his youth in Oakland before seeking adventure

EAST BAY

in the Yukon; he twice ran unsuccessfully for mayor on the Socialist ticket. **Jack London's Yukon Cabin** incorporates original timbers into a replica of the place London lived while prospecting for gold in Alaska. Next door, **Heinold's First and Last Chance Saloon** has changed little from the days when London drank there. The newer commercial development of Jack London Square is centered around an enormous Barnes & Noble bookstore, and hosts everything from farmers' markets to boat shows.

Jack London Museum and Bookstore: 30 Jack London Sq., Ste. 104, Jack London Village, Oakland, (510) 451-8218. This relatively new museum pays homage to one of America's most noted and prolific writers (and a one-time UC Berkeley student). It illustrates, through memorabilia and a collection of rare books, the history and impact of London and his contemporaries. • Tu-Sa 10:30am-6pm. Free admission but donations requested.

Ebony Museum of Art: 30 Jack London Village, Stes. 208-209, Oakland, (510) 763-0141. Upstairs from the Jack London Museum is this impressive collection of African-American antiquities. A highlight is founder and director Vernita's collection of slavery-era "soul food art": hand-painted jewelry and sculpture made from what she calls survival food—pig knuckles, peanuts, collard greens, and beef bones. The museum provides programs for Bay Area schools. • Tu-Su 11am-6pm. Admission by donation.

HOTELS & INNS

University Avenue in Berkeley contains blocks of budget motels that range from sketchy to decent. A general rule of thumb is that the closer the lodgings are to campus, the better their quality—with the exception of the national chain hotels sited directly on the waterfront.

Rates listed here are for a standard room, double occupancy. Note: If you're going to be in town at the time of Cal's Big Game (the weekend before Thanksgiving) or at graduation (mid-May), book accommodations well in advance.

Bancroft Club Hotel $$: 2680 Bancroft Way (College), Berkeley, (510) 549-1000, (800) 549-1002. This beautiful but dark hotel has 22 rooms, some with great views of the bay or the hills. Rooms are large and tastefully furnished to complement the late-1920s architecture. Rates include continental breakfast, but the hotel is next door to one of Berkeley's most popular cafés, Café Strada. $69-$109.

Bed and Breakfast Accommodations $$: 2235 Carleton St. (Shattuck/Telegraph), Berkeley, (510) 548-7556. Each room has a private entrance and private bath as well as a radio and TV. One features a large library; the other, a private deck. Discounts are offered for stays longer than seven days. $75-$85.

Berkeley City Club $$: 2315 Durant Ave. (Ellsworth), Berkeley, (510) 848-7800. Architecture buffs will want to stay in this Julia Morgan–designed inn. A private social club with 40 guest rooms, the tariff includes breakfast and access to the awe-inspiring indoor pool and fitness center. Even if you decide not to stay here, pay a visit just to appreciate the subtleties of Ms. Morgan's style. American Express cards are not accepted, and reservations are recommended. $80-90.

Berkeley Marina Marriott $$$: 200 Marina Blvd. (University), Berkeley, (510) 548-7920. Accommodations are predictable, but the rooms offer a view of either the hills or the water. Guests have use of the indoor pool, spa, and exercise facilities. This is the only major hotel in Berkeley, so be sure to make reservations well in advance. $94-$149.

Berkeley Travelodge $$: 1820 University Ave. (Grant), Berkeley, (510) 843-4262. A more expensive bet among the motels on University Avenue. You get HBO, coffee, and the peace of mind that comes with a national chain. $62-$84.

HOTELS & INNS

Claremont Resort and Spa $$$: Ashby and Domingo avenues, Oakland, (510) 843-3000. If it is luxury you want, head here. This elegant and immense (22 acres) East Bay institution offers commodious rooms that embody elegance. Every guest can enjoy the ten illuminated outdoor tennis courts, two heated pools, hot tubs, and saunas. In addition, there is a full European health and beauty spa, including aerobics classes, weight training, a beauty parlor, and a massage studio. $155-$720.

Days Hotel $$: 1603 Powell St. (Christie), Emeryville, (510) 547-7888. A reliable outpost of the national chain with two double beds and heated pool, Jacuzzi, in-room movies, and CNN. Conveniently located right off I-80. $79.

Dockside Boat and Bed $$$: 77 Jack London Square (Webster), Oakland, (510) 444-5858. A creative option in Jack London Square, where you can bunk on either a sailboat or motor yacht. On-board, catered candlelight dinners can be arranged. Prices vary according to the vessels, which differ in size and aesthetic quality. $95-$275.

Golden Bear Motel $: 1620 San Pablo Ave. (Cedar), Berkeley, (510) 525-6770. This AAA-rated lodge may be more expensive than the surrounding motels, but it's away from the busy University Avenue strip, on San Pablo at Cedar. There is a serviceable restaurant/coffee shop on the premises. $49.

Gramma's Rose Garden Inn $$/$$$: 2740 Telegraph Ave. (Stuart), Berkeley, (510) 549-2145. A Berkeley landmark as well as a beautiful bed and breakfast, these two picturesque mansions sit centrally on Telegraph Avenue only seven blocks from campus. Of the 40 rooms, many offer views of San Francisco and some have balconies. All are cozy, quiet, and nicely decorated. The breakfasts are generous California variations on the continental style. You should reserve at least three weeks in advance. $89-$175.

Hillegass House $$: 2834 Hillegass Ave. (Stuart/Russell), Berkeley, (510) 548-5517. A cozy B&B option. There are only four rooms in this turn-of-the-century building in the Elmwood residential district. The rooms are large and moderately priced, and the breakfasts are healthy, family-style offerings. A two-night minimum is required for weekend reservations. $70-100.

Hilton $$: 1 Hegenberger Rd. (I-880), Oakland, (510) 635-5000, (800) 445-8667. This sprawling facility near the Oakland Airport is agreeably landscaped, with most rooms opening onto an expansive grassy courtyard. You can enjoy a heated pool, a fitness center, and function and meeting rooms. $89-$126.

Holiday Inn $$$: 1800 Powell St. (I-80), Emeryville, (510) 658-9300. This link in a national chain has 280 newly renovated rooms, an outdoor pool, laundry services, and a jogging path. As one of the tallest structures in the area and located on the edge of the bay, the inn's rooms afford memorable views of the East Bay and San Francisco. If convention crowds scare you, stay away. $119-$149.

Hotel Durant $$$: 2600 Durant Ave. (Bowditch), Berkeley, (510) 845-8981. A popular hotel on the south side of campus, its 140 chambers are usually filled with business travelers and relatives of students. The rooms are moderately sized and rendered in a tasteful dark green. A complimentary continental breakfast is served in the downstairs restaurant, and conference and banquet facilities are available. $91-$101.

Hotel Shattuck $$: 2086 Allston Way (Shattuck), Berkeley, (510) 845-7300. If you're looking for an island of traditionalism in Berkeley, this downtown spot—just one block from campus—may fit the bill. There are 175 understated, quiet rooms in the 1910 historic hotel that's neighbored by a BART station. Continental breakfast and overnight parking are just two of the amenities offered. $69-$79.

Oakland Marriott $$$: 1001 Broadway (11th St.), Oakland, (510) 451-4000. Trustworthy, large-scale elegance in the heart of downtown Oakland, close to the waterfront, Jack London Square, BART, and the Civic Center. It's a bit on the expensive side for the services available, which include an outdoor pool, small workout room, and room service. $125-$150.

EAST BAY

The French Hotel $$: 1538 Shattuck Ave. (Cedar/Vine), Berkeley, (510) 548-9930. Near Berkeley's "Gourmet Ghetto" (Chez Panisse, Cheese Board, Peet's, etc.). The 18 rooms are on the smallish side, but they are comfortable (like home) and clean (unlike some homes). Bonus: The in-house café is a favorite gathering spot for North Berkeleyites, and its kitchen is the source of tasty room service. $85.

YMCA $: 2001 Allston Way (Milvia/Shattuck), Berkeley, (510) 848-6800. Never again doubt the veracity of the Village People; for budget accommodations in the East Bay, nothing beats the Y. It's especially ideal for the student traveler: a rock-bottom price for a central Berkeley location right next to BART and only a few blocks' walk from campus. The bedrooms are private, but the bathrooms are shared. All guests can take advantage of the extensive fitness facilities. The Y even accepts Visa and MasterCard. $33 double, $40 triple.

GETTING SETTLED

Bookstores

Barnes and Noble: 2352 Shattuck Ave. (Bancroft), Berkeley, (510) 644-0861. • Jack London Square, 98 Broadway (Embarcadero), Oakland, (510) 272-0120. Enormous branches of the national chain.

Black Oak Books: 1491 Shattuck Ave. (Vine/Rose), Berkeley, (510) 486-0698. A feast for the mind, with a good selection, helpful staff, and an impressive classics and literature sections. Dozens—if not hundreds—of portraits of authors line the walls, and chances are each of them has read at Black Oak at least once.

Borders Books & Music: 5800 Shellmound (Christie), Emeryville, (510) 654-1633. National chain.

Cody's Bookstore: 2454 Telegraph Ave. (Haste), Berkeley, (510) 845-7852. Started in the late 50s by West Virginia farm boy Fred Cody, the store has since become a legend. Cody's has over 250,000 titles (and will special order any book in print), a magazine rack with 1,500+ titles, and a knowledgeable staff to assist you in navigating the impressive stacks. Cody's also has over 15,000 children's books on the shelves.

Diesel—A Bookstore: 5433 College Ave. (Taft), Oakland, (510) 653-9965. An incredibly friendly place with a variety of new and used books, Diesel prides itself in offering something for everyone. The store is an old bowling alley on College Avenue in the Rockridge neighborhood. Offerings include a café with good eats and live music, and a selection of written and recorded books, including CD-ROMs.

Half-Price Books, Records, Magazines: 1849 Solano Ave. (Alameda/Colusa), Berkeley, (510) 526-6080. • 2525 Telegraph Ave. (Parker/Dwight), Berkeley, 843-6412. A sizable two-story shop that lives up to its name. Their selection is fantastic in all categories, and the staff is very willing to share their expertise. The Telegraph Avenue outpost is every bit as good as the Solano shop.

Moe's Books: 2476 Telegraph Ave. (Haste/Dwight), Berkeley, (510) 849-2087. Four floors of bibliophilic bliss, including an entire level devoted to rare and out-of-print books. Collectors come to cigar-chomping Moe Moskowitz's store first, which has been called the "yeastiest center of intellectual ferment" in Berkeley.

Small Press Distribution: 1814 San Pablo Ave. (Delaware/Hearst), Berkeley, (510) 549-3336. Another place worthy of a browse, they carry more than 200 quality titles, including an absolutely enormous selection of poetry and literary journals.

University Press Books: 2430 Bancroft Way (Telegraph/Dana), Berkeley, (510) 548-0585. While they don't stock books for specific courses, University Press Books does carry many excellent academic tomes from over 100 university presses.

CDs & Records

Amoeba Music: 2455 Telegraph Ave. (Haste), Berkeley, (510) 549-1125. The quintessential record shop for the quintessential college town, this colossal independent emporium boasts 100,000 new and used LPs, 75,000 used CDs, imports, videos, posters, and more. You get breadth over depth, with industrial, world jazz and zydeco (as well as standards like soul, rock, and pop). They also buy used records, even picking up large collections.

Borders: 5800 Shellmound (Christie), Emeryville, (510) 654-1633. National chain.

Half-Price Books, Records, Magazines: 1849 Solano Ave. (Alameda/Colusa), Berkeley, (510) 526-6080. • 2525 Telegraph Ave. (Parker/Dwight), Berkeley, (510) 843-6412. A good variety of new and used recordings of the gamut of musical genres at low prices. The Telegraph Avenue location specializes in classical and jazz on vinyl; Solano carries more pop CDs. (The latter also has a good collection of music mags from the days of yore, such as *Rolling Stone*.)

Hear Music: 1809 4th St. (Hearst), Berkeley, (510) 204-9595. You'll have a hard time tearing yourself away from Hear Music—their selection is inviting and extensive, and you can preview many discs on headphones that are integral to all the displays. They sell an eclectic range of tunes—from hula melodies to Johnny Cash—and display informative placards that profile specific artists and styles. The staff is genuinely friendly and helpful, and don't seem to mind that customers stay in the store for hours, moving from one set of headphones to the next.

Rasputin's Records: 2350 Telegraph Ave. (Channing), Berkeley, (510) 848-9005. This large, brutalist building is a stark composition of glass and steel, paying triumphant testament to the success of Berkeley music sales. Though Rasputin's used to favor pop and rock, it has now made a commitment to pursue a broader audience, expanding into folk, world beat, salsa, and other international forms. In addition to their fine selection of new items, there's also an excellent stock of used records and CDs.

Tower Classics: 2585 Telegraph Ave. (Parker), Berkeley, (510) 849-2500. Tower Records' sophisticated sibling is located a few blocks around the corner from its mainstream store (below). You'll find 100 percent classical music here, and plenty of it—the selection would impress even Mozart.

Tower Records: 2510 Durant Ave. (Telegraph), Berkeley, (510) 841-0101. • 5703 Christie Ave., Emeryville, (510) 652-7184. National chain featuring rock, pop, and other assorted new sounds.

Food & Wine

The supermarket scene in the East Bay is dominated by Safeway and Lucky stores, although in Berkeley and Oakland many smaller grocery chains (such as Andronico's), specialty markets, and even farmers' markets continue to provision many residents.

Acme Bread Company: 1601 San Pablo Ave., Berkeley, (510) 524-1327. Knowledgeable foodies come here for fantastic bread. Arrive early in the day, since they usually sell out by afternoon. The sourdough baguettes are chewy and perfect, and so are the loaves of the sour levain—the bread served at Café Fanny and Chez Panisse. (Acme breads are also available in many other food stores.)

Berkeley Bowl: 2777 Shattuck Ave., Berkeley. Meat dept. (510) 841-6346, produce dept. (510) 843-6929, seafood dept. (510) 548-7008. Berkeley Bowl is crowded and barn-like, housed in a former bowling alley. Despite its pedestrian appearance, it offers exotic produce, such as purple-spotted dragon-tongue beans. Bulk food, fresh seafood and meats, wines, coffee, cheeses, and packaged Asian foods are also specialties. The overall quality is high and prices are reasonable.

EAST BAY

Brothers' Bagels: 1281 Gilman St. (South), Berkeley, (510) 527-0272. Bakes and sells 14 varieties of bagels, cream cheese spreads, and smoked fish.

Canned Foods Grocery Outlet: 2001 4th St. (Addison), Berkeley, (510) 845-1771. For true bargain shopping, this outlet sells quantity canned, packaged, and frozen foods at often ridiculously low prices. The selection varies weekly, but you can get great deals on basic items like canned tomatoes, cereal, and odd wine lots.

Cheese Board: 1504 Shattuck Ave. (Vine), Berkeley, (510) 549-3183. You'll be greeted by delicious smells as you enter the door of this collectively run shop, which sells literally hundreds of imported and domestic cheeses. Ask for samples and advice from the staff if you feel overwhelmed by ten different kinds of chèvre. The Cheese Board has spawned its own brand of socially conscious customer service, offering a five percent discount "for those who need it" as well as for senior citizens. They also make delicious pizza and what some call the finest loaves of bread in the Bay Area. • Tu-F 7am-6pm; Sa 10am-5pm.

Farmers' Markets: Hosted by the Ecology Center, (510) 548-3333. Tuesday market: Derby St. between Martin Luther King Jr. Way and Milvia St. Summer 2pm-7pm; winter 1pm-dusk. • Saturday market: Center St. between Martin Luther King Jr. Way and Milvia St., behind City Hall. All year 10am-2pm. • Sunday market: Haste St. at Telegraph Ave., across from People's Park. May-Nov. 11am-3pm. For the freshest produce and best selection of organic fruits and vegetables, visit one of the Farmers' Markets. California farmers from as far away as Santa Cruz and the Central Valley bring seasonal produce, honey, herbs, and flowers to the open-air stalls.

G.B. Ratto & Co.: 821 Washington St. (8th St.), Oakland, (510) 832-6503. Every true food lover should experience G.B. Ratto and Co. The staff is brusque, the scales are huge, and the place is packed with every kind of international, imported, and ethnic foodstuff and spice imaginable.

Grace Baking Company: 1127 Solano Ave. (San Pablo), Albany, (510) 525-0953. Grace makes an extensive selection of filling breads, including sun-dried tomato, green onion walnut, and wild rice. They also make focaccia loaded with toppings and sold by the sheet or half-sheet, as well as myriad other delights, from delicious danish to cookies. Also in Rockridge Market Hall (see below).

Just Desserts/Tassajara Breads: 1823 Solano Ave. (Colusa), Berkeley, (510) 527-7344. • 2925 College Ave. (Ashby), Berkeley, (510) 841-1600. • 4001B Piedmont Ave. (40th St.), Oakland, (510) 601-7780. See San Francisco Food section for more information.

Kermit Lynch Wine Merchant: 1605 San Pablo Ave. (Cedar), Berkeley, (510) 524-1524. This West Berkeley store, located next to Café Fanny and Acme Bread, carries primarily French and Italian wines in the moderate-to-high price range. Shopping here requires a certain amount of faith: Kermit imports an eclectic selection of wines rarely seen in America, so you must rely on his taste more than your own knowledge. Fortunately, it's usually quite good, and the salespeople are helpful and knowledgeable.

Market Hall: 5655 College Ave. (Keith), Oakland, (510) 652-0390. Conveniently located across from the Rockridge BART station, the Hall houses nine specialty stores and the restaurant Oliveto all under one roof. Shoppers can nibble their way through the hall, sampling gourmet groceries from Grace Baking, Peaberry's Tea and Coffee, Paul Marcus Wines, Market Hall Produce, Pasta Shop Delicatessen, Enzo's Meat and Poultry, and Rockridge Fish Market. There is also a flower shop, Bloomies, and a catering service, Market Hall Caterers.

Monterey Fish Market: 1582 Hopkins St. (Monterey), Berkeley, (510) 525-5600. For quality swordfish and salmon, try this excellent fish market—and don't miss the live crabs and lobsters.

Monterey Market: 1550 Hopkins St. (Monterey), Berkeley, (510) 526-6042. The bustling Monterey Market is overflowing with produce. Located partially outdoors, it's loaded with the most incredible array of fruits and veggies ever seen in one place. The quantities are huge, the prices are great, and the selection is incomparable—for instance, Thai eggplant, ten varieties of exotic mushrooms, and mangoes from three different countries.

Noah's Bagels: 1883 Solano Ave. (Alameda), Berkeley, (510) 525-4447. • 3170 College Ave. (Alcatraz), Berkeley, (510) 654-0944. • 2344 Telegraph Ave. (Durant), Berkeley, (510) 849-9951. • 2060 Mountain Blvd. (La Salle), Oakland (510) 339-6663. • 4240 Hollis St. (42nd/43rd), Emeryville, (510) 652-6622. See San Francisco Food section for more information.

North Berkeley Wine Company: 1505 Shattuck Ave. (Vine), Berkeley, (510) 848-8910. Two doors down from Chez Panisse in the Gourmet Ghetto, this shop offers a nice selection of unusual bottled beer and an artful assemblage of California and imported wines at excellent prices.

Peet's Coffee and Tea: 2124 Vine St. (Shattuck/Walnut), Berkeley, (510) 841-0564. • 2916 Domingo Ave. (Claremont), Berkeley, (510) 843-1434. • 4050 Piedmont Ave. (Glen), Oakland, (510) 655-3228. • 1825 Solano Ave. (Colusa), Berkeley, (510) 526-9607. • 3258 Lakeshore Ave. (Lake Park), Oakland, (510) 832-6761. • 2066 Antioch Ct. (Mountain/Antioch), Oakland, (510) 339-6075. See San Francisco Food section for more information. The original store on Vine Street opened in 1966.

Whole Foods: 3000 Telegraph Ave. (Ashby), Berkeley, (510) 649-1333. Whole Foods, on the site of the lost-but-never-forgotten Co-op, has an unbeatable, upscale selection of organic and natural foods. See San Francisco Food section for more information.

Home Furnishings

Most of the chain stores described in the San Francisco Home Furnishings section have East Bay locations as well; check your local phone book for specific locations.

General Housewares

Crate and Barrel Outlet: 1785 4th St. (Hearst/Virginia), Berkeley, (510) 528-5500. See San Francisco Outlets section.

Z Gallerie: 1731 4th St. (Hearst/Virginia), Berkeley, (510) 525-7591. Z Gallerie's outlet on Fourth Street carries a fun selection of unique furniture and accessories, with some unbelievably stylish pieces at good prices.

Furniture: New

Amenities Futons: 1111 University Ave. (San Pablo), Berkeley, (510) 644-2311. For new and fluffy futons, you'll discover lots of attractive options here and a wide choice of frames.

Discount Depot: 2020 San Pablo Ave. (University), Berkeley, (510) 549-1478. Has great deals and a good selection on futons, frames, and accessories, as well as a standing offer to beat any advertised prices around.

Gorman & Son Furniture: 2599 Telegraph Ave. (Dwight), Berkeley, (510) 848-6094. Established in 1880, this is the oldest operating store in Berkeley, with fair prices on such student staples as wooden bookshelves, chairs, and desks.

Slater/Marinoff & Co.: 1823 4th St. (Hearst), Berkeley, (510) 548-2001. Whether you're in the market for a craftsman bedroom set or a wrought-iron chair for the garden, the looks are dazzling at Slater/Marinoff—and the price tags are equally eye-catching.

EAST BAY

Furniture: Used

As with most things, you can find the deals if you know the inside scoop, which begins with asking everyone you know whether they have anything they want to give you. Check out the classifieds in the *East Bay Express*, and don't forget the "free" category. The garage sales listed in the *Express* are perennial favorites for cheap furnishings. If antiques are really your game, take a stroll just beyond the flea market: 13 antique stores call the south Berkeley neighborhood home, including the **People's Bazaar**, a reasonable and popular option. For used furniture deals in truly serious quantities, make the thrift store rounds. (See also Thrift Store section.)

People's Bazaar: 3258 Adeline St. (Alcatraz), Berkeley, (510) 655-8008.

Housewares

Our Outlets section is a good place to begin your search. If you're really working on a bare-bones level, check out the Thrift Stores section for tips on the variety stores of the secondhand world, or try **Newberry's**.

Newberry's: 2036 Shattuck Ave. (Addison), Berkeley (510) 845-6353. Basics at bargain prices.

Sue Johnson Custom Lamps and Shades: 1745 Solano Ave. (Ensenada), Berkeley, (510) 527-2623. For wonderful handcrafted lamps of all descriptions, visit the charming Ms. Johnson in her custom lamp and shade shop. She designs gorgeous and touchable pieces using gingko leaves, antique bowls, and many other natural and vintage materials.

Trout Farm: 2179 Bancroft Way (Fulton), Berkeley, (510) 843-3565. A store in a category by itself, Trout Farm has some cool one-of-a-kind accessories and furniture from the 50s, not to mention strings of fish-shaped electric lights (to add that touch of romance mere candlelight can't provide).

Zosaku: 1780 4th St. (Delaware), Berkeley, (510) 524-7407. To find just the right snazzy something to impress important dinner guests or in-laws, step into Zosaku and pick out a present for yourself. Whether it's an ebony chess set or a water pitcher that resembles an iguana, it will definitely be well-designed, affordable, and perfectly unusual.

Thrift Stores

Berkeley Flea Market: 1937 Ashby Ave. (Shattuck), Berkeley, (510) 644-0744. No one should miss the Berkeley Flea Market—where else can you buy toilet brushes, kitchen sponges, incense, popcorn, and puppies all in the same place? Come for a weekend scene of wheeling and dealing on loads of new and used kitchen tables, bean bag chairs, and unfinished new wood furniture (mostly bookshelves). It's also an unexpected clothing resource, where you'll find African jewelry, Guatemalan shorts, and six-packs of men's athletic socks.

Berkeley Outlet: 711 Heinz Ave. (7th St.), Berkeley, (510) 549-2896. You'll discover serviceable used office furniture for no-nonsense prices in this mammoth, dusty warehouse.

Goodwill: 2925 East 4th St. (29th St.), Oakland, (510) 534-3037. • 1220 Broadway (12th St./13th St.), Oakland, (510) 834-6123. • 6624 San Pablo Ave., Oakland, (510) 428-4911. Goodwill operates three stores in Oakland. All have the usual smorgasbord of cheap sweatshirts, new hand lotions, and out-of-style designer jeans, but the East Fourth Street store also has Lucky McGilbert, the loquacious auctioneer for Goodwill As-Is merchandise. Stop by—you might find yourself the proud parent of anything from a wheelchair to a lava lamp.

Salvation Army: 1382 Solano Ave. (Ramona), Albany, (510) 524-5100. The Salvation Army runs a clean and inviting store that is *the* place for fabulous buys—rumor has it there have been cat fights over wingback chairs in the back room.

St. Vincent de Paul: 9235 San Leandro (98th St.), Oakland, (510) 639-4712. • 2009 San Pablo Ave., Berkeley, (510) 841-1504. • 2272 San Pablo Ave., Oakland, (510) 834-4647. St. Vincent's downtown Oakland store has more couches than a psychiatrist could use in a lifetime, and plenty of tables and chairs, all for the lowest of low prices. (They also deliver.) The East Oakland warehouse is equally well-endowed, and most weekdays at noon they hold a free-for-all auction for diehards.

Urban Ore: 1333 6th St. (Gilman), Berkeley, (510) 559-4450. Every secondhand junkie should visit Urban Ore, if only to see the yard full of hundreds of doors: hardwood, hollow core, screen, leaded glass…you name it. The selection isn't exactly upscale, but if you're refurbishing, there's no better place to find the toilet of your choice or the door frame of your dreams.

Outlets

As Berkeley continues to develop its wonderful mixed identity, outlet after outlet springs up to bring the best in consumer goods to the people. (Check out specific shopping categories in the Guide to pinpoint additional outlets that fit your needs.) Outdoor enthusiasts should take a trek through western Berkeley, where everything from socks to sleeping bags is available at discount prices.

CP Shades: 1811 4th St. (Hearst), Berkeley, (510) 843-0681. CP Shades sometimes has great deals on linen dresses and separates, all in that casual yet modern look.

Mishi: 801 Delaware St. (5th St.), Berkeley, (510) 525-1075. Mishi carries stylish but down-to-earth cotton combinations for women.

The North Face Factory Outlet: 1238 5th St. (Gilman), Berkeley, (510) 526-3530. See San Francisco Outlets section for more information.

Smith and Hawken Outlet Store: 1330 10th St. (Gilman), Berkeley, (510) 527-1076. Those into gardening and genteel tea sipping will get a kick out of Smith and Hawken. Their outlet prices on supplies, clothing, furniture, and plants sometimes dip well below retail.

Warm Things: 6011 College Ave. (Claremont), Berkeley, (510) 428-9329. As the name implies, Warm Things offers blankets, down pillows, and other comforts of life for less.

Weavers Outlet: 2570 Bancroft Way (Bowditch), Berkeley, (510) 540-5901. For casual cotton clothes by the barrel.

RESTAURANTS & CAFES

Ajanta ★ $/$$ 1888 Solano Ave. (Alameda), Berkeley, (510) 526-4373. This restful Indian eatery is named for Buddhist cave temples in India, and features beautiful, sensual reproductions of the murals found in the caves. Three special dishes from various regions of India are showcased each month. Regular items include tandoori fish and *jhinga malaidar*, prawns in a sauce of sour cream, onions, garlic, and spices. At least five vegetarian entrees are also offered, among them an excellent *bharwan baigan*, eggplant stuffed with nuts, tamarind, and spices. • Su-Th 11:30am-2:30pm, 5:30-9:30pm; F-Sa 11:30am-2:30pm, 5:30-10pm.

Au Coquelet ★ ¢ 2000 University Ave. (Milvia), Berkeley, (510) 845-0433. This café is multifaceted in both its cuisine and clientele. During the day, the restaurant caters to older patrons, who enjoy the buffet-style brunches, breakfasts, and lunches in the airy back room. After dark the front room fills with a younger crowd, and the brick walls and local art create a hip café atmosphere that suits them. The hollandaise egg spe-

EAST BAY

cials are popular with the weekend brunch customers, and the desserts, in particular the chocolate cheesecake, are terrific. Because Au Coquelet stays open later than any other Berkeley café (until 1:30am), it attracts the late-night film crowd streaming out of the UC Theater next door and plenty of students who ignore the No Studying signs. • M-F 6am-at least 1:30am; Sa-Su 8am-at least 1:30am.

Bay Wolf ★★★ $$$ 3853 Piedmont Ave. (Rio Vista), Oakland, (510) 655-6004. Beautiful and elegant, this is an ideal place for an intimate anniversary celebration or dinner with wealthy out-of-town relatives. The restaurant serves a mix of California and Mediterranean cuisines, punctuated with other regional American influences. The menu changes every two weeks, and might feature dishes of Rome or food of the southern United States. Start with a salad of red lettuce, nectarines, blue cheese, and hazelnuts, then move on to such entrées as crab cakes with black-eyed peas and peanut slaw. The staff is professional and helpful, and the deck in front is a nice place to sit on a warm night. • M-F 11:30am-2pm, 6-9pm; Sa-Su 5:30-10pm.

Bette's Oceanview Diner ★★ $ 1807 4th St. (Hearst), Berkeley, (510) 644-3230. A local favorite by the marina in West Berkeley, this classic diner dishes up all-American food and service. Take a seat at the counter and order up a stack of their famous pancakes or one of the fabulous egg concoctions. Breakfast is usually busiest, but you can also expect a buzz when the lunch crowd comes along. A jukebox and self-serve coffee will keep you entertained while you wait. If you're in a hurry, try Bette's To Go next door—same food, ready to travel. (The pancake mix and baked goods are also sold at local grocers.) • M-Th 6:30am-2:30pm; F-Su 6:30am-4pm.

Blondie's Pizza ★ ¢ 2340 Telegraph Ave. (Durant/Bancroft), Berkeley, (510) 548-1129. Like People's Park, Sather Tower, and the Naked Guy, Blondie's Pizza has come to symbolize Berkeley. For more than 15 years, this Telegraph Avenue mainstay has been serving up the biggest, greasiest, tastiest pizza in town. Check for the daily specials; you can usually get a slice, a drink, and indigestion all for under three bucks. • M-Th 10:30am-1am; F-Sa 10:30am-2am; Su 11am-midnight.

Blue Nile ★★ $ 2525 Telegraph Ave. (Dwight/Parker), Berkeley, (510) 540-6777. Consistently voted the best African restaurant in Berkeley, the Blue Nile specializes in authentic Ethiopian cuisine—so authentic that you use your fingers and bread to scoop up the food. Portions are huge. Bring your appetite and some friends; you'll have the most fun if you order several dishes and share. Try the Nile veggie combo platter, which includes lentil *wat*, split pea *wat*, *kinche, gomen*, and rice served with *injera* (Ethiopian bread). *Kitfo* is a platter of minced raw beef blended with spicy sauce, and includes *injera*, salad, and mixed vegetables. Chicken lovers should try *ye doro tibs*, tender chicken strips panfried and then simmered in sauce. Bamboo-covered walls, African travel posters, and marimba music conjure up images of Ethiopia's heyday. • M-Sa 11:30am-10pm; Su 5-10pm.

Brennan's ★★ $ 720 University Ave. (4th St.), Berkeley, (510) 841-0960. This venerable restaurant was founded by the Brennan brothers in 1878 as a livery and saloon, and now houses a down-home, all-American restaurant. The food here is strictly meat and potatoes, with some updated offerings like rotisserie chicken with garlic and thyme. Good bets are the turkey sandwiches and roast beef. The helpings are generous, the prices are remarkably low, and the atmosphere is unbeatably old-fashioned and inviting. Sip an Irish coffee at the huge bar and enjoy the eclectic crowd. • Daily 11am-9:30pm.

Brick Hut Café ★★ $ 2512 San Pablo Ave. (Dwight Way), Berkeley, (510) 486-1124. There's always a fun, alternative crowd rocking to Aretha at this funky café. The Brick Hut is owned and run by groovy women who have perfected the breakfast experience. Admire local art while savoring blueberry or walnut pancakes with real maple syrup. Or try their omelets (you can request Egg-Beaters instead of real eggs), home fries, or stick-to-the-ribs chili at lunch. • Su-Tu 7am-3pm; W-Sa 7am-3pm, 5-10pm.

RESTAURANTS & CAFES

Bucci's ★★ $$ 6121 Hollis St. (59th St./60th St.), Emeryville, (510) 547-4725. This quintessential Emeryville eatery is a favorite with angular artists and lumpy yuppies alike. The light, airy interior boasts an industrial chic, and the food is first-rate. The antipasti and pizzas live up to their billing, and just about anything on their light California-Italian menu is prepared to perfection—they have to maintain high standards in order to justify their attitude. Order at least one dessert to share for the table. • M-Th 11:30am-2:30pm, 5:30-9:30pm; F 11:30am-2:30pm, 5:30-10pm; Sa 5:30-10pm.

Cactus Taqueria ★★ ¢ 5525 College Ave. (Forest St.), Oakland, (510) 547-1305. Here is a spot that offers a refreshing break from the pretentious Euro-yuppiness of Oakland's Rockridge area. Decorated in festive Mexican colors, with piñatas hanging from the ceiling, terra-cotta floors, and brightly painted wood tables and chairs, the taqueria serves tasty burritos, soft tacos, *tortas*, and other Mexican specialties. The burritos, assembled while you wait, are some of the best in the Bay Area, with fresh fillings like chorizo, *pollo asado*, *carne asada*, vegetables, and more. On a sunny day, nothing is better than lounging at an outside table with a big, delicious burrito and a beer or *agua fresca*. • M-Sa 11am-10pm; Su 11am-9pm.

Café at Chez Panisse ★★★ $$ 1517 Shattuck Ave. (Cedar/Vine), Berkeley, (510) 548-5049. Chez Panisse started the whole California food revolution, but unlike most legends, it doesn't disappoint. This casual upstairs café supplements the downstairs restaurant and is surprisingly affordable, with a convivial atmosphere created by lots of Mission oak, copper lighting fixtures, obscure French posters, and distinguished professorial patrons. The menu is elegant and simple starters might include fresh figs with Parmesan, arugula, and virgin olive oil. For main courses, Niman-Schell Ranch steak with perfectly cooked fried potatoes is the ultimate carnivore's fantasy. If mussels appear on the menu, they'll be fresh and grit free, and might be steamed in a ginger-perfumed broth. Desserts should not be missed. Same-day lunch reservations; call after 4:30pm Monday through Thursday for a dinner reservation before 6pm and after 9pm; otherwise, wait for a table in the intimate bar. • M-Th 11:30am-3pm, 5-10:30pm; F-Sa 11:30am-4pm, 5-11:30pm.

Café de la Paz ★★ $ 1600 Shattuck Ave. (Cedar), Berkeley, (510) 843-0662. A most unusual North Berkeley eatery, Café de la Paz is an eclectic and adventurous discovery—Latin American cuisine with a vegetarian and California twist. Experience everything from tapas and tacos to organic salads, seasonal veggies (prepared with a mysterious blend of spices), and a creative array of chicken dishes. Try *empanada de pollo* (a tasty turnover), Argentine chicken *chimichurri*, or Brazilian *xim xim* (chicken served in a coconut-and-jalapeño sauce). Favorites include the savory seafood cakes with a mild, tangy orange-onion yogurt sauce, corn bread bursting with sweet corn kernels, and a wondrous wild-mushroom stew. Families will feel comfortable here, with a supply of crayons at every table. Ambience is cozy and brightly lit, with lots of greenery and a flowing fountain. Service is uneven, but the restaurant is still good. • M-Th 5:30-9:30pm; F-Sa 5:30-10pm; Su 5-9:30pm.

Café Fanny ★★ ¢ 1603 San Pablo Ave. (Cedar), Berkeley, (510) 524-5447. Tucked away in an unassuming little parking lot, this tiny café serves fabulous sandwiches, soups, and light fare. Named for the daughter of Alice Waters (of Chez Panisse fame), the café has a few counter seats and some outdoor tables. Lunch is busy, so you might have to wait for a spot on the shady, vine-covered patio. The soup is garnished with flowers, the staff is chic and cheerful, and the food is absolutely the best to be had for the price. Breakfast fare includes simple granolas and other café cuisine (and is served all day on Sunday), while lunch ranges from salads to sandwiches to goat-cheese creations. If you can't come up with the bucks for the Chez Panisse experience, make up for it by trying Café Fanny. • M-F 7am-3pm; Sa 8am-4pm; Su 9am-3pm.

EAST BAY

Café Intermezzo ★★ ¢ 2442 Telegraph Ave. (Haste), Berkeley, (510) 849-4592. This is the trendiest lunch spot in the Telegraph area for three reasons: the prices are low, the portions are huge, and the food is great. Specialties include sandwiches served on slabs of fresh wheat bread and salads that are so gigantic that two people would have a hard time finishing one. A good investment is the combination plate—for $4.25 you get enough soup, salad, or sandwich to feed you for two meals. During peak lunch hours, there is always a line out the door and a fight for tables, but service is quick and the diverse crowd is interesting to watch. • Daily 10am-10:30pm; open for coffee 7:30am.

Café Milano ★ ¢ 2522 Bancroft Way (Telegraph), Berkeley, (510) 644-3100. Conveniently located directly across from Sproul Plaza, this is where UC Berkeley students go to see and be seen. Grab a table on the balcony and watch the regulars play speed chess or the stylish young crowd mingle downstairs. At night the tables are crowded with students pretending to study, but expect a wait for a table almost any time of the day. The food—pastries, soups, salads—is uninspired, but prices are the lowest in town. The interior, a structure of brick, iron, and glass built from what was once an alleyway, is striking. Watch out, or you too will soon become a Milano junkie. • Daily 7am-midnight.

Caffè Strada ★ ¢ 2300 College Ave. (Bancroft), Berkeley, (510) 843-5282. This outdoor café is the perfect place to spend a sunny afternoon. Day and night the courtyard is crowded with caffeine addicts getting their fix under the trees. Most patrons are students, but there is also a large international contingency. After fighting for a table or bench space, you are likely to hear two or more languages being spoken at the tables crammed around yours. Strada serves espresso drinks, Italian sodas, and sinful pastries, and is responsible for popularizing the white chocolate bianca mocha. • M-Sa 6:30am-midnight; Su 7am-midnight.

The Cambodiana's ★★ $ 2156 University Ave. (Shattuck/Oxford), Berkeley, (510) 843-4630. Decorated in otherworldly shades of yellow and turquoise green, the atmosphere at this restaurant is surreal. The Cambodian entrées are equally atypical. Each dish is prepared in one of seven sauces, such as ginger blossom sauce, "the hunter's sauce for game," or *naga* princess sauce, "used in making food offerings for the temple." Marinated lamb chops are the specialty, and the owner claims they are the best in the Bay Area. Definitely an unusual dining experience. • M-Th 11:30am-3pm, 5-10pm; F 11:30am-3pm, 5-10:30pm; Sa 5-10:30pm; Su 5-9:30pm.

Cha-Am ★★ $ 1543 Shattuck Ave. (Cedar), Berkeley, (510) 848-9664. Although this restaurant sits, literally, in Chez Panisse's shadow, the food is a standout. Cha-Am loads its dishes with herbs, and the results are more strongly flavored than most. According to those who've been to Thailand, they are also more authentic than most. Don't miss the widely acclaimed soups: the *tom-ka gai*, chicken in a beautifully seasoned coconut milk broth, and the *tom-ka-talay*, the seafood version, are both good choices. Located in a converted house with a glassed-in front room, Cha-Am is just the place to chase away the culinary blahs. • M-Th 11:30am-4pm, 5-9:30pm; F-Sa 11:30am-4pm, 5-10pm; Su 5-9:30pm.

Chez Panisse ★★★★ $$$$ 1517 Shattuck Ave. (Cedar), Berkeley, (510) 548-5525. There's nothing that we can say about this Mecca of California cuisine that hasn't been said at least three times before. Go at least once in your life to experience food touched by the talented hands of Alice Waters and her apprentices. Her preparations are deceptively simple—a salad of mixed greens, corn and garlic soup, salmon with Zinfandel butter—and made with the best ingredients done perfectly. The prix fixe menu changes daily, but you don't get to choose anything other than the day you go. You also don't have to decide what tip to leave: a 15 percent service charge is added to the bill, European style. Fortunately, service is usually outstanding. Reservations are highly recommended, and are absolutely necessary on weekends far in advance. If you need more control over your destiny, or a lower price point, the café upstairs serves an à la carte lunch and dinner menu at lower prices. • M-Sa dinner seatings at 6pm, 6:15pm, 6:30pm, 8:30pm, 8:45pm, 9pm, and 9:15pm.

Christopher's Nothing Fancy Café ★ $ 1019 San Pablo Ave. (Monroe/Marin), Albany, (510) 526-1185. True to its name, Christopher's serves simple, fresh Mexican fare at very reasonable prices. From the outside, Christopher's looks like just another hole-in-the-wall along San Pablo Avenue. Inside, southwestern decor predominates, with a fireplace in one corner and a casual outdoor eating area with a tiny tiled fountain in another. Good bets are the veggie or chicken burrito, shrimp fajitas, and fish tacos. Load up on the fresh, self-serve salsa—it's excellent. Sierra Nevada and Späten are on tap, or go for one of several bottled Mexican beers. The margaritas are good, too; watch for peach, strawberry, or banana in addition to the traditional lime. If you're lucky, freshly baked cheesecake might be available for dessert. No credit cards. • M-Th 11:30am-9pm; F-Sa 11:30am-9:30pm; Su 5-9pm.

Citron ★★★ $$$ 5484 College Ave. (Lawton), Oakland, (510) 653-5484. Since it opened in 1992, Citron has become one of the top East Bay dining experiences. Chef Craig Thomas is an up-and-coming star, and the wait for a Saturday night reservation is sometimes a full month. The food is simple and beautifully prepared: the organic produce is usually selected just that morning, so you can expect to see interesting dishes on the varying menu. You might find balsamic-glazed sea bass with shelling beans, pancetta, and pickled onions, or perhaps cured roast pork loin with rustic new potatoes and spiced cherry sauce. • Daily 5:30-9:30pm.

Cuckoo's Nest ★★ $ 247 4th St. (Alice/Jackson), Oakland, (510) 452-9414. Forget you're in Oakland; pretend it's SoMa. Located in a post-industrial building filled with live-work lofts, the Cuckoo's Nest serves stellar café cuisine on long tables of Honduran mahogany. The decor features a cool slate floor, wall murals, and high ceilings. Bring a food dictionary to decipher the menu, which includes cambozola (triple-crème blue cheese), *bresaola* (air-cured beef), and cioppino. Wash it down with some good beer on tap. • M-F 7am-11pm; Sa 9am-11pm; Su 9am-2pm.

Espresso Roma ★ ¢ 2960 College Ave. (Ashby), Berkeley, (510) 644-3773. On the corner of College and Ashby, this spacious café offers the perfect spot for a latte and a read. Local artists' works adorn the sunny, sponge-painted walls, and large tables cater to studying students. The nontraditional soups, sandwiches, salads, pizzas, and calzones served here are well worth trying. Pizza with Yukon Gold potatoes, Asiago, and fresh rosemary or the panini with prosciutto, Fontina, and tomato are both good bets. The muffins come fat free, but the baked desserts are fresh and yummy. The scene is more lively in the evening when you might try one of 15 different beers, both European and locally brewed. • M-Th 6:30am-11pm; F 6:30am-midnight; Sa 7am-midnight; Su 7am-11pm.

Everett & Jones Barbeque ★ $ 1955 San Pablo Ave. (University), Berkeley, (510) 548-8261. Barbecued ribs, beef, chicken, and links are sold in this old corner joint on San Pablo. Get your barbecue, sandwiches, and side of potato salad to go. The only seating inside is two orange vinyl booths. Fueled by its established clientele, Everett & Jones recently celebrated its 20th anniversary. • Daily 11am-midnight.

Fatapple's Restaurant and Bakery ★ $ 1346 Martin Luther King, Jr. Way (Rose), Berkeley, (510) 526-2260. • 7525 Fairmont Ave. (Colusa), El Cerrito, (510) 528-3433. The worst part about Fatapple's is having to decide what to get: olallieberry pie or chocolate velvet pie, oatmeal banana pancakes or buttermilk waffles with blueberry sauce, one of the Bay Area's best burgers or vegetable polenta lasagna? The atmosphere is friendly and the air is filled with the unmistakable aroma of baked goods. This is an excellent place to have breakfast any day of the week, or linger over Sunday brunch. Park on any of the side streets in the mostly residential area. • Berkeley: M-F 6am-11pm; Sa-Su 7am-11pm. • EC: Daily 7am-9:30pm.

EAST BAY

Fat Slice Pizza ★ ¢ 2375 Telegraph Ave. (Channing), Berkeley, (510) 548-6479. The chief competition of Blondie's Pizza, Fat Slice offers the same fare at about the same price: a huge slice of pizza sets you back a dollar and some change. Berkeley connoisseurs differ on who makes the better pizza, but for value and portion size the difference is negligible. Fat Slice does tend to be a tad cleaner than Blondie's, and it has more seating. • Su-Th 10:30am-midnight; F-Sa 10am-2am.

Fenton's ★ $ 4226 Piedmont Ave. (Entrada), Oakland, (510) 658-7000. Fenton's is an East Bay institution, and everyone should make a visit at least once. The high ceiling, red Naugahyde booths, and tacky menu on the wall let you know this place has been around longer than you have. The menu consists of grilled sandwiches, soups, and sundaes. But who goes to Fenton's for the food? Ice cream, and lots of it, is the draw. Homemade flavors range from chocolate, vanilla, and butter pecan to espresso yogurt and champagne sherbet. The humongous sundaes, too big for the dish, may send you into hypoglycemic shock. • M-W 11am-11pm; Th-Sa 11am-midnight; Su 11:30am-midnight.

Flint's Bar-B-Q ★★ $ 6609 Shattuck Ave. (66th St.), Oakland, (510) 653-0593 • 3114 San Pablo Ave. (Market), Oakland, (510) 658-9912. The little take-out shack on Shattuck has just enough space for a barbecue pit, four employees, and the ever-present line of people waiting patiently for some of the East Bay's best barbecue. Not the place for weight watchers, the choices are limited to beef, pork, more beef, more pork, and chicken. The star is the 'Q, served blanketed with barbecue sauce (try the hot sauce), a side of potato salad, and a slice of Roman Meal bread. Be sure to try the beef links—they're outstanding. No credit cards. • W-Su 11am-11pm.

Gertie's Chesapeake Bay Café ★ $$ 1919 Addison St. (Milvia), Berkeley, (510) 841-2722. Crustacean cuisine in all its glory is served at this hard-to-find pink palace. Popular with the Berkeley Rep crowd, the atmosphere is fun, hip, and eclectic. Cross Street Market crab soup and Gertie's famous crab cakes are among the house specials. Also on the menu: littleneck clams, Eastern and Pacific Oysters, and Gertie's shrimp feed (shrimp steamed in beer). The wait staff is cheerful, and the desserts are fine. • M-Th 11:30am-2pm, 5:30-9:30pm; F 11:30am-2pm, 5:30-9:30pm; Sa 5:30-9:30pm; Su 4:30-9:30pm.

Ginger Island ★★ $$$ 1820 4th St. (Hearst), Berkeley, (510) 849-0526. When celebrity chef Bruce Cost took over the kitchen at Ginger Island (formerly the Fourth Street Grill), the food ranked among Berkeley's best. The bright, airy interior was revamped slightly, with a tropical motif, and the food a cross-cultural revelation. Bruce Cost has moved on, followed by a succession of chefs. The menu has become less interesting, featuring a global melange of cuisines rather than Cost's signature contemporary Asian dishes, prices have gone up, and consistency has been a problem. Choices might include Ginger Island wontons with hot vinegar-ginger sauce, Thai yellow curry noodles with sea scallops (ordered extra hot), or a hamburger. Try the Ginger Island homemade ginger ale. • Su-Th 11:30am-10pm; F-Sa 11:30am-11pm.

Great Wall ★ $ 6247 College Ave. (Claremont), Oakland, (510) 658-8458. The most interesting thing about Great Wall is the section of its menu titled "Vegetarian Meat & Chicken Specialties, Strictly Vegetarian." A mistake? Actually, no. Great Wall makes its "meat" from wheat gluten, shredding it into bite-sized pieces, deep-frying them into golden mounds, and serving them with the appropriate sauce, spice, nut, or vegetable. The result is surprisingly similar to the real thing. A strict vegetarian can safely order the cashew chicken or the pork with spicy garlic sauce. Fish and shellfish can also be found on the menu, along with an array of tofu and vegetable dishes. A dish called vegetable deluxe, which contains small, starchy, dumplinglike wheat gluten puffs, is particularly intriguing; for an appetizer, try the green bean ball soup. • Su-Th 11:30am-9:30pm; F-Sa 11:30am-10pm.

RESTAURANTS & CAFES

Homemade Café ★ $ 2454 Sacramento St. (Dwight), Berkeley, (510) 845-1940. Breakfast is served all morning and afternoon at this small, sunny restaurant in West Berkeley. Crammed with tables and colorful art, the café attracts crowds on weekend mornings who come for the omelets and hearty scrambles served with delicious home fries. Try the home-fry heaven, a decadent splurge with cheese, salsa, sour cream, and guacamole or pesto. The service is relaxed and easygoing; go ahead and help yourself to free coffee refills. No credit cards. • M-F 7am-2pm; Sa-Su 8am-3pm.

Hong Kong East Ocean ★★ $$ 3199 Powell St. (on the Marina), Emeryville, (510) 655-3388. This large, comfortable branch of a successful Hong Kong restaurant serves some of the area's best Cantonese food. At the same time you maneuver your chopsticks through a memorable meal, you can gaze out at a stunning view of the San Francisco skyline. As is typical of Cantonese restaurants, seafood dishes shine, with fresh ingredients plucked live from tanks and quickly wokked to perfection. Don't miss the fried calamari or anything with black cod. Weekend dim sum can be riotous, when throngs of Chinese patrons choose from a bewildering array of carts manned by a staff who speaks little English. Things are more restrained weekdays when the crowds are smaller and dim sum is ordered off a menu. • M-F 11am-2:30pm, 5-9:30pm; Sa-Su 10am-2:30pm, 5-9:30pm.

Joshu-Ya ★★ $ 2441 Dwight Way (Telegraph), Berkeley, (510) 848-5260. In the land of Joshu-Ya, the sushi boats are always full and tempting, and the dexterous sushi makers are always nimble fingered. For those squeamish about raw fish, try the wonderful grilled salmon dinners. A delicious, unusual dessert option is the fried green tea ice cream. During the summer, Joshu-Ya has outdoor seating in the tranquil front courtyard. • Tu-F 11:30am-2:30pm, 5-9:30pm; Sa-Su 5-10pm.

Juan's Place ★★ $ 941 Carleton St. (Sacramento), Berkeley, (510) 845-6904. Juan's is the liveliest Mexican restaurant this side of the bay. Tucked away in the industrial district, the clientele ranges from construction workers to businesspeople to students. With its casual, cantina-style decor, Juan's is relaxed and friendly. The portions are authentic and huge; be sure to try the chicken mole (usually listed as a special) and the *enchiladas rojas*. Juan's does not have a hard-liquor license, so the margaritas are made from wine and are tasty and refreshing. • M-F 11am-10pm; Sa-Su 2-10pm.

Juice Bar Collective ★ $ 2114 Vine St., Berkeley, (510) 548-8473. Blink and you might miss this tiny walk-up restaurant, with its single window and a few outdoor tables squeezed between two clothing stores. Renowned in Berkeley for their healthful, homemade lunches, the Juice Bar is a collective, and you can watch the members whip up pizzas, quiches, lasagna, sandwiches, and various other lunch items behind the counter. All the food is made in the store, including the baked goods and juices, and everything is fresh and organic. Portions are a bit small and pricy, but the food is terrific and the storefront is always crowded with eager lunchers. • M-Sa 10am-4:30pm.

King Dong ★★ $ 2429 Shattuck Ave. (Channing), Berkeley, (510) 841-6196. One of the best Chinese restaurants in Berkeley, King Dong offers excellent Hunan, Sichuan, and Mandarin dishes with no MSG. Dimly lit and air-conditioned, the dining room has a wonderfully subdued atmosphere, even when busy, and the service is impeccable. Most anything on the menu is worth trying, and the Hunan smoked pork, kung pao chicken, and the pot stickers come highly recommended. • Daily 11:30am-10pm.

Kirala ★★ $ 2100 Ward St. (Shattuck), Berkeley, (510) 549-3486. Kirala takes minimalism to the extreme—not even shoji screens or tatami mats are allowed in the converted garage-warehouse interior. You'll find a dozen tables, a sushi bar, and not much more. But it's still bright and cheery, with attentive service and fast, friendly sushi chefs. Fresh fish and lightly seasoned rice distinguish the sushi. Try the excellent *robata*-grilled items, and munch on the salted soybeans. • M 5:30-9:30pm; Tu-F 11:45am-2pm, 5:30-9:30pm; Sa 5:30-9:30pm; Su 5-9pm.

EAST BAY

La Méditerranée ★★ $ 2936 College Ave. (Ashby), Berkeley, (510) 540-7773. From the people who own the restaurants of the same name in San Francisco, this Berkeley version offers a pleasant atmosphere and an outdoor patio filled with tile-topped tables and plenty of greenery; a relaxing spot on a warm evening. See San Francisco section for review. • M-Th 10am-10pm; F-Sa 10am-11pm.

Lalime's ★★★ $$$ 1329 Gilman St. (Neilson/Peralta), Berkeley, (510) 527-9838. This tiny, flower-covered white stucco house is the perfect setting for a garden of gastronomic delights. While Mediterranean in concept, the ambitious menu strays to seared ahi tuna, duck foie gras, and medallions of lamb atop a squash and basil gratin. Desserts are equally delicious and original. A special-occasion place with an extensive and impressive list of beers, wines, and sherries. • M-Th 5:30-9:30pm; F-Sa 5:30-10pm; Su 5-9pm.

Lois the Pie Queen ★ $ 851 60th St. (Adeline), Oakland, (510) 658-5616. Dining with Lois and son Chris is a unique experience. Join them for breakfast, lunch, or Sunday dinner in their funky, triangle-shaped restaurant at the corner of Martin Luther King Jr. Way and 60th Street. The original decor features pink walls, black-and-white-checkered tablecloths, and a counter with chrome bar stools. Southern-style breakfasts, such as pork chops and eggs, are served with homemade biscuits and grits. The sweet potato, pecan, and other pies are sold by the slice or whole to take home. The Pie Queen does not accept checks or credit cards. • M-F 8am-2pm; Sa 7am-3pm; Su 7am-4pm.

Long Life Vegi House ★ $ 2129 University Ave. (Shattuck), Berkeley, (510) 845-6072. Long Life is a favorite restaurant among Berkeley residents and has received many awards for its Chinese-influenced cuisine. Vegetarians lay awake at night dreaming of the steaming dishes Long Life serves with the same passion carnivores feel for filet mignon. Even meat purists can't resist the huge plates (we're talkin' doggie bags here) of vegetables, tofu, and seafood served with complex and adventurous sauces. The claypot is a self-contained extravaganza of flavor and splendor. Giant rice plate lunches at this casual restaurant come with soup and an egg roll for about five dollars. Always a satisfying midday fix. • Daily 11:30am-9:30pm.

Nan Yang ★★ $ 6048 College Ave. (Claremont), Oakland, (510) 655-3298. The lights are bright, the decor simple, and the Burmese food fabulous. What more could you want? Start with the rich fish soup, served in the traditional manner on top of fried onions. Order the five-spice chicken, choose any of the garlic noodle dishes, and don't miss the curry—you'll begin planning a trip to Rangoon once you taste it. Service is fair, and you may have to wait for a table, but your taste buds will thank you. • Tu-F 11:30am-3pm, 5-10pm; Sa noon-10pm; Su noon-9pm.

O Chamé ★★★ $$ 1830 4th St. (Hearst), Berkeley, (510) 841-8783. For the most Zen-like of dining experiences, head for O Chamé, the renowned Japanese sanctuary on chic Fourth Street. The interior, with its polished wood chairs and tables, sponge-painted ceilings, and New Age music, glows with quiet elegance. Attentive wait staff glide gracefully around chopstick-wielding diners. The food is a perfectly balanced marriage of Japanese and California cuisine; the menu is small but varied. Try the appetizer of grilled shiitake and roasted red pepper (purists can partake of sashimi). A variety of cold or hot *soba* noodles dominate the entrée listings; the hot *soba* with tofu skins and spinach is delightful. Fish, poultry, and meat dishes from the wood oven are available daily. Dessert options range from fresh baked cookies to such delights as mango-rice tarts. Best of all, prices are reasonable for this sophisticated fare. • M-Th 11:30am-3pm, 5:30-9pm; F-Sa 11:30am-3pm, 5:30-9:30pm.

The Old Spaghetti Factory ★ $ 62 Jack London Square (Webster/Embarcadero), Oakland, (510) 893-0222. This charming pasta house, elaborately furnished in turn-of-the-century decor, is an enjoyable place for a good, inexpensive meal if you find yourself in Jack London Square. For value, it can't be beat. Complete meals for as little as five dollars come with salad, bread, ice cream, and a beverage. This is a great place to bring out-of-town visitors or a large group. • M-Th 11:30am-2pm, 5-9:30pm; F 11:30am-2pm, 5-10pm; Sa 5-10pm; Su noon-9:30pm.

Oliveto ★★★ $$ 5655 College Ave. (Shafter), Oakland, (510) 547-5356. Named for Italy's tree of life—the olive—this place seduces with its rustic northern Italian cuisine. When you sit down you're greeted with a plate of assorted olives and a basket of freshly baked bread. Since a group of refugees from Chez Panisse, Stars, and Campton Place moved into the kitchen, the food has improved dramatically. Conveniently located opposite the Rockridge BART station, the restaurant specializes in pasta, antipasti, hearty stews, risotto to write home about, and scrumptious homemade desserts. Those seeking a casual introduction can enjoy the café downstairs instead of the upstairs dining room. Warning: Split an appetizer and main dish; the portions are too bountiful to finish on your own. • M-F 11:30am-2pm, 5:30-10pm; Sa 5:30-10pm; Su 11am-2pm, 5:30-9pm.

Omnivore ★★ $$ 3015 Shattuck Ave. (Ashby), Berkeley, (510) 848-4346. This beautiful, intimate restaurant serves fresh California cuisine with Mediterranean, Asian, and French influences. A Japanese influence is also evident in the decor, which features rice-paper screens, wall sconces, and delicate flower paintings. Entrée choices include bouillabaisse and swordfish with a sauce of orange, ginger, and cilantro. The owner and staff make you feel like you're eating at a friend's house. • W-M 5:30-9:30pm.

Ozzie's Soda Fountain ★ $ Elmwood Pharmacy, 2900 College Ave. (Russell), Berkeley, (510) 843-1300. "A simple operation in a complex neighborhood" is how Ozzie describes his place. On Saturdays, buttermilk pancakes are served, and no one is allowed to leave hungry. Predictable items on the menu include double-decker sandwiches, grilled cheese, shakes, sundaes, and probably the cheapest cup o' joe in the East Bay (60 cents). Shake flavors are vanilla, chocolate, strawberry, coffee, mocha, cherry, and root beer. If you've got room, try the rocky road or chocolate cream cheese brownie. No credit cards. • Tu-Sa 10am-4pm.

Picante Taqueria ★★ $ 1328 6th St. (Gilman/Camelia), Berkeley, (510) 525-3121 Somewhere between a bar and a restaurant, this fun, upscale taqueria offers a wide selection of beers and Mexican entrées with the speed of a fast-food joint. You can watch sports or listen to live music (usually jazz or blues) while munching on the delicious vegetarian tamales or *enchiladas de pollo colorado* (spicy chicken). • Su-Th 11am-10pm; F-Sa 11am-11pm.

Plearn Thai Cuisine ★★★ $ 2050 University Ave. (Shattuck), Berkeley, (510) 841-2148. Perennially ranked the top Thai restaurant in the East Bay, Plearn earns its reputation by turning out a large assortment of richly seasoned food, with a particularly good selection of seafood dishes: don't miss the fiery *koong-ka-tee*, sautéed prawns in a coconut milk sauce, or any dish featuring green mussels. Curries are also delicious, although the selection is limited. Portions are on the small side. The large, airy restaurant looks more Californian than Thai, but can accommodate the throngs who flock here most nights. • Daily 11:30am-10pm.

Rin's Thai Cuisine ★ $ 12200 San Pablo Ave. (Nevin), Richmond, (510) 232-5542. This venture, opened by a Plearn alumnus, lacks ambience but features fresh, flavorful food. The decor is unremarkable, and the location, on a corner of San Pablo Avenue in Richmond, is less than scenic. Service is attentive, and the long menu offers something to please everyone. Vegetarians will appreciate the variety and flavor of the many meatless dishes such as green curry tofu, while carnivores will love items like the beef in peanut sauce. Prices are low, and tables are comfortably spaced. • M-F 11am-3pm, 5-9:30pm; Sa-Su 5-10pm.

Rivoli ★★★ $$ 1539 Solano Ave. (Peralta/Neilson), Berkeley, (510) 526-2542. M-This spare California-Mediterranean bistro had foodies swooning before it opened. The husband-and-wife team boasts an impressive resume: chef Wendy Brucker cooked at Square One before opening her own place, while Roscoe Skipper learned how to run a

EAST BAY

dining room at Square One and Masa's. Favorites from the frequently changing menu include portobello mushroom fritters with aioli and greens, braised lamb shanks with a Mediterranean mint-garlic yogurt sauce, stuffed pork chops with sweet potato gratin, and a slew of luscious desserts. • Th 5:30-9:30pm; F 5:30-10pm; Sa 5-10pm; Su 5-9pm.

Rockridge Café ★ $ 5492 College Ave. (Lawton/Forest), Oakland, (510) 653-1567. The food here is the kind you crave at weird hours of the night, whether it is the mushroom burgers, the Ben & Jerry's strawberry milk shakes, or the artichoke or lemon chicken calzones. The café is also known for its bang-up breakfast menu, complete with espresso drinks of every possible low-fat, nonfat, decaf, and caf combination. The atmosphere is homey, with works by local artists displayed on the walls. • M-Th 7:30am-10pm; F-Sa 7:30am-10:30pm; Su 8am-10pm.

Sabina Indian Cuisine ★ $ 1628 Webster St. (17th St.), Oakland, (510) 268-0170. If you find yourself in downtown Oakland at lunchtime, pop into this place. While the interior could use some refinishing and painting, you can't beat the $5.50 price tag for the all-you-can-eat, 11-course lunch buffet. They also have a fairly extensive à la carte menu, with tandooris, curries, vegetarian specialties, and saffron rice dishes. At dinner, prices go up a few dollars, although the menu remains the same. Daily 11:30am-2:30pm, 5-9:30pm.

Saul's ★ ¢ 1475 Shattuck Ave. (Vine), Berkeley, (510) 848-3354. If you're looking for a New York deli experience, head to Saul's, where the portions are huge, the service friendly and fast, and the prices reasonable. Every sandwich is giant; turkey, pastrami, and corned beef on fresh rye are all favorites. Salads are great, too, especially the Caesar, which is big enough to split. You can also get Noah's bagels and lox, and for the complete New York experience, an egg cream. Jars of crisp, savory pickles sit on every table, and kosher foods are sold here as well. • Daily 8am-9:30pm.

Saysetha ★ $ 6230 Telegraph Ave. (63rd St.), Oakland, (510) 653-2837. This small restaurant makes the best peanut sauce in town, along with exemplary pad Thai and great green curry chicken. Not every dish excels, so choose carefully. The decoration is standard Thai with an upscale touch, and the wait staff is masterful. Weekday lunch is a bargain. • M-Th 11:30am-2:30pm, 5-10pm; F 11:30am-2:30pm, 5-10:30pm; Sa 5-10:30pm; Su 5-10pm.

Skates on the Bay ★★ $$ 100 Seawall Dr. (University), Berkeley Marina, (510) 549-1900. Experience an unforgettable meal at this romantic restaurant with a breathtaking waterfront view. Skates is known for its enticing entrées of fresh fish and pastas, with generous portions big enough for two. Not hungry? Then sit at the expansive bar while waiters prepare sushi and skewered chicken appetizers. The cozy, comfortable atmosphere is further warmed by a fireplace and open ovens, where fabulous focaccia and muffins are baked. It's a challenge to choose from the creative brunch menu, which features such delectable dishes as *pain perdu* with fresh berries dressed with toasted almonds. • M-Th 11:15am-3pm, 5-10pm; F 11:15am-3pm, 5-10:30pm; Sa noon-3:30pm, 4-10:30pm; Su 10:15am-3pm, 4-10pm.

Sushi-Ko ★★ $$ 64 Shattuck Square (University), Berkeley, (510) 845-6601. Hidden behind a modest exterior in downtown Berkeley, this upscale Japanese restaurant is popular with high-class sushi fanatics. Watch the chefs in action at the small sushi bar, or sit in the stark dining room. It's easy to run up a huge bill if you try a variety of dishes, but you can have a reasonably priced dinner by ordering the combination plates, or dining before 7pm to get the early bird special, a full sushi dinner including salad and soup for $12.50. Try the Sushi-Ko roll, made from an interesting mix of tempura and avocado. • M-Th 11:30am-2pm, 5:30-9:30pm; F 11:30am-2pm, 5:30-10pm; Sa 11:30am-2:30pm, 5:30-10pm; Su 5-9pm.

Taiwan Restaurant ★★ $ 2071 University Ave. (Shattuck), Berkeley, (510) 845-1456. Delicious smells greet you at the door of this crowded, bustling Chinese restaurant. Choose from a wide array of dishes, including homemade fish ball soup, asparagus

RESTAURANTS & CAFES

beef, Taiwan spareribs, and crispy duck. The restaurant is loud and busy and the service can be harried, but the food is worth the wait for the devoted clientele composed of a cross section Berkeley residents. • M-Th 11:30am-midnight; F 11:30am-1am; Sa 10:30am-1am; Su 10:30am-midnight.

Thai Thai ★★ $ 1045 San Pablo Ave. (Marin), Albany, (510) 526-7426. Thai Thai, on San Pablo Avenue just south of Marin Avenue, serves lighter fare than many Thai restaurants in the area. The chef has cut back on salt and coconut milk and stepped up the seasoning, with satisfying and refreshing results. The sautéed vegetables are excellent, as are the lemon grass soup, curried duck, and barbecued pork. Particularly delicious as appetizers are the boneless chicken wings stuffed with pork and silver noodles. The spacious, muted interior is a welcome relief from the brass-elephant school of decor that most Thai places favor. • Tu-Th 11:30am-3pm, 5-9:30pm; F 11:30am-3pm, 5-10pm; Sa 5-10pm; Su 5-10pm.

Tomate ★★★ $ 2265 5th St. (Bancroft), Berkeley, (510) 549-9885. Tomate, located in the heart of industrial Berkeley, is owned and staffed by French people who find genuine joy in running a Berkeley café. The atmosphere combines rustic French style with industrial chic, resulting in an airy, spacious eating area with a cozy feel. Outdoor seating is ample, too. The food is consistently delicious, the service efficient and professional. Breakfast stars are homemade crêpes, croissants, and an assortment of warm, fragrant pastries. All sandwiches are served on crusty fresh bread; try the Provençal, served on a baguette, with roasted bell pepper, tomato, eggplant, and lemon dressing. The Greek salad is sensational. Watch for specials like barbecued chicken in sesame dressing with fresh basil, served on a baguette. No credit cards. • M-F 8am-3pm.

The Townhouse Bar and Grill ★★★ $$ 5862 Doyle St. (Powell), Emeryville, (510) 652-6151. Remade into a French bistrolike restaurant from a country-and-western dive bar, the Townhouse still has the rustic feel of the West. Done up with antiques and colorful modern paintings, the interior is casual and classic. The kitchen puts out multiethnic food, beautifully executed and wonderfully tasty. The menu ranges from gulf shrimp with Thai chili sauce to flank steak with black beans to risotto and shrimp brochettes with crispy leeks in a cognac cream sauce. For the less adventurous, the crab cakes, fried calamari, garlic fries, and burgers are good choices. The bar is still a great place for a martini or glass of wine. • M-Th 11:30am-2:30pm, 6-9:30pm; F 11:30am-2:30pm, 6-10pm; Sa 6-10pm.

Venezia ★★ $ 1799 University Ave. (Grant), Berkeley, (510) 849-4681. Enter Venezia, and you've stepped off a busy Italian *viale* to dine in a charming outdoor café, tucked away on a quiet side street. Trompe l'oeil scenes cover the walls, with a real-life laundry line stretching across one corner. The atmosphere may be an illusion, but the scrumptious *malfatti con funghi*, fried calamari, and *pasta alla puttanesca* are deliciously real. • M-Th 11:30am-2:30pm, 5:30-10pm; F 11:30am-2:30pm, 5-10pm; Sa 5-10pm; Su 5-9:30pm.

Walker's Pie Shop ★ $ 1491 Solano Ave. (San Pablo), Albany, (510) 525-4647. Celebrating its 30-year anniversary in 1994, Walker's Pie Shop is an East Bay institution. Wholesome, all-American meals in a homey, friendly atmosphere are what you'll find here. Offerings include soups, sandwiches, and hearty dinners such as fried chicken and prime rib served with soup, salad, rolls, vegetables, potato, and pie. The famous old-fashioned pies are available whole or by the slice; flavors include lemon chiffon, pecan, strawberry rhubarb, banana cream, and apple, of course. • Tu-Th 8am-3pm, 5-8pm; F-Sa 8am-3pm, 5-9pm.

Zachary's Chicago Pizza ★★ $ 1853 Solano Ave. (Alameda), Berkeley, (510) 525-5950. • 5801 College Ave. (Oak Grove), Oakland, (510) 655-6385. Zachary's serves Chicago-style "stuffed" pizza—a thick, orgiastic affair of rich cheese, sausages, and chunky tomatoes. A popular establishment, it has won top slice recognition from the *East Bay Express, San Francisco Chronicle, San Francisco Focus*, and its hordes of adoring customers. The line can be long, but it moves quickly and the wait is worth it. • Solano: Su-Th 11am-9:30pm; F-Sa 11am-10:30pm. • College: Su-Th 11am-10pm; F-Sa 11am-10:30pm.

EAST BAY
ARTS & ENTERTAINMENT

Amusements

Albany Bowl: 540 San Pablo Ave. (Carlson), Albany, (510) 526-8818. Run over to the Albany Bowl, don a pair of rented silly shoes, and listen to the video game explosions, the fervent slap of pinball flippers and, of course, the resounding crash of a mean strike. With 36 lanes, seven pool tables, a cocktail lounge, and a café, there's no reason to leave. • Daily 9am-1:30am.

City Rock: 1250 45th St. (Hollis), Ste. 400, Emeryville, (510) 654-2510. City Rock Indoor Climbing Center can give you some of the thrills and skills of rock climbing without the high winds and cold rain of the great outdoors. • M-F 11am-10pm; morning climbs M, W, F 6:30am-9:30pm; Sa-Su 10am-6pm.

Golden Gate Fields: 1100 East Shore Hwy. (Buchanan), Albany, (510) 559-7300. Put your money where your mouth is at Golden Gate Fields, where the thoroughbreds run from the end of January to the end of June. When the sun shines and the field is tight, the fun and excitement is contagious. Only a crowd with money on the line can cheer like this one does. Hours vary seasonally, so call for current post times.

Grand Slam USA: 5892 Christie Ave. (Powell), Emeryville, (510) 652-4487. Grand Slam's indoor baseball and softball batting cage facility has slam-dunk basketball and other games as well. • M-Sa, 11am-10pm; Su 11am-7pm.

Iceland: 2727 Milvia St. (Ward/Derby), Berkeley, (510) 843-8800. Iceland has open skating several times a week, and also rents skates. Hours vary.

Town and Country Billiards: 1551 University Ave. (Sacramento/California), Berkeley, (510) 549-1667. The folks here know how pool should be played: in a long, seedy room where smoke hangs thick under low lights and guys named Vinnie hustle games of 8-ball. There are over 20 tables, plus video games, nachos, snacks, and crummy domestic beer. Would you want it any other way? • Daily 11am-1am.

Entertaining Children

Adventure Playground: Berkeley Marina, University Ave. west of I-80, (510) 644-8623. Kids can be king of the mountain at Adventure Playground. You'll find paint, brushes, nails, and wood, so young'uns can improvise their own brand of architecture on the handmade ladders and forts. More cerebral children will want to investigate the nature center. • Summer hours M-F 9am-5pm; Sa-Su 11am-5pm. Winter hours Sa-Su 11am-5pm.

Ardenwood Historical Farm: 34600 Ardenwood Blvd. at Hwy 84, Fremont, (510) 796-0663. An historic farm where you can learn about early California in the days of European settlement. Staff and volunteers wear Victorian garb and cultivate the same crops that were grown a century ago; furthering the time traveling, visitors can watch demonstrations of farm chores and ride in horse-drawn trains and wagons. • April-November: Th-Su 10am-4pm, plus Memorial Day, Independence Day, Labor Day, and the first weekend in December. Admission: $6 adults; $3.50 ages 4-17; $4 seniors.

The Campanile: Sather Tower, University of California, Bancroft Way and Telegraph Ave., Berkeley, (510) 642-3666. See Berkeley Sightseeing.

Children's Fairyland: Lakeside Park, Lake Merritt, Grand Ave. and Bay Pl., Oakland, (510) 452-2259. This old-fashioned amusement park with a Mother Goose theme is ideal for three- to ten-year-olds. Children unlock story boxes on various sets and hear tales of the Crooked Old Man, Pinocchio, the Cow Who Jumped Over the Moon, and Snow White. The park is bright and cheerful, and features a merry-go-round, diminutive Ferris wheel, and bumper boats. • M-F 10am-4:30pm; Sa-Su 10am-5:30pm.

ARTS & ENTERTAINMENT

Codornices Park: 1201 Euclid Ave. (Eunice), Berkeley, (510) 644-6530. Codornices Park is a great place to romp in the fresh air, as well as a great place to work out with its basketball courts, baseball, softball, and soccer fields. Great picnic and BBQ facilities make this a fine site for birthday parties or other group actives.

Lawrence Hall of Science: Middle Centennial Dr., UC Berkeley Campus, (510) 642-5132, (510) 642-5133. Science fans shouldn't miss this interactive museum, where you can stop a laser beam with your bare hand, creep through a model of a DNA molecule, and navigate Columbus' voyage to the New World. The special robotics displays can be particularly exciting (past exhibits have included giant insects and dinosaurs which stomped, screeched, and roared to great effect). Other highlights are hairy tarantulas that crawl up your arm (kids like this), and computers that psychoanalyze on the spot. Perched high on the hill behind UC Berkeley, the views of the bay and civilization below are spectacular. Before leaving, walk down the hill just below the building and check out the wind pipes, where gusting breezes blow over a set of cylinders creating a natural symphony. • Daily 10am-5pm. $6 adults; $2 ages 3-6; $4 students and seniors.

Oakland Zoo: 9777 Golf Links Rd. (I-580), Oakland, (510) 632-9523. This stroller-friendly zoo set in the hills stresses the presentation of animals in their natural habitats. It features an open-air island for monkeys, an acre of roaming territory and a mud bath for the elephants, a eucalyptus grove for the pride of majestic lions, and much more. There's also a kiddie train ride, picnic areas, and a panoramic sky ride. • Daily 10am-4pm. $5 adults; $3 ages 2-14 and seniors. $3 parking.

Tilden Regional Park: Canon Dr. (off Grizzly Peak Blvd.), Berkeley, (510) 525-2233. There's no better way to pass a sunny day than in Tilden Regional Park, which stretches along the slopes surrounding Grizzly Peak and Canon Drive. Begin at the merry-go-round in the center of the park. Built by carousel connoisseur Herschel Spillman in 1911, this all-wood entertainer is a rotating piece of American heritage, with each animal a lovingly hand-carved work of art. Besides the horses, kids' favorite mounts are the chicken, frog, zebra, and sea monster. At the Little Farm, children mingle with Sweet Pea the cow, Flecka the goat, and the rest of the gang—burros, sheep, pigs, and more—in a pint-sized barnyard. Each year brings newborn kids, pups, and calves. A stone's throw away is a traditional pony ride ring. The steam trains, located at the park's south end, takes railroad aficionados of all ages for a 12-minute ride through the wilds of Tilden Park. (If you work up a little steam of your own, take a dip in nearby Lake Anza.) • Lake Anza, merry-go-round, and pony ride, daily 10am-5pm through the summer (and in warm weather); Sa-Su other months. Steam trains, noon-5pm M-F; Sa-Su 11am-6pm. Little Farm, daily 8:30am-3:30pm.

Movie Theaters

Act One/Two: 2128 Center St. (Shattuck), Berkeley, (510) 548-7200. The best local venue for art and foreign films.

Albany One/Two: 1115 Solano Ave. (San Pablo), Albany, (510) 524-5656. Downstairs shows mainstream films; upstairs is an intimate setting for foreign and art flicks.

California Cinema Center: 2113 Kitredge St. (Shattuck), Berkeley, (510) 848-0620. The California has one large theater and two smaller ones—the sound-sensitive will appreciate the thick, dampening walls. There's ample parking in a nearby lot (Oxford and Kitredge).

Grand Lake: Grand Ave. and Lake Park, Oakland, (510) 452-3556. A recent renovation of this 1926 theater has ensured its status as an historical landmark. A spacious, glorious, old-style theater complete with performances on the mighty Wurlitzer organ before weekend shows makes this Bay Area movie palace a must visit and a beautiful reminder of the silver screen's glamorous heritage. In addition to the main room, which accommodates nearly 1,000 people, there is a 500-seater and two smaller theaters.

EAST BAY

Pacific Film Archive: 2621 Durant St. (College), Berkeley, (510) 632-1124. In the University Art Museum is the world-famous Pacific Film Archive, with its outstanding library of Japanese and Eastern European films. Programs vary in everything save quality and creativity. Advance tickets are available.

Oaks: 1875 Solano Ave. (the Alameda), Berkeley, (510) 526-1836. Mainstream offerings on two screens.

Shattuck Cinema: 2230 Shattuck Ave. (Kitredge), Berkeley, (510) 644-3370. The best multiplex in the area, providing distinctive environments most large theaters lack. This eight-screener does it with custom-designed rooms, some decorated with Egyptian hieroglyphics, others are in vintage movie-palace style. Some of the screening rooms are quite small, but all are clean and comfortable.

United Artists Berkeley: 2274 Shattuck Ave. (Kitredge), Berkeley, (510) 843-1487. Expect sticky floors, gummy seats, and sound bleed. Audiences can be unruly at this seven-screen house—a fight in the audience ruined one evening.

United Artists Emerybay 10: 6330 Christie Ave. (Powell), Emeryville, (510) 420-0107. A large theater worth the trip, located in next door to the Emery Bay Public Market. All ten screens are decently sized; seating (complete with handy drink holders) is comfortable and the sound is excellent. No shortage of free parking, too.

UC Theater: 2036 University Ave. (Milvia/Shattuck), Berkeley, (510) 843-6267. It may command less attention, but the UC Theater in Berkeley predates the Grand Lake by 11 years. The cavernous (1,400 seat) venue specializes in non-conventional fare ranging from animated Japanese sagas to premiers of locally-made films to pop culture classics. It also schedules some fascinating themed series and festivals. For the sake of variety, movies rarely run more than two days. The exception is "The Rocky Horror Picture Show," which has run every Saturday at midnight for over 15 years.

Nightlife

An up-to-date source for finding out what's happening each weekend is the *East Bay Express*. Call BASS Tickets (510) 762-2277 for information on ticket availability for headlining acts as well as a listing of upcoming events.

Albatross: 2218 San Pablo (Hearst/Delaware), Berkeley, (510) 849-4714. This casual pub on San Pablo offers beer and wine, as well as dart boards and all the free popcorn you can handle.

Ashkenaz: 1317 San Pablo Ave. (Gilman), Berkeley, (510) 525-5054. Basically a big friendly shed where you and your friends can enjoy such diverse programs as flamenco, African rhythms, or zydeco.

Berkeley Community Theatre: Allston Way at Martin Luther King Jr. Way, Berkeley, (510) 845-2308. Hosts some mega-popular names. This venue may bring back memories of grade school auditorium experiences—it's an intimate setting, but the seating isn't always so great and it's hard to see the stage.

Berkeley Square: 1333 University Ave. (Sacramento), Berkeley, (510) 841-6555. Alternative sounds are pumped out of Berkeley Square, featuring bands with a Live-105 or KUSF following.

The Bison Brewery: 2598 Telegraph Ave. (Parker), Berkeley, (510) 841-7734. Probably the hippest of the local brew pubs, Bison attracts pierced and tattooed art-school bikers, slackers, and Deadheads. The striking space, with its high ceilings, giant brewing kettles, and upstairs balcony, is done in funky flea-market-meets-museum-of-modern-art decor. Servers are occasionally downright surly, but they're worth putting up with for the excellent homemade brews, which range from the typical (amber) to the bizarre (orange cardamon ale). Many evenings the Bison hosts live music. A small kitchen dishes up sandwiches, garlic bread, and pizza.

ARTS & ENTERTAINMENT

Caribee Dance Center: 1408 Webster St. (4th St.), Oakland, (510) 835-4006. International sounds, ranging from reggae to Brazilian pop.

Chalkers: 59th and Hollis sts., Emeryville, (510) 658-5821. This is not your cigar-chomping, seedy, fast-talking pool hall crowd—everything here is stylish, sophisticated, and low-key. The two-story interior is strategically sectioned into a series of rooms, each with a varying number of new oak tables and dart boards. You can concentrate on your game, then rest your weary arms at the bar and socialize with the ever-friendly patrons.

Eli's Mile High Club: 3629 Martin Luther King Jr. Way (36th St./37th St.), Oakland, (510) 655-6661. Where great blues bands sound off to a mixed and interesting crowd.

Freight and Salvage: 111 Addison St. (San Pablo), Berkeley, (510) 548-1761. Folk musicians, Irish duets, and swing-inspired groups, as well as your standard acoustic troubadours, play at this coffeehouse every night.

Jupiter: 2181 Shattuck Ave. (Allston/Center), Berkeley, (510) 843-8277. Just down the street from Triple Rock, Jupiter has quickly become a popular place to eat and drink with friends in an incredibly comfortable indoor (cozy pub) and outdoor (lovely courtyard) atmosphere.

Kimball's East: 5800 Shellmound St. (Christie), Emeryville, (510) 658-2555. Presents world-class jazz performers. Downstairs, Kimball's Carnival brings in Latin jazz acts.

Kip's: 2439 Durant Ave. (Telegraph), Berkeley, (510) 848-4340. For your standard college-hangout atmosphere, try Kip's, the Southside ruler of the sports bar scene and provider of great hamburgers.

La Peña Cultural Center: 3105 Shattuck Ave. (Ashby), Berkeley, (510) 849-2568. Berkeley's Latin American cultural center hosts a wide range of world music and jazz in a festive setting.

Larry Blake's: 2367 Telegraph Ave. (Durant), Berkeley, (510) 848-0886. Here the crowds get moving to jazz, reggae, blues, or rock played by live bands.

Pasand: 2282 Shattuck Ave. (Bancroft), Berkeley, (510) 848-0260. Serves hot jazz and spicy Indian food to packed crowds.

Spats: 1974 Shattuck Ave. (University/Berkeley), Berkeley, (510) 841-7225. A popular and charming place to take a date or meet up with friends, Spats resembles a comfy, yet exotic English sitting room and usually attracts a healthy, attractive crowd. The mixed-drink menu is extensive and unusual.

Starry Plough: 3101 Shattuck Ave. (Prince), Berkeley, (510) 841-2082. For a wide choice of musical options, try the Starry Plough, which, along with open-mike nights, offers everything from Welsh music (dance lessons included) to Beat-inspired jazz and funk bands.

The Stork Club: 380 12th St. (Webster/Franklin), Oakland, (510) 444-6174. Lying amidst the desolate wasteland that is Downtown Oakland is this gem of a bar and music venue, one of the Bay Area's best kept secrets. On one side of the center dividing wall sits the long bar, where the regulars who look like they haven't left their stools since the 50s nurse their bottled domestic beers. On the other side is a pool table, bright red leather booths, and at the very back, a tiny stage—surrounded by glitter, party favors, and Christmas lights—where excellent East Bay rock, punk, and avant-garde bands play to a young, hip, appreciative crowd. If this club were in San Francisco it would always be packed, but here you can usually get in and for five bucks soak in the laid-back atmosphere.

Tied House: 8 Pacific Marina (Triumph), Alameda, (510) 521-4321. See Peninsula Bar listing.

EAST BAY

Triple Rock: 1920 Shattuck Ave. (University/Hearst), Berkeley (510) 843-2739. The Berkeley brewpub that led to 20 Tank and Jupiter. This is a favorite all-day student hangout and all-around great place—you can even pull in some sun on the small rooftop deck.

Yoshi's Nitespot: 6030 Claremont Ave (College)., Oakland, (510) 652-9200. An Oakland jazz house and Japanese restaurant that regularly brings top international acts to the Bay Area for multi-night engagements. Yoshi's is moving to Jack London Square in the late spring of 1997.

Performing Arts

Berkeley City Ballet: 1800 Dwight Way, Berkeley, (510) 841-8913. This multiracial performing arts organization runs a ballet school and also graces the Zellerbach stage during the traditional December *Nutcracker* run. The young dancers perform chamber works commissioned from New York and beyond, in addition to the classics. In the spring, the company performs at the Berkeley Community Theater. Tickets $8-$10.

Berkeley Opera: 715 Arlington Ave., Berkeley, (510) 841-1903. The Berkeley Opera performs three times a year at the Julia Morgan Theater, with numerous chamber performances at the North Church and the Hillside Club Theater.

Berkeley Repertory Theater: 2025 Addison St. (Shattuck), Berkeley, (510) 845-4700. The crown jewel of the local scene, the Rep is one of the country's top regional theaters, frequently showered with accolades and awards. It features new works and what they call "reinvigorated classics," which sometimes bear little resemblance to the originals. Box office open noon-7pm daily.

Berkeley Symphony Orchestra: 2322 Shattuck Ave., Berkeley, (510) 841-2800. Renowned conductor Kent Nagano directs the Berkeley Symphony Orchestra in cutting-edge, 20th-century compositions, as well as a more traditional repertoire.

Cal Performances: (510) 642-9988. Cal Performances at UC Berkeley showcases some of the world's top artists and companies; past highlights have included performances by Baryshnikov and the companies of Alvin Ailey and Twyla Tharp. UC Berkeley students receive an unbelievable 50 percent discount on tickets and can also purchase $5 rush tickets 15 minutes prior to curtain time. Performances are held at the 2,000-seat Zellerbach Auditorium, the 700-seat Hertz Hall, and the 8,000-seat Greek Theater. Box office M-F 10am-5:30pm; Sa-Su 10am-4pm.

California Shakespeare Festival: Siesta Valley in Orinda, (510) 548-3422. A highly popular summer favorite, recently moved from Berkeley to a bucolic outdoor setting in Orinda. Shows sell out months in advance, so be sure to plan ahead.

Dimensions Dance Theatre: Alice Arts Center, 1428 Alice St., Suite 300, Oakland, (510) 465-3363. Dimensions traces the evolution of contemporary African-American dance. Live musicians accompany choreography by director Deborah Vaughan and company members. Tickets $8-$10.

Oakland Ballet: Paramount Theatre, 2025 Broadway (20th St.), Oakland, (510) 452-9288. The company is known for its unique style, which combines elements of classical European ballet with American and ethnic dance influences. Based in the sumptuously restored Paramount Theatre, the corps occasionally perform at the Concord Pavilion and Berkeley's Zellerbach Hall. Tickets range from $10 to $30, and discounts are available for students and seniors. The season runs from September through December.

Oakland East Bay Symphony: 1999 Harrison St., Ste. 2030, Oakland, (510) 446-1992. This symphony now calls the gorgeous art-deco Paramount Theatre home. Tickets run $10-$30, and if you plan on going more than once during the season, inquire about three-and four-concert subscription tickets for students and families, which amount to half-price performances. Rush tickets are also available at the door for students and seniors. Concerts are staged from January through April.

Oakland Ensemble Theatre: 1428 Alice St., Oakland, (510) 763-7774. The Ensemble Theatre of the Alice Arts Center is a top-quality African-American troupe which has been in operation since the 1970s.

Oakland Symphony Chorus: 6025 Rockridge Blvd., Oakland, (510) 444-5767. This chorus of 100 professional singers performs four or five times from September to June, often on holiday programs.

Trinity Chamber Concerts: 2320 Dana St., Berkeley, (510) 549-3864. Trinity Chamber Concerts holds vocal recitals with chamber orchestra accompaniment at the 200-seat Trinity Chapel.

UC Berkeley Music Department: Hertz Hall, UC Berkeley Campus, Bancroft Way and Telegraph Ave., (510) 642-4864. The UC Berkeley music department stages performances, including free noontime concerts, in Hertz Hall.

UC Berkeley Dramatic Arts Department: Performances in Zellerbach Playhouse and Durham Studio Theatre, (510) 642-1677, (510) 642-8276. There's no shortage of thespian activities at UC Berkeley. The Zellerbach Playhouse hosts the principal productions of the **Department of Dramatic Arts**—look for one well-known musical every summer. **Room Seven,** in the basement of Zellerbach, debuts smaller scale, student-directed plays. It's a "black box" type of theater—essentially an empty room that can be configured however the director wishes, so you never know what to expect. **The Joseph Wood Crutch Theater** on the Clark Kerr campus is a commodious auditorium particularly well-suited for talent shows, sorority romps, and the like. For tickets to all the campus venues, contact Cal Performances (some of the smaller productions do not offer tickets on an advance basis).

Westwind International Folk Ensemble: 5823 Patton St., Oakland, (510) 524-5333. Westwind has about 40 dancers, singers, and musicians who celebrate the folk traditions of North America, Europe, the Balkans, Russia, and the Middle East with drama, humor, stories, and song. Performances are held at the Julia Morgan Theater.

PARKS AND OPEN SPACES

The East Bay Regional Park District manages 73,000 acres of park lands and 1,000 miles of trails in Alameda and Contra Costa counties. Within its 47 parks you'll find ample opportunities for hiking, swimming, jogging, boating, fishing, and picnicking.

Aquatic Park: 7th and Heinz sts., Berkeley, (510) 843-2273. At this small strip of green paralleling I-80, bike and walking paths rim a long, narrow stretch of water popular with sculling teams, water-skiers, and migrating shorebirds.

Berkeley Marina: Off University Ave. west of I-80, (510) 644-6376. This breezy peninsula, with its pleasant grassy playgrounds and rocky inlets, is a popular kite-flying spot. Pack a picnic and watch the sailboats and windsurfers cavort.

Briones Regional Park: Orinda exit off Hwy 24, northwest on San Pablo Dam Rd., right on Bear Creek Rd., and 5 mi. to the park entrance, (510) 229-3020. An abundance of open space, lakes, challenging trails, and not a lot of people located between Lafayette and Martinez. Hiking trails offer views of Mount Diablo and the bay, as well as a good chance to observe deer and hawks amid the oak and grassland; herds of cattle are a reminder of the region's ranching heritage. There's also an archery range.

Crown Memorial State Beach: Shoreline Dr., Alameda, (510) 635-0138 ext. 2200. **Crab Cove Visitor Center:** 1252 McKay Ave., Alameda, (510) 521-6887. Although far enough removed from the bustle of Oakland, Crown Beach still feels somewhat urban. Its two and one-half miles of sandy shore faces the San Francisco skyline and is a popular promenade route on warm days. Anchoring the end of the park is Crab Cove, where you can wade in tide pools. A visitor center offers interpretive programs and explains bay ecology. • M-F 8:30am-5pm. Visitor Center W-Su 10am-4:30pm.

EAST BAY

Del Valle Regional Park: 7000 Del Valle Rd., off I-580 at N. Livermore exit, Livermore, (510) 373-0332. This spacious park in the Livermore hills is best known for its large, freshwater reservoir that attracts swimmers and windsurfers. Visitors so inclined can rent rowboats and sailboats for a day on the waves. The fishing is pretty good, too.

Anthony Chabot Regional Park (Lake Chabot): I-580 East to Fairmont Dr. exit east; merges with Lake Chabot Rd. to Anthony Chabot Regional Park, (510) 881-1833. High on a ridge, Lake Chabot is one of the most popular fishing spots in the East Bay. You can hire a canoe, rowboat, pedal boat, or electric boat. Sorry, there's no swimming allowed (so you better not fall overboard). For landlubbers, a paved bike path circles the lake. The park also offers serene picnic grounds set throughout its grasslands and forests. Other amenities include camp sites, a golf course, rifle and archery ranges, and an equestrian center.

Lake Temescal Recreation Area: Off Broadway at the Hwy 24 /Hwy 13 interchange, Oakland, (510) 635-0138. Swimming $2/day. This is one of the first regional parks in Oakland. The small "lake" is really a reservoir that was constructed in the 1800s. In summer months, the sandy beach on the east side of the water is frequently filled with kids and families. Year-round, visitors can hike the trail that wraps around the lake, fish for bass and trout, and picnic.

Mount Diablo State Park: North Gate Rd. off Walnut Ave. from Ygnacio Valley Rd. east of Walnut Creek, (510) 837-2525. Mount Diablo's height makes it an alluring place to visit at least once, but the oppressive summer heat and comparative lack of flora and fauna may exclude it from your list of favorite hiking jaunts. The 3,849-foot summit can be reached on foot by hiking up Mitchell Canyon, or you can drive to the top, where finding space in the parking lot can be problematic (especially on weekends). Mountain bikers can roll on the dirt roads to the west of North Gate and South Gate.

Redwood Regional Park: Off Skyline Blvd. and Redwood Rd. on the ridge east of Oakland, (510) 531-6417. Some of this park's trails are sheltered by 100-foot coastal redwoods, making these shady stretches a good choice for hot-weather hiking. (These trees are actually second-growth forests: the area was heavily logged in the mid-1800s.) A network of trails traverse a variety of landscapes: grassland, brush, madrone forest, and pine trees. Rare native trout still swim in Redwood Creek; fishing is prohibited. Other facilities include an equestrian site, archery range, and Roberts Recreation Area, which features a pool, playground, and picnic area.

Tilden Park and Nature Area: Off Wildcat Canyon Rd. in the hills above North Berkeley, (510) 525-2233. This incredible resource is located in a high valley adjacent to Berkeley. The most developed park in the region, Tilden counts among its attractions Lake Anza, a botanical garden, a children's park-within-a-park (featuring a merry-go-round, miniature trains, and hobby farm), a golf course, and an environmental education center, as well as hiking trails (some paved), and camping and picnic areas. Many short trails begin here, and several tree-lined meadows with tables and BBQ grills invite even the most city-worn Berkeley folk to picnic, fly a kite, or just lounge. Secluded Lake Anza is small but beloved, much in ye olde swimming hole mode. The visitor center (Tu-Su 10am-5pm) has free maps and information on all of the East Bay Regional parks.

Wildcat Canyon: Off McBryde Ave. and Arlington Blvd. east of Richmond, (510) 525-2233. Wildcat shares the hills and valleys east of Berkeley with Tilden Park, but is far less developed, offering primarily quiet hiking trails through dry hillsides and shady canyons.

Marin

Marin County is just north of San Francisco, extending from the Golden Gate Bridge up the coast to Bodega Bay and inland to the wine country. With the most hot tubs per capita in the United States, one of the highest per-capita income levels, and notable residents like the surviving members of the Grateful Dead and the principals at LucasFilms Productions, Marin has earned a reputation for being quintessentially Californian. It is also home to some of the most stunning scenery in the Bay Area. With such abundant open space and natural beauty, outdoor activities dominate the list of things to do in the county.

Basic Information

Golden Gate National Recreation Area: National Park Service, Building 201, Fort Mason, SF, (415) 556-0560. • M-F 9:30am-4:30pm.

Marin County Visitors Bureau: 30 N. San Pedro Rd. #150, San Rafael, (415) 472-7470. • M-F 8:30am-5pm.

Mill Valley Chamber of Commerce: 85 Throckmorton Ave., Mill Valley, (415) 388-9700. • M-F 11am-4pm.

Sausalito Chamber of Commerce: 333 Caledonia St., Sausalito, (415) 332-0505. • M-F 9am-5pm.

TRANSPORTATION

The drive to Marin from San Francisco will take you over the Golden Gate Bridge and onto Hwy 101, the main traffic artery through Marin and a major commuter route into the city during rush hour. Traffic headed south on Hwy 101 can also get ugly on weekend evenings, when all of the bikers, hikers, picnickers, and wine tasters are heading back into the city. From Hwy 101, Hwy 37 branches off to the northeast, toward the wine country of Sonoma and Napa. If you're in no hurry, Hwy 1, which clings to the coastline, is a scenic, if excruciatingly curvy and slow, alternative to Hwy 101.

Both Golden Gate Transit and Red and White Fleet provide ferry service from San Francisco to Marin; bus service is provided by Golden Gate Transit. The schedules are geared to commuters' needs, and serve most Marin cities and towns, and even some beaches. San Francisco has a city bus, the number 76, which goes to the Marin Headlands on Sundays. See Transportation chapter for more information on these companies and services.

Tiburon-Angel Island Ferry: (415) 435-2131. Family-run ferry located at 21 Main Street in Tiburon. Ferries to Angel Island run M-F 10am-3pm; Sa-Su 10am-5pm. Round-trip tickets to Angel Island are adults $6, children ages 5-11 $4, bikes $1.

Greyhound Bus: (800) 231-2222, (415) 453-0795. There is a terminal in San Rafael at 850 Tamalpais Street.

Airports

The Oakland (OAK) and San Francisco (SFO) airports are about the same distance from Marin. OAK offers the most budget flights, while more international flights leave from SFO. The distance makes taxis prohibitively expensive, but fortunately there are several other means available. See the Transportation chapter for more information about these airports and transportation companies.

MARIN

Taking public transportation to either of the airports is not a viable option unless you have little or no luggage. **Golden Gate Transit** will allow you to carry on only one small bag that will fit on your lap. There is no direct route to either of the airports. To get to SFO, take a Golden Gate Transit bus to the Transbay Terminal in San Francisco, and then transfer to a **SamTrans** bus to SFO. To get to OAK, take a Golden Gate Transit bus to the Transbay Terminal in San Francisco, and then transfer to an **AC Transit bus** or **BART**.

Shuttle services will save you from having to make endless connections, but door-to-door shuttles are pricy from Marin. **Marin Airporter** (415) 461-4222 has six pickup points in Marin and services SFO. The one-way fare is $11. **Marin Door-to-Door** (800) 540-4815 will pick you up at home and offers charters (1-7 passengers) to OAK for $75, and shuttle service to SFO for $30 for the first passenger and $12 for each additional passenger. The **Santa Rosa Airporter** (707) 545-8015 departs every hour on the hour 5am-10pm from the transportation station at 3rd Street and Heatherton in San Rafael. The one-way fare is $11 to SFO and $15 to OAK.

If you don't feel like waiting for a shuttle or making any connections, you can use one of the pricy car services that serve Marin. Be warned that this will cost you $50 to $140, depending on your departure point and the type of car. If you're stuck and need a ride, however, call one of the following, all of which service both SFO and OAK: **Associated Limousine Service** (415) 877-0433; **Paramount Limousine Service** (510) 569-5466; **Quicksilver Towncar Service** (415) 431-1600.

NEIGHBORHOODS & HOUSING

Marin is one of America's wealthiest counties and its housing prices are the highest in the Bay Area, so don't come looking for bargains. Residents enjoy plentiful open space, good schools, and a sophisticated country-suburban lifestyle. Generally, prices rise as the views of San Francisco improve, and fall as the commute to San Francisco becomes more stressful. Residents brag about their commute, but actually, Hwy 101 frequently is jam-packed from San Rafael to Novato, while the Golden Gate Bridge, $3 toll and all, is bumper to bumper even when it's not closed down by a head-on accident. The ferries, however, give bayside residents the most beautiful commute around.

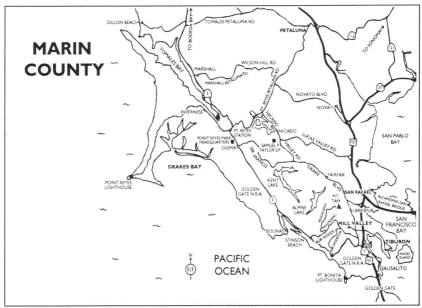

NEIGHBORHOODS & HOUSING

The southernmost city of Marin County, **Sausalito** is known more for its tourism and art festivals than as a place to live. Yet a smorgasbord of 7,300 characters has found a home in this beguiling community. There are a few different neighborhoods within the town limits. The southern sector represents the high end of real estate anywhere: some of these homes are not only aesthetic wonders in themselves, but offer priceless views of San Francisco, Angel Island, and the bay. Prices range from half a million to well over a million dollars. Moderately priced rentals are scarce. The next little hollow north, known as the Caledonia area, is more of an in-town community, with restaurants, shopping, and a movie theater. As you continue north, there are more affordable condominiums and even houseboats. The latter feature all the comforts of home except for the bonus of living on an ever-changing ecosystem. Overall, the rents in most of Sausalito are comparable with San Francisco, which is to say, expensive. But what you can't find across the bridge is the access to beautiful mountain trails and the bay. Public transportation is a breeze, with regular ferry and bus service from San Francisco easing the commute. One slight drawback: during the winter, the Marin Headlands keeps Sausalito shaded all afternoon. Another drawback for those seeking solitude: the steady stream of tourists that dominates town life.

When you finally find **Bolinas**, you might wonder if there's more to this infamous hermit town than a dusty little road with no parking and very few operating business. The town is located just north of Stinson Beach on Hwy 1, although the road signs are always taken down by residents to discourage visitors (go west just north of Bolinas Lagoon). The 1,100 voting residents oppose what they see as useless progress, which has resulted in an exclusive, albeit offbeat community. Even though some of the homes could be in *Architectural Digest*, most look modest from the outside. Many of the residents do not commute to work—they might not even work regular jobs: some are artists, some retired, some are independently wealthy. They all have one thing in common, however: the desire for peace and quiet.

Mill Valley, on the eastern slope of Mount Tamalpais, offers a small-town feel minutes away from city life. The typical landscape is redwood trees and wooded canyons. A popular place for both families and singles, homes are in the moderate range for Marin, $200,000 to $500,000 for a two- or three-bedroom house with a yard, garage, and all the amenities one needs to survive comfortably. Rental rates are on a par with San Francisco, although in Mill Valley, trees, quiet, and good weather come with the deal. The architectural style varies from postwar single-family starter homes to funky brown-shingled tree houses, with even some Mediterranean villas thrown in. There are no rules to define the type of people who choose to live in Mill Valley other than a general tolerance for their neighbors, however normal they may be. The downtown center is filled with interesting shopping, from retail chains like Banana Republic to unique boutiques. Fine restaurants and coffeehouses flourish here, relying on both locals and visitors. Along central Miller Avenue, there's great food shopping, restaurants, and bars. The commute to San Francisco via Golden Gate Transit bus is not bad. Mill Valley is an outdoorsman's haven. Opportunities for hiking and mountain biking are around every corner.

For the most part, **Tiburon** is a quiet, family-oriented suburb. The warm weather, comfortable lifestyle, scenic views, and good nursery and grammar schools are what draw people to this large peninsula jutting into the bay. The average home price is on the upper end of any market, floating between $700,000 and $1,000,000. There are some affordable condos and a few apartments to rent clustered around the main roads and commercial areas. Despite the distance from San Francisco, over 60 percent of the residents—mostly executive types—commute to the city for work. These commuters are well served by ferries. For the most part, the area is residential. There is a small business strip on the peninsula's southern end, near Belvedere, however. (**Belvedere**, a tiny spur of land, is Marin's smallest incorporated community and even more upscale than Tiburon.) Tiburon is one of the choicest places to live in Marin. Recreationally, Tiburon is on par with the rest of Marin, with the addition of the San Francisco Yacht Club for sailors and nearby Angel Island for a fun day trip.

MARIN

Corte Madera has a split personality, divided in half by Hwy 101. The eastern side offers the largest shopping plaza in Marin County, while the western end, in the shadow of Mount Tamalpais, is quiet and residential. The majority of its 8,700-odd residents are families. Corte Madera, along with its twin city, Larkspur, offers excellent elementary schools and little to no crime. The commute to San Francisco is not bad; depending on the traffic, it can take from 15 to 30 minutes on the bus or in a car. Most of the residences are single-family tract homes built between 1950 and 1970. Because of the community, some such abodes command a million-dollar price tag, although there are "affordable" three- or four-bedroom townhouses in the $450,000 price range. The rentals are comparable to nearby communities; a one-bedroom apartment runs from $750 to $1,500, depending on location and amenities.

A vacation-spot-cum-year-round residential area, **Larkspur** is an idyllic place to live. Known as Jagtown, in the early 1900s Larkspur earned a reputation for bars and carousing. One of its landmarks, the Lark Creek Inn, was a notorious haunted house known to the locals as the home of "Crazy Murphy." The 11,000-plus residents enjoy the same good schools and crime record as Corte Madera, since they share a police station and a school district. The homes above the highway are a mixture of middle-class homes interspersed with a few palatial estates. The prices vary with location, but are generally on the high end of the market. A woodsy feeling permeates the town, with redwoods lining the streets, especially Madrone and Baltimore. The commute is relatively quick to San Francisco by bus, car, or the Larkspur Ferry. The town's eastern section, which borders the bay, is newer, with apartments, condominiums, and Larkspur Landing, a very Marin-like open-air shopping center with Marin Brewing Company, A Clean Well Lighted Place for Books, and other retail options.

Incorporated in 1874, **San Rafael** is the county's financial, service, cultural, and economic hub and home to over 53,200 residents. Downtown reflects the charm of old Marin County, with beautiful Victorians and other stately buildings. Housing in the surrounding neighborhoods varies in price and style from ranch-style estates to condominiums. There are also a number of picturesque "starter homes" with yards and porches on tree-lined streets. The homes are well-priced for Marin, averaging $250,000 to $350,000. The rentals are also *relatively* manageable: a one-bedroom costs $650 to $875. Many residents actually work in San Rafael: job opportunities flourish because of the area's growing number of high-tech businesses and established financial and film companies.

Supporting San Rafael's reputation as a great place to raise a family is its great educational system, including nine elementary, two middle, and three high schools. There are also plentiful private and parochial schools. San Rafael is the center of the county's cultural activities. The Marin Center hosts national artists, as well as performances by the Marin Symphony, Marin Opera, Marin Ballet, and other local companies. Falkirk, San Rafael's community cultural center, and other community facilities frequently house theater performances, art exhibits, and music and dance events.

Sir Francis Drake Boulevard heads northwest from Hwy 101, becoming increasingly rural as it passes through a series of small communities. Quiet and pleasant, this part of Marin exemplifies serene living. **Ross** is hilly and calm; traffic on the streets is often in the form of nannies strolling with children. Found within this wealthy area are luxurious homes, many of them New England-style wood-shingled mansions. A golf course and art and garden center add to the comfort of living in Ross. One of the nation's best schools is located in here: the Ross Elementary School has consistently received wide praise.

Between Ross and Larkspur is **Kentfield**, another wealthy community. Close to majestic Mount Tamalpais, Kentfield has a "country" feeling, with homes set back from the town's main roads, nestled amid redwoods and pine trees. Less exclusive but high on charm is **San Anselmo**. The streets have sidewalks, and are lined with older, smaller homes in a variety of styles. Boasting to be California's "antique capital," San Anselmo is home to over 130 antique stores. San Anselmo Avenue features shops, delis, and cafés. **Fairfax** is a peaceful, close-knit community featuring miles of trails for biking, horse riding, and hiking. Many homes in this area are small and predate 1950; they make great fixer-uppers. If you're not seeking a house, apartments can be found near "downtown" Fairfax, along Sir Francis Drake Boulevard.

More rural **San Geronimo**, **Woodacre**, and **Lagunitas** round out the Sir Francis Drake area of Marin. Housing is mainly single-family units built into the hills or smaller structures that resemble summer cottages. Many trails wander through these hilly areas, providing hours of fun for locals who religiously engage in Marin's favorite pastimes—hiking and biking.

One of Marin County's most populous and affordable cities, **Novato** has been experiencing considerable growth in the past 25 years. While most residents live in the standard three-bedroom tract house, there are pockets of more upscale housing in Bahia Park and the woodsy area around Alameda del Prado. Off of Hwy 101 is a mall with standard stores such as Macy's and Costco, making life convenient for Novato residents (especially since the 28-mile drive to San Francisco seems much longer with traffic). In general, life is peaceful in Novato (there is hardly any crime). Novato schools are highly rated; in 1995, San Ramon School was certified by the state as "distinguished," and the Rancho Elementary School is so popular that parents must draw lots for admission during times of student overflow. If you have a cat, take note: a recent law requires cats be implanted with a microchip as an ID device, with the intention of reducing the number of strays in Novato that need to be killed. This might sound a bit Orwellian, but it is also evidence of the neatness and practicality that characterizes Novato.

SIGHTS & ATTRACTIONS

Marin Headlands ★★: Take Hwy 101 to Alexander Avenue, the first exit north of the Golden Gate Bridge. Go left under the highway and follow Conzelman Road up the hill. Encompassing most of the hills and valleys inland from the Pacific Coast north of the bridge, the Marin Headlands' grassy hills offer amazing views, while the valleys are filled with wildflowers and wildlife. The area is a war legacy, home to military installations active until the end of WWII. Battlements and bunkers still dot the hilltops.

Halfway up Conzelman Road, a dirt road on the left leads hikers and bikers down to **Kirby Cove**, a secluded beach almost under the bridge. **The Park Service** (415) 556-0560 allows group camping here. As you continue up Conzelman Road, bear left at the Y-intersection and continue to the top and **Battery 129**, a typical military relic. Hike up to the top of **Hawk Hill** for great views, but if it's a sunny weekend, expect a crowd. Continue on Conzelman west to **Point Bonita**. The still-functioning **Point Bonita Lighthouse** was one of the first to be built on the West Coast. The footpath leading to the lighthouse washed out during the 1993 rainy season, but has since been repaired; it is only open Sa-Su 12:30pm-3:30pm and for special guided tours; call the Headlands Visitors Center (see below) for schedules and reservations. The road past Point Bonita loops into Rodeo Valley, where you'll find **Rodeo Lagoon** (good for birding), **Rodeo Beach** (scenic but too rough to swim), and the **Marine Mammal Center** (415) 289-SEAL/7325, a hospital for marine critters that allows visitors.

Marin Headlands Visitors Center: Bunker Rd., at the end of Rodeo Valley, (415) 331-1540. Newly renovated, the center houses engaging hands-on exhibits in the historic Fort Barry Chapel. A small store sells maps and books about the area.

Sausalito ★: Take Hwy 101 to Alexander Avenue and follow it into town. Sausalito lies across Hwy 101 from the Headlands. Originally a fishing village and then an artists' retreat, Sausalito is now a typical tourist town. Located on the edge of the bay, it has a marina and a main commercial street lined with a variety of coffeehouses, waterfront restaurants, galleries, and T-shirt shops. Ferry service from San Francisco makes it particularly convenient for tired bikers looking for a shortcut back to the city.

Downtown offers shops and a boardwalk. On the water a little north of town sits a fascinating collection of **houseboats**, more house than boat (locals call them floating

MARIN

homes). Nearby at 2100 Bridgeway, there's the **San Francisco Bay Model** (see Amusements below). **Sea Trek Adventures** launches ocean kayaks for tours of Sausalito harbor and beyond. Their Full Moon Tour is a favorite. If you prefer sailing, try **Cass' Rental Marina**. For more information, see the Sailing and Kayaking sections.

Tiburon ★: Take Hwy 101 to Tiburon Boulevard east. A small pay-parking lot at the very end of the road is the best place to ditch your car. If you bike from San Francisco, follow the lovely bike path, which begins along Bridgeway in Sausalito and goes north along the bay to Tiburon Boulevard. A right turn leads you to town. There is also ferry service from San Francisco (see Ferries above). Spanish for "shark," Tiburon lies on a fin-shaped peninsula north of Sausalito. There isn't much in the way of tourist attractions; most people go to eat at one of the restaurants with a view of the bay and San Francisco (see Restaurants below). A small waterfront park has great views of San Francisco and inviting grass for picnics. The stores and galleries on **Ark Row** at the west end of Main Street will happily deplete your savings. **Windsor Vineyards** (800) 214-9463 has a tasting room and sales outlet at 72 Main Street.

Angel Island ★: Red and White Fleet ferries service Angel Island from San Francisco, the Tiburon-Angel Island Ferry runs from Tiburon (see Ferries above). Angel Island, the largest island in the San Francisco Bay, sits across from Tiburon. The **Visitors Center** (415) 435-1915 has historical displays documenting the military use of the island from the Civil War to its days as a Japanese internment camp in World War II. Today, Angel Island is best known for its hiking and biking. **Mount Hamilton** rises 800 feet, and offers excellent views of the area from a number of trails. The island is a great spot for a picnic away from the crowds. Other than the new **Cove Café**, there are few amenities available, so bring your own supplies.

Mill Valley ★: Take Hwy 101 to Tiburon Boulevard/East Blithedale exit and go west, following the signs to downtown Mill Valley. Once home to the mill that processed the huge trees used to build San Francisco, Mill Valley is now quintessentially Marin: a hip bedroom community with cute cottage houses, good food, coffee, and lots happening in the arts. Each autumn the **Mill Valley Film Festival** (415) 383-5256 brings the town to life. The town is also a convenient base of operations for expeditions to Mount Tam, which rises to the west.

Mount Tamalpais ★★: At 2,600 feet, Mount Tam dominates the landscape and offers spectacular views of the Bay Area, plus an enormous trail system. Within its vast expanse lie **Mount Tamalpais State Park** (415) 388-2070, **Muir Woods National Monument** (see below), and the **Marin Municipal Water District** (415) 924-4600 or (415) 459-5267. The diverse terrain includes redwoods, oak, and grassland. A quick way to sample Mount Tam is to drive to the top. Take Hwy 101 to Hwy 1, bear right on Panoramic Highway, and then following signs to Mount Tam and Muir Woods. At Pantoll Road, turn right and wind your way to the top. From the parking lot, walk up a short, steep dirt road for the ultimate view.

The extensive trail network on all sides of the mountain offers endless possibilities for exploring and lets you approach from any angle. The excellent Olmstead Bros. map, *Trails of Mount Tamalpais and the Marin Headlands*, is available in most bike shops and bookstores. Limited camping is possible. Bikes can be rented in San Anselmo at **Caesar's Cyclery**, 29 San Anselmo Avenue, (415) 258-9920. Close to the summit you will find the **Sydney B. Cushing Memorial Theater**, a 5,000-seat outdoor amphitheater that hosts musical productions by the **Mountain Play Association** (see Performing Arts below).

Muir Woods ★★: Take Hwy 101 to Hwy 1, bear right on Panoramic Highway, then turn left down Muir Woods Road. The park is about a mile down the road on your right, (415) 388-2595. One of the only places you can find old-growth, coastal redwoods in Northern California, Muir Woods is the forest primeval. The towering, thousand-year-old trees block out most of the sunlight, leaving the narrow valley lush and tranquil. Muir Woods attracts its well-deserved crowd; you can avoid the throngs

SIGHTS & ATTRACTIONS

somewhat by going during the week or in the winter, when the creeks are filled with water. A short loop winds its way along a stream bed among towering redwoods; this walk of less than an hour is what most visitors choose to explore, so even on weekends you can find solitude by taking the steeper trails away from the valley floor. **The Visitors Center** is open daily 8am-sunset.

Muir Beach ★: Take Hwy 101 to Hwy 1 and follow the signs. After six miles on Hwy 1 you will see the **Pelican Inn**. To reach Muir Beach, turn left. This small beach is located in an isolated, semicircular cove cut into the cliffs, with horse ranches and rugged hills in the background. The surf is generally too rough for swimming. A small grassy area has some picnic tables and barbecue grills.

Stinson Beach ★★: Follow directions to Muir Beach, but continue straight past the Pelican Inn for six miles and follow the signs to the left. Stinson is a very happening place; a wide spit of sand perfect for running, Frisbee, or sand castles. The parking lot has sheltered picnic spots, and a small settlement at the entrance includes shops and restaurants where you can fill out your picnic, rent a surfboard, or pop down oysters and beers under an umbrella. **Off the Beach Boats** (415) 868-9445 rents open-top kayaks for experts to use in the surf and the rest of us to use in Bolinas Lagoon; rates are about $20 for two hours, $35 all day. Be forewarned: Stinson Beach has a huge following, and on hot weekends traffic gets backed up for miles. You can avoid the crowds and find parking if you go early. Call ahead for fog, surf, and traffic information (415) 868-1922 or (415) 868-0942.

Point Reyes National Seashore ★★★: Take Hwy 101 to Sir Francis Drake Boulevard to Hwy 1, turn right and then immediately left, and follow the signs to the Park Headquarters. At the northern edge of Marin lies this spectacular park, ideal for hiking, camping, and beachcombing. The 75,000-acre expanse contains numerous well-marked trails through forest and coastal territory, while the ten-mile stretch of beach is full of caves, cliffs, waterfalls, and windy headlands.

Information is available at the **Bear Valley Visitors Center** (415) 663-1092. If you want to bike in Point Reyes, you can rent mountain bikes at **Trailhead Rentals** in Olema, 88 Bear Valley Rd., (415) 663-1958. Bike rentals are $6 per hour or $20 per day M-F; $24 per day Sa-Su. Call ahead for reservations and information. Tents, cameras, and binoculars can also be rented.

The **Visitors Center** is a good place to pick up maps or walk through the exhibits on park wildlife before setting out. Nearby is the **Earthquake Trail**, a **Miwok Village** re-creation, and **Morgan Horse Ranch**. The popular **Bear Valley Trail** leads hikers through four fairly flat miles to Arch Rock. From Arch Rock you can enjoy the beautiful view of the ocean, or take the lower trail to the beach and walk through Miller Cave if it's low tide. For a strenuous three-mile hike, take Bear Valley Trail to the Sky Trail, which ascends Mount Wittenberg, the highest point in Point Reyes. From there, you can continue down to the coast; then return either via the same route, or, to avoid Mount Wittenberg, along the beach to Arch Rock and back.

Point Reyes Lighthouse ★★★: Take Sir Frances Drake Boulevard to the end. The lighthouse sits at the very tip of the Point Reyes peninsula. It's the perfect spot for watching California gray whales during their biannual migrations. Late November through early January is best for sighting whales cruising south, while March and April are best for spotting them moving north. The lighthouse, located down a long set of stairs on a steep cliff, is open Th-M 10am-4:30pm; it is closed when the wind is too strong. The weather can be cold, foggy, and extremely windy, but when it's clear, the **views ★★★** are spectacular.

Drake's Bay Beach (watch for the left turn off Sir Francis Drake a few miles before the lighthouse) is located on the south side of the Point Reyes peninsula. The beach is backed by towering cream-colored cliffs. Along the way to the peninsula, you'll pass through the sleepy town of **Inverness**, which has bed-and-breakfasts, restaurants, and a grocery store. Alongside is Tomales Bay—calm, flat, and undeveloped.

MARIN
PLACES TO STAY

Camping & Hostels
Camping is available on most of the public lands in Marin. Many of the sites are walk-in, and most require reservations.

AYH Golden Gate Hostel: Fort Barry, Bunker Rd. in Rodeo Valley, Marin Headlands, (415) 331-2777. Located in the scenic but isolated Marin Headlands near Rodeo Beach and the visitors center. $12 dorm rooms, $35 for double room.

AYH Point Reyes Youth Hostel: Limantour Rd., Point Reyes National Seashore, (415) 663-8811. Located two miles from the ocean in a secluded valley near hiking trails and the estuary. You'll probably want to cook your own food here, but shop before you arrive, since the stores are an eight-mile trek from the hostel. Call for reservation information 8am-9:30am; 4:30pm-9:30pm. $10 adult, $5 children.

Destinet: (800) 444-7275. State Park Reservations.

Marin State Parks District Office: 1455A East Francisco Blvd., San Rafael, (415) 456-1286. Supervises local state parks: Samuel Taylor, Angel Island, and Mount Tamalpais. For reservations, call Destinet (see above). Open M-F 8am-5pm.

Point Reyes National Seashore: Bear Valley Visitors Center, Bear Valley Rd. just west of Olema, (415) 663-1092. Backpack sites only. Coast camp is shortest hike (two miles each way). Wildcat Camp is also near beach. Glen Camp and Sky Camp lie inland. Reservations required. For reservations, call M-F 9am-noon. Free.

Samuel Taylor State Park: Sir Francis Drake Blvd., Lagunitas, (415) 488-9897. Typical state park car camping: closely packed loops under the trees, plenty of facilities. Open Su-Th 8am-8:30pm; F-Sa 8am-10pm. For reservations, call Destinet (see above).

Steep Ravine Environmental Cabins: Mount Tamalpais State Park, Hwy 1, 1 mi. south of Stinson Beach. Rustic cabins on bluff overlooking ocean, with platform beds, woodstoves, and pit toilets. Water nearby, but no electricity. Camping allowed. (For reservations, call Destinet—see above—first thing in the morning, exactly eight weeks in advance.) $30 per cabin, $9 per campsite.

Hotels, Motels, Bed and Breakfasts

Bear Valley Inn Bed and Breakfast $$: 88 Bear Valley Rd., Olema, (415) 663-1777. Three-room Victorian ranch house in Olema one-half mile from the Point Reyes National Seashore. The staff promises to pamper guests with great food and old-fashioned hospitality. Rents mountain bikes, too. $70-$125; $10 off midweek.

Blackthorne Inn $$$: 266 Vallejo Ave., Inverness, (415) 663-8621. A unique lodging experience in a beautiful handcrafted tree house, complete with fireman's pole and spiral staircase, tucked in a secluded wooded canyon adjacent to the park. There are five rooms, a deck, a hot tub, and full breakfast served every morning. Hiking trails are nearby. $105-$185.

Casa Madrona $$$: 801 Bridgeway, Sausalito, (415) 332-0502. Deluxe, (mostly) historic inn built into hill above town. $105-$250.

Coastal Lodging of West Marin: (415) 485-2678, (415) 663-1351. Referrals for bed and breakfasts.

Courtyard By Marriott $$$: 2500 Larkspur Landing Cir., Larkspur Landing, (415) 925-1800, (800) 321-2211. National chain geared to business travelers, who will appreciate the access to ferries to San Francisco. $109-$145.

Inns of Point Reyes: (415) 485-2649, 663-1420. Referrals for bed and breakfasts.

Inverness Lodge/Manka's $$: Corner of Callendar and Argyle rds., Inverness, (415) 669-1034. Hunting lodge–style rooms and cabins, some with decks overlooking Tomales Bay. $85-$145; breakfast extra.

PLACES TO STAY

Mountain Home Inn $$$: 810 Panoramic Hwy., above Mill Valley, (415) 381-9000. Charming old lodge on slopes of Mount Tam. Some rooms offer fireplace and Jacuzzi. $131-$215.

Pelican Inn $$$: Hwy 1, Muir Beach, (415) 383-6000. Cozy, English-style pub, at entrance to Muir Beach. $140-$155 (includes full English breakfast); call 4 to 6 months in advance for Sa reservations!

Ten Inverness Way $$$: 10 Inverness Way, Inverness, (415) 669-1648. Built in 1904, a quaint four-room inn with a stone fireplace, a hot tub, a sun room, and a flower garden. Full breakfast is served. $110-$140.

Tiburon Lodge $$$$: 1651 Tiburon Blvd., Tiburon, (415) 435-3133. More of a 1950s motel than a lodge, but conveniently in the center of Tiburon. Also offers a pool and many spa rooms. Ask about their discount programs (AAA, off-season, etc.). $189-$319.

West Marin Vacation Rentals: 11150 Sir Francis Drake Blvd., Point Reyes Station, (415) 663-1776. Vacation home rentals.

Wyndham Garden $$: Hwy 101 at Northgate Dr., San Rafael, (415) 479-8800. All the predictability of a national chain. $79-$109.

GETTING SETTLED

Bookstores

A Clean Well Lighted Place for Books: 2417 Larkspur Landing Circle, Larkspur, (415) 461-0171. See San Francisco Bookstores.

Barnes & Noble: 2020 Redwood Hwy., Larkspur, (415) 924-1016. National chain.

Book Passage: 51 Tamal Vista Blvd., Corte Madera, (415) 927-0960. This local bookseller has been providing its customers with a café since before the trend become mandatory. The store specializes in travel guides, making it a good place to go before planning a trip. New and used books.

Borders Books & Music: 588 W. Francisco Blvd., San Rafael, (415) 454-1400. National chain with café.

Depot Bookstore & Café: 87 Throckmorton Ave., Mill Valley, (415) 383-2665. Located in an old railroad depot in the center of the town square, the Depot can't help but be a neighborhood gathering spot. The café gets most of the attention, although the tiny bookstore makes a nice spot to browse, and features a very Marin selection.

Food & Wine

The Marin grocery scene is dominated by Safeway and Lucky. In addition to the giants, Bell Market is a local chain with an area presence. Marin also has plenty of small, independent grocers and health-food stores, plus good farmers' markets.

Andronico's: 100 Center Blvd., San Anselmo, (415) 455-8186. See San Francisco Grocery Stores.

Asian Market: 5 Mary St., San Rafael, (415) 459-7133. Pan-Asian cooking supplies for chefs preparing Chinese, Japanese, Thai, or Vietnamese dishes. Mostly packaged foods, but some produce as well.

Marin French Cheese Factory: Petaluma-Point Reyes Rd., Petaluma, (707) 762-6001. They make Camembert, Schloss, and Brie cheeses under the Rouge et Noir label; sold along with other picnic foods. The factory and farm is set in a bucolic picnic area complete with a pond. Call for information about tours.

The Cheese Shop: 38 Miller Ave., Mill Valley, (415) 383-7272. A small store with a large cheese selection, as well as such accompaniments as bread, crackers, and wine.

MARIN

Johnson's Drake's Bay Oysters: 17171 Sir Francis Drake Blvd., turnoff 6 miles past Inverness on the way to the lighthouse, (415) 669-1149. At this bayside oyster farm, you can see how these delicacies are cultivated, then buy some to take home. Shucked oysters are sold by the pint or the quart; oysters in the shell go by the dozen or the thousand.

Mill Valley Market: 12 Corte Madera Ave., Mill Valley, (415) 388-3222. This grocery store caters to well-heeled Mill Valley gourmets in search of excellent cheese, pâté, and such. Complete a picnic by choosing from their extensive bread and wine selections.

Mollie Stone's Market: 100 Harbor Dr., Sausalito, (415) 331-6900. A Bay Area supermarket chain emphasizing a mixture of the sacred (health foods, organic produce) and the profane (Coke, Captain Crunch).

Perry's Deli: 246 E. Blithedale Ave., Mill Valley, (415) 381-0407. Great place for picnic supplies.

Real Food Company: 200 Caledonia St., Sausalito, (415) 332-9640. • 770 W. Francisco Blvd., San Rafael, (415) 459-8966. See San Francisco Food Stores.

Trader Joe's: Montecito Plaza, 337 3rd St., San Rafael, (415) 454-9530. See San Francisco Food Stores.

Whole Foods Market: 414 Miller Ave., Mill Valley, (415) 381-1200. See San Francisco Food Stores.

Farmers' Markets

Downtown San Rafael: 4th St. between Lootens and B sts., (415) 457-2266. Th 6-9pm April-October. Features live entertainment, from musicians to clowns.

Marin Civic Center: Civic Center Dr. off Hwy 101, (415) 456-3276. One of the Bay Area's most celebrated farmers' markets. Th 8am-1pm; Su 8am-1pm year-round.

Novato: Sherman Ave. between Grant and De Long aves., (415) 456-3276. Tu 4-8pm May-October.

The Village at Corte Madera: Paradise Dr. and Hwy 101, in the courtyard, (415) 456-3276. W 2-7pm May-October.

Home Furnishings

Most of the chain stores described in the San Francisco Home Furnishings section—Macy's, Crate & Barrel, Williams-Sonoma—have Marin locations as well; check your local phone book for specific locations.

RESTAURANTS & CAFES

Avenue Grill ★★ $$ 44 E. Blithedale Ave. (Sunnyside), Mill Valley, (415) 388-6003. The Avenue Grill brought upscale American food to Marin before it was commonplace, and still enjoys a loyal following despite claims of inconsistent execution. The large front windows brighten the convivial bistro setting, complete with requisite yellow walls and white tablecloths. The menu entices diners with inventive combinations like Pacific oysters with wasabi *mignonette* or grilled ono on a spinach and white bean salad with olive-pepper vinaigrette. On rainy days, turn to comfort foods like meat loaf with gravy and garlic mashed potatoes or barbecued honey-glazed pork loin with coleslaw. • Su-Th 5:30-10pm; F-Sa 5:30-11pm.

Bubba's Diner ★★ $$: 566 San Anselmo Ave. (Bridge), San Anselmo, (415) 459-6862. This tiny diner has been a runaway success, drawing huge crowds willing to wait for a seat in a Naugahyde booth or at the counter. Opened by a Lark Creek Inn alum, the menu focuses on upscale American comfort food, not greasy trucker fare. Tender pork chops with mashed potatoes show the elegant Lark Creek touch, as does the hamburger served on a fresh-baked bun with homemade mayonnaise. Finish with a milk shake or apple pie. Breakfast offers some of the best food—don't miss the pancakes—and longest lines. • M, W-Th 7:30am-2pm, 5:30-9pm; F 7:30am-2pm, 5:30-9:30pm; Sa 8am-2pm, 5:30-9:30pm; Su 8am-2pm, 5:30-9pm.

Buckeye Roadhouse ★★ $$$: 15 Shoreline Hwy. (Hwy 101), Mill Valley, (415) 331-2600. The Buckeye Roadhouse, along with Fog City Diner in San Francisco, Mustards Grill in Napa, and a growing list of others, is part of peripatetic chef Cindy Pawlcyn's burgeoning kitchen empire. It serves expensive new American cuisine—grilled pork chops with mashed potatoes, fantastic onion strings, strawberry shortcake—although not always as good as that found at some of her other outposts. If duck is on the menu, try it. The wait staff is professional, but highly sales oriented. Reservations recommended. • M-Th 11:30am-10:30pm; F-Sa 11:30am-11pm; Su 10:30am-10pm.

Cactus Café ★★ $: 393 Miller Ave. (La Goma), Mill Valley, (415) 388-8226. Cactus Café's highly rated, inexpensive Mexican food goes beyond basics with regional specialties like green chili polenta and *posole*. The simple, dinerlike setting is bright and festive, although you wouldn't guess it from the roadside location. Counter service only. • M-Th 11:30am-9:30pm; F 11:30am-10pm; Sa noon-10pm; Su noon-9pm.

Caffè Trieste ★ ¢: 1000 Bridgeway (Caledonia), Sausalito, (415) 332-7770. This suburban branch of the famous North Beach hangout serves the same fantastic, pricy cappuccino and cheesecake, plus decent pizza and pasta, in a cramped jumble of tiled tables. The low brick wall outside serves as a resting and posing point for the many bicyclists passing by. No credit cards. • Daily 7am-midnight.

Cantina ★ $: 651 E. Blithedale Ave. (Camino Alto), Mill Valley, (415) 381-1070. The Cantina chain of Mexican restaurants originated here, and boasts potent margaritas and live mariachi bands—one of the string players is the father of rock guitarist Carlos Santana. The food is standard Tex-Mex, but after a couple of margaritas, nobody notices. • Su-Th 11:30am-10pm; F-Sa 11:30am-11pm (food available until midnight in bar).

Chart House ★ $$: 201 Bridgeway (Richardson), Sausalito, (415) 332-0804. This pleasant outpost of the upscale surf-and-turf chain was formerly the Valhalla, one of the Bay Area's most famous brothels. Sally Stanford, a former madam, served as Sausalito's mayor in the 1970s. The waterfront location offers spectacular views of the bay. • M-Th 5:30-9:30pm; F 5:30-10pm; Sa-Su 5-10pm (later if they're busy).

Depot Bookstore and Café ★ ¢: 87 Throckmorton Ave. (Miller), Mill Valley, (415) 383-2665. This tiny café, located in a charming old train station in the center of town, got the bookstore-café combination down before Borders and Barnes & Noble moved it national. Inside you'll find a small, erudite bookstore and a basic café. If you take a table outside at which to devour your new book along with a latte and pastry, you'll have a view of local slackers playing hackey-sack on the square. Some locals feel success has led to high prices and negligent service, but they're still coming. • Daily 7am-10pm; food until 8:30pm.

Dipsea Café ★ $: 200 Shoreline Hwy. (Tennessee Valley Rd.), Mill Valley, (415) 381-0298. Most people come to this country cottage hall overlooking a breezy tidal inlet near the road to Tennessee Valley to enjoy home-cooked brunches, salads, and sandwiches. The walls are covered with pictures of the Dipsea Race, a grueling cross-country run from Mill Valley to Stinson Beach—and back for the Dipsea Double. Load up on carbs and give it a try. • M-F 7am-3pm; Sa-Su 7am-5pm.

Drake's Bay Beach Café ★ $: 1 Drake's Bay Beach Rd., Point Reyes National Seashore near lighthouse, (415) 669-1297. Warm and cozy, serving fried, barbecued, and stewed Johnson's oysters, along with more typical seaside café favorites. • Daily 10am-6pm (closed W in winter).

MARIN

Fabrizio's ★★ $$: 455 Magnolia Ave. (Ward/King), Larkspur, (415) 924-3332. Fabrizio's classic Italian fare won't surprise you, and the spare decor won't provide an evening's entertainment—unless you can make conversation out of blond wood and white tablecloths. But you also won't be disappointed by the well-done renditions of such classics as risotto Gorgonzola or veal piccata. Pastas are also respectable and moderately priced. Service is professional. • M-Sa 11:30am-10pm; Su 4-10pm.

Gatsby's ★ $: 39 Caledonia St. (Bridgeway), Sausalito, (415) 332-4500. No mint juleps here, Daisy. Just good pizza (and whole-wheat crust for the health-conscious). • M-Sa 11:30am-2:30pm, 5-10:30pm; Su 5-10:30pm.

Gira Polli ★★ $$: 590 E. Blithedale Ave. (Camino Alto), Mill Valley, (415) 383-6040. See San Francisco section for review. • M-Sa 4:30-9:30pm; Su 4-9pm.

Gray Whale Pub & Pizzeria ★ $: 12781 Sir Francis Drake Blvd., Inverness, (415) 669-1244. Pizza, beer, coffee drinks, and a variety of cakes, pies, and pastries. • M-F 11am-9pm; Sa-Su 10am-9pm.

Guaymas ★★ $$: 5 Main St. (Tiburon Blvd.), Tiburon, (415) 435-6300. Serves up good (although pricy) Mexican cuisine featuring fresh combinations unusual in these parts. Appetizers include an entire seafood section with two types of ceviche, grilled shrimp, and barbecued oysters with hand-cut salsa. The rest of the long menu specializes in tamales, mesquite-grilled meats and fish, and regional specialties like chicken mole. The large, bright dining area is big on ocher tile, but the real decoration is the stunning view of the bay, which you can admire from the patio on warm days. Sip a tasty margarita and mingle with the beautiful crowd. Reservations recommended for weekends. • M-Th 11:30am-10pm; F-Sa 11:30am-11pm; Su 10:30am-10pm.

Il Fornaio ★★★ $$: 223 Corte Madera Town Center (Paradise Dr.), Corte Madera, (415) 927-4400. The original Il Fornaio, done in trademark high style. See San Francisco section for review. • M-F 11:30am-10pm; Sa 10am-11pm; Su 9am-10pm.

Il Fornaio Panneteria ★ ¢: 1 Main St. (Tiburon Blvd.), Tiburon, (415) 435-0777. • 223 Corte Madera Town Center, Corte Madera, (415) 927-2300. In Tiburon, indulge in Il Fornaio's famous baked goods and panini in the bright corner café, or eat them on the lawn outside enjoying the view of Angel Island. • Tiburon: M-F 6:30am-8pm; Sa 7am-10pm; Su 7am-8pm. • CM: M-F 7am-6pm; Sa 7:30am-6pm; Su 7:30am-5pm.

Java ★ ¢: 320 Magnolia Ave. (King), Larkspur, (415) 927-1501. A hip coffeehouse and restaurant in an old brick train depot. Offerings include salads and light entrées from quesadillas to lasagna. Live music occasionally brightens the setting. • M 7am-3pm; Tu-Th 7am-10pm; F 7am-11pm; Sa 8am-11pm; Su 8am-8pm.

Jennie Low's Chinese Cuisine ★★ $: 38 Miller Ave. (E. Blithedale), Mill Valley, (415) 388-8868. • 120 Vintage Way (Rowland Blvd.), Novato, (415) 892-8838. Jennie Low's restaurants are a far cry from your basic Chinatown dives. While Jennie keeps busy working the large crowd, you can watch your food being prepared in the glass-fronted kitchen from your seat in the spotless, well-organized dining room. The menu is an eclectic mix of Cantonese, Mandarin, Hunan, and Sichuan dishes, all modified for suburban California tastes. The pot stickers come with either a pork or vegetarian filling. In addition to the standard kung pao chicken with peanuts, you can order a delicious pine nut chicken. Chili-hot string beans are particularly good. • M-Sa 11:30am-3pm, 4:30-9:30pm; Su 4:30-9:30pm.

Lark Creek Inn ★★★★ $$$: 234 Magnolia Ave. (William), Larkspur, (415) 924-7766. One of the most perfect places on earth. Situated in a Victorian house next to a wooded brook, the rustic dining room is understated and charming, the service is flawless, and the food is heavenly home cooking elevated to new heights: Yankee pot roast, oak-barbecued country spareribs with roasted potatoes, red garlic, and coleslaw, and homemade butterscotch pudding. Plus the best Sunday brunch ever. (The only distraction is the shameless hawking of Lark Creek Inn memorabilia on the menu.) Reservations a must on weekends. • M-Th 11:30am-2pm, 5:30-9:15pm; F 11:30am-2pm, 5-10pm; Sa 5-10pm; Su 10am-2pm, 5:30-8:45pm.

Left Bank ★★★ $$: 507 Magnolia St., (Ward), Larkspur, (415) 927-3331. This is the second restaurant of chef Roland Passot, whose La Folie in San Francisco has been consistently rated one the city's best for years. In keeping with the locale, this Marin venture is a large, casual brasserie—yellow walls, French posters, white tablecloths, and all. Simple classics dominate the menu: steak with *pommes frites,* roast chicken, duck confit, steamed mussels. The large patio makes a lovely al fresco dining spot. The reasonably priced wines match the affordable food. Reservations recommended. • M-Th 11:30am-11pm; F-Sa 11:30am-midnight; Su 11:30am-10pm.

Manka's Inverness Lodge ★★★ $$$: 30 Callendar Wy. (Argyle/Sir Francis Drake), Inverness, (415) 669-1034. Manka's California wild-game menu draws rave reviews for the excellent renditions of venison, elk, and wild boar, much of it cooked over an open grill. In keeping with its seaside locale, seafood is also excellent. The building is an old hunting lodge that captures the feel with roaring fires, overstuffed chairs, and board games from another era. Reservations recommended. • Daily 6-9pm.

Marin Brewing Company ★ $: 1809 Larkspur Landing Cir. (Sir Francis Drake), Larkspur Landing, (415) 461-4677. This large, immensely successful brew pub offers high-quality microbrews and a varied menu ranging from wood-fired pizza to Asian salads to pub grub. Located in the Larkspur Landing Shopping Center across from the ferry terminal, it attracts a loud after-work crowd. Reservations recommended if you want to bypass the bar on the way to your table. • Daily 11:30am-midnight.

Mikayla at Casa Madrona ★★ $$$$: 801 Bridgeway (Caledonia), Sausalito, (415) 331-5888. Casa Madrona's most noteworthy feature is the spectacular view of San Francisco Bay and the city itself. The food, a mix of California and Continental, is also quite good. Start with polenta with a wild mushroom sauce, then move on to grilled salmon with balsamic vinaigrette, striped bass with leek cream sauce, or rack of lamb. Meals are served in a romantic dining room. The perfect spot for a Sunday brunch, the room has a retractable roof for sunshine without blustery breezes. • M-Sa 6-9:15pm; Su 10:30am-2:30pm, 6-9:15pm.

Mill Valley Coffee Roastery $: 2 Miller Ave. (Throckmorton), Mill Valley, (415) 383-2912. Friendly local hangout for cappuccino and pastries. • M-Th 7am-9pm; F 7am-10pm; Sa 8am-10pm; Su 8am-9pm.

Mountain Home Inn ★★ $$: 810 Panoramic Hwy. (Hwy 1), Mill Valley, (415) 381-9000. On the slopes of Mount Tamalpais, the rustic Mountain Home Inn feeds hungry hikers and tourists great breakfasts on the weekends and dinners all week. Enjoy the view from the outdoor deck during the day and position yourself near the cozy fireplace in the evening. You pay for the wonderful atmosphere, but the food is pretty good, especially the brunches. Reservations recommended. • M-F 11:30am-3:30pm, 5:30-9:30pm; Sa-Su 8am-3:30pm, 5:30-9:30pm.

Parkside Café and Snack Bar ★★ $: 43 Arenal Ave. (Calle del Mar), Stinson Beach, (415) 868-1272. The Parkside Café is closer to the beach than any of the other Stinson Beach restaurants. In keeping with the local architectural canon, it's a small cottage with a large patio that appeals to the beach-bound crowd. Food is a cut above that offered by the neighbors, and consists of basic but fresh breakfasts and lunches, with inexpensive family Italian and seafood dinners. A snack bar dispenses burgers and fries to those who can't wait to start tanning. • Tu-W 7:30am-2pm; Th-M 7:30am-2pm, 5-9:30pm.

Pasticceria Rulli ★★ ¢: 464 Magnolia Ave. (Ward/King), Larkspur, (415) 924-7478. Duck back in time and enjoy cappuccino, gelato, panini, and gourmet northern Italian pastries in this cozy Victorian parlor replete with marble-topped tables and Florentine banquettes. The counter comes straight from a 19th-century soda shoppe. No credit cards. • M-Th 7am-7pm; F 7am-11pm; Sa 7:30am-11pm; Su 7:30am-7pm.

MARIN

Pelican Inn ★ $$$: 10 Pacific Wy. (Hwy 1 at Muir Beach turnoff), (415) 383-6000. A rambling Tudor-style bed and breakfast with an authentic British pub and rather formal dining room (tall folks will have to hunch down to avoid the low-timbered beams). Stop for a pint and some darts on your way back from the beach. Unfortunately, the food is as authentically British as the architecture: bangers and eggs, shepherd's pie, prime rib, and the like. On Sundays a lunch buffet is served. Be sure to wander the lovely gardens. Reservations only for groups of six or more. • Tu-F 11:30am-3pm, 6-9:30pm; Sa-Su 11:30am-3:30pm, 5:30-9:30pm.

Phyllis' Giant Burgers ★ $: 72 E. Blithedale Ave. (Forrest), Mill Valley, (415) 381-5116. The name says it all. • Daily 11am-9pm.

Rice Table ★★ $$: 1617 4th St. (G St.), San Rafael, (415) 456-1808. Indonesian food doesn't share the same high recognition level that Thai or Vietnamese food does in America, but this immensely popular restaurant is doing its part to change that. Many of the dishes on the short menu are familiar from other Southeast Asian restaurants: the ubiquitous *satay* skewered meat and chicken with peanut sauce, *lumpia* spring rolls, and hearty curries. *Rijstaffel*, a banquet of sampler dishes with rice, will look familiar to those who've been to Amsterdam, where this former colony's cooking enjoys a large following. The bright batik decorations in the rattan-lined room will make Deadheads feel at home. • W-Sa 5:30-10pm; Su 5-9pm.

Royal Thai ★ $$: 610 3rd St. (Irwin), San Rafael, (415) 485-1074. One of Marin County's most beloved restaurants, Royal Thai fits traditional Thai restaurant charm into a cozy Victorian house. The encyclopedic menu features an extensive range of dishes. Most dishes are pretty good, although the pad Thai is a standout. • M-F 11am-2:30pm, 5-10pm; Sa-Su 5-10pm.

Sam's Anchor Café ★ $$: 27 Main St. (Tiburon Blvd.), Tiburon, (415) 435-4527. Sam's is famous for the huge waterfront deck—featured in the movie *Nine Months*—where the Corona beer crowd comes to hang out and scarf burgers, fries, and deep-fried seafood. Its location also makes it a popular place for yachters to dock for snacks. At night, the seafood menu gets more expensive, but not necessarily better. Look for familiar combinations of pasta, steak, seafood, and chicken. • M-F 11am-10pm; Sa 10am-10pm; Su 9:30am-10pm.

Sand Dollar ★ $$: 3458 Hwy 1, Stinson Beach, (415) 868-0434. Quite the all-American beach restaurant with sandwiches, burgers, seafood, and pasta. The cozy bar inside is a local hangout—the gossip is juicier than the food—while the patio can be a scene for postfraternal San Francisco singles. Sit in the sun, sip a beer, and slurp some local oysters while you admire tan lines. • M-Th 11:30am-3pm, 5:30-9pm; F-Sa 11:30am-3pm, 5:30-9:30pm; Su 11am-3pm, 5:30-9:30pm.

Station House Café ★★ $$: 11180 Hwy 1 (2nd St.), Point Reyes Station, (415) 663-1515. Warm and homey, the Station House Café is a favorite for wholesome preparations featuring local ingredients, especially fresh seafood and delicious brunches. Some of the kitchen's classics include steamed mussels, barbecued oysters, and corn bread. The country-casual dining room is a welcoming spot for hungry hikers returning from a day in the park. The garden is perfect for dining al fresco. Reservations suggested on weekends. • Su-Th 8am-9pm; F-Sa 8am-10pm.

Stinson Beach Grill ★ $$: 3465 Hwy 1, Stinson Beach, (415) 868-2002. Burgers, seafood, and Southwest and Italian cuisines are all served in a beach house with a big deck. The food is passable, but most people come for the relaxing beach-hangout atmosphere after roasting in the sun or freezing in the fog. • M-Th 11:30am-9pm; F 11:30am-9:30pm; Sa-Su 11am-9:30pm.

Sweden House Bakery ★ $: 35 Main St. (Tiburon Blvd.), Tiburon, (415) 435-9767. Delicious, authentic, and pricy Swedish baked goods are available here, plus substantial breakfasts and sandwiches. Try the Swedish pancakes (rolled crêpes) served with lingonberries, or French toast made with Swedish limpa bread, apple butter, walnuts, sour cream, and syrup. The small waterfront patio offers a saner alternative to Sam's and Guaymas. • M-F 7:30am-7pm; Sa-Su 8am-8pm (later in summer).

Taqueria La Quinta ★ ¢: 11285 Hwy 1 (3rd St.), Point Reyes Station, (415) 663-8868. Point Reyes Station is an unlikely place for a budget-priced burrito shop, but here it is. It's not a Mission district taqueria, but it does a pretty good job with the basic soft tacos, burritos, and tostadas, and it's cheap and quick. No credit cards. • Su-M, W-Th 11am-8pm; F-Sa 11am-9:30pm.

Tutto Mare ★★ $$: 9 Main St. (Tiburon Blvd.), Tiburon, (415) 435-4747. Similar to Guaymas, but with an Italian fishing village theme. Sporting the same impressive views and outdoor deck, Tutto Mare appears to enjoy an equally enthusiastic following. The restaurant is split between the starkly casual downstairs "taverna," where diners pick from a limited menu of wood-fired pizzas, salads, and shellfish, and a more formal upstairs space with a full menu. Both dining rooms subscribe to the industrial chic school of decor, with expensive rustic wood furniture and open kitchens. The food follows the theme, featuring many unusual seafood and pasta dishes such as spaghetti with a cuttlefish ink sauce and tortellini filled with sardines, currants, fennel, and pine nuts. The food can be inconsistent, but most people are having too good a time to notice. • M-F 11:30am-10pm; Sa 11am-11pm; Su 11am-10pm.

ARTS & ENTERTAINMENT

Amusements

Bay Area Discovery Museum: 557 East Fort Baker (off Alexander Ave.), Sausalito, (415) 487-4398. Created solely with kids in mind, this museum, found under the north tower of the Golden Gate Bridge, features dozens of hands-on exhibits where children can engage in activities from rowing on a boat crew to exploring underneath a house. • Winter W-Su 10am-5pm; Summer Tu-Su 10am-5pm. Admission $6; free, under age 1; first Th of each month free.

San Francisco Bay Model: 2100 Bridgeway, Sausalito, (415) 332-3870. A working facsimile built by the Army Corps of Engineers to study the Bay. • Tu-Sa 9am-4pm. Free.

Scandia Family Fun Center: 5301 Redwood Rd. (Rohnert Park Expwy.), Rohnert Park, (707) 584-1361. One of the great joys of the 'burbs, this freeway-side place has a 36-hole miniature golf course, batting cages, video games, and all the other cheap fun you had as a kid. • M-F 10am-10pm; Sa-Su 10am-11pm. $5.50 adults; $3.50 ages 6-12 for a round of golf; $1.50 for 22 pitches.

Windsor Waterworks & Slides: 8225 Conde Ln. (Shiloh), Windsor, (707) 838-7760. • Summer M-F 11am-7pm; Sa-Su 10am-7pm. $11.95 adults; $10.95 ages 4-12; free under 4. Call for spring and fall hours.

Nightlife

Bar (with no name): 757 Bridgeway, Sausalito, (415) 332-1392. Popular local spot for drinks, sandwiches, and live music. Pleasant covered patio out back. There is no sign, as the name, or lack thereof, implies. Cash only.

Guaymas: See Restaurants section.

Margaritaville: 1200 Bridgeway, Sausalito, (415) 331-3226. Local branch of this chain of Mexican-themed party spots.

Marin Brewing Company: See Restaurants section.

New George's: 842 4th St., San Rafael, (415) 457-8424. One of Marin's premier spots for live rock and roll.

Sam's: See Restaurants section.

MARIN

Silver Peso Bar: 450 Magnolia Ave., Larkspur, (415) 924-3448. Dive bar and pool hall popular with slumming locals.

Smiley's Schooner Saloon & Hotel: 41 Wharf Rd., Bolinas, (415) 868-1311. *The* hangout in Bolinas.

Smitty's Bar: 214 Caledonia St., Sausalito, (415) 332-2637. An alternative to the no name.

Sweetwater: 153 Throckmorton Ave., Mill Valley, (415) 388-2820. A small saloon that hosts excellent live music, ranging from jazz to folk to Cajun. National acts, with prices to match.

The Two AM Club: 382 Miller Ave., Mill Valley, (415) 388-6036. This dive's cheap drinks and late hours draw a West Marin crowd.

Performing Arts

Marin Art and Garden Center: Sir Francis Drake Blvd., Ross, (415) 454-5597. For those interested in the visual arts, the Frances Young Gallery offers exhibitions; the Ross Valley Players stage productions here as well.

Marin Community Playhouse: 27 Kensington Rd., San Anselmo. (415) 456-5550. Films, lectures, dance, music, and drama productions are offered here year-round.

Marin County Civic Center: 3501 Civic Center Dr. (N. San Pedro Rd. exit off Hwy 101), San Rafael, (415) 499-6400, box office/events information (415) 472-3500. This Frank Lloyd Wright–designed municipal center houses county government offices, a theater, and the Marin Veterans Memorial Auditorium. All of the performing arts are showcased here. This is the home of the **Marin Symphony**, the **Marin Opera Company**, the **Marin Ballet**'s perennial production of "The Nutcracker," and the Golden Gate Geographic Travel Film Series.

Marin Theater Company: 397 Miller Ave., Mill Valley, (415) 388-5208. Over a quarter of a century old, this company offers drama classes for both children and adults and mounts many new plays.

Mountain Play Association: E. Ridgecrest Blvd., on Mount Tam, (415) 383-1100. Close to the summit of Mount Tam is the **Sydney B. Cushing Memorial Theater**, a 5,000-seat outdoor amphitheater that hosts excellent musical productions by the **Mountain Play Association** on the last two Sundays of May and the first four Sundays in June. Advance ticket purchases are usually necessary.

PARKS AND OPEN SPACES

Marin is an outdoorsperson's paradise. Most of the Sights & Attractions listed above involve hiking, biking, and the like, and many of the activities noted in the Sports chapter involve Marin parks and waters.

Peninsula & San Jose

The San Francisco Peninsula is a beautiful, 42-mile stretch of land dividing San Francisco Bay from the Pacific Ocean. The city of San Francisco occupies its narrow tip; from there the Peninsula widens on its way south, merging with the mainland below the bottom of the Bay in San Jose. The bay shore land is flat and low; moving west, the terrain rises steeply into the Santa Cruz Mountains, which comprise the Peninsula's spine. Beyond the mountains, the land drops down more gradually towards the Pacific.

From the beginning of European settlement until World War II, Peninsula land was cleared for grazing and farming, the Santa Cruz redwood forests were harvested and milled to supply building materials for the growing city of San Francisco, and small towns sprang up along the railway linking San Francisco and San Jose. The Santa Clara Valley was an agricultural community filled with orchards, while the northern Peninsula was a country playground for wealthy San Franciscans.

During WWII much of the Peninsula was used as a staging area for troops on their way to the Pacific. After the war, many who had worked in or passed through the area decided to settle down here, and the population exploded. This enormous growth spurt established much of the area's housing and determined its largely suburban character. The aerospace industry economy fueled this expansion, spearheaded by major corporations such as Lockheed and FMC. Stanford University's proximity gave the trend a technological bent, and sowed the seeds for the emergence of Silicon Valley. Most recently, the success of companies like Hewlett-Packard, Intel, and Apple Computer has powered the Peninsula's continuing growth, and as a result, San Mateo and Santa Clara counties now have some of the highest per capita incomes and housing prices in the nation.

Most of the region's residential development has taken place in the flatlands on the eastern half of the Peninsula. The corridor running south along Hwy 101 is densely settled, as is the stretch—seemingly punctuated by a Taco Bell every few miles—along El Camino Real (Hwy 82), which links Daly City with Santa Clara. Before WWII, each town between San Francisco and San Jose had its own unique identity; the rapid post-war population growth sent the communities sprawling into each other; little of their individuality survived. With the construction of I-280 paralleling the Santa Cruz Mountain foothills, expansion is now also creeping west, especially around San Jose. On the Peninsula's Pacific coast, development has been centered around Half Moon Bay, but for the most part, the area still remains blessedly and primarily agricultural.

Basic Information

The following tourist offices can give you maps and additional information about the region.

San Mateo County Convention and Visitors Bureau: 111 Anza Blvd., #410, Burlingame, (415) 348-7700. • M-F 8:30am-5pm.

San Jose Convention and Visitors Bureau: 333 W. San Carlos St., #1000, San Jose, (408) 295-9600, (800) SAN-JOSE/726-5673. • M-F 8am-5:30pm.

Convention and Visitors Bureau of Santa Clara: 1850 Warburton Ave., Santa Clara (408) 296-7111. • M-F 8am-5pm.

Palo Alto Chamber of Commerce: 325 Forest Ave., Palo Alto, (415) 324-3121. • M-F 9am-5pm.

PENINSULA & SAN JOSE

TRANSPORTATION

Arrival & Departure

Two major highways extend the length of the Peninsula, connecting San Jose to San Francisco. The primary commuter route, Hwy 101 slices through the heavily populated region along the bay, and is generally crowded and subject to frustrating delays. I-280 rolls through the Santa Cruz Mountain foothills to the west of most settlements, providing beautiful views and high speeds most of the way—in part because access between 280 and many Peninsula downtowns is via narrow, congested roads. Traffic sometimes becomes a problem north of I-380 and south from Cupertino to San Jose.

Only a few major roads connect Hwy 101 to I-280. I-280 itself traverses the Peninsula in the southern part of San Francisco. I-380 crosses at the narrowest point, near San Francisco airport. Hwy 92 runs through the middle of the Peninsula near San Mateo. Hwy 84 links the towns of Woodside and Redwood City. Newly completed Hwy 85 provides a loop west of San Jose from Mountain View to south San Jose.

Two major thoroughfares also connect the San Jose area to the East Bay: I-880 runs along the bay, and is frequently terribly congested; I-680 takes the inland route to Walnut Creek and beyond. Two bridges span the southern segment of the Bay. Hwy 92, the San Mateo Bridge, connects Foster City on the mid-Peninsula to Hayward. Hwy 84, the Dumbarton Bridge, ties Palo Alto and Menlo Park with Fremont. Both bridges collect the $1 toll only in the westbound direction, and both have formidable rush hour traffic. Hwy 237 crosses the mud flats at the southern end of the Bay, connecting Santa Clara to Milpitas. Hwy 17 winds and climbs southwest across the mountains to the coastal community of Santa Cruz.

Amtrak: (800) USA-RAIL/872-7245. Amtrak's San Jose station is located conveniently next to the downtown CalTrain station at 65 Cahill Street (between West Santa Clara and West San Fernando). There are no Peninsula stations. While no Amtrak trains serve San Francisco, Amtrak shuttle buses take passengers from Oakland to San Francisco.

Greyhound Bus: (800) 231-2222, (415) 495-1575. Greyhound has one depot in San Francisco's Transbay Terminal at First and Mission streets and another in downtown San Jose at 70 S. Almaden Avenue. There is also a secondary Peninsula stop at 400 West Evelyn Street in Sunnyvale.

Airports

Peninsula travelers have the distinct advantage of being able to utilize the small and convenient San Jose Airport (SJC). Flying in and out of SJC can cut back on the hassles involved in maneuvering around the larger airports, but there are fewer flights available, so you may need to utilize the San Francisco Airport (SFO) or Oakland Airport (OAK) at least occasionally. For residents of the northern Peninsula, SFO is the most convenient point of departure/arrival. See the Transportation chapter for more information about these airports and ground transportation options.

By Public Transportation

See Public Transportation section of Transportation chapter for additional tips on getting to the airport(s) without a car.

By Private Shuttle

There are several shuttle companies which service both SFO and SJC at fairly reasonable rates. A shuttle trip to OAK will be much more expensive. Be sure to call in advance to check prices and make a reservation.

Airport Connection: (408) 730-5555.

Bayporter Express: (415) 467-1800.
Express Airport Shuttle: (408) 378-6270.
South and East Bay Airport Shuttle: (800) 548-4664.
Super Shuttle: (415) 558-8500 (SFO and SJC only).
VIP Airport Shuttle: (408) 378-8VIP/8847 (SFO and SJC only).

Public Transportation

Santa Clara Transit Agency (TA) and San Mateo County (SamTrans) each operate municipal bus lines that together cover destinations from San Francisco to Gilroy, meeting in between at the Stanford Shopping Center. The Dumbarton Express bus connects Palo Alto to the East Bay via its namesake bridge. CalTrain runs commuter trains between San Francisco and San Jose (and even south to Gilroy), while Santa Clara TA operates light rail trains in San Jose and Santa Clara. Primarily, BART links San Francisco with the East Bay, but it is expanding service to the northern Peninsula: in addition to a Daly City station, BART has added a Colma stop, and plans for an airport connection or San Bruno station are on the drawing board. (See Transportation chapter for additional information.)

NEIGHBORHOODS & HOUSING

The volatile Silicon Valley economy drives the housing market in this region. While it has long been one of the nation's most expensive, it has significant ups and downs: housing prices dropped when defense contracts were cut back in the early 1990s, only to bounce back a few years later when hi-tech companies boomed.

Generally, as you ascend from the Bay up into the Santa Cruz Mountain foothills, house sizes and prices rise correspondingly. The following towns are listed in north-to-south geographic order; the estimated population is in parenthesis.

Although **Daly City (94,076)** is San Mateo County's largest city, it is really more a part of San Francisco than the Peninsula. Located just south of SF, it exhibits an urban diversity rare on the Peninsula, and even has a BART station, giving it immediate access to San Francisco. An influx of immigrants has given Daly City a large growth spurt; it now boasts a very cross-cultural population. The city is situated near a gap in the coastal mountains through which Pacific-bound planes taking off from nearby SFO pass; ocean winds and fog cross the gap going east. Typical for the northern Peninsula, housing prices are reasonable for the broad mix of homes and apartments, and the community's schools are varied.

Very few people actually live in **Colma (1,100)**, a town that's best known for its cemeteries. When San Francisco ran out of buildable terrain, it banned cemeteries and transferred all its dead to Colma; the city has been interring its departed there ever since. Other than burial grounds, Colma is home to such commercial developments as Auto Row on Serramonte Boulevard and the 280 Metro Center. A new BART station gives it excellent access to San Francisco.

Brisbane (3,000), a compact, blue-collar community, is best known for its office complexes east of Hwy 101. The moderately priced residential area—mostly pre-WWII single-family homes—is squeezed into an isolated valley on the steep slopes of San Bruno Mountain and further cut off from neighboring towns by a lagoon. Schools are above average for the northern Peninsula.

"South San Francisco the Industrial City," read the huge block letters emblazoned on a slope of San Bruno Mountain in a grand proclamation of turn of the century civic pride. Today in **South San Francisco (56,000)** you'll find more office parks and airport hotels than heavy industry, although there are still some printers and warehouses around. Some people might be disturbed by the ocean winds that whip through town, but South San Francisco's location near the airport and the intersection of Hwy 101 and I-380 enhances its commercial appeal. Although there's a beautiful, historic downtown along Grand Avenue between Airport Boulevard and Chestnut Avenue, most of the housing was erected after WWII. The neat, closely spaced, boxy houses and moderate prices are on a par with those in neighboring towns.

San Bruno (39,000) is located on the narrowest point on the Peninsula, where I-380 connects Hwy 101 to I-280. Commercial development dominates the eastern edge of town, which borders San Francisco Airport. San Bruno is also home to three shopping centers within a mile of each other: Tanforan Park, Bayhill Shopping Center, and Towne Center—although there is also an historic downtown along San Mateo Avenue, which is lined with small-town storefronts and international grocery stores. Office parks and industrial areas, including a huge Gap corporate campus, are also well represented. Housing prices and incomes in San Bruno are slightly higher than those found to the north. San Bruno fits into three school districts, with the best schools associated with San Mateo and Millbrae to the south.

Millbrae (21,100) lies in the shadow, if not the very flight path, of SFO. Industrial development associated with the airport runs along Hwy 101 while a mix of apartments and houses lines El Camino and larger single-family homes sit in the hills towards I-280. El Camino is a busy commercial strip with numerous Asian restaurants. A small downtown shopping area on Broadway parallel to El Camino has made a major step in establishing its credibility: it now has a Starbucks. Much of the housing was built in the postwar boom, and it is expensive. Millbrae schools are generally good.

As the northern Peninsula's prototypical exclusive, hillside residential community, **Hillsborough (10,700)** offers the an upscale mix of large homes, quiet streets, low crime, and excellent schools. It typically vies with Atherton for the highest average income and home prices on the Peninsula. Don't expect to see anybody strolling around town: sidewalks and street lights are prohibited.

While most Peninsula cities struggle to maintain one downtown, **Burlingame (27,000)** has two: one on Broadway, and the other on Burlingame Avenue. Credit CalTrain for giving Burlingame two rail stations, one for each area. Admittedly, the retail strip on Broadway is pretty small. The real action is on Burlingame Avenue between El Camino and the CalTrain station, where you'll find a bounty of restaurants, cafés, and retail shops. Around both downtowns you'll find quiet, suburban streets with a patchwork of houses and high-rise apartments. Burlingame single-family houses are generally imposing and expensive. The city has a reputation for stuffiness: one restaurant caused a huge outcry because its façade was painted blue. The eastern side of Burlingame along Hwy 101, especially on Bayshore Highway, is filled with commercial development serving the airport.

Although Redwood City is older and is the actual county seat, **San Mateo (85,500)** plays a more central role on the Peninsula: it's larger, located in the center of the county, has housing prices and incomes right at the county median, and boasts the region's main shopping center in Hillsdale Mall. The bustling downtown along Third and Fourth streets between El Camino and the CalTrain station has a diverse mix of restaurants, cafés, and shops, although competition from superstores and the mall has hurt some downtown businesses. San Mateo's neighborhoods are typical of the mid-Peninsula. Schools are generally good, with the high school especially well regarded.

The word "earthquake" carries a lot of weight in **Foster City (28,200)**: this lagoon community was created 30 years ago on landfill, the same stuff that turned to Jell-O under San Francisco's Marina district during the 1989 Loma Prieta quake. Residents, mostly highly educated professionals, insist that Foster City is designed to withstand temblors; in fact, Foster City held up in the '89 quake quite well. The town's developer, T. Jack Foster, created a modern suburban community with a centrally-planned combination of houses, town homes, offices, shopping centers, and parks. A population of professionals generates steep real estate prices, especially with regard to rental units.

Belmont (24,100) sits at the very geographic center of the Peninsula, halfway between San Francisco and San Jose, and epitomizes the quiet, upper-middle-class suburban bedroom community. Although single-family homes dominate the market, housing is slightly less expensive in Belmont than in neighboring San Carlos, and

NEIGHBORHOODS & HOUSING

apartments are more plentiful. Schools are generally very good. **San Carlos (25,700)** closely resembles Belmont—a comfortable small-town haven in the heart of the mid-Peninsula. The historic CalTrain station, built in 1888 in the Romanesque-influenced style of architect H. H. Richardson, is now a state historic landmark. Nearby on Laurel Street, the tiny downtown is slowly taking shape, with restaurants, bars, and cafés attracting pedestrian traffic.

Redwood City's (68,700) hard-working history goes back to the 1800s, when the city earned its name as a lumber town: redwood trees cut in the hills above what is now Woodside were processed in Redwood City and shipped through its port to San Francisco. Redwood City has redeveloped its historic downtown around Broadway and Main Streets, sprucing up the brick sidewalks and adding gas-lamp streetlights, and it's slowly coming to life. The city's latest project, Sequoia Station—a yuppie village-like shopping center with a Safeway, Starbucks, Noah's Bagels, Barnes & Noble, and more—is situated right at the CalTrain station, a boon for public transit. Redwood City is the San Mateo County seat, and many government offices, from the DMV to the courthouse, are also near downtown. One of the Peninsula's more ethnically diverse communities, Redwood City has an especially large Hispanic community; the retail strip along Middlefield Road between Hwy 84 and Fifth Avenue is lined with Mexican restaurants and markets. Housing is plentiful and generally less expensive than in surrounding communities. The schools are as diverse as the community.

One of the Bay Area's most aristocratic towns, **Atherton (7,200)** consists almost exclusively of large homes, many sizable enough to rightfully earn the sobriquet "mansion." Minimum lot sizes are strictly enforced, and absolutely no retail businesses are allowed. Its elementary schools are very highly rated; older students that stay in the public school system attend Menlo Atherton High, which is not as good. Among Atherton's celebrity population are investment tycoon Charles Schwab and baseball star Barry Bonds. The local CalTrain station has a residents-only parking policy.

Nestled in the wooded valleys of the Santa Cruz Mountains, **Woodside (5,000)** is best known as home of the horsey set—don't be surprised by the sight of country gentry trotting down the streets on their steeds. More of a village than a town, Woodside life centers around its historic downtown. There's not much else to the actual town, but the large areas of open space that surround it provide excellent trails for hiking, riding horses, and biking. The houses are hidden in the woods and hills. Many are full-blown mansions, replete with pools, tennis courts, and stables. Despite the town's high price tag, Woodside is much less ostentatious than nearby Atherton. There is a good elementary school, but older students attend Woodside High in Redwood City.

Menlo Park (28,000) pins its identity on a post-WWII vision of small-town America. The modest downtown centered around Santa Cruz Avenue still boasts old-time coffee shops serving grilled cheese sandwiches and independent drug stores where pharmaceuticals still outnumber cosmetics. Resisting the onslaught of the automobile, the town has narrowed El Camino Real from three lanes to two, causing an unfortunately modern inconvenience, the continuous traffic jam. The central part of town between Middlefield Road and Alameda de las Pulgas consists primarily of quiet tree-lined streets, modest ranch homes, and small apartment complexes dating from the 1950s. The area is popular with senior citizens, but many young families are attracted by the housing prices, which are somewhat below those of neighboring Palo Alto. Stanford University's influence is almost as strong here as in Palo Alto—you'll find many faculty families and quite good schools. The area east of Hwy 101 resembles East Palo Alto, with new industrial parks growing all over. The western side of town has been developed into a modern town-house community, Sharon Heights.

Portola Valley (4,300), a tiny enclave in the Santa Cruz Mountains above Stanford, provides a retreat for wealthy inhabitants to tend their gardens and horses. Surrounded by remote portions of the Stanford campus and acres of open space and parks, the seclusion is disturbed only by the packs of bicyclists who zip along the twisting mountain byways. As you might expect, housing consists primarily of large, expensive, contemporary homes set into the hillsides. When these houses are put up for rent, they are very popular with groups of Stanford students, especially if they have a hot tub. Schools are good, although the town is so small kids must go off to Woodside High in Redwood City.

With its long-standing ties to neighboring Stanford University, **Palo Alto (55,900)** has become a regional center, drawing visitors from all over the Peninsula to its many attractions. The vibrant downtown area along University Avenue between Middlefield and Alma has a remarkable number of restaurants, cafés, bookstores, and movie theaters, including the beautifully restored Stanford Theatre. (Teetotaler Leland Stanford would be appalled to watch young singles flock to the area's nocturnal hot spots.) Visitors are also drawn to the glittering Stanford Shopping Center. Palo Alto has mature neighborhoods with housing ranging from stately old shingled homes along the tree-lined streets south and east of downtown to bungalows south of campus to boxy ranch homes and apartment complexes on both sides of El Camino Real. As you would expect, the price tags per square foot for Palo Alto houses are among the highest in northern California. The tax base supports some of the best city services found anywhere; the school system is consistently top-rated (also reflecting Stanford's influence). Residents range from Stanford students to high-tech yuppies to longtime natives.

Located on the edge of the Bay at the base of the Dumbarton Bridge, **East Palo Alto (23,500)** was primarily ranch land until World War II. Things look different today as this small city, recently infamous for having the nation's highest per capita murder rate, struggles with urban problems such as crack and gangs. However, East Palo Alto proves that neighbors can pull together in the face of adversity: residents have the strongest sense of community on the Peninsula. Some parts of East Palo Alto are still dangerous and depressing, but the city does provide affordable housing in a region which has almost none. One of the Peninsula's most diverse communities, the residential section of town is a mix of the people who migrated to the area over the last fifty years.

Mountain View (67,500) recently remodeled its downtown along Castro Street between Central Expressway and El Camino Real, installing brick sidewalks, gas-lamp streetlights, and street-side trees. This has resulted in a restaurant boom along Castro and surrounding streets. Mountain View's first boom occurred after WWII, producing an abundance of modest ranch homes and boxy apartment buildings. This plentiful housing stock (affordable compared to nearby Palo Alto and Los Altos) attracts a diverse mix of singles to its apartments and young families to its homes. Mountain View has been especially popular with Hispanic immigrants. Adding to the family-friendly character, Mountain View has pretty good elementary schools and all the necessary modern conveniences in the plentiful new strip malls.

Los Altos (26,300) is a model upper-middle-class suburb, the kind of location you might see in a Driver's Ed film. Nice family homes with well-landscaped yards dot tree-lined streets. The quaint downtown village runs along Main Street across First, Second, and Third streets. The schools, especially the elementary ones, are excellent. However, modern times have invaded Los Altos. The coffee shops downtown are Starbucks and Peet's, and the real retail activity occurs in the strip malls along El Camino and San Antonio Road. Most important, modern-day real estate values in Los Altos are exorbitant, freezing out most young families and singles. As a result, the 1990 census reported that nearly one-third of the population was 55 or older.

The rolling hills provide exquisite views for those fortunate enough to live in **Los Altos Hills (7,500)**. These lucky few—average household income is triple the county average—enjoy large homes on large lots surrounded by a ring of open space preserves. This exclusively residential community has no town center or commercial activity. The K-12 school system also has a very good reputation.

Along with Cupertino and Santa Clara, **Sunnyvale (117,300)** lies at the heart of Silicon Valley; the city even maintains a patent library to keep the high-tech community pulsing. Vice President Al Gore singled out Sunnyvale as one of the most well-run cities in America. The heart of this neat, well-kept city is a pair of shopping malls, TownCenter and Town & Country. For those who prefer the Main Street model,

NEIGHBORHOODS & HOUSING

Sunnyvale's original downtown along Murphy Street (next to the CalTrain station) offers a few restaurants, cafés, and bars. The housing mode of choice is the multi-story condominium/town home, usually surrounded by enough convenience malls to meet all the basic needs. While Sunnyvale has a wide mix of residents, it's the young singles and young families who are most visible, especially on the tennis courts and in the pools of those condominiums. Housing prices are moderate by area standards (between Cupertino and Santa Clara). Schools are a mixed bag.

The influence of Apple Computer and the high-tech economy permeates **Cupertino (40,000)**. There aren't any futuristic monorails; rather, much of Cupertino has the look of a functional suburban boomtown, with large blocks of "townhominiums" and wide boulevards lined with an endless string of strip shopping centers. Apple's sprawling complex of buildings dominates a large area of town around De Anza Boulevard south of I-280, and Apple's ups and downs strongly impact the area's economy. Cupertino is more upscale than Sunnyvale and Santa Clara: homeowners outnumber apartment dwellers, housing is more expensive, schools better, and families older and more established.

Santa Clara (92,200) got a jump on the rest of Silicon Valley when the Spaniards founded Mission Santa Clara in 1777 near what was to become San Jose. Today, the mission site is home to Jesuit-run Santa Clara University, located in a setting as close to downtown as suburbia allows, albeit quite sparse. Nearby you'll find the city hall, the Triton Museum of Art, and a CalTrain station. The residential neighborhoods are older than those in Sunnyvale and Cupertino, and the area along Hwy 101 is heavily industrialized. Numerous ethnic restaurants and shops on El Camino reflect the residents' diverse backgrounds, including large Italian and Indian populations. Housing in Santa Clara is more affordable than in Sunnyvale or Mountain View. Families will find Santa Clara convenient to its most well-known attraction—Great America, a giant amusement park north of Hwy 101. Schools generally lag behind those of neighbors in Sunnyvale, Mountain View, and Cupertino.

San Jose (749,800) suffers in the shadow of San Francisco. While it lacks San Francisco's cosmopolitan attitude, San Jose actually outdoes its showy northern neighbor in many ways. San Jose was California's first city and first capital; it is now the Bay Area's biggest city, sprawling far and wide across the Santa Clara Valley where nothing but orchards once flourished. However, San Jose has maintained a rather suburban feel. Nevertheless, the ethnic diversity created by residents from all over the world, especially Latin America and Southeast Asia, makes the city rich in its own culture and history. Using wealth created by Silicon Valley's high-tech economy, San Jose created a glittering new downtown by redeveloping the area around Market and San Carlos streets. San Jose also has its own airport, museums, and performing arts companies. But along with size comes typical urban problems, and San Jose has struggled with crime, drugs, gangs, and deteriorating public schools. Housing runs the gamut, with prices being extremely variable from neighborhood to neighborhood, but still are generally lower than other South Bay cities. The school system does an admirable job by city standards, but as you might expect, they are not consistent in quality. Also typical of such a sprawling city, San Jose has terrible traffic problems and attendant smog. Recent improvements include a new light rail system and Hwy 85, connecting southern San Jose with Cupertino and Sunnyvale.

Campbell (36,000) is almost surrounded by San Jose; nevertheless, Campbell has carved out its own niche as a quiet, middle-class suburban community. It offers plenty of housing at lower prices than in most other Silicon Valley towns.

Saratoga (28,000), a former logging and resort town, has become one of the South Bay's most exclusive residential communities. Its location on the edge of the Santa Cruz Mountains, on the way to Saratoga Gap and Big Basin, once made it convenient for loggers and vacationers and now gives residents a nearby escape to the many parks along Skyline Drive. Downtown you'll find a quaint retail strip along Big Basin Way with lots of pricy continental restaurants, boutiques, and antiques shops. Even the strip malls are old-timey wooden buildings instead of characterless concrete.

While expensive single-family homes dominate the housing, they are modest compared to the mansions in other exclusive hillside communities. For those who can afford them, the schools are excellent.

Both the smallest city and southernmost prestige community in Santa Clara County, **Monte Sereno (3,100)** occupies a protected enclave between Saratoga and Los Gatos. Most of the details on housing, demographics, and so forth from Saratoga and Los Altos Hills apply to Monte Sereno as well. Although its character is closer to Saratoga, its commercial needs are met by nearby Los Gatos.

Los Gatos (27,400) has quieted down since the days when it was a rowdy logging town and stagecoach stop at the edge of the mountains. Fortunately, on its way to becoming a pricy bedroom community, it maintained many of its historic buildings, including those in the downtown area. In keeping with the theme, Old Town Shopping Plaza is housed in a former grammar school. Most schools in Los Gatos have fared better, and today they are considered excellent. While housing is generally expensive, there is enough variety in the size and types of units available for rent and sale to allow access to newcomers.

SIGHTS & ATTRACTIONS

In general, the Peninsula and San Jose lack the famous tourist destinations San Francisco offers. Most of this chapter is filled with interesting and exciting activities, from highbrow arts to lowbrow amusements, from bars to sports. But for those hard-to-please guests who want the kind of tourist attractions that come with colorful brochures and their own postcards, we've compiled the following list of attractions. Even blasé locals might be surprised to discover something new in these pages.

Filoli House and Gardens ★★: Cañada Rd., Woodside, (415) 364-2880. Built as a country retreat by San Francisco silver magnate William B. Bourn, Filoli (as in "To F*i*ght, to L*o*ve, to L*i*ve") became famous as the mansion in the opening shot of the 80s television series *Dynasty*. Designed by San Francisco architect Willis Polk and completed in 1917, the clematis-draped brick building was deeded to the National Trust for Historic Preservation in 1975. Unsupervised tours of the 43-room mansion on its 654-acre estate give you the opportunity to roam through the house at your own pace and linger in the various grand salons. The gardens, now reaching maturity, are laid out as a succession of outdoor rooms, each having its own design and personality. Throughout the seasons, the plantings provide an ever-changing palette of brilliant color nestled against the Santa Cruz Mountains. • Guided tours by reservation, Feb. to Nov. Tu-Th, Sa; call for current hours. Self-guided tours F-Sa 10am-2pm. $10.

HISTORIC PALO ALTO WALKING TOURS

In Palo Alto, you can catch a glimpse of the town's history beyond its glitzy shops and cafés. Docent-led tours of the downtown area provide enlightening stories about historic buildings such as the Hamilton Avenue Post Office and the Cardinal Hotel. The excursion begins at City Hall at 10am. There is also a tour of Professorville, the residential area bounded by Ramona, Waverley, Addison, and Kingsley streets. These old wooden houses, home to Stanford faculty, were built between 1890 and 1910. This walk begins at the corner of Bryant and Addison streets, also at 10am. Both tours are given on every Saturday and last one hour; a $2 donation is requested. Groups of six or more must make reservations. For more information, call the Chamber of Commerce at (415) 324-3121.

Also of interest to architecture buffs is the Hostess House, between El Camino and Alma next to the Palo Alto train station, which now houses the bustling restaurant MacArthur Park. Designed by Julia Morgan, court architect to the notorious empire builder William Randolph Hearst, it's worth stopping by to admire the graceful proportions and soaring interior.

SIGHTS & ATTRACTIONS

Lick Observatory ★: Mount Hamilton Rd. (off Alum Rock Rd.), San Jose, (408) 274-5061. The Observatory was created over a century ago by James Lick, a millionaire obsessed with the idea of life on the moon and set on gathering proof of his theory. After San Francisco rejected his observatory plans, he built it on Mount Hamilton. It takes about an hour to climb the windy road to the observatory by car, and the escorted tours of the telescopes and the panoramic views are quite interesting. • M-F 12:30pm-5pm; Sa-Su 10am-5pm. Free. Guided tour every half hour until 4:30pm.

NASA/Ames Research Center: Moffett Field (off Hwy 101), Mountain View, (415) 604-6497. Tour NASA's field laboratory and see a wind tunnel, gigantic flight hangar, and flight simulator laboratory. The two-hour tour covers about two miles of territory. • Tours by reservation only. Free.

Stanford Linear Accelerator (SLAC) ★: 2575 Sand Hill Rd., Menlo Park, (415) 926-2204. Tour the two-mile electron accelerator and receive a crash course in particle physics. Tours last two hours. • Tours by reservation. Free.

Stanford University Campus Tours: Meet in front of Memorial Hall, Stanford Campus, (415) 723-2560. Let friendly student guides familiarize you with the campus. Bubbling with information and anecdotes about campus history, guides lead an hour-long stroll by such campus landmarks as Memorial Church (restored following damage in the '89 quake) and the Rodin Sculpture Garden, featuring numerous works by the namesake sculptor (including the haunting *Gates of Hell*). • Tours daily 11am and 3:15pm, except during finals week, between sessions, and on some holidays. Free.

Winchester Mystery House ★: 525 S. Winchester Blvd., San Jose, (408) 247-2101. A taste of the bizarre. This 160-room maze underwent 24-hour-a-day construction at the behest of firearms heiress Sarah Winchester, who was convinced that such non-stop labor would appease the evil spirits she held responsible for the deaths of her husband and baby daughter. • Daily 9am-9pm. $12.95 adults; $9.95 seniors; $6.95 ages 6-12; free ages 5 and under. Admission includes hour-long guided tours.

Wineries ★★: While they lack the notoriety of wineries in Napa and Sonoma, South Bay wineries offer a closer opportunity to taste a variety of excellent vintages in more intimate settings. And don't underestimate the quality of these wines—Ridge in particular is known for its world-class reds. For additional information, contact the **Santa Clara Valley Wine Growers Association** at (408) 778-1555 or the **Santa Cruz Mountain Winegrowers Association** at (408) 479-9463.

David Bruce: 21439 Bear Creek Rd. (off Hwy 17), Los Gatos, (408) 354-4214. Picnic facilities. • Tasting daily noon-5pm. Free.

A LONG STRANGE TRIP

Sleepy, suburban Palo Alto and Menlo Park don't seem like the kind of towns to give rise to the Grateful Dead and LSD culture. But between 1961 and 1965, the original members of the band met each other and played in a variety of combinations under a couple of different names, eventually becoming the Grateful Dead. In fact, when the Dead hooked up with Ken Kesey and his Merry Pranksters, they gave the first "Acid Test" party in Palo Alto. Several of the musicians were locals: drummer Billy Kreutzmann attended Palo Alto High, as did harmonica player Ron "Pigpen" McKernan; guitarist Bob Weir lived in Atherton and spent a little time at Menlo-Atherton High. Although most of the places where they hung out are long gone, some still exist, albeit in new locations. Kepler's original location across El Camino was a hotbed of the Beat scene, and a favorite spot for Jerry Garcia and Pigpen. St. Michael's Alley has moved and changed names, but Palo Alto's original coffeehouse was one of the Dead's first venues. The VA hospital in Menlo Park where Kesey served as a guinea pig in army LSD tests still exists, although the drug research program, we presume, does not.

PENINSULA & SAN JOSE

J. Lohr: 1000 Lenzen Ave., San Jose, (408) 288-5057. • Tasting daily 10am-5pm; free. Tours Sa-Su 11am, 2pm.

Mirassou Champagne Cellars: 300 College Ave., Los Gatos, (408) 395-3790. • Tasting W-Su noon-5pm. Tours daily 1pm, 3pm unless production is in progress. Free.

Mirassou Vineyards: 3000 Aborn Rd., San Jose, (408) 274-4000. • Tasting M-Sa noon-5pm; Su noon-4pm. Free.

Ridge Vineyards: 17100 Montebello Rd., Cupertino, (408) 867-3233. Picnic facilities by reservation only. • Tasting Sa-Su 11am-3pm. Free.

Sunrise Winery: 13100 Montebello Rd., Cupertino, (408) 741-1310. Picnic facilities. • Tasting F-Su 11am-3pm. Free.

Museums

Barbie Doll Hall of Fame: 433 Waverley St., Palo Alto, (415) 326-5841. Come examine one of the most famous of contemporary cultural icons in a newly expanded collection of over 16,000 pieces. Check out nearly every Barbie product created since 1959 (the year of her birth), and see how the world of Barbie reflects almost every change in our popular culture. • Tu-F 1:30pm-4:30pm; Sa 10am-noon, 1:30pm-4:30pm. $4.

Children's Discovery Museum: 180 Woz Way (between Almaden and San Carlos), San Jose, (408) 298-5437. Get involved in the wonderful world of science in this participatory museum. Exhibits include a walk-through model of San Jose's city streets and underground, complete with traffic controls and waste-disposal systems that children can operate. • Tu-Sa 10am-5pm; Su noon-5pm. $6 adults; $5 seniors, $4 ages 2-18; children under 2 free. Parking $2.

Coyote Point Museum for Environmental Education: Coyote Point Dr., San Mateo, (415) 342-7755. Includes the two-acre wildlife habitat alive with badgers, otters, and other native animals; and the Environmental Hall, an 8,000-square-foot simulated walk from the San Francisco Bay to the Pacific coast. This museum also pays tribute to its California setting with computer games designed to educate players about the environment. • Tu-Sa 10am-5pm; Su noon-5pm. $3 adults; $1 ages 4-12, $2 seniors, ages 13-17, children under 6 free. Free first Wed of month. $4 vehicle fee.

Rosicrucian Egyptian Museum: Park and Naglee aves., San Jose, (408) 947-3636. Ancient history buffs and anyone who still believes in King Tut's curse will want to explore this museum, which contains more than 4,000 artifacts from Egypt, Assyria, and Babylonia. Highlights include human and animal mummies and a full-size replica of a nobleman's tomb. The museum also houses a planetarium. • Daily 9am-5pm. $6 adults; $4 students/seniors; children under 7 free. Free tours. Planetarium M-F only: $4 adults; $3.50 students/seniors; $3 ages 7-15.

San Jose Institute of Contemporary Art Galleries: 451 S. 1st St. San Jose, (408) 283-8155. Gallery space for changing exhibitions of cutting-edge artists. Look for exhibits like a multimedia depiction of "What Heaven Looks Like." • Tu-Sa noon-5pm. Free.

San Jose Museum of Art: 110 S. Market St., San Jose, (408) 294-2787. Focuses on art of the 20th century. Houses only a small permanent collection, but hosts some spectacular traveling exhibitions in its new 45,000-square foot wing. The first Sunday of every month kids and their escorts get in free. • Tu-Su 10am-5pm; Th 10am-8pm. $6 adults; $3 students/seniors; $3 ages 6-17; children under 5 free. Free first Th of month.

Stanford Museum and Gallery: Stanford University, (415) 723-4177. The museum, home to one of the world's largest collections of the works of August Rodin, is closed until 1998 due to damage from the 1989 Loma Prieta earthquake. However, the adjacent **Rodin Sculpture Garden** is still open and features numerous works by the namesake sculptor, including the haunting *Gates of Hell*. Visit at night when lighting dramatizes the sculptures. Other famous Rodin pieces are scattered around campus, including one of the nine replicas of *The Thinker*. The Stanford Gallery features exhibitions by artists ranging from Ansel Adams to Richard Diebenkorn to the graduating class of art students. • Tu-F, 10am-5pm; Sa-Su, 1pm-5pm; W, Sa-Su tours of garden at 2pm.

Tech Museum of Innovation: 145 W. San Carlos St., San Jose, (408) 279-7150. A Silicon Valley highlight designed to help visitors understand how technology works. Drive a Land Rover over a simulated Martian landscape, man the controls of life-size robots, and perform calculations on a nine-foot-square computer chip. • Tu-Su 10am-5pm. (July 1-Labor day M-Sa 10am-6pm; Su 10am-5pm.) $6 adults; $4 ages 6-18; free under 5.

Triton Museum of Art: 1505 Warburton Ave., Santa Clara, (408) 247-3754. This modern museum hosts a variety of changing exhibitions. It focuses on works by contemporary California artists, but also shows art from all over the world. • Tu 10am-9pm; W-Su 10am-5pm; admission varies.

HOTELS & INNS

Tariffs listed below are for the standard corporate rate during the week. Many hotels have a variety of rates, offering much more luxurious and expensive suites as well as discounts for weekends, big corporations, frequent flyers, AAA members, and more.

Brisbane to San Mateo

Best Western El Rancho Inn $$: 1100 El Camino Real, Millbrae, (415) 588-8500. This large motor inn has the pink-flamingos look to go with the pools, but the rooms are modern enough and it's cheaper than the airport hotels on the Bay. $75.

Crown Sterling Suites Hotel $$$: 150 Anza Blvd., Burlingame, (415) 342-4600. A huge airport hotel on the Bay. As the name implies, all accommodations are suites with separate living room area and feature refrigerator, coffee-maker, microwave, and sink. $119-$159.

Holiday Inn Express $$: 350 N. Bayshore Blvd., San Mateo, (415) 344-6376. Your basic motel, convenient to Hwy 101 and downtown San Mateo. $60-$70.

Hyatt Regency San Francisco Airport $$$: 1333 Bayshore Hwy., Burlingame, (415) 347-1234, (800) 233-1234. Classic Hyatt, with a large atrium lobby. Standard business-luxe rooms. $119-$190.

Marriott San Francisco Airport $$$: 1800 Old Bayshore Hwy., Burlingame, (415) 692-9100, (800) 228-9290. This comfortable upscale business hotel has a surprise—you can rent mountain bikes for local explorations along the Bay. $149.

Westin San Francisco Airport $$$$: 1 Old Bayshore Hwy., Millbrae, (415) 692-3500. A big airport conference hotel with a pool, spa, business services, and the like. $175-$190.

Belmont to Mountain View

Best Western Mountain View Inn $$$: 2300 El Camino Real, Mountain View, (415) 962-9912, (800) 785-0005. All the newly redecorated rooms and suites are tastefully furnished and include a refrigerator, microwave, coffee maker, and sitting areas. Enjoy your complimentary continental breakfast and then sweat it off in the pool and fitness center. $89-$200.

The Cardinal Hotel $$: 235 Hamilton Ave., Palo Alto, (415) 323-5101. This hotel features a high-ceilinged Spanish-style great hall as its lobby, with a buffed tile floor and baronial light fixtures. The hotel has been remodeled and the rooms sport a bright and cheerful new look, not to mention that they're clean and well kept. $50-$140.

Cowper Inn $$: 705 Cowper Ave., Palo Alto, (415) 327-4475. Want sublime, leafy, antiquey, New England ambiance? They provide porches for smokers and sherry in the parlor for everyone. $60-$110.

PENINSULA & SAN JOSE

Garden Court Hotel $$$$: 520 Cowper St., Palo Alto, (415) 322-9000. This is undoubtedly the executive choice in downtown Palo Alto. All those handsome young men in livery parking cars and hauling luggage will make any guest feel like a visiting dignitary. The rooms are pleasant and overscaled, outfitted with expensive (if somewhat standard) designer touches. Best of all, the room service is catered by Il Fornaio, one of Palo Alto's finest restaurants. $200-$245.

Holiday Inn Palo Alto $$$: 625 El Camino Real, Palo Alto, (415) 328-2800. The hotel recently underwent a major renovation, and rooms are still in pristine condition. There's a splendid pool in the courtyard, as well as Japanese water gardens on the grounds. The inn is just across El Camino from Stanford and thus often booked up, so plan ahead. $129-$163.

Hotel California $: 2431 Ash St., Palo Alto, (415) 322-7666. Each room is a bit different from the other, and each is attractively furnished with brass beds and the like. Breakfast is purchased at Harlan's Bakery downstairs using vouchers provided by the hotel. There's a central patio, a communal kitchen complete with microwave, a coin-operated washer and dryer, and a place to iron. $52-$65.

Hotel Sofitel San Francisco Bay $$$$: 223 Twin Dolphin Dr., Redwood City, (415) 598-9000, (800) 221-4542. A big, corporate hotel close to all the new industrial development along the Bay, especially Oracle (whose employees get special rates here). $155-$175.

Residence Inn Mountain View $$$: 1854 W. El Camino Real, Mountain View, (415) 940-1300. A Marriott property, this hotel is all suites and penthouses with working fireplaces. Guests are coddled with complimentary cocktails, valet laundry service, a "sport court," and a health club. 1-6 nights, $154; discounts for longer stays.

Stanford Park Hotel $$$$: 100 El Camino Real, Menlo Park, (415) 322-1234. A shingled brick and oak building that conjures up images of ye olde English inn. Somehow this luxury hotel feels as quiet as a country inn, despite that fact that it's smack dab on El Camino Real. The Stanford Park is very convenient to the Stanford Shopping Center and campus. $185-$235.

San Jose & South Bay

Best Western Downtown $$: 455 S. 2nd St., San Jose, (408) 298-3500. A basic downtown motel—more economical than the historic landmarks. $58-$68.

Cupertino Inn $$$: 10889 N. De Anza Blvd., Cupertino, (408) 996-7700. The Cupertino is very convenient for those trips to Apple Computer. Rates include breakfast and afternoon hors d'oeuvres. $125.

The Fairmont $$$$: 170 S. Market St., San Jose, (408) 998-1900. The centerpiece of San Jose's downtown redevelopment boasts over 500 luxury rooms, a rooftop pool, fitness center, and a variety of restaurants. $189-$204.

The Hensley House $$$: 456 N. 3rd St., San Jose, (408) 298-3537. This Victorian B&B in downtown San Jose offers private bathrooms, gourmet breakfasts, and afternoon hors d'oeuvres. $95-$155.

Hotel De Anza $$$: 233 W. Santa Clara St., San Jose, (408) 286-1000. A national historic landmark, this art deco hotel was recently restored as part of the renovation of downtown San Jose. $150-$175.

Hotel Sainte Claire $$$: 302 S. Market St., San Jose, (408) 295-2000, (800) 824-6835. This recently remodeled historic hotel is smaller than the Fairmont and quite luxurious. The Spanish-tiled interior courtyard is a distinctive touch, and the hotel houses a branch of the Il Fornaio restaurant chain. $135 and up.

The Inn at Saratoga $$$: 20645 4th St., Saratoga, (408) 867-5020, (800) 543-5020 (within CA), (800) 338-5020 (outside CA). Both business travelers and vacationers looking for a spa retreat will enjoy this tasteful, romantic inn overlooking Saratoga Creek. $150.

Madison Street Inn $$: 1390 Madison St., Santa Clara, (408) 249-5541. Period furnishings give this small Victorian B&B its charm, while modern touches such as a pool, hot tub, and excellent breakfasts add to the appeal. $60-$85.

Motel 6 $: 2560 Fontaine Rd., San Jose, (408) 270-3131. Your basic motel—it's cheap and south of downtown near Hwy 101 and Tully Road. $45-$50.

San Jose Hilton and Towers $$$$: 300 Almaden Blvd., San Jose, (408) 287-2100, (800) HILTONS/445-8667. One of the newest big hotels, the San Jose Hilton was built to serve the convention center. $170-$195.

Santa Clara Marriott $$$: 2700 Mission College Blvd., Santa Clara, (408) 988-1500. If you're heading to a convention in Santa Clara, this big corporate hotel can easily take care of you. $149.

GETTING SETTLED

The Peninsula and South Bay are largely suburban, residential areas; the locals shop primarily in regional malls and ubiquitous neighborhood strip centers. Nevertheless, many downtown areas near CalTrain stations have been revived into viable shopping districts reminiscent of the 1800s. You won't find huge stores like Macy's or J.C. Penny in any of these downtowns, but you will find many unique shops and boutiques, as well as plenty of cafés and restaurants.

Bookstores

A Clean Well Lighted Place For Books: Oaks Shopping Center, 21269 Stevens Creek Blvd., Cupertino, (408) 255-7600. See San Francisco Bookstores section for more information.

B. Dalton Bookseller: 20510 Stevens Creek Blvd., Cupertino, (408) 246-6760. • Eastridge Shopping Center, Tully Rd. and Capitol Expwy., San Jose, (408) 270-1070. • Oakridge Mall, Santa Teresa Blvd. and Blossom Hill Rd., San Jose, (408) 226-0387. • Valley Fair Shopping Center, Stevens Creek Blvd. and I-880, San Jose, (408) 246-6760. National chain.

Barnes and Noble: 1940 S. El Camino Real, San Mateo, (415) 312-9066. • Sequoia Station, 1091 El Camino Real, Redwood City, (415) 299-0117. • Hamilton Plaza, 1650 Bascom Ave., Campbell, (408) 369-9808. • 3600 Stevens Creek Blvd., San Jose, (408) 984-3495. National chain.

Books Inc.: Stanford Shopping Center, El Camino Real and Quarry Rd., Palo Alto, (415) 321-0600. • Near United Terminal in SFO, (415) 244-0610. See San Francisco Bookstores section for more information.

Borders Books & Music: 456 University Ave., Palo Alto, (415) 326-3670. • (408) 934-1180. See San Francisco Bookstores section for more information.

Crown Books: 1591 Sloat Blvd., Daly City, (415) 664-1774. • Super Crown, 765 Broadway, Millbrae, (415) 697-3224. • 590 Showers Dr., Mountain View, (415) 732-7057. • Super Crown, 789 E. El Camino Real, Sunnyvale, (408) 732-7057. • Super Crown, 19640 Stevens Creek Blvd., Cupertino, (408) 973-8100. • Super Crown, Main St. Shopping Ctr., Santa Teresa Blvd. and Blossom Hill Rd., San Jose, (408) 629-1033. • Westgate Shopping Ctr., 1600 Saratoga Ave., San Jose, (408) 374-9283. National chain.

Kepler's Books: 1010 El Camino Real, Menlo Park, (415) 324-4321. Kepler's boasts an enormous fiction selection that attracts readers from all over the South Bay and doubles as a hangout for literary types. Tables and chairs accommodate the hard-core browsers, while the more decisive can devour their purchases at the popular Café Borrone next door. Kepler's also sponsors frequent readings and book signings by visiting authors, all free. Kepler's Annex, on the other side of the café, sells remaindered books at bargain prices.

PENINSULA & SAN JOSE

Phileas Fogg's Books, Maps & More for the Traveler: Stanford Shopping Ctr., El Camino Real and Quarry Rd., Palo Alto, (415) 327-1754. If you're going on a journey, make this your first stop. It's worth it for the extensive map and guidebook selection.

Printers Inc.: 310 California Ave., Palo Alto, (415) 327-6500. • 301 Castro St., Mountain View, (415) 961-8500. This revered pair of stores boasts a large literature collection offering titles from both mainstream and small presses, a separate room for poetry and literary theory, and a large travel section. The Palo Alto shop has a spacious café next door, and the Mountain View shop has an outdoor patio. Printers Inc. also sponsors frequent readings and book signings by visiting authors.

Stacey's Bookstore: 219 University Ave., Palo Alto, (415) 326-0681. • 19765 Stevens Creek Blvd., Cupertino, (408) 253-7521. See San Francisco Bookstores section for more information.

Tower Books: 2727 S. El Camino Real, San Mateo, (415) 570-7444. • 630 San Antonio Rd., Mountain View, (415) 941-7300. National chain.

Waldenbooks: Tanforan Park, 1150 El Camino Real, San Bruno, (415) 583-7717. • 1354 Burlingame Ave., Burlingame, (415) 343-4231. • TownCenter, 2754 TownCenter Ln., Sunnyvale, (408) 739-9000. • Vallco Shopping Ctr., 10123 N. Wolfe Rd., Cupertino, (408) 255-0602. • Pavilion Mall, 150 S. Market St., San Jose, (408) 292-6416. • Eastridge Shopping Ctr., Tully Rd. and Capitol Expwy., San Jose, (408) 274-1301. National chain with smaller stores.

Food & Wine

The local grocery scene is dominated by two giants, Safeway and Lucky. They each have stores in virtually every city on the Peninsula. In addition to the giants, Bell Market is a local chain with an area presence. Many neighborhoods have preserved small, independent grocers, as well as a range of specialty, ethnic, and health food stores. Many cities also hold weekend farmers' markets from spring through the fall.

Beltramo's: 1540 El Camino Real, Menlo Park, (415) 325-2806. Beltramo's claims to have "one of the world's largest and finest selections of wines and spirits," stocks over 3,500 wines, and has one of the broadest inventories of beer around.

Cosentino's Vegetable Haven: South Bascom and Union aves., San Jose, (408) 377-6661. • 3521 Homestead Rd., Santa Clara, (408) 243-9005. For South Bay denizens, Cosentino's is *the* food emporium. In addition to the high-quality vegetables, Cosentino's has a great selection of bulk items, gourmet goods, and ethnic goodies—look for quinoa, couscous, specialty mustards, and a good selection of olive oils.

Cost Plus: 785 Serramonte Blvd., Colma, (415) 994-7090. • 68 Hillsdale Mall, El Camino Real and Hillsdale Blvd., San Mateo, (415) 341-7474. • 1910B El Camino Real, Mountain View, (415) 961-6066. • 4050 Stevens Creek Blvd., San Jose, (408) 247-3333. • 1084 Blossom Hill Rd. and Almaden Expwy., San Jose, (408) 267-6666. See San Francisco Food Stores section.

Draeger's Supermarket: 1010 University Dr., Menlo Park, (415) 688-0677. • 342 1st Street, Los Altos, (415) 948-4425. This upscale food emporium has a full-service butcher, an above-average produce department, and an extensive wine section. Draeger's carries a nice spread of domestic and imported cheeses. Draeger's also has a wonderful selection of European goods, including a score of olive oils, mustards, fine vinegars, and a stupendous deli.

Fiesta Latina: 1424 Cary Ave., San Mateo, (415) 343-0193. A very complete Latin American produce and dry goods market with many hard-to-find items. Fresh produce includes plantains, yucca, taro roots, and various fruits.

GETTING SETTLED

La Costeña: 2078 Old Middlefield Way, Mountain View, (415) 967-0507. La Costeña carries many Latin American products, especially for Mexican and Salvadoran cooking. The dried chilies and Mexican herbs are outstanding.

Monterey Market: Stanford Shopping Ctr., El Camino Real and Quarry Rd., Palo Alto, (415) 329-1340. People who seek out good produce and value prices swear by this festive market. The fresh, colorful offerings include Latin American staples like plantains and guava, and Asian essentials like bok choy and Chinese green beans, as well as a fine variety of exotic mushrooms. The prices are hard to beat for such top-of-the-line produce.

New Castro Market: 340 Castro St., Mountain View, (415) 962-8899. One of the best markets anywhere in the Bay Area for Asian groceries. The highlight of the store is probably the fish and meat department, which is as complete as any in the Bay Area. There is fresh fish and seafood especially for sushi. The noodle section fills an entire aisle with pastas from Taiwan, Japan, Vietnam, Thailand, and Korea.

Nishioka Brothers Fish Market: 665 N. 6th St., San Jose, (408) 295-2985. A complete Japanese food store with a wonderful selection of fresh and frozen fish for sushi.

Noah's Bagels: 1152 Burlingame Ave., Burlingame, (415) 342-8423. • 1067 El Camino Real, Redwood City, (415) 299-9050. • 746 Santa Cruz Ave., Menlo Park, (415) 326-4794. • 278 University Ave., Palo Alto, (415) 473-0751. • 15996 Los Gatos Blvd., Los Gatos, (408) 358-5895. See San Francisco Food Stores section.

Oakville Grocery: 715 Stanford Shopping Center, El Camino Real and Quarry Rd., Palo Alto, (415) 328-9000. Another upscale food emporium with a particularly nice wine stock (the proprietor owns the Joseph Phelps vineyard). The Oakville Grocery carries many domestic and imported cheeses at high prices, along with excellent breads and crackers. Well over a dozen olive oils, other gourmet oils such walnut and avocado, numerous vinegars, and dried exotic mushrooms can be found on these tempting shelves.

Peet's Coffee and Tea: 1305 Burlingame Ave., Burlingame, (415) 548-0494. • 899 Santa Cruz Ave., Menlo Park, (415) 325-8989. • 153 Homer Ave., Palo Alto, (415) 325-2091. • 367 State St., Los Altos, (415) 941-6522. • 798-1 Blossom Hill Rd., Los Gatos, (408) 358-6311. See San Francisco Food Stores section.

Race Street Fish & Poultry: 1935 W. El Camino Real, Mountain View, (415) 964-5811. Like the truly excellent fish and poultry market that it is, Race Street carries a great selection of seafood including crab, crawfish, shrimp, squid, octopus, oysters, mussels, and live lobsters. If you want chicken, rabbit, or duck, you got it, and Race Street can also handle special orders for game meats such as pheasant and quail.

Schaub's Meat, Fish & Poultry: 395 Stanford Shopping Ctr., El Camino Real and Quarry Rd., Palo Alto, (415) 325-6328. One of the best premium butcher shops on the Peninsula, offering a wide variety of fresh meats, including fish and seafood, as well as prepared rotisserie chicken and fajitas. They also carry a variety of terrific homemade sausages. Schaub's is a good bet for duck and rabbit, and the butchers can special order exotic game meats like pheasant and alligator.

Takahashi Market: 221 S. Claremont St., San Mateo, (415) 343-0394. This complete Japanese market sells fresh fish and all the necessary items for sushi. Check out the complete section of popular Chinese items including hoisin sauce, fermented black beans, and chili oils. Among the Southeast Asian goods on the shelves are fish sauce, dried lemongrass, laos powder, coconut milk, and dried galangal roots. There's even a selection of prepared Hawaiian foods, including *poi* and *lau-lau*.

Whole Foods: 774 Emerson St., Palo Alto, (415) 326-8566. • 15980 Los Gatos Blvd., Los Gatos, (408) 358-4434. See San Francisco Food Stores section.

PENINSULA & SAN JOSE

Home Furnishings

Most of the chain stores described in the San Francisco Home Furnishings section have Peninsula and San Jose locations as well; check the local phone book for specific locations.

Computers and Electronics

Anderson's: 901 El Camino Real, Redwood City, (415) 367-9400. • 999 El Camino Real, Sunnyvale, (408) 733-9820. • 606 Saratoga Ave., San Jose, (408) 554-1617. Go for the great selection of electronics at decent prices, and go especially for the frequent warehouse sales that'll get you reaching for your wallet.

Computer Attic Supercenter: 2750 El Camino Real, Redwood City, (415) 363-8100. This huge store carries Mac, Toshiba, IBM, and Compaq computers, as well as software, books, and hardware accessories galore. Service can be harried but the prices are usually good.

Fry's Electronics: 340 Portage Ave., Palo Alto, (415) 496-6000. • 1177 Kern Ave., Sunnyvale, (408) 733-1770. Fry's is a Silicon Valley institution. The former-supermarket-turned-electronics superstore carries Macs, IBMs, countless clones, numerous printers and monitors, and enough parts and accessories to build your own computer. They also carry all kinds of home electronics: stereos, portable stereos, VCRs, TVs, CD players, fax machines, telephones, and answering machines. Look for an especially large selection of telephone equipment and Walkman-type stereos.

Mateo Hi-Fi: 2207 S. El Camino Real, San Mateo, (415) 573-6506. Serious audiophiles might want to check out Mateo Hi-Fi (don't be put off by the funky pawn-shop storefront). They specialize in custom home design and installation, as well as mid-fi with some high-fi and specialty products, like in-wall speakers. You can always negotiate a good deal with their competent salespeople.

NCA Computer Products: 3825 El Camino Real, Palo Alto, (415) 493-2444. • 1202 Kifer Rd., Sunnyvale, (408) 739-9010. • 962 Blossom Hill Rd., San Jose, (408) 363-4600. Decor and sales assistance are sparse, but prices are absolutely rock bottom at this bare-bones computer supermarket, run in the same style as Fry's but with more focus on computers—mostly PC clones—and hardware components. They have a limited selection of software, mostly CD-ROMs.

Furniture

Cort Furniture Clearance Center: 2925 Meade Ave., Santa Clara, (408) 727-1470. Cort has quality new and used furniture, including some scratch-and-dent stuff.

Mattress Factory Outlet: 1970 W. El Camino Real, Mountain View, (415) 969-7580. Mattress Factory has a full line of mattresses, including national brands and discounted products.

Oprah House: 251 W. El Camino Real, Sunnyvale, (408) 730-1658. Oprah House carries a large selection of new, quality oak furniture at bargain basement prices.

Scandinavian Designs: 317 S. B Street, San Mateo, (415) 340-0555. Reasonably priced and good quality starter furniture; also children's furniture. Many pieces have the Euro-laminate look—lots of shelves, desks, dressers, and other basics.

Housewares

Most of the chain stores described in the San Francisco Home Furnishings section have Peninsula and San Jose locations as well; check the local phone book for specific locations.

Thrift Stores

Goodwill: 225 Kenwood Wy., South SF, (415) 737-9827. • 4085 El Camino Way, Palo Alto, (415) 494-1416. • 855 El Camino Real, Mountain View, (415) 969-3382. • 151 E. Washington Ave., Sunnyvale, (408) 736-8558. • 1125 Saratoga Sunnyvale Rd., Cupertino, (408) 252-3193. • 1579 Meridian Ave., San Jose, (408) 266-7151. • 1080 N. 7th St., San Jose, (408) 998-5774. This national institution known for its large selection at good prices has many area outlets. The Palo Alto store is chock-full of stuff, all of which is cheap and much of which is in extremely good condition, although clothing and odds and ends are the best finds. The Mountain View store is large, basic, and cheap. The Seventh Avenue store in San Jose is a wholesale outlet where junk that won't sell in other Goodwill stores is sold off by the barrel.

Pick of the Litter: 1801 S. Grant St., San Mateo, (415) 345-1024. This store gets its name from its beneficiary, the Peninsula Humane Society, but you won't find many dogs in its merchandise. This big, well-organized place sells it all, from furniture to books and records to clothes to housewares. Prices are low, but look for specials and sales to really save.

Salvation Army: 300 El Camino Real, San Bruno, (415) 583-3589. • 650 El Camino Real, Belmont, (415) 591-5499. • 1494 Halford Ave., Santa Clara, (408) 249-1715. • 660 Veterans Blvd., Redwood City, (415) 368-7527. • 4140 Monterey Rd., San Jose, (408) 578-1288. The reliable national institution.

Savers: 875 Main St., Redwood City, (415) 364-5545. • 60 S. Dempsey Rd., Milpitas, (408) 263-8338. • 2222 Business Cir., San Jose, (408) 287-0591. In Redwood City, you can find furniture on the second floor, while on the main floor you can browse through the huge and well-organized clothing and housewares collection. All the stores offer a good selection. For about $3 you can purchase a Chinese wok; you can get a nice set of glasses for around 99¢ each.

The Second Act: 12882 S. Saratoga-Sunnyvale Rd., Saratoga, (408) 741-4995. Second Act is the type of consignment shop you'd expect to find in a high-rent district like Saratoga, where the cast-off clothes and furniture are nicer than the new purchases down in the Valley. Prices are a good deal compared to what these garments cost new, but don't look for any dollar racks filled with Polo and Armani jackets.

This 'n' That Shop: 1336 5th Ave., Belmont, (415) 591-6166. For over 30 years this bargain Mecca has been reselling old clothes, housewares, books, and more to benefit the projects of Good Shepherd Episcopal Church. The store is only open a couple of days a week, and the low prices draw crowds.

Thrift Center: 1060 El Camino Real, San Carlos, (415) 593-1082. Thrift Center is as big and ramshackle a thrift store as you'll find anywhere, with everything from furniture to clothing to appliances. Prices are generally very low.

Flea Markets and Garage Sales

The classified ads in the local papers are a great resource for surprise finds. You'll see listings of secondhand goods, the week's flea markets and garage sales, and sometimes even a freebie section.

Capitol Flea Market: 3630 Hillcap Ave., San Jose, (408) 225-5800. 50¢ per person on Thursday, $1 per person on weekends. • Th 7am-5:30pm; Sa-Su 6am-5:30pm.

De Anza College Flea Market: 21250 Stevens Creek Blvd., Cupertino, (408) 864-8414. No entrance fee, parking $2. Over 800 stalls. • M-F 8:30am-3pm.

The Flea Market Inc.: 1590 Berryessa Rd., San Jose, (408) 453-1110. Plenty of parking. • W-Su 7am-6pm.

PENINSULA & SAN JOSE

RESTAURANTS & CAFES

Andalé Taqueria ★★ ¢ 6 N. Santa Cruz Ave. (Bean/Main), Los Gatos, (408) 395-4244. • 21 N. Santa Cruz Ave. (Bean/Main), Los Gatos, (408) 395-8997. • 209 University Ave. (Emerson), Palo Alto, (415) 323-2939. Some say these are the best of the fresh-Mex restaurants that are cropping up everywhere. The brightly painted, festive interiors put you in the mood for the first-rate, reasonably priced food. If you're in a burrito rut, try the chicken tamale. Margaritas are made with wine rather than tequila; sangria and beer are also served. No credit cards. • LG/6: Daily 11am-9pm. • LG/21: M-F 11am-10pm; Sa-Su 9am-10pm. • PA: Su-Th 11am-10pm; F-Sa 11am-11pm.

Bangkok Cuisine ★★ $ 407 Lytton Ave. (Waverley), Palo Alto, (415) 322-6533. • 5235 Prospect Rd., San Jose, (408) 253-8424. The full complement of Thai dishes can be found here. Among them are an ocean of seafood-oriented specialties, including sautéed shellfish with curry, sweet basil, and coconut milk and whole pompano deep-fried and topped with chili sauce. The portions are smallish and the tables packed together too tightly, but then again the food is above average. • PA: M-Sa 11am-3pm, 5-10pm; Su 5-10pm. • SJ: M-Th 11am-3pm, 5-9:30pm; F-Sa 11am-3pm, 5-10pm; Su 5-9:30pm.

Barley and Hopps ★★ $$/$$$ 201 South B St. (2nd Ave.), San Mateo, (415) 348-7808. The name Barley and Hopps tells you that this is a brew pub. The atmospheric interior—exposed brick walls, dark wood furniture, and trademark alabaster light fixtures—tells you it's owned by the same group that runs Capellini and the Buffalo Grill. And the three-story dining-and-entertainment center concept hints at the success of Palo Alto's Blue Chalk Café. The beer is pretty good, especially the India pale ale, and complements the hearty menu: lots of smoky barbecue, gourmet deep-dish pizza, and a mixture of burgers, fish, and the like. They brew their own root beer here, too, so save room for dessert and order up a float. After dinner, head upstairs for a cigar and a game of pool, or downstairs to Blues on B, the basement blues club. • M-Th 11:30am-3pm, 5-10pm; F-Sa 11:30am-3pm, 5-10:30pm; Su 11:30am-3pm, 5-9pm.

Basque Cultural Center ★★★ $$ 599 Railroad Ave. (Magnolia), South SF, (415) 583-8091. It's worth tracking down this out-of-the-way institution. Simple, delicious French Basque specialties are served family style in the comfortable dining room decorated with country French furniture, crisp white tablecloths, and dark wood beams. Meals start off with a tureen of soup, followed by a salad and two entrées, which might include red snapper Basque style or pepper steak with a satisfying black-pepper crust. The portions are huge. Reservations recommended. • Tu-F 11:30am-2:30pm, 5:30-9:30pm; Sa 5:30-9:30pm; Su 5-9pm.

Bella Saratoga/Bella Mia ★★ $$ 58 S. 1st St. (Santa Clara/San Fernando), San Jose, (408) 280-1993. • 14503 Big Basin Way, Saratoga, (408) 741-5115. Downtown Saratoga's most popular dining spot is located in a historic Victorian where you can enjoy a lazy Sunday brunch, complete with jazz and outdoor seating (weather permitting). The chef competes (and wins) in many of the pasta competitions held in the area. Some of his more stunning creations: salmon ravioli, oven-baked lasagna, and veal or chicken piccata. Indoors, the decor tends toward high Victorian—floral wallpaper, oak furniture, creaky stairs. A favorite pre-prom spot with high schoolers and a popular site for popping the question. After a second location in San Jose opened in 1993, it was sold to a new owner, and the original changed its name to Bella Saratoga. • SJ: M-Th 11am-10pm; F-Sa 11am-10:30pm; Su 10am-10pm. • Saratoga: M-Th 11:30am-9:30pm; F 11:30am-11pm; Sa 10am-10pm; Su 10am-9pm.

Bella Vista Restaurant ★★ $$$ 13451 Skyline Blvd. (Hwy 84), Woodside, (415) 851-1229. High up on top of Skyline Drive, the view from this woodsy retreat is unsurpassed, with the entire Peninsula and bay laid out before you. (Be sure to ask for a table with a view when you make your reservation.) A wood-burning fireplace, lots of rough-hewn wood, and white linen tablecloths create a rustic yet elegant ambience. The menu is classic Continental and expensive. • M-Th 5:30-9pm; F-Sa 5-9pm.

RESTAURANTS & CAFES

Beppo Little Italy ★★ $$$ 643 Emerson St., Palo Alto, (415) FAW-ZOOL/329-0665. Forget quiet trattorias—this bustling place is kitschy and fun. It's like eating at your Aunt Sophia's kitchen table with your cousin Vinnie. This new casual southern Italian restaurant brings the best of New York's Little Italy to Palo Alto: The generous pizzas, salads, pastas and desserts are served on platters for groups to share; Frank Sinatra and Dean Martin croon familiar Italian-American tunes; you'll leave feeling full and with a care package from "Nonni." Beppo's menu boasts hearty selections including calamari, spaghetti and meatballs, homemade ravioli, eggplant parmesan, thin-crust pizzas, and tiramisu. *Note:* No reservations...calling ahead up to one hour before you arrive can reduce the wait. • M-F 5pm-10pm; Sa-Su 5pm-11pm.

Bistro Elan ★★★ $$$ 448 California Ave. (El Camino/Ash), Palo Alto, (415) 327-0284. This bright, breezy bistro is uncharacteristically sophisticated for California Avenue, Palo Alto's "other" downtown. As with most new local bistros, the walls are honey yellow, a sophisticated eating bar (hammered tin) overlooks the open kitchen, and the attitude is casual but professional. The kitchen does an excellent job of turning out elaborately presented dishes like duck confit with potatoes and green beans, smoked salmon with wonton wrappers and wasabi, and pan-seared salmon with a Provençal artichoke ragout. Breads and desserts are baked on the premises. Reservations recommended. • M-F 11:30am-2pm; Tu-Sa 5:30-10pm.

Blue Chalk Café ★★★ $$ 630 Ramona St. (Hamilton/Forest), Palo Alto, (415) 326-1020. The Blue Chalk seats a huge crowd on two airy levels. More diners can enjoy the pleasant front patio in warm weather. The southern-influenced menu is excellent; specialties include a spicy seafood corn chowder, fresh catfish, and grilled-vegetable sandwiches. For gaming enthusiasts, pool tables occupy one room, while upstairs there's a shuffleboard table and dart boards. This isn't your typical pool hall scene, however: weekends it's packed with Silicon Valley swingles and there's not a surly bartender or tough biker in sight. Small but good beer selection on tap. • M-Sa 11:30am-2:30pm, 5-10pm; Su 5-10pm; bar menu M-Sa 2:30-5pm.

Buffalo Grill ★★ $$$ Hillsdale Mall, 66 31st Ave. (El Camino), San Mateo, (415) 358-8777. As its name suggests, this Pat Kuleto–designed destination departs wildly from his empire of Italian restaurants. The decor of this upscale and perpetually packed diner is over-the-top Western, with faux hunting trophies on the back wall and lighting fixtures shaped like buffalo horns alongside the booths. The food is equally tongue-in-cheek mock frontier with a Californian flourish. Entrées like a grilled chicken club sandwich with smoked bacon on sourdough and maple-cured pork chops with corn spoonbread and buttermilk onion rings draw a never-ending stream of society mavens and power lunchers during the day and crowds from all over the Peninsula at night. Anything from the grill is a sure bet, as are the gargantuan homemade desserts, which two or three diners can happily share. Reservations are a must. • M-Th 11:30am-2:30pm, 5-10pm; F-Sa 11:30am-2:30pm, 5-10:30pm; Su 5-9pm.

California Sushi and Grill ★★ $$ 1 E. San Fernando St. (1st St./2nd St.), San Jose, (408) 297-1847. • Red Lion Hotel, 2050 Gateway Pl. (Technology), San Jose, (408) 436-1754. Fresh, creative sushi preparations and fine teriyaki and tempura emerge from the kitchen at California Sushi and Grill, one of downtown San Jose's more pleasant dining spots. The cheerful interior is done up in pink, black, and white, with a few bamboo accents. Sit upstairs and you overlook the Gordon Biersch beer garden. All this and karaoke, too. A second location in the Red Lion Hotel offers the same fare. • M-F 11:30am-2pm, 5-9:30pm; Sa 5-9:30pm.

Capellini ★★ $$ 310 Baldwin Ave. (S. B St.), San Mateo, (415) 348-2296. The high-ceilinged downstairs dining room (designed by Pat Kuleto), with its dark wood bar and gleaming fixtures, reverberates with the din of local patrons. Try to sit on the loft level for a view of the goings-on. Bread served with excellent fruity olive oil starts things off; save space for the tasty pastas, salads, and main dishes. Good wine list. • M-F 11:30am-2pm, 5-10pm; Sa 5-10pm; Su 5-9pm; light menu M-F 2-5pm.

PENINSULA & SAN JOSE

Casa Vicky ★ ¢ 792 E. Julian St. (17th St.), San Jose, (408) 995-5488. One of the best values around. The delicious, spicy food at this self-service Mexican restaurant packs a lot of bang for the buck. You can eat solo for $2 to $4—an enormous tamale goes for $2, and a fiery chile relleno slathered in guacamole and sour cream is $3.50—or feed the entire family for just $13 with a whole mesquite-broiled chicken accompanied with rice, beans, chips, and salsa. Enjoy your meal outside on a nice day. • Daily 7am-10pm.

Chef Chu's ★★ $ 1067 N. San Antonio Rd. (El Camino), Los Altos, (415) 948-2696. Chef Chu's is a Peninsula institution, the kind of place where autographed photos of Brooke Shields and Gerald Ford hang on the wall. For every detractor who claims that standards have slipped, there's an equally adamant defender. We won't take sides, but we will say that there's still much here that's worth ordering, especially those old favorites, moo shu pork and wonton soup. With its landmark status, Chef Chu's is always crowded; expect to wait for a table most nights. • M-Th 11:30am-9:30pm; F 11:30am-10pm; Sa-Su noon-9:30pm.

Chez Sovan ★★★ $ 2425 S. Bascom Ave. (Dry Creek), Campbell, (408) 371-7711. • 923 13th St. (Hwy 101/E. Hedding), San Jose, (408) 287-7619. The original is located in a bleak San Jose neighborhood, but this shining star has expanded to additional quarters in Campbell. Mme. Sovan, the chef, serves some of the best Cambodian food on the Peninsula. Try the amazing chicken salad crunchy with peanuts, shredded vegetables, and thin noodles in a beguiling sweet-and-sour hot sauce—you'll crave it for weeks afterward. Curries are fiery and flavorful; grilled skewers of beef, pork, or chicken are redolent of the Cambodian grill. Friendly service. • Campbell: Su-Th 11am-9pm; F-Sa 11am-10pm. • SJ: M-F 11am-2:30pm.

Chez T.J. ★★★ $$$$ 938 Villa St. (Castro), Mountain View, (415) 964-7466. The interior of this restored Victorian bungalow is strictly Californian—peach walls, contemporary art, glass sculptures. Three prix fixe menus (from the seven-course *menu gastronomique* to the positively modest four-course *menu petit*) are offered nightly. Depending on the luck of the draw, you might be offered sea scallops in a potato crust with saffron sauce, venison with three-mushroom ragout, or monkfish in grape leaves. This is the type of place that serves palate-cleansing sorbets. Reservations required. • Tu-Sa 5:30-9pm.

Cho's ★ ¢ 213 California Ave. (Park), Palo Alto, (415) 326-4632. Palo Alto's premier dive for inexpensive dim sum. Mr. Cho himself has been serving pot stickers and pork buns to a retinue of regular customers for years, and his tiny store is a local institution. Only two small tables are available; get your food to go and sit in the nearby public plaza. No credit cards. • Daily 11:30am-7:30pm.

Dinah's Poolside Café ★ $ 4261 El Camino Real (San Antonio/Charleston), Palo Alto, (415) 493-4542. A Palo Alto weekend-brunch institution. Although you need a map and a compass to find this unpretentious dining spot (just turn in at the tiny sign and proceed to the rear of the parking lot and around the building), the wait for a table on a Sunday morning is every bit as long as it is at Hobee's. However, the wait is much more pleasant, since you can dangle your feet in the pool. The food is solidly American—fresh and plentiful, with a guaranteed lack of surprises. You'll leave satisfied, but it's the congenial surroundings and cheerful, family-style service that will keep you coming back. • Daily 6:30am-9:30pm.

Ecco Café ★★★ $$ 322 Lorton Ave. (Burlingame Ave.), Burlingame, (415) 342-7355. Self-taught chef Tooraj offers some of the most creative fine dining on the Peninsula. In an intimate dining room, he serves dishes that meld the freshest ingredients into subtle, balanced creations, some laced with lavender. Inventive standouts include a watercress and apricot soup and ahi tuna with an anchovy and olive compote. • M-F 11:30am-2pm, 5:30-10pm; Sa 5:30-10pm.

840 North First ★★ $$$ 840 N. 1st St. (Mission/Heading), San Jose, (408) 282-0840. San Jose's power elite flock here at lunchtime—you might spot the mayor or a gaggle

RESTAURANTS & CAFES

of lawyers on a lunch break from the courthouse. The sophisticated dining room, done up in grays and maroons with quirky modern light fixtures, is the ideal backdrop for business powwows. Italian and Asian influences prevail in the kitchen; pasta choices include shellfish linguine. Prawns with chili paste, sherry, and ginger are featured among the appetizers. Reservations a must at lunch. • M-F 11:30am-10pm; Sa 5-10pm.

Emile's ★★★ $$$$ 545 S. 2nd St. (William), San Jose, (408) 289-1960. Emile's has ruled the San Jose dining scene for nearly 20 years. Chef-owner Emile Mooser, the dapper Swiss-born and -trained chef, has a flair for public relations (expect to see him canvassing the dining room). The interior has a subdued elegance: an elaborate flower arrangement dominates the dining room, and an intricate, leaflike sculpture decorates the ceiling. Many of the dishes live up to Emile's vaunted reputation: grilled swordfish served with seafood risotto is perfectly cooked, and the osso buco is tender, rich, and flavorful. Finish off your meal with an ethereal Grand Marnier soufflé. • Tu-Th, Sa 6pm-reservations stop; F 11:30am-reservations stop, 6pm-reservations stop.

Empire Grill and Tap Room ★★ $$ 651 Emerson St. (Forest/Hamilton), Palo Alto, (415) 321-3030. This energetic, convivial eatery done up in forest green and lots of burnished wood was a hit the moment it opened its doors. Silicon Valley swingers flock to the long bar to down pints of Red Hook and Anchor Steam and survey the scene. On balmy evenings, the outdoor patio is an ideal spot for a date—the lighting is low, there's enough bustle to fill in the awkward stretches of silence, and the wait staff is discreet and good humored. The food's good, too, especially the designer pizzas and grilled fish specials. • M-Th 11:30am-9:30pm; F 11:30am-10:30pm; Sa-Su 11am-10pm.

Evvia ★★ $$ 420 Emerson St. (University/Lytton), Palo Alto, (415) 326-0983. Located in an elegant yet rustic Mediterranean space, Evvia brings Greek cuisine to its rightful place among the host of other national fares represented around Palo Alto. The menu has a range of dishes beyond the usual *spanakopitta* and moussaka, including roast chicken and lamb from the rotisserie and pasta dishes with a Greek twist. The *meze* platter has an arrangement of three tasty spreads, crispy, crackerlike pita bread, and several different dolmas filled with subtly spiced rice. The grilled lamb chops are delicious, although the pita pizzas need a bit more topping. Good deserts will have you bypassing the usual too-sweet baklava. The wine list combines California and Greek labels. • M-Sa 11:30am-3pm, 5:30-11pm.

Flea Street Café ★★ $$$ 3607 Alameda de las Pulgas (Avy), Menlo Park, (415) 854-1226. The ambience of a cozy country house and the cooking of enlightened chef and local celebrity Jesse Cool make this a must-visit. An omelet is not just an omelet here, but a concoction of stir-fried greens, roasted garlic, goat cheese, sun-dried tomato cream, and Yucatan sausage. Dinner selections include grilled salmon with buttermilk mashed potatoes. You get the satisfaction of eating organic produce, although good health comes at a fairly hefty price. Lunches are easier on the pocketbook. • Tu-F 11:30am-2pm; 5:30-9:30pm; Sa-Su 9am-2pm, 5:30-9:30pm.

Fook Yuen ★★★ $ 195 El Camino Real (Millbrae/Hillcrest), Millbrae, (415) 692-8600. A convenient, commodious, family-oriented restaurant serving high-quality Hong Kong–style cuisine. Fish is uniformly fresh, and barbecued meats are also recommended. Try the fabulous fried whole flounder and the Peking duck done to perfection. At times, the brightly lit dining room can be loud and cacophonous, but the service doesn't suffer. • M-Th 11am-2:30pm, 5:30-9:30pm; F 11am-2:30pm, 5:30-10pm; Sa 10am-2:30pm, 5:30-10pm; Su 10-2:30pm, 5:30-9:30pm.

Fuki-Sushi ★★★ $$$ 4119 El Camino Real (Ventura), Palo Alto, (415) 494-9383. A giant sushi spot with private tatami rooms: take off your shoes, sit on the floor (dangle your feet in the well), and sip sake served by a waitress in a kimono. Try the Japanese-style fondue called *shabu shabu*, which is a pot of boiling broth into which you dip cabbage, mushrooms, onions, and thinly sliced meat, and then dip the cooked morsels into a mustard sauce. Finish off the dish by drinking the broth. Open every day of the year. • M-F 11am-2pm, 5-10pm; Sa 5-10pm; Su 5-9:30pm.

PENINSULA & SAN JOSE

Gambardella's ★★ $$ 561 Oak Grove Ave. (El Camino/Merrill), Menlo Park, (415) 325-6989. Good, hearty southern Italian food served in an atmospheric wood-paneled dining room decorated with hundreds of old wine bottles. Specials might include lobster ravioli with Chardonnay cream sauce or petrale sole with spicy tomato sauce. A welcome respite from rampant trendiness, this place feels like it's been around for years. • Tu-Th 11:30am-2:30pm, 5:30-9:30pm; F 11:30am-2:30pm, 5:30-10pm; Sa 5:30-10pm; Su 5:30-9:30pm.

Ginger Club ★★★ $$ Stanford Shopping Center (El Camino/Quarry), Palo Alto, (415) 325-6588. Bruce Cost tested the concept of this tropical Southeast Asian restaurant at Ginger Island in Berkeley, which became a runaway success. Now, he has moved to the Peninsula and brought the same alluring cuisine, where it is being served in celebrated architect Mark Mack's colorful interior. Start with the club's very own ginger ale mixed with rum for a novel libation, and don't miss the curried noodles with scallops, a substantial portion of thick noodles and scallops dressed in a pungent, house-made Thai curry sauce. The wontons (both pork and vegetarian) and the ginger ice cream make standout bookends to the meal. • Su-Th 11:30am-9:30pm; F-Sa 11:30am-10:30pm.

Gombei Japanese Kitchen ★★ $ 1438 El Camino Real (Glenwood), Menlo Park, (415) 329-1799. • 193 E. Jackson St. (4th St./5th St.), San Jose, (408) 279-4311. You won't find any slimy, fishy things in this Japanese restaurant specializing in simple, light cooked dishes like teriyaki, tempura, *donburi* (rice bowls), and *udon* (noodle soup). A special salad of exotic Asian vegetables was a sculptural triumph one night, with a tangle of seaweed nestled among the various roots and unidentified vegetation. Looking into the open kitchen you'd think the meticulous chefs were assembling Swiss watches instead of meals. The waiting lines and largely Japanese crowd bode well for the food, but can often mean a wait. No credit cards. • MP: M-F 11:30am-2pm, 5-9:30pm; Sa 5-9:30pm; Su 5-9pm. • SJ: M-Sa 11am-2:30pm, 5-9:30pm.

Gordon Biersch Brewing Company ★★ $$ 640 Emerson St. (Hamilton/Forest), Palo Alto, (415) 323-7723. • 33 E. San Fernando St. (1st St./2nd St.), San Jose, (408) 294-6785. This upscale beer hall packs them in. The magic formula? Beer brewed on the premises, an attractive, on-the-prowl clientele, and an all-around stylish ambience. The long polished wood bar is favored by the young business set, especially on weekend evenings. The California cuisine has a mixed reputation, but burgers are always a good wager, and the garlic fries are delicious. • PA: Su-W 11am-10:30pm; Th-Sa 11am-11pm. • SJ: Su-Th 11am-10pm; F-Sa 11am-11pm.

Henry's World Famous Hi-Life ★ $ 301 W. Saint John St. (N. Almaden), San Jose, (408) 295-5414. Housed in a century-old roadhouse that was almost wiped out by the floods of '95, Henry's is a South Bay landmark. Smoky, white-oak barbecue is the specialty here. Choose from flavorful ribs served with a bowl of spicy sauce, teriyaki steak, or perhaps a side of mushrooms or barbecued onions. Pick a number and wait your turn in the dim, memorabilia-packed bar (an oil portrait of founder Henry Puckett presides over the merriment). • M 5-9pm; Tu-Th 11:30am-2pm, 5-9pm; F 11:30am-2pm, 4-10pm; Sa 4-10pm; Su 4-9pm.

Higashi West ★★★ $$$ 636 Emerson St. (Forest/Hamilton), Palo Alto, (415) 323-9378. Higashi West's dramatic interior features an indoor waterfall and soaring shoots of black bamboo. The menu is equally striking, featuring many daring East-West preparations. Try the garlic-crusted pork chops with green apple essence and wasabi mashed potatoes, or the Higashi West roll—smoked salmon wrapped around tiger shrimp and baked. The traditional sushi is well prepared and fresh, although pricy. The menu lists 13 varieties of sake. • M-Sa 5:30-10pm.

Hong Kong Flower Lounge ★★ $$ 1671 El Camino Real (Park Blvd.), Millbrae, (415) 588-9972. • 51 Millbrae Ave. (El Camino), Millbrae, (415) 692-6666. A celebrated tile-roofed temple with floor-to-ceiling windows on all three tiers. Ostentatious, yes, even gaudy, but somehow lovable. The Flower Lounge is best enjoyed by a group; reserve

RESTAURANTS & CAFES

one of the round tables by the window. The specialty here is Cantonese seafood: live prawns, crab, lobster, catfish, and ling cod are fished out of huge tanks to appear only moments later on your plate. The original location on El Camino is simpler. Service is aloof, to put it mildly, especially if you order in English. Dim sum every day. • M-F 11am-2:30pm, 5-9:30pm; Sa-Su 10:30am-2:30pm, 5-9:30pm.

Iberia ★★★ $$$ 190 Ladera Country Shopper, Alpine Rd., Portola Valley, (415) 854-1746. Regarded as one of the best restaurants on the Peninsula, Iberia prepares Spanish specialties in a beautiful setting. Spend a romantic evening in one of the indoor rooms or outside in the garden over large portions of terrific paella or seafood (you don't have to love garlic to love Iberia, but it helps). Many preparations, including flaming desserts, are orchestrated tableside, reinforcing an Old World feeling. • M-Sa 11:30am-2:30pm, 5:30-10pm; Su 11am-2pm, 5:30-10pm.

Il Fornaio Cucina Italiana ★★ $$ 327 Lorton Ave. (California), Burlingame, (415) 375-8000. • 520 Cowper St. (Hamilton/University), Palo Alto, (415) 853-3888. • 302 S. Market St. (San Carlos), San Jose, (408) 271-3366. See SF Restaurant section for review. • Burlingame: M-Th 11:30am-11pm; F 11:30am-midnight; Sa 8:30am-midnight; Su 8:30am-10pm. • PA & SJ: M-Th 7-10:30am, 11:30am-11pm; F 7-10:30am, 11:30am-midnight; Sa 8am-midnight; Su 8am-11pm.

JoAnn's Café ★★ $ 1131 El Camino Real (Arroyo), South SF, (415) 872-2810. This fabled Bay Area breakfast spot attracts hordes of omelet eaters on the weekends, so be prepared to wait for a table. The bright, airy interior is pleasant—try to snag a booth—and good background music (reggae, rock) serenades you as you peruse the long list of specialty egg dishes. Try the spectacular huevos rancheros or the seasonal berry hotcakes, or create your own omelet from a huge list of ingredients. This is home cooking like your mother never made. A popular spot for breakfast before heading to the ballpark for a Giants game. No credit cards. • M-F 7:15am-2:30pm; Sa-Su 8am-2:30pm.

Kitahama ★★ $$ 974 Saratoga-Sunnyvale Rd. (Bollinger), San Jose, (408) 257-6449. At this rigorously serene sushi establishment, a spalike ambience pervades the many dining areas. The main room features a light-wood sushi bar with tatami tables on the periphery. Another wing houses private tatami rooms (some with telephones). Yet another room houses a karaoke bar. Waitresses in traditional garb glide quietly through the restaurant, attending to your every need. The authentic sushi draws a crowd of appreciative Japanese who have made this into a private club of sorts for discriminating expatriates. • M-Sa 5pm-midnight; Su 5-9:30pm.

Krung Thai ★★★ $ 1699 W. San Carlos St. (Lee), San Jose, (408) 295-5508. Adventurous diners in the South Bay are no doubt familiar with the strip-mall genre of Asian restaurants. From the outside, Krung Thai seems a classic example: the cookie-cutter exterior and semiseedy location promise little. Don't be fooled. There is no better Thai food to be found anywhere (at least on this side of the Pacific). If you don't believe us, ask the customers, most of whom are Thai. But the secret is out, and you will be met by long lines snaking out the door on weekend evenings and at lunchtime. Inside, the dining room is narrow, crowded, and dimly lit. Once the food arrives, however, nothing else seems to matter. Fortunately, success hasn't spoiled the serving staff, who are friendly and solicitous. • M-F 11am-3pm, 5-10pm; Sa-Su 11am-10pm.

Kuleto's Trattoria ★★ $$ 1095 Rollins Rd. (Broadway), Burlingame, (415) 342-4922. See SF Restaurant section for review. • Su-Th 11:30am-10pm; F 11:30am-11pm; Sa 5-11pm.

La Fiesta ★★ $ 240 Villa St. (Calderon/Castro), Mountain View, (415) 968-1364. La Fiesta's drab exterior belies the festive interior, which features sombreros, piñatas, papier-mâché birds and fish, and a kitchenful of terra-cotta dishes suspended from the ceiling. A brightly colored, tiled bar occupies the center of the restaurant. Try the *mole poblano*, breast of chicken served with a heady mole sauce, or the *camarones picantes*, sautéed shrimp in a creamy chipotle and *guajillo* sauce. Portions are large. • Daily 11am-2pm, 5-9pm (later if busy).

PENINSULA & SAN JOSE

L'Amie Donia ★★★ $$$ 530 Bryant St. (University/Hamilton), Palo Alto, (415) 323-7614. Who would have imagined that a sterile café off University Avenue could be transformed into a warm, lively French bistro with little more than a bucket of yellow paint and the installation of a stylish wood and zinc bar? The perspicacious young Donia Bijan, who gained fame as chef at San Francisco's Sherman House and Brasserie Savoy, has savvy Peninsulans lining up for her expert renditions of traditional dishes like coq au vin, rabbit with mustard sauce, and *salade niçoise*. Desserts are a highlight. The front patio is pleasant on warm days, but the back patio is really a dumpster-filled alley—don't sit there. Reservations recommended. • Tu-F 11:30am-2pm, 5:30-11pm; Sa-Su 5:30-11pm.

Le Mouton Noir ★★★ $$$$ 14560 Big Basin Way (4th St./5th St.), Saratoga, (408) 867-7017. A perennial favorite (and perennial winner of the *San Francisco Focus* Best of Santa Clara County award), Le Mouton Noir serves imaginative French cuisine in a grandmother's parlor atmosphere. Pink and mauve accents and dried flowers abound. Start off with warm wild mushroom gateau (sautéed wild mushrooms in a light duck liver mousse) and move along to grilled beef tenderloin served with a port wine sauce, spicy mashed potatoes, and a green bean and shiitake stir-fry. • M-F 6-9:30pm; Sa 5:30-9:30pm; Su 5-9pm.

Left at Albuquerque ★★★ $ 1100 Burlingame Ave. (California), Burlingame, (415) 347-0111. • 445 Emerson St. (University/Lytton), Palo Alto, (415) 326-1011. The owners of the Blue Chalk Café have struck pay dirt again with this southwestern-style bar and restaurant. Bold desert art—black-and-white photos of rodeos and cowgirls, Navajo rugs, and more—and racks of tequila bottles furnish the long, thin space, which ends in an open kitchen against the back wall. The bar scene is wall-to-wall Silicon singles. The contemporary southwestern menu is flavorful, varied, with several tapas-sized dishes. The burritos are assembled from a wide range of meats, seafoods, and grilled vegetables, and the specials come with appetizing side orders such as lightly breaded onion rings or chipotle mashed potatoes. For drinks, margaritas are popular, as is just about every other tequila drink. A second location replaces Café Marimba in Burlingame, and a third on San Francisco's Union Street is in the works. No reservations accepted. • Daily 11:30am-10pm (appetizer, soup, and salad menu 3-4:30pm).

Little Garden ★★ $ 4127 El Camino Real (El Camino Way), Palo Alto, (415) 494-1230. Excellent Chinese-Vietnamese food in a Formica-table atmosphere. But where atmosphere is lacking, low prices usually follow, and you can dine sumptuously here on crackly imperial rolls and curried *kwo* noodle soup bristling with thread noodles and chicken, among other mysterious elements. Lemongrass chicken was a disappointment (the namesake ingredient was undetectable), but a healthy portion of moo shu pork made up for the omission. • M-Th 11:30am-2:30pm, 5-9:30pm; F-Sa 11:30am-2:30pm, 5-10pm; Su 5-9:30pm.

Los Gatos Brewing Co. ★★ $$ 130 N. Santa Cruz Ave. (Grays), Los Gatos, (408) 395-9929. A favorite haunt of beer drinkers and beach types alike in Los Gatos. Indoors, singles mingle over pints of the brewed-on-site ales. A long bar (salvaged from a St. Louis brothel) dominates one end of the soaring, barnlike space; another wall is occupied by a wood-burning oven for pizzas. The faux stone walls painted in earth tones add a rustic note. The menu features designer pizzas, pastas, and grilled meats, but beer is the draw here. • M-Th 11:30am-10pm; F-Sa 11:30am-11pm; Su 10:30am-10pm.

MacArthur Park ★★ $$ 27 University Ave. (El Camino), Palo Alto, (415) 321-9990. Housed in a handsome, rustic barn designed by Julia Morgan, MacArthur Park gives fidgety diners the option of doodling with crayons on the paper-draped tables as they wait for giant platters of ribs or mesquite-grilled chicken, sausages, or fish. Fish entrées are fresh and cleanly grilled, while barbecue options from the oak-fueled smoker require a dentist-style bib. Plentiful Sunday brunch buffet. • M-Th 11:30am-2:30pm, 5:30-10:30pm; F 11:30am-2:30pm, 5:30-11pm; Sa 5-11pm; Su 10am-2pm, 5-10pm.

RESTAURANTS & CAFES

Max's Bakery and Kitchen ★ $ 111 E. 4th Ave. (San Mateo Dr.), San Mateo, (415) 344-1997. See SF Restaurant section for review of Max's Eatz. This location is where the mammoth sweets for all the Max's restaurants in the Bay Area are baked. Sidewalk seating is available. • Su-Th 7am-8pm; F-Sa 7am-9pm.

Max's Opera Café ★★ $$ 711 Stanford Shopping Center (El Camino Real/Quarry), Palo Alto, (415) 323-6297. • 1250 Old Bayshore Hwy. (Broadway), Burlingame, (415) 342-6297. See SF Restaurant section for review. • PA: Su-Th 11:30am-10pm; F-Sa 11am-11pm. • Burlingame: Su-Th 6:30am-11pm; F-Sa 6:30am-midnight.

Menara Moroccan ★ $$ 41 E. Gish Rd. (N. 1st St.), San Jose, (408) 453-1983. You might wonder if this place is even open from its uninviting exterior. But once inside you'll think you've wandered onto the set of *Aladdin*. Be sure to go when the belly dancers are on duty—the audience participation can be almost as entertaining. The food is standard Moroccan. Caution: Seating is North African style, so this is not a place for the weak of knee or stiff of joint. • Daily 6-10pm.

Ming's ★★ $$ 1700 Embarcadero Rd. (E. Bayshore), Palo Alto, (415) 856-7700/7701. Ming's is one of the most well-regarded Chinese restaurants on the Peninsula, with a special room for power-lunching businesspeople. Everybody else dines in an elegant room done up in soft pink, green, and white, where the din during dim sum (served daily; try the crab claws and stuffed mushrooms) can be deafening. Hong Kong chefs prepare the southern Chinese cuisine according to traditional recipes, and the waiters complete the final assembly of some dishes before your eyes. Don't miss the famous chicken salad. • M-F 11am-3pm, 5-9:30; Sa 11am-3pm, 5-10; Su 10:30am-3pm, 5-9:30pm.

The Palace ★★ $$ 146 S. Murphy Ave. (Washington/Evelyn), Sunnyvale, (408) 739-5179. Big-city glitz comes to Silicon Valley in this swanky supper club, which offers dinner as well as jazz and musical events. Located in a restored Art Deco movie theater, the soaring two-tiered interior is an architectural extravaganza, with biomorphic silver-painted columns, wrought-iron accents, and sponge-painted orange walls. The ambitious tapas menu features ahi tuna carpaccio with deep-fried onion rings and sesame-ginger-soy vinaigrette, and crispy coconut prawns with mango mustard. Reservations recommended. • W-Sa 6-10pm.

Palermo ★★ $$ 452 University Ave. (Cowper/Waverley), Palo Alto, (415) 321-9908. • 394 S. 2nd St. (San Salvador), San Jose, (408) 297-0607. Big bites of garlic and ripe tomato punctuate most of Palermo's southern Italian dishes. Put simply, this is not subtle cuisine. The San Jose and Palo Alto locations differ wildly: The gargantuan San Jose facility encompasses three private banquet halls, a ballroom, a breezy outdoor courtyard, and even a wedding chapel, while the Palo Alto interior is small and cramped. • PA: M-Th 11:30am-2pm, 5-10pm; F 11:30am-2pm, 5-11pm; Sa 5-11pm; Su 5-10pm. • SJ: M-Th 11:30am-10:30pm; F 11:30am-11pm; Sa 4-11:30pm; Su 4-10pm.

Paolo's ★★★ $$$ 333 W. San Carlos St. (Woz Way), San Jose, (408) 294-2558. Among the notables who have dined on Paolo's acclaimed and inventive food are Joe DiMaggio, the Reagans, Frank Sinatra, and JFK. The chilled breast of rabbit stuffed with salsa verde and radicchio is one of the most novel concoctions, but innovative touches enliven even the more staid dishes, like beef tortellini in a béchamel sauce. Paolo's features European artwork on ocher sponge-painted walls and vaguely classical interior architecture. The atmosphere is more corporate than glitzy; at lunchtime there's even a *menu al professione*. Upstairs, you can enjoy an aperitif in the wine room or on the patio. • M-F 11am-2:30pm, 5:30-10pm; Sa 5:30-10pm.

Peninsula Fountain & Grill ★ $ 566 Emerson St. (Hamilton), Palo Alto, (415) 323-3131. You may experience the eerie feeling that you've stumbled onto the set of "Happy Days." The food recalls the '50s: juicy, enormous burgers, golden onion rings (delicious, if sometimes a bit on the greasy side), and tuna melts. The towering pies actually taste good (the apple in particular). Although the neon clock says "Eat and Get Out," the owners and the youthful wait staff are friendly to a fault. • M-W 7am-10pm; Th 7am-11pm; F 7am-midnight; Sa 8am-midnight; Su 8am-10pm.

PENINSULA & SAN JOSE

Pho Hua ★ $ 735 The Alameda (Stockton), San Jose, (408) 286-3481. *Pho* is the classic Vietnamese beef noodle soup, and this unpretentious diner serves it in style. Each order comes in a huge bowl, along with fresh herbs and hot sauce so that you can doctor it up to your own specifications. The Vietnamese owners have set up shop inside an old fast-foot drive-in just up the street from the new San Jose Arena. • Daily 9am-9pm.

Red Sea Restaurant ★ $ 684 N. 1st St. (Taylor), San Jose, (408) 993-1990. Housed in a homey California bungalow, the Red Sea is attractively decorated with African crafts and tapestries. The excellent East African food is served in big colorful mounds on top of the tangy, spongy Ethiopian bread called *injera*. You tear off a piece and use it to scoop up a serving of meat, lentils, greens, or mixed vegetables. The drink menu is fun, with its Ethiopian honey wine and some obscure African beers. Lots of good vegetarian options. Service is friendly. • M-Th 11am-2pm; 5-9pm; F-Sa 11am-2pm; 5-10pm.

Redwood Café and Spice Co. ★★ $ 1020 Main St. (Middlefield), Redwood City, (415) 366-1498. Blink and you might miss this gem, which is tucked away in a tiny Victorian in downtown Redwood City. It offers scrumptious omelets—try the one with smoked salmon and cream cheese—but not much for those who steer clear of eggs. All breakfasts are served with a basket of delicious, piping-hot bread and muffins. Service is friendly and homey. • Tu-F 7am-2:30pm; Sa-Su 8am-2pm.

71 Saint Peter ★★ $$ 71 N. San Pedro St. (St. John/Santa Clara), San Jose, (408) 971-8523. This intimate downtown spot manages to be rustic and elegant at the same time, with brick walls, exposed rafters, linen tablecloths, and flowers on every table. Chef Mark Tabak conjures up specialties such as filet mignon with blue cheese, pork loin with an herb crust, and excellent polenta. The perfect setting for a romantic rendezvous. • M 11:30am-2pm; Tu-F 11:30am-2pm, 5-10pm; Sa 5-10pm.

Stars Palo Alto ★★ $$$ 265 Lytton Ave. (Bryant/Ramona), Palo Alto, (415) 321-4466. San Francisco celebrity chef Jeremiah Tower opened the latest branch of his grand café on the site of the old Gatehouse Restaurant, and it's been an instant money magnet. To ensure patrons don't miss the splendor, the parking valets carefully arrange the Rolls-Royces, Jaguars, and Mercedes out front. The glamorous dining room, decorated with framed French posters and a long, polished wooden bar, leaves little evidence of the past (the patio has been transformed into an airy bar under a huge skylight). The restaurant is operated under a license from Tower rather than under his direct control, and service can be uneven. As with other Stars, the food can be overwrought, although some dishes are perfection, like the seared salmon served on a bed of lentils or the perfectly cooked steak served with a cognac sauce. Even when the food is merely good, dining at Stars is always an event, and a good excuse to dust off the Rolls. Reservations recommended. • M-Th 11:30am-2:30pm, 5:30-10:30pm; F-Sa 11:30am-2:30pm, 5:30-11pm; Su 10:30am-2:30pm, 5:30-10pm.

Stoddard's Brewhouse ★★ $$ 111 S. Murphy Ave. (Washington/Evelyn), Sunnyvale, (408) 733-7824. Opened by Bob Stoddard, former brew *meister* at the Tied House, the soaring two-story space houses a long, polished wood bar, wicker seating area, a downstairs dining room, and an upstairs aerie for quieter dining. Out back there's a beer garden in case you're restless. For starters, the hummus and eggplant with flat bread has become a quick success, while the roast chicken with garlic mashed potatoes and roasted corn is a good bet for an entrée. And oh, yes, the fresh-brewed ales are delicious. • M-Th 11:30am-2:30pm, 5:30-10pm; F 11:30am-2:30pm, 5-11pm; Sa noon-3pm, 5:30-10pm; Su 11:00 am-2:30pm, 5-9pm.

Sushi Ya ★★★ $$ 380 University Ave. (Waverley/Bryant), Palo Alto, (415) 322-0330. This tiny sushi bar serves excellent, still-quivering sushi and sashimi and is a favorite with visiting Japanese businessmen. If you're a sushi novice let Toshi, the sushi master, lead the way. He creates innovative presentations, and he'll put together a stunning sushi box to take out. There are only a few tables, so be prepared to wait or sit at the sushi bar. • M-F 11:30am-2pm, 5:30-9:30pm; Sa 5-9:30pm.

RESTAURANTS & CAFES

Taqueria La Bamba ★★ ¢ 2058 Old Middlefield Way (Rengstorff), Mountain View, (415) 965-2755. Huge burritos the size of a small loaf of bread and a limited menu with a Salvadorean touch are La Bamba's trademarks. The best strategy is to start with a *pupusa* (small, thick corn tortilla stuffed with pork and cheese) and move on to the first half of a hard-to-find vegetarian burrito. Save the other half for your next meal. Expect a brief wait during the lunchtime rush—you may have to scramble for one of the few chairs. No credit cards. • M-F 10am-9:30pm; Sa-Su 10-9pm.

Thepthai ★★ $ 23 N. Market St. (St. John/Santa Clara), San Jose, (408) 292-7515. A roaring success. The decor at this modest downtown restaurant is minimal—a few Christmas lights and a pagodalike folly. The food is the point here, though, with some of the most delectable Thai dishes around emerging from the kitchen. Pad Thai is the specialty; crunchy red cabbage, sprouts, cilantro, and lime distinguish this rendition. Other hits are the fried tofu appetizer with peanut sauce, the ginger chicken, and all the soups. • M-Th 11am-10pm; F-Su 10am-10pm.

The Tied House Café and Brewery ★ $/$$ 954 Villa St. (Shoreline/Bryant), Mountain View, (415) 965-BREW/2739. • 65 N. San Pedro Square (Santa Clara), San Jose, (408) 295-BREW/2739. An always-crowded beer hall big enough to accommodate an entire fraternity. A big-screen TV, darts, shuffleboard, kegs to go—what more could a frat brother ask for? Bar food, of course. Garlic onion rings, oyster shooters, and buckets of steamed clams (all mediocre) can be found on the menu, along with pizzas and pastas. Let's face it, though, the food here is secondary to the brews. Eight beers are served on tap, from Alpine Pearl pale to Ironwood dark. Order a sampler if you can't decide. • MV: M-Th 11:30am-10pm; F 11:30am-11pm; Sa 11:30am-10pm; Su 11:30am-9:30pm. • SJ: Su-Th 11:30am-9pm; F-Sa 11:30am-10pm.

2030 ★★★ $$ 2030 Broadway (Main/Jefferson), Redwood City, (415) 363-2030. Giant portions are the hallmark at this chic Redwood City dining spot. (One waitress explained that the chef is "a big guy who likes to eat a lot.") Entrées include a salad and a soup, so appetizers are irrelevant. Lamb loin chops with garlic and herbs are outstanding, as are the prawns with prosciutto, spinach, and mushrooms served over linguine. If you have room for dessert, try the vanilla bean crème brûlée. • M 11am-2:30pm, 5:30-9pm; Tu-Th 11am-2:30pm, 5:30-9:30pm; F 11am-2:30pm, 5:30-10pm; Sa 5:30-10pm; Su 5:30-9pm.

231 Ellsworth ★★★ $$$ 231 S. Ellsworth Ave. (2nd Ave./3rd Ave.), San Mateo, (415) 347-7231. Critics and patrons alike rave about this San Mateo restaurant, which serves some of the most innovative cuisine on the Peninsula. The two-tiered interior, done up in passé pink and aqua pastels, is uninspired. But the food more than makes up for any design lapses, and the four-course $30 prix fixe menu brings the classy food within reach of mere mortals. Appetizers in particular shine; try the sautéed sweetbreads if they're available. Contemporary French main courses include imaginatively prepared seafood, grilled meats, and homemade pasta. Order the luscious chocolate cake for dessert—it's heavenly. • M-F 11:30am-2pm, 5:30-9:30pm; Sa 5:30-10pm.

The Village Pub ★★★ $$$ 2967 Woodside Rd. (Mtn. Home Rd.), Woodside, (415) 851-1294. Don't let the folksy name deceive you. This is haute cuisine at the kind of high-rent prices you'd expect in Woodside. The interior is California-cottage style, with whitewashed walls and discreet framed prints. The menu changes daily, but it might include such highly evolved fare as sautéed crab cakes with corn relish and pepper essence, or steamed mussels with chipotle chili broth and cilantro. • M-Th 11:30am-2:30pm, 5:30-9:30pm; F 11:30am-2:30pm, 5:30-10pm; Sa 5:30-10pm; Su 5:30-9:30pm.

Willow Street Wood Fired Pizza ★★ $ 1072 Willow St. (Lincoln), San Jose, (408) 971-7080. Yuppie pizzas emerge from the roaring ovens at this bustling neighborhood dinner spot. Toppings include goat cheese and barbecued chicken, plus upscale versions of the basics, like plum tomatoes and basil. Pastas round out the offerings. Finish off your meal with an excellent tiramisù. • M-Th 11:30am-10pm; F-Sa 11:30am-11pm.

PENINSULA & SAN JOSE
ARTS & ENTERTAINMENT
Amusements

Bay Meadows: 2600 S. Delaware St., San Mateo, (415) 574-7223. When the sun is shining and the field is tight, you can't beat the track for fun and excitement: only a crowd with money on the line can cheer like this one does. Live horse racing throughout the year, but call for schedule (racing alternates with sister track Golden Gate Fields in Berkeley). Watch a simulcast when they're not running live.

(Paramount's) Great America: Great America Pkwy., Santa Clara, (408) 988-1800. (Take Hwy 101 South to Great America Parkway exit.) For man-made vertigo, you'll want to go to Great America, a full-blown amusement park in Santa Clara. The Edge has been replaced with the taller and scarier Drop Zone Stunt Tower, which drops riders from a height of 224 feet. Top Gun turns the traditional roller coaster on its head, and has you dangling below the tracks, rather than coasting on top. For those who'd rather keep than lose their lunch, there's Rip Roaring Rapids, a simulated white-water rafting ride (you'll get *very* wet), and completely unstrenuous attractions like an ice skating rink, singing and dancing performances, a dolphin show, and a seven-story movie screen. Films in the IMAX theater are included in the price of admission. Great America occasionally hosts popular music concerts, which cost $9 in addition to general admission. • Open March-October. Summer: Su-Th 10am-9pm; F-Sa 10am-11pm. Spring and fall: Sa-Su 10am-9pm. $27.95 ages 7-54; $13.95 ages 3-6; free ages 2 and under; $18.95 seniors. Season passes $58. Parking $5.

Hidden Villa: Rhus Ridge Rd. (off Moody Rd.), Los Altos Hills, (415) 949-8660. An educational working farm nestled on the edge of Rancho San Antonio Open Space Preserve. Check out the crops, learn how farms work, and pet the animals. Also houses an AYH Youth Hostel and a multicultural summer camp. • W-Su 9am-dusk; $3-$7 closed to public except specified weekends in the summer. Fee requested.

Ice Capades Chalet: 2202 San Mateo Fashion Island, San Mateo, (415) 574-1616. • Call for session schedule. Admission $5.50; skate rental $2. noon-5pm and 7:30-9:30pm daily.

Ice Center of San Jose: 1500 S. 10th St., San Jose, (408) 279-6000. New, dual-ice rink. Hours vary—call for session and lesson information. • General skating: $5.50 adults; $4.50 children; $2.50 skate rental.

Ice Oasis: 3140 Bay Rd., Redwood City, (415) 364-8090. Much improved after a renovation. They have various public sessions for skating as well as scheduled open hockey games. There's also a skating school for all levels and adult and youth hockey leagues. • $6 adults; $5 children 12 and under. Skate rental $2. Hours vary, call ahead.

Magic Edge: 1625 Shoreline Blvd., Mountain View, (415) 254-7325. Where else but Silicon Valley could you expect to find a virtual reality restaurant and bar? Look out, Red Baron—pray the flight simulators don't make you air sick. Reservations recommended. • M noon-11pm; Tu-Th 11am-11pm; F 11am-1am; Sa 10am-1am; Su 11am-10pm. $14.75 for a 12 minute "flight" and $19.75 for 20 minutes; additional $2 "membership" fee for first-timers.

Malibu Castle: 320 Blomquist St., Redwood City, (415) 367-1905. (Hwy 101 to Seaport Blvd., exit east to Blomquist). Rent some clubs and take a whack at one of the three 18-hole miniature golf course or grab a bat and take a few practice swings in the electronic batting cages. Malibu Castle also has a mini-prix for kids between 4'6" and 3'2". • Su-Th 10am-10pm; F-Sa 10am-midnight. $6 adults; $5 under 14 for golf; $1.50 for 20 pitches.

Malibu Grand Prix: 340 Blomquist St., Redwood City, (415) 366-6442. A dream come true for would-be Indy 500 racers (and fun for everyone else as well). Malibu has a fleet

ARTS & ENTERTAINMENT

of turbo charged go-carts and several different tracks of varying difficulties for child drivers, and regular cars for older motorists. After you've satisfied the speed demon in you, wander inside and regress for a while in the video arcade. • Su-Th 10am-10pm; F-Sa 10am-midnight. $3.19 for first lap; $2.95 for each lap after that. Requirements: 8 years old and 4'6" for go-carts; 18 years old and valid driver's license for regular cars.

Moonlight Lanes: 2780 El Camino Real, Santa Clara, (408) 296-7200. Check out their Saturday night rock and bowl: all the balls you can bowl from 10pm to 1am with full rock-club sound and light. Regular bowling the rest of the week.

Raging Waters: 2333 South White Rd. (Tully/Capitol), Lake Cunningham Regional Park, San Jose, (408) 270-8000. This water park, with lots of neon bathing suits and teeny-boppers, is especially fun with a large group of people. Slides with names like White Lightning, Blue Thunder, Rampage, and Serpentine will twist you, turn you, and finally throw you into a huge pool. Changing rooms, showers, and lockers available. • Open daily mid-June until September 10am-7pm. General admission $18.95; children under 42" $14.95; free ages 3 and under.

The Winter Lodge: 3009 Middlefield Rd., Palo Alto, (415) 493-4566. The only outdoor ice rink west of the Sierras is to be found right in Palo Alto. Call for session and lesson information. • Open October-April. Admission $5; skate rental $1.

Movie Theaters

Huge multiplexes dominate the mainstream-movie scene, and are found mostly near the major shopping malls. Check the local papers for listings of the latest Hollywood sensation. In addition, the following alternative theaters offer a good selection of independent and foreign flicks in charming and unique venues, as well as discounts on mainstream films which have been out a while.

Daly City to San Bruno

Burlingame Drive-In: Burlingame Ave. off Old Bayshore Hwy., Burlingame, (415) 343-2213. A funky, penny-wise option. Double features of first-run films play at this relic for an outmoded price, for those who are willing to forego state-of-the-art sound. $4.95.

Redwood City to Mountain View

Aquarius Cinemas: 430 Emerson St., Palo Alto, (415) 327-3240. Just off University Avenue, Aquarius shows those esoteric foreign films that are hard to track down elsewhere. $3.75 first show Sa-Su. $7.

Guild Theater: 949 El Camino Real, Menlo Park, (415) 323-6760. Shows artsy and foreign films in a slightly down-at-the-heels art-deco auditorium adorned with frayed velvet curtains (bring a sweater—this theater is mercilessly underheated). $7.

Palo Alto Square: 3000 El Camino Real (Page Mill Rd.), Palo Alto, (415) 493-1160. A spacious duplex showing a mix of commercial and art-house flicks. $7.

Park Theater: 1275 El Camino Real, Menlo Park, (415) 323-6181. Almost identical to its neighbor, the Guild. $7.

The Stanford Theater: 221 University Ave., Palo Alto, (415) 324-3700. The remodeled Stanford Theater presents double features of classic movies (along with a few old clunkers) in an elaborate art deco setting complete with live organ music. Showings follow monthly themes—Garbo, for example—and features change every few nights. $6 for double feature.

Sunnyvale to San Jose

Camera One: 366 S. 1st St., San Jose, (408) 998-3005. Art and foreign flicks. $6.75.

Camera Three: 288 S. 2nd St., San Jose, (408) 998-3300. Art and foreign flicks. $6.75.

PENINSULA & SAN JOSE

Capitol Drive-In: Capitol Expwy. and Monterey Rd., San Jose, (408) 226-2251. Double features of first-run films with FM radio sound. $4.95 per person.

Los Gatos Cinemas: 41 N. Santa Cruz Ave., Los Gatos, (408) 395-0203. Art, independent, and foreign films (part of the Camera chain). $6.75.

Towne Theatre: 1433 The Alameda, San Jose, (408) 287-1433. Art, independent, and foreign flicks (part of the Camera chain). $6.75.

Nightlife

Alberto's Club: 736 W. Dana St., Mountain View, (415) 968-3007. A top spot for an introduction to Latin American dance music, Alberto's has live salsa on Thursdays (lessons are included with the cover charge for early arrivals). Other nights you might find DJ dancing to salsa or occasionally other live music from reggae to samba.

Alpine Beer Garden: 3915 Alpine Rd., Portola Valley, (415) 854-4004. A former stagecoach stop and longtime standby that's still known primarily by its old nickname, Zott's (it was also formerly known as Risotti's). Gather up ten of your closest friends and plant yourselves at one of the dusty outdoor tables with a couple of pitchers some Saturday afternoon.

Blue Chalk Café: 630 Ramona St., Palo Alto, (415) 326-1020. One of downtown Palo Alto's most popular hangouts, The Blue Chalk has something to keep everyone entertained all night. The airy, two-level hall features an excellent restaurant, pool tables rented by the hour (or one "challenge" table for the hustlers in the crowd), dart lanes, a shuffleboard table, and a sports TV section. If all this activity makes you hungry, sit down for a delicious meal of updated Southern cuisine. A good mix of singles-scene energy and neighborhood hangout comfort.

Boswell's: Pruneyard Shopping Ctr., 1875 S. Bascom Ave. and Campbell Ave., Campbell, (408) 371-4404. In Campbell, you shouldn't be surprised to find your bars in shopping centers, although the slightly run-down Anglophile yard-sale theme differentiates Boswell's from its surroundings. Sibling to Woodside's Pioneer Saloon, Boswell's anonymous local bands keep the joint jumping with solid rock covers.

Britannia Arms: 5027 Almaden Expwy., San Jose, (408) 266-0550. • 1087 Saratoga-Sunnyvale Rd., Cupertino, (408) 252-7262. A pair of British theme pubs catering to the pints-and-darts crowd. You won't forget you're in the Valley, but with a good band and a delicious black and tan, you might be comfortable hanging out awhile.

British Bankers Club: 1090 El Camino Real, Menlo Park, (415) 327-8769. At the BBC, you can lounge in plush sofas and wingback chairs amid tapestries and chandeliers while sipping a cocktail in genteel fashion. Don't be intimidated by the somewhat older and obviously wealthier crowd that gathers here; the atmosphere can be a refreshing change from the noise of other bars, although it does occasionally get jolted up by live blues bands.

Café Quinn: Oaks Ctr., 21269 Stevens Creek Blvd., Cupertino, (408) 252-CAFÉ/2233. Live folk and jazz in an airy bistro café. Food and service are quirky, but tall windows and an outdoor patio make it a winner in warm weather.

City Pub: 2620 Broadway, Redwood City, (415) 363-2620. A hip and happening hangout in Redwood City's revived Old Downtown, where you can mingle with trendy Peninsulans sporting the latest Doc Martens and Gap flannels. Designer lighting highlights the restored brick, warm fireplace, and mod copper bar. Decent pub grub and an excellent selection of beer on tap.

The Dutch Goose: 3567 Alameda de Las Pulgas, Menlo Park, (415) 854-3245. A dark hole-in-the-wall with pinball machines, pool tables, and a small patio in the back. Eclectic menu mixing bags of peanuts, deviled eggs, burgers, and reasonably priced pitchers of good beer. A favorite hangout of Sun Microsystems' CEO Scott McNealy.

ARTS & ENTERTAINMENT

The Edge: 260 California Ave., Palo Alto, (415) 324-EDGE/3343. Primarily a dance club playing modern rock of the Live-105 variety (dress in black if you really want to fit in), The Edge also puts on concerts by hip local bands like American Music Club or national groups like Hole. Though this is one of the few places where the under-21 set can go for a good time, it's surprisingly not an exclusively teeny-bopper hangout.

Gordon Biersch Restaurant/Brewery: 640 Emerson St., Palo Alto, (415) 323-7723. • 33 E. San Fernando St., San Jose, (408) 294-6785. One of the first of the Peninsula brewpubs and the first catering right to the yuppie market. Rampant competition has cut the crowds a little, but no one else attracts as many suits after work. Beer brewed on the premises is fresh and delicious, and the upscale food is pretty good, especially in San Jose. San Jose has live jazz most nights. $8-$10 cover charge on Sundays.

JJ's Blues Stevens Creek: 3439 Stevens Creek Blvd., San Jose, (408) 243-6441. The lone survivor of the JJ's chain of the South Bay's premier blues clubs. Terrific blues bands, both local and national, keep the joint jamming.

Left at Albuquerque: 445 Emerson St., Palo Alto, (415) 326-1011. The owners of the Blue Chalk Café have struck pay dirt again with this southwestern-style bar and restaurant. Bold desert art—black-and-white photos of rodeos and cowgirls, Navajo rugs, potted cacti, and more—and racks of tequila bottles furnish the long, thin space, which ends in an open kitchen against the back wall. The bar scene is wall-to-wall Silicon singles, with talk of mountain bikes and stock options filling the air. Margaritas are popular, as is just about every other tequila drink (management boasts that if you can show proof of a brand of tequila it doesn't stock, you'll drink for free).

Mountain Charley's: 15 N. Santa Cruz Ave., Los Gatos, (408) 395-8880. Another hot spot for trendy rockers to hear local modern rock bands.

Oasis Beer Garden: 241 El Camino Real, Menlo Park, (415) 326-8896. Generations of graffiti carved into the hardwood tables and booths of the "O" attest to this bar's longtime popularity, especially with Stanford students. Beer by the pitcher and several TVs eternally tuned to sporting events make the Oasis a great place to hang out any night of the week. Also popular with local softball teams.

Oasis: 200 N. 1st St., San Jose, (408) 292-2212. Not to be confused with Menlo Park's Oasis bar, this SOFA sibling of The Edge in Palo Alto has lively dancing to modern mix, house, etc., as well as occasional live music. Look for a variety of promotions and cheap drink specials.

The Palace: 146 S. Murphy Ave., Sunnyvale, (408) 739-5179. Swanky supper club in a restored art deco movie theater featuring biomorphic silver-painted columns, wrought-iron accents, and orange-sponged walls. Live jazz Thursday nights, DJ dancing Fridays and Saturdays, and live Salsa Orquestra music on Wednesdays.

Pioneer Saloon: 2925 Woodside Rd., Woodside, (415) 851-8487. One of the best of the local joints, the Pioneer features a different band every night, and the tiny dance floor is usually packed with urban cowboys. Cover charge is around $3, but the beer is cheap and the atmosphere is relaxed.

Prince of Wales Pub: 106 E. 25th Ave., San Mateo, (415) 574-9723. San Mateo's oldest pub, with darts, foosball, and plenty of beer. Complete with outdoor patio for warm weather lounging.

Rose & Crown: 547 Emerson St., Palo Alto, (415) 327-ROSE/7673. Friendly and authentically smoky English pub setting, complete with British ales on tap, pub fare, and darts.

Saddle Rack: 1310 Auzerais Ave., San Jose, (408) 286-3393. Urban cowboys and real rednecks meet at the Saddle Rack, a country-western club that features a mechanical bull and free dance lessons. Rumor has it they once brought in a real bull, but it escaped and ran wild down the streets of San Jose.

South First Billiards: 420 S. 1st St., San Jose, (408) 294-7800. The San Jose outpost of San Francisco's successful South Beach Billiards follows the same formula: a clean, well-lit pool hall renting tables by the hour, serving up decent bar food, and pouring lots of good beer from the tap.

St. James Infirmary: 390 Moffett Blvd., Mountain View, (415) 969-0806. A bar known primarily for its street signs, sleds, and other odd adornments, including a 25-foot Wonder Woman statue which you can dance around at night when St. James turns into a dance club.

St. Michael's Art House Café: 806 Emerson St., Palo Alto, (415) 326-2530. This warm, homey café has been hosting talented local performers with a folk/bluegrass bent since the Warlocks played for Ken Kesey and the Merry Pranksters.

Stoddard's: 111 S. Murphy Ave., Sunnyvale, (408) 733-7824. Former Tied House brewmeister Bob Stoddard created this soaring monument to yuppie South Bay culture. This trendy brewpub gleams with polished wood, wall treatments à la Jackson Pollock, and singles heating it up after work. There's also a beer garden out back.

Tied House Café and Brewery: 954 Villa St., Mountain View, (415) 965-BREW/2739. • 65 N. San Pedro St., San Jose, (408) 295-BREW/2739. One of the best brewpubs around. Their beers are absolutely delicious, and you can watch the creation of these tasty quaffs in giant, gleaming vats. Tied House features seasonal beers and such libations as passion-fruit ale, wheat beer, and stout.

Toon's: 52 E. Santa Clara St., San Jose, (408) 292-7464. A downtown club featuring live music and a sense of humor. Lots of early drink specials. Wednesdays feature the popular local band The Gents.

Performing Arts

FYI San Jose: (408) 295-2265. Events line for San Jose activities.

Classical Music and Opera

Opera San Jose: Montgomery Theatre, W. San Carlos and S. Market sts., San Jose, (408) 437-4450. At the Montgomery Theatre you can attend the performances of Opera San Jose, a company developing young professional talent by producing classical works by composers such as Verdi, Rossini, and Mozart. • Box office M-F 9am-5pm.

Peninsula Civic Light Opera: San Mateo Performing Arts Center, 424 Peninsula Ave., San Mateo, (415) 579-5568. A very popular community theater group that appears at the San Mateo Performing Arts Center.

Peninsula Symphony Orchestra: (415) 574-0244. Performs alternately at the Flint Center and the San Mateo Performing Arts Center.

San Jose Symphony: (408) 288-2828. Attracts excellent soloists and guest conductors, and tickets tend to be a little less expensive than those for the San Francisco Symphony. Performances alternate between the Flint Center in Cupertino and the San Jose Center for the Performing Arts.

Stanford University: Braun Music Center, Stanford University, (415) 723-3811. Stanford plays host to an entire city's worth of performing groups. Look for a delightful Midsummer Mozart festival. For home-grown talent, the **Stanford Symphony Orchestra** and the **Symphonic Chorus** are excellent groups, particularly when they perform jointly. The **Chamber Chorale** is a smaller chorus that stages chamber music of every period from the Renaissance to the 20th century; most of the university's best singers have been involved with this outstanding group at one point or another.

West Bay Opera: (415) 321-3471. The West Bay Opera appears at the Lucie Stern Theatre in Palo Alto. The highly acclaimed company performs fully-staged operas for

ARTS & ENTERTAINMENT

two long weekends every October, February, and May, and shorter operatic pieces a few other times a year. Watch for student discounts on Thursday nights.

Dance

Janlyn Dance Company: (408) 255-4055. This modern dance company performs 20-35 times a year, makes guest appearances around the Peninsula, and has a special children's program for area schools.

Lively Arts at Stanford: Press Courtyard, Santa Teresa St., Stanford University, (415) 723-2551. The **Lively Arts at Stanford** routinely brings such well-known and innovative groups as MOMIX, Bebe Miller Dance Company, and Pilobolus to various venues on campus. Also, the Dance Division of the Stanford Athletics Department presents ballet, modern, jazz, and ethnic dance concerts throughout the year; the annual Spring Migration is a popular highlight. Information M-F 8am-5pm.

Peninsula Ballet Theatre: San Mateo Performing Arts Center, 600 N. Delaware St., San Mateo, (415) 343-8485. The only professional ballet company in the mid-Peninsula area draws consistently good notices for favorites such as *The Nutcracker* and *Giselle*.

San Jose Cleveland Ballet: Center for the Performing Arts, Almaden Blvd. and Park Ave., San Jose, (408) 288-2800. A joint venture between the cities of San Jose and Cleveland, which has received critical acclaim for its performances of new ballets and elegant renditions of the classics. The company performs from September to May at the San Jose Center for the Performing Arts.

Theatre

American Musical Theatre: (408) 453-7100. Performs traditional Broadway musicals on a large scale at the San Jose Center for the Performing Arts. Formerly named San Jose Civic Light Opera.

City Lights Theater Company: 529 S. 2nd St., San Jose, (408) 295-4200. A talented small company that produces an eclectic variety of contemporary plays.

Manhattan Playhouse: Manhattan Ave. and W. Bayshore Rd., E. Palo Alto, (415) 322-4589. This on-site company mounts only two shows a season, but it is worth the visit.

Mountain View Center for the Performing Arts: Mercy and Castro sts., Mountain View, (415) 903-6000. Hosts community theater, professional touring companies, and international artists and attractions.

Palo Alto Players: (415) 329-0891. The oldest group around; they put on six shows a year, notable for their consistent quality and reasonable ticket prices.

San Jose Repertory Theatre: (408) 291-2255. A professional outfit producing a combination of classics, old favorites, and also some original plays.

Saratoga Drama Group: (408) 255-0801. This group has been putting on two musicals a year for three decades and has a considerable following.

Stage One Theatre: (408) 293-6362. Produces cutting-edge contemporary theatre. Highlights include the South Bay premiere of *Jeffrey*.

Stanford University Department of Drama: Memorial Hall, Stanford University, (415) 723-2576. The Drama Department mounts several productions a year, directed by graduate students, in the Little Theatre in Memorial Hall and the Nitery in Old Union. The **Ram's Head Theatrical Society** (415) 723-0801 puts on three shows a year.

TheatreWorks: (415) 903-6000. TheatreWorks is a highly regarded and extremely popular local company that produces everything from Broadway musicals to staged readings of new works. Performs primarily at the Lucie Stern Theatre in Palo Alto and the Mountain View Center for the Performing Arts.

PENINSULA & SAN JOSE
PARKS & OPEN SPACES

The Peninsula has some of the Bay Area's most extensive open space, offering a wide variety of terrain. To the west, you can enjoy beautiful coastline and beaches and redwood forests. To the east, abundant and exotic waterfowl live on the shores of the San Francisco Bay. The following information covers some of the major parks in the Peninsula area, but there are always more gems out there. For additional information, contact any of the managing agencies or the **Trail Center** at 3921 E. Bayshore in Palo Alto, (415) 968-7065 (open Tu-F 11am-3pm); they can tell you all about local trails and trail activities, and also sell excellent maps. Most of our daytrips and weekend getaways (see Tahoe, Peninsula Coast, etc. sections) include information on outdoor excursions beyond the immediate area. A final word of caution: poison oak is rampant in most of these parks. Learn to recognize it!

City Parks

In addition to the many local neighborhood parks (check the front of your Yellow Pages for more information), some cities maintain larger parklands with regional appeal.

Foothills Park: 3300 Page Mill Rd. (entrance between Altamont and Moody rds.), Palo Alto, (415) 329-2423. Located halfway up Page Mill Road, this 1,400-acre nature preserve is open only to Palo Alto residents and their guests. Nature trails, hiking, picnicking, fishing, playing fields, car camping, and an interpretive center make Foothills a popular spot. Day use fee is $3 per automobile, $1 per bicycle.

Hakone Gardens: 21000 Big Basin Way, Saratoga, (408) 867-3438. One of the Emperor's former gardeners built this city park in 1917 as an exact reproduction of a Japanese Zen garden.

Palo Alto Baylands: Left at the east end of Embarcadero Rd., Palo Alto, (415) 329-2506. A beautiful spot for an easy walk or bicycle ride through 2,000 acres of salt marsh and sloughs. There is an astonishing variety of bird life here, and the sight of a great blue heron is impressive and far from rare. An interpretive center shows you where and what to look for.

Shoreline Park: 3070 N. Shoreline Blvd., Mountain View, (415) 903-6392. Small manmade park on a reclaimed landfill with Shoreline Amphitheatre, a golf course, a sailing lake, and many trails along the bay.

County Parks

Most county parks include picnic areas, bathrooms, a visitors center or park headquarters, comprehensive maps, the occasional playing field or playground, and readily-available rangers. **San Mateo County Parks and Recreation Department**, which covers the northern portion of the Peninsula and most of the coast north of Santa Cruz, can be reached at 590 Hamilton St., Redwood City, (415) 363-4020; reservations (415) 363-4021; TDD (415) 368-7807. **Santa Clara County Department of Parks and Recreation**, encompassing San Jose and the southern Peninsula, can be reached at 298 Garden Hills Dr., Los Gatos, (408) 358-3741; reservations (408) 358-3751.

Coyote Point County Recreational Area (San Mateo): Coyote Point Dr. from N. Bayshore Blvd., San Mateo, (415) 573-2592. A small, bayside park with swimming, trails, a marina, a boat ramp, and nature museum. Parking fee is $4.

Huddart County Park (San Mateo): King's Mountain Rd. 2 mi. west of Hwy 84, Woodside, (415) 851-1210. Once the hub of an extensive logging operation, Huddart Park is now heavily forested with second-growth redwoods. Shady trails wind through steep canyons, evergreen and oak forests, and flat chaparral and meadows. There are picnic grounds with barbecue pits, and a unique playground designed for the physi-

PARKS & OPEN SPACES

cally handicapped. Other attractions include hiking, equestrian trails, a whole-access trail, and hike-in group campsites. No dogs.

Memorial Park (San Mateo): Pescadero Rd., 6 mi. west of Alpine Rd., (415) 879-0212. One of the most beautiful of the inland coast-side parks. Particularly inviting is the swimming hole on Pescadero Creek, which is kept stocked with trout during the spring and summer. Enjoy the hiking, biking, and equestrian trails, as well as picnicking and car camping areas and a nature museum.

Pescadero Creek County Park (San Mateo): Camp Pomponio Rd. off Alpine Rd. west of Skyline Dr. (trails connect with Memorial and Sam McDonald County Parks and Portola State Park), (415) 879-0212. By far the largest of a cluster of three county parks with 7,500 acres. The hillsides are quite steep and feature lush redwood groves and open ridge tops with views of the ocean. Bicycles are allowed on fire roads. Trail camping is first-come, first-served.

Sam McDonald County Park (San Mateo): Pescadero Rd., 3 mi. west of La Honda, (415) 879-0212. Sam McDonald borders **Heritage Grove**, a stately 27-acre stand of old-growth redwood, and offers hiking and camping (car and trail). This park has 42 miles of hiking trails, permits biking on some fire roads, and facilities for picnicking and camping. The **Sierra Club Hikers' Hut** is a great place for group overnights; book far in advance through the Sierra Club, (415) 390-8411.

Sanborn Skyline County Park (Santa Clara): Skyline Blvd. between Hwy 9 and Hwy 17, (408) 867-9959. Steep, forested slopes set the background for hiking, biking, camping, an outdoor theater, and a youth hostel.

Stevens Creek County Park (Santa Clara): Stevens Canyon Rd., Cupertino, (408) 867-3654. Wooded canyons surrounding a reservoir offer good hiking, biking, horseback riding, and picnicking.

Upper Stevens Creek County Park (Santa Clara): Skyline Blvd., 1.5 mi. north of the Hwy 9 intersection, (408) 867-9959. Comprises 1,200 otherwise undeveloped acres with trails descending from Skyline Boulevard into Stevens Canyon and adjoining Open Space Preserves. Trails are open for hiking, biking, and horseback riding.

Open Space Preserves

There is an extensive green belt stretching along Skyline Boulevard (Hwy 35) from Hwy 92 west of San Mateo to Los Gatos. Trail maps can be obtained at the **Midpeninsula Regional Open Space District Office** at 330 Distel Circle in Los Altos, (415) 691-1200 (open weekdays 8:30am-5pm). There are two classes of preserves. Group A Preserves have fully-developed parking areas, well-maintained trails, and good signs. Printed brochures and maps are available at the entrance. Group B Preserves have little or no developed parking facilities and trails are limited. Preserves are located outside of city limits, so park addresses do not include a city.

El Corte de Madera (B): Skyline Blvd., 4 mi. north of Hwy 84, parking at Skeggs Point Overlook. Boasts a massive sandstone outcrop (accessible only on foot) and the Methuselah Tree, one of the oldest redwoods in the area. Due to recent logging, many of the trails here are dead-ends, and signage is insufficient at best, so prepare for a potentially long and confusing—but definitely beautiful—outing.

Long Ridge (B): Skyline Blvd., 3 mi. north of the intersection of Hwy 9 and Skyline Dr., parking on the east side of Skyline or the southeast corner of the intersection of Hwy 9 and Skyline. The rolling terrain along Skyline has a mix of oak, madrone, and fir, as well as grasslands with spectacular views of surrounding parklands. And don't forget some of the best legal single-track mountain biking trails in the area.

Monte Bello (A): Page Mill Rd., parking 1 mi. east of Skyline Blvd. on the south side. The largest MROSD preserve can boast excellent views of Santa Clara Valley from

PENINSULA & SAN JOSE

Black Mountain, which at 2,800 feet is the highest peak on the mid-Peninsula. The sag ponds formed along the San Andreas fault by the 1906 earthquake are no less admirable. A sign in the Page Mill parking area will help identify local summits, and a nature trail will help you identify natural inhabitants. Reservations required for the trail camp near Black Mountain.

Purisima Creek Redwoods (A): Skyline Dr., parking 4 mi. south of Hwy 92, parking for disabilities-access trail 6 mi. south of Hwy 92. (Alternate access from Hwy 1, one mile south of Half Moon Bay on Higgins-Purisima Rd.) Offers two magnificent redwood-filled canyons facing Half Moon Bay and a quarter-mile handicapped-access trail with restrooms and picnic tables.

Rancho San Antonio (A): Cristo Rey Dr. off Foothill Rd. (south of I-280), parking at Rancho San Antonio County Park. Accessible through Rancho San Antonio County Park, this preserve has excellent hiking trails up the foothills, with spectacular views of the Santa Clara Valley from the grassy plains at the summit. Bicycling is not permitted.

Windy Hill (A): Skyline Blvd., parking 2 mi. south of Hwy 84 on the east side. The most prominent bald spot along Skyline Ridge, the grassy knolls atop this park feature spectacular views of both the ocean and the bay. Hike one of three trails down the steep hillside into the lush creekside valley above Portola Valley.

State Parks

State parks are the most well-known, visited by tourists and locals alike, and provide all the amenities required by the RV set. The agency responsible for these parks is the **California Department of Parks and Recreation**, P.O. Box 2390, Sacramento, 95811, (916) 653-6995. They also have local district offices: (415) 726-8800 or (408) 429-2850. Reservations for camping at these parks or for other restricted programs are generally handled by **Destinet**, (800) 444-7275 or (619) 452-1950. Trail camps are usually first-come, first-served; otherwise reservations are made directly through the park.

Big Basin Redwoods State Park: Hwy 236 (runs right through the park), headquarters 9 mi. south of Boulder Creek, (408) 338-6132. Big Basin is California's first state park, now comprising 18,000 acres of magnificent old-growth redwoods. There is a hiking trail connecting Big Basin to Castle Rock State Park, 14 miles to the northeast, and another trail leads from the park headquarters down a rough but scenic drop to the ocean (together forming the Skyline to the Sea Trail). The park also offers camping (car and trail), a visitors center, and food service. Parking is $5.

Butano State Park: Cloverdale Rd., 3 mi. east of Hwy 1 and 5 mi. south of Pescadero, (415) 879-2040. Nearly 2,200 acres of steep coastal canyon with redwood forests, banana slugs, and chaparral ridges. Hiking here can be strenuous: the Año Nuevo trail (not for the weak of heart) leads to an overlook with a panoramic view of the ocean and Año Nuevo Island. The park offers camping (car and trail), picnicking, and hiking trails. Parking is $5.

Castle Rock State Park: Skyline Blvd., 2 mi. south of the intersection with Hwy 9, (408) 867-2952. Located on the crest of the Santa Cruz Mountains, Castle Rock boasts amazing sandstone formations popular with rock climbers, waterfalls, and canyons. It also has trail camping on a first-come, first-served basis. Day use fee runs $4 per vehicle.

Portola State Park: Portola State Park Rd., off Alpine Rd. 3 mi. west of Skyline Dr., (415) 948-9098. Deep in the folds of the Santa Cruz Mountains, wander among second-growth redwoods in this isolated park. Features include hiking, camping (car and trail), picnicking, a nature trail, museum, and visitors center. Parking is $5.

Getaways

MENDOCINO ★★

Mendocino is the jewel in the crown of the Northern California coast. Built on a wide bluff that juts out into the ocean, the town enjoys dramatic views of the gorgeous, rocky coastline on three sides. Mendocino looks like a Maine fishing village, with its white, New England-style houses and clapboard church. In keeping with this old-fashioned charm, few establishments post their street numbers, so pick up a good map before exploring. Throughout the summer and on holiday weekends, the community fills with tourists, so off-season visits are the most pleasant (and less likely to be fog-bound), though many visitors' services may be closed during mid-week.

Ten miles north of Mendocino is **Fort Bragg**, a large town catering to the lumber industry. Fort Bragg lacks the charm of its southern neighbor, but provides many of the everyday practicalities that are either unavailable or high-priced in Mendocino.

Fort Bragg-Mendocino Chamber of Commerce: (800) 726-2780, (707) 964-3153.

Getting There

To see as much as possible, take Hwy 1 in one direction and Hwy 101 the other. (Avoid following the former northward in the late afternoon—the sun can be a formidable adversary.) The most scenic route from San Francisco is to take the San Anselmo/Sir Francis Drake exit off Hwy 101 and go west on Sir Francis Drake Boulevard until it intersects Hwy 1 in Olema. From there, it's about three hours to Mendocino (see the *Inland Mendocino* section for inland directions, a somewhat quicker route). Without a car, your best bet is to rely on **Mendocino Transit Authority** (800) 696-4MTA/4682 or (707) 462-5765, which provides bus service to, from, and along the Mendocino coast; service includes a daily bus to Santa Rosa where you can use Golden Gate Transit or Amtrak buses to reach San Francisco (see Transportation chapter for more information on these companies).

Sights and Attractions

Parks and Preserves ★★

For information about these and other parks, contact the visitor center at Russian Gulch State Park (see below), open M-F 8am-5pm.

Mendocino Headlands State Park ★: (707) 937-5397. The Headlands wrap around the southwest side of the town, providing a spectacular landscape of sea stacks sculpted by dramatic waves. This spot is great for hiking, tide-pooling, and whale watching.

Van Damme State Park ★: Hwy 1 about 3 mi. south of Mendocino, (707) 937-4016. This park is made up of 1,800 acres covered with redwood trees and offers excellent camping (with a popular 71-site campground), a small beach for swimming, and several hiking trails that wind through pygmy forests, dense fern thickets, and a bog (the 2.5 mile Fern Canyon Trail is best). This park is especially popular with abalone divers. $5.

Russian Gulch State Park ★: Hwy 1 about 1.5 mi. north of Mendocino, (707) 937-5804. Home to the **Devil's Punch Bowl**, a blowhole that sends the surf shooting skyward when the ocean is stirred up. Camping is available (30 sites), and from the park's headlands overlooking a wide bay, you can observe migrating whales in the winter. $5.

GETAWAYS

Jug Handle State Reserve ★: Hwy 1 about 3 mi. north of Mendocino. Home to the "ecological staircase trail" that traces the geological and natural history of the area, from the beach to the redwoods. Here you can study 100-foot terraces carved by ocean waves, with each "step" 100,000 years older than the one below.

Mendocino Coast Botanical Gardens ★★: 18220 N. Hwy 1 about 7 mi. north of Mendocino, (707) 964-4352. This 17-acre park is an ideal place to explore the ecologically-rich coastal environment. You can enjoy the well-manicured gardens (with over 10,000 plant varieties) and spectacular bluff views in an hour's stroll, but spend an afternoon if you have time. $5.

MacKerricher State Park ★: Hwy 1 about 3 mi. north of Fort Bragg. This is the largest coastal state park in the area, featuring one of northern California's lengthiest beaches, stretches of wildflower fields, and a freshwater lagoon. Take the short trail to Laguna Point, where migrating whales can be spotted from December through April; it's also a good vantage point to watch harbor seals playing. MacKerricher also features a 140-site campground, complete with full bathroom facilities and beach access. $5.

Other Activities ★

Catch a Canoe & Bicycles, Too! ★: Just south of Mendocino at Comptche-Ukiah Road, (707) 937-0273. Rents and sells mountain bikes, canoes, and kayaks. Canoe trips from their dock on the Big River estuary provide glimpses of otters and blue herons, as well as secluded picnic spots along the river banks.

Charter Boats ★: Several sport-fishing and whale-watching charter boats are anchored in **Noyo Harbor**, just south of Fort Bragg. Optimal whale watching occurs between December and March; the best fishing is during the summer and fall, when the salmon are running. Many of the boats go out twice a day. Try **Anchor Charters** (707) 964-3854 with rates of $45 per person for fishing excursions (including poles and bait) and $20 per person for a two-hour whale watching trip.

Ricochet Ridge Ranch ★: 24201 N. Hwy 1 about 3 mi. north of Fort Bragg across from MacKerricher State Park, (707) 964-7669. Ricochet leads two-hour group horseback trips on the beach as well as private rides. Rides start at $26/person.

Skunk Train ★: Foot of Laurel St., Fort Bragg, (707) 964-6371. A good foggy day activity is a ride on the aptly-named Skunk Train, which pulls out of Fort Bragg from the California Western Railroad depot for a 40-mile scenic journey through towering redwood forests and over precarious gulches to Willits—where the skies could be cloud-free. The train makes day-long runs ($26), as well as half-day trips ($21).

Hot Tubs and Saunas ★: The local idiom for hot-tubbing on the North Coast is "soak." Beneath a renovated water tower next door to Café Beaujolais, **Sweetwater Gardens**, 955 Ukiah St., (707) 937-4140 offers massages for the hike-weary and private hot tubs for $9.50/hr per person. For end-of-the-day bonding, there's an enormous group tub where, for $7.50 per person, you can soak as long as you want. Bring your own towels and save a buck. • Open M-Th 2pm-11pm; F-Su noon-11pm.

Places to Eat

Albion River Inn ★ $$$: 3790 Hwy 1, Albion, (707) 937-1919. Diners come for the excellent meals and the panoramic views of the Pacific. Dishes tend toward simple preparations of fresh local ingredients—such as grilled salmon, roast chicken, and garlic mashed potatoes. Reservations recommended. • Su-Th 5:30-9pm, F-Sa 5-9:30pm.

Café Beaujolais ★★★ $$$: 961 Ukiah St. (School/Evergreen), Mendocino, (707) 937-5614. This famous restaurant (a favorite of Julia Child), located in a charming 1910 clapboard Victorian, is well worth a visit. Unfortunately, Margaret Fox's widely renowned breakfasts are no longer being served. Dinner, prepared under her husband Chris Kump's supervision, is more of a splurge. The eclectic, Asian-influenced California cuisine seems to have improved now that it's the sole focus of attention. Reservations recommended. Credit cards now accepted. • Daily 5:45-9pm.

Good Taste ¢: Little Lake and Lansing sts., Mendocino, (707) 937-0104. Gourmet picnic supplies. • Daily 10am-6pm.

D'Aurelio & Sons ★ $: 438 S. Franklin St. (Chestnut, behind Payless), Fort Bragg, (707) 964-4227. Good Italian food at reasonable prices. No credit cards. • Daily 5-9pm.

Ledford House ★ $$: 3000 N. Hwy 1, Albion, (707) 937-0282. The dining room offers great vistas of the coast from its perch on Salmon Point. House specialties are country French: rack of lamb, roast duck, and so forth, all in rich sauces. Romantic diners will want to sit by a window to bill and coo and enjoy the view. • W-Su 5-9pm.

Little River Inn ★ $$: 7751 Hwy 1, Little River, (707) 937-5942. An inn with a good reputation for its casual restaurant, and a long porch where you can sip a drink and watch the sunset with no obligation to dine later. Basic dishes might include red snapper with butter, lemon, and parsley, or charbroiled breast of chicken marinated in fresh ginger and soy sauce. The Swedish hotcakes are popular at breakfast. • M-Sa 7-10:30am, 6-9:30pm; Su 7am-1pm, 6-9:30pm.

Little River Restaurant ★★ $$$: 7750 N. Hwy 1 (attached to the market and post office), Little River, (707) 937-4945. Among the better coastside eateries, the Little River Restaurant serves sumptuous meals in a cozy atmosphere. Preparations taking advantage of fresh local ingredients include poached salmon with tarragon cream sauce, broiled quail with hazelnut-port sauce, and steamed mussels. You give up the spectacular views found at other establishments, but the first-class food is delicious compensation. The dining room seats only about a dozen, so reservations are a must. No credit cards. • Seatings at 6pm and 8:30pm; winter F-M; summer F-Tu.

MacCallum House Restaurant/Grey Whale Bar & Café ★★ $$$: 45020 Albion St. (Lansing), Mendocino, (707) 937-5763. A B&B that serves memorable meals. The dining area is split between the comfortable dining room and somewhat cramped café. Both share a menu of well-executed California cuisine. Hearty soups like seafood chowder and innovative pastas are the menu highlights. Entrées feature typical North Coast items like wild salmon and free-range chicken. Reservations recommended. • F-Tu 5:30-9pm.

Mendo Burgers ★ $: 10483 Lansing St. (Ukiah), Mendocino, (707) 937-1111. Serves every kind of burger under the sun, including veggie, beef, chicken, fish, and turkey versions. • M-Sa 11am-7pm; Su noon-5pm.

Mendocino Bakery & Café ★ ¢: 10485 Lansing St. (Ukiah), Mendocino, (707) 937-0836. The pastries here are every bit as fresh as the local gossip you're bound to catch a whiff of at this local favorite. • Daily 8am-6pm.

Mendocino Café ★ $: 10451 Lansing St. (Albion), Mendocino, (707) 937-2422. You can find some stellar offerings at reasonable prices here, although the waits can be long (reservations only for groups of five or more). The husband-and-wife owners comb the globe for new tastes which they successfully inject into their California cuisine repertoire. The Thai burrito is a tasty example of one such creation, as are the varied pastas. The place boasts a sunny deck to boot. • M-Th 11am-4pm, 5-9:30pm; F 11am-4pm, 5-10pm; Sa 10am-4pm, 5-10pm; Su 10am-4pm, 5-9pm.

Mendocino Market ¢: 699 Ukiah St., Mendocino, (707) 937-FISH/3474. Locals' choice for deli supplies and sandwiches. • Daily 10am-6:30pm.

Moosse Café ★★ $$: 390 Kasten St. (Albion), Mendocino, (707) 937-4323. Of course, in a place originally named the Chocolate Moosse Café, the desserts are sure to be decadently delicious. But this quaint restaurant also serves excellent appetizers and entrees. The mainly American menu includes salads, savory soups, pasta, and comfort foods such as roast chicken and short ribs. Lunch can be taken in Adirondack chairs in the front yard, and all dishes can be toted for a picnic in a park. No credit cards. • M-Th 11:30am-9pm; F 11:30am-10:30pm; Sa 10am-10:30pm; Su 9:30am-9pm.

North Coast Brewing Co. ★ $: 444 N. Main St. (Pine/Laurel), Fort Bragg, (707) 964-3400. This local brew pub serves excellent, freshly brewed beer; sample their renowned Red Seal ale. The food tends toward pub-grub standards like fish and chips, chili, and burgers. • Tu-F 5:30-9pm; Sa 5:30-10pm (longer hours during summer).

Tote Fête ¢: 10450 Lansing St., Mendocino, (707) 937-3383. Gourmet picnic fixings. • M-Sa 10:30-7pm; Su 10:30am-4pm.

Places to Stay

Since condo developments don't exist in the Mendocino architectural canon, and hotel chains have been banished, bed-and-breakfasts and quaint inns have a monopoly on accommodations. **Mendocino Coast Reservations** (707) 937-1913 handles bookings for about 20 B&Bs and a number of vacation homes in the area. For a comprehensive list of all lodging possibilities, contact the **Fort Bragg-Mendocino Coast Chamber of Commerce** at (800) 726-2780, they'll mail you brochures galore.

Most of the parks listed in the Parks & Preserves section above allow camping, though policies vary between different parks, and reservations are highly recommended. Call **Destinet** (800) 444-7275 or **Mendocino State Park Headquarters** (707) 937-5804.

Albion River Inn $$/$$$$: 3790 Hwy 1, Albion, (707) 937-1919. A gracious inn located on a bluff overlooking the Albion River. Twenty cottages on the river's edge offer deluxe accommodations, most with decks and some with Jacuzzis. $85-$225.

MENDOCINO

Brewery Gulch Inn $$: 9350 Hwy 1 off Brewery Gulch Ln., 1 mi. south of Mendocino, (707) 937-4752. Recognizable by the water tank on Hwy 1, this place is set amidst beautiful gardens. $85-$130.

Cypress Cove $$$: 4520 Chapman Dr., Mendocino, (707) 937-1456. Offering a view of Mendocino Bay and the town itself, each of these two modern suites offers a deck, fireplace, and kitchenette. They are superbly located one mile south of town, very convenient to outdoor activities such as golf and canoe rentals. $145-$170.

Glendeven Inn $$$: 8221 Hwy 1, Little River, (800) 822-4536, (707) 937-0083. A rustic country inn with well-kept grounds, hearty breakfasts, and an adjacent gallery with shows by local artists. $90-$200.

Heritage House $$$/$$$$: Hwy 1, Little River, (707) 937-5885. A renowned inn that requires guests to eat both breakfast *and* dinner in their restaurant. Cottages $125-$335 (inclusive of meals).

Inn at Schoolhouse Creek $$: 7051 Hwy 1, Little River, (707) 937-5525. Located south of town on Hwy 1, with three lodge rooms and two cottages which sleep four. $80-$130 on weekends; $65-$115 during the week.

John Dougherty House $$$: 571 Ukiah St. (Kasten), Mendocino, (707) 937-5266. A taste of New England, this 1867 Cape Cod-style house is located right in the midst of Mendocino village. The antiques are an elegant touch. $95-$165.

Jug Handle Farm & Nature Center ¢: Hwy 1 about 4 mi. north of Mendocino, (707) 964-4630, (707) 964-9912. The real lodging bargain in the Mendocino area is this spacious red farmhouse. They provide simple accommodations indoors, as well as campsites and primitive cabins nearby, for $15 per person per night ($10 with a student ID). Bring bedding or sleeping bags, towels, and anything else you might need. Bathrooms and showers are provided, and there is a kitchen available for guests' use. Everyone who spends the night is asked to perform an hour of work, which can mean chopping wood, sweeping, or gardening. Call ahead for reservations.

MacCallum House Inn $$$: 45020 Albion St. (Kasten/Lansing), Mendocino, (707) 937-0289. An interesting B&B, part of which occupies a restored barn. $75-$180.

McElroy's Inn $$: 998 Main St. (Evergreen), Mendocino, (707) 937-1734. A low-priced B&B located in the heart of town. $50-$75.

Mendocino Farmhouse $$: Comptche-Ukiah Rd., off Hwy 1, Mendocino, (707) 937-0241. This inland B&B offers privacy and a break from the fog. $80-$100.

Mendocino Hotel $$/$$$$: 45080 Main St. (Lansing/Kasten), Mendocino, (800) 548-0513, (707) 937-0511. A large Victorian establishment with high-end offerings. $50-$225.

Mendocino Village Inn $$: 44860 Main St. (Evergreen/Howard), Mendocino, (707) 937-0246. A cozy choice, this 1882 Victorian looks like it was transplanted right from Martha's Vineyard. $65-$90.

Ocean View Motel $$: 1141 North Main St., Fort Bragg, (707) 964-1951. Good prices and average accommodations. $45-$110.

Reed Manor $$$$: Little Lake St. and Palette Dr., Mendocino, (707) 937-5446. A recent construction (1990), this lodge offers its own breed of elegant accommodations. Some rooms have balconies overlooking either the ocean or the inn's lovely garden. $175-$375.

Sea Gull Inn $$: 44594 Albion St. (Lansing/Howard), Mendocino, (707) 937-5204. A charming, centrally-located hostelry with inexpensive accommodations in downtown Mendocino. $40-$150.

Stanford Inn by the Sea/Big River Lodge $$$: Comptche-Ukiah Rd., off Hwy 1, Mendocino, (800) 331-8884 or (707) 937-5615. The best features of a B&B with the

GETAWAYS

amenities of a larger hotel, including an indoor pool and hot tub, and resident llamas. Each room has a fireplace and TV. $140-$170.

Victorian Farmhouse $$: 7001 Hwy 1, Little River, (800) 264-4723 or (707) 937-0697. Known for its hospitality, coziness, and proximity to an ocean path. $80-$120.

Whitegate Inn $$$: 449 Howard St. (Ukiah), Mendocino, (707) 937-4892. This romantic inn offers little details that make a stay memorable: flowers, fruit, and chocolates in each guest room; wine and hors d'oeuvres every evening in the parlor. $95-$165.

Sonoma & Mendocino Coasts ★★

The coastline from Marin County to southern Mendocino County is sparsely populated, but dotted with state parks, public beaches, and a good supply of offbeat restaurants and lodgings. Hwy 1 rolls through the bucolic farms and pastures that border the **Pt. Reyes National Seashore,** and up along **Bodega Bay,** the setting for Alfred Hitchcock's *The Birds.* **Bodega Head** is known as a fine whale-sighting promontory in the wintertime.

Sonoma Coast State Beaches ★★: Once you've reached Bodega Bay, sandy beaches punctuate the coast every few miles and make inviting rest stops. For more information on Bodega Bay and the Sonoma Coast State Beaches, contact the **Salmon Creek Ranger Station** at (707) 875-3483.

Salt Point State Park ★: 25050 Hwy 1, Jenner, (707) 847-3221. Further north you'll find a primal landscape that is just beginning to recover from a recent fire. Within the park is the **Kruse Rhododendron State Preserve ★★,** with 300+ acres of wild rhododendrons (they're particularly spectacular in April and May). Look for the entrance on the east side of Hwy 1.

The Sea Ranch: (800) 842-3270, (707) 785-2371. An award-winning planned community with vacation homes for rent throughout the year. Close to the ocean, the **Sea Ranch Lodge** at 60 Sea Walk Drive also has rooms if you're not into group housing; tariffs run between $125 and $180.

Gualala: A bit further north, this town (pronounced wah-la-la) is the area's commercial center. Activities in the Gualala vicinity include horseback riding, wine tasting, and sea kayaking. **The Roth Ranch,** 37100 Old Stage Rd., (707) 884-3124, offers guided horseback rides through the Gualala River basin; $45 for the half-day ride. Call for directions. **Gualala Kayak** 39175 Hwy 1 (behind Don Berard Associates in the middle of Gualala), (707) 884-4705, features river and ocean kayaking excursions from $25 per person, and offers mid-week and group discounts. Open daily 8:30am to 5:30pm. The **Annapolis Winery,** 26055 Soda Springs Rd., (707) 886-5460, is set back seven miles in the hills high above the wind and fog. You'll find complimentary tastings and picnic grounds with a sunny view of the coast. Open M-Th noon to 5pm.

Places to Eat

Roadhouse Café ★ $: 6061 Hwy 1, Elk, (707) 877-3285. Locals come to this unprepossessing eatery—it's attached to the owner's husband's auto repair shop—for inexpensive, hearty breakfasts and lunches. No credit cards. • Summer: Tu-Sa 8am-2pm; Su 8am-1pm. Winter: Th-Sa 8am-2pm; Su 8am-1pm (call for winter hours)

St. Orres ★★★ $$$: 36601 S. Hwy 1, Gualala, (707) 884-3303. An eye-catching onion dome sits atop the towering, three-story wall of windows that dominates the dramatic dining hall in this inn. The French-meets-California cuisine relies heavily on complex game dishes like medallions of venison sauced with huckleberries and Zinfandel, and wild boar stuffed with dates and walnuts and served with apple ginger chutney. If you're looking for something less carnivorous, choose from lighter dishes that might include mussels on black pasta or a grilled vegetable tart. The wine list is excellent.

Make reservations well in advance, but if you get stuck with a late hour, come early anyway to catch the sunset from the porch. No credit cards. Reservations recommended. • Su-F 6-10pm; Sa 5:15-10pm.

Places to Stay

Elk Cove Inn $$$: 6300 S. Hwy 1, Elk, (707) 877-3321. This 1883 Victorian house features ocean views (there are also four freestanding cabins near the main building) and private access to an adjacent state beach. $98-$148.

Greenwood Pier Inn $$$: 5928 Hwy 1, Elk, (707) 877-9997. A cluster of cottages perched above a cut in the ocean cliffs. Gorgeous gardens and dazzling views complement the eclectic decor. $90-$195.

St. Orres $$/$$$: 36601 S. Hwy 1, Gualala, (707) 884-3303. The Russian-looking restaurant also offers inexpensive rooms and rustic, secluded cabins. $60-$150.

Sandpiper House Inn $$$: 5520 S. Hwy 1, Elk, (707) 877-3587. A charming 1916 ocean-front home, this inn offers private beach access and afternoon tea. $100-$195.

This is it! $$: Off Hwy 1 on Mtn. View Rd. btwn. Pt. Arena and Manchester State Beach, (707) 882-2320. A cottage in the redwoods with its own kitchenette and hot tub. $75.

Inland Mendocino ★

The other route to Mendocino involves more cross-country driving but the trip is about an hour shorter than the coastal trip. Stay on Hwy 101 to Cloverdale, where you pick up Hwy 128. This road winds through vineyards, serene golden hills, and redwoods as it cuts across the Anderson Valley. Once Hwy 128 hits the coast, it's just another ten miles north on Hwy 1 to Mendocino. To go to Hopland, continue on Hwy 101 past Cloverdale for about 15 miles. To then reach Mendocino, either backtrack to Cloverdale or continue north on Hwy 101 to Lakeport, where you follow Hwy 253 west until it meets Hwy 128 in Boonville.

Restaurants and Hotels

Boonville Hotel ★★★ $$$: 14050 Hwy 128 (Lambert), Boonville, (707) 895-2210. This southwestern-style hotel sports a lively, informal restaurant overlooking gardens. The kitchen serves an inventive menu that mixes the Old West with the new. Light eaters can enjoy gourmet pizzas, while those looking for more substantial offerings will enjoy chicken breast with corn-tomatillo-red pepper salsa, or pork tenderloin in a cumin, lemon, and mint marinade. Reservations recommended. • W-M 6-9pm; F-Su 11:30-2:30pm (June-Sept.), 6-9pm (year-round)

Buckhorn Saloon (Anderson Valley Brewing Company) ★ $: 14081 Hwy 128, Boonville, (707) 895-BEER/2337. Some scruffy locals add authenticity to this stalwart tavern, although the large redwood deck is a far cry from a grubby saloon. The Buckhorn is famous for serving some of the best microbrewed beer around. The country lunches and dinners—burgers, fish and chips, fresh fish—are well suited to the house libations. • Summer: M-F 11:30am-2:30pm, 5:30-8:30pm; Sa-Su 11:30am-8:30pm; Winter closed 2-3 days: Tu, W, and... (hey, it's the country).

Mendocino Brewing Company ★ $: Hwy 101, Hopland, (707) 744-1361. This brew pub is home to the ever-popular Red Tail Ale, as well as such other ornithological derivatives as Black Hawk Stout and Peregrine Pale Ale. With a laid-back, wisteria-draped, beer-garden atmosphere, this establishment has good bar food and music on Saturday nights. For dessert, stop next door at the Cheesecake Lady for a delicious slice of their namesake specialty. • Daily 11am-9pm; bar Su-Th until 11pm; F until midnight; Sa until 2am.

GETAWAYS

MONTEREY, CARMEL, & BIG SUR ★★

Monterey & Pacific Grove ★★

Monterey is home to the famous Cannery Row and the Monterey Bay Aquarium, as well as the many special events it hosts every year—including golf tournaments and jazz, blues, Dixieland, and squid festivals. The town also celebrates the famous people who once called the area home, including John Steinbeck and Robinson Jeffers.

Next to Monterey on the tip of its eponymous peninsula sits the city of Pacific Grove. Founded by Methodists in 1875, Pacific Grove has the distinction of being the last dry town in California, with alcohol legal only since 1969. It is nicknamed "Butterfly City, USA" because thousands of migrating monarch butterflies winter here.

Monterey Peninsula Chamber of Commerce: 380 Alvarado St., Monterey, (408) 649-1770. 24-hour information hotline. • Office open M-F 9am-5pm.

Tourist Information: (408) 624-1711; room reservations (800) 847-8066.

Getting There

Depending on traffic, it takes from two to two and a half hours to get to Monterey from San Francisco; tack on another 15 minutes if you're going to Carmel and an additional half hour to reach the heart of Big Sur. There are two routes: the first is I-280 to Hwy 17 south to Santa Cruz, then Hwy 1 south. This drive takes a little longer, but it is more scenic and there are other attractions along the way. A quicker alternative is to take Hwy 101 south to Hwy 156 south through Castroville, then Hwy 1 south.

Sights and Attractions

Cannery Row ★: Along the waterfront off Lighthouse Rd. just west of the Presidio, Monterey. Once known as the sardine capital of the world, Cannery Row is the street immortalized in John Steinbeck's novel of the same name. In 1945, Monterey's 19 canneries packed more than 235,000 tons of fish. Cannery Row still stands—but in its current incarnation as a shopping bazaar, now it's tourists that are packed together like sardines. A principal attraction is the Monterey Bay Aquarium (see below). Nearby sights include an historic carousel, wax museum, and **Fisherman's Wharf**, just off Del Monte Avenue. Some of the many restaurants and shops there have been operated by the same families for generations. From December to early April, whale-watching tours depart from the wharf for close-up views of the migrating sea mammals.

Monterey Bay Aquarium ★★: 886 Cannery Row, Monterey, (408) 648-4888; advance tickets (800) 756-3737. This state-of-the-art wonder provides a comprehensive view of the bay, from the sloughs to the deep sea. To the left of the entrance is the **California Kelp Forest** exhibit; don't miss feeding time at this 335,000-gallon tank. The latest addition to the aquarium is the **Outer Bay** exhibition, designed to simulate open ocean conditions in an enormous tank with tuna, ocean sunfish, and stingrays. Outside, take in the beauty of the bay itself and watch sea otters lounge on the rocks. • Daily 10am-6pm. $13.75 adults; $11.75 seniors, students, ages 13-17; $6 ages 3-12.

Monterey State Historic Park ★★: Around Custom House Plaza, Lighthouse Rd. and Del Monte Ave., Monterey, (408) 649-7118. This park manages a collection of historic structures located throughout the city. Stop by the headquarters at 20 Custom House Plaza behind Fisherman's Wharf for a free, self-guided tour map and listing of each building's hours. Included on the tour are several fine old adobes, some with beautiful patios and gardens. A $5 two-day pass covers admission to four houses. A walking tour ($2) leaves daily from Stanton Center on the Plaza at 10:15am, 12:30pm, and 2:30pm.

MONTEREY, CARMEL, & BIG SUR

Maritime Museum ★: Stanton Center, Custom House Plaza, Monterey, (408) 373-2469. Displays artifacts from Monterey's whaling days. • Daily 10am-5pm. $5.

Monterey Peninsula Museum of Art ★: 559 Pacific St., Monterey, (408) 372-5477. Has a diverse collection with an excellent selection of Western art, including several Charles M. Russell cowboy statues. • W-Sa 10am-5pm (third Th of the month until 7:30pm); Su 1-5pm. Free.

Colton Hall ★: Friendly Plaza, Pacific and Jefferson sts., Monterey, (408) 646-5640. An architectural gem well worth visiting, this is where California's first constitution was crafted in 1849.

Pacific Grove ★★: On the way to Pacific Grove, check out Ocean View Boulevard, also known as **Three-Mile Drive ★★** (begin at Cannery Row past the aquarium) for one of the best views of the region. Continuing beyond the aquarium you'll find the **American Tin Cannery**, 125 Ocean View, (408) 372-1442, with over 45 factory outlets. Further along the coast are **Shoreline Park**, **Marine Gardens Park**, and **Lover's Point**

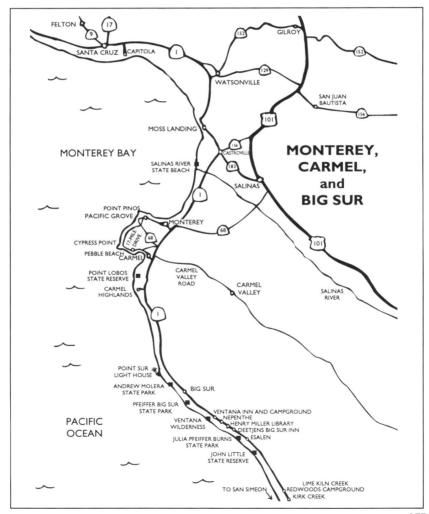

GETAWAYS

Beach, all great spots to picnic. Follow the ocean to **Point Piños Lighthouse and Museum**—(408) 375-4450 for private tours; (408) 648-3116 for group tours—the oldest operating lighthouse on the West Coast. Open to the public for tours Th-Su 1-4pm. **Doc's Great Tidepool**, a favored spot for microcosmic marine exploration, is at the base of the lighthouse. Check out more tide pools, as well as wind-sculpted cypress trees, at **Asilomar State Beach**.

Pacific Grove Museum of Natural History ★: Central and Forest aves. (turn on Forest from Lighthouse), Pacific Grove, (408) 648-3116. One of the finest natural history museums in the country, it highlights local species, including sea otters and over 400 varieties of birds; be sure to visit the Butterfly Tree. • Tu-Su 10am-5pm. Free.

17-Mile Drive ★: (408) 649-8500. You can get to this renowned attraction from Sunset Drive in Pacific Grove, Hwy 1 south of Monterey, or Ocean Avenue in Carmel. The famed scenery of this drive includes fancy houses, the golf courses in exclusive **Pebble Beach**, the picturesque lone cypress, and Crocker Grove, a 13-acre pine and cypress natural reserve. $7/car (refundable if you eat, play golf, shop, etc. along the way—keep any receipts).

Outdoor Activities ★

Monterey's **scuba diving** ★★ is ranked among the best in Northern California, and there are plenty of local dive shops ready to serve your needs. **Sea kayaking** ★★ is also very popular here, and there are several places that rent boats and offer tours. See Sports chapter for more information.

Boat Charters ★: **Monterey Sport Fishing**, 96 Fisherman's Wharf, (408) 372-2203, has various deep-sea fishing packages and also offers a 45-minute sightseeing cruise of Monterey Bay ($7 per person, weekends only) and seasonal whale-watching trips. **Randy's Fishing Trips**, 66 Fisherman's Wharf, (408) 372-7440, also offers numerous excursions.

Bicycle/Moped Rental ★: For the land-bound, biking and mopeding are popular and fun. **Monterey Moped Adventures**, 1250 Del Monte, (408) 373-2696, has both bikes and mopeds for rent (open weekends only). **Joselyn's**, 638 Lighthouse, (408) 649-8520), is another source for bicycle rentals. **Bay Bikes**, 640 Wave Street, (408) 646-9090 rents mountain bikes and surreys—four-person pedal bikes. You can take off right behind the store on a bike path that follows the coast to Pacific Grove and 17-Mile Drive.

Golf Courses ★★★

The Monterey area is a Mecca for world-class golf courses. See Golfing section for more information.

Places to Eat

Amarin Thai Cuisine ★ **$**: 807 Cannery Row, Monterey, (408) 373-8811. Traditional Thai specialties like satay, pad Thai, and curries, at decent prices in a casual atmosphere. • Daily 11am-9:30pm.

Clock Garden ★ **$**: 565 Abrego St., Monterey, (408) 375-6100. A great place to eat breakfast outdoors. The food is imaginative, delicious, and reasonably priced. • M-F 11am-3:30pm, 5-9pm; F-Sa 11am-3:30pm, 5-10pm.

The Fishwife at Asilomar Beach ★★ **$$**: 1996-1/2 Sunset Dr., Pacific Grove, (408) 375-7107. Seafood with a Caribbean flair. • W-M 11am-10pm (Su brunch begins 10am).

Gianni's Pizza ★ **$**: 725 Lighthouse Ave., Monterey, (408) 649-1500. The best pizza in Monterey—worth the wait. • Su-Th 4-10pm; F-Sa 11:30am-11pm.

Monterey's Fish House ★★ **$$**: 2114 Del Monte Ave., Monterey, (408) 373-4647. An East Coast–style seafood restaurant—basic but good. Grilled or blended with pasta, the fish is fresh and tasty. • M-F 11:30am-2:30pm, 5:30-9:30pm; Sa-Su 5:30-9:30pm.

MONTEREY, CARMEL, & BIG SUR

Montrio ★★ $$$: 414 Calle Principal, Monterey, (408) 648-8880. This former firehouse houses a pleasant restaurant serving California cuisine. Look for well-executed standards such as seared ahi tuna salad and grilled mahi mahi. • M-Th 11:30am-10pm; F-Sa 11:30am-11pm; Su 10am-10pm.

O'Kane's Irish Pub ★ $: 97 Prescott St., Monterey, (408) 375-7564. Irish hospitality is in abundance here. • Daily 11am-midnight.

Old Bath House Restaurant ★★ $$$: 620 Ocean View Blvd., Pacific Grove, (408) 375-5195. One of Pacific Grove's finest restaurants, it serves steak, chicken, seafood, and killer desserts in a charming Victorian overlooking the ocean. • M-F 5-10:30pm; Sa 4-10:30pm; Su 3-10:30pm.

Pepper's Mexicali Café ★★ $: 170 Forest Ave., Pacific Grove, (408) 373-6892. Good, authentic Mexican fare. • M, W-Sa 11:30am-10pm; Su 4-10pm.

Rappa's End of the Wharf ★ $$: Fisherman's Wharf, (408) 372-7562. Fresh seafood in a comfortable retreat from the wharf. • M-F 11am-9pm; Sa-Su 11am-9:30pm.

Roy's at Pebble Beach ★★★ $$$$: The Inn at Spanish Bay, 2700 17-Mile Dr., Pebble Beach, (408) 647-7423. Much acclaimed East-West cuisine from superstar chef Roy Yamaguchi. Never mind the great views, this is the kind of LA-style restaurant where all the glamorous fun is inside. Reservations recommended. • Daily 6:30am-10pm.

Spadaro's ★★ $$: 650 Cannery Row, Monterey, (408) 372-8881. Excellent Italian food served up with a spectacular view. • Daily 11am-3pm, 5-10pm.

Taqueria del Mar ★ ¢: 530 Lighthouse Ave., Pacific Grove, (408) 372-7887. Awesome burritos and other great Mexican dishes. • M-Sa 11:30am-8pm; Su 11:30am-4pm.

The Tinnery ★ $$: 631 Ocean View Blvd., Pacific Grove, (408) 646-1040. A bar featuring live entertainment nightly, and plenty of seafood. Also offers complete breakfasts. • M-F 8am-midnight; Sa-Su 8am-1am. Happy hour 4pm-6pm and 11pm-1am.

Toastie's Café ★ $: 702 Lighthouse Ave., Pacific Grove, (408) 373-7543. A great place for breakfast. • M 6am-3pm; Tu-Sa 6am-3pm, 5-9pm; Su 7am-2pm.

Warehouse Restaurant ★★ $$: 640 Wave St., Cannery Row, Monterey, (408) 375-1921. A very good Italian restaurant. • M-Th noon-10pm; F-Sa noon-11pm; Su 10am-10pm.

Whaling Station Inn ★★ $$$: 763 Wave St., Monterey, (408) 373-3778. Elegant setting for an excellent continental meal. • Daily 5-10pm.

Places to Stay

A midweek or off-season stay can be substantially cheaper.

Andril Fireplace Cottages $$: 569 Asilomar Blvd., Pacific Grove, (408) 375-0994. Cottages with fully equipped kitchens and fireplaces, set among the pines. $80-$110.

Asilomar Conference Center $$: 800 Asilomar Blvd., Monterey, (408) 372-8016. A historical landmark, right on the beach. Primarily for large groups; single rooms available. Reservations taken up to 30 days in advance. Breakfast included. $70-$90.

Beachcomber Inn $$: 1996 Sunset Dr., Pacific Grove, (408) 373-4769. Heated pool; a few rooms have kitchen facilities. $60-$118.

Best Western Lighthouse Lodge $$$: 1249 Lighthouse Ave., Pacific Grove, (408) 655-2111. A great view of (what else?) the lighthouse; Jacuzzis and in-room fireplaces. $79-$119, suites $185.

Californian Motel $$: 2042 N. Fremont St., Monterey, (408) 372-5851. Some rooms have kitchens, and there's a pool and a whirlpool. $39-$109.

Colton Inn $$$: 707 Pacific St., Monterey, (408) 649-6500. Rooms come with balconies, fireplaces, and whirlpool tubs. $77-$189.

GETAWAYS

Jabberwock $$$: 598 Laine St., Monterey, (408) 372-4777. A 1911 post-Victorian decorated in an *Alice in Wonderland* theme. Complimentary hors d'oeuvres and wine are served in the evening, and milk and cookies await you at bedtime. $100-$150.

Martine Inn $$$: 255 Ocean View Blvd., Pacific Grove, (408) 373-3388. A grand Mediterranean mansion overlooking the crashing surf. Full breakfast and afternoon wine and hors d'oeuvres included. $125-$230.

Merritt House $$$: 386 Pacific St., Monterey, (408) 646-9686. A charming historic adobe with 25 adjoining new units. All rooms have fireplaces. Breakfast included. $120-$200.

Monterey Bay Inn $$$: 242 Cannery Row, Monterey, (408) 373-6242, (800) 424-6242. A great location on the bay, plus a rooftop hot tub with a panoramic view. $119-$319.

Pacific Grove Motel $$: Lighthouse and Grove Acre aves., Pacific Grove, (408) 372-3218. Centrally located, with a pool and hot tub. Refrigerators in each room. $39-$139.

Sand Dollar Inn $$: 755 Abrego St., Monterey, (408) 372-7551. Offers a pool and spa, and includes continental breakfast. $64-$104.

Spindrift Inn $$$: 652 Cannery Row, Monterey, (408) 646-8900, (800) 424-6242. Pamper yourself with goose-down feather beds, fireplaces, and a rooftop garden. Complimentary continental breakfast and wine and cheese. $99-$189 for city views; $209-$289 for ocean views.

Terrace Oaks Inn $$: 1095 Lighthouse Ave., Pacific Grove, (408) 373-4382. Standard, reasonably priced lodging. $60-$82.

Carmel ★

Carmel is located on Hwy 1 just south of Monterey, and is known for its array of excellent restaurants, shops, and romantic inns and bed-and-breakfasts. Accordingly, most restaurants and hotels cater to those travelers with big bank accounts. Parking is very limited in the downtown area. Local ordinances prohibit house numbers and parking meters—but you can still get a ticket from the vigilant police.

Sights and Attractions

For more activities in the area, check out the **Sunset Cultural Center**, (408) 624-3996, located on San Carlos Street between Eighth and Ninth, or pick up a copy of the *Monterey Peninsula Review*, a free weekly newspaper that lists of the week's events.

Ocean Avenue ★: Carmel's main street is a window-shopper's delight, with countless specialty shops, art galleries, and boutiques. An art colony gone berserk (and a bit sour), you can't walk down a street in Carmel without encountering at least three galleries. Art lovers should investigate **Carmel Art Association Galleries** (408) 624-6176 on Dolores Street between Fifth and Sixth, which tastefully displays the work of local artists and hosts major traveling exhibits.

City Beach ★★: At the foot of Ocean Avenue, the town meets the sea, explaining the downtown area's official name, Carmel-by-the-Sea. Beautiful to look at, but rough for swimming. You'll find a less populated stretch of beach south on Scenic Road.

Tor House ★: 26304 Ocean View Ave., or off Stewart Way off Scenic Rd., (408) 624-1813; F-Sa call docent office, (408) 624-1840. The house of poet Robinson Jeffers. Jeffers built the home from rocks he carried up from the beach. Open only for guided tours given Fridays and Saturdays hourly between 10am and 3pm; reservations are suggested. No children under 12 allowed. $5.

Carmel Mission ★★: 3080 Rio Rd. (west of Hwy 1), (408) 624-3600. For a dose of California history, drop by the this mission, which has a baroque stone church completed in 1797, three museums, and fabulous gardens. Across the street is **Mission Trail Park**, 35 acres ready and waiting for hikers and mountain bikers.

Places to Eat

California Thai ★★★ $$: San Carlos St. at 4th, Carmel, (408) 622-1160. The name describes the food, where Thai food gets upscale California organic ingredients and styling. • Daily noon-3:30pm, 5-10pm.

Flaherty's ★★ $$: 6th St. between San Carlos and Dolores, Carmel, (408) 624-0311. Known as the best seafood place in town; expect to wait if you don't get there very early. • Daily 11:30am-9pm; oyster bar from 11:30am-10pm.

Flying Fish Grill ★★ $$$: Mission St. between Ocean and 7th, Carmel, (408) 625-1962. An intimate, upscale Japanese restaurant that isn't afraid to experiment with Western influences in its menu (desserts include crème brûlée). • Daily 5-10pm.

Friar Tucks ★ $: 5th Avenue and Dolores, Carmel, (408) 624-0311. One of the best breakfast deals around. The food is delicious, and the pub-like atmosphere lends itself well to the basic lunches. • Daily 6:30am-2pm.

Hog's Breath Inn ★ $$: San Carlos St. between 5th and 6th, Carmel, (408) 625-1044. This Clint Eastwood-owned establishment is moody, low-lit, and woody inside, but the outdoor patio is cheery and social, sporting multiple fireplaces and a bar. Free hors d'oeuvres buffet 4pm-6pm. • Daily 11:30am-3pm, 5-10pm.

Le Bistro ★ $: San Carlos between 5th and 6th, Carmel, (408) 624-6545. Burgers, soups, and sandwiches in a colorful atmosphere that includes a small garden. • M-Th 8am-3pm; Sa-Su 8am-7pm.

Places to Stay

Carmel Mission Ranch $$$: 26270 Dolores St., Carmel, (408) 624-6436. A rustic place replete with goats and grazing sheep, narrowly saved from condominium hell by none other than Clint Eastwood. Many cottages and rooms offer views of the ocean; continental breakfast included. $95-$225.

Carmel Valley Inn $$: Corner of Los Laureles Grade Rd. and Carmel Valley Rd., Carmel, (408) 659-3131, (800) 541-3113. Tennis courts, swimming pool, and hot tub. $69-$149.

Green Lantern $$: 7th and Casanova, Carmel, (408) 624-4392. Romantic rooms at reasonable prices. $75-$189.

Lincoln Green Inn $$$: Carmelo, between 15th and 16th, Carmel, (408) 624-1880. Excellent spot for couples and families. Cottages sleep four; almost all have fireplaces and full kitchens. $135 & up.

Pine Inn $$$: Ocean Ave. between Lincoln and Monteverde, Carmel, (408) 624-3851. "Carmel-Victorian" decor. Some rooms have ocean views. $100-$205.

Big Sur ★★★

Stretching along the mountains from Carmel south to San Simeon is the majestic coastline known as Big Sur. Seventy miles of cliff-hanging S-curves and switchbacks make up this part of the Pacific Coast Highway that runs perilously close to the ocean, with plenty of pull-offs to take in the **views** ★★★. The town of Big Sur is located about midway along the drive, but most people use "Big Sur" as a collective term for the whole magnificent landscape. There are several good camping areas, a few restaurants, and plenty of views and trails for hiking.

Big Sur Chamber of Commerce: P.O. Box 87, Big Sur CA, 93920, (408) 667-2100.

Big Sur Station: Hwy 1, one-half mi. south of Pfeiffer-Big Sur State Park, (408) 667-2423. A multi-agency ranger station with lots of information and maps for national forests and state parks. Also the place to go for Ventana Wilderness permits. • Daily 8am-6pm.

GETAWAYS

Pfeiffer-Big Sur State Park: (408) 667-2315. For information about Andrew Molera State Park, Garrapata State Park, Julia Pfeiffer Burns State Park, Pfeiffer-Big Sur State Park, and Point Sur Lighthouse State Park.

Sights and Attractions

The state and national parks offer plenty of opportunities for the solitude that first drew writer Henry Miller to Big Sur in the 1940s.

Point Lobos State Reserve ★★: Hwy 1, 3.5 mi. south of Carmel, (408) 624-4909. More than 1,250 magnificent acres of natural coastal and inland habitat. Hike along the reserve's numerous coastal and wilderness trails, check out the tide pools, or take a nature tour. Parking is very limited, so get there early; when the park is full you have to wait until a car exits before you can enter. • Daily 9am-7pm; gate closes at 6:30pm. $6.

Garrapata State Park ★: Hwy 1 about 6 mi. south of Carmel. There's a nice beach here and some high ground from which to watch whales in the winter, but there are few facilities and heavy winds.

Point Sur Lighthouse State Park ★: Hwy 1 about 19 mi. south of Carmel, (408) 625-4419, (408) 625-2006. This dramatically situated, historic lighthouse is maintained by the Coast Guard and can only be visited as part of a tour. Tours last over two hours, and visits by small children and the unfit are discouraged (some climbing required). Arrive at the gate early, since people are not permitted to enter or even wait outside the lighthouse if they miss the tour. • Tours Sa 10am, 2pm; Su 2pm; also some Wed. and special sunset and full-moon tours. $5.

Andrew Molera State Park ★: Hwy 1 about 22 mi. south of Carmel. Features a two-mile beach, a coastal sanctuary for seabirds, and walk-in campsites a few hundred yards from the dirt parking lot. Inside the campground, **Molera Trail Rides** (408) 625-8664 or (408) 659-0433, has two-hour rides at daybreak, afternoon, and sunset for $40-$50.

Pfeiffer-Big Sur State Park ★: Hwy 1 about 25 mi. south of Carmel on the east side of the highway, (408) 667-2315. The trails leading up into the mountains offer spectacular views of the Big Sur River gorge and the valley below, including the 60-foot **Pfeiffer Falls**. Provides access to Ventana Wilderness. $6.

Ventana Wilderness ★★: Access from Pfeiffer-Big Sur State Park. Inland from the state park is the largest protected area in Big Sur. Visitors need to have a free permit to hike, build fires, or camp within the preserve. These can be obtained, along with maps, at the **Big Sur Station** (see General Information above).

Pfeiffer Beach ★: Hwy 1 about 26 mi. south of Carmel. This small, popular cove is a good place to explore sea caves and watch divers.

Henry Miller Memorial Library ★: Hwy 1 about 28 mi. south of Carmel, (408) 667-2574. The unimposing wood structure houses Miller memorabilia—books, paintings, and photographs of Miller's friends and assorted wives.

Julia Pfeiffer Burns State Park ★: Hwy 1 about 36 mi. south of Carmel, (408) 667-2315. This park boasts the only California waterfall that drops directly into the sea. There are also walk-in campsites with limited facilities. Other state parks further south include **Lime Kiln State Park**, where you can spend about an hour or two hiking to ancient lime kilns, and then cool off in the waterfall. The park also has camping and beach access. $5.

Esalen Institute ★: Hwy 1 about 40 mi. south of Carmel, (408) 667-3000. Formerly a symbol of the 60s counterculture, but now a New Age retreat that bills itself as a "center to encourage work in the humanities and sciences that promotes human values and potentials." The beautiful encampment and cliffside baths are open to the curious public 1am-3:30am (yes, that's the wee hours of the morning), and reservations are required; call (408) 667-3047.

MONTEREY, CARMEL, & BIG SUR

Restaurants and Entertainment

Big Sur Lodge ★ $: Hwy 1, Pfeiffer-Big Sur State Park, (408) 667-2171. A rustic spot next to the Big Sur Campground. The food is much better than is found at typical park concessionaires, particularly the fresh-baked pies. • Daily 7am-10pm.

Center Deli ¢: Hwy 1, next to the post office, (408) 667-2225. A good place to pick up a sandwich and some fixings, but there is no seating on-site. • Daily 8am-8pm.

Coast Gallery Café ★ ¢: Hwy 1, 3 mi. south of Nepenthe, (408) 667-2301. Hot and cold sandwiches and a great view. • Daily 9am-5pm.

Deetjen's Big Sur Inn Restaurant ★★ $$: Hwy 1, (408) 667-2378. Wonderful brunches and dinners served in a country setting. Dinner reservations recommended. • Daily 8-11:30am, 6-8:30pm.

Fernwood Burger Bar ★ $: Hwy 1, 26 mi. south of Carmel, (408) 667-2422. A hopping place with occasional live music blasting through the redwoods. • Daily noon-11pm.

Nepenthe ★★ $$$/$$$$: Hwy 1, 30 mi. south of Carmel, (408) 667-2345. Once the haunt of literary loafer Henry Miller and stars Liz Taylor and Richard Burton, today's famous diners include the likes of Jane Fonda and Ted Turner. Exceptional views, of course, which greatly outdo the food. No reservations. • Daily 11:30am-10pm.

Post Ranch Inn ★★★ $$$$: Hwy 1, across from Ventana Inn, (408) 667-2200. An expensive, near-the-ocean experience of delicious California cuisine and phenomenal views. Reservations required. • M-F 5:30-9:30pm; Sa-Su noon-2pm, 5:30-9:30pm.

Ventana Inn ★★★ $$$$: Hwy 1, 28 mi. S. of Carmel, (408) 667-2331 or (408) 624-4812. Breathtaking views and prices to match, but if you decide to splurge you won't be disappointed. Coffee or tea on the deck gives a great overlook of the ocean. • Daily 11:30am-3pm, 6-9:30pm.

Places to Stay

Destinet: (800) 444-7275. State park campground reservations.

Big Sur Campground and Cabins $/$$$: Hwy 1, next to the River Inn, (408) 667-2322. Campgrounds and cabins, some with kitchens, nestled among the redwoods. Campsites $22 for two, $3 for each additional person; tent cabins $40 for two, $10 each additional; cabins $88-$143.

Big Sur Lodge $$: Located in Pfeiffer-Big Sur State Park, (408) 667-3100, (800) 424-4787 for reservations. Choose from 61 cottage-style rooms with either a deck or a porch. Some with kitchens and fireplaces. $79-$179.

Big Sur River Inn $$: Hwy 1, 25 mi. south of Carmel, (408) 667-2700. The first business you'll encounter in Big Sur Valley, with nice, clean, simple rooms. $88-$160.

Bottchers Gap Campground ¢: North of the Point Sur Lighthouse, Palo Colorado Rd. (Big Sur Station). Limited services and a first-come, first-served policy. $5.

Deetjen's Big Sur Inn $$: Hwy 1, (408) 667-2377. It's hard to imagine a more picturesque inn with its garden, ever-stoked fire, and hearty, inventive breakfasts. Two months' advance reservations recommended; call noon-4pm. $66-$121 and up.

Esalen Institute $$: Hwy 1, (408) 667-3000. Private or shared bunk-bed rooms available; meals included. Pool and hot tub. Reservations taken only a week in advance. $70-$125.

Fernwood Motel & Campground $/$$: Hwy 1 around 26 mi. south of Carmel, (408) 667-2422. Campsites for two $21, $4 each additional person (add $2 for electrical hookup); rooms $55-$74.

Kirk Creek Campgrounds ¢: Hwy 1, 15 mi. south of the Esalen Institute, (408) 385-5434 (U.S. National Forest Service). Policy is first-come, first-served at these campsites set on an open bluff above the ocean—go early in the afternoon, they usually fill up fast. Water, but no showers, phones, or electricity. $16.

Lime Kiln State Park: Hwy 1 about 55 mi. south of Carmel, (408) 667-2403. Situated in a canyon and surrounded by good hiking trails. Flush toilets and beach access. Advance reservations are a must and are handled through **Destinet**; call (800) 444-7275. $20-$23/site.

Post Ranch Inn $$$$: Hwy 1, (408) 667-2200. The newest resort in Big Sur. Its luxurious rooms are appointed with private fireplaces, Jacuzzis, and wet bars. The inn features neo-rustic lodgepole architecture among the redwoods, spectacular views, and plentiful spa services. $265-$525.

Ripplewood Resort $$: Hwy 1, (408) 667-2282. Some of these 16 well-kept cabins (nine of which are on the Big Sur River) have kitchens, fireplaces, and decks. $45-$80.

Riverside Campground & Cabins $/$$: Hwy 1, located on the Big Sur River, (408) 667-2414. No kitchens or fireplaces. Campsites $22 for two people, add $3 each additional person; cabins $50-$90.

Ventana Campground $: Hwy 1, (408) 667-2688. On the grounds of the Ventana Inn, so you're within reach of a meal or drink if those freeze-dried dinners aren't cutting it. $20 for two people. Reservations required, ten days' notice, and $20 deposit.

Ventana Inn $$$$: Hwy 1 about 30 mi. south of Carmel, (408) 667-2331, (408) 624-4812. A woodsy retreat, considered to be one of the finest in Northern California. Located high above the ocean, this sprawling, ranch-like compound is luxurious without being pretentious. Clothing-optional hot tubs and sun-bathing areas are only a sampling of the amenities available. $195-$550.

PENINSULA COAST ★★

The Peninsula coast that begins just south of San Francisco is replete with rolling hills, fields of artichokes, and gorgeous rugged beaches that draw surfers and beachcombers from far and wide. Sleepy towns like Pescadero, filled with ramshackle barns and Depression-era architecture, are more reminiscent of Tom Joad than Steve Jobs.

Half Moon Bay Chamber of Commerce: 520 Kelly Ave., Half Moon Bay, (415) 726-5202.

California State Parks District Office: 95 Kelly Ave., Half Moon Bay, (415) 330-6300. Manages state beaches along coast.

Pacifica to Half Moon Bay ★

If you need a break from sunny, warm weather, visit fog-bound Pacifica. To get to Pacifica, one of the first coastal towns south of San Francisco, take I-280 to Hwy 1 south. *Warning:* Hwy 1 normally continues south to Moss Beach and Half Moon Bay, but heavy rains can close the Devil's Slide portion of the road between San Pedro Point and Montara Beach (sometimes for months). When this happens, you must take I-280 to Hwy 92 west to Half Moon Bay to Hwy 1 north to reach Moss Beach and the surrounding area.

Beaches ★★: Pacifica is first and foremost a beach community. One of the first places you'll encounter there is **Sharp Park State Beach**, with a sandy beach and a picnic and barbecue area. Farther south on Hwy 1 is the smaller, semiprotected **Rockaway Beach**. The beach, which is framed between two outcroppings of rock, abuts a strip of hotels and restaurants. From Rockaway Beach, Hwy 1 winds up around **San Pedro Point**, a favorite with boogie-boarders and surfers. Just before you reach Montara Beach you will see **Gray Whale Cove**. This wonderful little spot is accessible only by a path down the cliffs, but the trip to this private, clothing-optional beach is well worth it. The next major stopping point is **Montara Beach**, a long, narrow stretch just off the highway framed by rocks and low cliffs.

PENINSULA COAST

Fitzgerald Marine Reserve ★: Off Cypress Ave., Moss Beach, (415) 728-3583. Hidden in Moss Beach, a tiny burg along the coast, is this vast and fascinating reserve. Its 30 acres of exposed reef at low tide make it one of the best places to explore tidepools on the coast. Adjacent to the Marine Reserve, in Princeton-by-the-Sea, is **Pillar Point Harbor**, embarkation point for deep-sea fishing and whale-watching tours. A fresh fish market and several seafood restaurants are also located at the harbor.

Half Moon Bay ★★

Half Moon Bay is the only incorporated city between Pacifica and Santa Cruz. This commercial center of the Peninsula coastline is currently experiencing a bit of a boom, resulting in growth at a rapid clip. Host of the enormously popular Half Moon Bay Pumpkin Festival every October, the town is the center of a rich agricultural economy that encompasses everything from Brussels sprouts to Christmas trees. To get there, take I-280 to Hwy 92 west. Hwy 92 cuts through the middle of town and ends at Hwy 1; beaches lie both north and south of that intersection.

Main Street ★: Originally known as Spanishtown, Half Moon Bay has a sleepy, historic Main Street lined with shops, restaurants, and inns. **The Spanishtown Historical Society/Half Moon Bay Jail** (415) 726-7084 at 505 Johnston Street offers walking tours on weekend afternoons (F-Su 1-4pm) that start at the old jail; reservations are recommended. It's definitely worth stopping on Main Street to check out the interesting stores and **galleries**. If you haven't brought your bike, visit **The Bicyclery** (415)

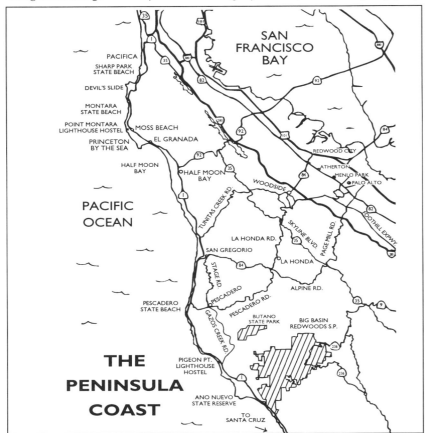

GETAWAYS

726-6000 at 432 Main Street. For $6 an hour, the friendly people at this bicycle store will supply you with mountain or road bikes, helmets, and locks. They're open M-F 9:30am-6:30pm; Sa 10am-5pm; Su 11am-5pm.

Beaches ★★: Beaches span the entire length of Hwy 1, but one of the largest continuous sandy stretches comprises **Half Moon Bay State Beach** (415-726-8820). There are many access points along Hwy 1 both north and south of Hwy 92, but the main entrance on **Francis Beach** is just south of Hwy 92 at Kelly Avenue. This beach is also the only one in the area that allows overnight camping. There's a $5 charge for parking your car during the day or overnight, but this fee also entitles you to park at any of the state parks on the coast. Other beaches around the area include **Elmar, Venice** (415) 726-5550**, Dunes, Naples,** and **Miramar,** each of which has a different personality and facilities, so check out a few sites before setting up for the day. You don't have to pay for parking at **Redondo Beach,** but you do have to pass along a lengthy, bumpy road and then scramble down the side of a cliff to reach the sand. The difficult access keeps down the crowds, however. Redondo Beach Road is a little south of Hwy 92.

Sea Horse Ranch/Friendly Acres Ranch ★: 1828 Cabrillo Hwy./Hwy 1, one mi. north of Hwy 92, (415) 726-8550. These twin local stables offer horse rentals and guides that will take you for a an hour-and-a-half trip along the coast for $35 one hour for $25, two hours for $40. The stables offer trail and beach rides for all levels of riding ability and are open daily from 8am-6pm.

Obester Winery ★: 12341 San Mateo Rd./Hwy 92, 1.5 miles east of Hwy 1, (415) 726-9463. Obester makes a nice Sauvignon Blanc that you can taste on the spot or save for a picnic. Open daily 10am-5pm. The surrounding area along Hwy 92 as you come into Half Moon Bay is replete with **nurseries**, offering everything from fresh-cut flowers to trees. It's a great place to browse for new additions to your yard or window box.

San Gregorio to Año Nuevo ★★

Beaches ★★: San Gregorio Beach (415) 726-7245 is located where Hwy 1 intersects Hwy 84, and is usually fairly crowded. Farther down Hwy 1 is **Pomponio Beach**, a good place to fish or have a picnic. **Pescadero Beach**, which also has nature trails and exhibits, is next to the 587-acre **Pescadero Marsh Natural Preserve**, where tidepools emerge along the rocky stretch at low tide. Other area beaches include **Pebble Beach** and rocky **Bean Hollow State Beach**. Admission to all beaches is $5, but one fee entitles you to park at any of the state parks on the coast for the whole day.

Butano State Park ★★: Cloverdale Rd., south of Pescadero, (415) 879-2040. If you're interested in a hike through the redwoods away from the coast, come here. This stretch of forest was lightly logged in the 1880s, and it features a stand of old-growth redwoods. Follow the Doe Ridge Trail for a hike through virgin timber. The facilities include walk-in and trail campsites, often full in spring and summer; advance reservations are a must (car/walk-in sites handled by **Destinet**, 800-444-7275; trail sites reserved through park office). $5/vehicle.

Año Nuevo Reserve ★★★: Hwy 1 about 30 mi. south of Half Moon Bay, (415) 879-0227, (415) 879-2025. By far the most interesting coastal area south of Half Moon Bay, and perhaps on the entire Peninsula. This area is home to enormous elephant seals that range from 8 to 18 feet long and can weigh as much as two and a half tons. The female seals come on shore in December to give birth, and then mate again while the male seals battle to establish breeding rights. Stellar sea lions and harbor seals breed on the beaches here at other times of the year, so it's always worth a visit. During the December to March breeding season, the reserve is only open to guided tours led by park rangers; advance reservations are a must (handled by **Destinet**, 800-444-7275). $5/vehicle.

Coastways U-Pick Ranch ★: across from Año Nuevo, (415) 879-0414. A farm where you can pick kiwifruits, olallieberries, and so forth, depending on the time of year. Enjoy your produce in the ranch's picnic area. Call first for harvest schedule.

Big Basin Redwood State Park ★★: Hwy 1 about 32 mi. south of Half Moon Bay, (408) 338-8860, (408) 425-1218. This part of Big Basin marks one end of the Skyline-to-the-Sea trail that begins at Waddell Beach and runs through the park to the top of the Santa Cruz Mountains on Skyline Drive. See Peninsula Parks.

Restaurants and Entertainment

Apple Jacks: Hwy 84, La Honda, (415) 747-0331. A venerable saloon where all types meet to drink and make merry. Live music includes blues and rock F-Sa nights and country and folk Su 4-8pm. • M-F noon-2am; Sa-Su 10am-2am.

Barbara's Fishtrap ★ $$: 281 Capistrano Rd. (off Hwy 1), Princeton-by-the-Sea, (415) 728-7049. Here you'll find some of the freshest fish, grilled or fried, on the San Mateo coast. While your California sensibilities steer you to the grilled fare, you won't be able to resist Barbara's great fried fish and tempura-style vegetables. Two can easily share the Fishtrap special, a heaping potpourri of fried calamari, scallops, shrimp, rockfish, and vegetables. The restaurant's large windows overlook the harbor, and a suitably nautical theme dominates inside. No credit cards. • Su-Th 11am-9:30pm; F-Sa 11am-10pm.

Chart House ★ $$$: 8150 Cabrillo Hwy./Hwy 1, Montara Beach, (415) 728-7366. Good, simple food, attentive service, and a spectacular sunset view of the beach make the Chart House a popular dinner destination with locals and tourists alike. The restaurant buys its excellent beef from Omaha; prime rib and "baseball sirloin teriyaki" are the best things on the menu. • M-F 5-9pm; Sa-Su 4-9:30pm.

Cunha's Country Store ¢: 448 Main St. (Kelly/Mill), Half Moon Bay, (415) 726-4071. Huge, cheap sandwiches, and everything from Jell-O to wild mushroom pasta. • M-Sa 8am-8pm; Su 8am-7pm.

Duarte's Tavern ★★ $$: 202 Stage Rd. (Pescadero Rd.), Pescadero, (415) 879-0464. Pescadero's most celebrated saloon for over a century. Now a respectable family seafood restaurant, the famous artichoke and green chili soups, garden-grown vegetables, delicious local seafood, and great pie give this place its well-deserved reputation as a wonderful stop back in time. If you're not in the mood for a full meal, sit at the counter and soak up the 1950s atmosphere over a piece of olallieberry pie and a cup of coffee. Reservations recommended on weekends. • Daily 7am-9pm.

Flying Fish Grill ★ $: 99 San Mateo Rd. (Corner of Hwy. 1 and Main St.), Half Moon Bay, (415) 712-1125. Standard fried fish and chips and interesting grilled seafood. • Tu-F 11am-8pm; Sa-Su 11am-8:30pm.

Half Moon Bay Coffee Company ★ ¢: 315 Main St. (Hwy 92), Half Moon Bay, (415) 726-1994. The home of huge slices of amazing pie. • M-F 6:30am-9pm; Sa-Su 7:30am-10pm.

McCoffee ★ ¢: 522 Main St. (Kelly), Half Moon Bay, (415) 726-6241. A good local joint to nurse espresso. • M-F 7am-6pm; Sa 8am-6pm; Su 9am-6pm.

Miramar Beach Inn ★ $$: 131 Mirada Rd., Miramar, (415) 726-9053. An historic roadhouse dating back to Prohibition, located right on the edge of the water. Decent seafood, steak, and pasta. • M-F 11:30am-3:30pm, 5:30-9pm; Sa 11am-3:30pm, 5-10pm; Su 10am-3:30pm, 5-10pm (hours vary depending on business).

Moss Beach Distillery ★ $$$: Beach Way (off Hwy 1 at Ocean Blvd.), Moss Beach, (415) 728-5595. The sign on Hwy 1 sums up the appeal of this Prohibition-era roadhouse: View, Food, Ghost. The restaurant boasts a large bar and deck area for viewing the Pacific sunset (blankets and heaters are provided). Young crowds mob the patio on sunny weekend afternoons, while live jazz plays inside. As you may have guessed, food isn't the main attraction. Mesquite-grilled fresh fish is the highlight of the menu, but there is a new emphasis on pasta. And yes, there is a ghost in residence: the "blue lady" even starred on an episode of "Unsolved Mysteries." • M-Sa noon-10pm; Su 10am-2:30pm, 4:30pm-10pm (bar menu available between meals).

GETAWAYS

Norm's Market ¢: 287 Stage Rd., Pescadero, (415) 879-0147. Great picnic fixings, fresh-baked bread, and an extensive wine cellar. M-Sa 10am-7pm; Su 10am-6pm.

Pasta Moon ★★ $$: 315 Main St. (Hwy 92), Half Moon Bay, (415) 726-5125. One of the better restaurants along the coast, Pasta Moon is cozy and quaint, albeit a bit cramped, with small town hospitality. Start with the assorted antipasti plate, which might include generous servings of grilled eggplant, roasted peppers, and more. Pastas are always a good bet, as are the seafood dishes. • M-Th 11:30am-2:30pm, 5:30-9:30pm; F 11:30am-2:30pm, 5:30-10pm; Sa noon-3pm, 5:30-10pm; Su noon-3pm, 5:30-9:30pm.

Phipps Ranch ¢: 2700 Pescadero Rd., Pescadero, (415) 879-0787. Seasonal produce, pick-your-own berries, and a petting zoo. • Daily 10am-7pm (except Thanksgiving Day and the week between Christmas and New Year's Day).

San Benito House ★★ $$$ (Deli $): 356 Main St. (Mill), Half Moon Bay, (415) 726-3425. Housed inside an historic inn in downtown Half Moon Bay, this quaint country-cottage dining room suits hotel guests shuffling in for breakfast and plenty of outsiders, too. Sunday brunch in the garden sets the tone for a day in the country. Candlelit dinners go beyond the standard slap-up seashore fare with imaginative California cuisine: grilled salmon on a bed of rice with gazpacho vinaigrette or roast chicken stuffed with hazelnuts, thyme, and mushrooms topped with orange cranberry *demi-glace*. • Th-Sa 5:30-9pm; Su 5:30-9pm. Deli 11am-3pm.

San Gregorio General Store $: Hwy 84 and Stage Rd., San Gregorio, (415) 726-0565. Everything you'll ever need—a bar, mercantile, bookstore, and music hall all in one. Bluegrass and Irish music starts at 2pm Sa-Su. • 9am-6pm daily (often Sa-Su later).

Sushi Main Street ★★ $$: 315 Main St. (Hwy 92), Half Moon Bay, (415) 726-6336. A hidden gem of a restaurant tucked inside the Tin Palace in Half Moon Bay. It's the coastside's only sushi choice, so it's fortunate that the fish is extremely fresh, creatively prepared, and inexpensive. Among the more inventive concoctions is the California-inspired tuna roll with macadamia nuts and avocado served on top of the chef's special sauce. • M-Sa 11:30am-2:30pm, 5-9pm; Su 5-9pm.

3 Amigos Taqueria ★ ¢: Kelly Ave. and Hwy 1, Half Moon Bay, (415) 726-6080. A fast-food atmosphere and great Mexican specialties. Cash only. • Daily 10am-10pm.

Two Fools ★ $: 408 Main St. (Kelly/Mill), Half Moon Bay, (415) 712-1222. The newest venture of established Peninsula chef Jesse Cool (of Flea Street Café) features a casual atmosphere and exceptionally fresh, stylishly prepared and presented organic salads, sandwiches, rotisserie chicken, and fish. Brunch and lunch fare includes healthy burritos with black beans and potatoes. The dinner menu focuses on hearty food to take out or eat in: fried chicken, shiitake mushroom stuffing, and great mashed potatoes. • M-F 11am-9pm; Sa-Su 9am-9pm.

Places to Stay

Cypress Inn $$$: 407 Mirada Rd., Half Moon Bay, (415) 726-6002, (800) 83-BEACH/832-3224. A cozy eight-room Santa Fe–style hideaway. Each room is impressively equipped with a fireplace and French doors that open onto a private deck with a view of the ocean. $150-$275.

Half Moon Bay State Beach ¢: Hwy 1 just south of Hwy 92 at Kelly Ave., Half Moon Bay, (415) 726-8820. There are 51 campsites located on the low bluff above the beach, all given out on a first-come first-served basis. You sign up on a waiting list starting at 8:30am and check back in the afternoon to see if you got a site. $15-$16/campsite.

Mill Rose Inn $$$: 615 Mill St., Half Moon Bay, (415) 726-9794. A romantic inn with attentive service. Enjoy an inviting English country garden setting. Separate entrances, private Jacuzzis, fluffy featherbeds, fireplaces, Champagne breakfasts, VCRs, and phones complete this luxurious picture. $165-$285.

SANTA CRUZ

Old Thyme Inn $$: 779 Main St., Half Moon Bay, (415) 726-1616. This charming downtown inn is cheerful and upbeat, with stuffed animals on every bed, and rooms named and decorated in an herbal theme. Weekdays $85-$165, weekends $105-$220.

Pigeon Point Lighthouse Hostel ¢: Pigeon Point Rd. and Hwy 1, Pescadero, (415) 879-0633. Made up of four buildings next to the still-functioning lighthouse, this hostel can house up to 50 people overnight. Reservations are recommended since rooms are sometimes booked months in advance. Check-in 4:30-9:30pm; closed 9:30am-4:30pm. $11 for AYH members, $14 for nonmembers.

Point Montara Lighthouse Hostel ¢: 16th St. and Hwy 1, Montara, (415) 728-7177. Check-in 4:30-9:30pm, closed 9:30am-4:30pm. A very interesting, inexpensive option featuring an outdoor hot tub and a functioning lighthouse. Rooms are booked weeks, if not months, in advance. $8 for AYH members, $10 for nonmembers.

SANTA CRUZ ★★

Idyllic Santa Cruz is southwest of the urban sprawl of the Bay Area, in redwood-covered hills that roll down to the sandy shores of the Pacific. With both the mountains and the ocean, Santa Cruz has unparalleled beauty and unlimited potential for outdoor activities. Far more than just a beach town, Santa Cruz offers a refreshing and peaceful atmosphere for all, a blend of the best of Northern and Southern California.

State Parks District Office: (408) 429-2850.
Santa Cruz Chamber of Commerce: (408) 423-1111.
Santa Cruz Visitors' Council: 701 Front St., Santa Cruz, (408) 425-1234. • M-Sa 9am-5pm; Su 10am-4pm.
Downtown Information: 1126 Pacific Ave., Santa Cruz, (408) 459-9486. Daily 10-8.

Getting There

The easiest way to get to Santa Cruz is by car. The most direct route is I-280 south to Hwy 17 west, which ends in Santa Cruz. (For a slight shortcut, from I-280 take Hwy 85 south to Hwy 17 west.) For a more scenic drive, take I-280 to Hwy 92 west to Hwy 1 south, a steep road that winds along the coast all the way to Santa Cruz.

The best method for getting to Santa Cruz sans car is to take CalTrain south all the way to the San Jose stop at 65 Cahill St. You should find a bus stop by the station where

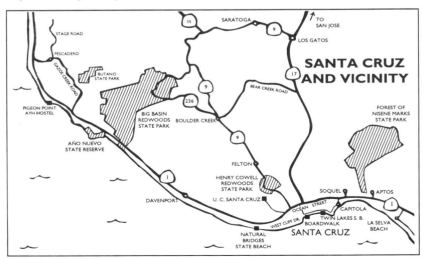

you can board the Amtrak bus called the "Santa Cruz Connector." For $5 ($8 round-trip) the bus will take you to the Metro Center in downtown Santa Cruz. Metro (408) 425-8600 provides Santa Cruz public transit, so you can then transfer to another bus depending on your final destination. The city of Santa Cruz has discontinued its free Beach Shuttle service. Instead, you can take bus #7 to the beach ($1/ride, $3/day pass).

Sights and Attractions

Santa Cruz Beach Boardwalk ★★: Beach St. at Riverside Ave., (408) 423-5590. The Boardwalk is a Coney Island-type amusement park—California's oldest—with a hair-raising, old-fashioned wooden roller coaster, a vintage, 85-year-old merry-go-round, and perhaps best of all, a collection of pinball machines and video games that includes all those classics which everyone else seems to have gotten rid of (Remember Joust?). The old rides can still offer a thrill—not the least because of their age—and are accompanied by the usual assortment of cotton candy and carny games. Cool off on the beach between rides. $17.95 day pass, individual rides $1.50-$3 each.

UC Santa Cruz ★: High St. at Bay Dr. on the hill above town. Central operator (408) 459-0111. Don't miss wandering around the redwood-shaded campus of UCSC. It is one of the smaller UC schools, and has perhaps the most beautiful campus of all nine schools. Enjoy the beautiful views of Monterey Bay from the athletic field, and the scent of both forest and ocean. The innovative **Shakespeare Santa Cruz** (408) 459-2121 series of plays, held in a wooded grove on the campus from July to September, shouldn't be missed. These interpretations of Shakespeare's plays are nontraditional and humorous, filled with drag queens and gender bending. Bring a blanket, a jug of wine, and a picnic. The truly adventurous should ask a student how to find **"Elfland"** and the **caves** located just across the Empire Grade.

Downtown Santa Cruz ★: Downtown centers around the outdoor **Pacific Garden Mall,** Pacific Ave. at Lincoln St., and offers a variety of intriguing bookstores, used-record stores, new-age crystal shops, as well as interesting cafés and restaurants. The atmosphere is upbeat—it's recovered from the devastating 1989 earthquake—but the number of languishing hippies and prepubescent panhandlers may at times make you think you're in the Haight. Book lovers will enjoy **Bookshop Santa Cruz** (408) 423-0900 at 1520 Pacific Ave., which has been in business since the 1960s and has everything from bestsellers to a gay and lesbian bulletin board. They're open daily 9am-11pm. Later in the day, visit **Kiva Hot Tubs** at 702 Water Street (408) 429-1142, which offers two outdoor tubs in a garden setting, as well as a dry redwood sauna. Two private tubs are also available. Clothing is optional; they're open Su-Th noon-11pm, F-Sa noon-midnight. Su 9am-noon it's reserved for women only.

Outdoor Activities

Beaches ★★★: The sandy beaches of Santa Cruz draw crowds from far and wide, especially on the weekends. If crowds and cotton candy aren't your thing, skip the Boardwalk and head across the San Lorenzo River toward Santa Cruz Harbor. **Sea Bright Beach ★★★** and **Twin Lakes State Beach ★★★** are two of the many pleasant places to enjoy the sand and sun, offering some of the best ocean swimming and bodysurfing in northern California. If you continue east from these beaches, you'll eventually come to **Capitola,** California's first seaside resort. Capitola is quaint, clean, and has great beach-side shopping; however, during the summer it can be just as crowded as Santa Cruz.

Heading west from the Boardwalk on West Cliff Drive, watch for the **Lighthouse Surfing Museum** (408) 429-3429 at Lighthouse Point, marked by a statue of a young surfer dude. They're open W-M noon-4pm. Lighthouse Point is a great place to watch the surfers below on **Steamer Lane,** or try the waves yourself. Surfing equipment and lessons are available at the north end of the boardwalk at **Cowell's Beach and Bikini,** 109 Beach St. (408) 427-2355. Just west of the Lighthouse, people gather daily at **It's Beach** to drum and dance at sunset. Continuing west from the point along West Cliff Drive, you'll find beautiful natural rock formations at **Natural Bridges State Beach** ★ (408) 423-4609, which is small and pretty, but has much colder, rougher water than the beaches to the east. Official parking is $6 ($5 seniors, $3 disabled); street parking outside the entrance is free but crowded. No dogs allowed.

Bike Path ★: A flat section of asphalt along West Cliff Drive between Natural Bridges and Capitola is perfect for rollerbladers, bikers, and joggers—no cars and lots of coastal scenery. Bring your bike. Rollerblades are available for rent at **Go Skate Surf and Sport**, at 601 Beach Street (408) 425-8578, open 10am-6pm daily (summer until 7pm), or rent a bike at **Pacific Avenue Cycles**, 709 Pacific Ave. (408) 423-1314.

Sea Kayaking ★: If you'd like to try a hand at sea kayaking, stop by **Venture Quest Kayak Rentals**, 125 Beach St. (408) 427-2267, open W-F 10am-5pm, Sa-Su noon-5pm, where they offer kayak rentals, lessons, and guided kayak tours of the area. **Adventure Sports**, 303 Potrero St., (408) 458-DO-IT/3648, also rents kayaks along with other water toys. Beginners are required to take an introductory class in basic paddling and safety before going out in a enclosed boat.

The Forest of Nisene Marks State Park ★: Aptos Creek Rd. off Soquel Dr. off Hwy 1, Aptos. This park has good hiking and mountain biking trails in a redwood forest.

Hwy 9 ★: Take a drive up Hwy 9 or Felton Empire Road to enjoy the redwoods and the small hippie towns along the way, such as **Felton**, **Ben Lomond**, and **Boulder Creek**. Another attraction in the Santa Cruz mountains is the wacky **Mystery Spot** ★, at 1953 North Branciforte Drive (408) 423-8897, a "natural phenomenon" where all laws of gravity are forgotten, balls roll uphill, and other bizarre events take place. Admission is $4, $2 for kids, and includes a bumper sticker; they're open 9am-8pm. About 30 minutes north of Santa Cruz on Hwy 236 lies **Big Basin Redwoods State Park** (see Peninsula Parks), with hiking, camping, and the gorgeous Berry Creek Falls.

Wineries ★

The Santa Cruz area, with almost two dozen wineries but without the crowds of Napa Valley, is a great destination for wine tasting.

Bargetto Winery: 3535-A N. Main St., Soquel, (408) 475-2258. Their tasting room is casual and packed with gourmet "foodstuffs." Enjoy the view of wooded Soquel Creek while you taste. The staff is passionate about their wines and loves to make recommendations. Bargetto is known for its fruit wines, such as olallieberry and apricot. Be sure to try the Chaucer's Mead. M-Sa 9am-5pm, Su 11am-5pm; tours M-F 11am and 2pm.

Bonny Doon: 10 Pine Flat Rd., Santa Cruz, (408) 425-3625. Wins honors for its Italian-style wines. Sep. 15-Apr. 15: Th-M noon-5pm. Apr. 16-Sep. 14: daily noon-5pm.

David Bruce Winery: 21439 Bear Creek Rd., Los Gatos, (408) 354-4214. Great winery for picnics. Daily noon-5pm.

Devlin Wine Cellars: 3801 Park Ave., Soquel, (408) 476-7288. Located on a 30-acre estate overlooking Monterey Bay. Try the champagne. Sa-Su noon-5pm.

Hallcrest Vineyards: 379 Felton Empire Rd., Felton, (408) 335-4441. Specializes in organic wines. Daily 11am-5:30pm.

Storrs Winery: 35 Potrero St., Santa Cruz, (408) 458-5030. Run by a husband-and-wife team who are both award-winning wine makers. F-M noon-5pm.

Restaurants and Entertainment

The Bagelry ✌: 320A Cedar St., Santa Cruz, (408) 429-8049. Fresh, inexpensive bagels made on the premises. Try the "slugs": large, misshapen bagels weighed down by "everything" (poppy and sesame seeds, onion, you name it). • M-F 6:30am-5:30pm; Sa 7:30am-5:30pm; Su 7:30am-4pm.

GETAWAYS

Balzac Bistro ★ **$$:** 112 Capitola Ave., Capitola, (408) 476-5035. European cuisine served in a casual atmosphere. The prices are great, and so is the British beer on tap. They also offer live jazz most nights. • Su-Th 4:30-10:30pm; F-Sa 4:30pm-midnight.

The Blue Lagoon: 923 Pacific Ave., Santa Cruz, (408) 423-7117. Behind the mirrored facade is a small, hopping dance club playing the latest techno and rave for a mostly gay and bisexual crowd. (But all are welcome.)

Benten ★★ **$$:** 1541 B Pacific Ave., Santa Cruz, (408) 425-7079. A cozy, clean place serving great Japanese food. • M, W-F 11:30am-2:30pm, 5:30-9pm; Sa-Su 12:30-9pm.

Caffè Lido ★ ¢: 110 Monterey Ave., Capitola, (408) 475-6544. Well-placed windows capture the afternoon sun and fill the main room with light. Rich desserts and strong espresso. • W-Th, Su 11:30am-9pm, F-Sa 11:30am-10pm.

Caffè Pergolesi ★ ¢: 418 Cedar St., Santa Cruz, (408) 426-1775. Bearing the name "Dr. Miller's," this artsy, Victorian house is the UCSC slacker place for desserts, espresso, and Indian Chai. (The owners scored on those dark-wood church pews in the side room.) There's a large, shady deck for whiling the hours away. • Daily 8am-midnight.

The Catalyst ★ **$:** 1011 Pacific Garden Mall, Santa Cruz, (408) 423-1338. The light, airy atrium is perfect for brunch. (Glance around. See all those plants? This used to be *the* fern bar in the 1970s). At night this is still the happening place. Play pool upstairs or check out the band in the back (anything from acoustic rock to hillbilly blues). This was the town's bowling alley in the 1950s. The stage sits where the pins used to fall. • Cover charge $1 and up; 21 and over. Shows start around 9:30pm.

Espresso Royale Café ★ ¢: 1545 Pacific Ave., Santa Cruz, (408) 429-9804. A great café with a peaceful garden courtyard to offset that coffee buzz. Hang with your laptop and check out the ever-changing art installations. Don't leave without trying the India Joze biscotti. • M-F 7am-midnight, Sa-Su 8am-midnight.

The Fog Bank ★ **$:** 211 Esplanade, Capitola, (408) 462-1881. A casual bar scene for grabbing a burger or sandwich. Sit at the outdoor bar to best survey the beach scene. • M-F 10am-11pm, Sa-Su 9am-2am.

India Joze ★★ **$:** Art Center, 1001 Center St., Santa Cruz, (408) 427-3554. Your friends will tire of hearing you rave about this place after your meal here. (Yes, the food is that good.) An extremely original restaurant serving spicy Middle Eastern and Asian cuisine. For added fun, the menu changes weekly. (And remember: leave room for the chocolate truffles.) • M-Sa 11:30am-2:30pm, 5:30-9:30pm; Su 10am-2:30pm, 5:30-9pm. Caffè Beppe serves light snacks daily 2:30-5:30pm.

Kuumbwa Jazz Center: 320-2 E. Cedar St., Santa Cruz, (408) 427-2227. A jazz bar popular with older locals and those "in-the-know." The small venue lends an intimacy to performances. • Cover $5 and up. Call for showtimes and scheduling.

Mr. Toots Coffeehouse ★ ¢: 221 Esplanade, Capitola, (408) 475-3679. A comfortable, earthy hang-out with live jazz/classical guitar nightly. Slouch around on garage-sale couches, get intellectual at the long study table, or head for the balcony out back and trip on the waves. • Su-Th 7:30am-midnight, F-Sa 7:30am-1am.

New Leaf ¢: 1134 Pacific Ave., Santa Cruz, (408) 425-5323. This small, well-stocked organic grocery and deli makes a fine place to pick up picnic fixings before heading to the beach or the hills. • Daily 9am-9pm.

Omei's ★★★ **$:** 2316 Mission St., Santa Cruz, (408) 425-8458. It doesn't look like much from the parking lot, but once inside, you'll find this romantic setting offers delicious Chinese food. • M-Th 11:30am-2pm, 5-9:30pm; F 11:30am-2pm, 5-10pm; Sa 5-10pm; Su 5-9:30pm.

The Red Room: 1003 Cedar St., Santa Cruz, (408) 425-0591. It's actually two rooms, complete with dance floor, bar, live music, and hoards of slacker-types on weekends.

Royal Taj ★ **$**: 270 Soquel Ave., Santa Cruz, (408) 427-2400. Reasonably priced Indian food served in peaceful and comfortable surroundings. A short walk from downtown. • Daily 11:30am-2:30pm; 5:30-10pm.

Santa Cruz Brewing Company and Front Street Pub ★ **$**: 516 Front St., Santa Cruz, (408) 429-8838. Great beer on tap, all brewed on the premises, and a pub menu. Live music some nights. • Su-Tu 11:30am-11pm; W-Sa 11:30am-midnight.

Santa Cruz Coffee Roasting Company ★ **¢**: 1330 Pacific Ave., Santa Cruz, (408) 459-0100. One of the original cafés downtown. Grab a cup of (individually brewed) joe and check out the scene from their patio. • M-Th 6:30am-11pm; Sa-Su 6:30-midnight.

Seabright Brewery ★ **$$**: 519 Seabright Ave., Santa Cruz, (408) 426-2739. Good place for drinks and outdoor dining. During warm days, the outdoor patio is jammed with rollerbladers, mountain bikers, beach goers, and locals who quaff steins, swap stories, and (possibly) exchange phone numbers. • Daily 11:30am-10pm.

Shadowbrook ★ **$$$**: 1750 Wharf Rd., Capitola, (408) 475-1511. A town classic. Always voted the city's "most romantic" dining spot. Take the single-car funicular from the upper terrace down to the restaurant. Or walk through the intriguing, garden-lined paths that lead to the dining room entrance. Be forewarned: The gorgeous setting overshadows the food (but not the prices). • M-Th 5:30-9:15pm; F 5-9:45pm; Sa 4-10:45pm; Su 10am-2:15pm, 4-9:45pm.

Tacos Moreno ★ **$**: 1053 Water St., Santa Cruz, (408) 429-6095. Inexpensive family-style Mexican food. Cash only. • Daily 11am-8pm.

Wharf House ★ **$$**: 1400 Wharf Rd., Ste. B, Capitola, (408) 476-3534. Built at the end of the 125-year old Capitola Wharf, this is a great place to catch outdoor jazz on weekends and enjoy the great view of the ocean. • Daily 8am-3pm, 5-10pm (earlier in winter).

Zackery's Restaurant ★★ **$**: 819 Pacific Ave., Santa Cruz, (408) 427-0646. Popular place with great healthy breakfasts. You may have to wait as long as an hour on the weekend, but the curry-tofu scramble is well worth it. • Tu-Su 7am-2:30pm.

Places to Stay

Camping & Hostels

Destinet State Parks Camping Reservations: (800) 444-7275.

New Brighton State Beach $: (408) 475-4850. From Santa Cruz, take Hwy 1 South to beach exit. This is a great wooded park with separate facilities for car and bike campers. $17 Su-Th, $18 F-Sa; extra cars $6; hikers and bikers $3, dogs $1. Day use $6.

Santa Cruz American Youth Hostel $: 321 Main St., Santa Cruz, (408) 423-8304. Dubbed "the friendliest hostel in the West," this small, charming, post-Victorian house attracts foreign travelers and backpackers in the summer. The hostel is a 10-minute walk from the downtown bus stop and has parking. $12. Call 8-10am or 6-10pm to reach a person instead of a message for reservations.

Hotels, Motels, and B&Bs

Babbling Brook Bed and Breakfast Inn $$$: 1025 Laurel St., Santa Cruz, (408) 427-2437. A restored country inn with 12 rooms, all boasting private baths and French decor. Fireplaces, private decks, and a garden stream contribute to the romantic setting. Located near the beach, shops, and boardwalk. $85-$165.

Cliff Crest Bed and Breakfast Inn $$$: 407 Cliff St., Santa Cruz, (408) 427-2609. A Queen Anne-style house with five rooms, one with a fireplace. Full breakfast is served in the rooms or the solarium, and wine and cheese are offered in the evenings. $95-$165.

GETAWAYS

The Darling House $$$: 314 West Cliff Dr., Santa Cruz, (408) 458-1958. An eight-room oceanside mansion dating from 1910, with antique furnishings. Continental breakfast is served in the dining rooms, and most rooms have a shared bath. $95-$225.

Inn Cal $$: 370 Ocean St., Santa Cruz, (408) 458-9220. It's 10 minutes from the Boardwalk, and has all the comforts of home (color TV, air conditioning, and telephones) but is a bit noisy due to the location. $35-$100.

Peter Pan Motel $$: 313 Riverside Ave., Santa Cruz, (408) 423-1393. A low-cost option near the beach and Boardwalk. $48-98.

Terrace Court $$: 125 Beach St., Santa Cruz, (408) 423-3031. A most excellent location directly across from the wharf. Rent a room on one of the two terraces facing the ocean. (Or stay in a poolside unit with a kitchenette.) The husband-and-wife management team will treat you like family. $90-$120 (summer); $80-$95 (winter).

TAHOE ★★

Lake Tahoe, the second deepest lake in the United States, is the center of the region known to many simply as "Tahoe." Rand McNally has named the area "America's Number One Resort Area," and justifiably so—there's skiing and snowboarding in the winter; hiking, camping, biking, water sports, and other outdoor activities in the summer; and gambling on the Nevada side year-round.

Most people break the area up into North Lake and South Lake. South Lake is centered around the towns South Lake Tahoe, California and adjacent Stateline, Nevada. This area embodies the honky-tonk hustle of Stateline's casinos, although it still has its share of outdoorsy activity with the lovely Desolation Wilderness and many state parks nearby. North Lake Tahoe commercial activity is less concentrated, spread out along the lake from the low-key resort town Tahoe City to pricy Incline Village (aka Income Village), and extending far from the lake to the Truckee-Donner Lake area, a mixture of old-West history and modern strip malls.

General Information

Road Conditions: California (800) 427-ROAD/7623. Nevada (702) 793-1313.

South Lake Tahoe Chamber of Commerce: 3066 L. Tahoe Blvd., South Lake Tahoe, (916) 541-5255. M-F 8:30am-5pm; Sa 9am-4pm. Visitor information.

South Lake Tahoe Visitors Authority: (800) AT-TAHOE/288-2463. Lodging reservations.

North Lake Tahoe Resort Association: 950 N. Lake Boulevard, Tahoe City, (916) 583-3494, (800) TAHOE-4U/824-6348. Visitor information M-F 8am-5pm. Lodging reservations: (800) 822-5959. M-F 7am-7pm (F until 6:30pm); Sa 9am-4pm; Su 9am-2pm.

North Lake Tahoe Chamber of Commerce: (916) 581-6900.

U.S. Forest Service Visitor Information: Hwy 89, 3 mi. north of the "Y" in S. Lake Tahoe, (916) 573-2674. Summer daily 8am-5:30pm; fall Sa-Su only; winter closed.

Getting There

When driving, take I-80 east to Sacramento; turn onto Hwy 50 to South Lake Tahoe or continue on I-80 toward Truckee and the North Shore. Reno is another 35 miles past Truckee. It can snow heavily without much warning at any time of the year; always carry chains. Also avoid leaving the Bay Area any time near 5pm on Friday.

Greyhound (800) 231-2222 or (702) 588-4645 runs a few daily buses to South Lake Tahoe, Truckee, and Reno from San Francisco; the one-way fare is around $21. **Amtrak** (800) 872-7245 runs from Oakland and San Jose to South Lake, Truckee, and Reno. Most trips involve a train to Sacramento and a bus to your destination, but an occasional train offering spectacular views goes all the way to Truckee and Reno (reservations required for this train). The round-trip fare to South Lake is around

$33, to Truckee around $53 (one-way fares are almost the same as round-trip). **South Lake Tahoe Airport** (916) 542-6180 is tiny. It is currently without commercial service, although flights are expected to resume around Christmas 1996. The airport is a short cab or shuttle-bus ride from South Lake Tahoe. There are frequent flights into **Reno Airport** (702) 328-6400, but it's an hour from Lake Tahoe, so you may have to rent a car or take a shuttle; try the **Tahoe Casino Express** (800) 446-6128, **Tours Unlimited** (916) 546-1355, **Budget Chauffer** (800) 426-5644, or **Aerotrans** (702) 786-2376.

Once in Tahoe, **TART**, Tahoe Area Regional Transit (916) 581-6365, offers bus service through the North Lake area, including winter ski area shuttles (ski and bike accessible). **STAGE**, South Tahoe Area Ground Express, (916) 573-2080, serves the South Lake Tahoe area with buses, tourist trolleys, and, for those far from bus lines, Bus Plus shuttle service.

Skiing & Snowboarding ★★

Because the Sierra is the first mountain range in from the coast, storms bring heavy, wet snows that are measured in feet, not inches. It's reasonable to expect snow from December to May. However, snowfall varies dramatically. During a bad year, ski areas might get 200 inches of snow, while during a good year they might get 600 inches.

The region offers a wide variety of skiing options, from huge resorts to tiny mom-and-pop hills. Tahoe also has many good cross-country ski resorts. **Royal Gorge** claims to be the largest in the United States. Many downhill resorts have trails, as do **Claire Tappaan Lodge** and **Alpine Skills Institute**. Many people prefer free "backwoods" skiing—you can often spot the trailhead by the cars parked on the side of the road. Many parking areas are part of California State Parks Sno-Park program, and require a permit; check with a local sports shop or call State Parks, (916) 653-6995. Stop in at any outdoors store for advice and trail maps. **Castle Peak** is a good starting point, just across I-80 from Boreal Ski Area (you can buy a Sno-Park permit at Boreal). In addition to shops at ski areas, there are rental shops in Truckee, Tahoe City, and South Lake.

Ski Club Hotline: (510) 827-4303. Lists phone numbers of various Bay Area ski clubs.

Alpine Meadows: Off Hwy 89 between Truckee and Tahoe City, (916) 583-4232, (800) 441-4423. The "other" large area in North Lake, but much smaller than Squaw. Offers ample variety, including steep chutes accessed by climbing. Well-sheltered in stormy weather. The last area to close in the spring. A local favorite, in part because of candid snow reports and retro feel, although opening the mountain to snowboarding may change this. 1,553' vert. $46 adult.

Boreal Ski Area: Just off I-80 at Boreal/Castle Peak exit, (916) 426-3666, (916) 426-1114. A little area that offers a good variety of runs for beginners and intermediates, and night skiing. Right off highway on top of Donner pass, so it's convenient and gets lots of snow. Popular with snowboarders, who should appreciate new, *lower* prices. Also owns **Soda Springs**, a tiny area off Hwy 40 near Norden. 600' vert. $27 adult.

Diamond Peak at Ski Incline: Off Hwy 28, Incline Village, Nevada, (702) 832-1126. 24-hour ski information: (702) 831-3211. Small area just across the state line. It's a bit harder to reach (which means smaller crowds) and can have good snow when other areas are lacking. Recently increased its skiable terrain, adding numerous expert runs at the top of the mountain. Cross-country area. 1,840' vert. $37 adult.

Donner Ski Ranch: Old Hwy 40 about 6 mi. from I-80 Soda Springs/Norden exit, (916) 426-3635. Mom-and-pop sized, but offers some good intermediate terrain, a homey atmosphere, and night skiing. 750' vert. $20 adult ($10 mid-week).

Heavenly Valley: Ski Run Blvd. from Hwy 50 in South Lake Tahoe or Tramway Dr. off Kingsbury Grade east of Stateline, (916) 541-SKII/7544, (916) 541-1330, (702) 586-7000. Huge resort claiming the most skiable terrain of any resort in the United States. Experts prefer the Nevada side. It also offers great views and is just minutes from the casinos and accommodations in Stateline. Suffers from overcrowding and a confusing trail network. 3,600' vert. $47 adult.

GETAWAYS

Homewood: Hwy 89, 6 mi. south of Tahoe City, (916) 525-2992, (916) 525-2900. Small area—although bigger than what you see from the road—with mostly intermediate runs and classic postcard views of Lake Tahoe. It may be the best place to ski on the weekends and is definitely an ideal place to learn to snowboard. 1,650' vert. $35 adult.

Kirkwood Ski and Summer Resort: Hwy 88 from the Central Valley, or 1/2 hour south of South Lake Tahoe off Hwy 89, (209) 258-6000, (415) 989-SNOW/7669. Medium-sized ski area with diverse terrain, including radical steeps and smaller crowds. High base elevation leads to drier snow. Cross country. 2,000' vert. $42 adult.

Mt. Rose Ski Resort: Rt. 431 near Incline Village, Nevada, (702) 849-0704, (800) SKI-ROSE/754-7673. Another small area across the state line offering a surprising amount of challenging terrain. Good on powder days. 1,450' vert. $38 adult.

Northstar-at-Tahoe: Hwy 267 between Truckee and North Lake Tahoe, (800) GO-NORTH/466-6784, (916) 562-1010, (916) 562-1330. Large, planned resort with the motto, "Northstar has it all," including luxury condominiums, cross-country, and a golf course. Medium-sized ski area with many beginner and intermediate cruising runs (locals call it Flatstar). 2,200' vert. $45 adult.

Royal Gorge: Off Old Hwy 40 from I-80 Soda Springs/Norden exit, (916) 426-3871. Huge cross-country ski area, with well-groomed tracks for kick-and-glide and skating. Serves all levels from beginners to competitive racers. Full-service lodge with rentals, lessons, and underfriendly employees. $19.50 adult.

Sierra at Tahoe: Off Hwy 50 between Echo Summit and South Lake Tahoe, (916) 659-7453. Formerly named Sierra Ski Ranch. Provides bowl skiing for intermediates and a nurturing atmosphere for beginners. 2,212' vert. $39 adult.

Squaw Valley: Hwy 89 between Tahoe City and Truckee, (916) 583-6985, (916) 583-6955. Squaw Valley is huge, offering everything from serious cliff jumping to gentle bunny hills. There's even a mountain-top outdoor skating rink, swimming pool, and bungee jumping. But be prepared for long lift lines on weekends, steep ticket prices, and a glitzy scene. The upper lifts are often closed on windy days. Squaw employees wear buttons that say "We Care," but everyone knows they don't. 2,850' vert. $46 adult.

Sugar Bowl Ski Resort: Old Hwy 40 about three miles from I-80 Soda Springs/Norden exit, (916) 426-3651. Medium-sized area with varied terrain. Ridge-top location draws good snow coverage. A recent expansion added road access to the Mt. Judah base area—good for those who don't like riding the creaky old gondola to the base lodge. Slow, old lifts stop a lot. 1,500' vert. $42 adult.

Tahoe Donner: Northwoods Blvd., north of I-80 from first Truckee exit, (916) 587-9444, (916) 587-9494. Tiny area associated with subdivision offering limited beginner and intermediate skiing. Family-oriented. Excellent cross-country area. $26 adult.

Warm-Weather Activities ★★

Parks and Beaches ★★

Much of the area around Lake Tahoe is public land; either State Park, National Forest, or local park. Most of the parks are open from approximately Memorial Day through Labor Day, weather permitting. **Donner Memorial State Park** (916) 582-7894, off I-80 on Donner Pass Road near Truckee, lies on the edge of **Donner Lake**. It's a beautiful spot for a short visit or camping, and there's even a museum which tells the Donner Party's grisly story—stranded pioneers reduced to cannibalism—open daily 10am to 5pm year-round. Off Hwy 89 along the west side of the lake, you'll find three state parks: **Sugar Pine Point** (916) 525-7982, **D. L. Bliss** (916) 525-7277, and **Emerald Bay** ★★ (916) 541-3030, home to shoreline beaches, camping, and trails. While at Emerald Bay, visit the Scandinavian mansion Vikingsholm. In **Lake Tahoe Nevada State Park** (702-831-0494) on the northeastern side of Lake Tahoe, you'll find **Sand Harbor**, a beautiful beach with shallow water that warms up enough for swimming. During the summer, Sand Harbor often hosts theater or music performances on its outdoor stage.

Desolation Wilderness ★★★: along the southwest side of Lake Tahoe. This magnificent area's austere beauty has much to offer day hikers and backpackers. There are four primary entry points: Emerald Bay and Fallen Leaf Lake off Hwy 89, and Echo Lake and Horsetail Falls off Hwy 50. It's one of California's most popular wilderness areas, so you won't find total solitude on the trail during summer weekends, but you will find crystal clear lakes nestled under ragged peaks and plenty of memorable vistas.

Aquatic Sports ★

Because Lake Tahoe is so large, it is always cold—the warmest it gets is 65 degrees—but never freezes over. However, the brave still swim, ski, sail, and otherwise indulge in the lake. Donner Lake is also cold, but popular for skiing and fishing.

Jet ski and **boat rentals** are a popular way to get out on the water for a few pricy hours. Reservations are recommended. On Tahoe's north shore, Kings Beach and

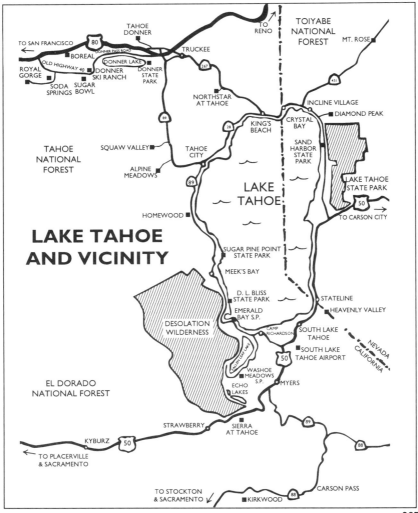

GETAWAYS

Tahoe City have the most active marinas. In King's Beach, try **North Tahoe Marina** (916) 546-8248, located at the Kings Beach marina (just west of Hwy 267), or **King's Beach Aquasports** (916) 546-AQUA/2782, on the east side of King's Beach. **Tahoe Paddle and Oar** (916) 581-3029, at the North Tahoe Beach Center across from Hwy 267, rents a variety of nonmotorized water toys. At the Tahoe City marina (central Tahoe City behind the Boatworks Mall), try **Lighthouse Watersports Center** (916) 583-6000 and **Tahoe Water Adventures** (916) 583-3225. On the west shore just south of Tahoe City in Sunnyside, **High Sierra Water Ski School** (916) 583-7417 has a variety of boats, including sailboats. In South Lake Tahoe, head for Timber Cove Marina on Lakeshore Boulevard at Park Avenue just west of the state line, where you'll find the **South Lake Tahoe Marina** (916) 541-6626, **Timber Cove Marina** (916) 542-4472 for jet skis; (916) 544-2942 for boats and canoes, and **Kayak Tahoe** (916) 544-2011. For a more relaxed exploration of the lake, hop on the glass-bottomed **Tahoe Queen** (916) 541-3364 or (800) 23-TAHOE/238-2463, at Hwy 50 and Ski Run Boulevard. They offer daily Emerald Bay cruises and sunset dinner-dance trips. The Emerald Bay trip costs about $14 for adults; the sunset cruise costs about $18 plus dinner.

Mountain Biking ★★★

There are a number of excellent rides throughout the Tahoe hills, free from all the rules and regulations prevalent in the Bay Area. Most Tahoe bike stores can give you advice on their favorite rides, but there is an endless supply of fire roads from which to choose. Serious riders should ask about the Flume Trail. Most of the bigger ski areas listed above open their trails to bikes in summer and offer bike rentals and even lift service (start with Squaw Valley and Northstar).

Rentals are available at those ski areas and at bike stores in Tahoe City, Truckee, and South Lake for about $20-$25/day. In downtown Tahoe City, try **Olympic Bicycle Shop** (916) 581-2500 at 620 North Lake Boulevard (just west of the Boatworks Mall) for higher performance gear or **Porter's Ski & Sport** (916) 583-2314 across the street at 501 North Lake Boulevard for basic bikes. In Truckee, **Dave's Summer Sports** (916) 582-0900 is at 10200 Donner Pass Road, just west of the downtown train station; Porter's has a second location in the Lucky Shopping Center on Hwy 89 just south of I-80. In South Lake Tahoe, bike rentals are available at **Tahoe Cyclery** (916) 541-2726, located at 3552 Hwy 50, **Anderson's** (916) 541-0500, located at 645 Emerald Bay Road (aka Hwy 89) at 13th Street, and **Sierra Cycleworks** (916) 541-7505 at 3430 Hwy 50.

Gambling ★

Nevada's casinos conspicuously mark the border between that state and California. (Remember that you must be 21 to get in.) Tahoe's casinos can offer some great deals (Reno's are the best!) including moderate room and meal prices and cheap entertainment in their lounges. Look for all-you-can-eat buffet specials for $5 or less.

On the south shore, **Caesar's**, **Harrah's**, and the other big-name casinos cater to visitors with lots of cash—they raise the minimum betting limits throughout the night. If you're looking to test the waters with small bets, find a $2 or $3 blackjack table at **Harvey's** or the **Horizon**, friendly, low-key places. Most casinos on the north shore are in Crystal Bay, Nevada. The biggest club on the north shore, however, is the **Hyatt**, which is off by itself in Incline Village.

Caesar's: 55 Hwy 50, Stateline, NV, (702) 588-3515, (800) 648-3353.

Crystal Bay: 14 Hwy 28, Crystal Bay, NV, (702) 831-0512.

Harrah's: Hwy 50, Stateline, NV, (702) 588-6611, (800) 648-3773.

Harvey's: Hwy 50, Stateline, NV, (800) 648-3361.

Horizon Resort Hotel Casino: Hwy 50, Stateline, NV, (702) 588-6211, (800) 648-3322.

Hyatt Regency Lake Tahoe Resort and Casino: 111 Country Club Dr. (at Lakeshore Dr.), Incline Village, NV, (702) 831-1111, (800) 233-1234.

Tahoe Biltmore Lodge and Casino: 5 Hwy 28, Crystal Bay, NV, (702) 831-0660, (800) BILTMORE/245-8667.

Restaurants and Entertainment

The Beacon ★★ $$: 1900 Jamieson Beach Rd. (off Hwy 89 at Camp Richardson), South Lake Tahoe, (916) 541-0630. Standard California fare along with its signature Rum Runner cocktail in a beachfront location. • Daily 11am-9pm.

Bridge Tender ★ $: 30 W. Lake Blvd. (Hwy 89), Tahoe City, (916) 583-3342. Live trees grow through the roof, and outdoor seating overlooks Fanny Bridge. Burgers, fries, and other pub grub. • Daily 11am-11pm; bar open until 2am.

Cantina Los Tres Hombres ★ $: 765 Emerald Bay Rd. (Hwy 89), South Lake Tahoe, (916) 544-1233. Margaritas and Mexican food. • Daily 11:30am-11pm.

Chart House ★★ $$$: 392 Kingsbury Grade, Stateline, NV, (702) 588-6276. Well-done surf-and-turf with great views of the lake. • Su-F 5:30-10pm; Sa 5-10:30pm.

Christy Hill ★★★ $$$$: 115 Grove St. off N. Lake Blvd. near marina), Tahoe City, (916) 583-8551. Creative California cuisine considered by many to be the finest in Tahoe. The multilevel dining room is located in a simply furnished house—lots of pink and gray—with the decorative emphasis on the spectacular lake views. • Tu-Su 5:30-9:30pm.

Donner Lake Kitchen ★ $: 13720 Donner Pass Rd., Truckee (behind Donner Pines Store along Donner Lake), (916) 587-3119. Popular local diner for home-style and Mexican breakfasts and lunches. Love the velvet paintings. Cash only. • Daily 7am-2pm.

Fire Sign Café ★★ $: 1785 W. Lake Blvd./Hwy 89, Tahoe Park (5 mi. south of Tahoe City), (916) 583-0871. A great spot for breakfast or a healthy lunch. Pleasant patio. • Daily 7am-3pm.

Frank's Restaurant ★ $: 1207 Emerald Bay Rd. (Hwy 89), South Lake Tahoe, (916) 544-3434. An amazing place for home-cooked breakfast. • M-Sa 6am-2pm; Su 7am-2pm.

La Hacienda del Lago ★ $: Boatworks Mall, 760 N. Lake Blvd. (Hwy 28), Tahoe City, (916) 583-0358. Tasty Mexican food and free-flowing margaritas at this festive local hangout. Happening night life. • Daily 11:30am-10pm.

Heidi's ★ $: 3485 Lake Tahoe Blvd. (Hwy 50), South Lake Tahoe, (916) 544-8113. They claim to serve "the best breakfast you'll ever have." Good lunches, too. • Daily 7am-2pm.

Jake's on the Lake ★★ $$: Boatworks Mall, 780 N. Lake Blvd. (Hwy 28), Tahoe City, (916) 583-0188. A swinging night spot ("snakes on the make"), with surprisingly good American food, especially seafood and pasta. • Daily 10am-10:30pm.

Lake Tahoe Pizza Co. ★ $: 1168 Emerald Bay Rd. (Hwy 50/89, just south of the Y), South Lake Tahoe, (916) 544-1919. Fantastic pizza place. • Daily 4-10pm.

O.B.'s Pub and Restaurant ★ $$/$$$: 10046 Commercial Row, Truckee, (916) 587-4164. A favorite among locals. Large, dark saloon serving a range of hearty American food from burgers to pasta to grilled salmon. • Daily 11:30am-10pm.

The Passage ★★★ $$$: Truckee Hotel, 1007 Bridge St. (at Commercial), Truckee, (916) 587-7619. Creatively prepared and presented California cuisine in a historic, candlelit dining room. Game specials can be superb. • M-Th 11:30am-3pm, 5:30-9:30pm; F-Sa 11:30am-3pm, 5:30-10pm; Su 10am-3pm, 5:30-9:30pm.

River Ranch Lodging and Dining ★★ $$/$$$: 2285 River Rd. (Hwy 89 at Alpine Meadows Rd.), Tahoe City, (916) 583-4264. Dark and cozy restaurant near Alpine Meadows with good basic food and great views of the Truckee River. If you don't want a serious meal, get a burger by the fireplace in the bar or out on the patio. • Patio Su-Th 11am-7pm; F-Sa 11am-8pm. Dining Room Su-Th 6-9:30pm; F-Sa 6-10pm.

Rosie's Café ★ $$: 571 North Lake Blvd. (Hwy 28), Tahoe City, (916) 583-8504. Eclectic, healthy menu in country saloon setting. Particularly good breakfasts. • M-F 8am-2:30pm, 5-9pm; Sa-Su 7:30am-2:30pm, 5-10pm.

GETAWAYS

Squeeze Inn ★ $: 10060 Commercial Row, Truckee, (916) 587-9814. Very popular local spot for great omelets (limitless variety of options), as well as other breakfast and lunch dishes. No credit cards. • Daily 7am-2pm.

Sunnyside Resort ★ $$: 1850 West Lake Boulevard, Tahoe City, (916) 583-7200. Sports a large deck on the lake and standard sandwich and burger fare. Especially pleasant for summer brunch. • M-Sa 10am-2pm, 5-10pm; Su 9am-2pm, 5-10pm (no breakfast and shorter dinner hours during winter).

Truckee Trattoria ★★ $$: Gateway Shopping Center, Hwy 89 at Old Hwy 40, Truckee, (916) 582-1266. Surprising find in a Safeway strip mall. Bright and clean setting for light California and Italian cuisine. Special entrées shine more than pastas. Liberal corkage policy. Reservations recommended. • Su, W-Th 5-9pm; F-Sa 5-9:30pm.

Wolfdale's ★★★ $$$: 640 N. Lake Blvd., Tahoe City, (916) 583-5700. Highly regarded Asian-California vegetarian cuisine. Reservations recommended. • Dinner W-M 6-whenever; nightly during summer.

Za's ★ $/$$: 395 N. Lake Blvd. (Hwy 28), Tahoe City, (916) 583-1812. A tiny local's favorite where the waitstaff remembers regulars. Za's bills itself as a simple Italian restaurant, and lives up to it with hearty basic pasta, calzone, and pizza laden with garlic. Hidden behind Pete & Peter's bar. • Su-Th 4:30-9:30pm; F-Sa 4:30-10pm.

Places to Stay

In addition to the places listed below, try the North and South Tahoe Visitors Bureaus, Chambers of Commerce, and Central Reservations numbers listed under *General Information* for most places to stay; they handle house and condo rentals, hotels, or inns. Also, **casinos** frequently offer good deals on weekend packages, figuring what you don't cough up in lodging you'll spend on gambling. **Renting houses** for a week or weekend is a good option for groups. Central Reservations' numbers should be able to handle short-term rentals. Many groups rent a house for the entire ski season. Tahoe realty companies have listings of available properties for short-term or seasonal rentals. The best bets for luxury accommodations are renting a nice condo (or house) or staying in one of the more upscale casinos such as the Hyatt.

Camping

Camping is available on most of the public lands around Tahoe, including the parks listed above. Most campgrounds are only open late spring and summer, although **Sugar Pine Point** and **Grover Hot Springs State Park** are both available for year-round camping. If you intend to camp in organized campgrounds between May and September, make reservations well in advance.

Destinet: (800) 444-7275. State Park campground reservations.
Biospherics: (800) 280-2267. Forest Service campground reservations.
Camp Richardson $/$$: Hwy 89, 2 mi. north of Hwy 50, South Lake Tahoe, (916) 541-1801. Private development with an 83-acre campground on the south shore that boasts 112 campsites with hot showers, a beach, a marina, and Nordic skiing in the winter. Lodging includes an inn as well as cabins (minimum one-week rental during summer). Campsites $17, lodge $64-84, cabins $495/week and up.

Hotels, Motels, and B&Bs

Alpine Skills International Lodge $/$$: Old Hwy 40 off I-80 at Norden/Soda Springs exit, (916) 426-9108. A mountaineering school that offers bunk-and-breakfast accommodations. Lodge open full-time Thanksgiving-mid-April; during course times June-September; closed spring and fall. $24 bunk bed; $75 double-occupancy room.

Best Western Truckee Tahoe $$: 11331 Hwy 267, 1.5 mi. south of Truckee, (916) 587-4525. Basic, clean, and comfortable, with pool, Jacuzzi, sauna, and skimpy continental breakfast. $69-$99.

Clair Tappaan Lodge $: Old Hwy 40 off I-80 at Norden/Soda Springs exit, (916) 426-3632. Run by the Sierra Club, this huge old building has dormitory-style rooms; price includes family-style meals. $33-$37/Sierra Club members, $37-$39/nonmembers.

Donner Country Inn $$: 10070 Gregory Place (Donner Lake Rd. at Donner Pass Rd.), Truckee, (916) 587-5574. Tiny, unassuming motel has comfortable rooms—some with wood-burning stoves. Minimum two night stay. $95.

Loch Leven Lodge $$: 13855 Donner Pass Rd., along Donner Lake, Truckee, (916) 587-3773. Lakeside lodge with a big deck and hot tubs. Some rooms have fireplaces or kitchenettes. Cash or checks only. $66-$136.

Squaw Valley Central Reservations: (800) 545-4350. Handles reservations for Squaw Valley and beyond. **Resort at Squaw Creek $$$$** is the newest, most deluxe property, although there are other, older facilities. Also handles condos and houses. $149-$325.

Super 8 Lodge $$: 11506 Deerfield Dr. (off Hwy 89 just south of I-80), Truckee, (916) 587-8888. Not charming, but convenient, with Jacuzzi and sauna. $68-$104.

Tahoe City Travelodge $$: 455 N. Lake Blvd., Tahoe City, (916) 583-3766, (800) 255-3050. Basic, clean, and comfortable, with pool. In town. $69-$105.

Trade Winds Motel $: 944 Friday Ave., Stateline, NV, (800) 628-1829. Two blocks from the casinos. Coffee makers, and a year-round spa and pool are included. $48-$98.

Truckee Hotel $$: 10007 Bridge St. (at Commercial Row), Truckee, (916) 587-4444, (800) 659-6921. A country-quaint historic building with reasonable prices (especially for European-style rooms). Breakfast included. $60-$115.

WINE COUNTRY ★★

The Napa and Sonoma Valleys are renowned as much for their scenic beauty as for their award-winning wines. In the Napa Valley, vineyards are scattered along a 35-mile stretch of land between the towns of Napa to the south and Calistoga (home of the hot springs and the bottled water) to the north. In between are Yountville, Rutherford, Oakville, and St. Helena; all quaint communities. The Sonoma Valley is less traveled than its neighbor, but is home to many quality wineries and other points of interest in the towns of Sonoma and Kenwood, and the small settlements in the Russian River Valley. Couples favor the region's numerous bed-and-breakfasts and intimate restaurants, which make for romantic (though often pricy) weekend retreats. For a most enjoyable visit, try to avoid going in summer, when temperatures regularly top 100 degrees, other tourists clog every and all spaces, and lodging prices skyrocket. Spring can be lush and fragrant, fall brings the excitement of the harvest, and winter offers peaceful seclusion (and off-season discount accommodations).

Napa ★★

Until Spanish explorers arrived in 1823, the Napa Valley was populated by the Nappa Indian tribe. American farmers began settling the region in the 1830s, and in 1833, George Calvert Yount (Yountville's namesake) planted the first vineyard in the valley. It was Charles Krug, however, who brought Riesling grapes to the area in 1861, launching the wine business in earnest.

Calistoga Chamber of Commerce: 1458 Lincoln Ave. #4, Calistoga, (707) 942-6333. • M-F 10am-4pm; Sa 10am-3pm.

Napa Conference & Visitors Bureau: 1310 Napa Town Center Mall, (downtown off 1st between Main and Franklin sts.), Napa, (707) 226-7459. • Daily 9am-5pm.

St. Helena Chamber of Commerce: 1010a Main St., St. Helena, (707) 963-4456. • M-F 10am-4:30pm.

GETAWAYS

Getting There

By car, follow Hwy 101 north over the Golden Gate Bridge. From Hwy 101, take Hwy 37 east to Hwy 121, to Hwy 29 north, which runs the length of the valley from Napa to Calistoga. It's about a one-hour drive from San Francisco to the city of Napa. For a less crowded route through the Napa Valley, travel along the Silverado Trail, which runs parallel to Hwy 29. Along this road you'll find a host of smaller wineries tucked into the wooded mountains that form Napa's eastern border. These wineries may be hard to find if you're not paying attention to the small blue road signs, but if you tear yourself away from the quiet beauty of the valley, you'll find them—many of them.

Napa City Bus: 1151 Pearl St., Napa, (707) 255-7631. Office M-F 8am-5pm; Sa 10am-3pm. Buses run M-F 6:45am-6:30pm; Sa 7:45am-5:30pm.

Napa Valley Wineries ★★

Many of Napa's wineries offer extensive, informative tours, and most charge a nominal fee for both the tour and tasting. Seasoned visitors take a comprehensive tour at one of the big wineries and then head to the smaller, less crowded wineries that have free tastings and unique wines not readily available in stores. The following list is just a sampling; while you are visiting, pick up one of the many free brochures listing other wineries galore.

Beringer Wine Estates: 2000 Main St./Hwy 29, St. Helena, (707) 963-7115, (707) 963-4812. Guided tours of the winery's caves and historic Germanic mansion, where tasting and purchasing take place. Tasting is complimentary (for a fee you can sample reserve wines). • Tours daily 9:30am-5pm. Tasting 10am-6pm. Group tours by reservation.

Charles Krug Winery: 2800 Main St./Hwy 29, St. Helena, (707) 963-5057. The valley's first winery, and a must-visit for its extensive, entertaining tour. Group tours by appointment. • Tasting daily 10:30am-5:30pm. $3 including glass (free on Wednesday). Tours Th-M 11:30am, 1:30pm, 3:30pm. $3, includes tasting.

Domaine Chandon: 1 California Dr., Yountville, (707) 944-2280. The place to visit if you get a kick from champagne—more accurately, sparkling wine—this vineyard is owned and operated by the French vintners Moet et Chandon, makers of Dom Perignon. Group tours by reservation. • Free tours daily 11am-5pm (W-Su in winter). Tasting 11am-6pm. $3.75-$5.50, depending on what's being poured.

Hakusan Sake Gardens: One Executive Way, Napa, (707) 258-6160. For a change of drink, visit this place for sake and a stroll in a beautiful Japanese garden. • Daily 10am-5pm for self-guided tours and tasting ($1 for four kinds of sake).

Hess Collection Winery: 4411 Redwood Rd., Napa, (707) 255-1144. A self guided tour of this renovated historic building and its immaculate premises, replete with an impressive contemporary art collection (in essence, a small museum) make a visit to this winery memorable. Tasting $2.50; museum free. • Daily 10am-4pm for tours and tasting.

Joseph Phelps Vineyard: 200 Taplin Rd., St. Helena, (707) 963-2745, (800) 707-5789. Informative tours and generous samples at one of the best-designed vineyards in the valley. Tours and tastings by appointment only. • M-Sa 9am-5pm; Su 10am-4pm.

Mumm Napa Valley: 8445 Silverado Trail, Rutherford, (707) 942-3434. The new kids on the champagne-makers' block, this winery offers enlightening tours every hour 11am-4pm (until 3pm in winter). To taste the wine you must purchase a glass or bottle of the bubbly—hardly a chore. • Daily 10:30am-6pm (10am-5pm in winter).

Robert Mondavi Winery: 7801 St. Helena Hwy./Hwy 29, Oakville, (707) 259-9463. A good place for first-time visitors to the valley, featuring a thorough, one-hour tour of the facilities. The tours are free, but you may have to wait quite a while to join one, since they fill up quickly (reservations suggested). You must take the tour to partake

WINE COUNTRY

of the complimentary tastes of regular wines, and reserve wine tasting is charged by the glass. Throughout the summer months, the winery is the site of a program of concerts and events. • Daily 9am-5:30pm; hourly tours summer 10am-4pm. Concert and event information: (707) 963-9617, ext. 4384.

Rutherford Hill Winery: 200 Rutherford Hill Rd. (off the Silverado Trail), Rutherford, (707) 963-7194. While the 30-minute tours here are free, you'll have to ante up for a barrel tasting of the outstanding Merlots. The $3 fee includes a keepsake glass. • Tasting and sales M-F 10am-4:30pm; Sa-Su 10am-5pm. Tours M-F 11:30am, 1:30pm, and 3:30pm, Sa-Su 11:30am, 12:30pm, 1:30pm, 2:30pm, and 3:30pm.

Stag's Leap Wine Cellars: 5766 Silverado Trail, Napa, (707) 944-2020. A small, unassuming place with great Cabernets and Chardonnays. Tastings are held throughout the day for $3 and include a glass. Free non-alcoholic beverages for designated drivers. • Daily 10am-4pm; tours by appointment only.

Sterling Vineyards: 1111 Dunaweal Ln., Calistoga, (707) 942-3344 Accessible to visitors by aerial tram; the views and scenery from this hilltop winery are amazing. Tasting and tram ride included in the $6 visitor fee ($3 for ages 3-18, free under 3). Self-guided tours. • Daily 10:30am-4:30pm.

Vichon Winery: 1595 Oakville Grade, Oakville, (707) 944-2811. A Mondavi-owned winery with some decent vintages and complimentary tasting (there's a fee for reserve wines). The shady picnic grounds that overlook the valley make this a nice place to stop for lunch, but they ask that you purchase a bottle of their vino in exchange for the setting. • Daily 10am-4:30pm.

Other Attractions ★

Hot Air Balloons ★: Take to the skies in a hot air balloon for a panoramic view of the valley. Though not for the frugal or the acrophobic, ballooning has become a popular and romantic tourist activity. Balloons typically depart at dawn, and most companies provide a champagne brunch afterward. Try **Above the West Ballooning** (707) 944-8638 and (800) NAPA-SKY/627-2759 in Yountville, or **Bonaventura Balloon Company** (707) 944-2822 and (800) FLY-NAPA/359-6272 in Napa. Flights start at $165-$185. Reservations are recommended on the weekend.

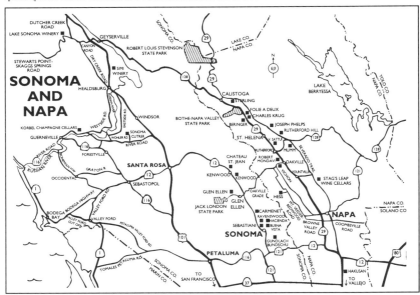

GETAWAYS

Horseback Riding ★: Landlubbers take heart—you can also see the countryside on horseback on a guided trail ride with **Sonoma Cattle Company**, (707) 996-8566. They operate concessions at three area parks: Bothe-Napa Valley State Park (see below), Sugarloaf Ridge State Park, and Jack London State Park (the latter two are in Sonoma). A 90-minute ride at Bothe costs $35, while two-hour treks at the other parks costs $40. Reservations are recommended on the weekend.

Bicycle Rentals ★: Athletic types may want to bring bikes and cycle through the flats of the valley. If you lack a bike or a way to transport your own, you can rent wheels at **St. Helena Cyclery**, 1156 Main St./Hwy 29, St. Helena, (707) 963-7736. Located in the heart of Napa Valley, it rents hybrids (a combination of a mountain and a road bike) for $7 per hour, $25 per business day. Prices include a lock, helmet, saddlebag, and water-bottle rack. • M-Sa 9:30am-5:30pm; Su 10am-5pm.

Bryan's Napa Valley Cyclery 4080 Byway East, Napa, (707) 255-3377, rents road bikes and hybrids for $4-6 per hour, $15-20 for an entire day. All-day guided cycle tours along the Silverado Trail are also available for groups of two to ten riders for $85 per person. Tours include bike rentals, and visits to three or four wineries with tastings and lunch. Make reservations at least four days in advance. • M-Sa 9am-6pm; Su 10am-4pm.

Bothe-Napa Valley State Park ★: Hwy 29 between St. Helena and Calistoga, (707) 942-4575. This park offers 1,800 acres of hiking amid redwoods, oaks, and wildflowers, as well as camping, picnicking, and a swimming pool. $5.

Robert Louis Stevenson State Park ★: Hwy 29, 5 mi. north of Calistoga, (707) 942-4575. Among the attractions at this park are an abandoned silver mine and the bunkhouse where the writer spent his honeymoon in 1880 and collected material for his novel *Silverado Springs*. There are no comfort facilities in the park (not even water or restrooms), but even so, make the climb to the 2,960-foot summit of **Mount St. Helena** (rumored to have been Stevenson's inspiration for Spyglass Hill in Treasure Island) for the breathtaking **view** ★★ of the Bay Area and the Sierra Nevada. Free.

Silverado Museum ★: 1490 Library Ln., St. Helena, (707) 963-3757. True Stevenson aficionados can also visit this museum, which is filled with manuscript notes and other memorabilia. The museum is located in the library in downtown St. Helena, so you can bone up on the author's works while you're there. • Tu-Su noon-4pm.

Taking the waters ★★: Don't leave Napa Valley without paying a visit to one of the many Calistoga spas and mineral baths. Indulgences range from basic mud and mineral baths to extras like herbal facials, acupressure, and manicures. The staff at **Calistoga Village Inn and Spa**, 1880 Lincoln Ave./Hwy 29, Calistoga, (707) 942-0991, will pamper you at reasonable prices, as will **Dr. Wilkinson's** 1507 Lincoln Ave., Calistoga, (707) 942-4102, which offers a two-hour mud bath/massage package for just $79. Overnight accommodations are available on the premises, but you don't have to be a guest to use the spa facilities—though you do need a reservation.

Old Faithful Geyser ★★: Hwy 29 to Tubbs Ln. (just north of Calistoga), (707) 942-6463. En route to the healing baths of Calistoga, take a detour to watch a different kind of steam bath. This natural wonder spews a 60-foot jet of boiling water into the air approximately every 40 minutes (emissions can vary quite a bit depending on the water level). • Daily 9am-6pm. Admission $5, seniors $4, ages 6-12 years $2, and under 6 free.

Places to Eat

Catahoula ★★★ $$$: 1457 Lincoln Ave. (Washington), Calistoga, (707) 942-2275. Owner-chef Jan Birnbaum escaped the constraints of big-city restaurants when he left San Francisco's Campton Place to open his own dining room in downtown Calistoga. This whimsical country venture assumes a canine theme—Catahoula is the state dog of Birnbaum's Louisiana birthplace—with photos of dogs on the walls, food in dog shapes, and a chic junkyard art motif. His southern menu takes mentor Paul Prudhomme's food uptown. Listed along with gumbo you'll find a crispy duck confit

WINE COUNTRY

salad with honey tangerines and candied onions. Definitely order dessert. Reservations recommended. • M, W-Th noon-2:30pm, 5:30-10pm; F noon-2:30pm, 5:30-10:30pm; Sa noon-3:30pm, 5:30-10:30pm; Su noon-3:30pm, 5:30-10pm (shorter in winter).

Foothill Café ★★ $$: J&P Shopping Ctr., 2766 Old Sonoma Rd., Napa, (707) 252-6178. This low-profile eatery is an enigma. Tucked into the back corner of a strip mall, this wonderful place was founded by a former sous chef at Masa's in San Francisco who wanted to provide first-class food for Napa Valley residents at less than first-class prices. It offers a limited menu of mostly barbecued and grilled items; the ribs are excellent, but don't miss anything that comes out of the oak oven, or the fresh fish specials. The bare, gray space is not much to look at, and service can be amateurish, but it all enhances the locals-only orientation. • W-Su 4:30-9:30pm; Th-F 11:30am-3pm.

French Laundry ★★★★ $$$$: 6640 Washington St. (Creek), Yountville, (707) 944-2380. After a long history as a low-key family operation with one sitting per evening, this restaurant was sold to Los Angeles chef Thomas Keller, who improved the already wonderful food and gave it a higher profile. Traditional ingredients and sauces are emphasized—duck confit, foie gras, salmon, caviar, *beurre blanc*—in elegant, creative, and perfectly executed combinations. The cottage-like atmosphere meshes with the authentic four- or five-course prix fixe tasting menus, although at $50 a head, not many *campagne* bumpkins can afford to eat here. Prepare to linger the evening, French style. • June-Oct.: daily 5:30-9:30pm; F-Su 12-1:30pm; closed Mon Nov-May.

Guigni's Grocery Good ¢: 1227 Main St./Hwy 29, St. Helena, (707) 963-3421. A good place for sandwiches, which can be eaten in the back room. • Daily 9am-5pm.

Meadowood Grille ★ $$: Meadowood Resort, 900 Meadowood Ln. (Silverado Trail), St. Helena, (707) 963-3646, (800) 458-8080. Choose one of the Grille's delectable sandwiches to savor in the sun after a round of golf or croquet on the manicured lawns. Although the prices are steep, the sylvan surroundings compensate for the dent in your wallet. Breakfast buffets are an extravagant start to a day of wine tasting. • Daily 7-11:30am, 11:30am-9:30pm.

Mustards Grill ★★★ $$: 7399 St. Helena Hwy./Hwy 29, (Yountville Cross), Yountville, (707) 944-2424. This upscale roadhouse, operated by the owners of San Francisco's Fog City Diner, has established itself as one of the most popular and well-known restaurants in the valley. Order crispy golden onion rings or sample nouvelle California cuisine—barbecued ribs, Asian marinated flank steak, or smoked duck with a coconut-almond sauce—while you survey the always-bustling scene. Reservations recommended. • Daily 11:30am-10pm.

Nation's Giant Hamburgers ★ $: 1441 3rd St. (School), Napa, (707) 252-8500. It's not much to look at, but the burgers are huge and delicious: a carnivore's dream come true. No credit cards. • Su-Th 6am-midnight; F-Sa 6am-2am.

Oakville Grocery Co. $: 7856 St. Helena Hwy. (Hwy 29), Oakville, (707) 944-8802. The gourmet's choice for picnic fixings. • Daily 10am-6pm.

Ristorante Piatti ★★ $$: 6480 Washington St. (Oak), Yountville, (707) 944-2070. A branch of this locally based chain of lively trattorias. The simple, bright dining rooms are casual and relaxed. Food tends to light preparations of Italian favorites. Try the ravioli in lemon sauce, the delightful mushroom risotto, or anything off the grill. Wood-fired pizzas are justifiably popular. Consistency has been a problem as the chain has grown. Wine prices are on the high side. Reservations recommended. • Summer: M-Th 11:30am-10pm; F-Su 11:30am-11pm; winter: M-Th until 9pm, F-Su until 10pm.

Terra ★★★★ $$$: 1345 Railroad Ave. (Hunt/Adams), St. Helena, (707) 963-8931. An elegant, sophisticated eatery perfect for a special dinner. The rustic stone building establishes a warm, intimate tone for chef Hiro Sone's fabulous cuisine. Raves keep coming for innovative combinations like duck liver wontons with wild mushroom sauce, duck breast with sun-dried cherries, or salmon in miso sauce. Sone's wife, Lissa Doumani, oversees the excellent desserts and service. The wine list is oriented toward splurges. Reservations recommended. • Su-M, W-Th 6-9pm; F 6-9:30pm; Sa 6-10pm.

GETAWAYS

Tra Vigne ★★★ $$$: 1050 Charter Oak Ave. (Hwy 29), St. Helena, (707) 963-4444. Don't pass up a delicious Italian meal with a California accent in this airy dining room, or on the sylvan patio. Mustards Grill's suave Italian sibling, Tra Vigne is sure to impress guests—even those from the big city. High-tech accouterments and soaring ceilings give the rustic, old stone building a trendy touch. The similarly cutting-edge menu includes gourmet pizzas, rustic pastas, and hearty meat dishes. Sometimes the food is more style than substance, but it's still a favorite with swinging young valley residents and visitors. Cantinetta Tra Vigne serves up pizza, sandwiches, and picnic fixings café-style or to go. Reservations recommended. • Daily 11:30am-10pm.

Wappo Bar Bistro ★★ $$: 1226-B Washington St. (Lincoln), Calistoga, (707) 942-4712. The name comes from a local Native American tribe, but the eclectic cuisine comes from all over the world. Mix New World specialties like chiles rellenos and empanadas with such old-country favorites as paella and Moroccan stew. The interior, with exposed wooden beams, rough wooden furniture, and tile floor has refreshingly few decorative flourishes. In true wine country fashion, a beautiful garden patio awaits fair-weather diners. • M, Th-Su 11:30am-3pm, 6-9:30pm; W 11:30-2:30pm.

Places to Stay

For more information and reservations, call **Napa Valley Reservations Unlimited** (707) 252-1985, located at 1819 Tanen Street in Napa, open M-F 9am-5pm. If you want to stay over a summer weekend, you may need to make reservations as far as two months in advance.

Auberge du Soleil $$$$: 180 Rutherford Hill Rd. (off Silverado Trail), Rutherford, (707) 963-1211. The place to go for very special occasions. Located in a secluded olive grove, rooms come with the works—fireplaces, terraces, sofas, king-size beds, and resplendent bathrooms. Facilities include a pool, hot tub, spa, and tennis. $175-$1200.

Bothe-Napa Valley State Park ¢: 3601 St. Helena Hwy. N./Hwy 29, St. Helena, (707) 942-4575. Call Destinet for reservations: (800) 444-7275. Facilities include hot water, restrooms, and showers. $15-$16 per campsite, $5 per extra vehicle.

Calistoga Ranch Campground ¢: 580 Lommel Rd., Calistoga, (707) 942-6565. A cheap stay, with showers available. Tent sites with elevated barbecue and picnic table $19 for four people, $2 each additional person. 28-day maximum stay.

Calistoga Spa and Hot Springs $$: 1006 Washington St., Calistoga, (707) 942-6269. Frequent discounts are offered—inquire when making reservations. Appointments must be made for the spa, which offers mud and mineral baths, massages, mineral water baths, and steam blanket wraps. With bath, kitchenette $78-$120.

Calistoga Village Inn and Spa $$: 1880 Lincoln Ave., Calistoga, (707) 942-0991. Sunken tubs, geothermal baths, whirlpools, and a swimming pool are included in the reasonable rates. With private bath $65-$150. No minimum stay.

Mountain Home Ranch $/$$: 3400 Mountain Home Ranch Rd. (off Petrified Forest Rd.), Calistoga, (707) 942-6616. Find seclusion at this rustic resort. Set on over 300 acres in the mountains above Calistoga, with its own natural sulfur spring, two swimming pools, tennis, volleyball, fishing, hiking trails, and a wisteria-draped family picnic area. Accommodations are available in the historic main lodge or in private cabins. An on-site restaurant serves California ranch cuisine. Perfect for family escapes. Open daily during summer; weekends spring and fall. $55-$165.

Napa Town & Country Fairgrounds ¢: 575 3rd St. (Silverado Trail), Napa, (707) 253-4900. RV campground. Water and electricity included. No reservations. Campsites $15.

Pink Mansion $$$: 1415 Foothill Blvd., Calistoga, (707) 942-0558. An elegant, restored mansion with in-house wine tasting and an indoor pool filled with local waters. Full breakfast included. $105-$175.

WINE COUNTRY

Shady Oaks Country Inn $$$: 399 Zinfandel Ln., St. Helena, (707) 963-1190. A quiet, romantic setting. Gourmet champagne breakfasts and wine and hors d'oeuvres every night add to the charm. $145-$175.

Triple S Ranch $: 4600 Mountain Home Ranch Rd. (off Petrified Forest Rd.), Calistoga, (707) 942-6730. Nine cabins located near the Old Faithful Geyser of California and numerous hiking trails—a true bargain for a double room. $42-$54.

Sonoma ★★★

When George Yount and Charles Krug were establishing Napa Valley as a wine-growing region, neighboring Sonoma County was undergoing chaotic times. The Russian, Mexican, and American governments were engaged in fierce territorial skirmishes over the region, until the United States finally took possession of Sonoma and its riches. Nowadays, the peaceful vineyards and scenic landscapes give little indication of the area's tumultuous past. Wineries in Sonoma County are centered in the Sonoma Valley, which is in the southern part of the county, and in northern Sonoma County around the town of Healdsburg and the Russian River Valley. Exploration of Sonoma requires an investigator's eye—the treasures abound, but you'll have to look a bit harder to find them, which makes it a more relaxed escape than Napa.

Sonoma County Visitors Bureau: 5000 Roberts Lake Rd. #A, Rohnert Park, (707) 935-0758, (707) 586-8100. Maps, brochures, and information on the wineries, including a tasting guide. • M-F 8am-5pm.

Sonoma Valley Visitors Bureau: 453 1st St. E., Sonoma, (707) 996-1090. Maps of Sonoma County. • Daily 9am-7pm; winter: 9am-5pm.

Getting There

The most direct route to the Sonoma Valley is via Hwy 101 across the Golden Gate Bridge. Continue on 101 to visit Healdsburg, Santa Rosa, and Sebastopol. If you want to head straight for the town of Sonoma, Hwy 37 to Hwy 121 to Hwy 12 is the quickest route. Sonoma is approximately one hour's drive from San Francisco.

Sonoma Wineries ★★

The vineyards of Napa may have brought California's wine country to prominence, but Sonoma is where it all began. Stories about the exact origins of the Golden State's wine business differ, but it seems to have taken root in 1823 at the vineyards of the Sonoma Mission. Wine making spread with arrival of the Hungarian immigrant Agoston Haraszthy, who brought thousands of vines back from Europe in 1861. The vineyards of Sonoma Valley and Northern Sonoma County still have a lot to offer to both the wine connoisseur and the dilettante, and unlike Napa, most wineries offer free tasting (although fewer tours and fancy visitor centers). When traveling through Sonoma, bear in mind that most of the wineries are not directly on the highway; keep your eyes open for the turnoffs, and don't hesitate to venture off into the countryside.

Buena Vista Winery: 18000 Old Winery Rd., Sonoma, (707) 938-1266. Self-guided tours through the historic stone winery, picnic spots, and a wine museum and gallery are some of the attractions beyond the internationally-acclaimed bottlings. • Daily 10:30am-4:30pm; winter: 10:30am-4pm.

Carmenet Vineyard: 1700 Moon Mountain Dr., Sonoma, (707) 996-5870. Tours and tastings are by appointment only, and well worth the call. The vista of the Mayacamas Mountains, underground aging caves, and the Sauvignon Blanc and Cabernet are all outstanding reasons for a visit. • M-Sa 10am-4pm; tours by appointment only.

Chateau St. Jean: 8555 Sonoma Hwy./Hwy 12, Kenwood, (707) 833-4134. The 1920s-inspired tasting room, complimentary samples, and picnic area make this a pleasant option. • Daily 10am-4:30pm.

GETAWAYS

Benzinger Family Winery: 1883 London Ranch Rd., Glen Ellen, (707) 935-4046. This ranch was once owned by General Vallejo and more recently was home to Glen Ellen Winery. Tasting is gratis, there's a free motorized tram tour of the vineyards, and picnic spots among the redwoods are inviting. • Tastings daily 10am-4:30pm; tours 12:30pm, 2pm, and 3:30pm.

Gundlach-Bundschu Winery: 2000 Denmark St., Sonoma, (707) 938-5277. A small, family-run winery known for its Merlot. Self-guided tours. • Daily 11am-4:30pm.

Kenwood Vineyards: 9592 Sonoma Hwy./Hwy 12, Kenwood, (707) 833-5891. Some of the excellent vintages made here are the product of grapes still grown on Jack London's estate in Glen Ellen. Comprehensive 30-45 minute tours are by appointment, and cost $3-$5—depending on which wines you choose to taste. (Staff permitting, a free, 15-minute mini-tour is available on a walk-in basis.) Tour participants receive a 20 percent discount on wine purchases. Tasting is complimentary and many weekends feature food and wine pairings. • Daily 10am-4:30pm.

Korbel Champagne Cellars: 13250 River Rd., Guerneville, (707) 887-2294. To get your fill of bubbles, brandy, and wine, visit this century-old winery. The picturesque place resembles a castle tucked away in the redwoods, and has a nice picnic area. • Tasting daily 9am-5pm (winter until 4:30pm); tours daily 10am-3:45pm (winter until 3pm).

Lake Sonoma Winery: 9990 Dry Creek Rd., Geyserville, (707) 431-1550. Its proximity to Warm Springs Dam and the Lake Sonoma Recreation Area make this a worthwhile to stop for the scenic views alone. An in-house deli offers fixings to accompany the family-produced vino for a picnic on the grounds. • Daily 10am-5pm.

Ravenswood Vintners: 18701 Gehricke Rd., Sonoma, (707) 938-1960. Noted for its big red vintages—their souvenir bumper sticker proclaims "No Wimpy Wines"—traditional production techniques, and summer weekend barbecues, this is a good place for a taste and a snack. Tours by appointment only. • Daily 10am-4:30pm.

Simi Winery: 16275 Healdsburg Ave., Healdsburg, (707) 433-6981. Two Italian immigrants began making wine here in 1876 and built the beautiful stone building in 1890. Now owned by the same French company as prestigious Moet-Hennessey, Simi offers three excellent guided tours per day, and tasting and picnicking on the grounds. • Tasting daily 10am-4:30pm; tours at 11am, 1pm, 3pm.

Viansa Winery: 25200 Arnold Dr./Hwy 121, Sonoma, (707) 935-4700. Ringed by outdoor picnic tables, this hilltop Mediterranean-style villa overlooks acres of vineyards. Complimentary wine tasting, plus an Italian food marketplace featuring terrific oils, spices, and dips, all of which can be liberally sampled. • Daily 10am-5pm.

Other Attractions ★

Sonoma Historic Park ★: Sonoma Plaza at 1st, Spain, and Napa sts., (707) 938-1519. A good place to start exploring is in the town of Sonoma, where many of the historic battles for control of the region took place. Sonoma Plaza was laid out in 1834 by General Mariano Guadalupe Vallejo, the Mexican commander charged with keeping the territory out of the hands of the Russians. Several historical landmarks comprise the park and are also sprinkled among the shops and restaurants that now line the square. Whichever monument you visit first, you will have to buy a ticket (adults $2, children $1), that is good for admittance to all the other sites. These include: **Sonoma Mission**, the last of the great California missions; the remaining portion of General Vallejo's first home, **La Casa Grande Indian Servants' Quarters**; the **Sonoma Barracks**, where Vallejo's troops were housed; and **Lachryma Montis**, the General's second, even more stately, home. • Daily 10am-5pm.

Sonoma Cheese Factory ★: 2 W. Spain St., Sonoma, (707) 938-5225. This fragrant store also fronts the Plaza, marking the spot Sonoma Jack cheese has been made from the same recipe since 1931. Kids especially like to watch the cheesemaking process. • M-F 8:30am-6pm; Sa-Su 8:30am-6:30pm.

WINE COUNTRY

Jack London State Historic Park ★: End of London Ranch Rd., Glen Ellen, (707) 938-5216. Heading north from Sonoma, be sure to visit Jack London State Historic Park, the writer's former ranch. Hiking and riding trails—horse rentals are available from Sonoma Cattle Company, (707) 996-8566—crisscross the ranch past old barns, pigpens, and the charred remains of Wolf House, which was to be London's home but was destroyed by fire shortly before he could move in. **The House of Happy Walls** was built by London's widow, Charmian, and now houses many of his manuscripts, notes, and personal effects. • Daily 9:30am-7pm; winter until 5pm. Entrance $5 per vehicle.

Snoopy's Gallery and Gift Shop: 1667 W. Steele Ln., Santa Rosa, (707) 546-3385. Before concluding that Sonoma County is too much like history class, recapture part of your childhood by visiting this emporium, owned and operated by the clever beagle's creator, Charles Schultz. This gallery boasts the world's largest collection of Peanuts memorabilia. • Daily 10am-6pm.

Bike Rental ★: If you'd like to cycle your way around the area, **Rincon Cyclery** (707) 538-0868 rents mountain bikes for $7/hour (two-hour minimum), or $25/day. Not too far from the bike trails of Annadel State Park, the shop is located at 4927 Sonoma Hwy 12 (at Middle Rincon) and is open M-F 10am-6pm; Sa 9am-6pm; Su 10am-5pm. You can also rent hybrid and tandem bikes at the **Spoke Folk Cyclery**, 249 Center St., Healdsburg, (707) 433-7171. Rates are $7/hour, $25 for the day. Hours are M, W-F 10am-6pm; Sa 10am-5pm; Su 11am-4pm.

Hot Air Ballooning ★: Sonoma has its share of hot air balloon operators eager to take you up for a champagne breakfast flight. **Once in a Lifetime Balloon Co.** (707) 578-0580 meets customers at the Santa Rosa airport and ends its flights with a tasty gourmet brunch. Rides cost about $165 per person, and reservations are required.

Canoe Rentals ★: Near Healdsburg, the Russian River's placid waters and forested banks are the perfect setting for a leisurely day of canoeing, swimming, and picnicking. Be warned, however: some folks come for a bucolic retreat, others to party their brains out. **Trowbridge Recreation**, 20 Healdsburg Ave., Healdsburg, (707) 433-7247, organizes canoe, kayak, and camping trips along the Russian River for groups. Trowbridge also rents canoes and kayaks: one day with a canoe is $39 and must be reserved in advance. You can also rent from **Burke's Canoe Trips** at 8600 River Rd. (Mirabel Rd.), Forestville, (707) 887-1222 and paddle the ten miles to Guerneville; bring a picnic lunch and make a day of it. A shuttle will take you back to Forestville. Two-person canoes rent for $30. Pick up canoes 9-10am. Weekend reservations are required

Places to Eat

Caffè Portofino ★★ $$: 535 4th St. (Mendocino/Santa Rosa), Santa Rosa, (707) 523-1171. This hopping Italian restaurant is known for its delicious stuffed artichokes and its loud singles bar. High ceilings, brick walls, and professional service give it that old country feeling. Strong flavors dominate the food, which includes such dishes as radicchio Gorgonzola salad and pasta with pesto and potatoes. Simple grilled meats and fish are good bets. Reservations recommended. • M-Th 11am-10pm; F-Sa 11am-11pm.

East Side Oyster Bar ★★ $$$: 133 E. Napa St. (1st St. E.), Sonoma, (707) 939-1266. Bring your eyeglasses to this trendy eatery: you'll need them first to read the lengthy descriptions of the innovative California preparations, then to admire their architectural presentations. Sturgeon is layered with a pumpkin-coriander seed crust and topped with a ginger-balsamic vinegar and herbed oil, all served atop steamed cucumbers. The parfait of Sonoma lamb includes slices of lamb, a mound of chick-pea mash, onion confit, plum tomato jam, and leeks. Some diners regret that some of the reviews of the restaurant have been better than the food. The parlor-sized dining room has a marble fireplace and simple arrangements of fresh flowers. The lovely back patio is well hidden; ideal for a discreet rendezvous. Reservations recommended. • M-Th 11:30am-2:30pm, 5:30-9pm; F-Sa 11:30am-2:30pm, 5:30-9:30pm; Su noon-3pm, 5:30pm-9pm.

GETAWAYS

John Ash & Co. ★★★ $$$$: 4330 Barnes Rd. (River), Santa Rosa, (707) 527-7687. This charming inn houses one of the wine country's premier restaurants. Created by local culinary giant John Ash (who now spends most of his time teaching cooking), the menu exhibits its strength in its mélange of cuisines. Fresh local ingredients—salmon, lamb, duck, greens—are mixed with ginger, butter, wine, wild mushrooms, and more. How about baked salmon wrapped in nori with sun-dried tomato compote? The prices are not for the faint of heart, but most consider a meal here worth every hard-earned penny. While you're splurging, try one of the older vintages on the wine list. The bar menu allows diners to sample the food without the sticker shock of the dining room. Reservations recommended. • M 5:30-9pm; Tu-F 11:30am-2pm, 5:30-9pm; Sa-Su 10:30am-2pm, 5:30pm-9pm; café menu available between meals.

La Casa ★ $: 121 E. Spain St. (1st St. E.), Sonoma, (707) 996-3406. This popular downtown spot serves passable Mexican food in an authentic Cal-Mex setting: dark wood, hand-painted tiles, the works. Wash down tacos and burritos with a tasty margarita and enjoy the low-key atmosphere. Reservations recommended. • Daily 11:30am-10pm.

Lisa Hemenway's ★★★ $$: 714 Village Ct., Montgomery Village (Farmers Ln./Sonoma Ave.), Santa Rosa, (707) 526-5111. It's hard to believe such a delightful gourmet restaurant could be hidden in a shopping mall. Lisa Hemenway, a veteran of John Ash's culinary empire who's been inspired by her travels around the world, has created a venue well suited to special-occasion dining. The light and airy dining room allows celebrants to relax and enjoy the eclectic cuisine based on fresh local ingredients. Start with crab cakes, oysters on the half shell, or a duck quesadilla, then enjoy Mongolian-style pork, vegetable tamales, or chicken breast with sun-dried cherries. Fill your picnic basket next door at Lisa Hemenway's Tote Cuisine. Reservations recommended. • M-Sa 11:30am-2:30pm, 5:30pm-9:30pm; Su 11:30am-2:30pm, 5-9pm.

Ristorante Piatti ★★ $$$: 405 1st St. W. (W. Spain St./W. Napa St.), Sonoma, (707) 996-2351. A breezy, modern Italian restaurant, twin to the Napa original. • M-Th 11:30am-10pm; F-Su 11:30am-11pm; winter, M-Th until 9pm, F-Su until 10pm.

World Famous Hamburger Ranch and Pasta Farm ★★ $: 31195 Redwood Hwy. N. (Hwy 128 West), Cloverdale, (707) 894-5616. No infusions, no exotica, no drizzled anything. Nothing but good food, with something for every palate: burgers, pastas, grilled cheese sandwiches. Summertime outdoor barbecues make a perfect family outing. • M-F 8am-9pm; Sa-Su 7am-9pm; F-Sa til 10pm in summer.

Places to Stay

Camping

Lake Sonoma/Warm Springs Dam ¢: 3333 Skaggs Springs Rd., Geyserville, (707) 433-9483. Drive-in campsites include access to hot showers. Drive-in sites $14 per night per vehicle; boat-in and backpacker sites $6. All sites first-come, first-served.

Spring Lake Park ¢: 5390 Montgomery Dr., between Howarth Park and Annadel State Park, Santa Rosa (707) 539-8092, (707) 539-8082. Campsites include access to hot showers. Sites $14, $4 extra vehicle. Reservations for May-September accepted beginning in January, and must be made two weeks in advance; unreserved sites available first-come, first-served. October-April, open weekends and holidays only.

Sugarloaf Ridge State Park ¢: 2605 Adobe Canyon Rd., Kenwood, (707) 833-5712. Reservations essential on weekends; call Destinet (800) 444-7275. Campsites $15-$16.

Hotels, Motels, and B&Bs

Best Western Garden Inn $$: 1500 Santa Rosa Ave., Santa Rosa, (707) 546-4031, (800) 528-1234. Landscaped grounds with two swimming pools. $61-$125.

Best Western Hillside Inn $$: 2901 4th St., Santa Rosa, (707) 546-9353, (800) 528-1234. Rooms with kitchens and two-bedroom family units. $65.

Glenelly Inn $$$: 5131 Warm Springs Rd., Glen Ellen, (707) 996-6720. Eight rooms with private baths and entrances, a garden, and an outdoor Jacuzzi. $105-$140.

Grape Leaf Inn $$$: 539 Johnson St., Healdsburg, (707) 433-8140. Seven rooms with private baths, whirlpool tubs for two, full breakfast in the morning, and wine and cheese at night. $90-$150.

Madrona Manor $$$$: 1001 Westside Rd., Healdsburg, (707) 433-4231. All 21 rooms have private baths; some have fireplaces. Enjoy the pool and gourmet restaurant. $140-$240.

Raford House $$$: 10630 Wohler Rd., Healdsburg, (707) 887-9573. An authentic Victorian farmhouse, complete with period furnishings, set on a hill among the vineyards. The seven guest rooms are cozy and private, and views from the deck are spectacular. $90-$145.

Santa Rosa Motor Inn $: 1800 Santa Rosa Ave., Santa Rosa, (707) 523-3480. Standard clean and spartan motel rooms. $35-$60.

Sonoma Mission Inn & Spa $$$/$$$$: 18140 Sonoma Hwy./Hwy 12, Boyes Hot Springs, (707) 938-9000, (800) 862-4945. This sprawling landmark offers all the amenities and pampering you'd expect of a big luxury hotel. The rooms are rather small, but expect to spend most of your time by the pool, in the spa, or on a golf or tennis course. (Unless you book a spa package, you must pay $10-$20 extra to use spa facilities, although use of the main pool is included with all room rates.) $115-$325.

YOSEMITE ★★★

Famous throughout the world, Yosemite National Park has stupendous scenery, challenging hikes, and, unfortunately, hordes of tourists—three and a half million a year. Yosemite Valley, the park's best-known attraction, inspired photographers Ansel Adams and Galen Rowell and the naturalist and Sierra Club founder John Muir. Sheer granite cliffs rise 3,000 feet above this scenic valley. Cascading down these cliffs are waterfalls that rank among the world's highest, most spectacular, and most visited—it isn't unheard of to be caught in traffic on a busy summer weekend. Try to see the valley in the spring (April or May) when the waterfalls are raging, the flowers are blooming, and free parking spots aren't as elusive as deer. In the summer, Tuolumne Meadows in the northern area of the park is an outstanding and less crowded place for walking, hiking, or climbing. In the fall, you can explore the Mist Trail without being trampled. The backcountry skiing in Yosemite is among the best in the Sierra, and there's both a touring center and a downhill area at Badger Pass, in the southern area of the park.

Yosemite National Park: P. O. Box 577, Yosemite, CA 95389; Operator/Recorded Announcements (209) 372-0264, 372-0200, 372-0209; Public Information (209) 372-0265; Wilderness Center (209) 372-0285; Permit Information (209) 372-0310; Wilderness Permit Reservations (209) 372-0740. • M-F 8am-5pm.

Backcountry Stations: Yosemite Valley (209) 372-0308. Tuolumne (209) 372-0309. • Su-F 7:30am-7:30pm; Sa 6:30am-7:30pm.

Tuolumne Visitors Center: Tuolumne Meadows, (209) 372-0263. • 9am-7pm daily.

Yosemite Concession Services: (209) 372-1000.

Yosemite Valley Visitors Center: (209) 372-0299. • Daily 8am-8pm summer, 9am-5pm winter.

Getting There

By car, plan on it taking three and one-half hours to Yosemite Valley from San Francisco. Take I-580 east toward Livermore, then I-205 east toward Stockton. I-205 runs into Hwy 120 East, which you follow all the way to Yosemite. Pay attention to the signs or you'll lose it: there's a tricky stretch where Hwys 108 and 120 split; you'll have

GETAWAYS

to take a right turn to stay on Hwy 120, which heads toward Chinese Camp, Groveland, Buck Meadows, and Yosemite.

Other mountain byways that enter the park from the west and south give you driving and scenic options through alternate park entrances. Hwy 140 enters through the town of El Portal, and Hwy 41 enters through the towns of Fish Camp and Mariposa. If you are lucky enough to enter on 41 at sunset, the view from the Wawona Tunnel is breathtaking.

If you're using public transportation, you'll have to be patient. **Via Yosemite**, (209) 722-0366, runs buses from Merced and Fresno Air Terminal to Yosemite (four times daily; $40 round-trip from Fresno; $33 round-trip from Merced). You can get to Merced and Fresno from the Bay Area by **Greyhound** (800) 231-2222 or **Amtrak** (800) 872-7245 bus.

Yosemite Valley ★★

Yosemite Valley, for all its splendor, is basically a human zoo—more Disneyland than natural escape. The best sightseeing is on the trails, so whether you hike, bike, ride, or ski, get away from the roads. All road signs and the park map (available at the entrance stations) lead you to the day-use parking lot in **Curry Village**, home to much of the valley's lodging and plenty of food concessions and shops. When exploring Yosemite Valley, park your car there and take the free and frequent **shuttle bus** to the Visitors Center and all other valley destinations.

El Capitan ★★★: As you drive into the valley, the first dramatic sight is this sheer rock wall, towering well over 3,000 feet above the valley. The best view from the valley is across a meadow on the north side of the road exiting the valley. The rock is nirvana for serious rock climbers who spend days hauling themselves up to the top (if you get close to the base, look out for climber waste).

Yosemite Village: The administrative center of the park. Timid visitors might start by dropping by the **Visitors Center** to learn about what they should be experiencing outside. Guided nature walks also leave from here. The **Ansel Adams Gallery** (209) 372-4413, a tribute to the photographer who made the park so famous, is open from 8am to 8pm in the summer, and 9am to 5pm in the winter.

Yosemite Concession Services offers a **guided bus tour**. Obtain more information at any of the information desks located at Yosemite Lodge, Curry Village, the Ahwahnee Hotel, and beside the Village Store, or by calling (209) 372-1240. Advance reservations are required. On the nights of a full moon and for two nights before, night tours through the valley floor are offered.

The Ahwahnee Hotel ★: A national historic landmark with lavish rooms and high rates, is well worth a look-in, if only for a walk through the grand common rooms. Built from native stones and logs, the hotel has an impressive fireplace, a huge dining hall with exposed log beams, and big windows to take in the sweeping vistas.

Glacier Point ★★★: If you'd prefer to see the valley from a different perspective, drive or hike from the valley to Glacier Point, where you'll have a bird's-eye view of the valley and Half Dome. The summer of 1996, an enormous chunk of rock fell from Glacier Point into the valley causing massive winds and killing one person. On the way back, be sure to stop at **Tunnel View ★★★** (a turnout at the eastern end of the Wawona Tunnel) and gaze at the valley, its cliffs and waterfalls, and the Sierras in the distance.

Hiking, Riding, & Climbing ★★★

Mist Trail ★★: This trail, which leads to Vernal Falls, got its name because the spray from the river it follows frequently soaks it and its travelers (making the ground slick). The trail starts from Curry Village, but you can take a shuttle bus all the way to Happy Isles. You can take a hike of any length; the trail follows a sparkling river up a scenic valley, so you don't have to get to any peak destination to make it worth your

YOSEMITE

while. **Vernal Falls** ★★ is a three-mile round trip, perfect for a half day. Though the trail is very popular, and initially paved like a freeway, it's well worth the effort. If you have the better part of a day, the Mist Trail continues past Vernal Falls to **Nevada Falls** ★★, a seven-mile round trip. The extra climb gives you views of a second, bigger waterfall and the valley.

Yosemite Falls ★★★: An even shorter walk is to the bottom of Yosemite Falls, only about half a mile, round trip. It doesn't sound like much, but it's impressive to stand at the base of the pounding water as it surges and sprays. During a full moon, when the falls are raging, one can even see "moonbows" at the base of the falls, a lunar rainbow of sorts. On a busy summer day it's not uncommon to see 20 tour buses parked at this trailhead across from the Yosemite Lodge, but don't be daunted—it's the only place for buses to park in the valley.

An enjoyable, but much more ambitious, hike is to the **top of Yosemite Falls** ★★★, 6.6 miles round trip. A nice extension to **Yosemite Point** ★★★ puts you on the rim above the valley across from Glacier Point. The trail is steep—it climbs over 3,000 vertical feet—and gives a good workout, so bring adequate food, water, and clothing.

Glacier Point ★★★: If you're feeling very ambitious, hike up to Glacier Point for breathtaking views. The trailhead is on the southern road in the valley, west of the Chapel. You can also take the shuttle bus up to Glacier Point, and hike back to the valley. Like the climb to Yosemite Point, this hike is a challenge.

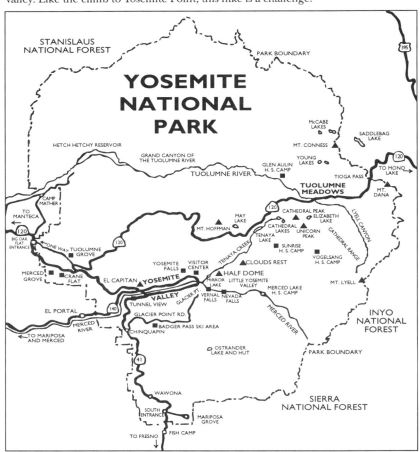

GETAWAYS

Half Dome ★★★: If you're truly hard core, hike Half Dome by the cables route—not an undertaking for the fainthearted. It's 16 miles round trip with a vertical gain of over 5,000 feet. The last half-mile is so steep that the Park Service has installed cables and steps. (Lightning storms are not uncommon; avoid being up there in a storm.) Start very early and bring warm, windproof clothing, lots of food and water, and rain gear.

Backpacking ★★★: The advantage of going on a multiday hike is that once you leave the valley, the crowds thin rapidly. The number of routes is virtually limitless, so buy a good topographic map and have some fun planning. Remember, all overnight trips in the park require a free permit, available at the backcountry stations around the park. Also, some trails have summer quotas, so call ahead for information on limits and reservations. Always hang your food in a tree or rent a bear box, lest the bears hold a midnight feast with your breakfast (most camping stores and rangers can explain the details). An enjoyable two- or three-day outing is a trek up the Mist Trail to Little Yosemite Valley. From camp you can do a day trip up Half Dome and return home, or, for an even longer trip, continue over Clouds Rest for one of the best views in the park. In the summer, a hiker's shuttle runs once a day from the valley to Tuolumne and back. It leaves the valley hotels around 8am, arrives in Tuolumne about two hours later, and continues all the way to Lee Vining on the East Side. It returns in the afternoon, stops in Tuolumne at 4pm and returns to the valley by 6pm. See the Wilderness Office or the Visitors Center for times and reservations.

Bike Rentals: If you'd prefer to see the valley on your own, but don't have the time for a tour on foot, Curry Village (209) 372-1000 rents bikes seasonally; open daily 8:30am-5:45pm. **The Yosemite Lodge** offers year-round rentals, as does **Lodge Bike Rentals**, across from parking lot for Yosemite Falls. They're open from 8:30am to 5:45pm daily, with the last rental out at 4:30pm; call (209) 372-1208 for details. Ride the eight miles of bike trails in the valley or venture onto the main road out of the valley. A popular destination is **Mirror Lake** ★ and Meadow, where you can gaze straight up at the massive, sheer cliff of Half Dome's north side. You're required to walk the last quarter of a mile to what remains of the lake (a fair amount during the spring runoff, very little in the late fall), a bit of an uphill.

Horseback Riding: If you give yourself at least a half day, why not saddle up? Yosemite Concession Services runs horse trips around the valley. This is a good option for folks who want a little adventure on horseback but are intimidated by the length or altitude gain in the trails.

Rock Climbing ★★★: Yosemite is one of the most challenging and scenic places to rock climb in the world, as the international mix of climbers in the park can attest. **The Yosemite Mountaineering School** (209) 372-1244 offers excellent classes for first-time climbers—call for schedules and rates. There are numerous books describing the many challenging routes in Yosemite. If you're a hard-core climber, scale El Capitan by the Nose Route, giving yourself five days. Don't forget to leave your fear behind.

Tuolumne Meadows ★★★

Unlike the valley, where temperatures can soar into the 90s (and the crowds seemingly into the millions), Tuolumne's altitude (8,000 feet) keeps the temperature bearable in the summer, and there are fewer people milling about. There are no "attractions," but hiking the trails around the heart of Tuolumne Meadows, watching birds of prey, enjoying the flora and fauna, and peering at the brightly clad climbers can be beautiful. A shuttle bus even allows you to park at the main lot and spend the day unencumbered by your automobile. **Tioga Road** crosses Tuolumne Meadows, leading to **Tioga Pass** on its way east to Mono Lake. The road is usually open June-November, depending on snowfall. **Olmstead Point** ★★★, located near the midpoint of Tioga Road, offers one of the park's best viewpoints looking down a dramatic valley towards Half Dome.

YOSEMITE

Hiking & Climbing ★★★: You should get a good, topographic trail map (the USGS Tuolumne Meadows is good, although private company maps are nice because they are often printed on durable plastic and show trail mileages). Remember, you need a permit (available at the Tuolumne Wilderness Office near the Tuolumne Meadows lodge) for all overnight trips. Also, bring enough cord and stuff sacks to hang your food at night or rent a bear box from the park—it's bulky, but it requires less strategic planning. **Young's Lakes** is a good day or overnight hike. It's a bit crowded but offers great views of the lakes, Ragged Peak, and Mt. Conness. Equine packers frequent the lakes, so pick another destination if you don't like horses. From Young's Lakes there's a Class 2 scramble leading up Mt. Conness. There's also a harder route (Class 2 to 3) from the other side, starting from Saddlebag Lake.

Mt. Hoffman offers one of the best views in Tuolumne. There's a moderately challenging trail from May Lake. **Elizabeth Lake** is popular and offers great views of the Clark Range and the Sierra. **Cathedral Peak** is a Class 4 climb, but it's reasonable for experienced rock climbers and provides great views. **Unicorn Peak** is a Class 3 scramble. **The Grand Canyon of the Tuolumne River** is spectacular in the spring and early summer when the water is high. You can reach it from Glen Aulin High Sierra Camp.

To get to **Mt. Dana**, a half-day climb, follow a footpath that runs from Tioga Pass (on Hwy 120 toward the East Side). Ice climbers may want to try a scenic, if not too challenging, 40-degree ice route on the northeast side. **Mt. Lyell**, the highest peak in the park, is a nice two-day, Class 3 climb. An ice ax, crampons, and a rope are advisable. To get to the base camp, hike up the beautiful **Lyell Canyon**, a worthwhile trip in itself.

Other Areas ★

Yosemite is also home to three **Sequoia Groves ★★**. Sequoia trees, cousins of the taller but less massive coastal redwood trees, are the largest living things on earth. **Tuolumne and Merced Groves ★** are near the Big Oak Flat entrance, on Hwy 120, and include the famous drive-through tree. The other grove is **Mariposa Grove ★★**, in the Wawona Basin (the south part of the park on Hwy 41). A tour bus will take you the final distance from the Mariposa Grove parking lot to the giant sequoias. This is an amazing place for a long walk and a picnic. **Wawona** is a much quieter area than the valley; you can also hike into Wawona Point and Chilnualna Falls.

Places to Eat

While there are several options for eating in and around the park, you may want to consider bringing your own food, a particularly good plan if you're heading for the back country. High prices and crowds are often more ominous than your appetite. But if you really need that hot meal and the camp stove isn't lighting, a foray into the eateries in the park will reward you with a hot meal—after a wait in line.

Ahwahnee Dining Room ★★ $$$: Ahwahnee Hotel, (209) 372-1488. This is a one of the priciest meals in the area, and one of the best. • Daily 7am-10:30am, 11:30am-3:30pm, 5:30pm-9pm.

Degnan's Deli ¢: Yosemite Village, (209) 372-1454. Good snacks and pizzas The grill upstairs is the best deal in town. • Daily 7am-10:30pm (Summer), 7am-8pm (Winter).

YOSEMITE BEARS

Everything you've heard about bears stealing picnic baskets is true. They are like huge cockroaches: they will find any way possible to get your food. A lone bear can easily consume a week's worth of menus in five minutes. Talk to a ranger or another expert to learn the proper techniques for hanging your food. You will need to bring 50 feet of rope and stuff sacks to bearproof your meal supplies. Better yet, rent one of the new bear canisters—heavy and bulky, but much more reliable for protecting your vittles.

GETAWAYS

Yosemite Lodge: ¢ (209) 372-1265. Cafeteria offerings. Daily 6:30am-10pm, 11:30am-3:45pm, 4:30pm-8pm. Also within the lodge: **Four Seasons** $ (209) 372-1269. Pretty good food at moderate prices. • Daily 7am-11am, 5pm-9pm. **Mountain Room Broiler** $$$ (209) 372-1281. Quality food at sequoia-sized prices. • Daily 5:30pm-10pm.

Places to Stay

Camping

For overnights on the trail, contact the **Wilderness Office** for free wilderness backpacking permits. For car camping, there are two types of campgrounds in the park: walk-ins (first come, first served), and those that require a reservation. The walk-ins tend to be filled to capacity in the peak season, so it's quite a gamble. The best way to get one is to be at the campground in the early morning on a weekday and grab a site just as someone is vacating it. The walk-in sites are **Hetch Hetchy, Tenaya** (on a lake close to Tuolumne Meadows), and **Sunnyside** (a climbers' hangout). From June 1 to September 15, there's a 7-day limit for Valley sites, and a 14-day limit outside the valley. At all other times of the year, there's a 30-day limit.

Reservation campgrounds are handled through a special **Destinet** office, which can be rather difficult to deal with. Reservations can be made no sooner than eight weeks beforehand, a task best done early in the morning. The campgrounds in the valley are **Upper Pines, North Pines, Lower Pines, Upper River, and Lower River.** They're all roughly the same. The best campgrounds along Tioga Pass Road in order of preference and distance from Tuolumne Meadows, are **Tuolumne, Porcupine Flat, Yosemite Creek, White Wolf, Tamarack Creek, and Hodgdon Meadow.** Three more options in the park are **Crane Flat** (on the Big Oak Flat Road), **Bridalveil Creek** (on the road to Glacier point), and **Wawona.**

Destinet (campground reservations): (800) 436-PARK/7275.

Yosemite Association: 5020 El Portal Rd., El Portal, (209) 379-2646, hut reservations (209) 372-0740. Mailing address: P.O. Box 230, El Portal, CA 95318. Manages Ostrander Hut reservations.

Lodging

Ahwahnee Hotel $$$$: Yosemite Park, (209) 372-1406. Rugged luxury, spectacular views, and conveniently located right in the Valley. $215 rooms, $500-$700 suites.

Buck Meadows Lodge $$: Hwy 120, Buck Meadows, (209) 962-6366. Located 30 miles from the park. Summer $50-$80; Winter $35-$65.

Cedar Lodge Resort $$$: Hwy 140, El Portal, (209) 379-2612. Just outside park. $80-$375.

Mariposa Inn $$: Hwy 140, Mariposa, (209) 966-4676. Located 43 miles from the park in downtown Mariposa, this six-room historic inn features a rear garden verandah and elegant design. Summer $75-$95; Winter $65-$85.

Tenaya Lodge $$$: Hwy 41, 2 mi. from the south entrance of the park, (209) 683-6555. Good restaurants, a convenient location, and clean, simple lodging. $70-$189.

The Redwoods $$/$$$: Wawona, (209) 375-6666. Books private homes for vacation rentals, with one- to six-room rentals available. Summer $88-$345; Winter $82-$325.

Yosemite Concession Services: Reservations (209) 252-4848. Handles reservations for all park lodging except camping. Includes Ahwahnee Hotel, Yosemite Lodge, Wawona Hotel, White Wolf Lodge, and the wood cabins and tent cabins in Curry Village.

Yosemite West $$: (209) 372-4240. Rents studio and loft condos year-round. Located near Chinquapin, which is inside the park between the Valley and Glacier Point. $79-$129 for two; $10 for each additional person.

INDEX

A
AAA 14
Aardvark 80, 82
AC Transit 17, 20, 184, 218
Academy of Sciences 59, 68, 70, 140
Adelaide Inn $ 72
African-American Cultural
  Society 54, 70
Airport Transportation 20-22,
  184, 217-218, 234-235
Airports 20, 184, 217-218, 234
Akiko's Sushi Bar ★★ $ 99
Alain Rondelli ★★★ $$$$ 99
Alamo Square Bed and Breakfast 61
Alamo Square Park 61
Albion Club 149
Albona ★★★ $$ 99
Alcatraz 19, 41, 51
Alexander's Books 81
Alta Plaza Park 33, 55, 172
American Express 9
Amsterdam Hotel $$ 73
Amtrak 20, 22, 183, 234
Anchor Brewing Company 69
Andalé Taqueria ★★ ¢ 99, 250
Angel Island 19, 51, 217, 222
Angkor Borei ★★ $ 99
Angkor Wat ★★★ $ 99
Ansel Adams Center for
  Photography 68, 71, 82
Appam ★★★ $$ 100
Aqua ★★★ $$$$ 100
Arabian Nights ★★★ $$ 100
Archbishops Mansion $$$ 61, 73
Ashkenaz 212
Asian Art Museum 47, 59, 68, 70
Automobile Rental 14
AYH Hostels 54, 73, 224, 260, 293

B
Bad Man Jose's ★★ ¢ 100
Bagdad Café 63
Bahia Cabana 149
Baker Beach 58, 161
(Plump Jack) Balboa Café ★ $$ 100
Balboa Café and Grill 149
Bambino's ★ $ 100
Barley and Hopps ★★ $$/$$$ 250
Barnes and Noble 81, 194, 245
Barney's ★★ $ 101
Bars & Clubs 149-159
BART 17
Basil Restaurant & Bar ★★ $$ 101
BASS Tickets 149, 212
Bay Area Discovery
  Museum 141, 231
Bay Wolf ★★★ $$$ 200
Beach Blanket Babylon 147
Beaches 58, 161-162, 269-270,
  274, 284-286, 290-291
Beat Books 82
Berkeley 163, 165, 183-216
Betelnut ★★ $$/$$$ 101

Bicycling 96, 162-166, 223, 270,
  278, 304, 309, 314
Big Nate's Barbeque ★★ $ 101
Big Sur 281-283
Bimbo's 365 Club 149
Bison Brewery 157, 212
Bistro Clovis ★★ $$ 101
Bistro Rôti ★★★ $$ 101
Bitter End 149
Bizou ★★ $$ 102
Black Oak Books 194
Black Thorn 149
Bluefish Cove 176
Bontà ★★ $$ 102
Boogaloos ★ $ 102
Bookstores 54, 81-83, 189, 194,
  225, 238, 245-246, 290
Borders 46, 81, 194-195
Bottom of the Hill 150
Boulevard ★★★ $$$ 102
Bound Together Collective 61
Box, The 158
Brady Acres $$ 73
Brain Wash 67
Brandy Ho's ★ $ 102
Brick Hut Café ★★ $ 200
Browser Books 81
Bruno's 150
Buca Giovanni ★★★ $$$ 103
Buddha Lounge 43

C
Cable Car Museum 49, 70
Cable car ride 40
Café, The 62-63, 158
Café Babar 150
Café Bastille ★★ $ 103
Café Claude ★★ $ 103
Café Du Nord 150
Café Fanny ★★ $ 201
Café Flore 63, 158
Café for All Seasons ★★ $$ 103
Café Jacqueline ★★★ $$$ 103
Café Kati ★★★ $$$ 103
Café Marimba ★★ $$ 104
Café Riggio ★★ $$ 104
Café Tiramisù ★★ $$ 104
Caffè Centro Marina ★ $$ 104
Caffè Centro South Park ★ ¢ 104
Caffè delle Stelle ★★★ $$ 104
Caffè Macaroni ★★★ $$ 104
Caffè Museo ★★ $ 105
Caffè Trieste ★ ¢ 87, 227
Cal. Academy of Sciences 59, 68
California Culinary Academy
  ★★ $$/$$$ 105
Calistoga 304, 306
CalTrain 17-22
Camping 95-97, 216, 221-224,
  266-269, 272, 281-282, 286,
  291, 293, 296, 300, 310, 316
Campton Place $$$$ 73, 105

Campton Place ★★★ $$$$ 105
Candlestick Point 181-182
Cannery, The 52
Canto Do Brazil ★ $ 105
Carmel 280-281
Carmen ★ ¢ 105
Carta ★★★ $$ 106
Cartoon Art Museum 68, 70, 141
Casa Aguila ★★★ $$ 106
Casanova's 158
Casinos 294-295, 298, 300-301
Castro 12, 27, 62-63, 158-159
Castro Theater 63, 144
Cha Cha Cha ★★★ $ 106
Chameleon 150
Chancellor Hotel $$$ 73
Chez Michel ★★★ $$$ 106
Chez Panisse ★★★★ $$$$ 202
Chez Panisse, the café ★★★ $$ 201
Chez Sovan ★★★ $ 252
Children's Discovery Museum 242
China Beach 58, 161
China Moon ★★★ $$$ 106
Chinatown 42-44
Chloe's Café ★★ $ 106
City Lights Bookstore 49-50, 81
Civic Center 46-47
Clean Well Lighted Place for
  Books 81, 225, 245
Cliff House 58
Club Townsend 158
Club Universe 158
Coastal Trail 58
Coco Club 158
Cody's Books 189, 194
Coit Tower 32, 40, 50-51
Columbus Books 83
Columbus Motor Inn $$ 73
Consulates 8
Country Station Sushi Café ★ ¢ 107
Crissy Field 30, 58, 164, 180-181
Cypress Club ★★★ $$$ 107

D
Dance 145-146, 214, 232, 265
Davies Symphony Hall 145
Days Inn San Francisco $$ 74
Delancey Street ★★★ $$ 107
Diesel—A Bookstore 194
Different Light
  Bookstore 63, 82, 158
DNA Lounge 150
Dog Eared Books 83
Doidge's Kitchen ★★ $ 107
Dol Ho ★ ¢ 107
Dolores Park 64, 172
Dolores Park Inn $$ 74
Duboce Triangle 27
DV 8 151

E
Ebisu ★★ $$ 107
Eddie Rickenbacker's 151

317

INDEX

Edinburgh Castle 151
El Rio 151
Elbo Room 151
Eleven Ristorante + Bar
 ★★ $$ 108, 151
Elite Café ★★ $$ 108
Eliza's ★★ $ 108
Embarcadero 39-40
Emerald Garden ★★ $$ 108
Emeryville 187, 193-195, 197, 210
Emporio Armani Café ★ $ 108
End Up 159
Enrico's ★★ $$ 108
Eos ★★★ $$$ 109
Escape from N.Y. Pizza ★ ¢ 109
Esperpento ★★ $ 109
Esprit Factory Outlet 68, 92
European Bookstore 82
Exploratorium 54, 68, 71, 98, 141

F
Fairmont Hotel $$$$ 48-49, 74
Farmers' Markets 84, 192, 196, 226
Fenton's ★ $ 204
Ferry Building 18-19, 40
Festivals 12, 64, 191
Fillmore 38, 53-54
Financial District 39, 41-42
Firefly ★★★ $$$ 109
Fisherman's Wharf 19, 50-52
 See also Northern Waterfront
500 Club 151
Flea Markets & Garage Sales 92, 249
Fleur de Lys ★★★★ $$$$ 109
Flying Saucer ★★★ $$$ 110
Fog City Diner ★★★ $$$ 110
Fook Yuen ★★★ $ 253
Fort Mason 41, 53-54, 70-71,
 147-148, 164, 180
Fort Point 58
42 degrees ★★★ $$$ 110
Fountain Court ★★ $ 110
Fringale ★★★ $$ 111

G
Galleries 44, 46, 65
Ganges ★ $ 111
Gaylord India ★★ $$$ 111, 137
Ghirardelli Square 52
Gira Polli ★★ $$ 111, 228
Goat Hill Pizza ★ ¢ 111
Gold Spike ★ $$ 111
Golden Gate Bridge 5, 41, 55, 58
Golden Gate Hotel $$ 74
Golden Gate National Recreation
 Area 53, 73, 161, 217
Golden Gate Park 29, 35-36, 41,
 56-57, 59-60, 68, 70-71, 139-140,
 162, 164, 166, 168, 170, 172,
 179-180
Golden Gate Transit 17-18, 20,
 68, 217-219, 269

Golden Turtle ★★ $$ 111, 138
Golf 58, 96, 141-142, 166,
 168-170, 266
Gordon Biersch Brewing
 Company ★★ $$ 112, 254
Gourmet Carousel ★★★ $ 112
Grace Cathedral 49
Grand Café ★ $$$ 112
Grant Plaza Hotel $ 74
Great America, Paramount's 260
Great Eastern ★★ $$ 112
Greek Theatre 160
Green Apple 83
Greens ★★★ $$ 112
Greyhound Bus 22, 183, 217, 234

H
Haas-Lilienthal House 54
Hahn's Hibachi ★★ ¢ 112
Haight 27, 29, 36, 38, 41, 57, 60-61
Half Moon Bay 12, 233, 268,
 284-289
Hamburger Mary's ★ $ 113
Harbor Village ★★ $$ 113
Harrington's Bar and Grill 152
Harry Denton's Starlight Rm. 152
Harvey Milk Plaza 62
Hawthorne Ln. ★★★ $$$$ 113
Hayes Street Grill ★★★ $$$ 113
Hayes Valley 38, 47, 61
Heights ★★★★ $$$$ 114
Helmand ★★ $$ 114
Hi-Ball Lounge 152
Holiday Inn $$$ 74
Home Furnishings 66, 88-92,
 197-199, 248-249
Home Plate ★★ $ 114
Horseback Riding 173, 267, 274,
 286, 304, 314
Horseshoe Tavern 152
Hospitals 7
Hot Air Ballooning 303, 309
Hotel Beresford $$ 75
Hotel Juliana $$$ 75
Hotel Milano $$$ 75
Hotel Monaco $$$$ 75, 112
Hotel Nikko $$$$ 75
Hotel Sheehan $$ 75
Hotel Triton $$$ 75
Hotel Utah Saloon Bistro 152
Hotels and Inns, SF 72-78
House of Nanking ★★ $ 114
Hunan Restaurant ★★ $ 114
Huntington $$$$ 48-49, 75
Hyatt-Regency $$$$ 76
Hyde Street Bistro ★★★ $$ 114
Hyde Street Pier 71

I
Il Fornaio ★★ $$ 114, 228, 255
Il Pollaio ★ ¢ 115
In-line Skating 59, 179-180
Inverness 223-226, 228-229

Ireland's 32 152

J
Jack London Village/
 Jack London Square 191-192
Jack's Bar 152
Jacks Elixir 152
Jackson Fillmore ★★★ $$ 115
Jackson Square 42, 79
Japanese Tea Garden ★★ 59
Japantown 11, 38, 53-55
Jewish Museum 71
Johnny Love's 152
Josie's Cabaret 147
Julie's Supper Club ★★ $$ 115
Jupiter 157, 213-214
Just Desserts 87, 124

K
Kabuki Hot Springs 55
Kabuki Movie Theater 11, 55
Kabuto Sushi ★★★ $$ 115
Kaffe Kreuzberg 67
Kan Zaman ★★ $ 115
Kate's Kitchen ★★★ $ 116
Kayaking 178-179, 274, 291,
 298, 309
Kepler's Books 245
Kezar 142, 153
Khan Toke Thai ★★★ $$ 116
Kilowatt Club 153
Kinokuniya 80, 82
Korean Buffet ★ $ 116
Krung Thai ★★★ $ 255
Kuleto's ★★ $$ 116

L
La Cumbre Taqueria ★★ ¢ 116
La Fiesta ★★ $ 255
La Folie ★★★★ $$$$ 116
La Méditerranée ★★ $ 117, 206
La Rondalla 153
La Taqueria ★★ ¢ 117
Laghi ★★★ $$$ 117
Lake Merritt 174-175, 187, 191, 210
Lands End 58, 162
Larkspur 18, 68, 163, 220
Last Day Saloon 153
Latin American Club 153
Lawrence Hall of Science 141, 211
Le Central ★★ $$$ 117
Le Mouton Noir ★★★ $$$$ 256
Le Soleil ★★ $ 117
Lee's Deli ★ ¢ 117
Left at Albuquerque
 ★★★ $ 256, 263
Leticia's ★ $ 118
Li Po Cocktail Lounge 43, 153
Liberty Café ★★ $$ 118
Liguria Bakery 50, 87
Lincoln Park 35, 58, 162, 169-170
Lion Pub 159
Little Italy Ristorante ★★ $$ 118

318

INDEX

Little Shamrock 153
Little Thai ★★ $ 118
Liverpool Lil's ★★ $$ 118
Lombard Street 30-31, 40, 49
Lone Palm 153
Lovejoy's Tea Room and Antiques 64
Lower Haight 37-38, 47, 61
Lucky 13 154
LuLu Bis ★★★ $$$ /
　LuLu Café ★★ $ 119
LuLu ★★★ $$ 119

M
M.H. de Young Museum 59, 71
MacArthur Park ★★ $$ 119, 256
Macondray Lane 40, 49
Mad Dog in the Fog 154
Maiden Lane 46
Mandalay ★★ $ 119
Mandarin Oriental $$$$ 42, 76
Mangiafuoco ★★ $$ 119
Manora's Thai Cuisine ★★ $ 119
Mansions Hotel $$$ 76
Marcus Books 82
Marin 18, 162-165, 217-232
Marin Brewing Company ★ $ 229
Marin Headlands 162, 221, 224
Marina 30, 41, 53-54
Marine World Africa USA 141
Mario's Bohemian Cigar Store
　★★ $ 120
Maritime Museum 71, 277
Maritime Natl. Historic Park 52
Mark Hopkins $$$$ 40, 48, 76
Masa's ★★★★ $$$$ 120
Matsuya ★★ $$ 120
Max's Diner ★ $ 120
Max's Eatz/Sweet Max's ★ ¢ 120
Max's Opera Café ★★ $$ 120, 257
McCormick & Kuleto's ★★ $$$ 119
Mel's Drive-In ★ $ 121
Mendocino 269-275
Mescolanza ★★ $$ 121
Mexican Museum 68, 71
Michelangelo Café ★★ $$ 121
Mick's Lounge 154
Midnight Sun 63
Mifune ★ $ 121
Mike's Chinese Cuisine ★★ $ 121
Milano Pizzeria ★ $ 121
Mill Valley 217, 219, 222
Millennium ★★ $$ 122
Miss Pearl's Jam House ★★ $$ 122
Mission 12, 26, 30-31, 34, 41, 64-66
Mission Dolores 64
Mission Rock Resort ★ $ 122
Mo's ★★ $ 122
Modern Times Bookstore 66, 80
Moe's Books 194
Monterey Bay 178, 276-283
Moose's ★★ $$/$$$ 122

Morrison Planetarium 70, 140
Moscone Convention Ctr. 35, 67
Mount Tamalpais 162-163, 165, 222
Mountain Biking 162, 267, 298
Movie Theaters 55, 63, 143,
　　211-212, 261-262
Muff Dive 158
Muir Beach 161, 223, 225, 230
Muir Woods 222
MUNI 17-19
Murals 41, 49, 51, 64-65, 68
Museo Italo Americano 71
Museums 70-72, 141, 188-189,
　　191, 242, 278
Myles O'Reilly's Pub 154
Mystery Bookstore 82

N
NAMES Project Foundation 62
Napa 301
Neecha Thai ★★ $ 123
New Dawn Café ★ ¢ 123
Nickie's BBQ 154
Nightlife 148-160, 212, 231, 262
Nippon Sushi (No Name) ★★ $ 123
Nob Hill 31, 48-49
Nob Hill Café ★★ $/$$ 123
Noc Noc 154
Noe Valley 31-32, 63-64,
Noe's Nest $$$ 76
North Beach 32, 40, 49-51
North Beach Pizza ★ $ 123
North Beach Rest. ★★ $$$ 124
North India ★★ $$ 124
Northern Waterfront 50-52
Novato 218, 221, 226, 228

O
O Chamé ★★★ $$ 206
Oakland 141-142, 163, 165, 183-216
Oakland Airport 20-22, 184, 193
Ocean Beach 58, 60, 162
Ocean Park Motel $$ 76
One Market ★★★ $$$ 124
Opera in the Park 12
Orphan Andy's ★ $ 124
Outlets 68-69, 80, 92-93, 197-199
(Bobby's) Owl Tree 154

P
Pacific Heights 33, 53-55
Pad Thai ★★ $ 124
Palace of Fine Arts 54
Palace of the Legion of Honor 41,
　　58, 70
Palio d'Asti ★★★ $$$ 124
Palomino ★★ $$ 125
Pane e Vino ★★★ $$ 125
Paradise Lounge 154
Paragon Bar and Café 155
Paramount Theatre 191, 214
Parking 14-15, 45
Parks 163-164, 170, 266-268, 274,
　　282, 284, 286

Pauline's Pizza Pie ★★ $ 125
Pebble Beach 168-170, 278-279, 286
Pelican Inn $$$ 223, 225, 230
Peninsula 18, 21-22, 141, 157,
　　163-165, 233-268
Petite Auberge $$$ 77
Phoenix 159
Picaro ★★ $ 125
Pier 23 155
Pier 39 40, 52, 140
Plough & Stars 155
Plump Jack 88, 100, 125
Plump Jack Café ★★ $$$ 125
Point Lobos State Reserve 176, 282
Point Reyes 223-224, 227
Postrio ★★★★ $$$$ 126
Potrero Hill 33, 67, 69, 171
Powell's Place ★ $ 126
Pozole ★ $ 126
Presidio 34-35, 56-58, 170
Printers Inc. 246

R
R & G Lounge ★★ $ 126
Radio Valencia ★ $ 126
Ramp, the ★ $ 126
Red Crane ★★ $ 127
Red Jack Saloon 155
Red Room 155, 292
Red Vic Moviehouse 144
Red Victorian $$ 77
Redwood City 237, 245, 247-249
Rendezvous du Monde ★★ $ 127
Richmond 35, 56-58
Rincon Center 67, 139
Ristorante Ecco ★★★ $$$ 127
River Rafting 173
Rizzoli 81
Road Biking 164-165
Rock Climbing 139, 268, 314
Rockridge 186, 194, 196
Roosevelt Tamale Parlor ★ ¢ 127
Rooster ★★ $$ 127
Rosmarino ★★★ $$$ 127
Roxie 66, 143, 145
Rubicon ★★★ $$$$ 128
Rumpus ★★★ $$ 128
Russian Hill 31, 48-49

S
Saigon Saigon ★★ $ 128
Sailing 173-175, 222, 266
SamTrans 17-18, 20-21, 184, 218
SF Art Institute 40, 49, 145
SF Art Institute Café ★★ ¢ 128
San Francisco Ballet 146-147
San Francisco Brewing Co. ★ $ 128
San Francisco Ctr. 46, 79-81, 90-91
SF Craft & Folk Art Museum 71
SF Intl. Airport 20-21
SF Intl. Film Festival 11, 143
San Francisco Museum of Modern
　Art (SFMOMA) 41, 68, 72

319

INDEX

San Francisco Opera 47, 68, 145
San Francisco Public Library 47
San Francisco Residence Club $$ 77
San Francisco Symphony 145-146
San Francisco Visitor Info. Ctr. 7, 45
San Francisco Zoo 36, 141
San Jose Airport 20-21, 184, 234
San Rafael 220, 224-226, 232
Sanppo ★★ $ 128
Santa Cruz 289-293
Sausalito 51, 219, 221-222, 224, 231-232
Savoy Tivoli 155
Scott's Seafood ★★ $$$ 129
Scuba Diving 176-177, 278
Sea Kayaking 178-179, 274, 278, 291
Sherman House $$$$ 77, 125, 256
Sir Francis Drake $$$ 77, 152
Skates on the Bay ★★ $$ 208
Skiing & Snowboarding 295
Slanted Door ★★★ $$ 129
Slim's 160
Slow Club ★★ $$ 129
Sol y Luna 155
Sonoma 274-275, 307-311
South of Market (SoMa) 35-36, 41, 66-69
South Park 67
South Park Café ★★★ $$ 129
Sparky's Diner 63
Spats 213
Spec's Adler Museum Café 155
Specialty's ★ ¢ 129
Splendido ★★★ $$$ 130
Sporting Goods 80, 95-96
St. Francis Hotel 45, 78
St. Mary's Cathedral 44
Stairways 31, 40, 49, 51
Stanford University 238, 241-242, 264-265
Stanyan Park Hotel $$ 77
Stars Café ★★ $$ 130
Stars ★★★ $$$$ 130
Steinhart Aquarium 70, 140
Stinson Beach 223
Stoyanof's ★★ $ 130
Straits Café ★★★ $$ 130
Stud 159
Sunset 36, 56-57
Suppenküche ★★ $$ 130
Sutro Baths 58, 164
Swan Oyster Depot ★★ $ 131

T

Tadich Grill ★★★ $$$ 131
Tahoe 297-302
Tai Chi ★★ $ 131
Taqueria El Balazo ★ ¢ 131
Taqueria San Jose ★★ ¢ 131
Tattoo Art Museum 72
Taxis 16, 217
Telegraph Avenue 189
Telegraph Hill 32, 40, 50-51

Temple Hotel $ 77
Tenderloin 7, 36-37, 46
Tennis 96-97, 166, 172, 193, 237, 239, 281, 306, 311
Thanya and Salee ★★ $$ 132
Theater 46, 65, 69, 147-148, 160, 191, 212, 214-215, 222, 232, 265
Thep Phanom ★★ $ 132
Thomas Cooke 9
330 Ritch Street 155
Thrift Stores 66, 91, 198, 249
Ti Couz ★★ $ 132
Tiburon19, 165, 217, 219, 222, 225
Tilden Regional Park 163, 165, 170, 190, 211, 216
Tillman Place Bookshop 82
Timo's ★★ $$ 132
Tin How Temple 44
TIX Bay Area 46, 147
Tomales Bay 178, 223-224
Tommaso's ★★ $$ 132
Tommy Toy's ★★ $$$$ 132
Ton Kiang ★★ $ 133
Tonga Room 40, 49, 74, 156
Top of the Mark 48
Toronado 156
Tosca Café 156
Trad'r Sam 156
Traffic Information Fastline 16
Transamerica Building 42
Transportation 13-22, 45, 68, 183-185, 217-219, 234-235, 269, 290, 294-295, 302, 312
Trattoria Contadina ★★ $$ 133
Travelodge $$ 78, 192, 301
Triple Rock 157, 213-214
Trocadero Night Club & Restaurant 156
Truly Mediterranean ★ ¢ 133
Tu Lan ★★ ¢ 133
20 Tank Brewery 156-157
2223 Market ★★ $$$ 133
Twin Peaks 63-64
Twin Peaks Tavern 63
Two Fools ★ $ 288

U

U-Lee Restaurant ★★ $ 134
U.S.S. Pampanito 72
UC Berkeley 185, 187-188, 215
UC Santa Cruz 290
UCSF Medical Center 7
Ultimate Frisbee 172
Underwater World 52, 142
Union Square 45-46, 79
Union Street Ale House 156
Universal Café ★★★ $$ 134
Up & Down Club 156

V

Val 21 ★★ $$ 134
Valentine's Café ★ $$ 134
Vertigo ★★★ $$$ 134
Vesuvio Café 40, 49, 156

Vicolo Pizzeria ★★ $ 135
Victorian homes 54, 60, 62-64
Victorian Inn on the Park $$$ 78
Villa Florence $$$ 78
Visitacion Valley 37
Vivande ★★★ $$$ 135
Vivande Porta Via ★★ $$ 135

W

¡Wa-Ha-Ka! ★ ¢ 135
Waldenbooks 82, 246
War Memorial Opera House 46, 145-146
Washington Square Park 50
Western Addition 37-38, 61
Westin St. Francis $$$$ 78
White Swan Inn $$$ 78
Willows Inn $$ 78
Winchester Mystery House 241
Windsurfing 181-182
Wine Country 301
Wineries 222, 241-242, 274, 286, 291, 302-303, 307-308
Women's Building 7, 65
Woodward's Garden ★★★ $$$ 135

Y

Yank Sing ★★ $$/$ 136
YaYa Cuisine ★★★ $$ 136
Yerba Buena Gardens/Center for the Arts 41, 67-68, 72, 147
YMCA 168, 194
Yosemite 311-316
Yoshi's Nitespot 214
Yuet Lee ★★ $ 136

Z

Zachary's Chicago Pizza ★★ $209
Zarzuela ★★ $$ 136
Zona Rosa ★ ¢ 136
Zuni Café and Grill ★★★ $$$ 136